Accounting for Canadian Colleges

THIRD EDITION

Ted Palmer

Vic D'Amico

Donna P. Grace

Toronto

Canadian Cataloguing in Publication Data

Palmer, Ted
Accounting for Canadian colleges
3rd ed.
ISBN 0-201-70306-8

1. Accounting. I. D'Amico, Victor L., 1936– . II. Grace, Donna P. III. Title

HF5635.P33 2001 657'.042 C00-930568-8

ISBN 0-201-70306-8

Vice President, Editorial Director: Michael Young
Acquisitions Editor: Samantha Scully
Marketing Manager: James Buchanan
Associate Editor: Veronica Tomaiuolo
Production Editor: Marisa D'Andrea
Copy Editor: Betty Robinson
Production Coordinator: Janette Lush
Page Layout: Paula Gray/Brian Taft/Artplus Ltd.
Permissions Research: Karen Becker
Art Director: Mary Opper
Interior Design: Dave Murphy
Cover Design: Dave Murphy
Cover Image: Masterfile

1 2 3 4 5 05 04 03 02 01

Printed and bound in USA.

Contents

Preface

CHAPTER 1
The Balance Sheet

UNIT 1 Financial Position 1
UNIT 2 Business Transactions 14

CHAPTER 2
Balance Sheet Accounts

UNIT 3 Recording Transactions in T-Accounts 24

CHAPTER 3
The Income Statement

UNIT 4 Preparing the Income Statement. 43
UNIT 5 Revenue and Expense Accounts 58

CHAPTER 4
The Journal and the Ledger

UNIT 6 The Journal 72
UNIT 7 Posting to the Ledger 77
UNIT 8 Source Documents 95

CHAPTER 5
The Work Sheet and Classified Financial Statements

UNIT 9 The Work Sheet 113
UNIT 10 Classified Financial Statements 122

CHAPTER 6
Completing the Accounting Cycle for a Service Business

UNIT 11 Adjusting the Books 133
UNIT 12 Work Sheets, Adjustments, Financial Statements . . . 144
UNIT 13 Adjusting and Closing Entries 161
INTEGRATIVE ACTIVITY 1 The Accounting Cycle/Westbrooke Cinema 179

CHAPTER 7
The Merchandising Company

UNIT 14 Merchandising Accounts 183
UNIT 15 Sales and Goods and Services Tax 214
UNIT 16 Bank Credit Cards 229

CHAPTER 8
The Subsidiary Ledger System

UNIT 17 The Three-Ledger System 243
UNIT 18 Accounting Systems 252

CHAPTER 9
The Special Journal System

UNIT 19 A Multi–Column Journal System 290
UNIT 20 Posting the Multi–Column Journal 298
UNIT 21 Purchases Journal 310
UNIT 22 Sales Journal 334
UNIT 23 Cash Receipts Journal 343
UNIT 24 Cash Payments Journal 350
INTEGRATIVE ACTIVITY 2 The Special Journal System/Marcov's Furniture . . . 367

CHAPTER 10
Cash Control and Banking

UNIT 25 Cash Control 373
UNIT 26 Checking Cash Records 389

CHAPTER 11
Completing the Accounting Cycle for A Merchandising Company

UNIT 27 Adjusting the Books 409
UNIT 28 Adjustments and the Work Sheet 425
UNIT 29 Financial Statements 435
INTEGRATIVE ACTIVITY 3 The Accounting Cycle/Metro Sales Co. 452

CHAPTER 12
Payroll Accounting

UNIT 30 Paying Employees 456
UNIT 31 Payroll Records and Journal Entries 482
INTEGRATIVE ACTIVITY 4 Payroll Accounting/Claymore Industries 499

CHAPTER 13
Accounting For Partnerships and Corporations

UNIT 32 Accounting for Partnerships 504
UNIT 33 Accounting for Corporations 525

PREFACE

The expectations and demands of the business world are continually in a state of change. In the field of accounting, employers require sound understanding of both accounting procedures and basic accounting principles, thinking skills, computer literacy, and well-developed personal characteristics.

This textbook, *Accounting for Canadian Colleges*, Third Edition, has been designed to meet these requirements, and is part of a complete first-year introductory accounting curriculum package for students who are not planning to specialize in accounting. Included are:

- A Textbook
- A set of Student Working Papers
- An Instructor's Manual that includes all the answers

ORGANIZATION OF THE TEXT

Accounting for Canadian Colleges, Third Edition, contains thirteen chapters that are divided into thirty-three units. Each unit presents learning objectives, the theory to be covered, review questions, and practical exercises.

The text introduces basic Generally Accepted Accounting Principles, where relevant, when presenting accounting procedures and practices to students. The theory is presented in such a way as to encourage clear understanding of the principles and purposes of accounting. Decision making based on the examination of financial data is encouraged throughout the text. *Accounting for Canadian Colleges*, Third Edition, uses a systems approach to illustrate the accounting procedures followed in the processing of data and in the control of company assets. Descriptions of accounting systems from real companies such as Warrendon Sports and Renfrew Printing are presented to further illustrate and reinforce accounting systems and procedures.

Relevant activities in various formats are a major method of reinforcing the accounting principles and procedures presented. In addition to questions and exercises at the end of each unit, summary application problems of varying degrees of difficulty are included at the end of each chapter. Major activities, called Integrative Activities, are interspersed throughout the text to reinforce student learning.

COMPUTER ACCOUNTING

Accounting for Canadian Colleges, Third Edition, provides computer exercises and projects as optional material in the Instructor's Manual. This material may be used for classes that have access to computer laboratories. The problems are designed to assist students in developing their decision-making, problem-solving, and analytical skills. Major activities in the text are also designed with an optional computer section.

Computer activities range from general computer literacy questions to applications on General Ledger, accounts receivable, and spreadsheet packages. Activities are designed to be completed both manually and on the computer, allowing students to compare the two methods.

All activities are generic and can be used with whatever software packages are available.

INTEGRATIVE ACTIVITIES

Four major activities are provided to reinforce students' knowledge of the accounting process. The activities can require both group and individual work in order to encourage the development of organizational skills, leadership qualities, and social interaction. Additional activities are provided in the Instructor's Manual.

GOODS AND SERVICES TAX AND HARMONIZED SALES TAX

Goods and Services Tax is used in the majority of provinces in Canada. Harmonized Sales Tax is used in the Atlantic provinces at the time of publication. You are strongly recommended to research subsequent changes by accessing the Canada Customs and Revenue Agency Web site at www.ccra-adrc.gc.ca. GST has been used primarily in the text with an HST supplement in the Instructor's Manual. In certain examples and exercises, the PST and/or GST have been deliberately omitted in order to focus attention on specific accounting concepts.

ACKNOWLEDGMENTS

I sincerely appreciate the materials, encouragement, and ideas provided to me in the preparation of *Accounting for Canadian Colleges,* Third Edition. Source documents, illustrations, and descriptions of accounting systems were supplied by Mary and Joseph Galotta, The Cascade Inn, Niagara Falls; Warren Creighton, Warrendon Sports, Ottawa; W. MacAdam, President, Renfrew Printing, Renfrew; W. Rorison, H. Prince, and R. Beaver, INCO Ltd., Sudbury; C. Smith, Accountant, Scotiabank, Ottawa; J. May, Canadian Tire Corporation; Dan O'Brien, Gold's Gym, St. Catharines; Dave Galotta, Scotiabank; Anne Martin, IBM; Nova Corporation; Len Webster, CGA Canada; T.G. O'Flaherty, Bedford Software Ltd.; A. Reynolds, Commodore Business Machines; Apple, Canada; Penny Lipsett, Xerox Canada; Canadian Institute of Chartered Accountants; Pat Holmes, Lochaven Financial Management; Janet Allen, KPMG; Maurice Pothier, CMA; my colleagues at BEC; and my co-authors Vic D'Amico and Donna Grace.

Finally, I am especially grateful for the editorial assistance and advice received from Samantha Scully and the understanding and encouragement shown by Donna's husband Michael, my son, Ryan, my mother, and Sherry, Rachael, and Kyle Campbell.

Ted Palmer

Donna Grace

REVIEWERS AND CONSULTANTS

Robert Dearden, *Red River College*

Vincent Durant, *St. Lawrence College*

Augusta Ford, *College of the North Atlantic*

Deb Otto, *Red Deer College*

Franc A. Weissenhorn, *Nova Scotia Community College, Halifax Campus*

CHAPTER 1

The Balance Sheet

UNIT 1 Financial Position

Learning Objectives

After reading this unit, discussing the applicable review questions, and completing the applications exercises, you will be able to do the following:

1. **DETERMINE** the financial position of a business.
2. **CLASSIFY** items as assets, liabilities, or owner's equity.
3. **CALCULATE** owner's equity.
4. **PREPARE** a balance sheet.
5. **USE** correct recording procedures.

FINANCIAL POSITION OF AN INDIVIDUAL

Susan Wu is a loan officer in a community branch of the Royal Bank of Canada. As part of her duties, she authorizes loans to individuals and to businesses wishing to borrow money.

Recently, a young person named Sherry Campbell visited Susan to apply for a loan. Sherry is a graduate of her local college's horticulture program and has been working for a landscaper for the past year.

Sherry has the entrepreneurial spirit — that is, she would like to own and run her own business. Although she is quite young, Sherry feels that her college training, combined with the practical experience that she has gained over the past year, will enable her to start her own successful landscaping business.

Sherry needs $10 000 in order to start the business and is applying to Susan's bank for a loan. In deciding whether to grant a loan, Susan examines the financial position of the applicant. This is what she does. First, she lists the items owned by the applicant:

Items Owned by Sherry Campbell	
Cash	$ 2 000
Government Bonds	5 000
Clothing	3 000
Furniture	10 000
Equipment	7 000
Automobile	10 000
	$37 000

A creditor is a person or business that has extended credit or loaned money.

Next, Susan lists what Sherry owes to creditors. Creditors are people or businesses that extended credit when items were purchased or who loaned money used to purchase possessions. These creditors must be paid before an individual has complete title to his/her possessions.

Debts Owed to Creditors by Sherry Campbell	
Credit Card Debt	$ 200
Student Loan	5 000
	$5 200

Now Susan determines the financial position of the applicant.

Calculation of Financial Position

Sherry's financial position is determined by making the following calculation:

Total Value of Items Owned	–	Total Owed to Creditors	=	Personal Net Worth
$37 000		$5 200		$31 800

Personal net worth is the difference between items owned and debts owed.

By calculating the cost of the items owned by an individual and subtracting the debts owed, it is possible to determine a person's net worth at any given time. The net worth represents the difference between the total owned and the debts owed. Thus, Susan has determined that Sherry Campbell's net worth is $31 800.

Accounting Terminology

The subject *accounting* is often called the *language of business.* An understanding of accounting terminology will help you in both your personal life and your business career. Starting with the items owned by Sherry, let's translate her financial position into the language of accounting.

Assets

In accounting, items of value owned by a business or person are called *assets.* The total of Sherry's assets is $37 000.

Assets are items of value owned by a business or person.

Liabilities

Debts or amounts owed to others by a business or a person are called *liabilities.* Sherry's liabilities total $5 200.

Liabilities are the debts of a business or person.

Personal Equity

Personal equity is a term that represents a person's net worth. Sherry's personal equity or net worth is $31 800. Because there is a substantial difference between Sherry's assets and liabilities, the bank gave her the loan. Sherry's very positive net worth indicated to the bank that Sherry has a secure financial position and should be able to repay the loan.

Personal equity is a person's net worth.

Accounting Equation

The financial position of a person or a business can be stated in the form of an equation called the *accounting equation:*

Assets = Liabilities + Equity

In Sherry's case, the accounting equation is:

$37 000 = $5 200 + $31 800

or $37 000 = $37 000

This accounting equation is the basis for much of the accounting theory you will learn.

Balance Sheet

Sherry's financial position is illustrated in Figure 1-1 in the form of a balance sheet. This is a financial statement that lists assets, liabilities, and personal equity (net worth) at a specific date.

FIGURE 1-1
Personal balance sheet

Sherry Campbell
Personal Balance Sheet
September 30, 2001

Assets		**Liabilities**	
Cash	$ 2 000	Credit Card Debt	$ 200
Government Bonds	5 000		
Clothing	3 000	Student Loan	5 000
Furniture	10 000	Total Liabilities	5 200
Equipment	7 000		
Automobile	10 000	**Personal Equity**	
		S. Campbell, Net Worth	31 800
Total Assets	$37 000	Total Liabilities and Personal Equity	$37 000

FINANCIAL POSITION OF A BUSINESS

The financial position of a business is determined in the same way as that described for Sherry Campbell. In the next few pages, we will examine the financial position and the balance sheet for a small business called Malibu Gym. Malibu Gym will be used in this text to demonstrate a variety of accounting procedures. This business will be followed from its formation through its first year of operation, thereby presenting an opportunity to examine both accounting and non-accounting procedures, problems, and decision making faced by all business proprietors.

Background Information

Hal O'Brien and his family opened Malibu Gym in Thorold, Ontario. Many factors were involved in Hal's decision to become an entrepreneur and open his own business.

Hal's background and continued interest in athletics, combined with his formal education, provided the expertise necessary to operate this type of business. His athletic background included playing professional hockey. Hal capitalized on his interest in athletics by completing a degree in physical education and returned to college to obtain a post-graduate diploma in business. A career as an accountant, combined with a hobby as a bodybuilder, provided him with additional experience that he could use in fulfilling his ambition to open a successful business in the field of fitness.

Hal felt that his unique background and interests, together with a capacity for hard work and a desire to succeed, qualified him to become a successful entrepreneur in the area of physical fitness. This idea was particularly appealing, given the increase in popularity of leisure and fitness-related activities. Hal decided to investigate the potential in the Niagara Region for opening a fitness centre for men and women. Through his former hobby of bodybuilding, he had become familiar with Malibu Gym, which had started in California and had spread across the United States and Europe but which had only begun to enter the Canadian market. Hal felt that the use of the Malibu name and promotional material would assist him in building a clientele for his gym, so he applied to become a licensee. A licensee pays a monthly fee to Malibu Gym International for the use of the Malibu name in a particular region of the country, but operates the business as his or her own. Because of Hal's background, he was approved as the licensee for the Niagara Region.

As with any business, starting this business required the owner to take risks in the hope of being successful. Hal collected all of his available cash and applied for a loan and mortgage from the bank to start his business. He decided he would work part-time at the fitness centre, and continue in his present position as an accountant. The Malibu Gym, Thorold, officially opened on July 1.

Purpose of Accounting

The purpose of accounting is to provide financial information for decision making.

The primary *purpose of accounting* is to provide financial information for decision making. In addition, accurate information is required for many purposes, including calculating income tax for Canada Customs and Revenue Agency. To fill this need, Hal had to develop an accounting system for Malibu. An accounting system is an organized method of performing accounting tasks. Every accounting system must:

- Record the day-to-day activities of the business.
- Summarize and report information in financial statements for analysis and decision making.

Introducing Generally Accepted Accounting Principles

It is very important to the users of accounting information, whether they are owners, creditors, bankers, or investors, that the information presented to them be prepared according to a common set of rules. Only in this way can users compare the data of various businesses to make decisions. Generally Accepted Accounting Principles (GAAP) and their underlying concepts provide a set of consistent rules used by all accountants in order to prepare financial statements such as the balance sheet. In Canada, the Canadian Institute of Chartered Accountants (CICA) publishes a *Handbook* containing these principles. Where appropriate throughout this text, a simplified version of GAAP and concepts will be discussed in order to assist you in understanding the significance of the accounting procedures that you are undertaking.

Generally Accepted Accounting Principles (GAAP) are standard rules and guidelines.

Business Entity Concept

In this chapter, the study of accounting will begin with a look at the balance sheet, which is one of the financial statements for Malibu Gym. It should be pointed out at this time that the financial data for the business must be kept *separate* from Hal's personal financial data in order to prepare accurate financial statements. Each business should be considered as a separate unit or *entity* for the purpose of keeping accounting records. This is known as the *business entity concept.*

COMPANY BALANCE SHEET

The financial position of Malibu Gym on opening day is shown in Figure 1-2 in a balance sheet. Just as with the personal balance sheet shown for Sherry Campbell, a company balance sheet is a formal report or statement showing the financial position of a business at a certain date. It lists assets, liabilities, and owner's equity. Owner's equity is an accounting term for the owner's claim against the assets of the company.

A balance sheet is a financial statement that lists the assets, liabilities, and owner's equity at a specific date.

Owner's equity is the owner's claim against the assets of the company.

FIGURE 1-2

Company balance sheet

Malibu Gym
Balance Sheet
July 1, 2001

Assets		Liabilities	
Cash	$ 5 000	Accounts Payable	$ 4 000
Accounts Receivable	6 000	Bank Loan	65 000
Office Supplies	500	Mortgage Payable	80 000
Land	25 000	Total Liabilities	149 000
Building	110 000		
Training Equipment	94 500	**Owner's Equity**	
		O'Brien, Capital	92 000
Total Assets	$241 000	Total Liabilities and Owner's Equity	$241 000

The company's financial position can also be described in terms of the accounting equation:

Assets	=	Liabilities	+	Owner's Equity
$241 000	=	$149 000	+	$92 000
$241 000	=	$241 000		

In this equation, the two sides balance. The left side ($241 000) equals the right side ($241 000).

Notice that the balance sheet also balances. The total of the left side equals the total of the right side. This is why it is called a *balance sheet.*

Accounting Terms

Notice also that accounting terminology is used for all items on the balance sheet. The amount owed by customers for memberships, $6 000, is called *Accounts Receivable.* The amount owed as debts to creditors, $4 000, is *Accounts Payable.* The loan (mortgage) owed on the building, $80 000, is *Mortgage Payable.*

Balance Sheet Preparation

The opening balance sheet for Malibu Gym will be used as an example to discuss the correct format and procedures followed to prepare a balance sheet. This is known as a formal report since it is prepared according to a specific set of rules, outlined in the following steps.

Step 1: Prepare Statement Heading

The three-line heading is centred at the top of the page and is designed to provide information in this sequence:

Line 1: Who? — Malibu Gym — business name
Line 2: What? — Balance Sheet — statement name
Line 3: When? — July 1, 2001 — date of statement

Step 2: List Assets

The assets are listed on the left side of the page. Before the assets are totalled, the liabilities must be listed and totalled. Then, if required, the necessary number of blank lines must be inserted before the owner's equity section and before the assets total so that the final totals on both sides of the statement will be on the same line.

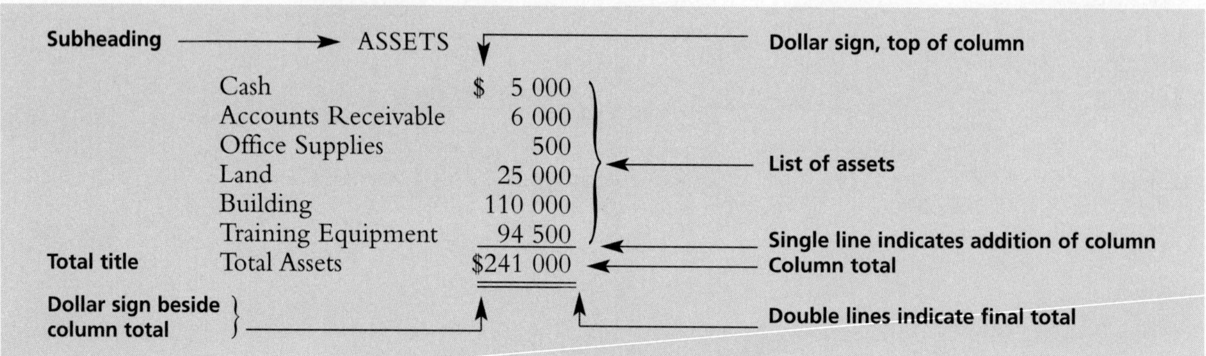

Step 3: List Liabilities

The liabilities are listed and totalled on the right side of the page:

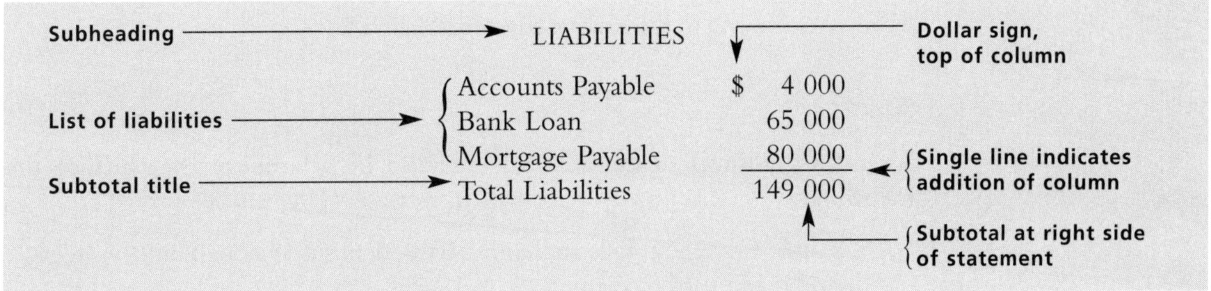

Step 4: Show Owner's Equity

The owner's equity section, showing the owner's investment, is on the right side of the page after the liabilities section. As explained previously, the final totals of each side must be on the same line. This allows for an attractive presentation of the information and emphasizes the fact that the left side of the balance sheet equals the right side, that is, A = L + OE.

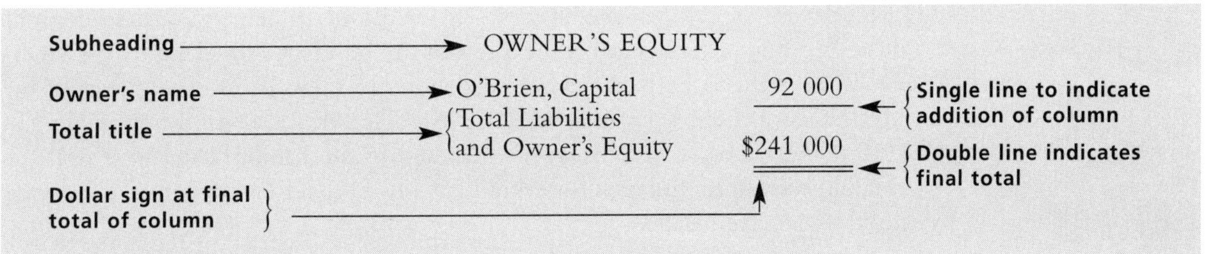

Facts to Remember

The total assets and the total liabilities and owner's equity are written on the same line:

Total Assets	$241 000	Total Liabilities and Owner's Equity	$241 000

The appearance of the balance sheet is very important since the statement may be viewed by a variety of people inside and outside the business. Statements such as this create an impression regarding the business and should be prepared as attractively and accurately as possible. In addition to the specifications for balance sheet preparation given in the examples, the following requirements should be considered:

(1) No abbreviations should be used in the statement.
(2) The statement should contain no corrections.
(3) For the balance sheet, dollar signs should be placed as follows:

- Beside the first figure in each column.
- Beside the *final* total on both sides of the statement.

Additional Accounting Terminology

Earlier in the chapter, you started to build your accounting vocabulary by learning what assets, liabilities, and equity were. Here is additional information regarding these terms as they relate to the balance sheet for Malibu Gym.

Assets

Assets are resources or items of value owned by a business. They include the following:

- **Cash:** Currency (bills and coins), bank deposits, cheques, money orders, and credit card receipts.
- **Accounts Receivable:** The total amount due from debtors (customers). Debtors are persons or businesses that owe a business money as a result of purchasing goods or services on credit. The amount is normally due within 30 days.
- **Office Supplies:** Items purchased for use within the business office.

Liabilities

Liabilities are the debts of the business. The creditors who are owed these amounts are said to have a claim against the assets of the business. This claim by the creditors is the right to be paid the amount owing to them before the owner of the business can benefit from their sale. For example, Malibu Gym lists a building at $110 000 as an asset. A mortgage is included in the liabilities at $80 000. If the building were sold, the creditor would have to be paid in full before the owner could obtain the balance.

Liabilities include items such as:

- **Accounts Payable:** The total amount owed to the creditors for the purchase of goods or services of the business. These amounts are normally due in 30 days.
- **Bank Loan:** The amount of loans owing to the bank. These loans vary in length of time (1–5 years). Some bank loans are "demand" loans and are due whenever payment is demanded by the bank.
- **Mortgage Payable:** The amount borrowed from financial institutions usually to purchase buildings or land. The lender has the right to obtain control of the property in the event that the borrower fails to repay the debt. Since this liability is normally large in amount, the time to repay is longer than other liabilities (for example, 25 years).

Equities

Equities are claims against the assets of a company

The assets are listed on the left side of the balance sheet. On the right side are the claims against the *assets*. These claims are called *equities.*

The *liabilities* section lists the claims of the creditors. The *owner's equity* section lists the owner's claim. The owner's claim is what the company is "worth to the owner," or the net worth. It is listed on the balance sheet using the word "Capital" beside the owner's name (see *O'Brien, Capital* — page 5). The owner's equity is the difference between the assets and the liabilities (OE = A – L).

Order of Items on the Balance Sheet

The assets and liabilities on the balance sheet are listed in a particular order.

Assets

Assets are listed in the order of liquidity. This is the order in which they would likely be converted to cash. Using the balance sheet for Malibu Gym as an example, the order would be Cash, Accounts Receivable, and Office Supplies, since this is the order in which these items could be converted to cash. After assets such as Cash, Accounts Receivable, and Office Supplies comes a different type of asset — assets that *last a long time* and are used for a long period of time to operate the business. Examples include Land, Building, and Training Equipment. They are listed in order of useful life to the business with the longest lasting first:

Liquidity order is the order in which assets can be converted into cash.

ORDER OF ASSETS		REASONS
Cash	$ 5 000	Most liquid asset.
Accounts Receivable	6 000	Received within 30 days.
Office Supplies	500	Easily converted to cash.
Land	25 000	Assets listed in order of length of
Building	110 000	useful life in the business. Longest life
Training Equipment	94 500	listed first and shortest life last.

Liabilities

Liabilities are listed according to payment due date from most recent to longest term. This is known as the *maturity date rule.*

The maturity date rule specifies that liabilities are listed according to the date they are due to be paid.

ORDER OF LIABILITIES		REASONS
Accounts Payable	$ 4 000	Payable within 30 days.
Bank Loan	65 000	Payable usually within 1–5 years.
Mortgage Payable	80 000	Payable usually within 25 years.

Valuation of Items on the Balance Sheet

All of the items on the balance sheet have a dollar value. There are accounting rules governing the methods used to assign dollar values. One of them is the cost principle.

Cost Principle

Assets are valued according to the *cost principle.* When assets are obtained, they are recorded at the actual cost to the business. This figure is never changed even though the owner might think that the value of the assets has increased.

Users of the Balance Sheet

For a variety of reasons, a number of people and organizations could be interested in the financial position of a business. The following chart provides a brief introduction to users of a balance sheet and lists reasons for their interest. When you consider the number of users of this financial information and the importance of the decisions they are making, it is easy to see why it is essential to employ the most objective, accurate data available in preparing the balance sheet.

USERS	REASONS FOR INTEREST
Owner	Indicates his or her claim on the assets. Comparing balance sheets at different points in time will show whether or not the financial position is improving.
Creditors	Companies considering extending credit or loaning money are interested in liquid assets available to meet payments as well as claims on assets.
Investors	Investors investigate the financial position of a business as one of the factors they consider in deciding whether or not to invest in the business. They want to protect their investment and are interested in much the same information as are creditors.
Government	Government departments need information for policy decision making, statistical reports, and taxation.

COMMON RECORDING PRACTICES

There are several common recording practices followed by most accountants. They are described and illustrated below:

(1) When ruled accounting paper is used, dollar signs and decimals are not required.
(2) A single line indicates addition or subtraction.
(3) Double lines indicate final totals.

ASSETS			
Cash		500	00
Accounts Receivable	1	200	75
Equipment	5	000	00
Total Assets	6	700	75

← Ruled accounting paper

← A single line indicates addition or subtraction

← Double lines indicate final totals

(4) When ruled accounting forms are not used, dollar signs and decimals are used.
(5) Dollar signs are placed before the first figure in a column and beside final column totals when accounting forms are not used.

ASSETS	
Cash	$ 500.00
Accounts Receivable	1 200.75
Equipment	5 000.00
Total Assets	$6 700.75

(6) Abbreviations are not used on financial statements unless the official name of the company contains an abbreviation. For example, Lumonics Inc. *does* contain a short form (Inc.) in its official name and should be written as *Lumonics Inc.* Goldcorp Investments Limited should not be written in short form since the company uses *Limited*, not Ltd., as part of its official name.

(7) Accounting records must be neat and legible. They are used by many people and are kept for a long period of time. They are either printed, keyed, or written in ink. Care must be taken to write numbers and words clearly and legibly.

REVIEW QUESTIONS

1. What is meant by "financial position"?
2. Define asset and give an example of an asset.
3. (a) Define liability and give an example.
   (b) Define owner's equity.
4. What is the accounting equation?
5. What is the balance sheet?
6. Why did Hal O'Brien decide to go into business for himself? What risks did he take?
7. How is the owner's equity calculated?
8. In what order are assets listed on the balance sheet?
9. In what order are liabilities listed on the balance sheet?
10. What does a single ruled line on a financial statement indicate? What do double lines mean?
11. What is meant by "Generally Accepted Accounting Principles"?
12. What is the business entity concept?
13. What is the cost principle?

PROBLEMS: APPLICATIONS

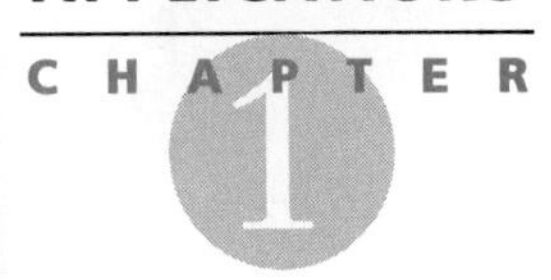

1. Complete the following equations in your study guide or notebook

A	=	L	+	OE
$ 75 000		$25 000		$50 000
?		80 000		35 000
110 000		49 000		?
65 000		43 000		?
80 000		43 000		?

2. Classify the following items as assets, liabilities, or owner's equity:

Cash
Bank Loan
Equipment
Land
Mortgage
Furniture
Owner's Investment in the Business
Accounts Receivable

3. The balance sheet items for the Tidey Company are listed in random order below.
   (a) Prepare lists of the assets, the liabilities, and the owner's equity.
   (b) Complete the accounting equation for the Tidey Company in your study guide or notebook, following the format shown below.
   Assets $____ = Liabilities $____ + Owner's Equity $____

Cash	$21 500
Building	60 000
Land	35 000
Bank Loan	9 500
Mortgage	40 000
Equipment	20 000
S. Tidey, Capital	87 000

4. The balance sheet items for the Repar Company at October 31, 2001 are listed in random order below.
   (a) Prepare lists of the assets, the liabilities, and the owner's equity.
   (b) Complete the accounting equation for the Repar Company in your study guide or notebook, following the format shown below:
   Assets $____ = Liabilities $____ + Owner's Equity $____

Building	$70 000
Cash	11 500
Land	25 000
Bank Loan	9 500
Mortgage	38 000
Equipment	15 000
Repar, Capital	77 000
Accounts Receivable	7 000
Accounts Payable	4 000

5. Using the format in Figure 1-1 (page 3) and Figure 1-2 (page 5), prepare a balance sheet for Repar Company (refer to exercise 4 above).

6. The balance sheet items for Nakhooda Real Estate are listed below. Prepare a balance sheet dated September 15, 2001 listing assets and liabilities in correct order.

Cash	$ 2 500
Accounts Receivable	?
Office Equipment	5 000
Bank Loan	3 500
Accounts Payable	3 000
Building	55 000
J. Nakhooda, Capital	45 000
Land	25 000
Mortgage Payable	40 000
Supplies	1 600

7. Chili Pepper is a restaurant owned by Michael Kurri. The restaurant's assets and liabilities on June 30, 2001 are as follows:

Cash	$ 19 000
Food Supplies	3 000
Restaurant Supplies	5 000
Furniture and Fixtures	50 000
Land and Building	190 000
Payable to Suppliers	12 000
Mortgage Payable	85 000
Bank Loan	23 000

(a) Calculate Kurri's equity.
(b) Prepare a balance sheet.

8. The assets and liabilities of Susan Baird, a lawyer, are as follows on April 30, 2001:

Cash	$12 000
Due from Clients	35 000
Office Supplies	2 800
Office Equipment	28 000
Bank Loan	15 500
Owed to Creditors	6 000

(a) Classify each item as an asset or a liability.
(b) Calculate Baird's equity.
(c) Prepare a balance sheet.

UNIT 2 Business Transactions

Learning Objectives

After reading this unit, discussing the applicable review questions, and completing the applications exercises, you will be able to do the following:

1. **RECORD** transactions affecting assets, liabilities, and owner's equity on a transaction sheet.
2. **PROVE** the arithmetical accuracy of a transaction sheet.
3. **PREPARE** a balance sheet from a completed transaction sheet.

INTRODUCING TRANSACTIONS

The balance sheet for Malibu Gym was prepared on July 1, 2001. Events will occur in the business after this date that will change the value of the balance sheet items. For example, customers will pay the remainder owing on their memberships, equipment will be purchased for the business, and payments will be made to creditors. All of these events are examples of transactions.

A business transaction is an exchange of things of value.

A *transaction* is an event occurring during the operation of a business which results in a financial change. A business transaction always includes an exchange of things of value:

Transaction

Something of value is given ⟷ Something of value is received

The balance sheet provides a detailed picture of the financial position on a certain date. This same information is presented in summary form by the accounting equation:

Assets = Liabilities + Owner's Equity

To assist in the examination of transactions and their effect on the balance sheet, a *transaction analysis sheet* will be used. This places the balance sheet items in equation form in order to more easily examine the effect of transactions on these items as well as on the equation. Transaction analysis sheets are not used in business, but the technique of analysis developed by their use will be useful throughout your career.

A number of common transactions will be analyzed and recorded for Malibu Gym. This example will begin with the information found on the July 1, 2001 balance sheet; it will conclude with the preparation of a new balance sheet at the end of this accounting period. The term "accounting period" refers to the length of time between the preparation of financial reports. This time varies from monthly to annually, depending on many factors such as business size and current need for the data contained in the reports.

The accounting period is the period of time covered by financial statements.

USING A TRANSACTION ANALYSIS SHEET

The first step in preparing a transaction analysis sheet is to restate the balance sheet in balance sheet equation form on the transaction analysis sheet. Figure 1-3 below shows the July 1 balance sheet for Malibu Gym.

FIGURE 1-3
July 1 balance sheet

Malibu Gym
Balance Sheet
July 1, 2001

Assets		Liabilities	
Cash	$ 5 000	Accounts Payable	$ 4 000
Accounts Receivable	6 000	Bank Loan	65 000
Office Supplies	500	Mortgage Payable	80 000
Land	25 000	Total Liabilities	149 000
Building	110 000		
Training Equipment	94 500	**Owner's Equity**	
		O'Brien, Capital	92 000
Total Assets	$241 000	Total Liabilities and Owner's Equity	$241 000

Figure 1-4 on page 17 is a transaction analysis sheet containing the opening balance information. Notice that the left side contains the assets and the right side the liabilities plus owner's equity.

The following transactions will cause changes in items on the balance sheet:

Jul. 1 Purchased new training equipment for $4 000 cash.
5 Bought office supplies for $55, on credit, from Central Supply Co.
10 Received $4 000 cash from customers (various accounts receivable) who owed money.

These transactions must now be analyzed to determine the changes in value caused to the items on the balance sheet. The changes will then be recorded on the transaction analysis sheet.

Transaction Analysis

Transaction 1: Asset Purchased for Cash

Jul. 1 Purchased new training equipment for $4 000 cash.

The following questions are asked to assist in analyzing a transaction:

(a) Which items change in value as a result of the transaction?
(b) How much do the items change?
(c) Do the items increase or decrease in value?
(d) After the change is recorded, is the equation still in balance?

In the first transaction, *Training Equipment* and *Cash* will change. Training Equipment will increase since the company now owns more equipment. Cash will *decrease* by $4 000 since the company has spent money. Notice how these changes are shown on the transaction analysis sheet in Figure 1-5 on page 17. After the transaction is recorded, the total assets ($241 000) still equal the liabilities plus owner's equity ($241 000).

Transaction 2: Asset Purchased on Credit

Jul. 5 Bought office supplies for $55, on credit, from Central Supply Co.

Which items on the balance sheet change? Do they increase or decrease? If you said the asset, *Office Supplies, increases* by $55 and the liability, *Accounts Payable*, also *increases* by $55, you were correct. Look at how this transaction is recorded on the transaction analysis sheet in Figure 1-6. Is the equation still in balance? If you add up the asset balances after the second transaction, you will get a total of $241 055. The liabilities and owner's equity now total $241 055. The equation is still in balance.

Transaction 3: Cash Received from Customers

Jul. 10 Received $4 000 cash from customers (various accounts receivable) who owed money.

Which items change? Do they increase or decrease? Look at Figure 1-7 to see how this transaction is recorded. Is the equation still in balance?

Additional Transactions

Look at the next four transactions. For each of them, ask yourself which items change. Do they increase or decrease?

Jul. 15 Sold some unused equipment for $400 cash.
18 Paid $375 cash to Central Supply Co. in payment of an account payable that had become due.
21 Owner invested an additional $1 800 cash in the business.
25 Purchased equipment from Niagara Sport Ltd. at a cost of $3 000. Of the total price, $2 000 was paid in cash and $1 000 will be paid in 30 days.

Now look at Figure 1-8, on page 18, and follow the recording of each of these transactions. Note that the final transaction involves changes in three items.

PREPARING A NEW BALANCE SHEET

The completed transaction analysis sheet now contains the changes caused by the July transactions. The equation is still in balance; that is, the total of the left side equals the total of the right side. The new balances are used when the new balance sheet is prepared on July 31, 2001. Figure 1-9 below shows the July 31 balance sheet.

FIGURE 1-9
July 31 balance sheet

Malibu Gym
Balance Sheet
July 31, 2001

Assets		Liabilities	
Cash	$ 4 825	Accounts Payable	$ 4 680
Accounts Receivable	2 000	Bank Loan	65 000
Office Supplies	555	Mortgage Payable	80 000
Land	25 000	Total Liabilities	149 680
Building	110 000		
Training Equipment	101 100	**Owner's Equity**	
		O'Brien, Capital	93 800
Total Assets	$243 480	Total Liabilities and Owner's Equity	$243 480

FIGURE 1-4
Transaction analysis sheet – opening balances

	ASSETS						=	LIABILITIES			+	OWNER'S EQUITY
	Cash	Accts. Rec.	Off. Supps.	Land	Bldg.	Train. Equip.		Accts. Pay.	Bank Loan	Mtge. Pay.		O'Brien, Capital
Bal.	$5 000	$6 000	$500	$25 000	$110 000	$94 500	=	$4 000	$65 000	$80 000	+	$92 000

FIGURE 1-5
Transaction analysis sheet – July 1 transaction

	ASSETS						=	LIABILITIES			+	OWNER'S EQUITY
	Cash	Accts. Rec.	Off. Supps.	Land	Bldg.	Train. Equip.		Accts. Pay.	Bank Loan	Mtge. Pay.		O'Brien, Capital
Bal.	$5 000	$6 000	$500	$25 000	$110 000	$94 500	=	$4 000	$65 000	$80 000	+	$92 000
Jul. 1	–4 000					+4 000						
New Bal.	1 000	6 000	500	25 000	110 000	98 500	=	4 000	65 000	80 000	+	92 000

FIGURE 1-6
Transaction analysis sheet – July 5 transaction

	ASSETS						=	LIABILITIES			+	OWNER'S EQUITY
	Cash	Accts. Rec.	Off. Supps.	Land	Bldg.	Train. Equip.		Accts. Pay.	Bank Loan	Mtge. Pay.		O'Brien, Capital
Bal.	$5 000	$6 000	$500	$25 000	$110 000	$94 500	=	$4 000	$65 000	$80 000	+	$92 000
Jul. 1	–4 000					+4 000						
New Bal.	1 000	6 000	500	25 000	110 000	98 500	=	4 000	65 000	80 000	+	92 000
Jul. 5			+55					+55				
New Bal.	1 000	6 000	555	25 000	110 000	98 500	=	4 055	65 000	80 000	+	92 000

FIGURE 1-7
Transaction analysis sheet July 10 transaction

	ASSETS						=	LIABILITIES			+ OWNER'S EQUITY
	Cash	Accts. Rec.	Off. Supps.	Land	Bldg.	Train. Equip.		Accts. Pay.	Bank Loan	Mtge. Pay.	O'Brien, Capital
Bal.	$5 000	$6 000	$500	$25 000	$110 000	$94 500	=	$4 000	$65 000	$80 000	$92 000
Jul. 1	−4 000					+4 000					
New Bal.	1 000	6 000	500	25 000	110 000	98 500	=	4 000	65 000	80 000	92 000
Jul. 5			+55					+55			
New Bal.	1 000	6 000	555	25 000	110 000	98 500	=	4 055	65 000	80 000	92 000
Jul. 10	+4 000	−4 000									
New Bal.	5 000	2 000	555	25 000	110 000	98 500	=	4 055	65 000	80 000	92 000

FIGURE 1-8
Transaction analysis sheet July 15 25 transactions

	ASSETS						=	LIABILITIES			+ OWNER'S EQUITY
	Cash	Accts. Rec.	Off. Supps.	Land	Bldg.	Train. Equip.		Accts. Pay.	Bank Loan	Mtge. Pay.	O'Brien, Capital
Bal.	$5 000	$6 000	$500	$25 000	$110 000	$94 500	=	$4 000	$65 000	$80 000	$92 000
Jul. 1	−4 000					+4 000					
New Bal.	1 000	6 000	500	25 000	110 000	98 500	=	4 000	65 000	80 000	92 000
Jul. 5			+55					+55			
New Bal.	1 000	6 000	555	25 000	110 000	98 500	=	4 055	65 000	80 000	92 000
Jul. 10	+4 000	−4 000									
New Bal.	5 000	2 000	555	25 000	110 000	98 500	=	4 055	65 000	80 000	92 000
Jul. 15	+400					−400					
New Bal.	5 400	2 000	555	25 000	110 000	98 100	=	4 055	65 000	80 000	92 000
Jul. 18	−375							−375			
New Bal.	5 025	2 000	555	25 000	110 000	98 100	=	3 680	65 000	80 000	92 000
Jul. 21	+1 800										+1 800
New Bal.	6 825	2 000	555	25 000	110 000	98 100	=	3 680	65 000	80 000	92 800
Jul. 25	−2 000					+3 000		+1 000			
New Bal.	$4 825	$2 000	$555	$25 000	$110 000	101 100	=	$4 680	$65 000	$80 000	$93 800

$243 480 = $149 680 + $93 800

$243 480 = $243 480

ACCOUNTING TERMS

Accounting	The "language of business." The purpose of accounting is to provide accounting information for decision making.
Accounting Equation	Assets = Liabilities + Owner's Equity.
Accounting System	Organized method of performing accounting tasks.
Accounts Payable	Amount owed to suppliers of the business for the purchase of goods or services on credit.
Accounts Receivable	Total amount due from customers.
Assets	Resources or items of value owned by a business or person.
Balance Sheet	Financial statement that lists assets, liabilities, and owner's equity at a specific date.
Business Entity Concept	Each business should be considered as a separate unit or entity for the purpose of keeping accounting records.
Capital	Owner's net worth found in the Owner's Equity section of the balance sheet.
Cost Principle	Assets are recorded at the actual cost to the business.
Debtors	Persons or businesses that owe a business money as a result of purchasing goods or services on credit.
Entrepreneur	A person who organizes and operates a business.
Equities	Claims against the assets. Found on the right side of the balance sheet.
Financial Position	Listing of the assets, liabilities, and equity of a person or business.
Generally Accepted Accounting Principles	Consistent accounting rules published by the Canadian Institute of Chartered Accountants needed to prepare financial statements.
Liabilities	Debts or amounts owed to others by a business or person.
Liquidity	The order in which assets would likely be converted into cash.
Maturity Date Rule	Liabilities are listed on the balance sheet according to payment due date from most recent to longest term.
Owner's Equity	Difference between the assets and liabilities of a business.
Personal Equity	The difference between personal assets and personal liabilities.

REVIEW QUESTIONS

UNIT

1. Define the term "transaction."
2. What four questions are asked when analyzing a business transaction?
3. Define the term "accounting period."

PROBLEMS: APPLICATIONS

CHAPTER

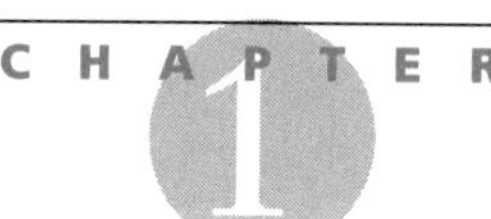

9. For each of the items listed below, give an example of a business transaction that will have the desired effect on the accounting equation:

   (a) Increase an asset and increase owner's equity
   (b) Increase an asset and decrease an asset
   (c) Increase an asset and increase a liability
   (d) Decrease an asset and decrease a liability
   (e) Increase a liability and decrease a liability

10. The June 30 balance sheet for Y. Bissonette Secretarial Service is shown below.

Yolanda Bissonette Secretarial Service Balance Sheet June 30, 2001			
Assets		**Liabilities**	
Cash	$ 4 500	Accounts Payable	$ 3 000
Accounts Receivable	5 000	Mortgage Payable	45 000
Office Supplies	6 000	Total Liabilities	48 000
Building	95 000	**Owner's Equity**	
		Y. Bissonette, Capital	62 500
Total Assets	$110 500	Total Liabilities and Owner's Equity	$110 500

The following transactions occurred in July:

July 4 Paid $800 cash on some accounts payable.

15 Received $1 200 cash from an account receivable.

20 Purchased office supplies for $1 000 on credit (payment is due in 30 days).

29 The owner, Y. Bissonette, invested an additional $2 500 in the business.

(a) Place the June 30 balances on a transaction sheet.
(b) Record the transactions on the transaction sheet. Follow the format of the transaction sheet in Figure 1-8. Be sure that the total assets equal the total liabilities and owner's equity after each transaction.
(c) In your study guide or notebook, complete the equation on July 31 following this format:
Assets $____ = Liabilities $____ + Owner's Equity $____
(d) Prepare a new balance sheet on July 31.

11. Mail-O-Matic Printing produces a variety of advertising materials such as brochures and flyers and distributes them door-to-door for retail stores. The March 1 balance sheet for Mail-O-Matic Printing and several transactions that occurred during March are given below.

(a) Complete a transaction sheet for Mail-O-Matic.
(b) Prepare a new balance sheet on March 31.

Mail-O-Matic Printing Balance Sheet March 1, 2001			
Assets		**Liabilities**	
Cash	$ 24 000	Accounts Payable	$ 16 500
Accounts Receivable	23 000	Bank Loan	20 000
Printing Supplies	18 900	Total Liabilities	36 500
Equipment	97 000	**Owner's Equity**	
		S. Zimic, Capital	126 400
Total Assets	$162 900	Total Liabilities and Owner's Equity	$162 900

Mar. 1 Purchased $850 worth of printing supplies from Cooper Products, on credit.

10 Some of the printing supplies bought on March 1 were damaged when received. Returned $150 worth of damaged supplies to Cooper for credit.

15 Paid $1 700 to Clear Chemicals Ltd., a supplier, to reduce balance owing.

26 Purchased a new $15 000 copier from Conway Manufacturers. A down payment of $3 000 cash was made, and the balance of $12 000 is to be paid later.

31 Made a $2 000 payment on the bank loan.

12. The following is the balance sheet for Fisher's Body Repairs as of September 1:

Fisher's Body Repairs
Balance Sheet
September 1, 2001

Assets		**Liabilities**	
Cash	$ 6 500	Accounts Payable	$ 3 400
Accounts Receivable	15 300	Bank Loan	1 500
Equipment	56 000	Total Liabilities	4 900
		Owner's Equity	
		L. Fisher, Capital	72 900
Total Assets	$77 800	Total Liabilities and Owner's Equity	$77 800

The following transactions took place during September:

Sept. 3 Received $650 cash from K. Bell, a customer.

4 Purchased a new $1 500 air compressor from K.D. Manufacturers, on credit.

5 Borrowed $2 000 cash from bank.

8 Paid $800 to General Auto Parts, a supplier, to pay off some of the balance owing to them.

15 Made a $600 cash payment on the bank loan.

20 The owner, L. Fisher, invested a further $3 000 in the business.

(a) Prepare a transaction sheet for Fisher's Body Repairs and record the transactions.

(b) After the last transaction has been recorded, prepare the accounting equation to prove the accuracy of your work.

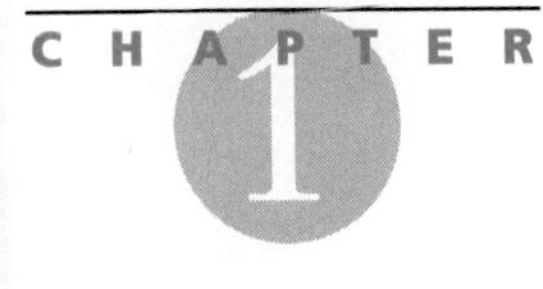

1. The completed transaction sheet for Metro Cleaners is on page 23. For (a) to (f), describe the transactions that must have occurred in the business to produce the changes shown on the transaction sheet.

   Example:

   (a) Cash increased by $500 as a result of the collection of $500 from a customer (an account receivable).

2. At first glance, the following balance sheet for Dart Company may appear to be correct, but it has several major and minor errors.

   (a) List the errors.
   (b) Prepare a correct balance sheet.

Dart Company December 31, 2001			
Assets		**Liabilities**	
Cash	$ 3 500	Bank Loan	$ 44 400
Truck	10 600	Accounts Payable	3 600
Building	152 000		
Less Mortgage	76 000		
Land	42 300		
Equipment	5 100	Dart Co. Capital	89 500
	$137 500		$137 500

3. There are several mistakes in the set-up and content of this balance sheet. Can you locate them?

M. Mancini & Company Balance Sheet March 31, 2001			
Assets		**Liabilities**	
Cash	2 000	Accounts Receivable	3 000
Accounts Payable	2 000	Equipment	6 000
Supplies	1 000	Bank Loan	30 000
Building	90 000	Total Liabilities	39 000
		Owner's Equity	
		M. Mancini, Capital	68 000
Total Assets	95 000	Total Liabilities and Owner's Equity	106 000

	ASSETS									=	LIABILITIES			+	OWNER'S EQUITY
	Cash		Accts. Rec.		Clean. Equip.		Bldg.		Land		Accts. Pay.		Mtge. Pay.		Kitt, Capital
Bal.	$5 000	+	$2 000	+	$7 500	+	$42 000	+	$18 000	=	$750	+	$38 000	+	$35 750
(a)	+500		−500												
New bal.	5 500	+	1 500	+	7 500	+	42 000	+	18 000	=	750	+	38 000	+	35 750
(b)	−700				+1 500						+800				
New bal.	4 800	+	1 500	+	9 000	+	42 000	+	18 000	=	1 550	+	38 000	+	35 750
(c)	+2 000														+2 000
New bal.	6 800	+	1 500	+	9 000	+	42 000	+	18 000	=	1 550	+	38 000	+	37 750
(d)	−800										−800				
New bal.	6 000	+	1 500	+	9 000	+	42 000	+	18 000	=	750	+	38 000	+	37 750
(e)	+300		+700		−1 000										
New bal.	6 300	+	2 200	+	8 000	+	42 000	+	18 000	=	750	+	38 000	+	37 750
(f)	−2 000												−2 000		
New bal.	4 300	+	2 200	+	8 000	+	42 000	+	18 000	=	750	+	36 000	+	37 750

CHAPTER 2

Balance Sheet Accounts

UNIT 3 Recording Transactions in T-Accounts

Learning Objectives

After reading this unit, discussing the applicable review questions, and completing the applications exercises, you will be able to do the following:

1. **RECORD** the opening balances on a balance sheet in a T-account ledger.
2. **ANALYZE** transactions to determine which accounts are changed and whether the changes are recorded as debits or credits.
3. **RECORD** transactions in T-accounts.
4. **CALCULATE** the balances in accounts.
5. **PREPARE** a trial balance to verify the mathematical accuracy of the ledger.
6. **PREPARE** a balance sheet from the trial balance.

INTRODUCING T-ACCOUNTS

Transaction analysis sheets were used in Chapter 1 to demonstrate the process of analysis necessary to record changes in the balance sheet items caused by business transactions. In actual practice, the use of a transaction analysis sheet is impractical due to the large number of financial events occurring each day in a business. A more efficient method of collecting, recording, and summarizing these events is to keep a separate record of the changes for each item. This record is called an *account*. In order to introduce the concepts and practices involved in recording data in accounts, a simplified form of this record, called a T-account, will be used in this chapter.

An account is a form in which changes caused by transactions are recorded.

For every item on the balance sheet, an account is prepared. As transactions occur, the changes that happen as a result of these transactions are recorded in accounts. Following is an example of a T-account. It is shaped like a "T" and has two sides just like a balance sheet prepared in account format:

Account Title	
Left Side	Right Side
Debit	Credit

Debit is the accounting term used for the *left side* of the account. *Credit* is the accounting term used for the *right side* of the account. Following is an account used to record transactions involving cash. It has a debit (left) side and a credit (right) side. One side is used to record increases in cash, that is, money received, and the other side is used to record decreases in cash, that is, money paid out.

Debit refers to the left side of an account. Credit refers to the right side of an account.

Cash	
Debit	Credit

T-accounts are not needed in business but are often used by accountants for their rough work when analyzing transactions. They are used at this time to introduce a number of basic accounting procedures and concepts.

On the next few pages, we will examine the use of accounts by recording transactions for Malibu Gym. As a first step, look again at the July 31 balance sheet for Malibu Gym shown in Figure 2-1.

Recording Balances in Accounts

A separate account is required for each asset, for each liability, and for the owner's equity on the balance sheet. For Malibu Gym, ten accounts are required because there are six assets, three liabilities, and one equity account. These ten accounts are shown a little further ahead in Figure 2-2 on page 27. The beginning amounts on the balance sheet are called *balances*. For each item on the balance sheet, the balance is recorded in a T-account. The Cash account is shown on page 27 after the beginning balance has been recorded. Since Cash appears on the left side of the balance sheet, the beginning balance for cash is recorded on the left side of the Cash account. This rule applies to all asset accounts.

There is a separate account for each asset and liability and for the owner's equity.

Asset balances are recorded on the left side of asset accounts.

FIGURE 2-1
July 31 balance sheet

Malibu Gym Balance Sheet July 31, 2001			
Assets		**Liabilities**	
Cash	$ 4 825	Accounts Payable	$ 4 680
Accounts Receivable	2 000	Bank Loan	65 000
Office Supplies	555	Mortgage Payable	80 000
Land	25 000	Total Liabilities	149 680
Building	110 000		
Training Equipment	101 100	**Owner's Equity**	
		O'Brien Capital	93 800
		Total Liabilities	
Total Assets	$243 480	and Owner's Equity	$243 480

Since assets are located on the left side of the balance sheet, the beginning balance of an asset is recorded on the left or debit side of its account.

Cash			
Jul. 31	4 825		

Liability balances are recorded on the right side of liability accounts.

Since liabilities are located on the right side of the balance sheet, the opening balance of a liability account is placed on the credit (right) side of the liability account. For the same reason, the opening balance for the owner's equity account is placed on the credit side of its account. This rule applies to all liability and owner's equity accounts.

Since liabilities and owner's equity are located on the right side of the balance sheet, their opening balances are recorded on the credit or right side of their accounts.

INTRODUCING LEDGERS

A ledger is a group of accounts.

A ledger is the place where the accounts are found. It may be in the form of a book containing pages for each account in a manual accounting system, or stored on disk or tape for computerized accounting systems. The accounts in the ledger are designed to collect the data concerning changes in value of each item on the balance sheet on an individual basis.

Opening the Ledger

The balance sheet shown on page 27 can be visualized as a large "T" with the assets on the left and the liabilities and owner's equity on the right. This will help you remember that asset accounts normally have debit balances (balances shown on the left side of the T-account), while liabilities and owner's equity accounts have credit balances (balançes shown on the right side of the T-account).

In order to open the ledger, these steps should be followed:

- Place the account name in the middle of each account.
- Record the date and balance from the balance sheet in the account on the appropriate side.

The ledger for Malibu Gym is shown in Figure 2-2 on page 27. A separate account has been opened for each item on the balance sheet.

Left Side		Right Side	
Assets		**Liabilities**	
Cash	$ 4 825	Accounts Payable	$ 4 680
Accounts Receivable	2 000	Bank Loan	65 000
Office Supplies	555	Mortgage Payable	80 000
Land	25 000	Total Liabilities	149 680
Building	110 000		
Training Equipment	101 100	**Owner's Equity**	
		O'Brien, Capital	93 800
Total Assets	$243 480	Total Liabilities and Owner's Equity	$243 480

Now let's analyze Figure 2-2. Since assets are found on the left side of the balance sheet, the value of each asset account has been recorded on the left or debit side of the account. Since liabilities are found on the right side of the balance sheet, the value of each liability account has been recorded on the right or credit side of the account. Since owner's equity is found on the right side of the balance sheet, the value of the owner's equity account has been recorded on the right or credit side of the account.

Total of debit balances must equal total of credit balances. Note that if the debit balances are added together, they equal the total of the credit balances.

Debits:

$4 825 + $2 000 + $555 + $25 000 + $110 000 + $101 100 = $243 480

Credits:

$4 680 + $65 000 + $80 000 + $93 800 = $243 480

This is known as having the ledger in balance. This relationship must continue as transactions are recorded, in keeping with the important principle of double-entry accounting.

Cash			
Jul. 31	4 825		

Accounts Receivable			
Jul. 31	2 000		

Office Supplies			
Jul. 31	555		

Land			
Jul. 31	25 000		

Building			
Jul. 31	110 000		

Training Equipment			
Jul. 31	101 100		

Accounts Payable			
		Jul. 31	4 680

Bank Loan			
		Jul. 31	65 000

Mortgage Payable			
		Jul. 31	80 000

O'Brien, Capital			
		Jul. 31	93 800

FIGURE 2-2
Ledger for Malibu Gym showing balances in each account

Double-Entry Accounting

One of the most important principles of accounting is the *double-entry principle*. For each transaction, a debit amount equal to a credit amount must be recorded in the accounts. Thus, all transactions are recorded in one or more accounts as a debit and in one or more accounts as a credit. The total of the debit amounts must always equal the total of the credit amounts for each transaction.

Double-entry accounting requires a debit amount equal to the credit amount for each transaction.

RECORDING TRANSACTIONS IN ACCOUNTS

These steps are followed in analyzing transactions and recording them in accounts:

- **Step 1:** Determine *which* accounts change in value as a result of the transaction. Note that two or more accounts will change in value as a result of each transaction.
- **Step 2:** Identify the *type of account* that has changed. Is the account that has changed an asset, a liability, or an owner's equity account?
- **Step 3:** Decide whether the change is an *increase* or a *decrease* in the account.
- **Step 4:** Decide whether the change is recorded as a *debit* or a *credit* in the account. Note that the ledger must remain in balance.

The following transactions for Malibu Gym occurred during August 2001. These transactions will be analyzed and entered in the ledger to illustrate how the four steps described previously are followed. As you read the examples, note that each transaction has a debit amount that is equal to the credit amount. Note also that the debit portion of the entry is always shown before the credit portion.

Transaction Analysis

Transaction 1

Aug. 2 Received $500 cash from members as payments on memberships.

Assets increase on the debit side.

The two accounts that are affected are Cash and Accounts Receivable. The Cash account is increased with a debit for the following reasons:

- Cash is an asset.
- The asset Cash is increasing (money has been received).
- Assets are found on the left side of the balance sheet and increase on their debit (left) side.

The $500 increase is recorded in the Cash account as illustrated below:

Cash

Jul. 31	4 825		
Aug. 2	500		

Assets decrease on the credit side.

The asset, Accounts Receivable, is also affected. The balance for this asset decreases because customers have paid some of the amount owing by them. An account *decreases* on the side *opposite* to its opening balance. The decrease in Accounts Receivable is recorded as a credit, as shown below:

Accounts Receivable

Jul. 31	2 000	Aug. 2	500

Here is a summary of how this transaction was recorded:

ACCOUNT AFFECTED	TYPE OF ACCOUNT	INCREASE/DECREASE	DEBIT/CREDIT	
Cash	Asset	Increase	Debit	$500
Accounts Receivable	Asset	Decrease	Credit	500

Notice that in recording the transaction, there is a debit of $500 and a credit of $500. A general rule for recording transactions can now be stated:

Accounts increase on the same side as they appear on the balance sheet and they decrease on the opposite side.

Following are four specific statements based on this general rule:

(1) If assets increase, the amount is recorded on the debit side.
(2) If assets decrease, the amount is recorded on the credit side.
(3) If liabilities or owner's equity increases, the amount is recorded on the credit side.
(4) If liabilities or owner's equity decreases, the amount is recorded on the debit side.

Transaction 2

Aug. 5 Purchased $25 worth of office supplies from a creditor, Central Supply Co., with 30 days to pay.

Which accounts are changed by this transaction? What type of accounts are they? Do they increase or decrease, and are they debited or credited to record the changes? The answers to these questions will help you to understand how this transaction is recorded.

The asset account Office Supplies increases because the company now has more supplies. Assets are found on the left side of the balance sheet; therefore, the increase in supplies is recorded on the debit (left) side of the Office Supplies account.

The company now owes more money to an account payable. Therefore, the liability account Accounts Payable increases. Since liabilities are found on the right side of the balance sheet, the liability Accounts Payable increases on the credit (right) side. The transaction is shown recorded in the accounts below:

Liabilities increase on the credit side.

Office Supplies			Accounts Payable		
Jul. 31	555			Jul. 31	4 680
Aug.5	25			Aug.5	25

Here is a summary of how this transaction was recorded:

ACCOUNT AFFECTED	TYPE OF ACCOUNT	INCREASE/DECREASE	DEBIT/CREDIT	
Office Supplies	Asset	Increase	Debit	$25
Accounts Payable	Liability	Increase	Credit	25

An asset increased by $25 and was debited. A liability increased by $25 and was credited. There was a debit of $25 and an equal credit of $25.

Transaction 3

Aug. 5 Paid $705 now due to Equipment Unlimited for goods previously purchased but not paid for.

Can you determine which account is debited? Which account is credited? The asset Cash decreases because money was paid out. Assets decrease on the credit side; therefore Cash is credited.

Liabilities decrease on the debit side.

The liability Accounts Payable also decreases because less money is now owed to the creditor. Liabilities decrease on the debit side; therefore, Accounts Payable is debited. This transaction is shown in the accounts below.

Accounts Payable

Debit		Credit	
Aug. 5	705	Jul. 31	4 680
		Aug. 5	25

Cash

Debit		Credit	
Jul. 31	4 825	Aug. 5	705
Aug. 2	500		

Here is a summary of how this transaction was recorded:

ACCOUNT AFFECTED	TYPE OF ACCOUNT	INCREASE/DECREASE	DEBIT/CREDIT	
Accounts Payable	Liability	Decrease	Debit	$705
Cash	Asset	Decrease	Credit	705

An asset decreased by $705 and was credited. A liability decreased by $705 and was debited. Therefore, the ledger remains in balance. The total of the debits will still equal the total of the credits.

Transaction 4

*Aug. 7 **Purchased three new exercycles for $545 each (total of $1 635). Cash down payment of $535 made. Remaining amount ($1 100) to be paid at a later date.***

This transaction involves changes in three accounts. They are the assets Cash and Training Equipment and the liability Accounts Payable. Can you determine the debits and credits?

Training Equipment increases by $1 635. Cash decreases by $535. Accounts Payable increases by the amount still owing, $1 100. This is how the transactions are recorded in the accounts:

Training Equipment

Debit		Credit	
Jul. 31	101 100		
Aug. 7	1 635		

Cash

Debit		Credit	
Jul. 31	4 825	Aug. 5	705
Aug. 2	500	7	535

Accounts Payable

Debit		Credit	
Aug. 5	705	Jul. 31	4 680
		Aug.5	25
		7	1 100

Here is a summary of how this transaction was recorded:

ACCOUNT AFFECTED	TYPE OF ACCOUNT	INCREASE/DECREASE	DEBIT/CREDIT	
Training Equipment	Asset	Increase	Debit	$1 635
Cash	Asset	Decrease	Credit	535
Accounts Payable	Liability	Increase	Credit	1 1000

Remember that assets are recorded at cost price whether or not they are fully paid for at the time of purchase. The asset increase of $1 635 (debit) is balanced by an asset decrease of $535 (credit) and a liability increase of $1 100 (credit). Therefore, the ledger remains balanced. The total debits are equal to the total credits.

Transaction 5

*Aug. 7 **Owner invested an additional $5 000 in the business.***

This transaction causes the company's cash to increase. It also causes the owner's equity to increase because the business is now worth more. The two accounts that change, Cash and O'Brien, Capital, are shown on the following page.

Cash

Jul. 31	4 825	Aug. 5	705
Aug. 2	500	7	535
7	5 000		

O'Brien, Capital

		Jul. 31	93 800
		Aug. 7	5 000

Here is a summary of how this transaction was recorded:

ACCOUNT AFFECTED	TYPE OF ACCOUNT	INCREASE/DECREASE	DEBIT/CREDIT	
Cash	Asset	Increase	Debit	$5 000
O'Brien, Capital	Owner's Equity	Increase	Credit	5 000

Note that the proprietor's investment of additional cash increases the owner's equity. The company's Cash account increases by $5 000 (debit), and this is balanced by the owner's equity account increase of $5 000 (credit). Therefore, the ledger remains in balance.

CALCULATING NEW BALANCES IN THE ACCOUNTS

The accounts in the ledger of Malibu Gym now contain the opening balances from the July 31, 2001 balance sheet plus entries to record changes in value of these accounts up to Aug. 7, 2001. In order to determine the new balance in the accounts, the following calculations are made for each account:

(1) Add up the debit side of the account.
(2) Add up the credit side of the account.
(3) Subtract the smaller amount from the larger and place the answer on the larger side of the account. This is the new balance for the account. Two examples are provided on below:

The difference between the two sides of an account is called the account balance.

Cash

Jul. 31	4 825	Aug. 5	705
Aug. 2	500	7	535
7	5 000		1 240 ← **Credit Total**
Debit Total →	10 325		
Balance	9 085		

Accounts Payable

Aug. 5	705 ← **Debit Total**	Jul. 31	4 680
		Aug. 5	25
		7	1 100
		Credit Total →	5 805
		Balance	5 100

The account balance is placed on the side of the account with the highest total.

Note that the final balance in the Cash account was placed on the debit side and the Accounts Payable balance was placed on the credit side. The balances are always placed on the side of the account that has the larger total. For assets, this is usually the debit side; for liabilities and owner's equity, this is usually the credit side. The ledger for Malibu Gym would appear as shown in Figure 2-3 after the August 7 balances have been calculated for all of the accounts.

FIGURE 2-3
Ledger for Malibu Gym with balances calculated in each account

Cash

Jul. 31	4 825	Aug. 5	705
Aug. 2	500	7	535
7	5 000		1 240
	10 325		
Balance	9 085		

Accounts Payable

Aug. 5	705	Jul. 31	4 680
		Aug. 5	25
		7	1 100
			5 805
		Balance	5 100

Accounts Receivable

Jul. 31	2 000	Aug. 2	500
Balance		1 500	

Bank Loan

		Jul. 31	65 000
		Balance	65 000

Office Supplies

Jul. 31	555		
Aug. 5	25		
Balance	580		

Mortgage Payable

		Jul. 31	80 000
		Balance	80 000

Land

Jul. 31	25 000		
Balance		25 000	

O'Brien, Capital

		Jul. 31	93 800
		Aug. 7	5 000
		Balance	98 800

Building

Jul. 31	110 000		
Balance	110 000		

Training Equipment

Jul. 31	101 100		
Aug. 7	1 635		
Balance	102 735		

PREPARING A TRIAL BALANCE

A trial balance is a list of the ledger account balances. The total of the debit balances should equal the total of the credit balances.

In order to prove the mathematical accuracy of our calculations, a trial balance is prepared to verify that the total debits are still equal to the total credits in the ledger. The trial balance is a list of all of the accounts with their current balances. They are listed in the order that they appear in the ledger. Two columns are required to prepare the trial balance. The first column is used to record the debit balances and the second column is used to record the credit balances. Since the trial balance is used within the business, it is an informal statement compared to the balance sheet, which is considered to be a formal financial statement. Because the trial balance is an informal statement, it is possible to use abbreviations. However, the statement should still be prepared as neatly as possible.

The trial balance for Malibu Gym, dated August 7, 2001, is shown in Figure 2-4. The format for the trial balance is as follows:

Heading

Line 1: Who? — Malibu Gym
Line 2: What? — Trial Balance
Line 3: When? — August 7, 2001

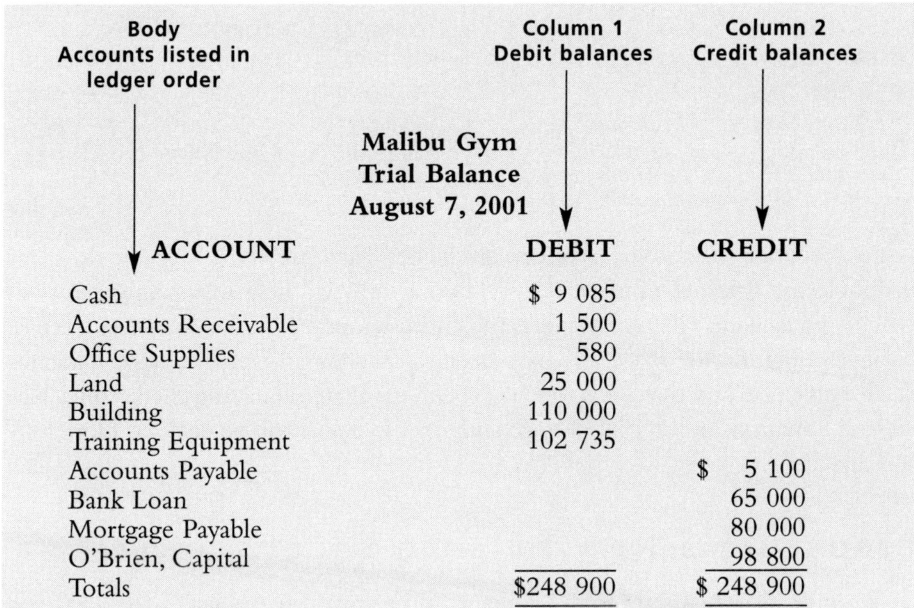

Malibu Gym
Trial Balance
August 7, 2001

ACCOUNT	DEBIT	CREDIT
Cash	$ 9 085	
Accounts Receivable	1 500	
Office Supplies	580	
Land	25 000	
Building	110 000	
Training Equipment	102 735	
Accounts Payable		$ 5 100
Bank Loan		65 000
Mortgage Payable		80 000
O'Brien, Capital		98 800
Totals	$248 900	$ 248 900

FIGURE 2-4
Trial balance for Malibu Gym

Limitations of the Trial Balance

The trial balance simply indicates the mathematical accuracy of the ledger. It shows that the total debits equal the total credits. It verifies that a debit amount was recorded for each credit amount; that is, that the principle of double-entry accounting was followed. However, the trial balance does not indicate if the wrong accounts were used in recording a transaction.

If, for example, the first transaction given in this unit was recorded incorrectly by reversing the debit and credit, the error would not be discovered on a trial balance. In that first transaction, $500 cash was received from members who owed Malibu Gym payments on their memberships. The transaction was analyzed correctly as:

Cash	Debit	$ 500
Accounts Receivable	Credit	500

If this was mistakenly recorded as:

Accounts Receivable	Debit	$ 500
Cash	Credit	500

the error would not be discovered on a trial balance.

Examine the two accounts involved as they are shown below. The Aug. 2 entry for $500 is incorrectly recorded as a credit in the Cash account. It is also incorrectly recorded as a debit in Accounts Receivable:

Cash

Jul. 31	4 825	Aug. 2	500*
Aug. 7	5 000	5	705
	9 825	7	535
			1 740
Balance	8 085		

Accounts Receivable

Jul. 31	2 000	
Aug. 2	500*	
Balance	2 500	

*Incorrect entry

The $8 085 balance of the Cash account is $1 000 too low. The $2 500 balance of the Accounts Receivable account is $1 000 too high. However, the trial balance will balance mathematically because the errors offset each other. The totals on the trial balance are the same but two accounts are incorrect. Here is a summary:

REFERENCE	CORRECT BALANCE	INCORRECT BALANCE	DIFFERENCE
Cash account	$ 9 085	$ 8 085	–$1 000
Accounts Receivable account	1 500	2 500	+ 1 000
Trial balance	$248 900	$248 900	No change

Note that when the amount is placed on the opposite side in the account, the error is double the original amount. Remembering this will help in locating errors, as will be discussed in Chapter 4. It is sufficient to remember at this time that the trial balance only indicates that there have been equal debit and credit entries made for each transaction and that no errors have been made in calculating the account balances. Limitations of the trial balance and error location will be covered more fully in Chapter 4.

Preparing a New Balance Sheet

To provide a formal statement of financial position on August 7, 2001, a new balance sheet, as prepared from the information contained in the trial balance, is shown in Figure 2-5:

FIGURE 2-5
August 7 balance sheet

Malibu Gym
Balance Sheet
August 7, 2001

Assets		Liabilities	
Cash	$ 9 085	Accounts Payable	$ 5 100
Accounts Receivable	1 500	Bank Loan	65 000
Office Supplies	580	Mortgage Payable	80 000
Land	25 000	Total Liabilities	150 100
Building	110 000		
Training Equipment	102 735	**Owner's Equity**	
		O'Brien, Capital	98 800
Total Assets	$248 900	Total Liabilities and Owner's Equity	$248 900

SUMMARY OF DEBIT AND CREDIT THEORY

- Double-entry accounting requires that, in recording transactions, the total of the debit amounts must always equal the total of the credit amounts.
- Assets are located on the left side of the balance sheet. Asset accounts increase on the debit (left) side and decrease on the credit (right) side.
- Liabilities and owner's equity are located on the right side of the balance sheet. Liability and owner's equity accounts increase on the credit (right) side and decrease on the debit (left) side. These concepts, known as the rules of debit and credit, are summarized in the following chart:

Assets		=	Liabilities		+	Owner's Equity	
Debit	Credit		Debit	Credit		Debit	Credit
Increase	Decrease		Decrease	Increase		Decrease	Increase

- A trial balance proves the mathematical accuracy of the ledger. It does not indicate that transactions were all correctly recorded as debits and credits.

SUMMARY OF ACCOUNTING PROCEDURES

Figure 2-6 summarizes, in chart form, the important accounting procedures and concepts that have been covered in this chapter.

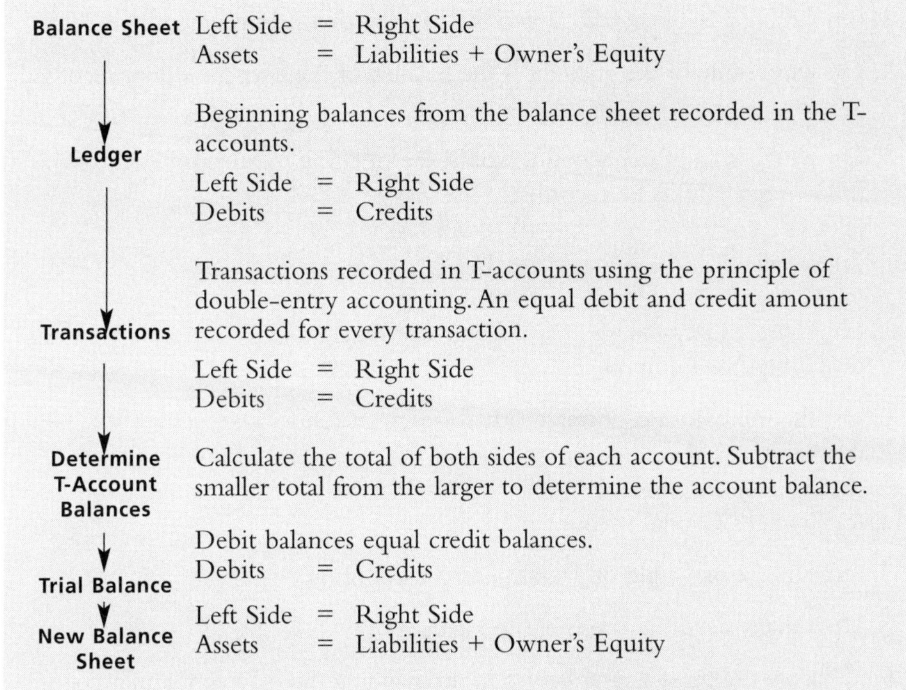

FIGURE 2-6
Summary of accounting procedures discussed in this chapter

ACCOUNTING TERMS

Account	A form in which changes caused by business transactions are recorded.
Account Balance	The difference between the debit and credit sides of an account.
Analyzing Transactions	Determining which accounts are debited and credited in order to record transactions.
Asset Accounts	Accounts found in the asset section of the balance sheet.
Balance Sheet Accounts	A separate account is required for each asset, liability, and owner's equity on the balance sheet.
Credit	Right side of an account.
Debit	Left side of an account.
Double-Entry Accounting	All transactions are recorded in one or more accounts as a debit and one or more accounts as a credit. The total debit amount must equal the total credit amount.
Ledger	A group of accounts. It may be found in various forms such as a book, computer, tape, or disk.
Liability Accounts	Accounts found in the liability section of the balance sheet.
Open the Ledger	Enter the balances as shown on the balance sheet in the accounts found in the ledger.
Owner's Equity Accounts	Accounts found in the owner's equity section of the balance sheet.
T-Account	A T-shaped account.
Trial Balance	A list of ledger account balances. The total of the debit balances should equal the total of the credit balances. This indicates the mathematical accuracy of the ledger.

REVIEW QUESTIONS

UNIT 3

1. What is the meaning of each of the following?
   (a) Account
   (b) Debit
   (c) Credit
   (d) Ledger
2. On which side of the account is the balance of an asset recorded? Why?
3. On which side of the account is the balance of a liability recorded? Why?
4. On which side of the account is the balance of the owner's equity recorded? Why?
5. On which side of the account would the opening balance for each of the following accounts be recorded?
   (a) Cash
   (b) Supplies
   (c) Mortgage Payable
   (d) Accounts Payable
   (e) Computer Equipment
   (f) Bank Loan
   (g) Land
   (h) Building
   (i) Delivery Truck
   (j) Owner, Capital
6. List the increase and decrease side for each of the following:
   (a) Asset account
   (b) Liability account
   (c) Owner's Capital account
7. Explain the principle of double-entry accounting.
8. How many accounts are there in a ledger?
9. What are the three steps followed in determining the balance for an account?
10. (a) What is a trial balance?
    (b) What does a trial balance indicate?

PROBLEMS: APPLICATIONS

CHAPTER 2

1. The April 1 balance sheet for the New San Juan Restaurant is shown below.
   (a) Open accounts in a ledger for each of the assets and liabilities and for the owner's equity. You will need seven T-accounts.
   (b) Record the April 1 balances in the accounts.

New San Juan Restaurant
Balance Sheet
April 1, 2001

Assets		Liabilities	
Cash	$ 4 000	Accounts Payable	$ 16 000
Supplies	10 000	Mortgage Payable	83 000
Building	200 000	Total Liabilities	99 000
Equipment	50 000		
		Owner's Equity	
		G. Alvarez, Capital	165 000
Total Assets	$264 000	Total Liabilities and Owner's Equity	$264 000

2. High-Rise Cleaners has contracts to wash the windows of large office buildings. Using the information from their balance sheet, set up accounts and record the opening balances.

High-Rise Cleaners
Balance Sheet
May 1, 2001

Assets		**Liabilities**	
Cash	$12 500	Accounts Payable	$ 2 700
Cleaning Supplies	4 400	Bank Loan	6 300
Equipment	15 000	Total Liabilities	9 000
Truck	28 500		
		Owner's Equity	
		B. Hill, Capital	51 400
Total Assets	$60 400	Total Liabilities and Owner's Equity	$60 400

3. Calculate the balance for each of the following accounts using the procedure shown on page 31.

Cash

1 800	250
400	750
2 000	

Accounts Receivable

2 000	500
4 200	350
1 800	50

Accounts Payable

300	300
	450
	75

4. Bradley Air Service provides aviator training and leases or rents aircraft. The transactions on the following page occurred during the first week of November. Analyze each transaction using the format indicated in the example. List the debit part of the entry before the credit part.

Example:

TRANSACTION	ACCOUNT AFFECTED	TYPE OF ACCOUNT	INCREASE/ DECREASE	DEBIT/CREDIT
Nov. 1	Bank Loan	Liability	Decrease	Debit $600
	Cash	Asset	Decrease	Credit 600

Nov. 1 Made the regular monthly payment of $600 on the bank loan.

2 Purchased a new air pump from Cadence Industries for $1 700, payment to be made later.

4 Secured a further bank loan of $16 000 to pay for future purchases of aircraft.

5 Purchased a new aircraft worth $24 000 from Airways Manufacturing by paying a $14 000 down payment with the $10 000 balance to be paid later.

7 Received $3 500 cash from L. Rosewood, a customer.

5. (a) The New San Juan Restaurant had the following transactions to record during the first week of April. Analyze each transaction using the format indicated in this chapter. List the debit portion of the entry before the credit portion. The April 1 transaction is done for you as an example.

Apr. 1 Purchased a new oven from Restaurant Supplies for $1 780 on credit.

2 Made the regular monthly payment of $1 080 on the mortgage.

3 Paid $1 300 to reduce the balance owing to Wholesale Foods Limited.

5 Purchased a new table and four chairs from Owen Furniture for a $1 280 cash down payment and $320 due in 30 days.

6 Owner, G. Alvarez, invested an additional $6 000 cash in the business.

Example:

TRANSACTION	ACCOUNT AFFECTED	TYPE OF ACCOUNT	INCREASE/ DECREASE	DEBIT/CREDIT
Apr. 1	Equipment	Asset	Increase	Debit $1780
	Accounts Payable	Liability	Increase	Credit 1780

(b) Now record the Apr. 1–6 transactions in the ledger accounts prepared for exercise 1.
(c) Calculate the new balance for each of the accounts.
(d) Prepare a trial balance.

6. In the ledger you opened for High-Rise Cleaners in exercise 2:

(a) Record the following transactions.
(b) Prepare a trial balance on May 9, 2001.

May 4 Bought soap, towels, and other cleaning supplies for $550 cash.

6 Bought a new hoist for the scaffolds. The hoist is valued at $4 500. A down payment of $1 800 was made today with the remainder to be paid at a later date.

8 Cash of $1 800 was paid to the bank to reduce the bank loan.

9 Mr. Hill invested $2 500 of his personal savings in High-Rise Cleaners.

7. Clare's Beauty Salon has been in operation for a number of years. The March 1 balance sheet for the business is shown on the next page.

(a) Prepare T-accounts for Clare's Beauty Salon using the accounts and balances given in the March 1 balance sheet.

Clare's Beauty Salon
Balance Sheet
March 1, 2001

Assets		Liabilities	
Cash	$ 4 800	Accounts Payable	$ 800
Accounts Receivable	3 600	Bank Loan	2 700
Supplies	2 400	Mortgage Payable	88 000
Land	30 000	Total Liabilities	91 500
Building	90 000		
Equipment	40 000	**Owner's Equity**	
		C. Williams, Capital	79 300
		Total Liabilities	
Total Assets	$ 170 800	and Owner's Equity	$170 800

(a) Record the March transactions listed below in the accounts.
(b) Calculate the account balances and prepare a trial balance on March 7, 2001.

Mar. 2 Purchased shampoo, hair spray, etc., from Beauty Products, $300 on credit.

3 Received $75 credit for supplies purchased yesterday. Order incorrectly filled.

4 Received $2 500 cash from customers who paid their accounts.

4 Made the regular $700 payment on the mortgage.

5 Bought four hair dryers worth $12 000 from Beauty Products. The business made a $4 000 cash deposit on the dryers and the balance was to be paid later.

6 Obtained a bank loan of $10 000, part of which will be used to pay for the hair dryers.

7 Paid Beauty Products $9 025, payment in full of the amount owing to them.

8. Shirley Mullane, CGA, operates a single proprietorship offering a wide range of accounting services to her clients. The balance sheet for this firm on June 30 is shown below.

(a) Open a T-account ledger for Shirley Mullane Accounting Services using the accounts and balances provided in the June 30 balance sheet.
(b) Record the July transactions listed in the ledger.

Shirley Mullane Accounting Services
Balance Sheet
June 30, 2001

Assets		Liabilities	
Cash	$ 4 200	Accounts Payable	$ 3 750
Accounts Receivable	6 500	Taxes Payable	830
Office Supplies	2 700	Bank Loan	8 520
Land	25 500	Mortgage Payable	44 000
Building	75 000	Total Liabilities	57 100
Training Equipment	42 100	**Owner's Equity**	
		S. Mullane, Capital	98 900
		Total Liabilities	
Total Assets	$ 156 000	and Owner's Equity	$156 000

(c) Calculate the account balances and prepare a trial balance on July 7, 2001.

July 1 Received cheques from clients totalling $500 in the mail today in payment of amounts previously billed.

1 Made regular monthly payment of $220 on the bank loan.

2 Purchased a new computer system for the office from Computer Accounts Co. for $9 250. A down payment of $2 500 was made today, and the balance will be due in 30 days.

3 The owner, S. Mullane, invested an additional $2 500 in the business.

4 Paid $750 to various creditors to reduce balances owing to them.

5 Purchased additional supplies for the computer system for $600 cash.

5 Returned $75 worth of supplies for a cash refund since they were unsuitable.

6 The owner had recently purchased a laser printer for personal use. Since the firm required a similar piece of equipment, the owner decided to place this printer in the business on a permanent basis instead of buying another one for the business after incurring the expense of the computer system. The printer cost S. Mullane $1 800. (Note: This transaction represents an additional investment by the owner in the business.)

PROBLEMS: CHALLENGES

1. The following accounts contain a series of transactions for Disk Jockeys Unlimited. For each of the entries labelled (a) to (e), indicate how accounts have changed and describe the transaction that must have occurred to cause the entry. Use a chart similar to the one below where transaction (a) has been done for you.

Example:

TRANSACTION	ACCOUNT AFFECTED	TYPE OF ACCOUNT	INCREASE/ DECREASE	DEBIT/CREDIT
(a)	Accounts Payable	Liability	Decrease	Debit $ 150
	Cash	Asset	Decrease	Credit 150

Paid an account payable.

Cash

Balance	1 500	(a)	150
(b)	300	(d)	100
		(e)	250

Truck

Balance	7 500		

Accounts Receivable

Balance	1 000	(b)	300

Accounts Payable

(a)	150	Balance	500
(e)	250	(c)	500
		(d)	300

Tapes

Balance	2 000		
(d)	400		

Bank Loan

		Balance	2 500

Equipment

Balance	5 500		
(c)	500		

Potter, Capital

		Balance	14 500

2. The T-accounts below contain a number of transactions for Action Auction Sales. For each of the entries labelled (a) to (f), indicate how the accounts have changed and the transaction that must have taken place to generate the entry. The chart below, with transaction (a) done as an example, will assist you in describing the transactions correctly.

Example:

TRANSACTION	ACCOUNT AFFECTED	TYPE OF ACCOUNT	INCREASE/ DECREASE	DEBIT/CREDIT
(a)	Cash	Asset	Increase	Debit $12 000
	V. Henry, Capital	Owner's Equity	Increase	Credit 12 000

Since the Cash and Capital accounts both increased, the owner must have invested cash in the business.

Cash

(a)	12 000	(b)	750
(f)	6 500	(c)	1 000
		(d)	1 750

Accounts Payable

(d)	1 750	(c)	2 000
		(e)	5 000

Supplies

(b)	750		

Bank Loan

		(f)	6 500

Furniture

(c)	3 000		

V. Henry, Capital

		(a)	12 000

Equipment

(e)	5 000		

3. Dr. E. Kingsbury has the following account balances on September 30, 2001. The balances have been listed in no particular order: Cash $35 000; due to suppliers $4 000; Equipment $130 000; due from patients $6 000; Bank Loan $7 000; due from Provincial Health Plan $14 000; Dr. E. Kingsbury, Capital $176 000; Medical Supplies $2 000.

   (a) Open a T-account ledger in the correct order from the balances listed above.
   (b) Record the following October transactions in the ledger.
   (c) Prepare a trial balance.
   (d) Prepare a balance sheet on October 13, 2001.

   Oct. 2 Dr. Kingsbury invested an additional $50 000 cash in the business to assist in financing a new office.

   3 C. Patten, a patient, paid $65 (an amount owed).

   4 Bought surgical bandages and other medical supplies from Medical Suppliers, $78 on credit.

   5 Returned $43 worth of supplies to Medical Suppliers because they were not the type ordered.

   6 Paid $110 to Pharmaceutical Products, a creditor, to reduce the amount owing to it.

   7 Made the regular $300 payment on the bank loan.

   8 Received a cheque from the Provincial Health Plan for $12 500.

   9 Dr. Kingsbury located a satisfactory office building for his practice. The property cost $292 000, with the land worth $150 000 and the building worth the remainder ($142 000). A mortgage was secured from Canada Trust for $200 000, and the balance was paid in cash.

   10 Purchased a new computer and printer from Ace Computers for $3 500 cash.

   12 Purchased the software necessary for the computer from the same supplier for $1 500, on credit.

   13 Sold an old printer for $150 cash.

4. The ledger accounts of Bagels Galore contain the following balances on April 30 of this year. Prepare a trial balance with the accounts arranged as shown below. Fill in the missing amount for Capital.

Accounts Payable	$ 4 000
Accounts Receivable	1 500
Baking Equipment	22 500
Baking Supplies	3 500
Bank Loan	11 500
Building	105 000
Capital	?
Cash	6 000
Delivery Trucks	45 000
Land	20 000
Mortgage Payable	95 000

CHAPTER 3

The Income Statement

UNIT 4 Preparing the Income Statement

Learning Objectives

After reading this unit, discussing the applicable review questions, and completing the applications exercises, you will be able to do the following:

1. **CLASSIFY** items as revenue or expenses.
2. **PREPARE** an income statement.
3. **EXPLAIN** the accrual basis of accounting for revenue and expenses.
4. **PREPARE** an income statement and report form of balance sheet from a trial balance.

REVIEWING THE PURPOSE OF ACCOUNTING

In Chapter 1, the purpose of accounting was expressed as a system designed to provide information that is used to make decisions. This involves two types of accounting activity:

- Recording daily transactions
- Preparing reports that summarize daily transactions

In Chapters 1 and 2, you learned how daily business transactions were recorded and how a statement called a balance sheet was prepared. The balance sheet presented the assets, liabilities, and owner's equity at a specific date. In this chapter, you will expand your knowledge of business transactions and learn how and why a second financial statement, called an *income statement*, is prepared.

PROFIT AND LOSS

People go into business for themselves for a variety of reasons. Hal O'Brien, the owner of Malibu Gym, Thorold, started his business:

- To use his personal talents and abilities to the fullest
- To achieve a pride of ownership of his own business
- To gain the satisfaction of building a successful business
- To earn a profit on his investment of money and labour

Once Malibu Gym was established, it grew and became successful as a result of the owner's hard work and business knowledge. One of the major criteria of success for a business is its profitability. A business cannot survive for very long unless it earns a profit.

Defining Profit and Loss

Profit is the increase in owner's equity resulting from the successful operation of a business.

Profit is the increase in owner's equity that results from successful operation of a business. In this chapter, we will determine how to calculate whether a business is profitable. When a business is not successful, a loss occurs and owner's equity decreases.

A business sells goods or services.

Revenue is amounts earned by the business from the sale of goods or services normally sold during the routine operation of the business.

A business sells *goods* such as cameras, automobiles, clothes, and furniture or it sells *services* like television repairs, transportation, and hair styling. The money or the promise of money received from the sale of goods or services is called *revenue*.

Expenses are the costs of items or services used up in the routine operation of the business.

In order to sell goods and services, money is spent to operate the business. Money is spent on salaries, advertising, deliveries, and many other things required to run a business. These items are called *expenses*. Take the case of a television set that has a selling price of $500. The seller has to spend $400 in order to sell the TV. When the TV is sold, does the seller make a profit or is there a loss? There is a profit of $100.

Net income is the difference between revenue and expenses when revenue is greater than expenses.

As the television example illustrates, when the revenue is greater than the expenses there is *profit*. The term *net income* is the preferred accounting term for profit. Net income occurs when the revenue is greater than the expenses:

Revenue – Expenses = Profit or Net Income

Net loss is the difference between revenue and expenses when expenses are greater than revenue.

However, the total of the expenses may be greater than the revenue, then the result is called a loss or *net loss*:

Revenue – Expenses = Loss or Net Loss

The following equation mathematically illustrates how the net income or net loss on the sale of the television set is determined:

Revenue (Selling Price)	–	Expenses (All Expenses)	=	Net Income or Net Loss
$500	–	$400	=	$100 Net Income
500	–	550	=	(50) Net Loss

Notice that the $50 loss is shown in brackets. The use of brackets to indicate a loss is a commonly accepted procedure in accounting.

THE INCOME STATEMENT

An Income statement is a financial statement which presents the revenue, expenses, and net income/loss for a specific period of time.

In Chapter 1, we prepared a financial statement called a balance sheet in order to show the financial position of Malibu Gym at a certain date. The second major financial statement that every business prepares is called an *income statement*. This statement summarizes the items of revenue and expense and determines the net income or loss for a stated period of time. This period of time is called an *accounting period*. The accounting period may be a week, month, quarter, year, or any other regular period of time. The *time-period principle* requires the definition and consistent use of the same period of time for the accounting period. This allows the owners and other users of the financial statements to compare data for similar periods of time. For example, the owner can determine if the business is as profitable this year as in previous years if one year is used as the accounting period.

The accounting period is the period of time covered by the financial statements.

The time-period principle is the definition and consistent use of the same period of time for the accounting period.

A synonym for accounting period is *fiscal period*. Businesses prepare statements on a yearly basis for tax purposes. The statements prepared for this purpose are said to be prepared for the fiscal year. This fiscal year may or may not coincide with a calendar year. For example, a company's fiscal year may extend from July 1:Year 1 to June 30: Year 2, while the calendar year starts January 1:Year 1 and ends December 31:Year 1.

Income Statement Preparation

An income statement prepared for Malibu Gym for the month of September 2001 will be used to discuss the correct format and procedures followed to prepare a formal financial statement. This income statement is shown in Figure 3-1 below.

FIGURE 3-1
September Income Statement

Malibu Gym Income Statement For the Month Ended September 30, 2001		
REVENUE		
Members' Fees	$16 500	
Tanning Bed Rental	2 650	
Towel Rental	150	$19 300
EXPENSES		
Salaries Expense	5 850	
Advertising Expense	3 450	
Telephone Expense	290	
Maintenance Expense	1 720	
Licence Expense*	1 100	
Interest Expense	1 500	
Laundry Expense	95	14 005
Net Income		$ 5 295

* *Licence Expense is the amount that is paid to the parent company for the exclusive rights to the Malibu Gym name in the Niagara Region.*

The four steps followed in preparing an income statement are described below.

Step 1: Prepare Statement Heading

The three-line heading is centred at the top of the page and is designed to provide information in this sequence:

Line 1: Who? — Malibu Gym
Line 2: What? — Income Statement
Line 3: When? — For the month ended September 30, 2001

Note: The income statement provides data for a given time period (week, month, year), while the balance sheet provides data on a specific date. The income statement loses its usefulness if the accounting period is not specified. Thus, if Line 3 was omitted from our example, we would have no way of knowing whether the net income $5 295 was for a week, month, or year. The owner would have a very different reaction when reading the statement if the income shown was for a week versus a year.

Step 2: Prepare Revenue Section

The revenue received from the business operations is listed under the subheading Revenue. The largest revenue item is usually listed first. The revenue is totalled, and the total is placed in the right column:

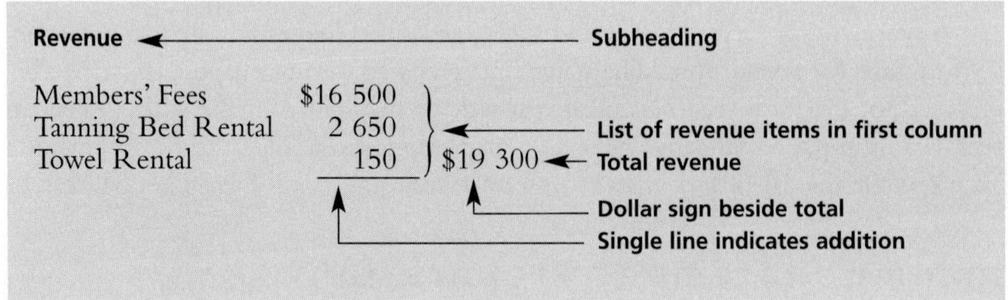

Step 3: Prepare Expenses Section

The expense items are listed in the order in which they appear in the ledger:

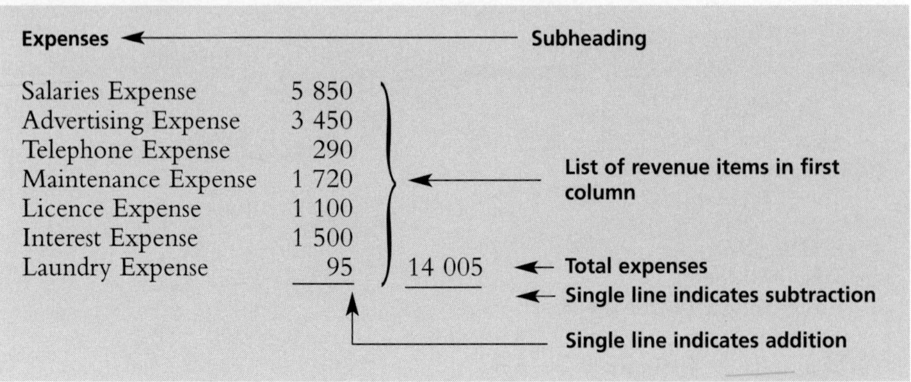

Step 4: Determine Net Income or Net Loss

The difference between total revenue and total expenses is the *net income* or the *net loss*. There is a net income (profit) when the total revenue is greater than total expenses. There is a net loss when the expenses are greater than the revenue.

In Figure 3-1 there is a net income of $5 295. This is determined by subtracting the expenses from the revenue ($19 300 – $14 005 = $5 295). Notice in Figure 3-1 that there is a dollar sign beside the net income and the net income is ruled with a double line. Double lines are ruled below the net income or net loss. They indicate the final total.

Facts to Remember

For the income statement, dollar signs should be placed as follows:

- Beside the first figure in each column
- Beside the net income or net loss figure at the bottom of the statement

ACCURACY OF THE INCOME STATEMENT

It is important when determining the net income for an accounting period to include only revenue earned during that period and only expenses incurred to produce that revenue. The net income or loss calculated will then accurately reflect only the business activities that took place during that period of time. This comparison of the revenue for a specific accounting period with the related expenses for the same period is called the *matching principle*. In this text, two simple rules will assist you in recording the appropriate revenue and expenses for an accounting period.

The matching principle requires that costs recorded for expenses be matched with revenue generated during the same time period.

Rules for Recording Revenue and Expenses

1. Revenue Is Recorded as It Is Earned.

Revenue is recorded when the service is performed or goods are shipped to a customer even if cash has not been received. For demonstration purposes regarding this point, we will consider the accounting methods in a legal firm.

During the first week in June, lawyer Patricia Little performed a variety of services for a number of clients. Some of the clients paid cash for services totalling $1 500. The remainder of the clients were billed $3 500 for the services. The total revenue recorded for June was $5 000 even though only $1 500 cash was received:

Services Performed and Paid For in Cash	+	Services Performed on Credit	=	Total Revenue
$1 500		$3 500		$5 000

What is the effect of earning this revenue on the accounting equation of Patricia Little's law firm?

	A		=	L	+	OE
Cash:	+	$1 500	=	No Change	+	$5 000
A/R:	+	3 500				

When revenue is earned, it produces an increase in owner's equity.

Revenue increases owner's equity

2. Expenses Are Recorded When the Cost Is Incurred.

Expenses decrease owner's equity.

Expenses are the costs incurred to generate the revenue. Expenses are recorded when the cost is incurred whether paid in cash or on credit. In normal practice, the receipt of a bill for the expense item provides evidence that the expense was incurred and should be recorded. A separate account is kept in the ledger for each of the expenses, as explained further in the next unit. The transactions are recorded in the expense accounts whether they are cash transactions or credit transactions. Remember, expenses are recorded as they are incurred. When expenses are incurred, they produce a decrease in owner's equity.

Accrual Basis of Accounting

A business that records revenue when earned and expenses when incurred is using the *accrual basis of accounting*. This method produces an accurate picture of profitability for an accounting period because it matches revenue earned with the expenses necessary to produce the revenue during the accounting period. The accrual basis of accounting will be used throughout this book.

FURTHER STUDY OF OWNER'S EQUITY

Introducing the Owner's Drawings Account

At the beginning of the chapter, it was indicated that one of the reasons people start their own business is to earn a profit and increase the value of the owner's equity. The owner of the business may make a regular practice of withdrawing money or other assets for personal use. This withdrawal of assets decreases the value of the owner's equity. This event is similar to an expense transaction since owner's equity is reduced. However, as you know, expenses are only recognized if the cost was incurred to produce revenue. Therefore, the withdrawal of assets by the owner is not an expense. This transaction is recorded in an account called Drawings. Since the withdrawal of assets affects the owner's investment, the owner's Drawings account is an equity account. This account appears in the equity section of the ledger and decreases owner's equity on the balance sheet. The Drawings account normally has a debit balance since withdrawals by the owner decrease owner's equity.

The owner's Drawings account records the withdrawal of assets from the business by the owner.

The owner's Drawings account is debited whenever assets are withdrawn by the owner for personal use. Examples of this are:

- Withdrawal of cash
- Removal of merchandise for personal use
- Taking of equipment from the business for personal use
- Using company funds for personal expenses of the owner or the owner's family

P. Little, Drawings	
Debit	Credit
Withdrawals are recorded as debits because they *decrease* capital.	

On October 15, for example, P. Little, the owner of a business, withdrew $1 000 cash from the business for personal use. The effect of this withdrawal is illustrated by these T-accounts:

P. Little, Drawings		Cash	
Oct. 15 1 000			Oct. 15 1 000

Owner's Salary

A salary may be paid by a business to the person who owns that business. However, for income tax purposes, the business may not record the payment in an expense account such as the Salaries account. Therefore, payment of wages or salaries to the owner must be recorded in the owner's Drawings account.

Drawings Account in the Ledger

The study of the ledger can now be summarized. You have learned that a *ledger* is a group of accounts. In the ledger, there is one account for each asset, for each liability, and for the owner's equity. As transactions occur, the changes caused by the transactions are recorded in these accounts. There is also an account required in the ledger for each revenue account, for each expense account, and for the Drawings account.

At the end of the accounting or fiscal period, a trial balance is prepared. The assets, liabilities, and owner's equity accounts (including the Drawings account) are used to prepare the balance sheet. The revenue and expense accounts are used to prepare the income statement. A complete summary of some typical ledger accounts, the account classifications, and the financial statements prepared from these accounts is shown in Figure 3-2 on page 50.

Equity Accounts on the Balance Sheet

The owner's Capital account and the owner's Drawings account appear in the owner's equity section of the balance sheet. The Capital account is a record of the owner's investment in the business. It is the owner's claim against the assets. The Capital account increases if there is a net income earned or if the owner increases the assets of the business by further investment in the business. The Capital account decreases if there is a net loss or if the owner withdraws assets from the business for personal use. The owner's Drawings account is used to record the withdrawals. The results of increases or decreases in the Capital account are shown in the equity section of the balance sheet.

Figures 3-3, 3-4, and 3-5, on page 51, show the owner's equity section of three balance sheets. On the October balance sheet shown in Figure 3-3, the business had a net income of $3 000; the owner, P. Little, withdrew $1 000 for personal use; and the Capital account increased, by $2 000, to $22 000. Notice how three money columns are used to record this information.

FIGURE 3-2
Ledger containing asset, liability, owner's equity, revenue, and expense accounts

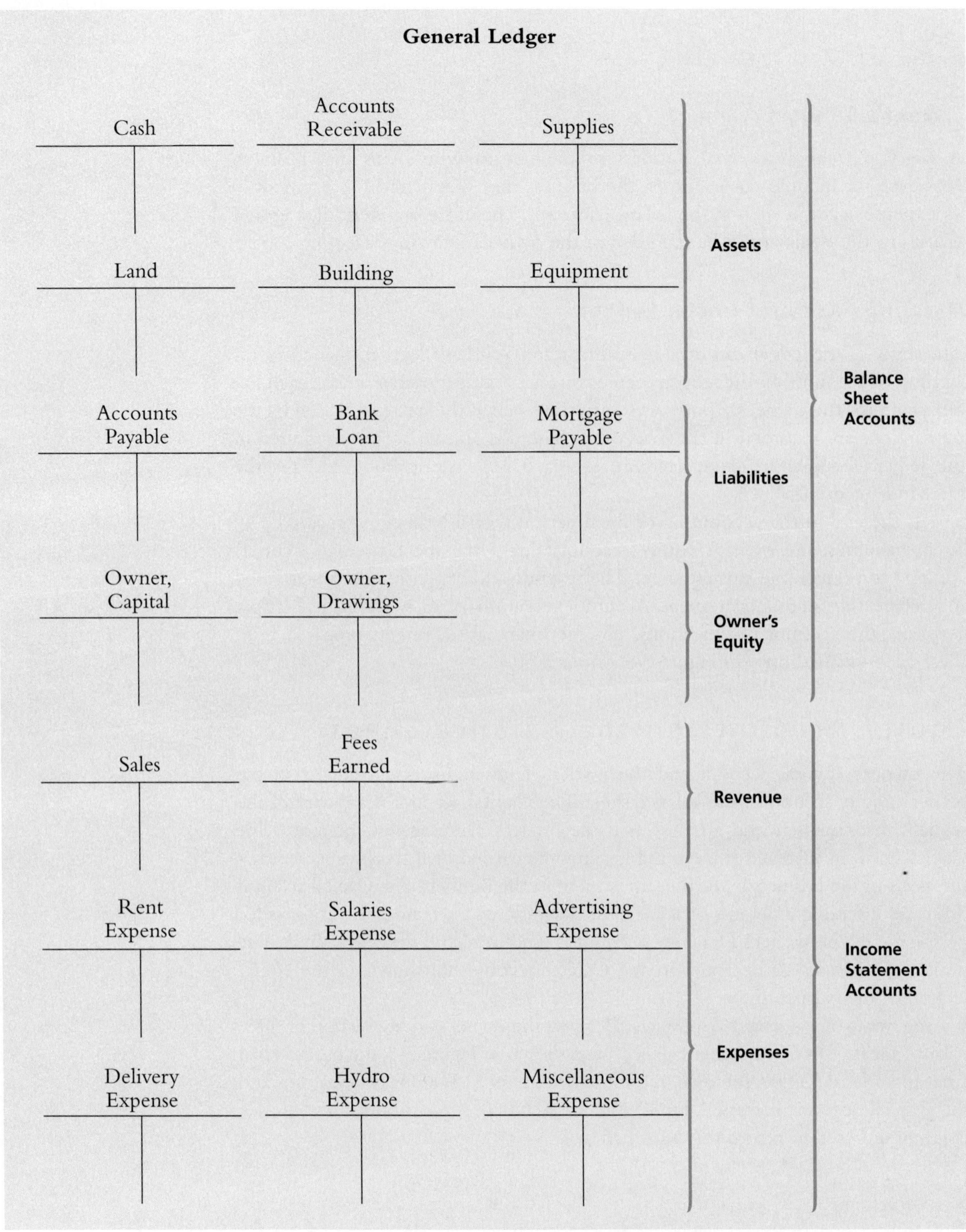

Owner's Equity			
P. Little, Capital October 1		$20 000	
Add: Net Income for October	$3 000		
Less: P. Little, Drawings	1 000		
Increase in Capital		2 000	
P. Little, Capital October 31			$22 000

FIGURE 3-3
Capital increases when withdrawals are less than net income.

In the November balance sheet shown in Figure 3-4, the Capital account decreased because the owner withdrew $1 500 while the net income was only $1 000. The result was a decrease in Capital of $500. Again, three money columns are used to show the changes in Capital.

Owner's Equity			
P. Little, Capital November 1		$22 000	
Add: Net Income for November	$1 000		
Less: P. Little, Drawings	1 500		
Decrease in Capital		500	
P. Little, Capital November 30			$21 500

FIGURE 3-4
Capital decreases when withdrawals are greater than net income.

In the December balance sheet shown in Figure 3-5, the Capital account decreases because of a net loss of $500 and drawings of $800. The total decrease in Capital is $1 300. Therefore, Capital decreases from $21 500 to $20 200.

Owner's Equity			
P. Little, Capital December 1		$21 500	
Less: Net Loss for December	$500		
Less: P. Little, Drawings	800		
Decrease in Capital		1 300	
P. Little, Capital December 31			$20 200

FIGURE 3-5
Capital decreases when there is a loss and the owner has withdrawn assets.

REPORT FORM OF THE BALANCE SHEET

The concept to be introduced now in this chapter is a new form for writing a balance sheet. Up to this point, the *account form* of balance sheet has been used. The account form of balance sheet was essential to establishing the concept:

Left Side = Right Side

From this concept, the accounting equation was established:

Assets = Liabilities + Owner's Equity

The accounting equation is an inflexible rule and the basis of the double-entry accounting system.

The account form of the balance sheet lists the assets on the left side and the liabilities and owner's equity on the right side.

The balance sheet does not usually appear in the account format, however. Another form of balance sheet is the *report form* (see Figure 3-6 on page 52). In the report form, the assets, liabilities, and owner's equity are listed vertically. The report form is easier to prepare since there is no need to move lines of figures in order to have the final balances appear opposite each other. In addition, it presents information in a format that is useful for statement analysis.

The report form of the balance sheet lists the assets, liabilities, and owner's equity vertically.

In Figure 3-6, of course, the first step involved in deriving the accounting equation, Left Side = Right Side, no longer applies because the balance sheet is written *vertically,* and there is no left side and right side. Remember that the accounting equation still applies:

Assets	=	Liabilities	+	Owner's Equity
$247 785		$157 630		$90 155

Facts to Remember

A slight modification of the rule given in Chapter 1 for the placement of dollar signs on the balance sheet is now required. For the report form of the balance sheet, dollar signs should be placed as follows:

- Beside the first figure in each column in both sections of the statement
- Beside the final total in both sections of the statement

FIGURE 3-6
Report form of balance sheet

Malibu Gym Balance Sheet September 30, 2001			
Assets			
Cash		$ 7 325	
Accounts Receivable		2 000	
Office Supplies		725	
Land		25 000	
Building		110 000	
Training Equipment		102 735	
Total Assets			$247 785
Liabilities and owner's equity			
Liabilities			
Accounts Payable		$ 12 630	
Bank Loan		65 000	
Mortgage Payable		80 000	
Total Liabilities			$157 630
Owner's Equity			
O'Brien, Capital September 1		86 860	
Add: Net Income for September	$5 295		
Less: O'Brien, Drawings	2 000		
Increase in Capital		3 295	
O'Brien, Capital September 30			90 155
Total Liabilities and Owner's Equity			$247 785

PREPARING FINANCIAL STATEMENTS FROM THE BALANCE SHEET

Figures 3-7, 3-8, and 3-9 illustrate how the financial statements are prepared from the trial balance, in this order:

Trial Balance → Income Statement → Balance Sheet

First, Figure 3-7 shows all of the accounts on the trial balance.

Remember that the trial balance is a list of the accounts and balances from the ledger in ledger order. The accounts are arranged in the ledger with the balance sheet accounts preceding the income statement accounts. However, since you must calculate the net income/loss for the accounting period in order to complete the equity section of the balance sheet, the income statement is prepared before the balance sheet.

FIGURE 3-7
Trial balance containing all ledger accounts

Malibu Gym Trial Balance October 31, 2001			
Balance Sheet Accounts	Cash	$ 7 650	
	Accounts Receivable	2 700	
	Office Supplies	695	
	Land	25 000	
	Building	110 000	
	Training Equipment	102 735	
	Accounts Payable		$ 11 600
	Bank Loan		63 000
	Mortgage Payable		80 000
	O'Brien, Capital		90 155
	O'Brien, Drawings	1 200	
Income Statement Accounts	Members' Fees		14 600
	Tanning Bed Rental		725
	Towel Rental		160
	Salaries Expense	3 850	
	Advertising Expense	2 880	
	Telephone Expense	190	
	Maintenance Expense	650	
	Licence Expense	1 100	
	Interest Expense	1 500	
	Laundry Expense	90	
		$260 240	$260 240

Figure 3-8 is the income statement which is prepared using the revenue and expense accounts.

FIGURE 3-8
Income statement

Malibu Gym Income Statement For the Month Ended October 31, 2001		
Revenue		
Members' Fees	$14 600	
Tanning Bed Rental	725	
Towel Rental	160	$15 485
Expenses		
Salaries Expense	$ 3 850	
Advertising Expense	2 880	
Telephone Expense	190	
Maintenance Expense	650	
Licence Expense	1 100	
Interest Expense	1 500	
Laundry Expense	90	10 260
Net Income		$ 5 225

Remember that even though Drawings has a debit balance, it is not an expense account and is not included on the income statement. Drawings will be used along with the net income ($5 225) in the equity section of the balance sheet.

Figure 3-9 is the balance sheet. It contains assets, liabilities, and owner's equity accounts. It is prepared in the *report form*.

FIGURE 3-9
Report form of balance sheet

Malibu Gym
Balance Sheet
October 31, 2001

Assets			
Cash		$ 7 650	
Accounts Receivable		2 700	
Office Supplies		695	
Land		25 000	
Building		110 000	
Training Equipment		102 735	
Total Assets			$248 780
Liabilities and owner's equity			
Accounts Payable		$ 11 600	
Bank Loan		63 000	
Mortgage Payable		80 000	
Total Liabilities			$154 600
Owner's Equity			
O'Brien, Capital October 1		90 155	
Add: Net Income for October	$5 225		
Less: O'Brien, Drawings	1 200		
Increase in Capital		4 025	
O'Brien, Capital October 31			94 180
Total Liabilities and Owner's Equity			$248 780

REVIEW QUESTIONS UNIT 4

1. Name two financial statements.
2. Write definitions for each of the following:
   (a) Revenue
   (b) Expense
   (c) Net income
   (d) Net loss
3. What is the purpose of the income statement?
4. What are the three parts of the heading of an income statement?
5. What are the two main sections of the body of the income statement?
6. How is the net income determined?
7. When is there a net loss?
8. Write definitions for:
   (a) Income statement
   (b) Accounting period
   (c) Balance sheet
9. List the four steps followed in preparing an income statement.
10. What is the time-period principle?

11. Explain the matching principle.

12. Explain the accrual basis of accounting.

13. (a) Give an example of a transaction that is recorded in the owner's Drawings account.
    (b) On which financial statement does the owner's Drawings account appear?

14. In which account is a payment of a salary to the owner recorded?

15. Which financial statement is prepared first? Why?

16. What is the difference between the account form and the report form of the balance sheet?

PROBLEMS: APPLICATIONS

CHAPTER 3

1. Classify the following accounts as an asset, a liability, owner's equity, a revenue, or an expense; (a) has been done for you as an example.

(a) Bank Loan	(f) Cash
(b) Commissions Earned	(g) Accounts Payable
(c) Salaries	(h) Building
(d) Accounts Receivable	(i) Fees Earned
(e) Owner, Capital	(j) Advertising Expense

   Example:
   (a) Bank loan — Liability

2. Calculate the net income or net loss for each of the following; then identify the accounting period.

(a)	Revenue for September	$ 90 000
	Expenses for September	79 000
(b)	Revenue for 6 months	329 000
	Expenses for 6 months	362 000
(c)	Revenue for the year	600 000
	Expenses for the year	375 000
(d)	Revenue for Jan. 1–Mar. 31	295 000
	Expenses for Jan. 1–Mar. 31	230 000
(e)	Revenue for October	69 250
	Expenses for October	81 300

3. Prepare an income statement for Dr. Leon Winters for the year ended December 31, 2001 by using the following accounts from the ledger: Income from Fees $225 000; Investment Income $11 200; Automobile Expense $3 800; Supplies Expense $4 600; Rent Expense $24 000; Salaries Expense $47 000; Donations Expense $4 500; Utilities Expense $7 000; Insurance Expense $6 500; Miscellaneous Expense $5 000.

4. Prepare an income statement for Burnaby Cleaners for the month ended April 30, 2002 by using the ledger accounts given here in random order: Salaries Expense $4 000; Advertising Expense $1 500; Telephone Expense $750; Delivery Expense $2 000; Cleaning Revenue $12 000; Office Expense $3 000; Repairs Revenue $2 000; Rent Expense $5 000.

5. (a) From the trial balance for Morrison Moving, classify each account as an asset, a liability, an owner's equity, a revenue, or an expense, and indicate whether it appears on the balance sheet or on the income statement.

   Example:
   Cash — an asset that appears on the balance sheet.

   (b) Using the appropriate accounts, prepare an income statement for Morrison Moving for the year ended June 30, 2000.

Morrison Moving
Trial Balance
June 30, 2000

Account title	Debit	Credit
Cash	$ 27 000	
Accounts Receivable	65 000	
Land and Buildings	175 000	
Equipment	65 200	
Accounts Payable		$ 26 000
Bank Loan		31 000
A. Morrison, Capital		200 000
Storage Fees Revenue		28 500
Moving Service Revenue		185 000
Salaries Expense	95 300	
Truck Expense	34 000	
Utilities Expense	9 000	
	$470 500	$470 500

6. Complete the following chart by indicating the increase or decrease in Capital and showing the amount of the Capital.

BEGINNING CAPITAL	NET INCOME	NET LOSS	DRAWINGS	INC. OR DEC. IN CAPITAL	ENDING CAPITAL
(a) $10 000	$1 000	—	$ 500	?	?
(b) 25 000	1 000	—	1 500	?	?
(c) 18 000	—	$2 000	600	?	?
(d) 12 000	3 000	—	1 000	?	?

7. Prepare the owner's equity section of the balance sheet for each of the following three months for Dr. W. Lucey.

(a) Capital Balance January 1	$38 000
Net Loss for January	4 000
Drawings for January	6 000
(b) Capital Balance February 1	?
Net Income for February	2 000
Drawings for February	5 000
(c) Capital Balance March 1	?
Net Income for March	5 000
Drawings for March	4 500

8. Perfect Cruises had the following assets and liabilities at the beginning and the end of fiscal year April 30, 2002:

	Assets	Liabilities
May 1, 2001	$62 000	$47 000
April 30, 2002	93 000	59 000

Calculate the net income (or net loss) for the year using the following unrelated scenarios:

(a) The owner made an additional investment of $12,000 but made no withdrawals during the year.
(b) The owner withdrew $18 000 during the year but made no additional investments.
(c) The owner withdrew $2 000 per month and made an additional investment of $45 000.

9. (a) Prepare the income statement for Mazzone Enterprises from the trial balance given for the month ended April 30, 2001.
(b) Prepare a report form balance sheet for Mazzone Enterprises on April 30, 2001

Mazzone Enterprises Trial Balance April 30, 2001		
Cash	$ 4 500	
Accounts Receivable	14 800	
Office Supplies	2 000	
Office Equipment	9 600	
Furniture and Equipment	16 500	
Accounts Payable		$ 5 400
Bank Loan		10 000
P. Mazzone, Capital		29 450
P. Mazzone, Drawings	2 500	
Commissions Earned		12 500
Salaries Expense	5 000	
Office Expense	1 850	
General Expense	600	
	$57 350	$57 350

UNIT 5 Revenue and Expense Accounts

Learning Objectives

After reading this unit, discussing the applicable review questions, and completing the applications exercises, you will be able to do the following:

1. **ANALYZE** transactions involving assets, liabilities, equity, revenue, and expense accounts.
2. **RECORD** the transactions in ledger accounts.
3. **PREPARE** financial statements from a trial balance.

In order to have the information necessary to prepare an income statement, accounts must be kept for the revenue and expense data for the accounting period. As you learned in Unit 4, the General Ledger must contain all the accounts required to prepare both financial statements: the balance sheet and the income statement. It will contain asset, liability, and owner's equity accounts for the balance sheet. It will also contain revenue and expense accounts for the income statement. The ledger will include these in the order shown:

General Ledger

TYPE OF ACCOUNT	USE
Asset Liability Owner's Equity	Preparation of balance sheet
Revenue Expense	Preparation of income statement

INCOME STATEMENT ACCOUNTS

There are two main sections in the body of the income statement, the *revenue* section and the *expense* section. For each item of revenue, there is an account in the ledger. For each item of expense, there is an account in the ledger.

Revenue Accounts

Revenue is the proceeds arising from the sale of goods or services to customers. Revenue is generated in different ways in various types of businesses. A fitness centre obtains revenue from members' fees; a real estate firm earns commissions from selling houses; professionals such as lawyers, accountants, and doctors earn fees from their clients for their services; a company selling a product earns sales revenue.

A separate revenue account is set up for each distinct type of revenue earned by a company. Therefore, the type of revenue earned determines the type and number of revenue accounts necessary to accurately collect and summarize the revenue data.

Expense Accounts

Expenses are the costs incurred to generate the revenue. A separate expense account is set up for each major type of expense. Therefore, the number and type of the expense accounts will be determined within each individual business according to its requirements. The major criteria used to decide whether a separate expense account is needed are: (1) frequency of usage, and (2) dollar value of expenditure. For each expense item that occurs frequently, a separate account is set up in the ledger. A separate account is also set up for any items that involve large amounts of money. Small expenditures that occur infrequently are normally collected in one or more non-specific accounts, such as Miscellaneous Expense or General Expense.

Rules of Debit and Credit for Revenue and Expense Accounts

In Chapter 2, the procedure for entering transactions in the balance sheet accounts was explained as summarized in Figure 3-10.

The procedure for recording transactions that affect revenue and expense accounts will now be demonstrated.

Assets		=	Liabilities		+	Owner's Equity	
Debit Increase	Credit Decrease		Debit Decrease	Credit Increase		Debit Decrease	Credit Increase

Assets originate on the left side of the balance sheet. Because they originate on the left side, they increase on the left (debit) side of accounts and decrease on the right (credit) side of accounts.

Liabilities and owner's equity originate on the right side of the balance sheet. Because they originate on the right side, they increase on the right (credit) side of accounts and decrease on the left (debit) side of accounts.

FIGURE 3-10
Theory summary for recording debits and credits in balance sheet accounts

Before a transaction can be recorded in the accounts, it is necessary to determine whether the account will be debited or credited. As was shown earlier, net income and revenue increase owner's equity. Owner's equity is increased on the credit side. Therefore, when revenue occurs, it is recorded on the credit side of the revenue account

Revenue is recorded on the credit side.

Owner's Equity	
Debit Decrease	Credit Increase **Revenue increases owner's equity.**

Expenses decrease owner's equity.

Expenses are recorded on the debit side.

A net loss and expenses decrease owner's equity. Owner's equity is decreased on the debit side. Therefore, when expenses occur, they are recorded on the debit side of the expense accounts.

Owner's Equity

Debit Decrease **Expenses decrease owner's equity.**	Credit Increase

Debits and credits in revenue and expense accounts are determined by the effect of each transaction on owner's equity. *Revenue increases equity and is recorded as a credit. Expenses decrease equity and are recorded as debits.* These points are illustrated in Figure 3-11 and Figure 3-12 below.

Reason for Revenue and Expense Accounts

If revenue increases equity, expenses decrease equity, and net income is eventually added to the owner's equity on the balance sheet, why are revenue and expense accounts necessary? Why not enter transactions directly into the equity account?

FIGURE 3-11
Determining debits and credits in revenue and expense accounts

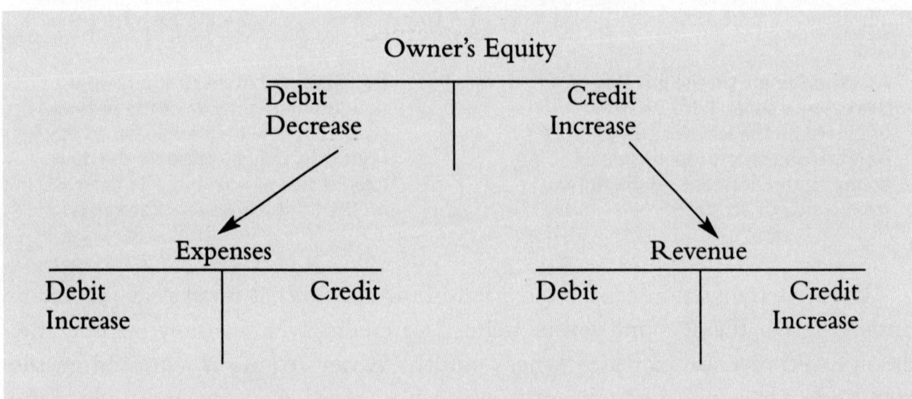

FIGURE 3-12
Theory summary for recording debits and credits in income statement accounts

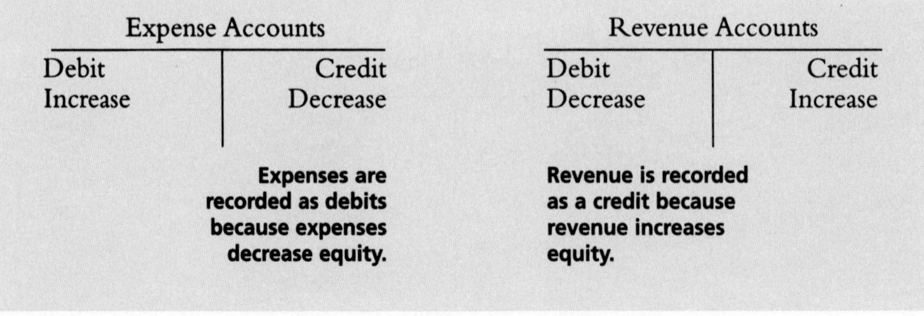

The answer is that one of the main purposes of accounting is to provide information to management about the operations of the business. Separate accounts for items of revenue and expense show at a glance which accounts are bringing in the company's revenue and which expenses are increasing too rapidly. Individual accounts for revenue and expenses provide managers with detailed information that helps them to make decisions about the business they are running and to control expenses, increase revenue, and operate the business effectively.

Transaction Analysis

As you have already learned, at least two accounts are involved in every business transaction. There is an equal debit amount recorded for every credit amount. In this chapter, you will see that the same principles of double-entry accounting apply when recording transactions involving revenue and expense accounts. For every debit amount, an equal credit amount is recorded. The transactions in this chapter will involve five types of accounts: asset, liability, equity, revenue, and expense.

Following are six transactions for lawyer P. Little. Examine carefully how each transaction is analyzed and the position of the debit and the credit in the T-accounts.

Transaction 1: Asset and Revenue Transaction

Jul. 1 Received $175 cash from client for drawing up new will.

The accounts affected are Cash and Fees Earned. Cash is an asset that increases. Therefore, the account should be debited. By completing the performance of a service, the firm earned revenue in the form of fees. Since revenue increases owner's equity, the revenue account Fees Earned would be credited.

Cash

Debit		Credit	
Jul. 1	175		

Fees Earned

Debit		Credit	
		Jul. 1	175

ACCOUNT AFFECTED	TYPE OF ACCOUNT	INCREASE/DECREASE	DEBIT/CREDIT
Cash	Asset	Increase Debit	$175
Fees Earned	Revenue	IncreaseCredit	175

Transaction 2: Asset and Revenue Transaction

Jul. 2 Billed client fee of $1 200 for legal services required to close purchase of new home.

The accounts affected are Accounts Receivable and Fees Earned. Accounts Receivable is an asset that increases. Therefore, the account is debited. By performing a service, the firm earned revenue. Revenue should be recorded when the service is completed whether the bill is paid or not. Since revenue increases owner's equity, it is credited on Jul. 2.

Accounts Receivable

Debit		Credit	
Jul. 2	1 200		

Fees Earned

Debit		Credit	
		Jul. 1	175
		2	1 200

ACCOUNT AFFECTED	TYPE OF ACCOUNT	INCREASE/DECREASE	DEBIT/CREDIT	
Accounts Receivable	Asset	Increase	Debit	$1 200
Fees Earned	Revenue	Increase	Credit	1 200

Transaction 3: Asset and Asset Transaction

Jul. 3 Received $600 from client as partial payment of $1 200 billed on Jul. 2.

The accounts affected are Cash and Accounts Receivable. This transaction does *not* involve revenue because the revenue was previously recorded in Fees Earned on Jul. 2. The asset Cash increases and is debited. The asset Accounts Receivable decreases and is credited.

Cash

Debit		Credit	
Jul. 1	175		
3	600		

Accounts Receivable

Debit		Credit	
Jul. 2	1 200	Jul. 3	600

ACCOUNT AFFECTED	TYPE OF ACCOUNT	INCREASE/DECREASE	DEBIT/CREDIT	
Cash	Asset	Increase	Debit	$ 600
Accounts Receivable	Asset	Decrease	Credit	600

Transaction 4: Expense and Asset Transaction

Jul. 4 Paid $95 to Bell Canada for telephone bill received today.

The accounts affected are Telephone Expense and Cash. The cost of the telephone is incurred in order to produce revenue and should be recognized as an expense when the bill is received. The expense decreases owner's equity and should be debited. Cash is an asset that decreases and should be credited.

Telephone Expense

Debit		Credit	
Jul. 4	95		

Cash

Debit		Credit	
Jul. 1	175	Jul. 4	95
3	600		

ACCOUNT AFFECTED	TYPE OF ACCOUNT	INCREASE/DECREASE	DEBIT/CREDIT	
Telephone Expense	Expense	Increase	Debit	$ 95
Cash	Asset	Decrease	Credit	95

Transaction 5: Expense and Liability Transaction

Jul. 5 Received a bill from the Calgary Herald for $150 for advertising the new location of the practice. The terms of payment allow 30 days to pay. The bill will be paid later.

The accounts affected are Advertising Expense and Accounts Payable. The cost of advertising was incurred to produce revenue and is an expense. It should be recorded upon receipt of the bill whether or not the bill is paid. Since an expense decreases owner's equity, it should be debited. Accounts Payable is credited since it is a liability that increases.

Advertising Expense

Debit		Credit	
Jul. 5	150		

Accounts Payable

Debit		Credit	
		Jul. 5	150

ACCOUNT AFFECTED	TYPE OF ACCOUNT	INCREASE/DECREASE	DEBIT/CREDIT	
Advertising Expense	Expense	Increase	Debit	$ 150
Accounts Payable	Liability	Increase	Credit	150

Transaction 6: Liability and Asset Transaction

Jul. 6 Paid $100 to Calgary Herald as partial payment of its bill for $150 received on Jul. 5.

The accounts affected are Accounts Payable and Cash. Notice that even though a bill is paid, an expense does not result. The expense was recorded when the bill was received on Jul. 5. This is a simple payment of an account payable. Accounts Payable is a liability that decreases and is debited. Cash is an asset that decreases and is credited.

Accounts Payable

Debit		Credit	
Jul. 6	100	Jul. 5	150

Cash

Debit		Credit	
Jul. 1	175	Jul. 4	95
3	600	6	100

ACCOUNT AFFECTED	TYPE OF ACCOUNT	INCREASE/DECREASE	DEBIT/CREDIT	
Accounts Payable	Liability	Decrease	Debit	$ 100
Cash	Asset	Decrease	Credit	100

The six transactions described above were analyzed and recorded in a systematic fashion. The answers to the following four questions helped to correctly record the transactions:

- What accounts were affected?
- Were the accounts assets, liabilities, owner's equity, revenue, or expense accounts?
- Did the accounts increase or decrease?
- Were the accounts debited or credited?

SUMMARY OF DEBIT AND CREDIT THEORY

Accurate recording of transactions is based on the rules of debit and credit. The basis for recording transactions in balance sheet and income statement accounts is shown below.

Balance Sheet Accounts

The debits and credits for balance sheet accounts are determined by the accounting equation:

Assets		=	Liabilities		+	Owner's Equity	
Debit Increase	Credit Decrease		Debit Decrease	Credit Increase		Debit Decrease	Credit Increase

The following rules are based on the equation:

(1) Assets are on the left side of the equation.
(2) Asset accounts increase on the left or debit side.
(3) Asset accounts decrease on the right or credit side.
(4) Liabilities and owner's equity are on the right side of the accounting equation.
(5) Liabilities and owner's equity accounts increase on the right or credit side.
(6) Liabilities and owner's equity accounts decrease on the left or debit side.

Income Statement Accounts

The income statement accounts (revenue and expenses) have debits and credits determined by their effect on equity:

Owner's Equity	
Debit	Credit
Decrease	Increase
Expenses	Revenue

The following rules are based on the equity account:

(1) Equity increases on the right, or credit, side.
(2) Revenue increases equity.
(3) Revenue is recorded on the credit side of revenue accounts.
(4) Equity decreases on the left, or debit, side.
(5) Expenses decrease equity.
(6) Expenses are recorded on the debit side of expense accounts.

ACCOUNTING TERMS

Accounting Period The period of time covered by the financial statements.

Accrual Basis of Accounting A commonly used method of accounting where revenue is recorded when earned and expenses when incurred.

Balance Sheet Accounts Asset, liability, and owner's equity accounts found in the General Ledger.

Equity Accounts The owner's Capital and Drawings accounts.

Expense Cost of items or services used up in the routine operation of the business.

Financial Statements Income statement and balance sheet.

Fiscal Period A synonym for accounting period.

Income Statement A financial statement that summarizes the items of revenue and expense and determines the net income or loss for a stated period of time.

Income Statement Accounts Revenue and expense accounts found in the General Ledger.

Loss Decrease in owner's equity that results from unsuccessful operation of a business.

Matching Principle Comparison of only the revenue earned during a specific accounting period with only the expenses for the same period of time in order to obtain an accurate net income.

Net Income Occurs when revenue is greater than expenses for the accounting period.

Net Loss Occurs when expenses are greater than revenues for the accounting period.

Owner's Drawings Account Used to record the withdrawal of assets by the owner for personal use. This withdrawal decreases the value of owner's equity.

Profit	Increase in owner's equity that results from successful operation of a business.
Report Form of Balance Sheet	Lists the assets, liabilities, and owner's equity vertically.
Revenue	Amounts earned by a business from the sale of goods or services normally sold during the routine operation of the business.
Time-Period Principle	Requires the definition and consistent use of the same period of time for the accounting period.

REVIEW QUESTIONS

1. (a) Does revenue increase or decrease owner's equity?
   (b) Do expenses increase or decrease owner's equity?
2. (a) What is the increase side for revenue accounts? Why?
   (b) What is the increase side for expense accounts? Why?

PROBLEMS: APPLICATIONS

10. Following are some of the accounts found in the ledger of Almond Nursery School: Cash; Accounts Receivable; Playground Equipment; Accounts Payable; L. Almond, Drawings; Fees Earned; Advertising Expense; Automobile Expense; Salaries Expense. Referring to these accounts, analyze the transactions shown below for this business. Use the format demonstrated in this chapter to assist you. List the debit portion of the entry before the credit portion. Transaction (a) has been done for you as an example.

    (a) Received $225 cash for a client's weekly nursery school fees.
    (b) Paid $35 cash for gas used in transporting children to school.
    (c) Received a bill from the *Standard* for $125 for advertising.
    (d) Purchased a new swing set for the playground from School Supply for $1 600 on credit.
    (e) Paid the weekly salary of $3 000 to the staff.
    (f) The owner, L. Almond, withdrew $750 for personal use.
    (g) Paid the $125 bill received previously from the *Standard*.

    Example:

TRANSACTION	ACCOUNT AFFECTED	TYPE OF ACCOUNT	INCREASE/ DECREASE	DEBIT/CREDIT
(a)	Cash Fees Earned	Asset Revenue	Increase Increase	Debit $ 225 Credit 225

11. Record the following transactions in the ledger of N. Doresco Ltd. containing five T-accounts. The names of the accounts are: Cash; Accounts Receivable/B. Irwin; Accounts Receivable/B. Hodge; Accounts Receivable/B. Ianizzi; Sales.

Feb. 1 Sold goods for cash, $1 800.

3 Sold goods on account to B. Irwin $1 400.

4 Sold goods on account to B. Hodge $1 900.

5 Sold goods to B. Ianizzi, $460; terms half cash, balance on account.

8 B. Hodge returned $150 worth of the goods sold Feb. 4. The goods were not what was ordered.

9 Received $700 from B. Irwin.

12. Record the following transactions in a ledger with these eight accounts: Cash; Equipment; Accounts Payable/Acme Ltd.; C. Clarke, Capital; C. Clarke, Drawings; Salaries; Advertising Expense; Rent Expense.

Mar. 1 C. Clarke invested $21 000 cash in a business.

2 Paid $210 cash to the *Bowmanville Chronicle* for advertising.

3 Bought equipment worth $6 000 on account from Acme Ltd.

6 Paid rent, $1 600.

7 Paid Wilco Printers $250 cash for advertising circulars.

8 Paid salaries, $1 900 cash.

8 Paid $1 500 cash to Acme Ltd. on account.

9 C. Clarke withdrew $800 cash for personal use.

13. Conradi's Service Centre repairs automobiles on a cash or credit basis. Accounts in the ledger include: Cash; Accounts Receivable; Tools; Accounts Payable; P. Conradi, Capital; P. Conradi, Drawings; Repair Service Revenue; Advertising Expense; Rent Expense; Telephone Expense. Transactions that occurred during June are given below.

(a) Record the transactions in a T-account ledger.
(b) Prepare a trial balance.

Jun. 2 Paid the monthly rent of $4 000 to Deneer Co.

3 Repaired the car of a client, Jim Jones, and billed him $835.

4 Purchased a new set of tools for $1 575 on credit from Tool Supply.

6 Received a bill for $475 from the *Gazette* for advertising.

6 Paid Auto Supply $1 000 for amounts owing to them.

7 Paid the telephone bill received today, $85.

10 The owner, P. Conradi, withdrew $900 for his own use.

11 Received $215 cash from a customer for a tune-up and oil change done today.

11 Received $245 cash from a customer who was sent a bill last month.

14. Record the following transactions in a ledger for Stokes Driving School with these accounts: Cash; Accounts Receivable/L. Starr; Equipment; Automobiles; Accounts Payable/Grant's Esso; R. Stokes, Capital; Revenue from Lessons; Salaries Expense; Advertising Expense; Automobile Expense; Utilities Expense.

Apr. 1 R. Stokes invested $35 000 cash.

2 Purchased equipment for $3 500 cash.

4 Purchased two cars from Dardick Motors for $42 000 cash.

5 Received $1 100 cash from customers taking driving lessons.

7 Paid $700 cash for instructor's salary for the first week.

9 Paid $57 cash to the telephone company.

10 Received $800 cash from customers taking driving lessons.

11 Issued a bill of $150 to L. Starr, a customer who is taking lessons but will pay at a later date.

11 Received a bill for $75 from Grant's Esso for gas and oil used by cars.

12 Paid $135 cash for hydro and electricity.

13 Sent a $290 cheque to the *Daily Star* for advertising space.

14 Received $150 cash from L. Starr in payment of bill sent previously.

(a) Balance the accounts and prepare a trial balance.
(b) Prepare an income statement for the two weeks ended April 14.

15. Eight transactions were recorded in the following T-account ledgers. Describe each transaction; include the dollar amount in your answer.

Cash

(a)	25 000	(b)	3 000
(e)	315	(g)	500
(h)	125		

Accounts Receivable

(f)	275	(h)	125

Dental Supplies

(d)	1 800		

Dental Equipment

(c)	8 500		

Accounts Payable

		(d)	1 800

Bank Loan

		(c)	8 500

Owner, Capital

Debit		Credit	
		(a)	25 000

Owner, Drawings

Debit		Credit	
(g)	500		

Dental Fees Income

Debit		Credit	
		(e)	315
		(f)	275

Rent Expense

Debit		Credit	
(b)	3 000		

1. The Blacksox are a minor league professional baseball team owned by Dave Howes. A partial list of the accounts used by the team is as follows: Cash $10 000; Equipment; Accounts Payable; Bank Loan; D. Howes, Capital; D. Howes, Drawings; Gate Receipts; Parking Revenue; Concession Revenue; Advertising Expense; Players' Salaries Expense; Interest Expense; Rent Expense; Transportation Expense. Set up the T-account ledger for the Blacksox Baseball Club Inc., and record the cash balance and the following transactions.

May 1 D. Howes, the owner, invested an additional $38 000 in the team.

1 Received a bill from the *Gazette* for advertising. The bill for $750 is due in 30 days.

2 Purchased a new speaker system for the field from Electronics Inc. Paid $500 cash and the remaining $1 800 is to be paid in 30 days.

2 Paid the players' salaries for the week, $29 400.

3 The game today produced gate receipts $4 500, parking revenue $490, and concession revenue $1 575.

4 Signed a new player to a standard player's contract calling for a payment of $750 per week for the remainder of the season. The player will join the club for tomorrow's game.

4 Made the regular monthly payment on the bank loan. The payment consisted of $1 500, of which $300 was interest and $1 200 was used to reduce the amount of the loan.

4 Today's game generated gate receipts of $4 100, parking revenue $425, and concession revenue $1 300.

4 Paid rent on the stadium for the last two games. The rent was calculated on the basis of 10 percent of gate receipts.

5 The owner, D. Howes, withdrew $850 in order to make the monthly payment to GMAC on his personal car loan.

5 Received a bill today from Buckley's Transit for the bus used on the last road trips, $3 100. Sent a cheque in full payment.

2. On April 1, Ted's Golfing School had the following accounts, some with balances and some without: Cash $3 000; Accounts Receivable/P. Moores $150; Accounts Receivable/L. Troop; Equipment $4 700; Accounts Payable/Jack's Repair Shop $750; T. Craig, Capital $7 100; Fees Income; Advertising Expense; Rent Expense; Equipment Repairs Expense; Utilities Expense.

   (a) Set up the General Ledger for Ted's Golfing School on April 1 and record the following transactions.
   (b) On April 12, balance the accounts and prepare a trial balance, an income statement for the two weeks, and a balance sheet.

   Apr. 2 Received $400 cash from customers for golfing lessons.

   2 Issued a bill for $115 to L. Troop for lessons that will be paid for later.

   3 Paid $1 400 cash to United Realty for the monthly rent.

   4 Received $75 cash from P. Moores.

   5 Received a $215 bill from Jack's Repair Shop for repairing equipment.

   8 Received $2 000 cash from customers for lessons.

   8 Issued another $45 bill to L. Troop for lessons.

   9 Received $75 cash from P. Moores who paid the balance of money owed by him.

   10 Received a $575 bill for a piece of equipment bought from Jack's Repair Shop. The amount is to be paid at a later date.

   12 Paid $90 cash for electricity and water.

   12 Paid $450 cash to Jack's Repair Shop to reduce balance owing for work done.

   12 Paid $355 cash to the *Gazette* for advertising.

3. On November 1, the Luckville Beavers Hockey Team, owned by R. Branch, had the following accounts, some with balances and some without: Cash $12 000; Accounts Receivable/Stokes Dept. Stores; Equipment $4 000; Bus $15 000; Accounts Payable/Klaman Motors $5 300; R. Branch, Capital $25 700; Ticket Sales; Income from Concessions; Players' Salaries Expense; Bus Maintenance Expense; Arena Rental Expense; Advertising Expense.

   (a) Set up the General Ledger for the hockey team, on November 1, and record the transactions given below for the month of November.
   (b) On November 30, balance the accounts and prepare a trial balance, an income statement for the month, and a balance sheet.

   Nov. 2 Received $120 000 cash from sales of season's tickets.

   4 Purchased equipment for $5 000 cash.

   8 Received a $250 bill from Klaman Motors for repairs to the team bus.

9 Issued a bill of $2 400 to Stokes Department Stores who bought a block of 500 tickets for the team's opening home game. (The store will use the tickets for promotional purposes.)

10 Paid $425 rental fee for use of the arena for the last two weeks of practice.

14 Issued cheques for $18 000 to pay the players' salaries for the past two weeks.

16 Paid $350 cash to KCV TV for advertising the first home game on November 26.

17 Paid $515 to the *Daily Reporter* for advertising.

20 The week's sale of tickets for the opening game brought in $3 800.

24 Paid $80 cash for gas and oil for the bus on the first away-from-home game.

26 Received a further $8 700 cash for ticket sales on the opening game.

28 Paid $2 700 cash to the arena for rental for the last two weeks.

29 Issued cheques for $13 700 to pay the players' salaries for the rest of the month.

4. The T-accounts shown on page 71 contain a series of transactions for Hagadorn Realty. For each of the labelled entries, indicate how the accounts have changed and the transaction that must have occurred to generate the entry. The following chart, with transaction (a) done as an example, will assist you in completing the question.

TRANSACTION	ACCOUNT AFFECTED	TYPE OF ACCOUNT	INCREASE/ DECREASE	DEBIT/CREDIT
(a)	Cash Accounts Receivable	Asset Asset	Increase Decrease	Debit $ 500 Credit 500

Cash increased and Accounts Receivable decreased. Therefore an account receivable was collected.

Cash

Balance	2 500	(b)	200
(a)	500	(d)	650
(f)	3500	(g)	1 200
(i)	2 000	(h)	115
		(j)	175

J. Hagadorn, Drawings

(b)	200		

Accounts Receivable

Balance	3 500	(a)	500
(c)	1 500		

Commissions Earned

		(c)	1 500
		(f)	3 500

Office Furniture

Balance	8 000		

Office Salaries

(d)	650		

Office Equipment

Balance	12 000		

Advertising Expense

(e)	500		

Accounts Payable

		Balance	1 700
		(e)	500

Rent Expense

(g)	1 200		

Bank Loan

		Balance	9 000

Telephone Expense

(h)	115		

J. Hagadorn, Capital

		Balance	15 300
		(i)	2 000

Utilities Expense

(j)	175		

CHAPTER 4

The Journal and the Ledger

UNIT 6 The Journal

Learning Objectives

After reading this unit, discussing the applicable review questions, and completing the applications exercises, you will be able to do the following:

1. **EXPLAIN** the purpose of a journal.
2. **RECORD** transactions in a General Journal.
3. **EXPLAIN** the use of a compound entry.

Imagine a business, such as a major department store, that has a very large number of accounts. Now imagine that a $500 error was made in recording one of the transactions in the ledger accounts. The debit of $500 was placed in the wrong account. How would the $500 error be traced? The accountant would have to go through all the accounts until the incorrect entry was located. The debit and credit parts of the transaction would be in widely separated parts of the ledger, and it could take a long time to locate the error. This type of difficulty is eliminated by the use of a *journal*.

INTRODUCING THE JOURNAL

The *journal* records all parts of a transaction in one place. The date, debit, credit, and an explanation for each transaction are recorded together. Transactions can be conveniently located because they are recorded *chronologically,* that is, in the order in which they take place. The main journal of a business is often called the *General Journal.* Other types of journals will be discussed in later chapters.

A journal is a record of transactions recorded in chronological order (date order).

A journal is sometimes called a *book of original entry* because it is where transactions are first recorded. Transactions may be written in a journal manually or they may be prepared using a computer.

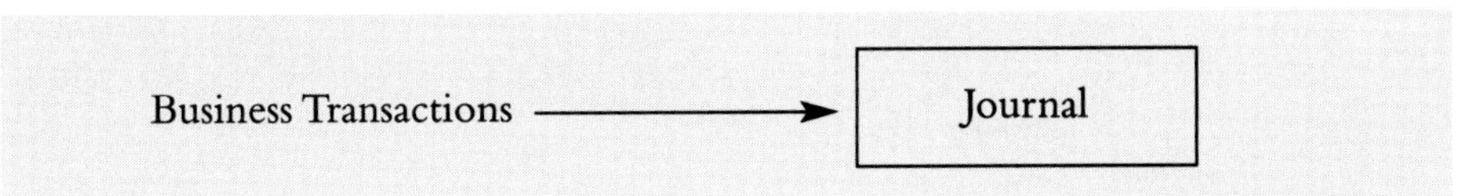

FIGURE 4-1
Transactions are first recorded in a journal.

Journal Entries

Each transaction recorded in a journal is called an *entry.* The process of recording transactions in a journal is called *journalizing.* Each journal entry has four parts as shown in Figure 4-2:

Journalizing is the recording of transactions in a journal.

- Date of the transaction
- Account debited and amount
- Account credited (indented) and amount
- Explanation giving details of the transaction

Sample Transactions

Figure 4-2 illustrates how the following four transactions appear when they are recorded in the General Journal:

Oct.	1	***Sold services for $900 cash.***
	3	***Paid $400 for advertising.***
	5	***Paid secretary's salary, $700.***
	6	***Purchased a new office computer for $4 500. A cash down payment was made today of $1 000 and the remaining $3 500 will be paid to COMCO in 30 days.***

In the previous chapters you learned to analyze transactions and record them directly in T-accounts. Many businesses, however, first record entries in a journal when the transaction occurs. They later transfer the information to the ledger account. This second step is explained in Unit 7.

In T-account form the first transaction would be recorded as follows:

Cash		Sales	
Oct. 1 900			Oct. 1 900

In Figure 4-2, the same transaction is shown in the journal. Notice that in the journal Cash is debited $900 and Sales is credited $900 just as in the accounts.

FIGURE 4-2
Transactions recorded in a General Journal

GENERAL JOURNAL					PAGE 3
DATE		PARTICULARS	P.R.	DEBIT	CREDIT
2001					
Oct.	1	Cash		900	
		Sales			900
		Sold services to R. Heino for			
		Cash, Sales Slip 1.			
	3	Advertising Expense		400	
		Cash			400
		Paid cash for newspaper ad,			
		Cheque 1.			
	5	Salaries Expense		700	
		Cash			700
		Paid secretary's weekly salary,			
		Cheque 2.			
	6	Office Equipment		4 500	
		Cash			1 000
		Accounts Payable/COMCO			3 500
		Purchased a computer,			
		Cheque 3 — 30 day account.			

Notice that in the General Journal illustrated in Figure 4-2, debits and credits are determined according to the same rules as those you learned in previous chapters. Note also that there is a consistent procedure for recording debits and credits in the General Journal. An entry such as the transaction on October 6, which shows more than one debit or credit, is called a *compound entry*. All entries must have equal debit and credit amounts.

A compound entry is an entry that has more than one debit or more than one credit.

Journal Recording Procedures

There are four steps in recording transactions in a journal. All of them are shown in Figure 4-2.

Step 1: Record the Date

The year, month and day are shown on each journal page.

In a journal, the first entry on each page must show the year, the month, and the day. Only the day of the month needs to be recorded for other entries on the page unless the month changes before a page is completed. In that event, the new month is shown in the date column.

Step 2: Record the Debit

The debit is shown first.

The name of the account debited is written next to the date. It should be written exactly as it appears in the ledger. For example, if cash is received, the appropriate account title would be Cash, not Cash Received. The dollar amount of the debit is written in the debit column.

Step 3: Record the Credit

The credit is indented.

The credit is recorded on the next line. It is indented about the same as a paragraph indent in order to distinguish it visually from the debit. The dollar amount is written in the credit column.

Step 4: Record the Explanation

On the next line, starting at the margin, an explanation of the transaction is written. The invoice or cheque number is included.

Advantages of the Journal

Although transactions may be recorded directly into the ledger accounts, many businesses prefer to record transactions in a journal first for the following reasons:

A journal presents a history of all the company's transactions.

- The complete transaction is recorded in one place.
- The use of a journal reduces errors. When entries are recorded directly into ledger accounts, it is easy to make a mistake by recording two debits and no credits or by recording only the debit or only the credit. Such errors are less likely to occur in a journal, but if they do, they are easy to spot. A quick check of each page in a journal will reveal any entry that does not show a debit and an equal credit.
- A journal represents a chronological history of all the business transactions recorded by date.
- A journal makes it possible to determine the daily, weekly, or monthly volume of business and to identify busy periods more easily.
- A convenient picture of each day's business is provided.

Double-Entry Accounting

You have already learned that when recording a transaction the debit amount(s) recorded must always equal the credit amount(s). This principle applies even if more than two accounts are used in recording the transaction. You will continue to apply the principle of double-entry accounting as you learn to use a journal. Look again at the journal entries in Figure 4-2. Notice that for every entry, the debit (left side) equals the credit (right side).

1. What is a journal?
2. Why is a journal sometimes called a book of original entry?
3. What is a journal entry?
4. What is journalizing?
5. What is a compound entry?
6. Name the four parts of a journal entry.
7. Which part of a journal entry is indented?
8. (a)Describe four advantages of using a journal.
   (b)In what order do entries appear in a journal?
9. Explain the principle of double-entry accounting.

PROBLEMS: APPLICATIONS

1. Journalize the following transactions for the Rialto Theatre, using these accounts: Cash; A. Renner, Capital; Ticket Sales; Refreshment Sales; Salaries Expense; Film Rental Expense; Hydro Expense; Advertising Expense.

May	1	A. Renner invested $85 000 cash.
	4	Ticket sales for the week, $25 000.
	4	Refreshment sales for the week, $6 100.
	7	Paid for film rental, $13 500 cash.
	7	Paid salaries, $3 300 cash.
	10	Paid the *Citizen* for newspaper advertising, $1 500.
	11	Paid the hydro bill, $525 cash.

2. Journalize the following transactions for Forsyth Day Care Centre, using these accounts: Cash; Equipment; Accounts Payable/Sears; E. Forsyth, Drawings; E. Forsyth, Capital; Day Care Fees; Salary Expense; Advertising Expense; Utilities Expense; Food Expense.

Aug.	1	E. Forsyth invested $15 000 cash.
	4	Purchased new equipment for the centre; $600 in cash was paid immediately and the remaining $2 200 was charged to the centre's account with Sears.
	5	Food items for the children's lunches this week were purchased for $425 cash.
	6	Paid $150 for classified advertising in the *Tribune.*
	7	Paid salaries for the week, $2 500 cash.
	7	E. Forsyth withdrew $825 cash.
	7	Collected fees from parents for the week, $4 200 cash.

3. Journalizc the following transactions for the Stokes Driving School, using these accounts: Cash; Accounts Receivable/L. Starr; Equipment; Automobiles; Accounts Payable/Grant's Esso; R. Stokes, Capital; Revenue from Lessons; Salaries Expense; Advertising Expense; Automobile Expense; Utilities Expense.

Apr.	1	R. Stokes invested $62 000 cash.
	2	Purchased equipment for $2 700 cash.
	4	Purchased two cars from Dardick Motors for $27 000 cash each.
	5	Received $1 500 cash from customers taking driving lessons.
	7	Paid $2 800 cash for instructors' salaries for the week.
	9	Paid $85 cash to the telephone company.
	10	Received $1 800 cash from customers taking driving lessons.
	11	Issued a bill for $300 to L. Starr, a customer who is taking lessons but will pay at a later date.
	11	Received a bill from Grant's Esso for gas and oil, $510.

12 Paid $275 cash for hydro and electricity.

13 Sent a $350 cheque to the Daily Star for advertising space.

14 Received $300 cash from L. Starr, to pay off amount owing for lessons.

4. Journalize the following transactions in a General Journal. Select appropriate accounts for each transaction. Note: This firm keeps a separate account for each account receivable and each account payable.

Oct. 1 G. Sloan invested $11 000 cash in a business.

2 Sold services worth $600 to D. Ferris, for cash.

3 Sold services to W. Anderson, $375 on credit.

4 Sold services to T. Tidey, $825 on credit.

5 Received $175 cash from W. Anderson as part payment of amount owing.

8 Received $825 cash from T. Tidey in full payment of amount owing.

8 The owner, G. Sloan, paid the office rent for the month, $1 750, out of a personal bank account (not the company account).

9 Purchased a new computer from Office Systems for $3 300. They required a 10-percent down payment today and the remainder within 30 days.

10 Received the hydro bill, $357, to be paid in 10 days.

UNIT 7 Posting to the Ledger

Learning Objectives

After reading this unit, discussing the applicable review questions, and completing the applications exercises, you will be able to do the following:

1. **USE** a chart of accounts.
2. **POST** journal entries to ledger accounts.
3. **PREPARE** the opening entry.
4. **PREPARE** trial balances in three forms:
   - Formal trial balance
   - Informal listing of debits and credits
   - Calculator tape listings
5. **LOCATE** errors.
6. **DEFINE** posting, journal, chart of accounts.

The General Journal is a systematic record of all transactions. It shows the accounts debited and credited for every transaction in the order in which the transactions occur. However, the General Journal does not provide the balance for each account. The General Journal does not tell the accountant how much cash is on hand, and it also does not record the balance of each of the items that will appear on the financial statements. This type of information is found in the accounts in the ledger. The information in the General Journal (as well as the other journals to be discussed later in the book) is transferred to the ledger by a process called *posting.*

Posting is the transfer of information from a journal to the ledger.

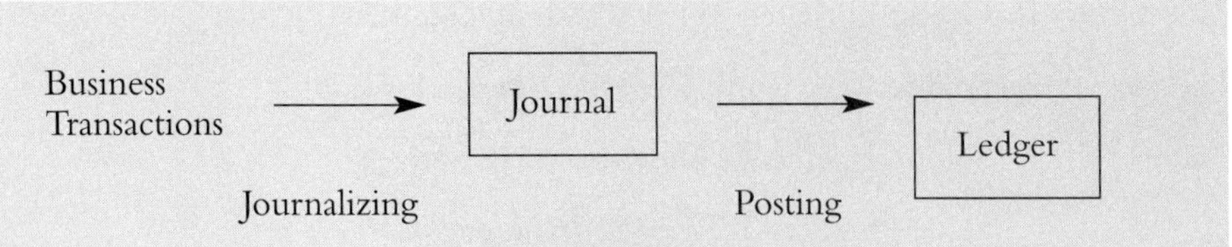

FIGURE 4-3
Posting is the transfer of information from a journal to the accounts in the ledger.

INTRODUCING THE BALANCE-COLUMN FORM OF LEDGER ACCOUNT

The T-account was introduced in Chapter 2 as a simple form of recording transactions in ledger accounts. It is an ideal form for learning the rules of debit and credit, but the T-account is not very practical for use in business. The balance in the account is not available for reference after each transaction. The most widely used form of account is the *balance-column account,* which is sometimes called a three-column account.

In Figure 4-4 a number of transactions are recorded in a Cash T-account. Exactly the same transactions appear in Figure 4-5 in the form of a balance-column account. Why is it called a balance-column form of account?

FIGURE 4-4
Transactions recorded in a Cash T-account

Cash			
Nov. 1	2 000	Nov. 3	150
3	75	6	200
5	100		350
	2 175		
Balance	1 825		

FIGURE 4-5
Transactions shown in Figure 4-4 recorded in a balance-column ledger account

ACCOUNT Cash NO. 100

DATE	PARTICULARS	P.R.	DEBIT	CREDIT	DR. CR.	BALANCE
2001						
Nov. 1		J1	2 000		DR.	2 000
3		J1	75		DR.	2 075
3		J1		150	DR.	1 925
5		J2	100		DR.	2 025
6		J3		200	DR.	1 825

Compare the information in the T-account in Figure 4-4 with the same information shown in the balance-column form of account in Figure 4-5. Notice that in the balance-column form of account a running balance is provided on each line. The accountant can see at a glance how much cash the company has at the close of each transaction. The DR./CR. (debit/credit) column indicates that the balance in the example is a debit balance; that is, the debits are larger than the credits. Although entries in the account on November 3 and 6 are credits, the DR./CR. column on these dates indicates that the balance is still a debit balance. The DR./CR. column of the account also indicates the column of the trial balance in which the account will appear. Since the $1 825 balance in the Cash account in Figure 4-5 is a DR. (debit), the Cash account balance would be listed in the debit column of the trial balance.

The DR./CR. column indicates whether the account balance is a debit or a credit.

Notice that each account is numbered. In Figure 4-5, the Cash account is number 100. The accounts are filed numerically in the ledger.

POSTING TO A BALANCE-COLUMN FORM OF LEDGER ACCOUNT

Figure 4-6 shows how a $900 General Journal entry is posted to the Cash account in the balance-column form of ledger account.

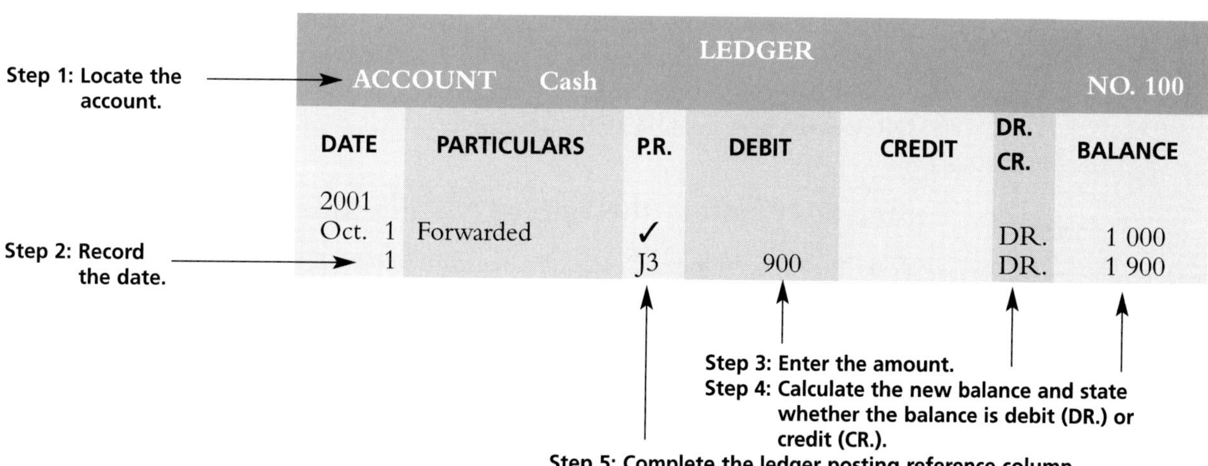

LEDGER

ACCOUNT Cash NO. 100

DATE	PARTICULARS	P.R.	DEBIT	CREDIT	DR. CR.	BALANCE
2001						
Oct. 1	Forwarded	✓			DR.	1 000
1		J3	900		DR.	1 900

Step 1: Locate the account.
Step 2: Record the date.
Step 3: Enter the amount.
Step 4: Calculate the new balance and state whether the balance is debit (DR.) or credit (CR.).
Step 5: Complete the ledger posting reference column.

GENERAL JOURNAL PAGE 3

DATE	PARTICULARS	P.R.	DEBIT	CREDIT
2001				
Oct. 1	Cash	100	900	
	Sales			900
	Sold services to R. Heino, for cash, Sales Slip 1.			

Step 6: Complete the journal posting reference column.

FIGURE 4-6
Steps for posting the journal to the ledger

Steps in Posting

To avoid mechanical errors in the posting procedure, follow these steps, which are illustrated in Figure 4-6.

Step 1: Locate the Account

Look at the name of the account to be posted to and locate that account in the ledger. On October 1 in Figure 4-6, that account is Cash.

Step 2: Record the Date

The transaction date is recorded in the account. The month and year need not be repeated if they are already recorded on that page of the account.

Step 3: Enter the Amount

The amount of $900 is recorded in the debit column of the account.

Step 4: Calculate the New Balance

Since the previous balance was $1 000 (debit) and another debit of $900 is being entered in the account, the new balance is $1 900 (debit). The two debits are added ($1 000 + $900) because they are on the same side of the account, the debit side. Record the new balance of $1 900 indicating that it is a debit balance (DR.). The DR. is written in the DR./CR. column.

Step 5: Complete the Ledger Posting Reference Column

Enter the General Journal page number from which the amount was posted (J3) in the posting reference (P.R.) column of the ledger account. The page number is preceded by the letter J to indicate that the amount came from the journal. The (✓) in the posting reference column indicates the forwarded balance came from a previous ledger page rather than the journal.

Step 6: Complete the Journal Posting Reference Column

Copy the account number (100) from the ledger account into the posting reference column of the General Journal. This number indicates that the amount in the General Journal has been posted to the ledger in account 100.

Figure 4-7 shows the General Journal and the Sales account after the credit has been posted to the Sales account. The six steps in posting have all been repeated. What does the number 400 in the journal posting reference column represent? What does J3 in the account posting reference column indicate?

GENERAL JOURNAL				PAGE 3
DATE	PARTICULARS	P.R.	DEBIT	CREDIT
2001				
Oct. 1	Cash	100	900	
	Sales	400		900
	Sold services to R. Heino, for cash, Sales Slip 1.			

LEDGER						
ACCOUNT Sales						NO. 400
DATE	PARTICULARS	P.R.	DEBIT	CREDIT	DR. CR.	BALANCE
2001						
Oct. 1		J3		900	CR.	900

FIGURE 4-7
Posting to the Sales account

Posting References

Numbers in the posting reference columns serve an important purpose. They are cross references that link particular journal entries to corresponding postings in the ledger accounts.

A journal page number in the ledger account posting reference column indicates where more information about the transaction can be found. For instance, the information explaining the transaction with R. Heino (Figure 4-6) can be located by referring to page 3 of the General Journal.

The ledger account number in a journal posting reference column indicates that the amount has been posted. It tells the accounting clerk where he or she left off in posting to the ledger.

Periodically, all companies have their records audited by an outside accountant. An *audit* is a systematic check of accounting records and procedures. The cross reference provided by posting reference numbers helps the auditor to check the accuracy of the journalizing and posting of transactions. The posting reference numbers allow the transactions to be traced from a journal to the ledger and also from the ledger to a journal.

Figure 4-8 represents page 12 of a General Journal used by Martin Painting Contractors. Figure 4-9 is a portion of the company's ledger to which the transactions have been posted. Trace the transactions from the General Journal to the ledger. The posting reference column will help you.

OPENING THE BOOKS

Figures 4-8 and 4-9 illustrated how routine transactions are recorded in the General Journal and then are posted to a ledger. The special procedures followed when a business first begins operations will now be examined.

FIGURE 4-8
Page 12 of the General Journal for Martin Painting Contractors

GENERAL JOURNAL — PAGE 12

DATE	PARTICULARS	P.R.	DEBIT	CREDIT
2001				
Nov. 1	Cash	100	1 300	
	Sales	400		1 300
	Sold services to W. Mason, Sales Slip 49.			
3	Advertising Expense	500	275	
	Cash	100		275
	Paid *Ottawa Journal* for a newspaper advertisement, Cheque 15.			
5	Salaries Expense	502	250	
	Cash	100		250
	Paid secretary's salary, Cheque 16.			
6	Cash	100	700	
	Sales	400		700
	Painted house for M. Blais, Sales Slip 50.			

FIGURE 4-9
Portion of the ledger for Martin Painting Contractors affected by the transactions in Figure 4-8

ACCOUNT Cash — NO. 100

DATE	PARTICULARS	P.R.	DEBIT	CREDIT	DR. CR.	BALANCE
2001						
Nov. 1	Forwarded	✓			DR.	4 000
1		J12	1 300		DR.	5 300
3		J12		275	DR.	5 025
5		J12		250	DR.	4 775
6		J12	700		DR.	5 475

ACCOUNT Sales — NO. 400

DATE	PARTICULARS	P.R.	DEBIT	CREDIT	DR. CR.	BALANCE
2001						
Nov. 1		J12		1 300	CR.	1 300
6		J12		700	CR.	2 000

ACCOUNT Advertising Expense — NO. 500

DATE	PARTICULARS	P.R.	DEBIT	CREDIT	DR. CR.	BALANCE
2001						
Nov. 3		J12	275		DR.	275

ACCOUNT Salaries Expense — NO. 502

DATE	PARTICULARS	P.R.	DEBIT	CREDIT	DR. CR.	BALANCE
2001						
Nov. 5		J12	250		DR.	250

The Opening Entry

A special entry, called an *opening entry,* is prepared when a business first begins operations. Following are the procedures K. Martin used when starting a painting business.

The opening entry records the assets, liabilities, and owner's equity when a business first begins operations.

On September 1, K. Martin borrowed money from a bank and started a painting business. He invested $4 000 cash, a small truck worth $6 500, and equipment worth $1 900. The assets of the new business are:

Cash	$ 4 000
Equipment	1 900
Truck	6 500
Total	$12 400

The business has one liability:

Bank Loan	$5 000

Martin's equity is calculated by applying the equation:

A	=	L	+	OE
$12 400		$5 000		$7 400

Martin's equity is $7 400.

To open the books of the business, the General Journal is set up, and the business' assets, liability, and owner's equity are recorded. The first entry, as illustrated in Figure 4-10, is called the *opening entry.*

GENERAL JOURNAL					PAGE 1
DATE		PARTICULARS	P.R.	DEBIT	CREDIT
2001					
Sep.	1	Cash		4 000	
		Equipment		1 900	
		Truck		6 500	
		Bank Loan			5 000
		K. Martin, Capital			7 400
		Started a painting business with the above assets, liability, and owner's equity.			

FIGURE 4-10
Opening entry in the General Journal for Martin Painting Contractors

Notice that the opening entry shows three debits and two credits with the three debit amounts ($12 400) equal to the two credit amounts ($12 400). You learned in Unit 6 that an entry that shows more than one debit or credit is called a compound entry. Remember, however, that all entries must have equal debit and credit amounts. After the opening entry is journalized, the daily entries of the business can be recorded.

Opening Ledger Accounts

Next, the ledger is prepared by opening accounts required to post the opening entry (Figure 4-10). As business transactions occur, they are journalized. As new accounts are required, they are opened in the ledger. Follow these procedures when opening a new balance-column account:

(1) Write the name of the account to the right of the word "account."

(2) Write the account number at the far right on the top line.

(3) Write the date in the date column.

(4) Write "Opening Balance" on the first line in the column identified by the heading "particulars." This will help distinguish the opening entry from the changes that will occur in the account as business transactions take place.

(5) Write J1 for General Journal page 1 in the posting reference column.

(6) Record the amount in the correct debit or credit column.

(7) Enter the balance in the balance column.

(8) Depending on the balance, write DR. or CR. in the DR./CR. column.

(9) Enter the ledger account number in the posting reference column of the General Journal.

(10) Insert the account in numerical sequence in the ledger.

Figure 4-11 (on page 85) shows the posting of the opening entry to the ledger accounts. For each item in the opening entry, an account has been prepared. Notice that "Opening Balance" has been written in the particulars column and that the six steps in posting have been followed.

GENERAL LEDGER

ACCOUNT Cash						NO. 100
DATE	PARTICULARS	P.R.	DEBIT	CREDIT	DR. CR.	BALANCE
2001						
Sep. 1	Opening Balance	J1	4 000		DR.	4 000

ACCOUNT Equipment						NO. 141
DATE	PARTICULARS	P.R.	DEBIT	CREDIT	DR. CR.	BALANCE
2001						
Sep. 1	Opening Balance	J1	1 900		DR.	1 900

ACCOUNT Truck						NO. 142
DATE	PARTICULARS	P.R.	DEBIT	CREDIT	DR. CR.	BALANCE
2001 Sep. 1	Opening Balance	J1	6 500		DR.	6 500

ACCOUNT Bank Loan						NO. 221
DATE	PARTICULARS	P.R.	DEBIT	CREDIT	DR. CR.	BALANCE
2001 Sep. 1	Opening Balance	J1		5 000	CR.	5 000

ACCOUNT K. Martin, Capital						NO. 300
DATE	PARTICULARS	P.R.	DEBIT	CREDIT	DR. CR.	BALANCE
2001 Sep. 1	Opening Balance	J1		7 400	CR.	7 400

FIGURE 4-11
Ledger after posting the opening entry

CHART OF ACCOUNTS

Each account in the ledger has an account title and an account number. Accounts are placed in the ledger in numerical sequence so that they may be located quickly. A list of the account names and numbers – called a *chart of accounts* – is used by accounting employees. The chart of accounts is an aid in deciding which accounts may be used when transactions are journalized and in locating accounts when posting to the ledger.

A chart of accounts is a list of the names and account numbers of all the accounts in the ledger.

The accounts in the ledger are numbered in the same order as they appear on the balance sheet and income statement. Notice that in the chart of accounts for Martin Painting Contractors (Figure 4-12) a series of numbers is assigned to each type of account:

100–199	Asset accounts	400–499	Revenue accounts
200–299	Liability accounts	500–599	Expense accounts
300–399	Owner's equity accounts		

In large companies, a four-digit series of numbers may be required to cover all the accounts. For example, asset accounts might be numbered 1000–1999, and liability accounts might be numbered 2000–2999. This system is suitable for a business with a large number of accounts. In computer accounting, the account number becomes a numeric code and is used in place of the account title when journalizing transactions. Only the number is entered on the keyboard. The account name then automatically appears on the screen.

FIGURE 4-12
Chart of accounts for Martin Painting Contractors

Martin Painting Contractors
Chart of Accounts

Assets

100 Cash
110 Accounts Receivable/A. Baker
111 Accounts Receivable/L. Carter
131 Painting Supplies
141 Equipment
142 Truck

Liabilities

200 Accounts Payable/International Paints
201 Accounts Payable/Hardware Supply Corp.
221 Bank Loan
231 Mortgage Payable

Owner's Equity

300 K. Martin, Capital
301 K. Martin, Drawings

Revenue

400 Sales

Expenses

500 Advertising Expense
501 Rent Expense
502 Salaries Expense

FORWARDING PROCEDURE

The active accounts of a business show many transactions recorded on the pages of the ledger. When an account page is filled, a new page is opened according to the following procedure:

(1) Head up a new page using the same account name and number (Figures 4-13 and 4-14).
(2) Write "Forwarded" on the last line of the old page in the particulars column (Figure 4-13).

FIGURE 4-13
Ledger page that has been filled and forwarded

ACCOUNT Accounts Receivable/L. Carter NO. 111

DATE	PARTICULARS	P.R.	DEBIT	CREDIT	DR. CR.	BALANCE
2001						
Nov. 3	Opening Balance	J1	1 200		DR.	1 200
3		J1	500		DR.	1 700
4		J1		1 000	DR.	700
5		J2	100		DR.	800
5		J2		300	DR.	500
6		J3	400		DR.	900
7		J3	2 300		DR.	3 200
7	Forwarded	J3		3 050	DR.	150

(3) On the first line of the new page, write the date (year, month, day), "Forwarded" in the particulars column, and the balance in the balance column. Indicate the type of balance. Place a check mark in the posting reference column as shown in Figure 4-14.

FIGURE 4-14
New ledger page

ACCOUNT Accounts Receivable/L. Carter						NO. 111
DATE	PARTICULARS	P.R.	DEBIT	CREDIT	DR. CR.	BALANCE
2001 Nov. 7	Forwarded	✓			DR.	150

Note that aside from the "Opening Balance" and "Forwarded" notations, the particulars column is seldom used. If further information is required about a transaction, use the posting reference numbers to trace the entry back to the General Journal where more detailed information can be found.

REVIEWING THE TRIAL BALANCE

At regular intervals, usually monthly, a trial balance is prepared. A trial balance is proof of the mathematical accuracy of the ledger. As you learned in Chapter 2, a trial balance is a list of the debit account balances and the credit account balances. The total of the debit balances should equal the total of the credit balances. The formal trial balance for Martin Painting Contractors is illustrated in Figure 4-15.

A trial balance is proof of the mathematical accuracy of the ledger.

FIGURE 4-15
Formal trial balance

Martin Painting Contractors
Trial Balance
November 30, 2001

ACCOUNT TITLE	ACC. NO.	DEBIT	CREDIT
Cash	100	$ 1 200	
Accounts Receivable/A. Baker	110	295	
Accounts Receivable/ L. Carter	111	150	
Equipment	141	2 250	
Truck	142	6 500	
Accounts Pay./International Paints	200		$ 695
Accounts Pay./Hardware Supply Corp.	201		315
Bank Loan	221		5 000
K. Martin, Capital	300		4 385
		$10 395	$10 395

Forms of the Trial Balance

The trial balance may take several forms:

- Formal trial balance (Figure 4-15)
- List of the debit and credit account balances in which the debits total equals the credits total (Figure 4-16)
- Machine tape listing the account balances in which the debits minus the credits equal zero (Figure 4-17)

FIGURE 4-16
List form of trial balance — total debits equal total credits

Martin Painting Contractors
Trial Balance
November 30, 2001

DEBIT	CREDIT
$ 1 200	$ 695
295	315
150	5 000
2 250	4 385
6 500	
$10 395	$10 395

FIGURE 4-17
Machine tape form of trial balance — debits minus credits equal zero

Martin Painting Contractors
Trial Balance
November 30, 2001

```
      0
1 200 +
  295 +
  150 +
2 250 +
6 500 +
  695 –
  315 –
5 000 –
4 385 –
      0
```

DEALING WITH ERRORS

Avoiding Posting Errors

By following the six steps in posting given previously, the following types of errors can be avoided:

- Not posting an entire transaction
- Not posting either the debit or credit part of a transaction
- Posting to the correct side but to the wrong account
- Posting to the wrong side of an account
- Calculating the balance incorrectly
- Transposing figures (posting 96 instead of 69)

Locating Trial Balance Errors

The trial balance is a test or trial to prove that the ledger is mathematically in balance. If the totals of the debit and credit columns of the trial balance are not the same, the error must be located before the financial statements are prepared.

Locating errors can be very discouraging and time-consuming. The suggestions that follow represent procedures for identifying the type of error that has occurred and methods for tracking it down.

(1) Add the columns over again and check for arithmetic errors.
(2) Determine the difference between the debit and credit totals.
(3) If the difference is 1, 10, 100, etc., there may be an addition or subtraction error.
(4) Check to see if an account in the ledger with the same balance as the difference (Step 2) has been omitted from the trial balance.
(5) Divide the difference (Step 2) by 2. Look for that amount on the wrong side of the trial balance.
(6) If the difference is divisible evenly by 9, the error may be due to a transposition of numbers (for example 97 written as 79).
(7) Check to see if the amount of the difference has been omitted when it was posted from a journal to the ledger.
(8) If the error still escapes you:
   (a) Check each balance in each column in the ledger.
   (b) Check the posting reference column of each journal to locate unposted items.
   (c) Recheck each posting.
(9) If you still have not found the error — relax! Go on with something else, then return later with a clear frame of mind and try again.

Example of a Transposition Error

Following is a list of debits and credits from a trial balance. The totals do not balance because an error has been made. The debit total is $2 075 and the credit total is $2 165.

DEBIT	CREDIT
$ 150	
400	
560	
200	
765	
	$ 495
	1 670
$2 075	$2 165

In order to find the error, the following is done:

(1) Re-add the columns to ascertain if an addition error has been made.
(2) Determine the difference. The difference between the debit total ($2 075) and the credit total ($2 165) is $90.
(3) Is the difference divisible by 9, evenly? Since the difference is divisible by 9 evenly (90 ÷ 9 = 10), the error may be a transposition error. That is, numbers may be reversed.

(4) Check each number for a reversal. A check of each ledger account balance indicates that an account balance of $560 was incorrectly written. It should be $650. The 5 and the 6 have been transposed.

The correct trial balance follows.

DEBIT	CREDIT
$ 150	
400	
650	
200	
765	
	$ 495
	1 670
$2 165	$2 165

Correcting Errors

The accepted method of correcting errors is to rule out the mistake and to rewrite the correction:

~~265~~ *256*

Some businesses insist that all corrections be initialled:

~~159~~ *195* *C.D.*

Correcting Journal Entries

Suppose the following entry had been made in the journal and posted to the ledger accounts:

Jun. 2	Equipment	50	
	Cash		50
	Cheque 141, purchase of equipment.		

The amount of the entry should have been $500. One method of correcting this error is to cancel the entry and re-enter the transaction. This is done as illustrated below.

Cancel the entry:

Jun. 3	Cash	50	
	Equipment		50
	To cancel the Jun. 2 entry for Cheque 141, incorrect amount.		

Re-enter the transaction:

Jun. 3	Cash	500	
	Equipment		500
	Cheque 141, purchase of equipment.		

Checking for Accuracy

When using a calculator to check calculations, follow these procedures (see Figure 4-18):

(1) Clear the calculator.
(2) Enter the data.
(3) Label the tape.
(4) If the totals being checked do not balance, audit the tape by checking the numbers on the tape against the source. This step will locate errors made in entering numbers on the machine keyboard.
(5) Staple the labelled tape to the material being checked.

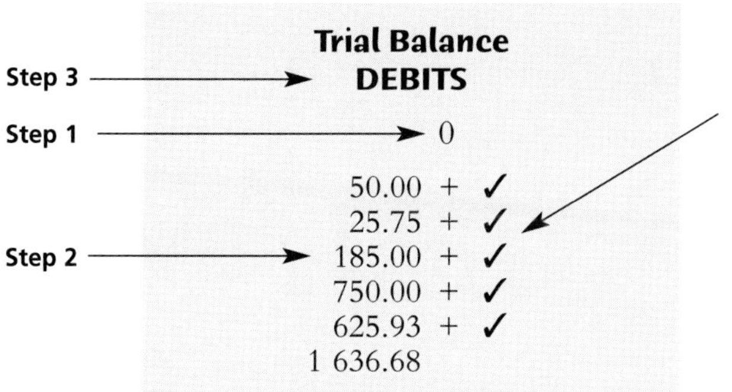

FIGURE 4-18
Checking a trial balance by calculator

Checking Accounts

The balance of an account may be checked on a calculator by entering each debit with the plus (+) key and each credit with the minus (–) key. Take the total after the last entry. Figure 4-19 below illustrates this procedure.

Another method of checking accounts is to use the subtotal or equals key to check the balance column after each entry (Figure 4-20). This technique specifically identifies the line on which an error may occur.

Cash Account

2 190.00	+
2 190.00	+
25.00	=
2 215.00	
2 215.00	–
395.00	=
1 820.00	
1 820.00	–
620.00	=
1 200.00	
1 200.00	+
895.60	=
2 095.60	
2 095.60	–
8.70	=
2 086.90	
2 086.90	+
699.20	=
2 786.10	

FIGURE 4-20
Subtotal method

ACCOUNT Cash NO. 100

DATE	PARTICULARS	P.R.	DEBIT	CREDIT	DR. CR.	BALANCE
2001						
Nov. 1	Forwarded	✓			DR.	2 190.00
2		J16	25.00		DR.	2 215.00
3		J16		395.00	DR.	1 820.00
5		J16		620.00	DR.	1 200.00
5		J17	895.60		DR.	2 095.60
5		J17		8.70	DR.	2 086.90
5		J18	699.20		DR.	2 786.10

Cash Account

0	
2 190.00	+
25.00	–
395.00	–
620.00	+
895.60	–
8.70	+
699.20	=
2 786.10	

FIGURE 4-19
Checking accounts by calculator

INTRODUCING THE ACCOUNTING CYCLE

The accounting cycle is the set of accounting procedures performed in each accounting period.

You have seen that business transactions are first recorded in a journal and are then posted to the ledger. If the ledger is in balance, the financial statements (the income statement and the balance sheet) are then prepared. These steps are completed in sequence in each accounting period and together are called the *accounting cycle.*

FIGURE 4-21
Accounting cycle

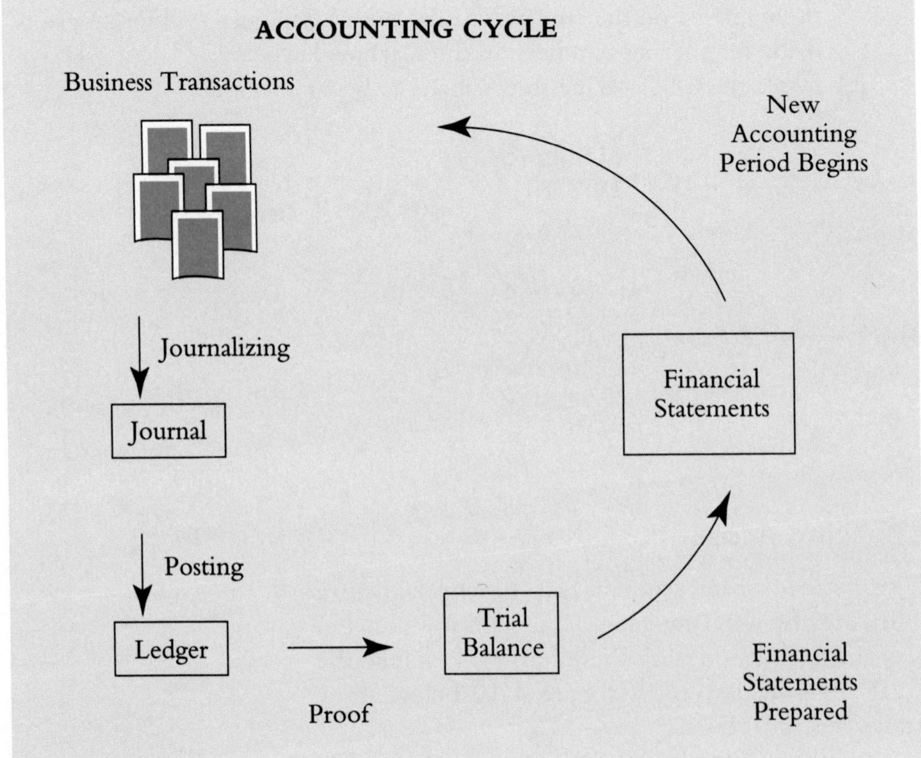

REVIEW QUESTIONS UNIT 7

1. What is posting?
2. What are the six steps followed in posting?
3. What is written in the posting reference column of a journal and a ledger?
4. What is an opening entry?
5. What is a chart of accounts?
6. What is the accounting cycle?
7. An account with a $600 debit balance is incorrectly placed on the trial balance as a $600 credit.
   (a) State how much the difference will be between the trial balance debit and credit totals.
   (b) How is such an error identified?
   (c) What is a transposition error? Give an example.

8. (a) The difference in the totals of a trial balance is $100. What type of error has probably been made?
   (b) If the difference is $270, what type of error may have been made?

PROBLEMS: APPLICATIONS

CHAPTER 4

5. (a) The following Cash account has incomplete DR./CR. and balance columns. Prepare a copy of the account, completing the DR./CR. column and the balance column on each line of the account.
   (b) Assume that the account page for Cash is filled. Apply the forwarding procedure and forward the balance to a new account page for Cash.

ACCOUNT Cash NO. 100

DATE		PARTICULARS	P.R.	DEBIT	CREDIT	DR. CR.	BALANCE
2001							
Dec.	1	Forwarded	✓			DR.	4 261.00
	2		J16	200.00		DR.	4 461.00
	2		J16		175.00	DR.	4 286.00
	3		J16	162.50			.
	3		J16	843.75			
	4		J17		53.17		
	5		J17	86.19			
	5		J17		2 433.70		

6. On May 1, M. Conway, an architect, opened a business. A chart of accounts for the business is given below.
   (a) Journalize the May transactions using accounts from the chart of accounts.
   (b) Open ledger accounts using account titles and numbers from the chart of accounts.
   (c) Post the General Journal entries.
   (d) Prepare a trial balance.

100	Cash
110	Accounts Receivable/Bak Contractors
141	Office Equipment
142	Automobile
200	Accounts Payable/Ajax Motors
300	M. Conway, Capital
400	Fees Earned
505	General Expense
507	Rent Expense
508	Salaries Expense
510	Telephone Expense

May 1 M. Conway invested $25 000 cash in an architectural consulting business.

2 Bought office equipment, $4 500 cash.

3 Bought an automobile for business from Ajax Motors Ltd. on credit. The cost price of the car was $26 900.

4 Received $650 cash for services provided to a customer.

5 Sent a bill for $1 000 to Bak Contractors for services provided.

5 Paid the May rent, $1 200 cash.

5 Paid office salaries, $1 425.

5 Paid $75 for the installation of a telephone.

7. An accounting clerk has prepared three mini trial balances that do not balance. Calculate the difference in the debit and credit totals and indicate the probable type of error made by the clerk in each case.

(a)

DEBIT	CREDIT
$ 3 000	
1 000	
700	
420	
	$ 2 950
	2 170
$5 120	$5 020

(b)

DEBIT	CREDIT
$200	
300	
50	
	$ 75
	25
	300
	200
$550	$600

(c)

DEBIT	CREDIT
$ 3 000	
1 000	
700	
240	
	$ 2 950
	2 170
$4 940	$5 120

8. The Supplies account shown below contains a number of errors.

(a) List the errors.
(b) Prepare a corrected Supplies account.

ACCOUNT Supplies **NO. 102**

DATE	PARTICULARS	P.R.	DEBIT	CREDIT	DR. CR.	BALANCE
2001						
Oct. 1	Forwarded	✓			DR.	2 300
2		J3		300	CR.	2 000
3		J3	400		DR.	2 400
4		J3	250		DR.	2 650
5		J3	150		DR.	2 500

9. Ahmad Nauman opened an insurance agency on August 1 with the following assets and liabilities: Cash $2 500; Equipment $5 500; Building $105 000; Land $25 000; Bank Loan $8 000; Mortgage $85 000; A. Nauman, Capital $45 000. Record the opening entry for the business in a General Journal.

10. Bonnie Gordon opened a secretarial service business on April 1 with the following assets and liabilities: Cash $2 500; Equipment $4 300; Bank Loan $3 800.

(a) Prepare an opening entry in a General Journal. (Remember that your entry must balance.)
(b) The following events, on page 95, occurred in April. Journalize the items in the books of the company. Revenue should be recorded in the Fees from Clients account.

Apr. 1 Paid the first month's rent on the office, $800 cash.

1 Completed keying a report for a client, J. Jamison, and mailed the bill for $250.

2 Received a bill from the *Express* for advertising, $155.

3 Purchased office supplies from Beatties Stationery, $180 on credit.

4 Received $115 cash from a client for work completed today.

5 Mailed a cheque drawn on the company bank account, $630 to pay Ms. Gordon's apartment rent.

8 J. Jamison paid the bill issued Apr. 1 in full.

9 Returned $65 box of envelopes purchased Apr. 3 to Beatties Stationery because they were the incorrect size. Beatties agreed to give us a credit for the amount. (This means the firm now owes Beatties $65 less as a result of the transaction.)

10 Paid the *Express* bill of Apr. 2.

11 Paid Beatties in full.

UNIT 8 Source Documents

Learning Objectives

After reading this unit, discussing the applicable review questions, and completing the applications exercises, you will be able to do the following:

1. **IDENTIFY** and **RECORD** source documents.
2. **EXPLAIN** why source documents are prepared for every transaction.

As business transactions occur, information about the transactions is recorded on some form of business document. For example, when a cash sale is made, a sales slip is prepared. A copy is given to the customer and a copy is kept by the seller. The accountant for the seller uses the sales slip as the source of information that a sale has been made. The accountant for the buyer uses the copy of the same document as a source of information that a purchase has been made. This is where the term *source document* comes from. The most commonly used source documents will be described in this chapter.

A source document is any business form that is the original source of information.

Source documents are proof that a business transaction did in fact occur. A document is a concrete object. The source document is generally prepared with at least two copies. The two parties to a transaction, generally the seller and the buyer, each receive an exact copy. An important principle of accounting is:

A source document must be prepared for every business transaction.

CASH SALES SLIPS

Figure 4-22 on the next page is a cash sales slip used by many retail stores. Three copies of the cash sales slip are prepared when a cash sale is made. These are distributed as follows:

- Copy 1: Given to the customer.
- Copy 2: Used by the accounting department of the seller to record the transaction.
- Copy 3: Kept in a numerical file which serves as a record of all cash sales. Every sales slip must be accounted for in this file.

This entry is made by the seller's accountant from Copy 2:

May	21	Cash	24.89	
		Sales		24.89
		Sales Slip 43785.		

It should be noted that in actual practice, groups of sales slips would be combined and an entry similar to the preceding one would be made to record the total of the group of slips.

The buyer uses Copy 1 as the source of information to record this entry:

May	21	Building Repairs Expense	24.89	
		Cash		24.89
		Purchased paint for cash.		

The diagram shown below in Figure 4-23 illustrates how both the buyer and the seller use copies of the same source document to record a transaction:

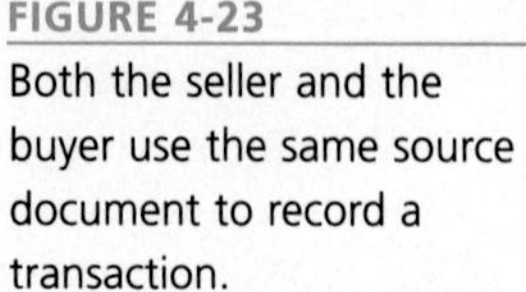

FIGURE 4-23

Both the seller and the buyer use the same source document to record a transaction.

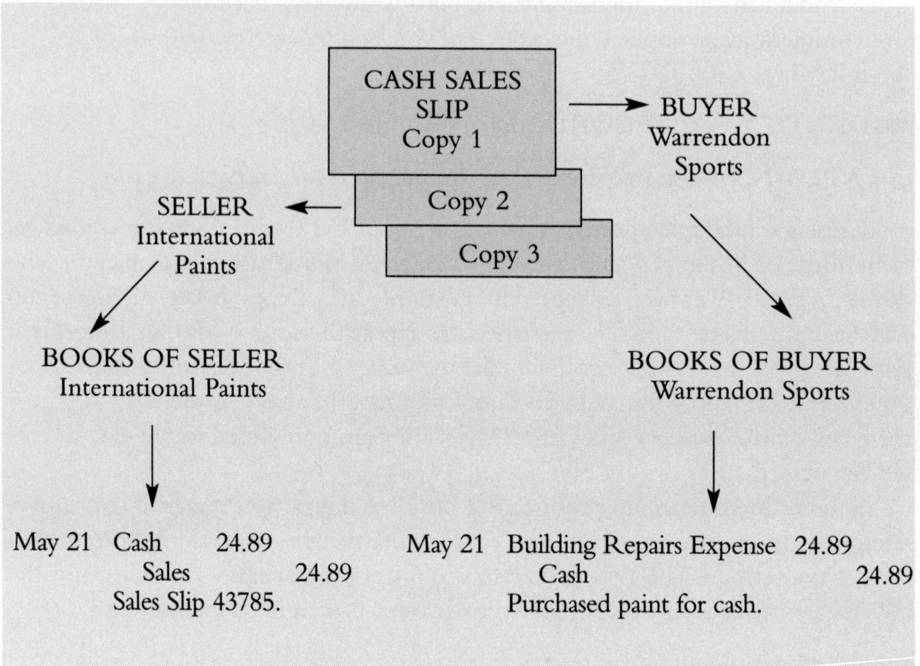

160 SPRUCE STREET OTTAWA, ONT. K1R 6P2 TEL (613) 236-0716

CASH SALE

VENTE AU COMPTANT

International Paints (Canada) Limited

Marine, Industrial, Railway, Aircraft & Household Finishes

DATE May 21 2001

NAME / NOM Warrendon Sports

ADDRESS / ADRESSE 2579 Base Line Rd., Ottawa, Ont. K2H 7B3

CODE NUMBER NUMÉRO DU CODE		ORDERED COMM	UNIT SIZE FORMAT	DESCRIPTION	UNIT PRIX L'UNITÉ	AMOUNT MONTANT	
CM 230000		1	1 L	Exterior Paint		24	89
CASH ✓	CHX.	REF.		CHEQUE	PROV. TAX TAXE PROV.		
SALESPERSON VENDEUR/EUSE		R.H.			TOTAL	24	89

43785 **CUSTOMER'S COPY / COPIE DU CLIENT**

FIGURE 4-22
Cash sales slip — a source document used by retail stores

SALES INVOICES

Figure 4-24 is an example of another source document called a *sales invoice.* It is the bill of sale or simply the bill completed by the seller and given to the buyer as a record of a credit sale. A *credit sale* is one in which the customer agrees to pay at a later date. Other terms used to describe a credit sale are *charge sale* or *on account sale.*

The selling company makes several copies of the sales invoice and distributes them as follows:

- Copies 1 and 2: Sent to the customer.
- Copy 3: Used by the accounting department of the seller as the source of information to record the transaction.
- Copy 4: Kept by the sales department as a record of the sale.
- Copies 5 and 6: Given to the shipping department of the seller. Copy 5 is used to pack and label the shipment. Copy 6 is placed inside the shipment as a packing slip. The packing slip tells the customer what should be in the shipment.

FIGURE 4-24
Sales invoice with details of a charge sale

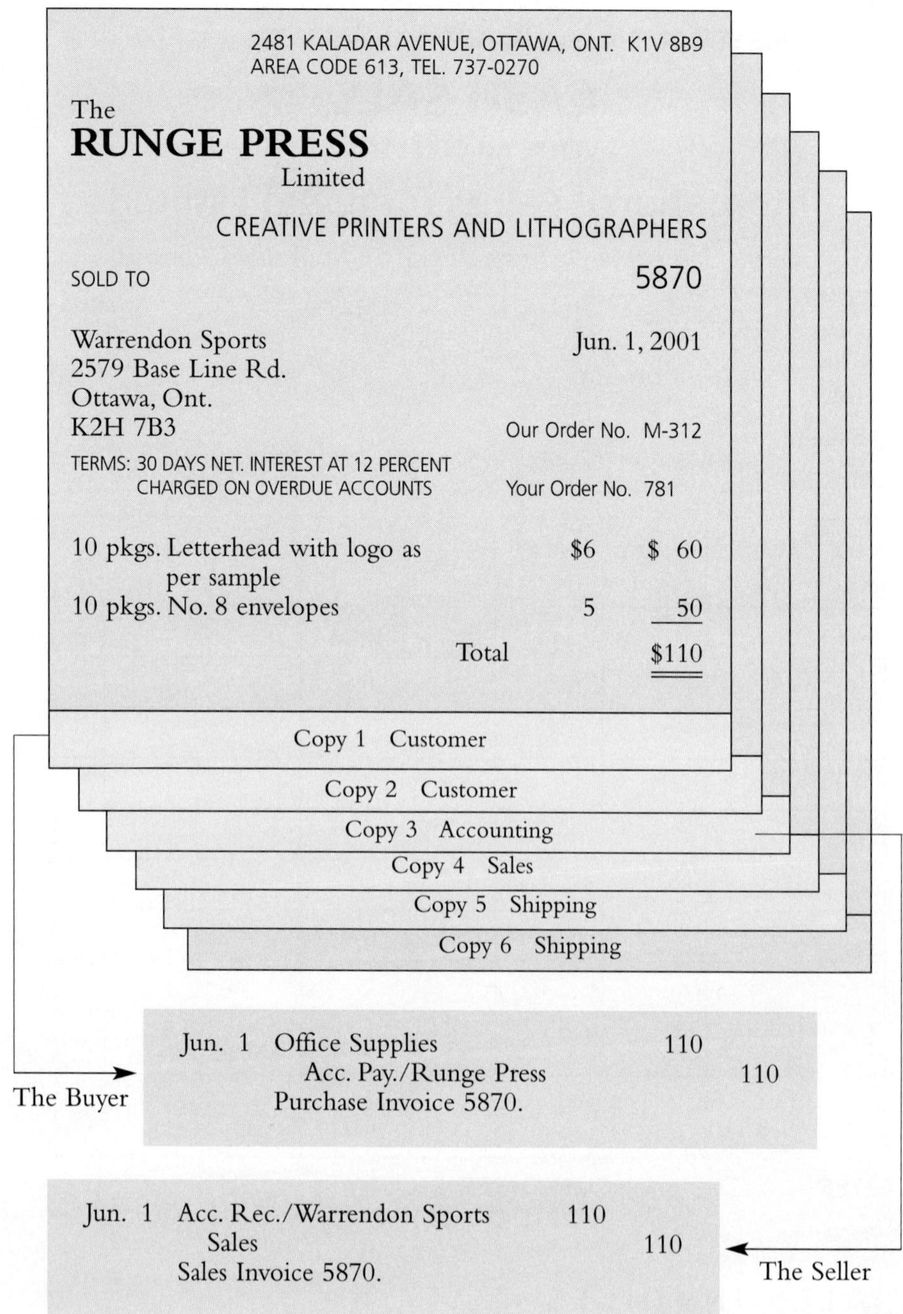
2481 KALADAR AVENUE, OTTAWA, ONT. K1V 8B9
AREA CODE 613, TEL. 737-0270

The
RUNGE PRESS
Limited

CREATIVE PRINTERS AND LITHOGRAPHERS

SOLD TO 5870

Warrendon Sports
2579 Base Line Rd.
Ottawa, Ont.
K2H 7B3

Jun. 1, 2001

Our Order No. M-312

TERMS: 30 DAYS NET. INTEREST AT 12 PERCENT CHARGED ON OVERDUE ACCOUNTS

Your Order No. 781

10 pkgs. Letterhead with logo as per sample	$6	$ 60
10 pkgs. No. 8 envelopes	5	50
Total		$110

This entry is made by the accounting department of the seller from Copy 3:

Jun.	1	Accounts Receivable/Warrendon Sports	110	
		Sales		110
		Invoice 5870, letterhead paper and envelopes.		

PURCHASE INVOICES

Look again at Figure 4-24. What is the name of the seller? The buyer? To the seller, Runge Press, this is a *sales invoice* and Copy 3 of this sales invoice is used to prepare the entry shown at the bottom of page 98. To the buyer, Warrendon Sports Ltd., this is a *purchase invoice.* Copies 1 and 2 are records of what Warrendon has purchased and indicate how much is owed to the seller.

When must Warrendon Sports Ltd. pay the $110? What happens if the invoice is not paid on time? The buyer, Warrendon Sports, would make this journal entry to record the purchase invoice:

Jun.	1	Office Supplies	110	
		Accounts Payable/Runge Press		110
		Purchased stationery, Invoice 5870, net 30 days.		

You can see that the same document is used to record the sale by the seller and the purchase by the customer. As has been stated, the sellers call their document a *sales invoice* and the buyers call their copy a *purchase invoice.*

CHEQUES

Cheques Paid

On June 1, Warrendon Sports bought $110 worth of office supplies from the Runge Press. The terms of payment were net 30 days. This means that the $110 must be paid within 30 days from the date of the invoice. On June 30, Warrendon Sports prepared Cheque 1624 illustrated in Figure 4-25.

The cheque form consists of two parts, the cheque itself and an attached portion, which provides the details to explain why the cheque was written. The original cheque form is sent to Runge Press. The attached portion and/or a photocopy of the cheque is kept by Warrendon Sports and is the source document for this transaction. The cheque copy is used by Warrendon's accountant to record this entry:

Jun.	30	Accounts Payable/Runge Press	110	
		Cash		110
		Issued Cheque 1624 to pay Invoice 5870.		

Cheques Received

Cheque 1624 is mailed to Runge Press. When it is received by Runge Press, the cheque is separated from the record portion (bottom half). The cheque is endorsed with a restrictive endorsement (deposit only to the account of Runge Press) and immediately deposited in the Runge Press' bank account.

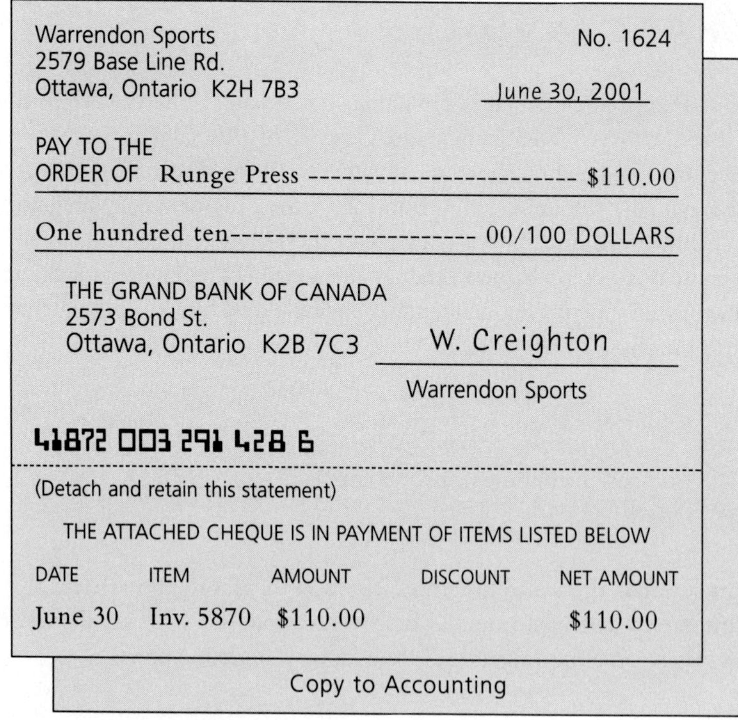
Warrendon Sports
2579 Base Line Rd.
Ottawa, Ontario K2H 7B3

No. 1624

June 30, 2001

PAY TO THE
ORDER OF Runge Press ------------------------ $110.00

One hundred ten---------------------- 00/100 DOLLARS

THE GRAND BANK OF CANADA
2573 Bond St.
Ottawa, Ontario K2B 7C3

W. Creighton
Warrendon Sports

41872 003 291 428 6

(Detach and retain this statement)

THE ATTACHED CHEQUE IS IN PAYMENT OF ITEMS LISTED BELOW

DATE	ITEM	AMOUNT	DISCOUNT	NET AMOUNT
June 30	Inv. 5870	$110.00		$110.00

Copy to Accounting

FIGURE 4-25
Cheque issued by Warrendon Sports

An *endorsement* is the signature placed on the back of a cheque by the person or company depositing the cheque. A *restrictive endorsement* is used to control what will happen to the funds from the cheque. The record portion of the cheque is used to prepare the following entry:

Jul.	2	Cash	110	
		Accounts Receivable/Warrendon Sports		110
		Received Cheque 1624 for Invoice 5870.		

List of Cheques Received

Companies that receive a large number of cheques each day prepare a list of the cheques. The cheques are then deposited in the bank. The list is used by the accountant to prepare the journal entries to record the money received and to lower the amounts owing on the customer accounts.

FURTHER FACTS ABOUT SOURCE DOCUMENTS

Prenumbered Source Documents

Source documents are prenumbered, and every document must be accounted for. The numbering of documents is a control procedure designed to prevent errors and losses due to theft or the use of false documents. Source documents are kept on file and must be made available to persons who have the authority to check a company's records. These include:

- Owners and managers of the business
- Outside accountants hired to check the records
- Federal income tax personnel
- Provincial sales tax and Department of Labour personnel
- Officials of the courts

Source documents are an important part of a company's accounting system. Every business should take care to produce neat, legible documents that are numbered and filed in a well-organized manner.

Source Documents as Evidence for Transactions

Source documents provide evidence that a transaction has actually occurred. If a check is made on a company's accounting records, the company must be able to prove that the transactions did happen. Source documents such as cash sales slips, sales invoices, and purchase invoices provide the necessary proof.

Further checks on the accuracy of a company's records can be made by comparing the source document copies of both the buyer and the seller. The information on the documents should be the same.

The Concept of Objectivity

The dollar values used in transactions should be determined in a very objective way. The source documents provide objective, verifiable evidence to support the value placed on transactions.

A company could overstate the value of its assets by recording them at a high value. This would make the company appear to be more valuable than it really is. To avoid such situations, accountants follow the concept of objectivity.

The concept of objectivity requires evidence to support the value used to record transactions.

Summary

Remember that, as has already been stated, it is an important principle of accounting that:

A source document must be prepared for every business transaction.

The chart on the following page summarizes the source documents used in this chapter:

Source Document	Business Transaction
Cash sales slip	Cash sale to a customer
Sales invoice	Sale on account to a customer
Purchase invoice	Purchase on account
Cheque paid	Payment made to a creditor (account payable)
Cheque received	Payment received from a customer (account receivable)

ACCOUNTING TERMS

Accounting Cycle The accounting cycle is the set of accounting procedures performed in each accounting period.

Balance-Column Form of Account A form of account that shows a continuous balance after each transaction.

Book of Original Entry The journal is referred to as the book of original entry. Transactions are recorded in the journal as they occur.

Cash Sales Slip Source document for a cash sale.

Compound Entry An entry that has more than one debit or more than one credit.

Concept of Objectivity Dollar values used in recording transactions should be verified by objective evidence such as source documents.

General Journal The main journal of a business.

Journal A record of transactions recorded in chronological (date) order.

Journal Entry Each transaction recorded in a journal.

Journalizing Process of recording transactions in a journal.

Opening Entry Records the assets, liabilities, and owner's equity when a business first begins operation.

Posting Transfer of information from a journal to the ledger.

Posting Reference Column Indicates where more information regarding the entry can be located.

Purchase Invoice Source document for a purchase on credit.

Sales Invoice Source document for a sale on credit.

Source Document A business form that is the original source of information for a transaction.

Transposition Where numbers are reversed, such as writing 89 rather than 98.

1. (a) What is a source document?
   (b) Give four examples of source documents.
   (c) Why are source documents prenumbered?
   (d) Name a source document for each of the following:
      (i) Cash sale
      (ii) Sale on account
      (iii) Purchase on account
      (iv) Payment by cheque
2. Explain the concept of objectivity.

11. For the Birchwood Manufacturing Company invoice shown below, answer the following:
   (a) Who is the seller?
   (b) Who is the buyer?
   (c) What is the invoice number? Invoice date? Invoice total?

BIRCHWOOD MANUFACTURING COMPANY
WOODEN THREAD SPOOLS AND WOOD TURNINGS
MANDEVILLE, BERTHIER COUNTY, QUEBEC J0K 1L0

VIA C.P. EXPRESS
SHIP TO WABASSO LTD. **INV. NO.** 20529
ADDRESS 2069 LINCOLN ST.
WELLAND, ONTARIO
L3B 4R8

INVOICE DATE	SHIPPING DATE	CUST. ORDER NO.	OUR ORDER NO.	CUST. PROV. SLS. TAX LIC. NO.
Nov. 6, 2002	Nov. 7, 2002	6821	20529	0231

SOLD TO SAME AS SHIP TO

PACKAGES	DESCRIPTION	QUANTITY PER PKG.	QUANTITY TOTAL	PRICE	TOTAL
1	4 cm WOOD SPOOLS	200	200	$0.16	$32
1	2.5 cm WOOD SPOOLS	100	100	0.11	11
	TOTAL				$43

TERMS: NET 30 DAYS F.O.B. OUR MILL.
1 1/2% MONTHLY SERVICE CHARGE ON PAST DUE ACCOUNT. **INVOICE — SALES**

1. (a) Using the trial balance on the following page, open the accounts in the ledger for Carlo's TV Repairs.
   (b) At the end of each day, Carlo Amato does his accounting from the source documents that he received or issued on that day. Record the source documents for November 15 in the General Journal. Assign page 26 to the General Journal. The source documents are shown on pages 104 to 106.

Carlo's TV Repairs Trial Balance November 15, 2001			
ACCOUNT TITLE	**ACC. NO.**	**DEBIT**	**CREDIT**
Cash	100	$14 000.00	
Accts. Rec./B. Dover	110	647.43	
Accts. Rec./Drive-Inn Motor Hotel	111	198.76	
Accts. Rec./L. Mansfield	112	325.50	
Equipment	141	25 000.00	
Truck	142	17 000.00	
Accts. Pay./Electronics Suppliers	200		$ 2 047.50
Accts. Pay./Poulin's Service Stn.	201		1 276.89
Bank Loan	221		10 000.00
C. Amato, Capital	300		43 847.30
Sales	400		0
Hydro Expense	504	0	
Truck Expense	506	0	
Equipment Repairs Expense	507	0	
		$57 171.69	$57 171.69

Sales Invoices:

INVOICE
Carlo's TV Repairs
1750 Elgin Street, Winnipeg, Manitoba R3E 1C3

DATE: Nov. 15, 2001
INV. NO: 1501
TERMS: Net 30 days

SOLD TO:

B. Dover
141 Dynes Road
Winnipeg, Manitoba R2J 0Z8

RE: C.R.A. Colour TV

Labour	$160.00
Parts	89.85
	$249.85

AMOUNT OF THIS INVOICE: $249.85

INVOICE
Carlo's TV Repairs
1750 Elgin Street, Winnipeg, Manitoba R3E 1C3

DATE: Nov. 15, 2001
INV. NO: 1502
TERMS: Net 30 days

SOLD TO:

Drive-Inn Motor Hotel
1460 River Road
Winnipeg, Manitoba R2M 3Z8

RE: TVs in rooms 117, 119, and 212

Labour	$356.00
Parts	137.50
	$493.50

AMOUNT OF THIS INVOICE: $493.50

Purchase Invoices:

ELECTRONICS SUPPLIERS
147 Industrial Blvd., Winnipeg, Manitoba R2W 0J7
Tel. 475-6643 **Terms:** Net 15 days

Montreal
Toronto
Winnipeg
Vancouver

SOLD TO	**SHIP TO**
Carlo's TV Repairs 1750 Elgin Street Winnipeg, Manitoba R3E 1C3	SAME

Prov. Sales Tax No.	**Date Invoiced**	**Invoice No.**
435 70913	11/12/2001	7463

Quantity	**Description**	**Unit Price**	**Amount**
1	Equipment	$453.90	$453.90
		Pay this amount	$453.90

INVOICE
Poulin's Service Station
1553 Park Drive, Winnipeg, Manitoba R3P 0H2

Date: Nov. 13/2001 **Terms: Net 15 days** **Inv. No. B-151**

Part No.	**Part Name**	**Total**
X340	Oil Filter	$ 11.29
	4 L oil	10.50
316-092	Spark plugs	15.90

Make: GMC Truck
Licence: A-4597
Name: Carlo's TV Repairs
Address: 1750 Elgin Street
Winnipeg, Manitoba
R3E 1C3

WORK COMPLETED	AMOUNT
Oil Change	
Tune-Up	$ 63.00
TOTAL LABOUR	$ 63.00
PARTS	37.69
PAY THIS AMOUNT	$100.69

Cheques issued:

Carlo's TV Repairs
1750 Elgin Street.
Winnipeg, Manitoba R3E 1C3

No. 347

Nov. 15 2001

PAY TO THE
ORDER OF Electronic Suppliers ------------------------------ $2,047.50

Two thousand and forty-seven -------------------------- 50/100 DOLLARS

THE ROYAL BANK OF CANADA
3017 Lelland Road
Winnipeg, Manitoba R2K 0J7

Carlo Amato

Carlo's TV Repairs

21639 003 416 285 9

(Detach and retain this statement)

THE ATTACHED CHEQUE IS IN PAYMENT OF ITEMS LISTED BELOW

DATE	ITEM	AMOUNT	DISCOUNT	NET AMOUNT
Oct. 28	Inv. 7393	$2,047.50		$2,047.50

Carlo's TV Repairs
1750 Elgin Street.
Winnipeg, Manitoba R3E 1C3

No. 348

Nov. 15 2001

PAY TO THE
ORDER OF Winnipeg Hydro ------------------------------------ $79.50

Seventy-nine -- 50/100 DOLLARS

THE ROYAL BANK OF CANADA
3017 Lelland Road
Winnipeg, Manitoba R2K 0J7

Carlo Amato

Carlo's TV Repairs

21639 003 416 285 9

(Detach and retain this statement)

THE ATTACHED CHEQUE IS IN PAYMENT OF ITEMS LISTED BELOW

DATE	ITEM	AMOUNT	DISCOUNT	NET AMOUNT
Nov. 15	Inv. B-741	$79.50		$79.50

Cash receipts:

Daily Cash Receipts Nov. 15, 2001		
CUSTOMER	**INVOICE**	**AMOUNT**
L. Mansfield	1370	$ 225.50
Drive-Inn Motor Hotel	1269	398.76
Cash sales		1 156.63
		$1 780.89

(c) In the General Journal, record the Nov. 16 source documents listed below.

(d) Post the General Journal to the ledger and prepare a trial balance.

Nov. 16 Sales invoices issued to:
L. Mansfield, No. 1503, $477;
Drive-Inn Motor Hotel, No. 1504, $573.60.

Purchase invoice received from:
Electronic Suppliers, No. 7533, $550.80 for servicing the equipment.

Cheques issued to:
Poulin's Service Station, No. 349, $276.89 on account;
Electronic Suppliers, No. 350, $453.90 on account.

Cash received:
B. Dover, $147.43;
Drive-Inn Motor Hotel, $293.50;
Cash sales, $1453.70

2. Following is the October 1 balance sheet for the Valley Motel owned by Jacqui Lebrun.

Valley Motel Balance Sheet October 1, 2003			
Assets		**Liabilities**	
Cash	$ 14 000	Accounts Payable/	
Supplies	12 000	Acme Supply	$ 5 000
Office Equipment	12 000	Bank Loan	25 000
Furniture	20 000	Mortgage Payable	80 000
Automobile	28 000	Total Liabilities	110 000
Building	150 000		
		Owner's Equity	
		J. Lebrun, Capital	126 000
Total Assets	$236 000	Total Liabilities and Owner's Equity	$236 000

The chart of accounts contains the accounts shown on the balance sheet plus the following:

301	J. Lebrun, Drawings	502	Salaries Expense
400	Room Rentals	503	Telephone Expense
500	Advertising Expense	505	Utilities Expense
501	General Expense	506	Automobile Expense

(a) Journalize the opening entry.
(b) Journalize the October transactions using account titles found in the balance sheet and in the chart of accounts.
(c) Open the ledger accounts.
(d) Post the opening entry and the October General Journal entries.
(e) Prepare a trial balance.
(f) Prepare the October financial statements.

Oct. 1 Paid $110 cash for automobile expenses.

2 J. Lebrun withdrew $240 cash for personal use.

3 Paid $2 000 cash to Acme Supply to reduce the amount owing to Acme.

4 Paid $275 cash for the month's telephone charges.

5 Received cash, $3 750, for room rentals for the week.

8 Purchased cleaning supplies from Acme Supply, $160, but did not pay for them.

10 Paid $280 cash for repairs to Lebrun's personal car.

11 Bought a computer for the office for $3 000 cash.

12 Received cash, $2 100, for room rentals for the week.

12 Paid $42 cash for postage stamps (General Expense).

12 Paid the hydro bill, $290 cash, and the water bill, $175 cash.

15 Paid $245 cash for the printing of an advertising brochure.

15 Paid $150 for a small advertisement in the local newspaper.

16 Paid $300 cash to J. Lebrun, the owner, for her own use.

16 Paid salaries for the first half of the month, $2 200 cash.

18 The bank sent a memorandum (letter) informing J. Lebrun that $350 had been taken out of the business bank account to pay for interest on the bank loan. (Open a new account numbered 507 for Interest Expense.)

19 Received $3 250 cash for room rentals for the week.

22 Received a $450 bill from Acme Supply for new linen and towels.

23 Received an $85 bill from Kelly Motors for gasoline and oil used in the business car. (A new account will have to be opened for Kelly Motors.)

25 Paid $500 cash to Acme Supply, on account.

26 Received $2 525 cash for room rentals for the week.

31 Paid salaries for the rest of the month, $2 850 cash.

31 Sold an old typewriter for $50. The typewriter was included in the Office Equipment account at $200. (You will need to set up a new account called Loss on Sale of Equipment.)

3. Helen Young operates a real estate agency which earns money from three sources:

- Commissions earned on sales of property
- Management fees
- Investment income

The management fees are a result of renting and maintaining homes and condominiums for owners who are not living in them but who lease them to others. For a fee, H. Young manages such properties for the owners. The company has invested past net incomes (profits) in stocks and bonds. Interest and dividends received on these investments are recorded in the Investment Income account.

(a) Record the January transactions on page 17 of a General Journal. Use the accounts from the chart of accounts on the next page.

Jan. 2 Received $3 400 cash as a commission for handling the sale of a house.

2 Paid $2 100 cash for the month's rent for the office.

3 Received a bill from Tom's Service Centre for $475 for gas, oil, and repairs to the company automobile. The bill is not to be paid until Jan. 15.

5 Received a bill for $210 for the printing of letterhead, envelopes, and sales contract forms from Willson's Stationery. This bill is to be paid on Jan. 15.

6 Paid $190 cash for a new filing cabinet for the office.

8 Sold an old filing cabinet to a friend for $20. This cabinet was recorded in the Furniture and Equipment account at the original cost price of $175.

8 Received $8 000 cash, commission for a sale of property.

8 Paid office salaries, $1 400.

11 Paid $290 cash for newspaper advertising.

12 Received a $450 cash fee for renting a home owned by a client.

13 H. Young, the owner, withdrew $1 200 for personal use.

14 Received commissions totalling $15 500 from the sale of properties.

14 Paid $275 cash for telephone bill.

15 Paid Tom's Service Centre $475 for the invoice received on Jan. 3.

15 Paid Willson's Stationery $210 for the invoice received on Jan. 5.

15 Paid $150 for the hydro bill.

15 Donated $40 to a charitable organization.

15 Received $90 in dividends from investments owned.

15 Purchased $2 800 worth of Government of Canada bonds.

15 Paid office salaries, $1 400.

15 Paid $5 000 in commission to H. Young Agency's salespeople.

100	Cash	401	Management Fees Earned
131	Office Supplies	402	Investment Income
141	Furniture and Equipment	500	Advertising Expense
142	Automobile	501	Automobile Expense
170	Investments	502	Commissions Expense
200	Accounts Payable/ Tom's Service Centre	503	Rent Expense
		504	Salaries Expense
201	Accounts Payable/ Willson's Stationery	505	Telephone Expense
		506	Utilities Expense
300	H. Young, Capital	507	Miscellaneous Expense
301	H. Young, Drawings	508	Loss on Sale of Furniture and Equipment
400	Commissions Income		

(b) Open a ledger using the chart of accounts.

(c) Record the January 1 balances that follow in the ledger accounts. (Record the date, balance, and put a check mark (✓) in the posting reference column.)

Cash	$ 9 500
Office Supplies	1 700
Furniture and Equipment	5 900
Automobile	24 100
Investments	20 000
H. Young, Capital	61 200

(d) Post the January 1–15 General Journal entries.

(e) Prepare a trial balance.

(f) Prepare an income statement.

(g) H. Young asks you, her accountant, to devise a statement that would show her the change in her equity for this accounting period. Prepare the statement.

4. Judy James began a business called The Easy Weight Loss Salon on February 1, 2001. Several transactions were completed during the month. Judy's knowledge of accounting is very limited, but she knows how to record journal entries and prepare a trial balance. Presented below are the journal entries and the trial balance for the February business.

Date	Account	Debit	Credit
Feb. 1	Cash	50 000	
	J. James, Capital		50 000
2	Rent Expense	2 500	
	Cash		2 500
3	Insurance Expense	550	
	Cash		550
4	Salon Furniture	3 000	
	Salon Equipment	15 000	
	Bank Loan		18 000
4	Salon Supplies	1 700	
	Accounts Payable		1 700
5	Advertising Expense	1 200	
	Cash		1 200
6	Judy officially opened her business		
7	Cash	150	
	Service Revenue		150
8	Accounts Receivable	275	
	Service Revenue		275
9–14	Cash	1 200	
	Accounts Receivable	2 700	
	Service Revenue		3 900
14	Salaries Expense	1 400	
	Cash		1 400
14	Accounts Payable	1 700	
	Cash		1 700
15	Cash	225	
	Service Revenue		225
17	Salon Supplies	1 100	
	Accounts Payable		1 100
19	Cash	275	
	Accounts Receivable		275
19	Accounts Receivable	180	
	Service Revenue		180
20	Advertising Expense	1 500	
	Cash		1 500
23	Cash	1 700	
	Accounts Receivable		1 700

24–28	Cash	2 100	
	Accounts Receivable	3 200	
	Service Revenue		5 300
27	Cash	180	
	Accounts Receivable		180
28	J. James, Drawings	1 300	
	Cash		1 300
28	Bank Loan	1 000	
	Cash		1 000
28	Salaries Expense	1 400	
	Cash		1 400

Note: Each journal entry would normally include an explanation; these were omitted to conserve space.

Trial Balance The Easy Weight Loss Salon February 28, 2001		
Cash	$41 280	
Accounts Receivable	4 200	
Salon Supplies		$ 2 800
Salon Furniture	3 000	
Salon Equipment	15 000	
Accounts Payable		1 100
Bank Loan		1 700
J. James, Capital		50 000
J. James, Drawings		1 300
Service Revenue		10 030
Rent Expense	2 500	
Insurance Expense	550	
Advertising Expense		2 700
Salaries Expense	2 800	
	$69 330	$69 630

Judy remembers that a trial balance should balance and realizes that the one she prepared must have at least one error.

(a) To help Judy find the mistakes, open a ledger and post the entries to the accounts. Use the following accounts:

100	Cash	300	J. James, Capital
110	Accounts Receivable	301	J. James, Drawings
121	Salon Supplies	400	Service Revenue
131	Salon Furniture	500	Rent Expense
141	Salon Equipment	501	Insurance Expense
200	Accounts Payable	502	Advertising Expense
220	Bank Loan	503	Salaries Expense

(b) Prepare a correct trial balance.

CHAPTER 5

The Work Sheet and Classified Financial Statements

UNIT 9 The Work Sheet

Learning Objectives

After reading this unit, discussing the applicable review questions, and completing the applications exercises, you will be able to do the following:

1. **EXPLAIN** the function of a work sheet.
2. **PREPARE** a work sheet when given a trial balance.
3. **PREPARE** an income statement and a balance sheet from a work sheet.

Figure 5-1, on the next page, illustrates the steps in the accounting cycle as they have been described up to this point. The end of the fiscal period is a particularly important time for accountants because they do a great deal of work at that time. They must prove the mathematical accuracy of the ledger by preparing a trial balance; then they prepare the income statement and the balance sheet. As an aid in avoiding errors and to help organize their work, accountants use a device called a work sheet.

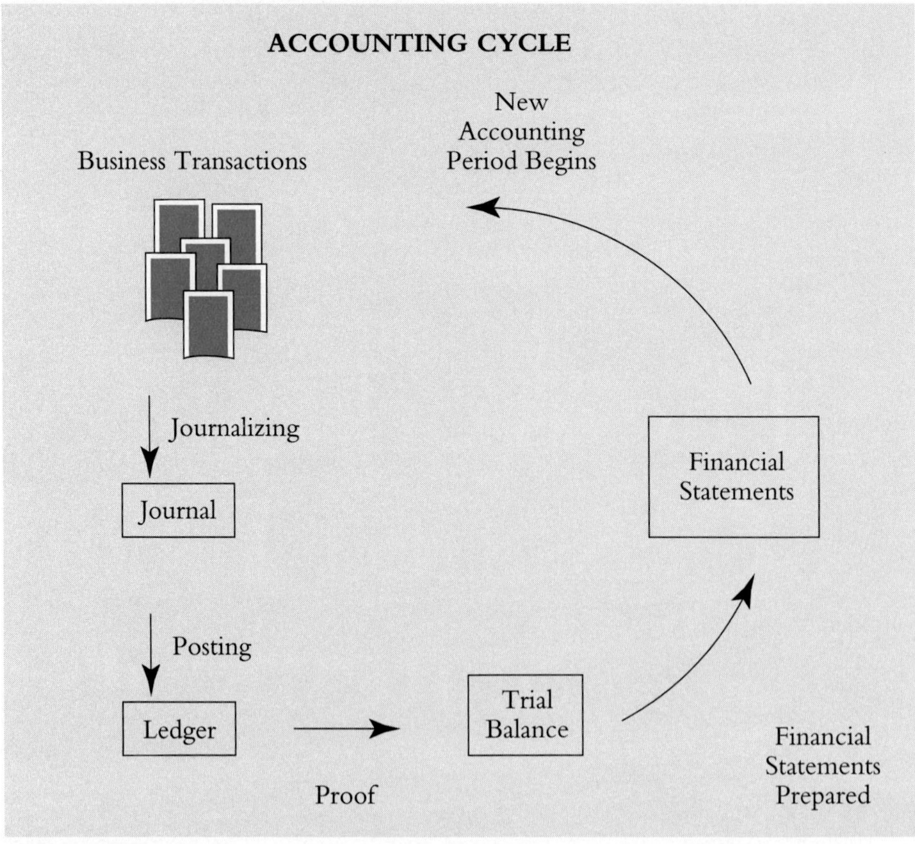

FIGURE 5–1
Steps in the accounting cycle covered to this point

INTRODUCING THE WORK SHEET

A work sheet is a device that organizes accounting data required for the preparation of financial statements.

A *work sheet* is a device that organizes accounting data required for the preparation of financial statements. It is one of the few forms that may be completed in pencil since it is not part of permanent accounting records. It is designed to discover and to eliminate errors before they become part of permanent records. The work sheet represents a rough draft of the work completed at the end of the accounting cycle and is sometimes called the accountant's working papers. It is not a formal statement provided for management, for the owners, or for persons interested in the financial position of the business.

Figure 5-2, below, illustrates the basic principles of the six-column work sheet. All the account balances are taken from the ledger and written on the work sheet in the trial balance section. The account balances are then transferred to either the income statement section or the balance sheet section of the work sheet.

FIGURE 5–2
Basic principles of the six-column work sheet

Account Title	Acc. No.	Trial Balance Debit	Trial Balance Credit	Income Statement Debit	Income Statement Credit	Balance Sheet Debit	Balance Sheet Credit
Assets		XX				XX	
		XX				XX	
Liabilities			XX				XX
			XX				XX
Owner's Equity			XX				XX
Revenue			XX		XX		
Expenses		XX		XX			

Steps in Preparing a Work Sheet

Figure 5-3, on page 116, is Malibu Gym's work sheet prepared for the month of November. It has three sections in the body of the statement: trial balance, income statement, and balance sheet. Each of the three sections has two money columns: a debit column and a credit column. See if you can follow the steps required to complete the work sheet shown in Figure 5-3.

Step 1: Write the Heading

Write the main heading showing who, what, and when across the top of the work sheet. Notice that the date line indicates the length of time covered by the accounting period — one month in this example.

Step 2: Record the Trial Balance

Record the balances from all the ledger accounts on the work sheet. Add the debit column balances and the credit column balances. The debit and credit columns should show the same totals.

Step 3: Transfer the Balance Sheet Items

The first accounts on the trial balance are assets, liabilities, and owner's equity. These are transferred to the balance sheet section of the work sheet. For example, the Cash debit of $7 800 is extended to the debit column of the balance sheet section since Cash is an asset. Extend the remaining assets, the liabilities, and equity accounts to the appropriate debit or credit column of the balance sheet section.

Step 4: Transfer the Income Statement Items

The revenue and expense accounts on the trial balance are now transferred. The Members' Fees account is a revenue account with a credit balance of $17 030. This amount is transferred to the credit column of the income statement section. The remaining revenue and expense accounts are transferred to the income statement section. The expense accounts have debit balances and are transferred to the debit column.

Step 5: Complete the Income Statement Section

The new income or net loss is now determined by doing the following:

- Rule a single line and add the income statement debit and credit columns.
- In Figure 5-3, the debit total is $10 790 and the credit total is $17 740.
- Write the totals below the single line.
- Determine the difference between the two columns. In Figure 5-3, the debit total (expenses) of $10 790 is subtracted from the credit total (revenue) of $17 740. Write the difference on the smaller side (see the $6 950 amount in Figure 5-3).

FIGURE 5-3
Steps in preparing a work sheet

Step 1: Write the heading

Malibu Gym
Work Sheet
For the month ended November 30, 2001

Step	ACCOUNT TITLE	ACC. NO.	TRIAL BALANCE DEBIT	TRIAL BALANCE CREDIT	INCOME STATEMENT DEBIT	INCOME STATEMENT CREDIT	BALANCE SHEET DEBIT	BALANCE SHEET CREDIT
Step 2: Record the trial balance	Cash	100	7 800				7 800	
	Accounts Receivable	101	2 600				2 600	
	Office Supplies	110	695				695	
Step 3: Transfer the balance sheet items	Land	120	25 000				25 000	
	Building	121	110 000				110 000	
	Training Equipment	122	102 735				102 735	
	Accounts Payable	200		10 700				10 700
	Bank Loan	221		63 000				63 000
	Mortgage Payable	231		80 000				80 000
	O'Brien, Capital	300		90 680				90 680
Step 4: Transfer the income statement items	O'Brien, Drawings	301	2 500				2 500	
	Members' Fees	400		17 030		17 030		
	Tanning Bed Rental	401		560		560		
	Towel Rental	402		150		150		
	Salaries Expense	500	4 650		4 650			
	Advertising Expense	501	2 700		2 700			
Step 5: Complete the income statement section	Telephone Expense	502	190		190			
	Maintenance Expense	503	600		600			
	Licence Expense	504	1 100		1 100			
	Interest Expense	505	1 500		1 500			
Step 6: Complete the balance sheet section	Laundry Expense	506	50		50			
			262 120	262 120	10 790	17 740	251 330	244 380
	Net Income				6 950			6 950
Step 7: Rule the work sheet					17 740	17 740	251 330	251 330

In Figure 5-3, is there a profit or a loss? If the credit column exceeds the debit column, a net income has been made during the accounting period. The amount of this net income is entered below the total of the debit column, so that when these two amounts are added, the two columns are equal. "Net income" is written in the account titles section opposite the amount of the net income. If the debit column exceeds the credit column, a net loss has occurred. The difference between the two columns is written in the credit column opposite the words "Net loss."

Step 6: Complete the Balance Sheet Section

Rule a single line and total the columns in the balance sheet section. Enter the *net income* amount below the total of the *credit* column of the balance sheet section. The *net income* represents the increase to the owner's equity for the period. If there has been a net loss, enter the amount of the *loss* below the *debit* column total. If the amount of the net income or net loss added to the column total makes the column equal to the other column total in the balance sheet section, the work sheet is mathematically correct.

Net income increases owner's equity.

Net loss decreases owner's equity.

Step 7: Rule the Work Sheet

Rule double lines below the totals to indicate completion and proof that the work is mathematically correct.

Recording a Net Loss on a Work Sheet

Figure 5-4, below, illustrates a work sheet that has a net loss. (Only part of the work sheet is shown.) Following is a description of how a loss is handled:

- Obtain the amount of the loss by subtracting the smaller total, revenue ($75 000), from the larger, expenses ($83 000). The difference, or net loss ($8 000), is written under the credit (revenue) total.
- Write "Net loss" in the account title section on the same line as the loss ($8 000).
- Enter the loss in the balance sheet section column.
- Rule double lines.

FIGURE 5-4

Recording a net loss on a work sheet

Brulé Services
Work Sheet
For the Month Ended October 31, 2001

	ACC.	TRIAL BALANCE		INCOME STATEMENT		BALANCE SHEET	
ACCOUNT TITLE	NO.	DEBIT	CREDIT	DEBIT	CREDIT	DEBIT	CREDIT
Cash	100	5 000				5 000	
Accounts Receivable	101	10 000				10 000	
Maintenance Expense	510	2 000		2 000			184 000
		259 000	259 000	83 000	75 000	176 000	184 000
Net Loss					8 000	8 000	
				83 000	83 000	184 000	184 000

USING THE WORK SHEET

The completed work sheet is used to prepare the financial statements at the end of the fiscal period.

When the work sheet is complete, it contains, in an organized, systematic, and convenient form, all the information that the accountant needs to prepare formal financial statements.

Preparing the Income Statement

The information from the income statement section of the work sheet is used to prepare the formal income statement. When the credit column of this section shows a greater total than the debit column, the amount of the difference is the *net income.* When the debit column exceeds the credit column, the difference is called *net loss.* When the formal income statement is complete, the conclusion (net income or net loss) should be the same as the matching conclusion on the work sheet.

The *income statement* shows the operating results for a business over a period of time. Figure 5-5, below, is the income statement of Malibu Gym for the month of November. Notice that the heading clearly shows the period of time covered by the statement.

The information for the body of the income statement is taken from the income statement section of the work sheet. The *revenue* information is found in the credit column of that section. The *expense* data are found in the debit column. The net income of $6 950 appears both on the work sheet (Figure 5-3) and the income statement (Figure 5-5).

FIGURE 5-5
Income Statement

Malibu Gym
Income Statement
For the Month Ended November 30, 2001

Revenue		
Members' Fees	$17 030	
Tanning Bed Rental	560	
Towel Rental	150	$17 740
Expenses		
Salaries Expense	4 650	
Advertising Expense	2 700	
Telephone Expense	190	
Maintenance Expense	600	
Licence Expense	1 100	
Interest Expense	1 500	
Laundry Expense	50	10 790
Net Income		$ 6 950

Preparing the Balance Sheet

A *balance sheet* presents the financial position of a business at a specific date. Figure 5-6 is the balance sheet of Malibu Gym prepared on November 30. It shows the assets, liabilities, and owner's equity at that specific date.

Just as the information for the income statement originated in the work sheet, so does the information for the balance sheet. Notice that in Figure 5-6 all the data used on the balance sheet came from the balance sheet section of the work sheet. Notice also that the net income of $6 950 increases the Capital in the owner's equity section of the balance sheet. The balance sheet in Figure 5-6 has been prepared in the report form.

FIGURE 5-6
Balance Sheet

Malibu Gym Balance Sheet November 30, 2001			
Assets			
Cash		$ 7 800	
Accounts Receivable		2 600	
Office Supplies		695	
Land		25 000	
Building		110 000	
Training Equipment		102 735	
Total Assets			$248 830
Liabilities and Owner's Equity			
Liabilities			
Accounts Payable		$ 10 700	
Bank Loan		63 000	
Mortgage Payable		80 000	
Total Liabilities			$153 700
Owner's Equity			
O'Brien, Capital November 1		90 680	
Add: Net Income for November	$6 950		
Less: O'Brien, Drawings	2 500		
Increase in Capital		4 450	
O'Brien, Capital November 30			95 130
Total Liabilities and Owner's Equity			$248 830

1. What is a work sheet?
2. What three items of information are included in the work sheet heading?
3. What fiscal period (accounting period) is covered by the November work sheet for Malibu Gym, Figure 5-3?
4. What are the three major sections in the body of a work sheet?
5. Which accounts from the trial balance are extended to the balance sheet section of the work sheet?
6. Which accounts from the trial balance are extended to the income statement section of the work sheet?
7. When the debit column total of the income statement section of the work sheet is greater than the credit column total, what is the difference called?
8. When the credit column total of the income statement section is greater than the debit column total, what is the difference called?
9. When is a work sheet considered to be mathematically correct?

10. Why is the net income from the income statement section of the work sheet transferred to the credit column of the balance sheet section of the work sheet?

11. What is the difference between the report form and the account form of the balance sheet?

12. Prepare a diagram illustrating the steps in the accounting cycle.

PROBLEMS: APPLICATIONS

1. Following is a list of account titles. Prepare a form like the one in the example and indicate on which statement section and in which column of the work sheet each account would appear. The first one, Cash, is done for you.

ACCOUNT TITLE	INCOME STATEMENT		BALANCE SHEET	
	DEBIT	CREDIT	DEBIT	CREDIT
Cash			✓	
Supplies				
Rent Expense				
W. Nguyen, Capital				
Office Equipment				
Accounts Payable				
Advertising Expense				
Light, Heat, Water Expenses				
Bank Loan				
Sales				
Accounts Receivable				
Investment Income				
Land				
W. Nguyen, Drawings				
Loss on Sale of Equipment				

2. Prepare a work sheet for the month of May from the following trial balance:

M. Oliwa
Trial Balance
May 31, 2001

ACCOUNT TITLE	ACC. NO.	DEBIT	CREDIT
Cash		$ 3 000	
Accounts Receivable		4 300	
Equipment		6 200	
Accounts Payable			$ 2 500
M. Oliwa, Capital			6 000
Sales			8 600
Salaries Expense		1 800	
General Expense		800	
Advertising Expense		1 000	
		$17 100	$17 100

3. Prepare a work sheet for the month of July from the following trial balance:

B. Irwin
Trial Balance
July 31, 2000

ACCOUNT TITLE	ACC. NO.	DEBIT	CREDIT
Cash		$12 000	
Accounts Receivable		8 000	
Equipment		36 500	
Accounts Payable			$12 500
B. Irwin, Capital			35 000
Sales			21 500
Salaries Expense		9 200	
General Expense		1 800	
Advertising Expense		1 500	
		$69 000	$69 000

4. Prepare a work sheet for the month of November from the trial balance that follows:

J. Kowalchuk
Trial Balance
November 30, 2002

ACCOUNT TITLE	ACC. NO.	DEBIT	CREDIT
Cash		$ 14 000	
Accounts Receivable		17 350	
Supplies		9 600	
Equipment		18 000	
Delivery Truck		78 000	
Accounts Payable			$ 12 450
Loan Payable			17 000
J. Kowalchuk, Capital			105 000
J. Kowalchuk, Drawings		13 000	
Sales			92 700
Salaries Expense		60 000	
Rent Expense		8 000	
Miscellaneous Expense		5 400	
Office Expense		2 550	
Telephone Expense		1 250	
		$227 150	$227 150

5. Prepare a work sheet for the month of March from the trial balance that follows:

D. Leung Enterprises
Trial Balance
March 31, 2001

ACCOUNT TITLE	ACC. NO.	DEBIT	CREDIT
Cash		$ 15 000	
Accounts Receivable		4 350	
Supplies		1 160	
Building		105 000	
Equipment		31 700	
Accounts Payable			$ 2 500
Bank Loan			21 000
Mortgage Payable			57 000
D. Leung, Capital			81 595
D. Leung, Drawings		3 900	
Sales			17 500
Salaries Expense		9 900	
Miscellaneous Expense		2 500	
Office Expense		3 420	
Telephone Expense		435	
Advertising Expense		2 230	
		$179 595	$179 595

UNIT 10 Classified Financial Statements

Learning Objectives

After reading this unit, discussing the applicable review questions, and completing the applications exercises, you will be able to do the following:

1. **PREPARE** a classified balance sheet.
2. **DEFINE** current and capital assets and current and long-term liabilities.
3. **PREPARE** supporting schedules for financial statements.

The purpose of financial statements is to provide financial information about a company to owners, management, creditors, and government. By classifying items on the statements into special categories, it is possible to provide more information and to provide it in a way that is more easily interpreted.

CLASSIFIED BALANCE SHEET

In Figure 5-7, balance sheet information from the previous unit is presented in classified balance sheet format to answer the following questions:

- Which debts must be paid within a year?
- Is there sufficient cash (or assets) on hand to pay debts?
- Which debts must be paid in future years?

Look at Figure 5-7 and answer the preceding questions.

FIGURE 5-7
Balance Sheet

Malibu Gym Balance Sheet November 30, 2001			
Assets			
Current Assets			
Cash		$ 7 800	
Accounts Receivable		2 600	
Office Supplies		695	
Total Current Assets			$ 11 095
Capital Assets			
Land		25 000	
Building		110 000	
Training Equipment		102 735	
Total Capital Assets			237 735
Total Assets			$248 830
Liabilities and Owner's Equity			
Current Liabilities			
Accounts Payable			$ 10 700
Long-Term Liabilities			
Bank Loan		$ 63 000	
Mortgage Payable		80 000	
Total Long-Term Liabilities			143 000
Total Liabilities			153 700
Owner's Equity			
O'Brien, Capital November 1		90 680	
Add: Net Income for November	$6 950		
Less: O'Brien, Drawings	2 500		
Increase in Capital		4 450	
O'Brien, Capital November 30			95 130
Total Liabilities and Owner's Equity			$248 830

Assets and Liabilities

The balance sheet of Malibu Gym illustrated in Figure 5-7 includes the standard classifications usually found on balance sheets. The assets are divided into two main groups: *current* and *capital*. The liabilities are divided into two groups: *current* and *long-term*.

Current Assets

Current assets are listed in order of liquidity.

Liquidity order is the order in which assets may be converted into cash.

Assets that are converted into cash in the ordinary course of business, usually within one year, are called *current assets*. The list that follows provides some examples and the order in which current assets usually appear. They are listed in *order of liquidity,* that is, the order in which assets may be converted into cash.

CURRENT ASSETS

Cash
Government Bonds
Marketable Securities
Accounts Receivable
Merchandise Inventory
Prepaid Expenses

Government Bonds and Marketable Securities are easily converted into cash. For that reason, they are placed immediately after Cash in the current assets section of the classified balance sheet. Accounts Receivable, debts that most customers pay within 30 days, come next.

The Merchandise Inventory account records the value of merchandise on hand for sale to customers.

Merchandise Inventory is an asset account used to record the value of merchandise on hand for sale to customers. When the merchandise is sold, cash will be eventually received for it. For that reason, Merchandise Inventory is listed after Accounts Receivable.

Prepaid expenses are expense payments made in advance.

Prepaid Expenses are items such as Prepaid Rent and Prepaid Insurance. They represent the value of insurance policies owned by the company and rental leases for which payment has been made in advance. Although they are not generally converted into cash in the normal operations of the business, they could be if necessary. For example, many insurance policies have a cash value equal to the value of the unused portion. A company in need of cash could "cash in" an insurance policy. Prepaid Expenses are listed after Cash, Government Bonds, Marketable Securities, Accounts Receivable, and Merchandise Inventory on the balance sheet.

Capital Assets

Capital assets are assets such as land, buildings, equipment, and trucks that are used in operating the business and that have a long life. This section of the balance sheet may also be titled "plant and equipment." The capital assets that have the longest life are generally listed first.

CAPITAL ASSETS

Land
Building
Equipment
Delivery Trucks

Capital assets are recorded using the price at which they were purchased (cost principle). This is a standard principle used by all accountants.

Current Liabilities

The term *current liabilities* generally refers to liabilities that must be paid within a year or less. If possible, current liabilities are listed in the order that they are to be paid.

Current liabilities are liabilities due to be paid within a year.

CURRENT LIABILITIES

Salaries Owing
Accounts Payable
Taxes Payable
Loans Payable

Long-Term Liabilities

Long-term liabilities are liabilities that are not due to be paid for at least a year. A loan payable in two years and a mortgage payable in 25 years are examples of long-term liabilities.

Long-term liabilities are liabilities that are not due to be paid for at least a year.

Owner's Equity Section of the Balance Sheet

The owner's equity in a business increases when the business operates profitably. Owner's equity decreases when there has been a net loss and when the owner withdraws assets from the business.

The owner's equity section of the balance sheet in Figure 5-7 is an example of equity increasing as a result of Malibu Gym earning a net income that is greater than the owner's withdrawals from the business. Figure 5-8, below, shows how the equity section of a balance sheet is set up to record a net loss.

It is possible for a business to earn a net income yet still have a decrease in owner's equity. This happens when the withdrawals by the owner are greater than the net income. Figure 5-9 illustrates the set-up of the equity section when withdrawals are greater than net income.

OWNER'S EQUITY			
O'Brien, Capital November 1		$99 245	
Less: Net Loss for November	$1 200		
Less: O'Brien, Drawings	1 800		
Decrease in Capital		3 000	
O'Brien, Capital November 30			$96 245

FIGURE 5-8
Net loss

OWNER'S EQUITY			
O'Brien, Capital November 1		$99 245	
Add: Net Income for November	$1 000		
Less: O'Brien, Drawings	1 800		
Decrease in Capital		800	
O'Brien, Capital November 30			$98 445

FIGURE 5-9
Withdrawals greater than net income

SUPPORTING STATEMENTS AND SCHEDULES

In addition to the basic income statement and balance sheet, a number of additional statements or schedules may be used to provide financial information.

Statement of Owner's Equity

The statement of owner's equity describes the changes in owner's equity for the accounting period.

The statement of owner's equity is an example of a *supporting statement*. This statement provides the owner of the business with the data regarding the change in value of the owner's equity for an accounting period. It is prepared separately from the balance sheet. The owner's equity balance at the end of the period is shown on the balance sheet instead of the full calculation. Figure 5-10 illustrates a statement of owner's equity.

FIGURE 5-10
Statement of Owner's Equity

Malibu Gym Statement of Owner's Equity For the Month Ended November 30, 2001			
O'Brien, Capital November 1		$90 680	
Add: Net Income for November	$6 950		
Less: O'Brien, Drawings	2 500		
Increase in Capital		4 450	
O'Brien, Capital November 30			$95 130

The balance sheet for Malibu Gym in Figure 5-7 could have been presented with the separate statement of owner's equity shown in Figure 5-10. In such a case, the final balance of the O'Brien, Capital account, $95 130, would be shown on the balance sheet in place of the complete equity calculation. This is illustrated in the balance sheet in Figure 5-11 on the following page.

Schedule of Accounts Receivable

A supporting schedule provides details about an item on a main statement.

Supporting schedules are used to provide details about an item on a main statement. An example of a supporting schedule is the schedule of accounts receivable, shown in Figure 5-12 on page 127. It provides a listing of the individual accounts receivable and the amounts owed. This provides the details regarding the Accounts Receivable total on the balance sheet. In Figure 5-11, the Accounts Receivable total on the balance sheet is $2 600. Further information about the amount owed by each customer is found on the schedule (Figure 5-12). Notice that the total of the schedule, $2 600, is the same as the Accounts Receivable total on the balance sheet (Figure 5-11).

Supporting schedules and statements may be prepared whenever the accountant feels they would provide additional useful information for the readers of the financial statements.

FIGURE 5-11
Balance Sheet

Malibu Gym Balance Sheet November 30, 2001		
Assets		
CURRENT ASSETS		
Cash	$ 7 800	
Accounts Receivable	2 600	
Office Supplies	695	
Total Current Assets		$ 11 095
CAPITAL ASSETS		
Land	25 000	
Building	110 000	
Training Equipment	102 735	
Total Capital Assets		237 735
Total Assets		$248 830
Liabilities and Owner's Equity		
CURRENT LIABILITIES		
Accounts Payable		$ 10 700
LONG-TERM LIABILITIES		
Bank Loan	$ 63 000	
Mortgage Payable	80 000	
Total Long-Term Liabilities		143 000
Total Liabilities		$153 700
OWNER'S EQUITY		
O'Brien, Capital November 30		95 130
Total Liabilities and Owner's Equity		$248 830

FIGURE 5-12
Schedule of Accounts Receivable

Malibu Gym Schedule of Accounts Receivable November 30, 2001	
B. Adams	$ 250
C. Bartoshewski	250
L. Foster	200
W. Lane	200
D. McIssac	300
K. Owen	100
R. Rand	200
G. Singh	250
B. Taylor	250
H. Vanede	300
K. Wier	100
A. Wong	200
Total Accounts Receivable	$2 600

ACCOUNTING TERMS

Classified Balance Sheet Items on the balance sheet are placed in categories to provide additional information to statement users.

Current Assets Assets that are/could be converted to cash within one year.

Current Liabilities Liabilities due to be paid within one year.

Capital Assets Assets that have a long life and contribute to the business for more than one year.

Long-Term Liabilities Liabilities that are not due to be paid for at least a year.

Schedule of Accounts Provides list of individual accounts receivable and amounts owed in order to provide details regarding the accounts receivable total on the balance sheet.

Statement of Owner's Equity Provides information regarding the change in value of the owner's equity for an accounting period.

Supporting Schedule Provides details about an item on a main statement.

Work Sheet A device that organizes accounting data required for the preparation of financial statements.

REVIEW QUESTIONS

1. What is a classified financial statement?
2. Explain the following terms:
   (a) Current asset
   (b) Capital asset
   (c) Liquidity order
   (d) Current liability
   (e) Long-term liability
3. Explain the cost principle as it is applied to capital assets on the balance sheet.
4. What effect does a withdrawal of assets from the business by the owner have on owner's equity?
5. (a) What effect does a net loss have on the owner's equity?
   (b) What effect does a net income have on the owner's equity?

6. Classify each of the following as a current asset, fixed asset, current liability, or long-term liability:

(a) Accounts Receivable
(b) Land
(c) Bank Loan (6 months)
(d) Office Supplies
(e) Delivery Truck
(f) Prepaid Rent
(g) Automobile
(h) Mortgage Payable
(i) Taxes Owing
(j) Government Bonds
(k) Accounts Payable

7. The completed work sheet for the month of January for D. Lo, a lawyer, is shown below. Prepare the income statement and classified balance sheet.

D. Lo
Work Sheet
For the Month Ended January 31, 2000

ACCOUNT TITLE	ACC. NO.	TRIAL BALANCE		INCOME STATEMENT		BALANCE SHEET	
		DEBIT	CREDIT	DEBIT	CREDIT	DEBIT	CREDIT
Cash		3 000				3 000	
Accounts Receivable		500				500	
Office Equipment		6 000				6 000	
Automobile		10 000				10 000	
Willson Supply Ltd.			400				400
D. Lo, Capital			17 700				17 700
Fees Income			4 000		4 000		
Automobile Expense		100		100			
Rent Expense		800		800			
Salaries Expense		1 200		1 200			
General Expense		500		500			
		22 100	22 100	2 600	4 000	19 500	18 100
Net Income				1 400			1 400
				4 000	4 000	19 500	19 500

8. Trial balance figures for May and June for a business owned by T. Hood are shown on page 130.

(a) Prepare a work sheet, an income statement, a statement of owner's equity, and a balance sheet for May.
(b) Prepare a work sheet and financial statements for June (including a statement of owner's equity).

9. (a) Using the trial balance at the bottom of page 130, prepare a work sheet for the three months ended September 30, 2001 for the Cedar Hill Golf Club.
(b) Prepare an income statement, a statement of owner's equity, and a classified balance sheet.

	MAY		JUNE	
Cash	$5 000		$4 000	
Accounts Receivable	7 000		6 000	
Prepaid Insurance	800		600	
Land	30 000		30 000	
Building	90 000		90 000	
Furniture	5 000		5 000	
Accounts Payable		$4 000		$ 3 000
Taxes Owing		2 000		2 000
Bank Loan (2 year)		15 000		14 000
Mortgage Payable		40 000		38 000
T. Hood, Capital		75 000		76 800
T. Hood, Drawings	4 500		6 500	
Sales		22 000		26 100
Salaries Expense	12 000		14 000	
Delivery Expense	1 200		900	
Utilities Expense	700		700	
Advertising Expense	1 100		1 400	
Miscellaneous Expense	300		200	
Insurance Expense	400		600	
	$158 000	$158 000	$159 900	$159 900

Cedar Hill Golf Club
Trial Balance
September 30, 2001

ACCOUNT TITLE	ACC. NO.	DEBIT	CREDIT
Cash		$ 4 000	
Supplies		7 500	
Land		200 000	
Equipment		30 000	
Accounts Payable			$ 2 000
Bank Loan			92 000
G. Thompson, Capital			101 000
G. Thompson, Drawings		6 000	
Membership Fees			114 000
Salaries Expense		50 000	
Maintenance Expense		2 500	
Utilities Expense		7 000	
Office Expense		2 000	
		$309 000	$309 000

1. Below is the December 31 trial balance for the Cedar Hill Golf Club.
   (a) Prepare a work sheet for the three months ended December 31, 2001.
   (b) Prepare an income statement.
   (c) Why do you think the operating results for this three-month period are different from the three-month period in exercise 9 on page 129?

Cedar Hill Golf Club Trial Balance December 31, 2001			
ACCOUNT TITLE	**ACC. NO.**	**DEBIT**	**CREDIT**
Cash		$ 3 500	
Supplies		2 000	
Land		200 000	
Equipment		30 000	
Accounts Payable			$ 1 000
Bank Loan			90 000
G. Thompson, Capital			147 500
G. Thompson, Drawings		4 000	
Membership Fees			22 000
Salaries Expense		12 000	
Maintenance Expense		6 000	
Insurance Expense		1 500	
Utilities Expense		1 000	
Office Expense		500	
		$260 500	$260 500

2. A work sheet for Expert Real Estate is presented on page 132. Certain amounts are missing or misplaced. Determine the amounts that should be entered into these spaces.

Expert Real Estate Work Sheet For the Year Ended December 31, 2001						
ACCOUNT	TRIAL BALANCE		INCOME STATEMENT		BALANCE SHEET	
TITLE	DEBIT	CREDIT	DEBIT	CREDIT	DEBIT	CREDIT
Cash					7 500	
Fees Receivable					5 000	
Office Supplies	1 400					
Office Furniture	7 000					
Office Equipment					11 000	
Land	40 000					
Building					145 000	
Accounts Payable						2 300
Taxes Owing		3 500				
Bank Loan		11 500				
Mortgage Payable						110 000
M. Dennis, Capital		87 000				
M. Dennis, Drawings					18 000	
Commissions Income				78 900		
Salaries Expense	42 000					
Advertising Expense			7 200			
Telephone Expense	2 800					
Utilities Expense	1 300					
Insurance Expense		3 600				
Miscellaneous Expense		1 400				
		293 200		78 900		214 300
Net						

CHAPTER 6

Completing the Accounting Cycle for a Service Business

UNIT 11 Adjusting the Books

Learning Objectives

After reading this unit, discussing the applicable review questions, and completing the applications exercises, you will be able to do the following:

1. **EXPLAIN** why adjustments are necessary.
2. **PREPARE** adjusting entries for prepaid expenses.
3. **RECORD** amortization for the accounting period.

The basic accounting cycle was introduced in the first five chapters of this text. In this chapter, the accounting procedures performed at the end of the accounting cycle will be introduced. These procedures include adjustments, financial statements, and closing the books.

One of the main purposes of accounting is to provide information for decision making. The information is presented in the form of financial statements. If decisions are to be made based on data in the financial statements, it is essential that the statements be as accurate as possible.

INTRODUCING ADJUSTMENTS

Revenue from one period and expenses from the same period are matched together to determine net income or net loss.

The purpose of adjusting the books is to ensure that the accounts and financial statements are accurate.

It is not enough that the debits equal the credits and that the statements are mathematically correct. They must also be accurate.

Many transactions are begun in one accounting period but have an effect for several accounting periods. It is essential that all revenue and expenses be recorded. In addition, the matching principle discussed in Chapter 3 requires that the revenue of a particular accounting period be matched with the expenses of the same accounting period to produce an accurate picture of profitability. All asset, liability, and equity account balances must be correct. The purpose of adjusting the books is to ensure that the account balances and the financial statements are accurate.

Therefore, it is important that the account balances are accurate. The balance sheet must show, as accurately as possible, the value of all the assets, liabilities, and equity accounts at the end of the fiscal period. The income statement must accurately present the revenue and expenses for the fiscal period it covers.

Adjusting the Books

Suppose that employees work overtime or earn bonuses that have not been recorded by the end of the fiscal period. What will be wrong with the financial statements? Both the income statement and the balance sheet will be incorrect.

The expenses will be too low because the Salaries Expense does not include the overtime. This failure to accurately match the expense of this accounting period with the revenue earned will result in the income statement's understating expenses and showing a net income that is overstated.

The liabilities will be incorrect because the debt owing to the workers, called Salaries Payable, will not be shown on the balance sheet. This will result in the total liabilities of the company being understated.

It is necessary to adjust the books to ensure that all accounts have correct balances. In this chapter, some of the accounts of a business called Management Consultant Services will be examined, and the adjustments to the accounts which are required before the financial statements are prepared will be described. J. Turner is the owner of Management Consultant Services. This business provides management advice to other companies and is located in a rented office.

PREPAID EXPENSES

Prepaid expenses are expense payments made in advance.

Prepaid expenses are current assets.

In Chapter 3, expenses were defined as the cost of items used up in operating a business. Payments made in advance for items such as rent, insurance, and supplies are called *prepaid expenses*. Often, the payments are made in advance for more than one fiscal period. Prepaid expenses are items of value. They are assets.

Prepaid expenses are considered to be assets — items of value owned — until they are used up or no longer have value. For example, office supplies are assets as long as they are owned by a business and are unused. Once they have been used, they no longer have value and therefore are no longer assets. They have changed to expenses.

When prepaid expenses such as office supplies are purchased, they are recorded as assets. When they are used, the value of the assets has changed by the amount used and the asset accounts should be decreased. Since they have changed to expenses, the amount used should be recorded in an appropriate expense account. This change from prepaid asset to expense may occur on a regular basis; however, the actual recording of the change is normally made at the time financial statements are prepared in order to ensure their accuracy. At the end of the accounting period, entries are made to record the conversion of prepaid assets to expenses in order to correct the account balances for the balance sheet and to record the appropriate expense for the period on the income statement. These entries are called *adjusting entries.* The adjusting entries involve a change in both an income statement account (revenue or expense) and a balance sheet account (asset or liability).

Prepaid Rent

The rental lease of J. Turner's business, Management Consultant Services, requires that rent of $2 000 a month be paid in advance for three months. Therefore, on April 1, a cheque for $6 000 is issued in payment of the April, May, and June rents. Because the rent is being paid in advance for three months, Rent Expense is not debited. Instead, an account called *Prepaid Rent* is debited.

At the end of April, Management Consultant Services prepares financial statements covering one month. Should Prepaid Rent be shown as a current asset with a value of $6 000? The answer is no. After one month, one-third of the asset Prepaid Rent has been used. The business has used up one-third, or $2 000, of the value of the prepaid rent. The value of the prepaid rent must be reduced by $2 000 if the asset Prepaid Rent is to be correct. It is now worth $4 000, not $6 000.

Furthermore, since $2 000 of the rent has been used, an expense of $2 000 must be recorded. The following entry, called an *adjusting entry*, is made:

Apr. 30	Rent Expense	2 000	
	Prepaid Rent		2 000
	To record one month's Rent Expense.		

This adjusting entry has two effects:

- It records the Rent Expense for April.
- It decreases the asset Prepaid Rent by $2 000.

The entry in T-account form is:

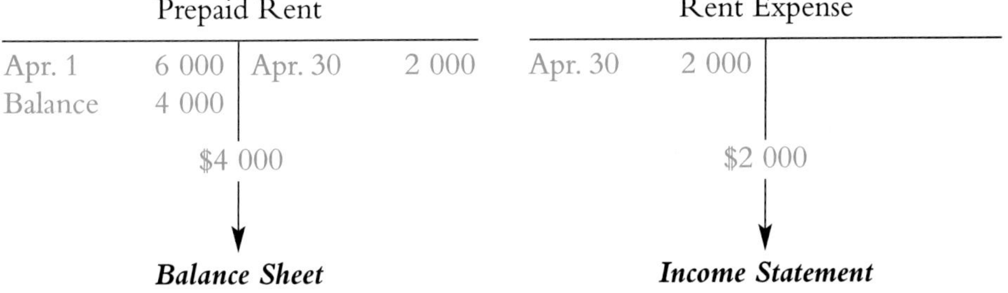

When the financial statements for the month ended April 30 are prepared, Rent Expense of $2 000 will be shown on the income statement. Prepaid Rent of $4 000 will appear on the balance sheet. If this adjusting entry were not made, the expenses would be too low and, as a result, the net income would be too high. Also, the assets would be too high.

Supplies

The Supplies account is another prepaid expense. At the beginning of April, supplies worth $900 are purchased by Management Consultant Services. These supplies will last for several fiscal periods.

Each working day in April, small amounts of the supplies are used up. The Supplies account is not decreased because it would be time-consuming and inconvenient to record a decrease in the Supplies account every time supplies were used. Thus, the Supplies account is deliberately allowed to become incorrect. However, at the end of April, when financial statements are prepared, the Supplies account must be adjusted. This is how it is done.

First, a count of all supplies left on April 30 is made. The value of the unused supplies is $600. Then, the amount of supplies used is determined by this calculation:

Supplies purchased	$900
Less: Supplies left	600
Supplies used	$300

Supplies Expense is the value of supplies used.

The value of supplies used is the Supplies Expense. The asset Supplies should be decreased by the amount used. The following adjusting entry is made:

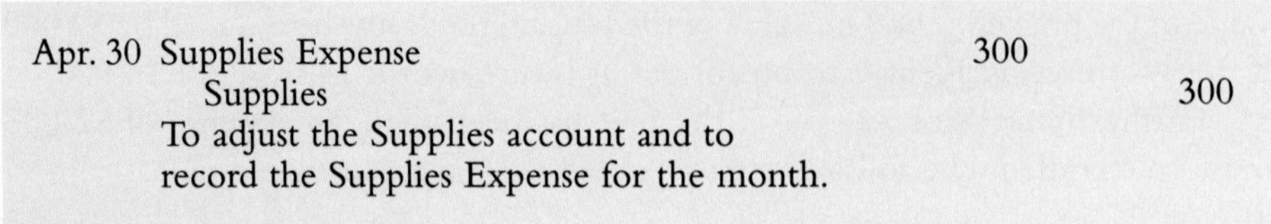

Apr. 30	Supplies Expense	300	
	Supplies		300
	To adjust the Supplies account and to record the Supplies Expense for the month.		

The effect of this adjusting entry is shown in these T-accounts:

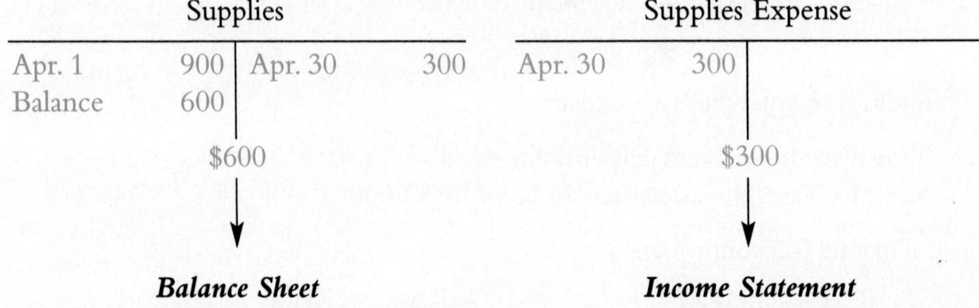

When the April 30 financial statements are prepared, the asset Supplies, with a value of $600, appears on the balance sheet. The Supplies Expense of $300 appears on the income statement.

Prepaid Insurance

On April 1, a comprehensive insurance policy covering fire, theft, and accidental damage to all office furniture and equipment is purchased. The cost of the insurance for one year is $1 200.

At the end of April, one month's insurance has been used and must be recorded as an expense. The cost of one month's insurance is 1/12 of $1 200, or $100. This adjusting entry is made:

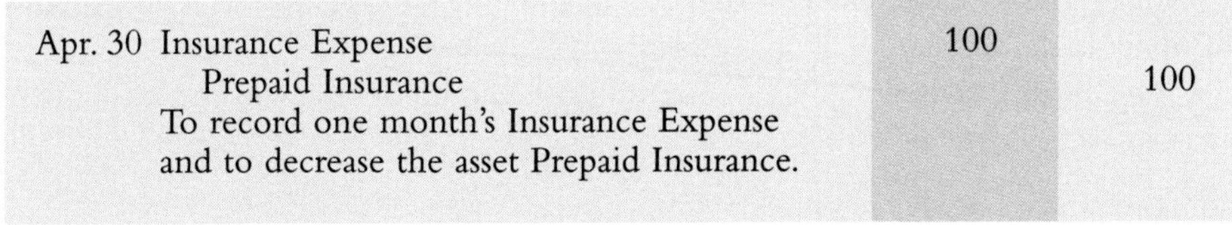

Apr. 30	Insurance Expense	100	
	Prepaid Insurance		100
	To record one month's Insurance Expense and to decrease the asset Prepaid Insurance.		

The effect of this adjusting entry is shown in these T accounts:

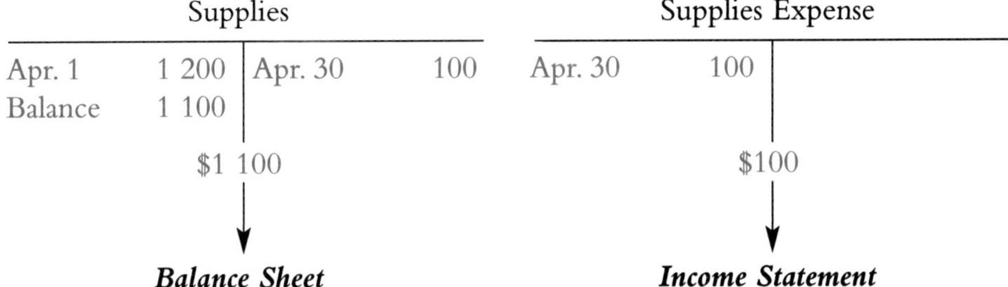

On the April financial statements, Prepaid Insurance of $1 100 appears in the asset section of the balance sheet. Insurance Expense of $100 appears on the income statement.

INTRODUCING AMORTIZATION

Management Consultant Services purchased office equipment for $12 000 on January 1. This purchase is recorded by decreasing Cash and increasing the capital asset account Equipment.

The equipment will be used to help operate the business. Typewriters, calculators, and computer equipment are only some of the equipment used by companies. Such equipment is necessary for the operation of most businesses.

Early in this text, you learned a simple definition of an expense: money spent on things used to operate a business over the years. Since the equipment is used up in operating the business, it does in some way contribute to the expenses of the business. For example, Management Consultant Services may estimate that the equipment purchased will probably last for five years. After that time, it will be worthless. The $12 000 spent on the equipment will have been used up.

An expense is the cost of items used to produce the revenue for a business.

However, the equipment does not suddenly become worthless — it loses value each year. The cost of the equipment should be assigned or allocated as an expense to each year's operation. Each year, part of the equipment cost should become an expense.

This allocation of the cost of the capital asset as an expense during the accounting period when the asset is used to produce revenue is consistent with the matching principle. There is a cost of using capital assets during an accounting period to produce the revenue for that accounting period. This cost should therefore be shown as an expense on the income statement for that period.

Recording Amortization

Amortization is the allocation of the cost of an asset to the fiscal periods in which it is used.

The assignment of costs, or division of the initial cost over the life of the asset, is called *amortization*. By dividing the initial cost ($12 000) over the life (five years) of the equipment, the amortization figure would be $2 400 each year. This assumes that the equipment is worthless after five years and has no *scrap value* or *trade-in value.*

Amortization is an expense and appears on the income statement.

The allocation of the cost of assets is recorded in an expense account called Amortization Expense. The amortization or using up of capital assets is an expense of operating a business.

The entry to record the amortization of the equipment at the end of the first year is:

Dec. 31 Amortization Expense — Equipment	2 400	
Accumulated Amortization — Equip.		2 400
To record amortization for the year.		

After this entry has been posted, three accounts relating to the equipment and its amortization are affected:

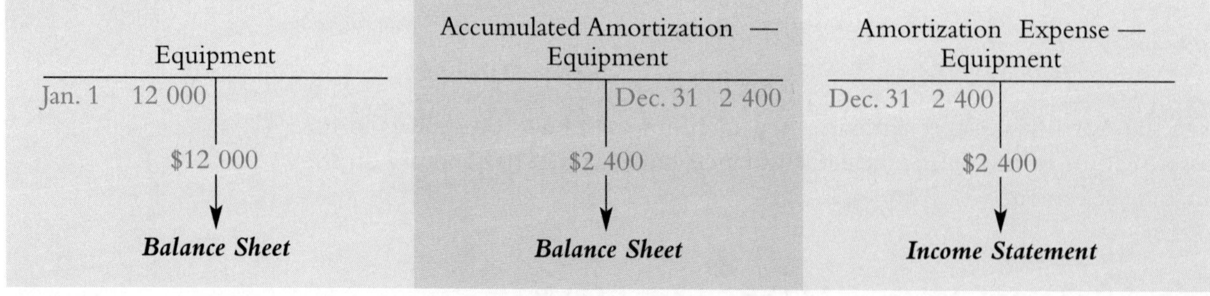

Accumulated amortization appears on the balance sheet.

The Amortization Expense — Equipment account appears on the income statement in the expense section. Both Equipment and Accumulated Amortization — Equipment appear on the balance sheet. They are in the capital assets section. Accumulated Amortization is a deduction from Equipment as shown in the partial balance sheet in Figure 6-1.

FIGURE 6-1
Accumulated Amortization appears in the capital assets section of the balance sheet

Management Consultant Services Partial Balance Sheet December 31, 2000		
Capital Assets		
Equipment	$12 000	
Less: Accumulated Amortization	2 400	9 600

Amortization is a method of spreading the cost of a capital asset over the life of the asset. It is a process of converting the cost of capital assets into expenses over the time the asset will make a contribution to the business. There is a separate Amortization Expense account and a separate Accumulated Amortization account for each group of capital assets such as Buildings, Equipment, Delivery Trucks, and Machinery. Once an asset has been amortized 100 percent, no further amortization is allowed. Suppose an asset costs $10 000 and, over the years, 20 percent is deducted each year. When the Accumulated Amortization account reaches $10 000, no further amortization is available.

You might ask why it is necessary to use an Accumulated Amortization account. Why not simply credit Equipment to show the decrease in its value? The use of the Accumulated Amortization account as well as the asset account Equipment provides two types of information. One is the *original cost* of the equipment. This is found in the asset account Equipment. The other is the *total amount of amortization* recorded over the years. Accounts such as Accumulated Amortization are set up to record subtractions from related accounts. These valuation, or contra, accounts reduce the value of assets on a balance sheet.

Valuation, or Contra, Accounts

The Accumulated Amortization account is sometimes called a *valuation account* because it is used to arrive at the value of an asset. It is also known as a *contra asset account* because it has a credit balance rather than the normal debit balance found in most asset accounts. It has a credit balance because it is subtracted from the value of an asset to show the correct net balance sheet value or *book value.*

Book value is the cost of an asset minus the accumulated amortization.

When an asset is purchased, it is recorded at its cost price. Each year, amortization builds up in the Accumulated Amortization account. The book value of the asset is the cost minus the accumulated amortization. This value is the value according to the books of the company. It is not the actual value, which is the amount received if the asset is sold.

Look again at Figure 6-1. In the fixed asset section of the balance sheet, Equipment is shown at its cost price of $12 000. The accumulated amortization to date of $2 400 is subtracted to arrive at a book value of $9 600. However, amortization is not valuation. The fact that in Figure 6-1 a current figure of $9 600 is shown for the equipment does *not* mean that the equipment is worth $9 600. It does *not* mean that the equipment can be sold for $9 600. The figures simply mean:

- That the equipment cost $12 000
- That amortization of $2 400 has been recorded
- That $9 600 remains to be amortized

The term "book value" is used to describe the $9 600 unamortized cost.

Contra accounts provide information to the reader of the financial report. It is clear that the equipment cost was $12 000, that the amortization charged to date is $2 400, and that additional amortization charges are available in the future. The net or book value of Equipment shown on the balance sheet is $9 600. The $9 600 represents the unamortized value of this fixed asset at the end of the fiscal period.

METHODS OF CALCULATING AMORTIZATION

There are several methods for calculating amortization. The two methods that will be discussed in this chapter are:

- Straight-line method
- Declining-balance method, fixed percentage

Straight-Line Method

The straight-line method of amortization allocates the same amount of amortization to each fiscal period.

A widely used method of calculating amortization is the *straight-line method.* As shown in Figure 6-1, the equipment depreciated $2 400 per year.
Calculation:

$$\frac{\text{Cost}}{\text{Number of years of use}} = \frac{12\ 000}{5} = \$2\ 400/\text{year}$$

After five years, a total of $12 000 amortization will have been recorded (5 × 2 400 = 12 000). Each year, the same amount of amortization, or $2 400, is recorded. The table in Figure 6-2 summarizes the calculation of amortization by the straight-line method. The rate is established by using the following calculations:

$$\frac{100\%}{\text{Number of years of use}} = \frac{100\%}{5} = 20\% \text{ per year}$$

FIGURE 6-2
Amortization by the straight-line method

Amortization Schedule — Equipment Straight-Line Method			
Year	**Calculation**	**Amortization Expense**	**Accumulated Amortization**
1	20% × $12 000	$ 2 400	$ 2 400
2	20% × 12 000	2 400	4 800
3	20% × 12 000	2 400	7 200
4	20% × 12 000	2 400	9 600
5	20% × 12 000	2 400	12 000
		$12 000	

Declining-Balance Method, Fixed Percentage

The straight-line method of amortization allocates an equal amount of amortization to each fiscal period. It can be argued that this is not accurate because amortization is greatest in the first few years of an asset's life. For example, an automobile's amortization is greatest in its first year.

The declining-balance method of amortization allocates a greater amount of amortization to the first years of an asset's life.

A greater amount of amortization is allocated to the first years when the *declining-balance method* is used. Suppose that equipment, worth $12 000, is amortized using the declining-balance method. Each year, a fixed percentage, for example, 20 percent of the declining balance, is charged. The table in Figure 6-3, below, shows the calculation of amortization using the declining-balance method.

FIGURE 6-3
Amortization by the declining-balance method

Amortization Schedule — Equipment Declining-Balance Method			
Year	**Unamortized cost**	**Amount of amortization 20%**	**Declining balance, end of year**
1	$12 000.00	$2 400.00	$9 600.00
2	9 600.00	1 920.00	7 680.00
3	7 680.00	1 536.00	6 144.00
4	6 144.00	1 228.80	4 915.20
5	4 915.20	983.04	3 932.16

Notice that each year, as the asset grows older, the amortization is smaller. The cost of the fixed asset is never completely written off as long as the asset is being used. However, each year's amortization is progressively smaller.

Journal Entries for the Declining-Balance Method

The adjusting entry used for the declining-balance method of amortization must show a different amount each year:

Year 1	Amortization Expense — Equipment	2 400	
	Accumulated Amortization — Equip.		2 400
	To record the first year's amortization.		
Year 2	Amortization Expense — Equipment	1 920	
	Accumulated Amortization — Equip.		1 920
	To record the second year's amortization.		

Amortization and Income Taxes

Two methods of calculating amortization have been described. However, for income tax purposes in Canada, the declining-balance method must be used. This method is called *capital cost allowance* under the *Income Tax Act*.

For income tax purposes, amortization is called capital cost allowances.

The maximum percentage of amortization (capital cost allowance), as well as the method used, is controlled by the government. Assets are grouped into classes and a maximum percentage of amortization allowed for income tax purposes is set for each class. A few of the classes are shown in Figure 6-4 below. Complete information can be found on the Canada Customs and Revenue Agency Web site, www.rc.gc.ca.

FIGURE 6-4
Amortization for income tax purposes

Class	Capital cost allowance description of asset	Maximum percentage
1	Buildings (Brick)	4%
8	Machinery and equipment	20%
10	Trucks, tractors, automobiles, trailers, buses, wagons	30%

Figure 6-4 describes only a few assets and their maximum percentage rates of capital cost allowance. The income tax regulations provide a listing of all types of assets and the classes to which they belong. The rates vary from 4 percent a year for Class 1 to 100 percent for Classes 12 and 29. Class 1 includes items such as buildings. Class 12 includes tools and dental instruments costing less than $200 and some types of computer software.

Land is not amortizable.

It is important to note that land is not amortizable. For income tax purposes, a business may not claim amortization expense (capital cost allowance) on land. Land has an unlimited life — it does not wear out or deteriorate. Unlike a building or equipment, it does not eventually have to be replaced. Because land is so permanent, it is not an asset for which amortization is recorded.

1. (a) What is meant by the term "adjusting the books"?
   (b) Why are adjustments necessary?
   (c) List three parties that would be interested in studying accurate financial statements for a company.
2. (a) What type of accounts are prepaid expenses?
   (b) On which financial statement do they appear?
3. (a) Why is the account Supplies allowed to become incorrect?
   (b) Why is it not credited each time supplies are used?
   (c) On which financial statement does the account Supplies appear? On which statement is Supplies Expense found?
4. (a) What type of account is Prepaid Insurance?
   (b) What type of account is Insurance Expense?
5. Define amortization.
6. Which assets amortize?
7. On which financial statement do Amortization Expense and Accumulated Amortization appear?
8. "Amortization is not valuation." What does this mean?
9. Two methods of calculating amortization are the straight-line method and the declining-balance method. Explain each of them.
10. What is capital cost allowance?
11. For income tax purposes, which method of amortization must be used?
12. What is a contra, or valuation, account? Give an example.

1. Set up T-accounts for Cash, Prepaid Rent, and Rent Expense.
   (a) In the T-accounts, record the following entry: June 1, cheque No.467 for $4 800 was issued to Triangle Realtors as advance payment for four months' rent.
   (b) On June 30, record an adjustment for one month's rent expense.
   (c) Indicate what type of accounts Prepaid Rent and Rent Expense are, and indicate the financial statement on which each appears.
2. The asset account Supplies had a balance of $700 at the beginning of the fiscal period. At the end of the fiscal period, an inventory shows supplies worth $125 on hand.
   (a) What was the value of supplies used during the fiscal period?
   (b) What is the Supplies Expense for the fiscal period?
   (c) What should the balance in the asset account Supplies be at the end of the fiscal period?
   (d) Prepare the adjusting entry to record the supplies used.
   (e) What is the amount of the Supplies Expense that will appear on the income statement?
   (f) What is the value of the asset Supplies that will appear on the balance sheet?

3. On July 1, a one-year insurance policy was purchased for $1 224 cash. Prepare the July 31 adjusting entry to record one month's insurance expense.

4. Prepare adjusting entries for the month of January for the following:

   (a) Balance of Supplies account on January 1: $700. Supplies on hand on January 31: $200.
   (b) Rent was paid for three months on January 1, $2 700.
   (c) A 12-month insurance policy was purchased on January 15, for $1 200.

5. Three accounts related to the fixed asset account Automobile (which was bought one year ago) follow:

Automobile		Accumulated Amortization — Automobile		Amortization Expense — Automobile	
Jan. 1 24 000					

   (a) On December 31, prepare the General Journal adjusting entry to amortize the automobile for one year at the rate of 30 percent.
   (b) Post the entry to T-accounts.
   (c) Give the accounts and balances that appear in the balance sheet and the income statement.

6. It has been estimated that equipment bought for $30 000 will have a useful life of six years, at which time it will be thrown away.

   (a) Using the straight-line method of amortization, what will be the amount of amortization each year?
   (b) Complete your own copy of the following chart for a period of six years.

Year	Value at beginning of year	Amortization for the year	Accumulated amortization	Book value at end of year
1	$30 000	$5 000	$5 000	$25 000
2				
3				
4				
5				
6				

   (c) How would the equipment appear in the fixed asset section of the balance sheet at the end of year five? year six?

7. (a) Make your own copy of the chart on page 144 and complete the chart for the amortization of equipment, purchased for $60 000, that amortizes at the rate of 20 percent a year on the declining balance.
   (b) Show the journal entries required to record the amortization expenses in the first four years.

Year	Value at beginning of year	Amortization for the year	Accumulated amortization	Book value at end of year
1	$60 000	$	$	$
2				
3				
4				

8. Priddle Plumbing prepares monthly financial statements. Capital assets owned by the company include Equipment valued at $24 000 and Delivery Truck worth $18 000. Accumulated Amortization on the truck is $4 500. Prepare adjusting entries to record one month's amortization, using the declining-balance method. The rate of amortization for one year for the equipment is 20 percent, and for the truck, 30 percent.

UNIT  12 Work Sheets, Adjustments, Financial Statements

Learning Objectives

After reading this unit, discussing the applicable review questions, and completing the applications exercises, you will be able to do the following:

1. **PREPARE** adjustments on a work sheet for prepaid expenses and amortization of fixed assets.
2. **COMPLETE** an eight-column work sheet.
3. **COMPLETE** a ten-column work sheet.
4. **PREPARE** financial statements from a work sheet.

So far in this chapter you have learned:

- That adjustments are necessary if financial statements are to be correct
- How to adjust prepaid expenses such as Supplies, Rent, and Insurance
- How to adjust fixed assets by recording Amortization Expense

Adjustments are first prepared on the work sheet.

In this unit, you will learn how the adjustments are prepared on the work sheet and how the financial statements are prepared.

EIGHT-COLUMN WORK SHEET

The trial balance for Management Consultant Services is shown in Figure 6-5, on page 146, on an eight-column work sheet. In Chapter 5, you learned how a six-column work sheet is used to help organize the financial statements. The trial balance is written on a work sheet. The accounts on the trial balance are then transferred to either the income statement section or the balance sheet section of the work sheet. The revenue and expense items are transferred to the income statement section. The difference in the totals of the income statement section is the net income or the net loss for the accounting period. The difference in the totals of the balance sheet section is also the net income or the net loss. This difference should, of course, be the same as that obtained in the income statement section.

The eight-column work sheet serves the same purpose. It is prepared in the same way as a six-column work sheet, but an *adjustments* section is added. It is also used by the accountant to rough out or plan the necessary adjustments so that the financial statements will be correct. There are four sections on an eight-column work sheet, as shown in Figure 6-5:

- Trial balance section
- Section to plan the adjustments
- Income statement section
- Balance sheet section

In the next few pages, the work sheet will be completed for Management Consultant Services. The period of time covered by this work sheet will be one full year. The first step in preparing the work sheet is to gather the information required to complete the adjustments. This information includes the following:

- A count made of all supplies on hand shows $400 worth left on December 31.
- On January 1, a three-year insurance policy was purchased. One year of the policy is now expired.
- The balance in the Prepaid Rent account represents a payment on October 1 for the October, November, and December rents.
- The equipment amortizes 20 percent a year. The declining-balance method is used.

Using this information, the adjustments are prepared on the work sheet.

PREPARING ADJUSTMENTS

In this example, four accounts need to be adjusted. They are:

- Supplies
- Prepaid Insurance
- Prepaid Rent
- Equipment

Supplies

The asset account Supplies has a $1 000 balance. However, the inventory taken at the end of the fiscal period indicates only $400 worth of supplies are left. This means that $600 worth of supplies has been used and should be recorded as an expense.

FIGURE 6-5
Eight-column work sheet

Management Consultant Services
Work Sheet
For the year ended December 31, 2001

	ACCOUNT TITLE	ACC. NO.	TRIAL BALANCE		ADJUSTMENTS		INCOME STATEMENT		BALANCE SHEET		
			DEBIT	CREDIT	DEBIT	CREDIT	DEBIT	CREDIT	DEBIT	CREDIT	
1	Cash	100	13 000								1
2	Accounts Receivable	110	7 000								2
3	Supplies	131	1 000								3
4	Prepaid Insurance	132	900								4
5	Prepaid Rent	133	5 100								5
6	Equipment	141	12 000								6
7	Acc. Amort. — Equip.	142		2 400							7
8	Accounts Payable	200		1 000							8
9	Bank Loan	221		3 000							9
10	J. Turner, Capital	300		10 400							10
11	J. Turner, Drawings	301	15 000								11
12	Fees Earned	400		144 000							12
13	Salaries Expense	500	89 500								13
14	Utilities Expense	501	1 300								14
15	Rent Expense	502	15 300								15
16	Miscellaneous Expense	503	700								16
17			160 800	160 800							17

Supplies purchased	$1 000
Supplies left	400
Supplies Expense	$ 600

It is necessary to record the Supplies Expense of $600 and to decrease the asset Supplies by $600. This is done by debiting Supplies Expense and crediting Supplies. Figure 6-6, on page 148, shows how this adjustment is prepared on the work sheet.

In preparing the adjustment, it is necessary to add the account Supplies Expense to the bottom of the trial balance because the account Supplies Expense does not appear on the trial balance. The new account Supplies Expense is debited $600 in the adjustments debit column. The asset Supplies is reduced by entering a credit of $600 in the adjustments credit column on the same line as Supplies. The effect of this adjustment, in T-account form, is:

Supplies

Dec. 31	1 000	Dec. 31	600
Balance	400		

Supplies Expense

Dec. 31	600		

This adjustment decreases the asset Supplies by $600 to the correct balance of $400. It also records the amount of supplies used ($600) in the Supplies Expense account.

Prepaid Insurance

In January, a $900, three-year insurance policy was purchased. At the end of the current year, two years of insurance remain. One-third of the policy has expired or been used up, and it is necessary to reduce the Prepaid Insurance by $300 ($1/3 \times 900 = 300$) and record an expense of $300. This is done by adding the account Insurance Expense to the work sheet. A debit of $300 is written beside Insurance Expense in the adjustments debit column. The asset Prepaid Insurance is reduced by entering a credit of $300 in the adjustments credit column opposite Prepaid Insurance. The work sheet in Figure 6-7, on page 150, illustrates how Prepaid Insurance is adjusted.

The effect of this adjustment is to lower the asset Prepaid Insurance to $600 and to record the Insurance Expense for one year of $300.

Prepaid Rent

On October 1, rent of $5 100 was prepaid for October, November, and December. On December 31, the rent for those three months is no longer prepaid. It has been used up and an expense must be recorded.

Since there is already a Rent Expense account on the trial balance, all that is required to adjust Prepaid Rent is to decrease the asset by a credit of $5 100. The rent expense for the three months is recorded by debiting Rent Expense $5 100. Because the rent is no longer prepaid, the effect of the credit to Prepaid Rent is to reduce this asset to zero. Figure 6-8, on page 151, illustrates the rent adjustment.

FIGURE 6-6
The adjustment for Supplies is shown on lines 3 and 18 of the work sheet.

Management Consultant Services
Work Sheet
For the Year Ended December 31, 2001

	ACCOUNT TITLE	ACC. NO.	TRIAL BALANCE		ADJUSTMENTS		INCOME STATEMENT		BALANCE SHEET		
			DEBIT	CREDIT	DEBIT	CREDIT	DEBIT	CREDIT	DEBIT	CREDIT	
1	Cash	100	13 000								1
2	Accounts Receivable	110	7 000								2
3	Supplies	131	1 000			(a) 600					3
4	Prepaid Insurance	132	900								4
5	Prepaid Rent	133	5 100								5
6	Equipment	141	12 000								6
7	Acc. Amort. — Equip.	142		2 400							7
8	Accounts Payable	200		1 000							8
9	Bank Loan	221		3 000							9
10	J. Turner, Capital	300		10 400							10
11	J. Turner, Drawings	301	15 000								11
12	Fees Earned	400		144 000							12
13	Salaries Expense	500	89 500								13
14	Utilities Expense	501	1 300								14
15	Rent Expense	502	15 300								15
16	Miscellaneous Expense	503	700								16
17			160 800	160 800							17
18	Supplies Expense	504			(a) 600						18

Equipment

Capital assets such as Equipment amortize each year. Equipment may be amortized at a rate of up to 20 percent a year. For income tax purposes, the declining-balance method must be used. The year's depreciation on Equipment using a 20 percent rate on the declining balance is $1 920.

To record the amortization, a debit is entered in the Amortization Expense — Equipment account and a credit is entered in the Accumulated Amortization — Equipment account. It is necessary to add Amortization Expense — Equipment to the work sheet. This account is debited $1 920 in the adjustments debit column. The Accumulated Amortization — Equipment account is credited $1 920 in the adjustments credit column. Figure 6-9, on page 152, illustrates this adjustment.

Coding the Adjustments

Four adjustments have now been made on the work sheet and placed in the adjustments section; each adjustment has been *coded.* For example, the supplies adjustment has an (a) beside the debit and an (a) beside the credit. The other adjustments were labelled (b), (c), and (d), respectively. These labels ensure that there is a debit for every credit and provide a reference for checking the adjustments.

The mathematical accuracy of the adjustments section of the work sheet is proven by adding the two columns. The debit column total should equal the credit column total. If this is the case, the columns are double-ruled.

COMPLETING THE WORK SHEET

After the adjustments have been completed and the adjustments columns totalled, the items on the trial balance are transferred to either the income statement or balance sheet sections of the work sheet. The income and expenses are transferred to the income statement section. The assets, liabilities, and equity accounts are transferred to the balance sheet section.

For example, Figure 6-9 shows that Cash, $13 000, is transferred to the balance sheet debit column (line 1). Accounts Receivable, $7 000, is also transferred to the balance sheet debit column (line 2). However, there is a complication on line 3 of the work sheet. The asset Supplies has a debit of $1 000 and a credit of $600 in the adjustments section. The difference between a debit of $1 000 and a credit of $600 is $400. Because Supplies is an asset account, the $400 balance is transferred to the balance sheet debit column.

Prepaid Insurance is handled in the same way as Supplies. The difference between the $900 debit and the $300 credit is $600. This amount ($600) is transferred to the balance sheet debit column (line 4). On line 5, the difference in the Prepaid Rent account is zero (5 100 debit – 5 100 credit = 0). Therefore, there is no balance shown in the balance sheet section for Prepaid Rent. There is no change in the Equipment account. Thus $12 000 is transferred to the balance sheet debit column (line 6). On line 7, there are two credits for Accumulated Amortization — Equipment. These are added and the balance, $4 320, is transferred to the balance sheet credit column. Accounts Payable, Bank Loan, and J. Turner, Capital are all transferred to the balance sheet credit column, and J. Turner, Drawings is transferred to the balance sheet debit column.

FIGURE 6-7
The adjustment for Prepaid Insurance is shown on lines 4 and 19.

Management Consultant Services
Work Sheet
For the Year Ended December 31, 2001

ACCOUNT TITLE	ACC. NO.	TRIAL BALANCE DEBIT	TRIAL BALANCE CREDIT	ADJUSTMENTS DEBIT	ADJUSTMENTS CREDIT	INCOME STATEMENT DEBIT	INCOME STATEMENT CREDIT	BALANCE SHEET DEBIT	BALANCE SHEET CREDIT	
1 Cash	100	13 000								1
2 Accounts Receivable	110	7 000								2
3 Supplies	131	1 000			(a) 600					3
4 Prepaid Insurance	132	900			(b) 300					4
5 Prepaid Rent	133	5 100								5
6 Equipment	141	12 000								6
7 Acc. Amort. — Equip.	142		2 400							7
8 Accounts Payable	200		1 000							8
9 Bank Loan	221		3 000							9
10 J. Turner, Capital	300		10 400							10
11 J. Turner, Drawings	301	15 000								11
12 Fees Earned	400		144 000							12
13 Salaries Expense	500	89 500								13
14 Utilities Expense	501	1 300								14
15 Rent Expense	502	15 300								15
16 Miscellaneous Expense	503	700								16
17		160 800	160 800							17
18 Supplies Expense	504			(a) 600						18
19 Insurance Expense	505			(b) 300						19

FIGURE 6-8

The adjustment for Prepaid Rent is shown on lines 5 and 15.

Management Consultant Services
Work Sheet
For the Year Ended December 31, 2001

	ACCOUNT TITLE	ACC. NO.	TRIAL BALANCE DEBIT	TRIAL BALANCE CREDIT	ADJUSTMENTS DEBIT	ADJUSTMENTS CREDIT	INCOME STATEMENT DEBIT	INCOME STATEMENT CREDIT	BALANCE SHEET DEBIT	BALANCE SHEET CREDIT	
1	Cash	100	13 000								1
2	Accounts Receivable	110	7 000								2
3	Supplies	131	1 000			(a) 600					3
4	Prepaid Insurance	132	900			(b) 300					4
5	Prepaid Rent	133	5 100			(c) 5 100					5
6	Equipment	141	12 000								6
7	Acc. Amort. — Equip.	142		2 400							7
8	Accounts Payable	200		1 000							8
9	Bank Loan	221		3 000							9
10	J. Turner, Capital	300		10 400							10
11	J. Turner, Drawings	301	15 000								11
12	Fees Earned	400		144 000							12
13	Salaries Expense	500	89 500								13
14	Utilities Expense	501	1 300								14
15	Rent Expense	502	15 300		(c) 5 100						15
16	Miscellaneous Expense	503	700								16
17			160 800	160 800							17
18	Supplies Expense	504			(a) 600						18
19	Insurance Expense	505			(b) 300						19

FIGURE 6-9
Completed work sheet

Management Consultant Services
Work Sheet
For the Year Ended December 31, 2001

ACCOUNT TITLE	ACC. NO.	TRIAL BALANCE DEBIT	TRIAL BALANCE CREDIT	ADJUSTMENTS DEBIT	ADJUSTMENTS CREDIT	INCOME STATEMENT DEBIT	INCOME STATEMENT CREDIT	BALANCE SHEET DEBIT	BALANCE SHEET CREDIT	
1 Cash	100	13 000						13 000		1
2 Accounts Receivable	110	7 000						7 000		2
3 Supplies	131	1 000			(a) 600			400		3
4 Prepaid Insurance	132	900			(b) 300			600		4
5 Prepaid Rent	133	5 100			(c) 5 100					5
6 Equipment	141	12 000						12 000		6
7 Acc. Amort. — Equip.	142		2 400		(d) 1 920				4 320	7
8 Accounts Payable	200		1 000						1 000	8
9 Bank Loan	221		3 000						3 000	9
10 J. Turner, Capital	300		10 400						10 400	10
11 J. Turner, Drawings	301	15 000						15 000		11
12 Fees Earned	400		144 000				144 000			12
13 Salaries Expense	500	89 500				89 500				13
14 Utilities Expense	501	1 300				1 300				14
15 Rent Expense	502	15 300		(c) 5 100		20 400				15
16 Miscellaneous Expense	503	700				700				16
17		160 800	160 800							17
18 Supplies Expense	504			(a) 600		600				18
19 Insurance Expense	505			(b) 300		300				19
20 Amort. Expense — Equip.	506			(d) 1 920		1 920				20
21				7 920	7 920	114 720	144 000	48 000	18 720	21
22 Net Income						29 280			29 280	22
23						144 000	144 000	48 000	48 000	23

Fees Earned, on line 12, is the revenue of Management Consultant Services and is transferred to the income statement credit column.

Salaries Expense, Utilities Expense, and Miscellaneous Expense did not require adjustment and are transferred to the income statement debit column. Rent Expense on line 15 has two debits. These are added and the total of $20 400 appears in the income statement debit column. At the bottom of the work sheet are found the remaining expenses, including Supplies Expense, Insurance Expense, and Amortization Expense — Equipment, which required adjustments. These expenses are transferred to the income statement debit column.

Determining the Net Income or Net Loss

After all the amounts have been transferred to either the balance sheet or income statement sections, it is quite simple to determine the net income or net loss. First, add the income statement debit and credit columns and then find the difference between them. This difference is the net income or the net loss. There is net income if the credit column total is bigger than the debit column total. Conversely, there is net loss if the debit column has a bigger total than the credit column. Looking at Figure 6-9, it can be seen that the credit column total of the income statement section is bigger and thus shows a net income ($29 280).

Next, add the balance sheet debit and credit columns and determine the difference between them. The difference is the net income or net loss. There is net income if the debit column total is bigger than the credit column total, and net loss if the credit column total is the larger of the two. Notice that the debit column total in Figure 6-9 is bigger and the difference is the same as the difference in the income statement columns — both differences are $29 280. This should come as no surprise because both differences are measuring the same thing — net income.

Balancing the Work Sheet

After the net income (or net loss) has been determined, the amount (in this example $29 280) is added to the smaller column total of both the income statement and the balance sheet sections of the work sheet. The net income figure is added to both the debit side of the income statement section and to the credit side of the balance sheet. A net loss would be added to the credit side of the income statement section and to the debit side of the balance sheet section. The columns are then double-ruled as shown in Figure 6-9.

Steps in Preparing the Eight-Column Work Sheet

To summarize, these are the steps followed when preparing an eight-column work sheet:

(1) Write the heading on the work sheet.
(2) Write the trial balance on the work sheet.
(3) Gather the data needed to prepare the adjustments.
(4) Prepare the adjustments and total, balance, and rule the adjustment columns.
(5) Transfer all items to either the income statement or balance sheet columns.
(6) Total the income statement and balance sheet columns and determine the net income or net loss.
(7) Balance and rule the work sheet.

TEN-COLUMN WORK SHEET

Many businesses use a ten-column work sheet instead of the eight-column work sheet. The extra two columns are used to prepare an "adjusted trial balance." This trial balance is prepared on the work sheet after the adjustments have been completed. It is prepared to ensure that the ledger accounts are still in balance; that is, to ensure that the debit balances equal the credit balances. If the ledger is still in balance, then the accountant proceeds to complete the work sheet. The work sheet for Management Consultant Services is shown in Figure 6-10, on page 155, using the ten-column format. Notice that the adjusted trial balance section comes after the adjustments section and before the financial statement sections.

Steps in Preparing the Ten-Column Work Sheet

These steps are followed when completing a ten-column work sheet:

(1) Write the heading on the work sheet.
(2) Write the trial balance on the work sheet.
(3) Gather the data needed to prepare the adjustments.
(4) Prepare the adjustments and total, balance, and rule the adjustment columns.
(5) Transfer all items to the adjusted trial balance columns and recalculate the balances where necessary. Total, balance, and rule the adjusted trial balance columns.
(6) Transfer all items from the adjusted balance to either the income statement or the balance sheet columns.
(7) Total the income statement and balance sheet columns and determine the net income or net loss.
(8) Balance and rule the work sheet.

PREPARING THE FINANCIAL STATEMENTS

When the work sheet has been completed, the formal financial statements are prepared. All the information necessary for the preparation of the income statement is found on the work sheet in the income statement columns. Similarly, all the necessary data for the balance sheet is found on the work sheet in the balance sheet columns.

Figures 6-11 and 6-12 (page 156) illustrate the financial statements prepared from the completed work sheet. Note the following about the two statements:

- The new expenses resulting from the adjustments are included on the income statement. These are Supplies Expense, Insurance Expense, and Amortization Expense — Equipment.
- The Accumulated Amortization is shown as a subtraction from Equipment in the capital asset section of the balance sheet.

FIGURE 6-10
Ten-column work sheet

Management Consultant Services
Work Sheet
For the Year Ended December 31, 2001

	ACCOUNT TITLE	ACC. NO.	TRIAL BALANCE DEBIT	TRIAL BALANCE CREDIT	ADJUSTMENTS DEBIT	ADJUSTMENTS CREDIT	ADJUSTED TRIAL BALANCE DEBIT	ADJUSTED TRIAL BALANCE CREDIT	INCOME STATEMENT DEBIT	INCOME STATEMENT CREDIT	BALANCE SHEET DEBIT	BALANCE SHEET CREDIT	
1	Cash	100	13 000				13 000				13 000		1
2	Accounts Receivable	110	7 000				7 000				7 000		2
3	Supplies	131	1 000			(a) 600	400				400		3
4	Prepaid Insurance	132	900			(b) 300	600				600		4
5	Prepaid Rent	133	5 100			(c) 5 100							5
6	Equipment	141	12 000				12 000				12 000		6
7	Acc. Amort. — Equip.	142		2 400		(d) 1 920		4 320				4 320	7
8	Accounts Payable	200		1 000				1 000				1 000	8
9	Bank Loan	221		3 000				3 000				3 000	9
10	J. Turner, Capital	300		10 400				10 400				10 400	10
11	J. Turner, Drawings	301	15 000				15 000				15 000		11
12	Fees Earned	400		144 000				144 000		144 000			12
13	Salaries Expense	500	89 500				89 500		89 500				13
14	Utilities Expense	501	1 300				1 300		1 300				14
15	Rent Expense	502	15 300		(c) 5 100		20 400		20 400				15
16	Miscellaneous Expense	503	700				700		700				16
17			160 800	160 800									17
18	Supplies Expense	504			(a) 600		600		600				18
19	Insurance Expense	505			(b) 300		300		300				19
20	Amort. Expense– Equip.	506			(d) 1 920		1 920		1 920				20
21					7 920	7 920	162 720	162 720	114 720	144 000	48 000	18 720	21
22	Net Income								29 280			29 280	22
23									144 000	144 000	48 000	48 000	23

FIGURE 6-11
Income statement prepared from the work sheet

Management Consultant Services Income Statement For the Year Ended December 31, 2001		
Revenue		
Fees Earned		$144 000
Expenses		
Salaries Expense	$89 500	
Utilities Expense	1 300	
Rent Expense	20 400	
Miscellaneous Expense	700	
Supplies Expense	600	
Insurance Expense	300	
Amortization Expense — Equipment	1 920	114 720
Net Income		$ 29 280

Book Value of Assets

The concept of "book value" is an important one in accounting. In Unit 11, you learned that the book value is the amount remaining after the accumulated amortization has been subtracted from the cost price of a capital asset.

The book value of Equipment owned by Management Consultant Services is $7 680. This is the net value of the asset. It is determined by subtracting the Accumulated Amortization from the cost of the asset. The book value should not be confused with the market value or cost of the asset. It is simply the remaining value of the asset that has not yet been converted to expense (i.e., the unamortized value).

FIGURE 6-12
Balance sheet prepared from the work sheet

Management Consultant Services Balance Sheet December 31, 2001			
Assets			
Current Assets			
Cash		$13 000	
Accounts Receivable		7 000	
Supplies		400	
Prepaid Insurance		600	
Total Current Assets			$21 000
Capital Assets			
Equipment		12 000	
Less: Accumulated Amortization		4 320	
Total Capital Assets			7 680
Total Assets			$28 680
Liabilities and Owner's Equity			
Current Liabilities			
Accounts Payable		$ 1 000	
Bank Loan		3 000	
Total Current Liabilities			$ 4 000
Owner's Equity			
J. Turner, Capital January 1		10 400	
Add: Net Income for the Year	$29 280		
Less: J. Turner, Drawings	15 000		
Increase in Capital		14 280	
J. Turner, Capital December 31			24 680
Total Liabilities and Owner's Equity			$28 680

REVIEW QUESTIONS

UNIT 12

1. (a) What are the two new columns added to an eight-column work sheet?
   (b) For what purpose are the two new columns used?
2. How is the net income or net loss determined on the work sheet?
3. When there is a net loss, which column of the income statement section of the work sheet is greater? Which column of the balance sheet section is greater when there is a net loss?
4. When there is a net income, to which columns on the work sheet is the amount of the net income added?
5. List the seven steps in preparing an eight-column work sheet.
6. How is the book value of an asset determined? Give an example.

PROBLEMS: APPLICATIONS

CHAPTER 6

9. The trial balance for Forsythe Enterprises follows. Prepare an eight-column work sheet for the year ended December 31, 2001, using the additional information given.

Additional Information:

- Supplies on hand at December 31 are valued at $900.
- The declining-balance method of amortization is used, and Equipment amortizes at the rate of 20 percent per year.

Forsythe Enterprises
Trial Balance
December 31, 2001

ACCOUNT TITLE	ACC. NO.	DEBIT	CREDIT
Cash	100	$ 12 000	
Accounts Receivable	110	4 000	
Supplies	131	1 700	
Equipment	141	18 000	
Accumulated Amortization — Equip.	142		$ 6 480
Accounts Payable	200		2 000
E. Forsythe, Capital	300		33 600
E. Forsythe, Drawings	301	19 080	
Sales	400		66 000
Salaries Expense	500	44 000	
Rent Expense	501	4 000	
Telephone Expense	502	1 400	
Miscellaneous Expense	503	900	
Office Expense	504	3 000	
		$108 080	$108 080

10. The trial balance for Music Man DJ follows. Prepare an eight-column work sheet for the year ended December 31, 2002, using the additional information given.

Additional Information:

- Supplies on hand at December 31 are valued at $150.
- The declining-balance method of amortization is used, and Equipment amortizes at the rate of 20 percent per year.

Music Man DJ Trial Balance December 31, 2002			
ACCOUNT TITLE	ACC. NO.	DEBIT	CREDIT
Cash	100	$ 4 000	
Accounts Receivable	102	3 000	
Supplies	131	700	
Equipment	141	20 000	
Accumulated Amortization — Equip.	142		$ 7 200
Accounts Payable	200		1 500
M. Bathurst, Capital	300		15 300
M. Bathurst, Drawings	301	8 000	
Sales	400		62 000
Salaries Expense	500	42 000	
Rent Expense	501	4 000	
Telephone Expense	502	400	
Miscellaneous Expense	503	900	
Office Expense	504	3 000	
		$86 000	$86 000

11. Prepare an eight-column work sheet for Elan Group Consultants using the trial balance on page 159 and additional information below. The fiscal period is one year.

    Additional Information:

    - Supplies on hand on December 31 are valued at $450.
    - The three-year insurance policy was purchased on January 1 for $2 700.
    - The declining-balance method of amortization is used to record amortization for Office Equipment (20 percent per year) and Automobile (30 percent per year).

12. Prepare a ten-column work sheet for Crowland Grange Travel Service, for March, using the trial balance on page 159 and additional information below.

    Additional Information:

    - Crowland Grange Travel prepares a work sheet each month.
    - Supplies on hand at the end of March are worth $900.
    - The declining-balance method of amortization is used to record amortization for Office Equipment (20 percent per year) and Automobile (30 percent per year).

Elan Group Consultants Trial Balance December 31, 2003			
ACCOUNT TITLE	ACC. NO.	DEBIT	CREDIT
Cash	100	$ 6 500	
Accounts Receivable	102	17 000	
Supplies	131	2 000	
Prepaid Insurance	132	2 700	
Office Equipment	141	11 000	
Acc. Amortization — Office Equip.	142		$ 3 760
Automobile	143	12 000	
Acc. Amortization — Automobile	144		5 760
Accounts Payable	200		1 500
K. Mullane, Capital	300		28 280
K. Mullane, Drawings	301	18 000	
Fees Income	400		122 000
Salaries Expense	500	80 000	
Rent Expense	501	7 200	
Automobile Expense	502	800	
Utilities Expense	503	1 100	
Office Expense	504	3 000	
		$161 300	$161 300

Crowland Grange Travel Service Trial Balance March 31, 2000			
ACCOUNT TITLE	ACC. NO.	DEBIT	CREDIT
Cash	100	$ 12 000	
Accounts Receivable	102	22 000	
Supplies	131	4 000	
Office Equipment	141	15 000	
Acc. Amortization — Office Equip.	142		$ 5 000
Automobile	143	9 000	
Acc. Amortization — Automobile	144		4 800
Accounts Payable	200		2 000
Bank Loan	220		3 000
P. Smythe, Capital	300		31 500
P. Smythe, Drawings	301	15 000	
Sales	400		105 000
Advertising Expense	500	3 500	
Salaries Expense	501	57 000	
Rent Expense	502	9 800	
Office Expense	503	4 000	
		$151 300	$151 300

13. Prepare a ten-column work sheet for Wiebe Consultants using the trial balance and additional information given. The fiscal period is one year.

Additional Information:

- Supplies on hand at December 31 are valued at $550.
- A three-year insurance policy was purchased on March 1 for $4 500.
- The declining-balance method of amortization is used to record amortization for Office Equipment (20 percent per year) and Automobile (30 percent per year).

Wiebe Consultants Trial Balance December 31, 2002			
ACCOUNT TITLE	ACC. NO.	DEBIT	CREDIT
Cash	100	$ 14 500	
Accounts Receivable	110	17 000	
Supplies	131	2 000	
Prepaid Insurance	132	4 500	
Office Equipment	141	16 000	
Acc. Amortization — Office Equipment	142		$ 3 200
Automobile	143	22 000	
Acc. Amortization — Automobile	144		6 600
Accounts Payable	200		11 500
D. Wiebe, Capital	300		53 680
D. Wiebe, Drawings	301	24 000	
Fees Income	400		126 620
Salaries Expense	500	80 000	
Rent Expense	501	14 200	
Automobile Expense	502	2 800	
Utilities Expense	503	1 600	
Office Expense	504	3 000	
		$201 600	$201 600

14. Rita Lynch opened a beauty salon on March 1, 2000. Presented below is a list of selected accounts, with their normal debit and credit balances, from the December 31, 2000 trial balance and adjusted trial balance. Prepare the adjusting entries that would explain the differences between the two trial balances.

	TRIAL BALANCE	ADJUSTED TRIAL BALANCE
Cash	$ 8 150	$ 8 150
Accounts Receivable	0	200
Prepaid Rent	9 600	1 600
Prepaid Insurance	3 000	500
Salon Supplies	1 720	750
Salon Furniture	21 000	21 000
Accumulated Amortization — Salon Furniture	0	1 750
Accounts Payable	0	515
Interest Payable	0	185
Salaries Payable	0	1 400
Bank Loan	35 000	35 000
R. Lynch, Capital	77 500	77 500
R. Lynch, Drawings	8 600	8 600
Service Revenue	68 500	68 700
Salaries Expense	14 000	15 400
Rent Expense	0	8 000
Insurance Expense	0	2 500
Salon Supplies Expense	9 830	10 800
Amortization Expense — Salon Furniture	0	1 750
Interest Expense	1 850	2 035
Utilities Expense	5 150	5 665

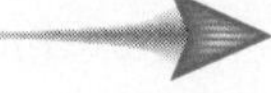

UNIT 13 Adjusting and Closing Entries

Learning Objectives

After reading this unit, discussing the applicable review questions, and completing the applications exercises, you will be able to do the following:

1. **PREPARE** adjusting entries from a work sheet.
2. **EXPLAIN** how closing entries update the Capital account and prepare revenue and expense accounts for entries of the next accounting period.
3. **CLOSE** revenue, expense, Drawings, and income summary accounts.
4. **EXPLAIN** why asset, liability, and Capital accounts are not closed.

The books of a company consist of the various journals and ledgers. The work sheet is not part of a company's permanent records. The work sheet is used by the accountant as an aid in organizing data used to prepare the financial statements.

The ledger accounts must be updated to be in agreement with the adjusting entries on the work sheet.

In the example used in this chapter, the assets Supplies, Prepaid Insurance, Prepaid Rent, and Accumulated Amortization — Equipment were adjusted. Changes were made in some expenses, and three expenses were added: Insurance Expense, Supplies Expense, and Amortization Expense — Equipment. All these adjustments were made on the work sheet. The accounts themselves in the ledger have not as yet been changed. The ledger accounts are incorrect and must be changed to reflect the adjustments made on the work sheet. The purpose of *adjusting entries* is to record the adjustments in the ledger accounts.

Adjusting entries are necessary to record the adjustments in the ledger accounts.

ADJUSTING ENTRIES

The recording of adjusting entries is quite simple because the adjustments have already been made on the work sheet. It is only necessary to record the adjustments in journal form and to post them to the ledger.

When the adjustments were made on the work sheet, they were coded (a), (b), (c), and (d). The debit and credit for the Supplies adjustment were coded (a). By referring to the work sheet and finding the (a) adjustment (Figure 6-9 on page 152), this entry is journalized:

Dec. 31	Supplies Expense	600	
	Supplies		600
	To record supplies used.		

Similar entries are recorded in the General Journal for each of the adjustments. These are shown in Figure 6-13.

FIGURE 6-13
General Journal entries to record the adjustments

DATE	PARTICULARS	P.R.	DEBIT	CREDIT
2001				
Dec. 31	Supplies Expense		600	
	Supplies			600
	To record supplies used.			
31	Insurance Expense		300	
	Prepaid Insurance			300
	To record the Insurance Expense for the year.			
31	Rent Expense		5 100	
	Prepaid Rent			5 100
	To record Rent Expense for three months.			
31	Amortization Expense — Equip.		1 920	
	Acc. Amortization — Equipment			1 920
	To record one year's amortization, declining-balance method.			

FIGURE 6-14
Partial General Ledger in T-account form before end-of-year adjustments have been posted

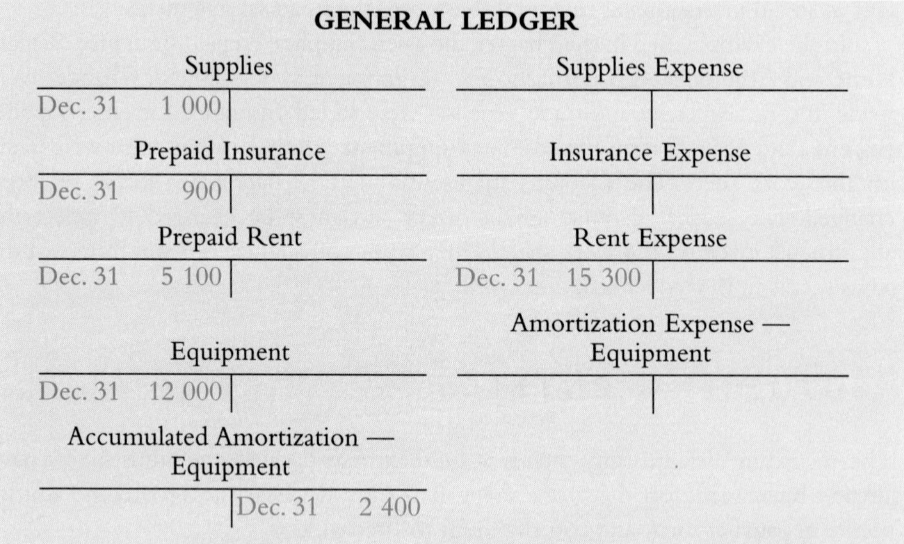

Posting the Adjusting Entries

After the adjusting entries have been journalized, they are posted to the General Ledger. Some of the General Ledger accounts of Management Consultant Services are shown in Figure 6-14, above. These T-accounts contain the end-of-the-fiscal-period balances found on the trial balance before adjustments have been made.

In the accounts shown in Figure 6-14, several expense accounts have no balance. If the adjustments were not journalized and posted, Supplies Expense, Insurance Expense, and Amortization Expense — Equipment would all have nil balances at the end of the fiscal period. That would be wrong since supplies were used, insurance did expire, and amortization is an expense. As well, the balance of $15 300 in the Rent Expense account would be incorrect since it would not include the $5 100 rent for the last three months.

Figure 6-15 on the following page is the partial General Ledger showing the accounts after the adjusting entries have been posted. Can you trace the entries from the General Journal in Figure 6-13 to this ledger?

FIGURE 6-15
Partial General Ledger in T-account form after end-of-year adjustments have been posted

GENERAL LEDGER

Supplies

Dec. 31	1 000	Dec. 31	600
Balance	400		

Supplies Expense

Dec. 31	600		

Prepaid Insurance

Dec. 31	900	Dec. 31	300
Balance	600		

Insurance Expense

Dec. 31	300		

Prepaid Rent

Dec. 31	5 100	Dec. 31	5 100
Balance	0		

Rent Expense

Dec. 31	15 300		
31	5 100		
Balance	20 400		

Equipment

Dec. 31	12 000		

Amortization Expense — Equipment

Dec. 31	1 920		

Accumulated Amortization — Equipment

		Dec. 31	2 400
		31	1 920
		Balance	4 320

Adjusted Trial Balance

After posting the adjusting entries, the accountant may wish to prepare an adjusted trial balance to verify that the ledger is still mathematically correct before preparing the financial statements.

The balances shown in the accounts in Figure 6-15 are the adjusted balances. They appear on the financial statements shown in Figures 6-11 and 6-12. Can you find each of them? What would be wrong with the income statement if adjustments had not been made? What would be wrong with the balance sheet if adjustments had not been made?

CLOSING ENTRIES

Introducing Closing the Books

The income statement is a means of calculating the net income or net loss for a specific accounting period. The financial data required to determine the net income (or net loss) are found in the revenue and expense accounts.

When one accounting period ends and a new one begins, the revenue and expense accounts should show *zero* balances so that in the new accounting period they contain only data that refer to the new period. This allows the calculation of a net income for the new period. When preparing an income statement, you learned that it is important that revenue for each accounting period is matched with expenses for that accounting period to determine the net income or loss.

In order to ensure this is the case, the revenue and expense accounts are reduced to zero by a process called *closing the books.* At the end of each accounting period, the balances of the revenue and expense accounts are reduced to zero so that they are ready to accumulate data for the next accounting period. For this reason, they are known as *temporary accounts.* They contain information for the current accounting period only. They do not carry their balances forward to the next accounting period.

Revenue and expense accounts are known as temporary accounts.

Asset, liability, and owner's equity accounts are known as permanent accounts.

Asset, liability, and owner's equity accounts are known as *permanent accounts.* Their balances are carried forward from accounting period to accounting period.

Purpose of Closing the Books

Revenue and expense accounts are closed at the end of each accounting period.

As has been stated, the process of reducing revenue and expense accounts to a zero balance is known as *closing the books.* Generally, the accounts are closed once a year, although some businesses perform this procedure more frequently. Closing the books serves two purposes:

(1) To prepare the revenue and expense accounts for the next accounting period by reducing them to zero
(2) To update the owner's equity account

Updating the Owner's Equity Account

Before closing entries are prepared, the owner's Capital account does not include the net income or net loss and withdrawals by the owner (Drawings account). When the balance sheet is prepared, the owner's Capital account is adjusted by the amount of the net income or loss and withdrawals. A net income is added to the Capital account. A net loss and withdrawals are subtracted from the Capital account.

The closing entries update the Capital account in the ledger. They increase or decrease the Capital account's balance by the amount of the net income or net loss. Closing entries also decrease the Capital account by the amount the owner has withdrawn from the business for personal use (Drawings account). The closing entries result in the Capital account being brought into agreement with the balance sheet. The Capital account has now been updated.

Income Summary Account

Revenue and expense accounts are closed by transferring their balances to an account called Income Summary. This procedure is illustrated in Figure 6-16 on the following page. The credit balance in the Income Summary account indicates a net income was earned.

When the revenue and expense account balances have been transferred to the Income Summary account, the balance of this account is the net income or net loss. The balance in the Income Summary account should be the same as the net income (or net loss) shown on the work sheet.

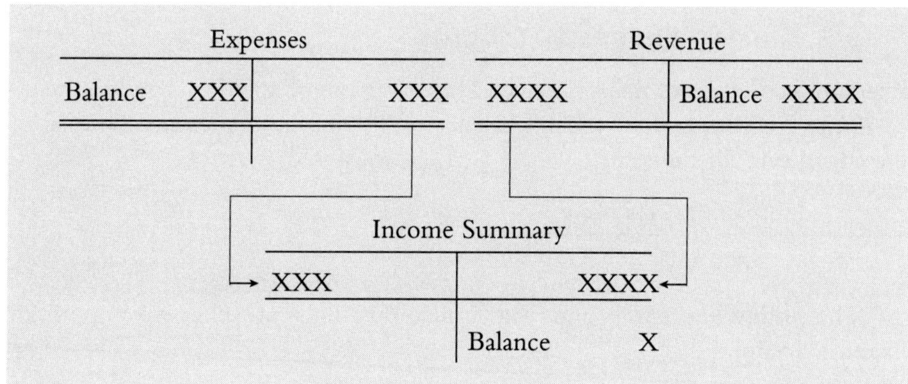

FIGURE 6-16
Closing the revenue and expense accounts to the Income Summary account

Steps in Closing the Books

The closing of revenue and expense accounts is first recorded in the form of debits and credits in the General Journal. These journal entries are called closing entries. After journalizing, the closing entries are posted to the General Ledger accounts. The four steps required to close the books follow.

Step 1: Closing Revenue Accounts

Revenue accounts have credit balances. The following Sales account shows a credit balance of $20 000 that represents the total sales for the year:

Sales	
	Dec. 31 20 000

To close the Sales account means to reduce it to zero and to transfer the balance to the Income Summary account. This procedure is illustrated by the following journal entry:

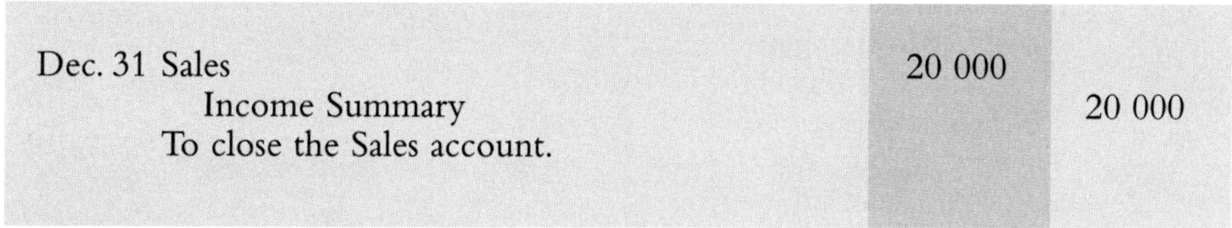

Dec. 31 Sales	20 000	
Income Summary		20 000
To close the Sales account.		

The following T-accounts illustrate the effect of this entry on the two accounts:

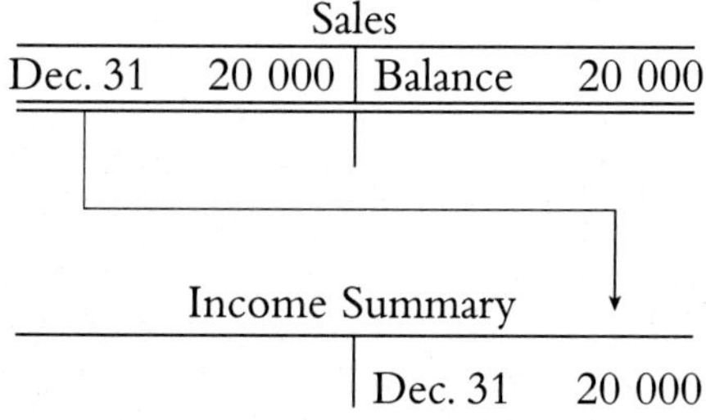

Step 2: Closing Expense Accounts

Expense accounts have debit balances. The Advertising Expense account illustrated in the T-account shows a debit balance of $3 000 that represents the total of the advertising for the year:

Advertising Expense	
Dec. 31 3 000	

The following entry and the T-accounts illustrate the closing of an expense account:

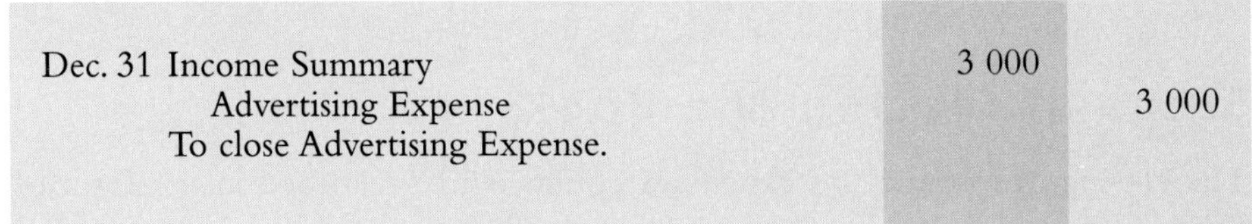

		Debit	Credit
Dec. 31	Income Summary	3 000	
	Advertising Expense		3 000
	To close Advertising Expense.		

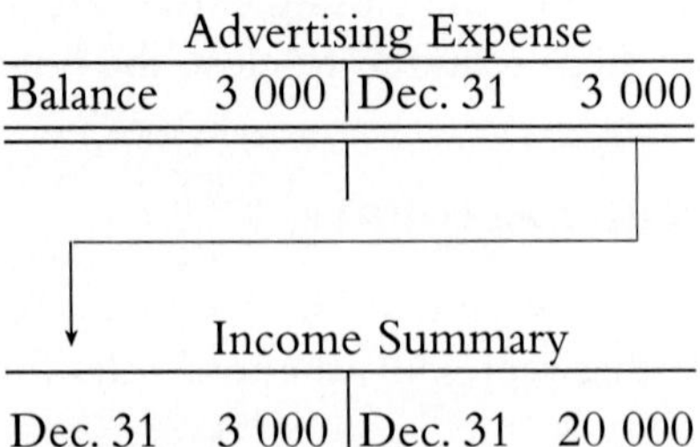

Each expense account in the ledger is closed in the same way. If a business has four expense accounts, they can be closed with four individual entries similar to the one for closing the Advertising Expense account. However, it is much simpler to make one compound entry such as the following:

		Debit	Credit
Dec. 31	Income Summary	14 000	
	Advertising Expense		3 000
	Salaries Expense		10 000
	Telephone Expense		500
	General Expense		500
	To close the expense accounts.		

Step 3: Closing the Income Summary Account

After the entries to close the revenue and expenses have been posted, the Income Summary account contains the revenue for the period on the credit side and the expenses for the period on the debit side. Since the credit side is larger, the $6 000 balance represents the net income for the period.

Income Summary	
Dec. 31 14 000	Dec. 31 20 000
	Balance 6 000

The net income of $6 000 earned for the period increases the owner's equity or, in other words, the net income belongs to the owner. The balance of the Income Summary accounts is therefore transferred to the owner's Capital account by this closing entry:

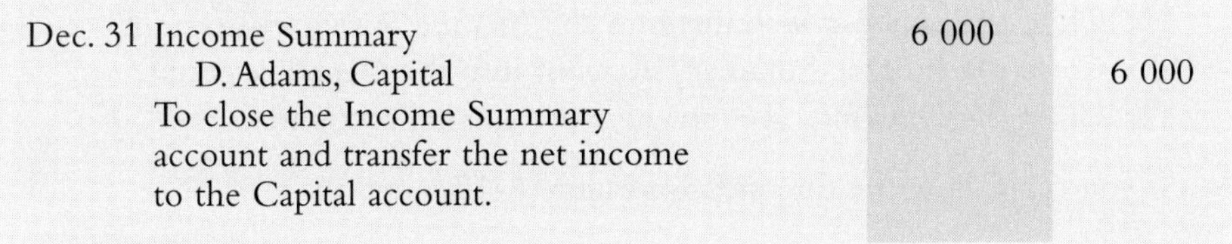

Dec. 31	Income Summary	6 000	
	D. Adams, Capital		6 000
	To close the Income Summary account and transfer the net income to the Capital account.		

The following T-accounts illustrate the effect of this entry on the two accounts:

Income Summary

Dec. 31	14 000	Dec. 31	20 000
31	6 000	Balance	6 000

D. Adams, Capital

		Balance	17 000
		Dec. 31	6 000

This entry increases the balance of the owner's Capital account by $6 000, the amount of the profit (net income) for the accounting period.

Step 4: Closing the Drawings Account

During the accounting period, withdrawals of cash and other assets by the owner are recorded in the owner's Drawings account. Since withdrawals by the owner affect the owner's investment, the Drawings account is closed with the following entry:

Dec. 31	D. Adams, Capital	2 000	
	D. Adams, Drawings		2 000
	To close the Drawings account.		

The following T-accounts illustrate the effects of this entry:

D. Adams, Drawings

Balance	2 000	Dec. 31	2 000

D. Adams, Capital

Dec. 31	2 000	Balance	17 000
		Dec. 31	6 000
		Balance	21 000

This entry reduces the owner's Capital account by $2 000, the amount that has been withdrawn from the business by the owner. Since the owner has withdrawn assets from the business, the owner's equity is decreased. The effect of this entry is to decrease the Capital account.

After these last two entries have been posted, the Income Summary account has been closed (reduced to zero), the Drawings account has been closed, and the Capital account has been updated so that it agrees with the balance for Capital shown on the balance sheet.

Summary

In summary, there are four steps involved in closing the books:

(1) Close the revenue accounts into the Income Summary account.
(2) Close the expense accounts into the Income Summary account.
(3) Close the Income Summary account into the Capital account.
(4) Close the Drawings account into the Capital account.

See if you can follow the four steps in Figure 6-17.

FIGURE 6-17
Closing the books

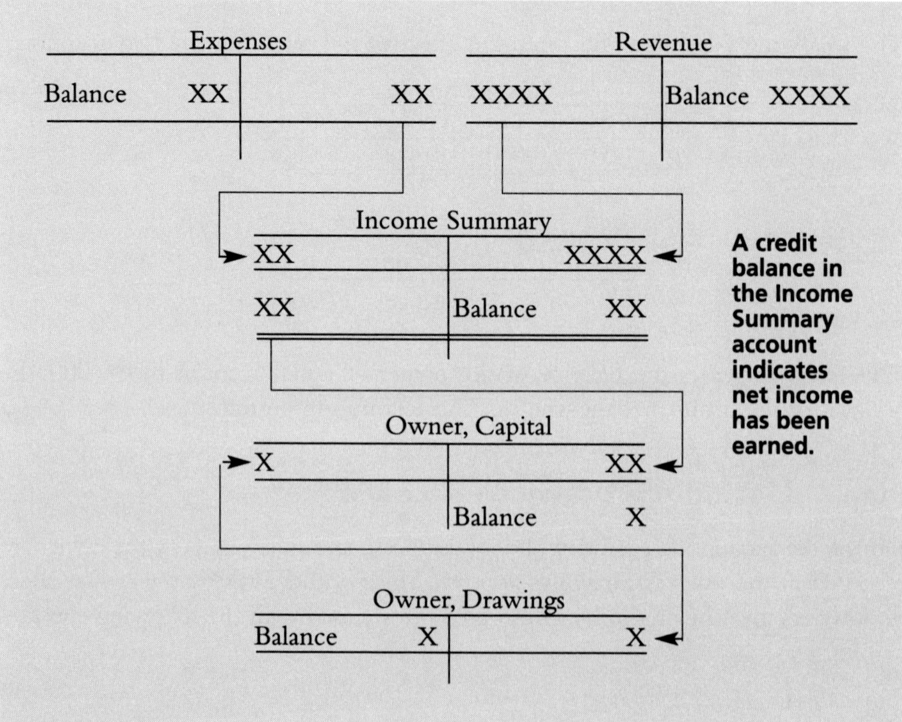

Closing the Books from the Work Sheet

The completed work sheet for Management Consultant Services is found in Figure 6-9. The revenue and expense accounts are found in the income statement columns of the work sheet. If you examined the ledger *before* closing the books, you would see that J. Turner's Capital account has a balance of $10 400. The balance sheet shown for Management Consultant Services in Figure 6-12 shows the actual Capital balance on December 31 to be $24 680. Why does the ledger balance not agree with the balance sheet? How will the closing entries bring them into agreement? As we journalize and post the closing entries, remember the purposes served by these entries.

Reviewing the Purpose of Closing Entries

Two main purposes are served by closing entries:

(1) Revenue and expense accounts are prepared for the next accounting period.
(2) The Capital account is updated.

Closing Revenue Accounts

On the work sheet (Figure 6-9), the revenue account Fees Earned has a credit balance of $144 000. To reduce it to zero, the Fees Earned is debited $144 000. This closing entry is journalized:

Dec. 31	Fees Earned	144 000	
	Income Summary		144 000
	To close the revenue account.		

Closing Expense Accounts

There are seven expenses in the debit column of the income statement section of the work sheet. Each is credited to reduce it to zero. This entry is journalized:

Dec. 31	Income Summary	114 720	
	Salaries Expense		89 500
	Utilities Expense		1 300
	Rent Expense		20 400
	Miscellaneous Expense		700
	Supplies Expense		600
	Insurance Expense		300
	Amortization Expense — Equip.		1 920
	To close the expense accounts.		

Updating the Equity Account

There are two entries required to update the owner's equity account. The first is to transfer the net income or net loss to the Capital account from the Income Summary. The net income of $29 280 earned during the year increases the owner's Capital account. In very simple terms, the net income belongs to the owner. For this reason, the net income is credited to the owner's Capital account. This increases the owner's Capital. If there was a net loss, Capital would be decreased. This entry is journalized:

Dec. 31	Income Summary	29 280	
	J. Turner, Capital		29 280
	To transfer net income to the owner's Capital account.		

A second entry involving owner's equity is needed to close the Drawings account into the Capital account. This entry is journalized:

Dec. 31	J. Turner, Capital	15 000	
	J. Turner, Drawings		15 000
	To close the Drawings account into the Capital account.		

The closing entries just described are all recorded in the General Journal. The sources of information are the income statement columns of the work sheet except for the Drawings account, which is found in the balance sheet columns of the work sheet.

After the closing entries have been journalized, they are posted to the General Ledger. Selected ledger accounts from the General Ledger are shown below and on following two pages in Figure 6-18. This ledger contains the adjusting entries and the closing entries that have been posted from the General Journal. All the revenue and expense accounts have a zero balance. They are double-ruled and are now ready to receive data for the new fiscal period. Notice that the Drawings account and the Income Summary account are also closed. The asset, liability, and owner's Capital accounts are *not* closed. Their balances continue into the next fiscal period.

Asset, liability, and owner's Capital accounts are not closed at the end of a fiscal period.

FIGURE 6-18

Partial General Ledger for Management Consultant Services after adjusting and closing entries have been posted

ACCOUNT Cash — NO. 100

DATE	PARTICULARS	P.R.	DEBIT	CREDIT	DR. CR.	BALANCE
2001						
Dec. 31		✓			DR.	13 000

ACCOUNT Supplies — NO. 131

DATE	PARTICULARS	P.R.	DEBIT	CREDIT	DR. CR.	BALANCE
2001						
Dec. 31		✓			DR.	1 000
31	Adjusting Entry	J34		600	DR.	400

ACCOUNT Prepaid Insurance — NO. 132

DATE	PARTICULARS	P.R.	DEBIT	CREDIT	DR. CR.	BALANCE
2001						
Dec. 31		✓			DR.	900
31	Adjusting Entry	J34		300	DR.	600

ACCOUNT Equipment — NO. 141

DATE	PARTICULARS	P.R.	DEBIT	CREDIT	DR. CR.	BALANCE
2001						
Dec. 31		✓			DR.	12 000

ACCOUNT Accumulated Amort. — Equipment — NO. 142

DATE	PARTICULARS	P.R.	DEBIT	CREDIT	DR. CR.	BALANCE
2001						
Dec. 31		✓			CR.	2 400
31	Adjusting Entry	J34		1 920	CR.	4 320

ACCOUNT Accounts Payable NO. 200

DATE	PARTICULARS	P.R.	DEBIT	CREDIT	DR. CR.	BALANCE
2001						
Dec. 31		✓			CR.	1 000

ACCOUNT J. Turner, Capital NO. 300

DATE	PARTICULARS	P.R.	DEBIT	CREDIT	DR. CR.	BALANCE
2001						
Dec. 31		✓			CR.	10 400
31	Net Income for Year	J35		29 280	CR.	39 680
31	Drawings	J35	15 000		CR.	24 680

ACCOUNT J. Turner, Drawings NO. 301

DATE	PARTICULARS	P.R.	DEBIT	CREDIT	DR. CR.	BALANCE
2001						
Dec. 31		✓			DR.	15 000
31	Closing Entry	J35		15 000		0

ACCOUNT Income Summary NO. 302

DATE	PARTICULARS	P.R.	DEBIT	CREDIT	DR. CR.	BALANCE
2001						
Dec. 31	To Close Fees Earned	J35		144 000	CR.	144 000
31	To Close Expenses	J35	114 720		CR.	29 280
31	To Close Inc. Summary	J35	29 280			0

ACCOUNT Supplies Expense NO. 504

DATE	PARTICULARS	P.R.	DEBIT	CREDIT	DR. CR.	BALANCE
2001						
Dec. 31	Adjusting Entry	J34	600		DR.	600
31	Closing Entry	J35		600		0

ACCOUNT Insurance Expense NO. 505

DATE	PARTICULARS	P.R.	DEBIT	CREDIT	DR. CR.	BALANCE
2001						
Dec. 31	Adjusting Entry	J34	300		DR.	300
31	Closing Entry	J35		300		0

ACCOUNT Amortization Expense — Equipment						NO. 506
DATE	PARTICULARS	P.R.	DEBIT	CREDIT	DR. CR.	BALANCE
2001						
Dec. 31	Adjusting Entry	J34	1920		DR.	1 920
31	Closing Entry	J35		1 920		0

Post-Closing Trial Balance

The post-closing trial balance is prepared after the closing entries have been posted to the General Ledger.

The post-closing trial balance contains only asset, liability, and Capital accounts.

After the adjusting and closing entries have been posted to the General Ledger, a post-closing trial balance is prepared (Figure 6-19). The purpose of this trial balance is to prove the mathematical accuracy of the General Ledger. If the debit total equals the credit total, the ledger is assumed to be *in balance.* It is ready for the next fiscal period. The post-closing trial balance is quite a bit shorter than other General Ledger trial balances. This is because it contains only asset, liability, and Capital accounts with balances. The revenue, expense, and Drawings accounts have been reduced to zero and do not appear on this final trial balance.

FIGURE 6-19
Post-closing trial balance prepared after the closing of the books

Management Consultant Services Post-Closing Trial Balance December 31, 2001			
ACCOUNT TITLE	ACC. NO.	DEBIT	CREDIT
Cash	100	$13 000	
Accounts Receivable	102	7 000	
Supplies	131	400	
Prepaid Insurance	132	600	
Equipment	141	12 000	
Accumulated Amortization — Equip.	142		$ 4 320
Accounts Payable	200		1 000
Bank Loan	221		3 000
J. Turner, Capital	300		24 680
		$33 000	$33 000

Effect of a Net Loss

How is the closing process affected when a business has a net loss? Revenue and expense accounts are closed as already described in this chapter. However, because there is a loss, the owner's Capital account will decrease. Look at this example:

Expenses		Revenue		Owner, Capital	
Dec. 31 50 000			Dec. 31 47 200		Dec. 1 100 000

As you can see, the expenses are greater than the revenue. The first two entries are shown as follows:

		Debit	Credit
Dec. 31	Revenue	47 200	
	Income Summary		47 200
	To close the revenue accounts.		
31	Income Summary	50 000	
	Expenses		50 000
	To close the expense accounts.		

After these entries have been posted, the Income Summary account has a debit balance of $2 800 — this is a net loss. What effect will this loss have on the owner's Capital account?

Expenses

Debit		Credit	
Dec. 31	50 000	Dec. 31	50 000

Revenue

Debit		Credit	
Dec. 31	47 200	Dec. 31	47 200

Income Summary

Debit		Credit	
Dec. 31	50 000	Dec. 31	47 200
Balance	2 800		

Owner, Capital

Debit		Credit	
		Dec. 1	100 000

The entry to close the Income Summary account and to transfer the loss to the Capital account is shown below:

		Debit	Credit
Dec. 31	Owner, Capital	2 800	
	Income Summary		2 800
	To close the Income Summary account and to transfer the loss to the Capital account.		

The owner's Capital account has now been updated. The Capital balance has been decreased by the net loss suffered during the accounting period.

Income Summary

Debit		Credit	
Dec. 31	50 000	Dec. 31	47 200
		31	2 800

Owner, Capital

Debit		Credit	
Dec. 31	2 800	Dec. 1	100 000
		Balance	97 200

At the beginning of the accounting period, Capital was $100 000. At the end of the period, Capital has decreased to $97 200 because of the net loss.

Additions to the Accounting Cycle

Figure 6-20 illustrates the accounting cycle with the addition of the adjusting and closing entries and the post-closing trial balance.

FIGURE 6-20

The accounting cycle is a continuous process

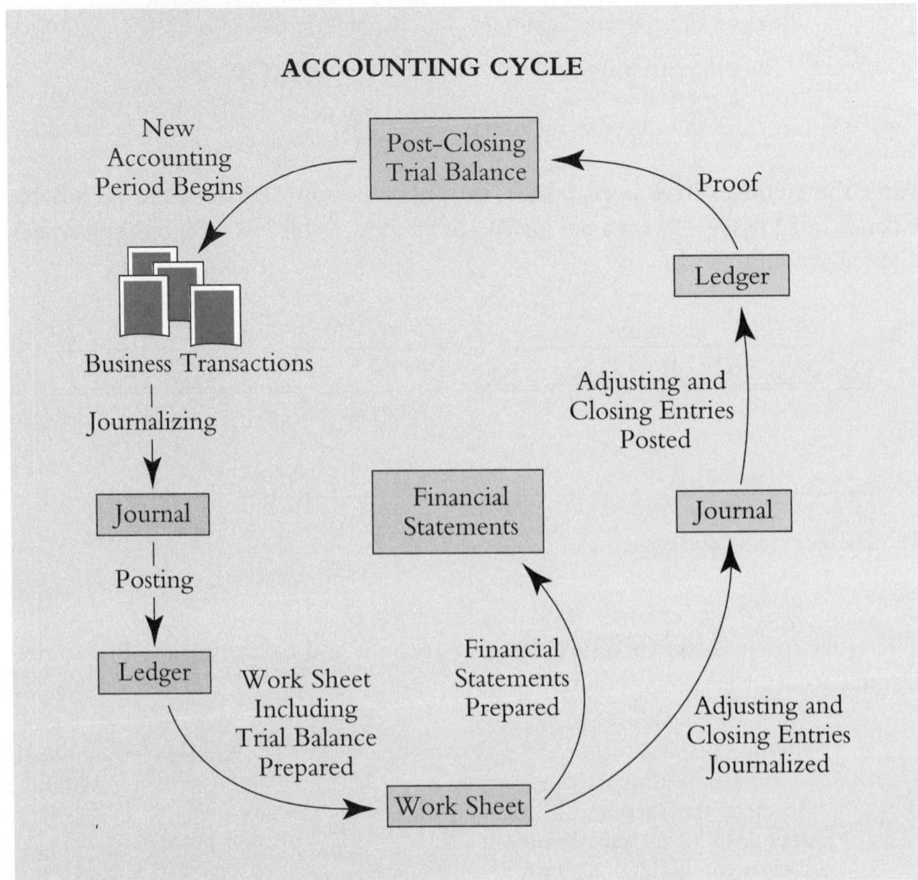

ACCOUNTING TERMS

Accumulated Amortization A contra-asset account on the balance sheet that shows the total amount of amortization recorded to date over the life of the asset.

Adjusted Trial Balance Verifies that the ledger is mathematically correct after the adjusting entries are posted.

Adjusting Entries Journal entries made at the end of the accounting period to ensure the balances in the ledger accounts are accurate before the financial statements are prepared.

Adjusting the Books Journal entries made at the end of an accounting period to ensure that the account balances and the financial statements are accurate.

Amortization The allocation of the cost of an asset to the fiscal periods in which it is used.

Amortization Expense An expense on the income statement that represents the cost of an asset allocated to that accounting period.

Book Value	Cost of an asset minus the accumulated amortization.
Capital Cost Allowance	The term used for amortization under the Income Tax Act. The declining-balance method using specified percentages must be used in the calculation.
Closing the Books	The process of preparing the revenue and expense accounts for the next accounting period by reducing them to zero and updating the owner's equity account.
Contra Accounts	Reduce the value of assets on the balance sheet.
Declining-Balance Method of Amortization	A method of calculating amortization in which the amortization allowance is a constant percentage of the book value of the asset.
Eight-Column Work Sheet	A sheet that contains columns for trial balance, adjustments, income statement, and balance sheet. It is used to rough out the adjustments and organize the financial statements.
Income Summary Account	A temporary account used during the process of closing the books to collect the revenue and expenses of the period and transfer the net income or loss to the owner's Capital account.
Post-Closing Trial Balance	Verifies that the ledger is mathematically correct after the closing entries have been posted. It contains only asset, liability, and Capital accounts.
Prepaid Expenses	Expense payments are made in advance. They are current assets.
Prepaid Insurance	Insurance premiums paid in advance.
Prepaid Rent	Rent paid in advance.
Straight-Line Method of Amortization	A method of calculating amortization that allocates the same amount of amortization to each fiscal period.
Ten-Column Work Sheet	Similar to an eight-column work sheet but also contains adjusted trial balance columns to ensure the accounts remain balanced after adjustments are calculated.
Valuation Account	An account used to arrive at the net value of an asset.
Work Sheet Code	As adjustments are made on the work sheet, they are coded by letter.

REVIEW QUESTIONS

1. Why is it necessary to record adjusting entries in the journal?
2. What two purposes are served by closing the books?
3. What type of accounts are closed?
4. (a) Which accounts are permanent accounts?
   (b) Which accounts are temporary accounts?
5. Is a revenue account debited or credited in order to close the revenue account?
6. In order to close an expense, is a debit or a credit necessary in the expense account?

7. Into which account are revenue and expenses closed?

8. Into which account are the Income Summary account and the Drawings account closed? Why?

9. What is the purpose of the post-closing trial balance?

10. Which accounts appear on the post-closing trial balance?

15. Refer to the work sheet completed in exercise 9 for Forsythe Enterprises and record the adjusting entries in a General Journal.

16. Refer to the work sheet in exercise 11 for Elan Group Consultants and record the adjusting entries in a General Journal.

17. Use the T-account ledger below to:

    (a) Prepare Jan. 31 closing entries in a journal and post them to the T-accounts in the ledger.
    (b) Calculate the final balance on Jan. 31 in the Pat Holmes, Capital account.

Pat Holmes, Capital 300	
	Jan. 31 60 000

Pat Holmes, Drawings 301	
Jan. 31 3 000	

Income Summary 302	

Sales 400	
	Jan. 31 45 000

Advertising Expense 500	
Jan. 31 2 000	

Auto Expense 501	
Jan. 31 1 000	

General Expense 502	
Jan. 31 3 000	

Rent Expense 503	
Jan. 31 5 000	

Salaries Expense 504	
Jan. 31 24 000	

18. The completed six-column work sheet for J. Fioravanti is shown on the following page.

    (a) Open a ledger using the accounts and balances on the trial balance and account 302, Income Summary.
    (b) Prepare closing entries in a General Journal.
    (c) Post the closing entries to the ledger.
    (d) Prepare a post-closing trial balance.

J. Fioravanti
Work Sheet
For the Month Ended April 30, 2001

ACCOUNT TITLE	ACC. NO.	TRIAL BALANCE DEBIT	TRIAL BALANCE CREDIT	INCOME STATEMENT DEBIT	INCOME STATEMENT CREDIT	BALANCE SHEET DEBIT	BALANCE SHEET CREDIT
Cash	100	2 000				2 000	
Accounts Receivable	101	4 300				4 300	
Equipment	110	6 200				6 200	
Accounts Payable	200		2 500				2 500
J. Fioravanti, Capital	300		5 000				5 000
Sales	400		8 000		8 000		
Salaries Expense	500	1 200		1 200			
General Expense	501	800		800			
Advertising Expense	502	1 000		1 000			
		15 500	15 500	3 000	8 000	12 500	7 500
Net Income				5 000			5 000
				8 000	8 000	12 500	12 500

1. Refer to exercise 9, Forsythe Enterprises.
   (a) Prepare the closing entries in a journal.
   (b) What should the balance in the Income Summary account be after closing the revenue and expense accounts?
   (c) What will the new balance be in Forsythe Capital after the closing entries have been posted?
2. The trial balance for Music Man DJ is shown below.
   (a) Open a ledger using the accounts and balances on the trial balance and account 302, Income Summary.
   (b) Journalize the adjusting and closing entries for the month of December.
   (c) Post the closing entries.
   (d) Prepare a post-closing trial balance.

Refer to Chapter 6, Unit 12, exercise 10.

Music Man DJ
Trial Balance
December 31, 2002

ACCOUNT TITLE	ACC. NO.	DEBIT	CREDIT
Cash	100	$ 4 000	
Accounts Receivable	102	3 000	
Supplies	131	700	
Equipment	141	20 000	
Accumulated Amortization — Equip.	142		$ 7 200
Accounts Payable	200		1 500
M. Bathurst, Capital	300		15 300
M. Bathurst, Drawings	301	8 000	
Sales	400		62 000
Salaries Expense	500	42 000	
Rent Expense	501	4 000	
Telephone Expense	502	400	
Miscellaneous Expense	503	900	
Office Expense	504	3 000	
		$86 000	$86 000

3. The trial balance for Crowland Grange Travel Service is shown below.
   (a) Open a ledger using the accounts and balances on the trial balance and account 302, Income Summary.
   (b) Journalize the adjusting and closing entries for the month of March.
   (c) Post the closing entries.
   (d) Prepare a post-closing trial balance.

Crowland Grange Travel Service
Trial Balance
March 31, 2000

ACCOUNT TITLE	ACC. NO.	DEBIT	CREDIT
Cash	100	$ 12 000	
Accounts Receivable	102	22 000	
Supplies	131	4 000	
Office Equipment	141	15 000	
Acc. Amortization — Office Equip.	142		$ 5 000
Automobile	143	9 000	
Acc. Amortization — Automobile	144		4 800
Accounts Payable	200		2 000
Bank Loan	220		3 000
P. Smythe, Capital	300		31 500
P. Smythe, Drawings	301	15 000	
Sales	400		105 000
Advertising Expense	500	3 500	
Salaries Expense	501	57 000	
Rent Expense	502	9 800	
Office Expense	503	4 000	
		$151 300	$151 300

4. Listed below are the month-end closing entries for The Dental Clinic, which were prepared by an inexperienced accountant. Upon review of these entries you discover a number of errors.

Jun. 30	Dental Fees Earned	9 800	
	Salaries Payable	1 650	
	Utilities Expense	635	
	Amortization Expense	1 300	
	Owner, Drawings	2 000	
	Income Summary		15 385
Jun. 30	Income Summary	9 170	
	Salaries Expense		3 300
	Rent Expense		1 800
	Accounts Payable		2 740
	Insurance Expense		550
	Dental Supplies Expense		780
Jun. 30	Owner, Capital	6 215	
	Income Summary		6 215

Prepare the correct closing entries for The Dental Clinic.

INTEGRATIVE ACTIVITY 1

THE ACCOUNTING CYLE

Westbrooke Cinema

INTRODUCTION

This activity includes all the steps in the accounting cycle covered to this point in *Accounting for Canadian Colleges*. It is a comprehensive review of Chapters 1 to 6. There are five parts to the project — Parts A, B, C, and optional parts D and E.

Part A: The first task is to complete the work sheet and financial statements for the month of January and then prepare and post adjusting and closing entries and prepare a post-closing trial balance. You are given the January 31 trial balance from which to work.

Part B: In this part you will journalize the February transactions, post to the ledger accounts, and prepare a trial balance.

Part C: Your next job is to complete the work sheet, financial statements, adjusting and closing entries, and post-closing trial balance for February.

Optional — Financial Analysis

Part D: The next task is to examine the financial results for the theatre for two months and to make recommendations to the owners.

Optional — Computer Accounting

Part E: If you have access to a computer accounting system, your teacher may have you complete this project using the computer.

Part A

The Westbrooke Cinema rents its premises from the Westbrooke Shopping Centre. The business has been open for a month, and the management wishes to find out if the business has made a profit or a loss. Using the additional information and the trial balance provided, do the following:

1. Complete an eight-column work sheet.
2. Prepare the monthly financial statements.
3. Set up a General Ledger with the appropriate accounts and balances.
4. Journalize and post the adjusting and closing entries.
5. Prepare a post-closing trial balance.

Additional Information:

- The straight-line amortization method is used by Westbrooke Cinema. The equipment amortizes 20 percent per year. (Note: Calculate the amortization to the nearest dollar value.)
- Rent was prepaid for three months on January 1.
- Insurance was prepaid for one year effective January 1.
- Supplies on hand January 31 were valued at $380.

Westbrooke Cinema
Trial Balance
January 31, 2001

ACCOUNT TITLE	ACC. NO.	DEBIT	CREDIT
Cash	100	$ 5 953	
Prepaid Rent	115	6 000	
Prepaid Insurance	116	1 800	
Supplies	117	620	
Equipment	120	89 563	
Accounts Payable	200		$ 890
Bank Loan	201		10 387
V. Schultz, Capital	300		94 312
V. Schultz, Drawings	301	1 600	
Ticket Sales	400		15 593
Confectionery Income	401		2 607
Salaries Expense	500	6 801	
Advertising Expense	501	2 563	
Film Rental Expense	502	3 563	
Cleaning Expense	503	850	
Telephone Expense	504	95	
Equip. Repairs & Maintenance Expense	505	2 293	
Film Transportation Expense	506	248	
Heating Expense	507	858	
Electricity and Water Expense	508	632	
General Expense	509	350	
		$123 789	$123 789

Additional Accounts:

Accumulated Amortization — Equipment	121
Income Summary	302
Amortization Expense — Equipment	510
Rent Expense	511
Insurance Expense	512
Supplies Expense	513

Part B

The following source documents came across the desk of the accountant during the month of February. Do the following:

1. Journalize the source documents and post to the General Ledger.
2. Prepare a trial balance.

Feb. 7 Cash register tapes from the box office for the week showing transactions No. 5345 to No. 6253 for total sales of $2 858. The money was deposited in the bank account.

Weekly sales report for the confectionery showing a net income of $225. The money was deposited in the bank account.

Purchases invoices received from:

Electronics Canada Ltd., $256 for final adjustments to the projector;

The Daily Sentinel, $750 for newspaper advertisements.

Cheques issued to:

City Hydro, No. 375, $350 for electricity and water;

Bell Canada, No. 376, $45.

Feb. 14 Cash register tapes from the box office for the week showing transactions No. 6254 to No. 8871 for total sales of $7 534.

Weekly sales report for the confectionery showing a net income of $612.

Purchases invoices received from:

International Film Distributors, $1 289 for rental of the film shown from Feb. 1 to 7;

Commercial Cleaners Ltd., $420 for cleaning the premises in the first half of the month.

Cheques issued to:

Craig Stationers, No. 377, $35 for supplies;

International Film Distributors, No. 378, $890 on account;

V. Schultz, the owner, No. 379, $400 for drawings;

Employees, No. 380 to 390, for a total of $2 890 for salaries from Feb. 1.

Feb. 21 Cash register tapes from the box office for the week showing transactions No. 8872 to No. 11 608 for total sales of $8 132.

Weekly sales report for the confectionery showing a net income of $657.

Purchases invoices received from:

Air Canada, $178 for transportation of film;

CCHH Radio and TV, $371 for spot advertising;

Stinson Fuels, $356 for heating oil.

Cheques issued to:

Electronics Canada Ltd., No. 391, $256 on account;

The Daily Sentinel, No. 392, $750 on account;

Triangle Office Supply, No. 393, $445 for supplies.

Feb. 28 Cash register tapes from the box office for the week showing transactions No. 11 609 to 14 142 for total sales of $7 483.

Weekly sales report for the confectionery showing a net income of $589.

Purchases invoices received from:

International Film Distributors, $2 658 for rental of film from Feb. 8 to 28;

Commercial Cleaners Ltd., $435 for cleaning of premises.

Cheques issued to:

Commercial Cleaners Ltd., No. 394, $420 on account;

V. Schultz, the owner, No. 395, $400 for personal drawings;

Employees, No. 396 to No. 406, for a total of $2 635 for salaries from Feb. 15.

Part C

Using the additional information given, complete the following procedures for the end of February:

1. Prepare an eight-column work sheet.
2. Prepare the financial statements.
3. Journalize and post the adjusting and closing entries.
4. Prepare a post-closing trial balance.

Additional Information:

- Supplies on hand, February 28, were valued at $390.

Part D — Optional — Financial Analysis

1. On behalf of the owner, V. Schultz, prepare a short written report for use in answering the following questions:

   (a) Is the business profitable at this time?
   (b) Is the profitability increasing or decreasing?
   (c) If the business were to apply for a $20 000 bank loan to purchase further equipment, would it be approved? Concentrate your response on the ability to repay the loan and the bank's chance of recovering its money if the firm cannot meet its loan payments.
   (d) Has the value of the business increased or decreased over the first two months of operation?
   (e) Should the present method of operating the confectionery be changed? G. Jones has submitted a proposal to V. Schultz to take over operation of the confectionery in the theatre and to pay Westbrooke Cinema 25 percent of sales. At present, the salary for the booth operator is $200 per week and the cost of the merchandise sold represents approximately 50 percent of the sales revenue. (Example: Sales 300 × 0.50 = 150 = cost of merchandise sold.) Based on this information and the confectionery income for the first two months, Schultz would like an opinion on whether it would be more profitable to run the booth or to lease it to Jones.

Part E — Optional — Computer Accounting

1. Use a computer to record the February transactions.
2. Print the journal, ledger, and trial balance.
3. Record the adjusting entries.
4. Print the adjusting entries and the financial statements.
5. Record the closing entries.
6. Print the ledger and the post-closing trial balance.

CHAPTER 7

The Merchandising Company

UNIT 14 Merchandising Accounts

Learning Objectives

After reading this unit, discussing the applicable review questions, and completing the applications exercises, you will be able to do the following:

1. **NAME** and **DEFINE** the function of the three major types of companies.
2. **PREPARE** a schedule of cost of goods sold.
3. **PREPARE** an income statement for a merchandising business.
4. **RECORD** transactions for a merchandising business including the following accounts: Sales, Sales Returns and Allowances, Sales Discounts, Purchases, Purchases Returns and Allowances, Purchases Discounts, Transportation-in, and Delivery Expense.

TYPES OF BUSINESS OPERATIONS

Service Companies

A service company sells services.

Up to this point, accounting procedures have been illustrated mainly by reference to businesses such as a fitness centre, motel, cinema, contractor, doctor, etc. All of these businesses offer services to their customers. They do not sell products like mouthwash or tires; they sell services and are called *service companies.*

FIGURE 7–1

There are three basic types of business operation — service, merchandising, and manufacturing companies.

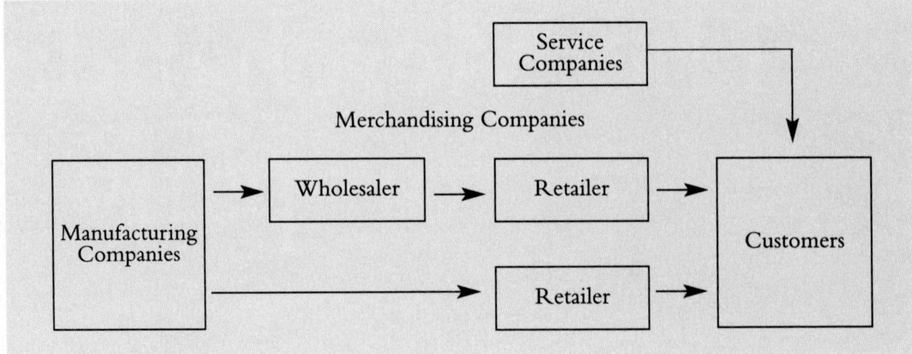

Merchandising Companies

A merchandising company sells a product.

Many businesses sell products, not services, and are known as *merchandising companies.* Both wholesalers and retailers are included in this group. Retailers usually buy merchandise from wholesalers or manufacturers and sell it to their customers at a price that covers their costs and provides a net income.

Manufacturing Companies

A manufacturing company makes a product.

A firm that converts raw materials into saleable products is called a *manufacturing company*. Usually, a manufacturer sells products to merchandising companies such as retailers and wholesalers.

Warrendon Sports: A Merchandising Company

Goods bought for resale are called merchandise.

The accounting procedures of a merchandising company are a little different from those of a service company. The difference can be illustrated by examining Warrendon Sports, a retail store located in Ottawa.

The Merchandise Inventory account represents the total dollar value of goods on hand for sale.

Warrendon Sports buys bicycles, hockey equipment, baseball equipment, and hundreds of other sporting goods from manufacturers such as Spalding, CCM, Winwell, Slazenger, and a variety of wholesalers. The goods bought from these manufacturers and sold to Warrendon's customers are called *merchandise.* The total dollar value of goods on hand for resale is found in an account called *Merchandise Inventory.*

DETERMINING THE NET INCOME FOR A MERCHANDISING COMPANY

In Chapter 3, you learned that expenses are the cost of goods or services used in the operation of a business. To calculate the net income for a service business, expenses are subtracted from the revenue. This calculation is illustrated by the equation:

Revenue – Expenses = Net Income

A merchandising company must buy and pay for the merchandise it sells as well as pay the expenses of operating the business. The following two equations illustrate how net income is calculated for a merchandising company:

Revenue	–	Cost of Goods Sold	=	Gross Profit
Gross Profit	–	Expenses	=	Net Income

Net income occurs when revenue from sales exceeds both the cost of goods sold and the operating expenses.

The preparation of the income statement for a merchandising enterprise is a little more complicated than for a service business. Figure 7-2, below, shows an income statement for a merchandising company. Notice that there are three sections in the body of the statement — revenue, cost of goods sold, and operating expenses. Can you locate the following equations on the income statement, Figure 7-2?

Revenue	–	Cost of Goods Sold	=	Gross Profit
$64 000		$34 000		$30 000
Gross Profit	–	Expenses	=	Net Income
$30 000		$13 600		$16 400

One of the major expenses for a merchandising company is the cost of the goods that it buys for resale. Since the cost of goods sold is a major expense, it receives special attention on the income statement or in a separate schedule.

Warrendon Sports Income Statement For the Month Ended May 31, 2001		
Revenue		
Sales		$64 000
Cost of Goods Sold		
Cost of Goods Sold (per schedule)		34 000
Gross Profit		30 000
Operating Expenses		
Advertising Expense	$2 400	
Delivery Expense	700	
Office Expense	400	
Miscellaneous Expense	500	
Rent Expense	2 600	
Salaries Expense	5 400	
Utilities Expense	1 600	
Total Expenses		13 600
Net Income		$16 400

FIGURE 7-2
Income statement for Warrendon Sports

SCHEDULE OF COST OF GOODS SOLD

A schedule is a supporting statement providing details of an item on a main statement.

A *schedule* is a supporting statement providing details of an item or items on a main statement.

In the income statement format used by Warrendon Sports, a single total, $34 000, appears in the cost of goods sold section. This total includes all the costs involved in purchasing the merchandise to be sold. It is arrived at by the completion of the *schedule of cost of goods sold* as illustrated in Figure 7-3. The use of this schedule simplifies the presentation of the income statement.

FIGURE 7–3
Schedule of cost of goods sold for Warrendon Sports

Warrendon Sports Schedule of Cost of Goods Sold For the Month Ended May 31, 2001		
Merchandise Inventory, May 1	$ 16 000	
Add: Purchases	36 000	
Total Cost of Merchandise	52 000	
Less: Merchandise Inventory, May 31	18 000	
Cost of Goods Sold		$34 000

Preparing a Schedule of Cost of Goods Sold

The steps followed in preparing a schedule of cost of goods sold can be illustrated as follows:

Beginning Merchandise Inventory	+	Purchases of Merchandise	=	Cost of Merchandise Available for Sale	–	Ending Merchandise Inventory	=	Cost of Goods Sold

However, there are several other items that affect the cost of goods sold. These include:

- Purchases returns and allowances
- Purchases discounts
- Transportation-in

How do each of these items affect the total cost of merchandise? Figure 7-4, the expanded schedule of cost of goods sold, contains each of these additional items.

Purchases Returns and Allowances

If goods that have been purchased and recorded in the Purchases account are *returned*, the cost of purchases decreases. The *Purchases Returns and Allowances account* is used to record such returns. On the schedule of cost of goods sold (Figure 7-4), the amount shown for the Purchases Returns and Allowances account is a subtraction.

Purchases Discounts

When a cash discount off the invoice price is received, the discount is recorded in the *Purchases Discounts account.* The cost of the merchandise decreases because of the discount received. Therefore, on the schedule, Figure 7-4, the amount shown for the Purchases Discounts account is subtracted from the Purchases account.

FIGURE 7-4
Expanded schedule of cost of goods sold including net purchases calculation and transportation cost

Warrendon Sports Schedule of Cost of Goods Sold For the Month Ended June 30, 2001				
Merchandise Inventory, June 1			$ 18 000	
Add: Purchases		$42 400		
Less: Purchases Returns				
and Allowances	$8 000			
Purchases Discounts	400	8 400		
Net Purchase Cost		34 000		
Add: Transportation-in		2 000		
Total Cost of Merchandise Purchased			36 000	
Cost of Merchandise Available for Sale			54 000	
Less: Merchandise Inventory, June 30			22 000	
Cost of Goods Sold				$32 000

Net Purchase Cost

The Purchases account figure less the Purchases Returns and Allowances account figure and the Purchases Discounts account figure equals net purchase cost. The calculation is shown below:

Calculation of Net Purchases		
Purchases		$42 400
Less: Purchases Returns and Allowances	$8 000	
Purchases Discounts	400	8 400
Net Purchase Cost		$34 000

Transportation on Purchases

The cost of merchandise purchased for resale is increased by the cost of transporting the merchandise to the retailer's place of business. *Transportation-in, Transportation on Purchases,* or *Freight-in* is the account used to record this cost. Figure 7-4 shows how the transportation cost is added to the net purchases total. The $2 000 transportation cost is added to $34 000 (net purchase cost) to arrive at a total of $36 000, called *total cost of merchandise purchased.*

MERCHANDISE INVENTORY

The *Merchandise Inventory account* contains the total dollar value of goods on hand for resale (merchandise). The schedule of cost of goods sold contains the inventory value at the beginning of the accounting period (beginning inventory) and at the end of the accounting period (ending inventory). The dollar value of inventory may be determined in two ways: *the perpetual inventory method* and *the periodic inventory method.*

Perpetual Inventory Method

The perpetual inventory method is a continuous record of all merchandise on hand

A *perpetual inventory system* is commonly used by retailers who need to know exactly how much of each item of merchandise is on hand. Under this system, records are kept for each individual item the company sells. The record, often called a *stock card,* is updated each time the item is purchased or sold. The company normally sells a low number of "high priced" items such as cars or appliances.

However, the system is also used by retailers who have computerized point-of-sale terminals. When a customer at a store takes an item to a computerized cash register, the clerk uses a scanner to record the sale on the cash register tape. At the same time, the computer deducts the item purchased from the stock or inventory so that a continuously updated record of items of merchandise is available. The accounting system used for the perpetual inventory method is fully explained later in this unit.

Periodic Inventory Method

The *periodic inventory method* is used by retailers who do not feel it necessary to keep a continuously updated record of items of merchandise. We will discuss in detail the accounting procedures and entries required for this method throughout this text unless the perpetual method is specifically identified.

If a business sells a large quantity of relatively low-priced merchandise, such as candy or potato chips in a variety store, it is not practical to record the number of each item bought and sold during the accounting period. These retailers usually determine the amount of each item on hand and the cost of the merchandise only at the end of the period when the cost is needed in order to prepare financial statements.

A physical inventory is a count of all goods on hand.

Businesses using the periodic inventory system determine the value of the ending inventory by taking a physical inventory. A *physical inventory* simply means counting all the various types of merchandise on hand. The value of this inventory is then determined by multiplying the quantity of each item by its cost price and adding the cost of all the various units together.

The total value of the merchandise on hand is recorded in the Merchandise Inventory account. The value of the inventory is used on both the schedule of cost of goods sold (Figure 7-4) and the balance sheet (Figure 7-5).

The Merchandise Inventory account balance appears in the current assets section of the balance sheet as shown in Figure 7-5:

FIGURE 7-5
The Merchandise Inventory account balance is shown in the current assets section of the balance sheet.

Warrendon Sports Partial Balance Sheet June 30, 2001		
Assets		
Current Assets		
Cash	$ 8 000	
Accounts Receivable	54 000	
Merchandise Inventory (at cost)	20 000	
Office Supplies	2 000	
Total Current Assets		$84 000

CHART OF ACCOUNTS FOR A MERCHANDISING BUSINESS

As you have learned, the income statement for a merchandising company contains a new expense section — the cost of goods sold section. For each item in this section, there is an account in the General Ledger. Figure 7-6 lists the accounts usually found in the General Ledger of a merchandising company.

FIGURE 7-6
Chart of accounts for a merchandising company

Merchandising Company Chart of Accounts		
SECTION	**NO.**	**TITLE**
(1) Assets	101	Cash
	110	Accounts Receivable
	120	Merchandise Inventory
	125	Office Supplies
	126	Store Supplies
	150	Building
	151	Equipment
	160	Land
(2) Liabilities	200	Accounts Payable
	205	PST Payable
	206	GST Payable
	207	GST Refundable
	210	Bank Loan
	250	Mortgage Payable
(3) Owner's Equity	300	Owner, Capital
	301	Owner, Drawings
	302	Income Summary
(4) Revenue	400	Sales
	401	Sales Returns and Allowances
	402	Sales Discounts
(5) Cost of Goods Sold	500	Purchases
	501	Purchases Returns and Allowances
	502	Purchases Discounts
	503	Transportation-in
	550	Cost of Goods Sold
(6) Expenses	600	Advertising Expense
	601	Delivery Expense
	602	Miscellaneous Expense
	603	Office Expense
	604	Salaries Expense
	605	Utilities Expense

Notice that there are six sections in the General Ledger of a merchandising company: assets, liabilities, owner's equity, revenue, cost of goods sold, and expenses. The General Ledger of a service business has only five sections. It does not have a cost of goods sold section. Most, but not all, of the new merchandising accounts are found in the new section — the cost of goods sold. The new merchandising accounts are shown in Figure 7-6 and include:

NEW MERCHANDISING ACCOUNTS

120	Merchandise Inventory	500	Purchases
205	PST Payable	501	Purchases Returns and Allowances
206	GST Payable	502	Purchases Discounts
207	GST Refundable	503	Transportation-in
400	Sales	550	Cost of Goods Sold
401	Sales Returns and Allowances	601	Delivery Expense
402	Sales Discounts		

DEBIT AND CREDIT RULES FOR MERCHANDISING ACCOUNTS

In this chapter, you will learn additional debit and credit rules for the accounts of a merchandising company. The rules are based on the equation:

Assets = Liabilities + Owner's Equity

You will remember that income statement accounts are related to the owner's equity account. The two basic principles determine the debit and credit rules for the new accounts:

- Revenue increases owner's equity.
- Expenses decrease owner's equity.

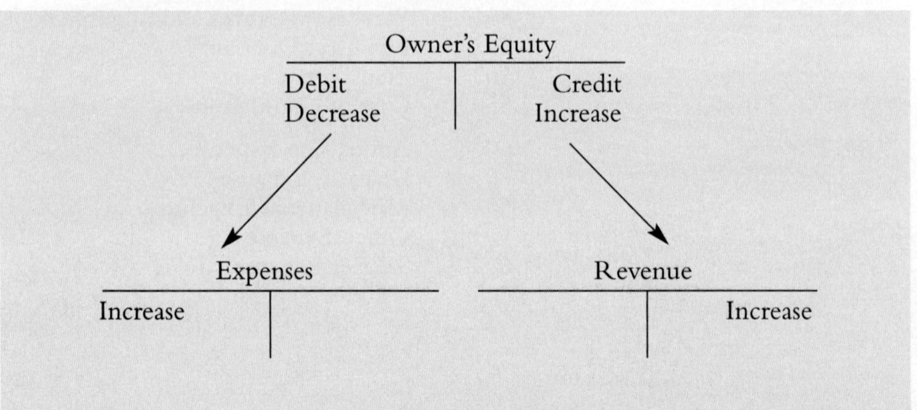

- Expenses decrease owner's equity and are recorded as debits. Expense accounts increase on the debit side and decrease on the credit side.
- Revenue increases owner's equity and is recorded as a credit. Revenue accounts increase on the credit side and decrease on the debit side.

INCOME STATEMENT ACCOUNTS

The income statement in Figure 7-2 demonstrates the three sections of the statement for a merchandising enterprise and the calculations necessary to determine net income. This section of the unit will discuss the new accounts necessary to record the sale and purchase of merchandise for a merchandising company.

Revenue Section of the Income Statement

In order for a business to record a net income (have a net profit), the revenue from sales must exceed the cost of goods sold and the operating expenses (rent, advertising, light, heat, salaries, etc.). Figure 7-7 is the revenue section for Warrendon Sports for June:

Warrendon Sports Partial Income Statement For the Month Ended June 30, 2001		
Revenue		
Sales		$62 000
Less: Sales Returns and Allowances	$1 500	
Sales Discounts	500	2 000
Net Sales		$60 000

FIGURE 7-7
Revenue section of the income statement

RECORDING REVENUE ACCOUNT TRANSACTIONS

Sample transactions involving Warrendon Sports' revenue accounts follow.

Sales

Sales means the amount of cash sales and credit sales made by the business during the accounting period. When merchandise is sold to a customer, it is recorded in the Sales account.

Transaction 1: Cash Sale

Jun. 1 Cash register total for the day, $4 250.

Cash sales are entered into the cash register or computerized point-of-sale terminal at the time of the sale. At the end of the day, a total is obtained and is recorded by journal entry:

Jun. 1	Cash	4 250	
	Sales		4 250
	To record cash sales for Jun. 1.		

Transaction 2: Credit Sale

Jun. 2 G. Giles purchased a pair of skates and three hockey sticks, $150 on account.

This transaction is recorded as follows:

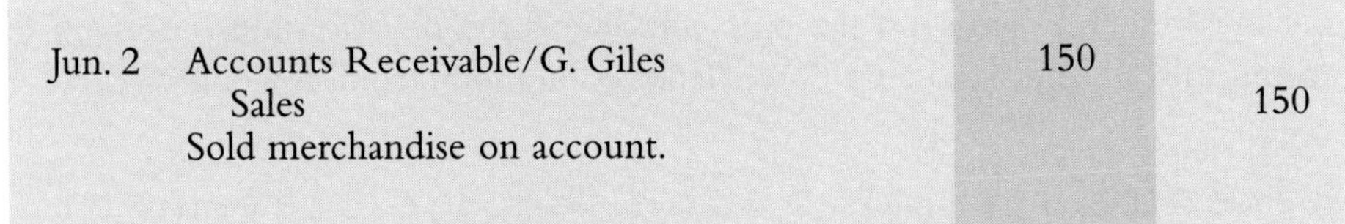

Jun. 2	Accounts Receivable/G. Giles	150	
	Sales		150
	Sold merchandise on account.		

The first two transactions are shown in the T-accounts below:

Cash				Accounts Receivable/G. Giles				Sales			
Jun. 1	4 250			Jun. 2	150					Jun. 1	4 250
										2	150

Sales Returns and Allowances

There is always the chance that the buyer of merchandise may not be satisfied with the goods received. The goods may be the wrong size or colour; they may be defective; or they may be unsatisfactory for other reasons. Either the goods are returned to the seller for a full refund, or the seller gives the customer an allowance on the selling price. Normally, a customer is given a cash refund if the merchandise was paid for, and a credit to his or her account if the merchandise was purchased on account and the bill is unpaid.

The Sales Returns and Allowances account is used by the seller to record merchandise returned by a customer.

The account *Sales Returns and Allowances* is used to record a return of merchandise by the customer. Since this, in effect, cancels all or a portion of a previous sale, this transaction reduces sales revenue. The Sales Returns and Allowances account is often called a *contra revenue account* because its debit balance is the *opposite* of the credit balance of the revenue account, Sales. The Sales account could be debited to record these transactions, but most retailers use a Sales Returns and Allowances account in order to have separate information in this important area. It is important since an increase in sales returns and allowances results in a decrease in the revenue for the period. Continued increases in returns may indicate a number of problems such as poor handling of merchandise, shipping problems, or problems with the quality of the merchandise.

Transaction 3: Sales Return on a Credit Sale

Jun. 3 G. Giles returned one defective hockey stick, priced at $15, from merchandise purchased on Jun. 2.

This transaction represents a sales return from a credit customer. Therefore, the customer's account balance must be reduced (credit) and the amount recorded as a sales return and allowance. The Sales Returns and Allowances account is debited to record a reduction in revenue (contra revenue) as a

Jun. 3	Sales Returns and Allowances	15	
	Accounts Receivable/G. Giles		15
	Goods returned by G. Giles.		

This transaction is shown in the following T-accounts:

Sales Returns and Allowances				Accounts Receivable/G. Giles			
Jun. 3	15			Jun. 2	150	Jun. 3	15

Transaction 4: Sales Return on a Cash Sale

Jun. 4 Customer returned merchandise worth $25 with the cash sales slip for a refund. The goods were bought for cash on Jun. 1.

Since the customer originally paid for the merchandise, a cash refund is given. The journal entry would be as follows:

Jun. 4	Sales Returns and Allowances	25	
	Cash		25
	Goods returned for cash refund.		

This transaction is shown in the T-accounts below:

Sales Returns and Allowances				Cash			
Jun. 3	15			Jun. 1	4 250	Jun. 4	25
4	25						

A sales return represents a decrease in revenue and is recorded as a debit. Since revenue accounts like Sales increase on the credit side, they decrease on the debit side. The amount of the Sales Returns and Allowances account is subtracted from the Sales account figure in the revenue section on the income statement (see Figure 7-7).

Credit Invoices

All business transactions must be supported by an original source document. The source document that is completed when goods are returned is the *credit invoice* as shown in Figure 7-8. The credit invoice is prepared by the seller, in this case Warrendon Sports, and sent to the customer, G. Giles. A copy is kept by the seller and used as the basis for the entry reducing the customer's account and for recording the sales return in the Sales Returns and Allowances account. A credit invoice provides the details about a reduction in a customer's account, the amount, the reason, and the original invoice number.

A credit invoice is a source document issued by the seller to indicate the amount of credit allowed to a customer for returned or defective goods.

The credit invoice and its copy are used by both the seller and the buyer to prepare an entry to record the return. The seller records a sales return, and the buyer records a purchases return. Other terms used for credit invoice are *credit memorandum* and *credit note.*

FIGURE 7–8
Credit invoice recording goods returned by G. Giles

WARRENDON SPORTS
2579 Base Line Road
Ottawa, ON K2H 7B3
Tel: 684-1287 Fax: 684-5381

CREDIT INVOICE

Sold To
G. Giles
32 Cleary Ave.
Ottawa, ON K2A 4A1

No. 149
Date June 3, 2001

Quantity	Description	Unit Price	Amount
1	Re: Our Invoice 896-defective hockey stick	$15	$15
	CREDIT		

Sales Discounts

Cash discounts are offered to encourage early payment of customer account balances.

The second item that results in a reduction in sales is a cash discount given to customers for prompt payment. A discount given to a customer for early payment is called a *sales discount.* Such discounts are indicated in the *terms of sale* agreed upon between the seller and the customer.

Terms of Sale

The invoice sent by the supplier to the buyer contains the agreed-upon terms for payment of the items purchased. If payment is to be made immediately, the terms are *cash* or *cash on receipt of invoice.* If the buyer is allowed a period of time for payment, the terms are said to be *on account,* or *on credit,* and the sale is called a credit sale. Some firms offer the same terms to all customers. Other firms offer a variety of terms to customers. Here is a list of some commonly used terms of sale:

- **C.O.D.:** Payment must be made when the goods are delivered (cash on delivery).
- **Receipt of invoice:** Payment is to be made when the invoice is received.
- **Net 30:** The full amount of the invoice is due 30 days from the invoice date.
- **EOM:** Payment is due at the end of the month.
- **10th following:** Payment is due on the tenth day of the following month.
- **2/10, n/30:** The buyer may deduct a 2 percent discount from the invoice amount if payment is made within 10 days from the date of the invoice. The full amount (net) is due in 30 days if the buyer does not pay within 10 days.
- **1/10, n/30 EOM:** A 1-percent discount may be taken if payment is made within 10 days. The full amount must be paid within 30 days after the end of the month.

It is common practice for firms to negotiate the terms of sale with their customers. Favourable terms, for example 60 days, may be offered to a valued customer. Less favourable terms may be offered to customers who buy small amounts of goods or services or who have a very poor record of paying amounts owed. You have just learned that sellers offer discounts to customers to encourage early payment of account balances. Transactions 5 and 6 are examples of a sale to a customer involving a discount for early payment of the invoice.

Transaction 5: Credit Sale Offering Sales Discount

Jun. 5 Sold merchandise to W.P. Mulvihill, Invoice 907, terms 3/10, n/30, $620 on account.

To encourage early payment, terms of 3/10, n/30 were offered to Mulvihill. On Jun. 5, Warrendon's accounts appeared as follows, in T-account form:

Accounts Receivable/ W.P. Mulvihill			Sales		
Jun. 5	620			Jun. 5	620

Transaction 6: Recording the Sales Discount

Jun. 15 Received cheque for $601.40 from W.P. Mulvihill in payment of Invoice 907.

Mulvihill decided that it was worth paying within 10 days because it meant a saving of $18.60 ($0.03 \times 620 = 18.60$). Therefore, on Jun. 15, exactly 10 days from the date of the invoice (Jun. 5), payment of $601.40 was made to Warrendon. Warrendon received the cheque, and it was recorded in their accounts as follows, in T-account form:

Cash			Sales Discounts			Acc. Rec./W.P. Mulvihill		
Jun. 15	601.40		Jun. 15	18.60		Jun. 5	620.00	Jun. 15 620.00

Note that the Sales Discounts account is debited. The debit represents a decrease in revenue; therefore, Sales Discounts is a contra revenue account like Sales Returns and Allowances. The company has lost or given away $18.60 in order to encourage early payment. Note also that Mulvihill's account is credited for the full amount owing, $620, even though only $601.40 was received from Mulvihill. The $601.40 cancels the full amount owing of $620.

Sales discounts decrease owner's equity and are recorded as debits.

In General Journal form these entries would appear as follows:

Date	Account	Debit	Credit
Jun. 5	Accounts Receivable/W.P. Mulvihill	620.00	
	Sales		620.00
	Invoice 907, terms 3/10, n/30.		
15	Cash	601.40	
	Sales Discounts	18.60	
	Accounts Receivable/W.P. Mulvihill		620.00
	Cash received for Invoice 907.		

After these two entries are posted, there is a zero balance in the Mulvihill Accounts Receivable account.

Sales discounts reduce the total revenue that will be received from sales. Since a reduction in revenue decreases Capital, discounts given to customers are recorded as debits in the Sales Discounts account. The amount of the Sales Discounts account is subtracted from the Sales account figure on the income statement, as shown in Figure 7-9.

FIGURE 7–9

The total of sales discounts and sales returns and allowances is subtracted from sales.

Warrendon Sports Partial Income Statement For the Month Ended June 30, 2001		
Revenue		
Sales		$62 000
Less: Sales Returns and Allowances	$1 500	
Sales Discounts	500	2 000
Net Sales		$60 000

For the month of June, Warrendon's total sales were $62 000. However, since some customers returned merchandise (sales returns of $1 500), the amount of sales for the month must be decreased by $1 500. Also, since sales discounts of $500 were given to customers for early payment, sales must be decreased by $500.

On the income statement, Figure 7-9, the total of sales returns and allowances and sales discounts, $2 000 ($1 500 + $500), is subtracted from sales in the revenue section. The result, $60 000, is called *net sales.*

Relationship Between Sales Discounts and Sales Returns

When merchandise is returned to a supplier as unsuitable, a credit invoice (also called a credit memorandum) is issued to the customer. The discount period for that original sales invoice is calculated from the date of the credit invoice. Following is an example illustrating this type of situation.

On June 5, Warrendon Sports sold $500 worth of sports equipment to the Parks and Recreation Commission with terms of 2/10, n/30. When the goods were received by Parks and Recreation, it was discovered that part of the order was different merchandise than ordered and was returned. A credit invoice for $100 was issued by Warrendon on June 10. Can you determine by which date the original invoice must be paid to take advantage of the discount?

The discount period begins from the date of the credit invoice, which is June 10. If the invoice is paid 10 days from June 10, the discount may be taken by the customer.

Disallowance of Sales Discounts

If a payment is received from a customer after the discount period, but with the discount subtracted, it is necessary to inform the customer that the discount is disallowed. The amount of the discount is still owed by the customer and remains as a balance on the customer's account.

RECORDING COST OF GOODS SOLD ACCOUNT TRANSACTIONS

In the next part of this unit, the rules of debit and credit for the cost of goods sold accounts will be described. Some sample transactions for Warrendon Sports follow.

Purchases

The *Purchases account* is used to record the cost of merchandise bought for resale. The cost of goods purchased is one of the major costs of operating a merchandising business. Because costs (like expenses) decrease the net income and ultimately decrease owner's equity, the Purchases account is debited when merchandise for resale is purchased.

The cost of merchandise purchased for resale is recorded in the Purchases account.

Transaction 7: Cash Purchase of Merchandise

Jun. 8 Purchased sports equipment from CCM, $500 cash.

For this transaction, Warrendon Sports issues a cheque in payment. The two accounts involved are Cash and Purchases. Cash, an asset, decreases and is credited. Purchases, a cost account, is debited because it reduces owner's equity. In General Journal format, the entry is:

Jun. 8	Purchases	500	
	Cash		500
	Purchased sports equipment for cash from CCM.		

This transaction is shown in the T-accounts below:

Purchases				Cash			
Jun. 8	500					Jun. 8	500

Transaction 8: Credit Purchase of Merchandise

Jun. 9 Purchased tennis equipment from Spalding Ltd., net 30, $200 on account.

The two accounts involved are Purchases and Accounts Payable/Spalding Ltd. Spalding Ltd. is a liability account; it increases and is credited. Purchases is a cost account and it is debited because it reduces owner's equity. Following is the journal entry to record the transaction:

Jun. 9	Purchases	200	
	Accounts Payable/Spalding Ltd.		200
	Purchased tennis equipment, terms of payment net 30 days.		

This transaction is shown in the T-accounts below:

Purchases				Accounts Payable/Spalding Ltd.			
Jun. 8	500					Jun. 9	200
9	200						

Recognition of Costs

As indicated earlier in this text, costs and expenses are recorded when incurred, not when paid. Therefore, both cash and credit purchases are recorded in the Purchases account in order to obtain the correct balance for purchases for the accounting period.

Purchases Returns and Allowances

The Purchases Returns and Allowances account is used by the buyer to record the return of goods.

If the merchandise purchased from suppliers is unsuitable for resale, it is returned. The accounting entries and procedures for purchases returns are similar to sales returns. When the purchaser returns merchandise, a cash refund is given for items previously paid for, and a credit is given for unpaid invoice items. A *Purchases Returns and Allowances account,* often called a *contra cost account* because it reduces the cost of a purchase, is used to record the returns on the books of the purchaser.

Transaction 9: Goods Returned for Cash Refund

Jun. 10 Returned to the supplier merchandise worth $100, purchased for cash on Jun. 8 from CCM. Received refund cheque for $100 from CCM.

To record this transaction, Cash, an asset, is increased with a debit of $100. Purchases Returns and Allowances, because it is a contra cost account, is credited $100. This transaction results in an increase in equity, and therefore the Purchases Returns and Allowances account is credited. The journal entry is as follows:

Jun. 10	Cash	100	
	Purchases Returns and Allowances		100
	To record cash refund received from CCM.		

T-accounts for this transaction are shown below:

Cash		Purchases Returns and Allowances	
Jun. 10 100			Jun. 10 100

Transaction 10: Goods Returned for Credit

Jun. 11 Returned to Spalding Ltd. defective tennis equipment purchased for $200, on account, on Jun. 9. Received Credit Invoice 981 for $200 from Spalding Ltd.

The Accounts Payable account Spalding Ltd. decreases and is debited. The Purchases Returns and Allowances account is credited because it decreases Purchases. Following are the journal entry and the T-accounts:

Jun. 11	Accounts Payable/Spalding Ltd.	200	
	Purchases Returns and Allowances		200
	To record Credit Invoice 981 for the return of defective merchandise.		

Accounts Payable/ Spalding Ltd.			
Jun. 11	200	Jun. 9	200

Purchases Returns and Allowances			
		Jun. 10	100
		11	200

Credit Invoice

The source document that is completed when goods are returned is the credit invoice. The credit invoice is prepared by the seller and sent to the customer. The seller keeps a copy and uses it to enter the amount by which the customer's account is reduced. As well, the seller uses the credit invoice to record the return of merchandise in the Sales Returns and Allowances account. The purchaser, on the other hand, uses the credit invoice to record the purchase return in its books.

Purchases Discounts

Just as Warrendon offers discounts to its customers for early payment of bills, it receives discounts for the same reason from its creditors. When Warrendon receives such a discount, it is called a *purchases discount*. The next two transactions illustrate how purchases discounts are recorded.

Transaction 11: Credit Purchase with Purchases Discount Available

Jun. 12 Received Purchase Invoice 4918 for $500 from Spalding Ltd., terms 2/15, n/30.

Warrendon checked the invoice for accuracy and, since the merchandise was received in good condition, the invoice was approved for payment. Warrendon's accounts recording the invoice appeared as follows, in T-account form:

Purchases			
Jun. 12	500		

Accounts Payable/ Spalding Ltd.			
		Jun. 12	500

Transaction 12: Recording the Purchases Discount

Jun. 27 Sent cheque for $490 to Spalding Ltd. in payment of Invoice 4918.

When Invoice 4918 was received, it was placed in a date file in a folder dated June 27. Then, on June 27, when the cheque for $490 was prepared and sent to Spalding Ltd., it was recorded in Warrendon's accounts as follows, in T-account form:

Accounts Payable/ Spalding Ltd.			
Jun. 27	500	Jun. 12	500

Cash			
		Jun. 27	490

Purchases Discounts			
		Jun. 27	10

In General Journal form, these two entries would be made as follows:

Jun. 12	Purchases	500	
	Accounts Payable/Spalding Ltd.		500
	Invoice 4918, terms 2/15, n/30.		
27	Accounts Payable/Spalding Ltd.	500	
	Cash		490
	Purchases Discounts		10
	Paid Invoice 4918, less 2 percent discount.		

Purchases discounts increase owner's equity and are recorded as credits.

Purchases discounts reduce the total cost of goods purchased and are recorded as credits in the Purchases Discounts account. The Purchases Discounts account, like the Purchases Returns and Allowances account, is often called a contra cost account because it reduces the cost of a purchase.

The account Purchases Discounts appears in the schedule of cost of goods sold, where it is subtracted from the cost of purchases. This is illustrated in the schedule of cost of goods sold in Figure 7-10.

Transportation on Purchases

The Transportation-in account records the transportation charges on merchandise purchased.

The cost of merchandise purchased for resale is increased by the cost of transporting the merchandise to the retailer's place of business. *Transportation-in* or *Transportation on Purchases* is the account used to record this cost. Figure 7-10 shows how transportation adds to the final cost of goods purchased during the accounting period.

FIGURE 7-10

Expanded schedule of cost of goods sold including net purchases calculation and transportation cost

Warrendon Sports
Schedule of Cost of Goods Sold
For the Month Ended June 30, 2001

Merchandise Inventory, June 1			$18 000	
Add: Purchases		$42 400		
Less: Purchases Returns and Allowances	$8 000			
Purchases Discounts	400	8 400		
Net Purchase Cost		34 000		
Add: Transportation-in		2 000		
Total Cost of Merchandise Purchased			36 000	
Cost of Merchandise Available for Sale			54 000	
Less: Merchandise Inventory, June 30			22 000	
Cost of Goods Sold				$32 000

Transaction 13: Transportation-in

Jun. 14 Received $55 invoice from CN Express, net 30, for transportation of merchandise purchased.

The invoice received from CN Express is to cover the cost of transporting merchandise from a manufacturer to Warrendon's store. Since this transaction adds to the costs of operating the business, owner's equity is reduced and therefore the Transportation-in account is debited. The liability account Accounts Payable/CN Express increases and is credited. The company has incurred more costs and has another debt. The transaction is shown on the following page in General Journal and T-account form:

Jun. 14	Transportation-in	55	
	Accounts Payable/CN Express		55
	Invoice from CN for the transportation of merchandise purchased.		

Transportation-in		Accounts Payable/CN Express	
Jun. 14 55			Jun. 14 55

Delivery Expense

The cost of delivering merchandise to customers is recorded in the Delivery Expense account. This account appears in the expenses section of the income statement as shown in Figure 7-11, on page 202.

Transaction 14: Delivery Expense

Jun. 18 Paid $75 to a local cartage firm for delivering merchandise sold to customers.

The expense of delivering goods to customers is recorded in the Delivery Expense account. Delivery Expense reduces owner's equity and is debited. The asset Cash decreases and is credited. This transaction is shown below in General Journal and T-account form:

Jun. 18	Delivery Expense	75	
	Cash		75
	Cash payment for the delivery of goods to customers.		

Delivery Expense		Cash	
Jun. 18 75			Jun. 18 75

The 14 sample transactions described in this unit involved the new accounts used by merchandising. Look at Figure 7-10, the schedule of cost of goods sold, and Figure 7-11, the income statement. Can you locate the new accounts? What effect do they have on the statements?

DEBIT AND CREDIT SUMMARY

Several new income statement accounts have been introduced in this chapter. Figure 7-12, on page 202, summarizes the recording of debits and credits in these new accounts.

Transactions involving five of the new accounts normally cause a decrease in owner's equity. These accounts are Delivery Expense, Purchases, Transportation-in, Sales Returns and Allowances, and Sales Discounts. These five accounts usually have a debit balance.

In previous chapters, you learned that transactions involving the Sales account increase the owner's equity and are recorded as credits. Transactions for two other accounts — Purchases Returns and Allowances and Purchases Discounts — also increase the owner's equity and are recorded as credits.

FIGURE 7-11
Income statement for a merchandising company

Warrendon Sports Income Statement For the Month Ended June 30, 2001			
Revenue			
Sales		$62 000	
Less: Sales Returns and Allowances	$1 500		
Sales Discounts	500	2 000	
Net Sales			$60 000
Cost of Goods Sold			
Cost of Goods Sold (per schedule)			32 000
Gross Profit			28 000
Operating Expenses			
Delivery Expense		2 400	
Office Expense		800	
Miscellaneous Expense		600	
Rent Expense		2 400	
Salaries Expense		2 600	
Utilities Expense		400	
Total Expenses			9 200
Net Income			$18 800

FIGURE 7-12
Summary of debits and credits for the new accounts introduced in this chapter

Owner's Equity

Debit	Credit
These accounts normally decrease owner's equity and have debit balances.	**These accounts normally increase owner's equity and and have credit balances.**
Purchases: X (debit)	Sales: X (credit)
Delivery Expense: X (debit)	Purchases Returns and Allowances: X (credit)
Transportation-in: X (debit)	Purchases Discounts: X (credit)
Sales Returns and Allowances: X (debit)	
Sales Discounts: X (debit)	

1. A business may be classified according to what it does. A company that sells services to customers is called a service business. Name two other types of businesses and describe what they do.
2. Prepare a list of firms in your area. The list should include the names of five companies in each of the three classifications identified in question 1.
3. (a) Which account is debited when merchandise is purchased?
   (b) In which account does the value of the merchandise on hand appear?
4. Name the statement (balance sheet, income statement, or schedule of cost of goods sold) and section of the statement in which each of the following items appears. The first item is done for you as an example.

   Example:

ITEM	STATEMENT	SECTION
(a) Cash	balance sheet	current asset

   (b) Accounts Receivable
   (c) Sales
   (d) Office Supplies
   (e) Purchases
   (f) Sales Returns and Allowances
   (g) Salaries Expense
   (h) Purchases Returns and Allowances
   (i) Delivery Expense
   (j) Transportation-in
   (k) Building
   (l) Beginning Inventory
   (m) Ending Inventory
   (n) Sales Discounts
   (o) Purchases Discounts
5. Indicate whether each of the following increases or decreases the cost of the merchandise:

   (a) Transportation-in
   (b) Purchases returns and allowances
   (c) Purchases discounts
6. Explain the difference between a periodic inventory system and a perpetual inventory system.
7. (a) Which account is debited when a customer returns merchandise bought on credit because the merchandise is unsatisfactory? Which account is credited?
   (b) Which account is debited when a cash refund is given to a customer for returned merchandise? Which account is credited?
8. Does the balance in the Sales Returns and Allowances account increase or decrease revenue?
9. What source document is prepared when goods are returned for credit?
10. (a) Do sales discounts increase or decrease revenue?
    (b) Are sales discounts recorded as debits or credits? Why?

11. We sold merchandise worth $1 000 to R. Heidebrecht. The terms of sale were 3/10, n/30. We received a cheque for $970 from Heidebrecht within 10 days. When recording the $970 cheque, is Heidebrecht's account credited for $1 000 or $970?
12. Why do businesses offer cash discounts when the final effect is a reduction in net revenue?
13. A cash discount is recorded in the books of the buyer and seller. What account would be used to record the discount in the ledger of (a) the buyer, and (b) the seller?
14. What effect does a return have on the discount period offered by a business?
15. What is the difference between the Purchases account and the Office Supplies account?
16. What is the difference between the Purchases account and the Merchandise Inventory account?
17. What account is debited for each of the following items purchased by Johnson's Hardware?

    (a) 1 desk and chair for the office
    (b) 10 ladders
    (c) 1 box of continuous computer paper
    (d) 2 000 bags for the check-out counter
    (e) 150 lengths of rope for clothes lines

18. What is the difference between the Delivery Expense account and the Transportation-in account?
19. Name the increase side (debit or credit) for each of the following accounts and give a reason for your answer:

    (a) Purchases
    (b) Delivery Expense
    (c) Transportation-in
    (d) Purchases Returns and Allowances
    (e) Sales Returns and Allowances
    (f) Purchases Discounts
    (g) Sales
    (h) Sales Discounts

PROBLEMS: APPLICATIONS

1. In January, Pelican Gifts had net sales of $6 900 and cost of goods sold of $3 100.

    (a) What is the gross profit?
    (b) If expenses totalled $2 100, what is the net income or net loss?

2. In February, Pelican Gifts' net sales were $5 600 and the cost of goods sold was $3 400. Expenses totalled $1 840.

    (a) What is the gross profit for the month?
    (b) What is the net income or the net loss for the month?

3. Pelican Gifts' March figures were net sales $2 700, cost of goods sold $1 200, total expenses $1 750.
   (a) What is the gross profit?
   (b) What is the net income or net loss?
4. Complete the following equations by supplying the missing term in each one:
   (a) Net Sales – Cost of Goods Sold = ?
   (b) ? – Sales Returns and Allowances – Sales Discounts = Net Sales
   (c) Net Income + Operating Expenses = ?
   (d) Cost of Goods Sold + Ending Inventory = ?
   (e) Beginning Inventory + ? – Purchases Returns and Allowances – Purchases Discounts + Transportation-in = Cost of Goods Purchased
5. The cost accounts of Conway Variety follow. Prepare a schedule of cost of goods sold for each of the following months.
   (a) Feb. 1: Inventory $2 000; Purchases $4 500; Feb. 28 Inventory $3 000.
   (b) March 1: Inventory $3 500; Purchases $2 900; Purchases Returns and Allowances $300; Purchases Discounts $100; Transportation on Purchases $190; March 31 Inventory $3 100.
6. Conway Variety uses a periodic inventory system.
   (a) How would the March 31 inventory value of $3 100 be determined if this was the end of the fiscal year and financial statements were being prepared?
   (b) How would the April 1 inventory total be determined?
7. Prepare the revenue section of the income statement for Conway Variety on March 31 from the following information:
   - Sales Discounts $210
   - Sales $31 000
   - Sales Returns and Allowances $490
8. (a) The documents on page 206 were issued by Warrendon Sports.
      (i) What kind of source documents are they?
      (ii) Prepare journal entries to record them.
   (b) Record the transactions listed on page 207 in a journal for Warrendon Sports. Use the accounts Cash, Accounts Receivable, Sales, and Sales Returns and Allowances.

WARRENDON SPORTS

2579 Base Line Road
Ottawa, Ontario K2H 7B3

INVOICE Order No.

SOLD TO

Woodroffe High School
2410 Georgina Drive
Ottawa, Ontario K2B 7M8

SHIP TO

Same

Date Jan. 4, 2000 **Invoice No.** 26 **Terms** Net 30 days **Cash** **Charge**

Quantity	Description	Unit Price	Amount
30	Hockey Sticks	$25	$750

WARRENDON SPORTS

2579 Base Line Road
Ottawa, Ontario K2H 7B3

CREDIT INVOICE

SOLD TO

Woodroffe High School
2410 Georgina Drive
Ottawa, Ontario K2B 7M8

No. 18

Date Jan. 10, 2000

Quantity	Description	Unit Price	Amount
5	Re: Our Invoice 26 — hockey sticks received in damaged condition	$25	$125

CREDIT

Mar. 1 Cash register summary:
Cash received from cash sales, $1 350.

2 Sales invoices:
No. 301, Nepean Hockey Association, $1 950;
No. 302, Laurier High School, $850;
No. 303, S. Edgerton, $85.

3 Cash refund slip:
No. 29, for $87, refund for the return of a pair of children's skates.

8 Cash register summary:
Cash received from cash sales, $2 120.

9 Credit invoices:
No. 89, for $250, hockey jackets returned by Nepean Hockey Association — wrong size.

10 Sales invoices:
No. 304, Kanata Tennis Club, $875;
No. 305, H. Burger, $63.

15 Cash receipts:
Cheques received from Nepean Hockey Association ($1 700) and S. Edgerton ($85).

9. (a) On what date is the amount to be paid for each of the following invoices? Discounts are not to be taken. In your notebook, use a third column headed "Payment Date" to record your answers.

Invoice Date	Terms
August 5	EOM
August 6	n/30
August 8	n/60
August 14	15 EOM
August 17	2/10, n/30
August 19	C.O.D.
August 20	Receipt of invoice
August 25	1/10, n/30

(b) Determine the amount of the discount, the last day for obtaining the discount, and the amount to be paid for each of the following. All invoices are paid on the last day of the discount period. Record your answer in columns headed:

- Discount Date
- Amount to Be Paid
- Amount of Discount

Amount of Invoice	Terms	Invoice Date
$120	2/10, n/30	August 1
500	1/15, n/30	August 2
380	3/10, n/60	August 5
250	2/10, n/30	August 12
195	1/10, n/60	August 25

10. (a) Set up the following T-accounts for Parker's Men's Wear:

    101 Cash

    112 Accounts Receivable/C. Baker

    113 Accounts Receivable/A. Jonsson

    114 Accounts Receivable/T. Mathews

    401 Sales

    402 Sales Returns and Allowances

    403 Sales Discounts

    (b) Journalize and post the following source documents. Use page 94 for the General Journal.

    Oct. 10 Sales invoices issued to:
    A. Jonsson, No. 1035 for $3 250, terms 2/10, n/30;
    C. Baker, No. 1036 for $709, terms 2/10, n/30;
    T. Mathews, No. 1037 for $1 750, terms 2/10, n/30.

    14 Credit invoice issued to A. Jonsson, $650 for goods returned. Goods were sold to Jonsson on Oct. 10. It was agreed to change the discount period to date from Oct. 14.

    17 Cheque received from C. Baker, $694.82 for Invoice 1036.

    20 Cheque received from T. Mathews, $1 715 for Invoice 1037.

    24 Cheque received from A. Jonsson, $2 548 for Invoice 1035 less credit invoice $650, and less discount.

    (c) Calculate the net sales for the two-week accounting period.

11. Which of the following transactions should be recorded in the Purchases account for Lepp Hardware?

    (a) Purchase of advertising in the *St. Catharines Standard*
    (b) Purchase of a new salesperson's car from Nemeth Motors
    (c) Purchase of 12 snowblowers from John Deere for a special pre-winter sale
    (d) Purchase of a new liability insurance policy
    (e) Payment of three months' advance rent on the building

12. The following source documents have been received by Warrendon Sports.

    (a) Identify the source documents.
    (b) Prepare a General Journal entry to record each source document.

BROOMBALL MANUFACTURING

331 Marion Street
Oshawa, Ontario L1J 3A8

SOLD TO	SHIPPED TO	WI-60505
Warrendon Sports 2579 Base Line Road Ottawa, Ontario K2H 7B3	Same	PLEASE QUOTE THIS NUMBER WHEN REFERRING TO OR PAYING THIS INVOICE

SHIP VIA	PPD.	COLL.	CUSTOMER'S ORDER NO.	TERMS	SALESPERSON	DATE MO.	DAY	YEAR
Pick-up			1214	Net 30 days	Phone	12	10	2000

NO.	DESCRIPTION	QUANTITY	UNIT	AMOUNT
25	Pairs of Broomball shoes	25	$80	$2 000
			PLEASE PAY THIS AMOUNT	$2 000

WILSON OFFICE SUPPLIERS

6350 Main Street
Ottawa, Ontario K1S 1E7

	SHIP TO	INVOICE NUMBER
Warrendon Sports 2579 Base Line Road Ottawa, Ontario K2H 7B3	Same	T110982

DATE	SHIP VIA	ORDER NUMBER	TERMS
Dec. 22, 2000	--	1215	n/30

QUANTITY ORDERED	QUANTITY SHIPPED	PRODUCT NO.	DESCRIPTION	UNIT PRICE	AMOUNT
1	1		IBM PS/2 Personal Computer	$4 350	$4 350

THIS IS YOUR INVOICE
NO OTHER WILL BE SENT

SPORTING EQUIPMENT

347 Tachereau Blvd.
Montréal, Québec H2C 3B3

SOLD TO Warrendon Sports
2579 Base Line Road
Ottawa, Ontario K2H 7B3

SHIPPED TO Same

INVOICE NUMBER TR89-6153

Cust. Order No.	Our Order No.	Date Received	Date Shipped	Shipped Via	Invoice Date
1190	16150	Dec. 13, 2000	Jan. 4, 2001	Our Truck	Jan. 10, 2001

Terms	F.O.B.	Salesperson
Net 30 days		

Qty.	Description	Price	Total
50	Dolphin Clear Goggles	$15.50	$775.00

PRICES SUBJECT TO CHANGE WITHOUT NOTICE

ORIGINAL INVOICE

OVERLAND TRANSPORT

MONTREAL
OTTAWA
TORONTO

HEAD OFFICE:
1473 Blake Road
Montréal, Québec H3J 1E4

Shipper:

Broomball Manufacturing
331 Marion Street
Oshawa, Ontario L1J 3A8

Consignee:

Warrendon Sports
2579 Base Line Road
Ottawa, Ontario K2H 7B3

TERMS Net 30 days **DATE** Dec. 12, 2000 **INV. NO.** CK 4376

Quantity	Containers	Mass	Rate	Amount
3	Boxes	20 kg	$3.75/kg	$75.00

Pay this amount $75.00

CITY DELIVERY

576 Blythe Rd.
Ottawa, Ontario K2A 3N6

Charge	**Deliver to**
Warrendon Sports 2579 Base Line Road Ottawa, Ontario K2H 7B3	Carleton Broomball League 1476 Braeside Street Ottawa, Ontario K1H 7J4

INV. NO. T-7437 **TERMS** Net 30 days **DATE** Dec. 20, 2000

Description	**Amount**
5 Boxes	$55.65

CREDIT INVOICE

SPORTING EQUIPMENT

347 Tachereau Blvd.
Montréal, Québec H2C 3B3

SOLD TO Warrendon Sports
2579 Base Line Road
Ottawa, Ontario K2H 7B3

January 12, 2001

CREDIT NUMBER 1195

WE CREDIT YOUR ACCOUNT AS SPECIFIED BELOW

Re: Invoice TR89-6153, dated January 10, 2001

6 damaged Dolphin Goggles @ $15.50	$93.00
TOTAL CREDIT DUE	$93.00

13. Journalize the following transactions for Warrendon Sports. Use the accounts Cash, Accounts Payable, Purchases, Purchases Returns and Allowances, Transportation-in, Sales Returns and Allowances, Delivery Expense.

Mar. 1 Purchases invoices:
Cooper Bros., $825.60 for hockey sticks;
CN Express, $112.50 for transportation charges on purchases.

2 Cheque copies:
No. 94, to Dinardo Delivery, $275 for delivery charges on sales to schools;
No. 95, to Merivale High School, $143 for return of unordered sporting goods.

10 Cheque copies:
No. 96, to Spalding Bros., $425 on account;
No. 97, to Tanyss Imports for tennis shoes, $627.50.

15 Purchases invoices:
Hofstra Ltd., $1 873 for skis;
Smith Transport, $92.75 transportation charges on purchases;
Dinardo Delivery, $210.20 for delivery of goods to customers.

16 Credit note:
Cooper Bros., $116 for goods returned to them because they were received in a damaged condition.

14. Following are the March sales figures for Warrendon Sports: Sales $28 300; Sales Returns and Allowances $1 300; Sales Discounts $275.

(a) What is the net sales total for March?
(b) Determine the cost of goods for March for Warrendon Sports from the following:
Beginning Inventory $35 000; March Purchases $17 600; Purchases Returns and Allowances $1 300; Transportation-in $875; Ending Inventory $37 000.
(c) Determine the March gross profit for Warrendon Sports using the answers from parts (a) and (b) of this exercise.

15. (a) Prepare a schedule of cost of goods sold for Warrendon Sports for May from the following figures:
Beginning Inventory $37 900; Purchases $18 800; Purchases Returns and Allowances $800; Purchases Discounts $210; Transportation-in $975; Ending Inventory $35 900.
(b) Prepare an income statement for Warrendon Sports for May using the cost of goods sold from part (a) and the following figures:
Sales $38 750; Sales Returns and Allowances $950; Sales Discounts $180; Salaries $6 800; Rent $1 850; Delivery Expense $900; Other Expenses $2 100.

16. The Children's Boutique had the following transactions occur during March of this year:

Mar.	2	Purchased \$2 500 merchandise from Les Petits Enfants; terms 2/10, n/30.
	3	Sold \$270 merchandise to B. Comeau; terms EOM.
	4	Paid \$375 freight charges on the Mar. 2 purchases.
	4	Sold \$54 merchandise for cash.
	6	Returned \$250 merchandise to Les Petits Enfants; received a credit memo.
	8	Sold \$380 merchandise to M. Tompkins; terms 2/10, n/30.
	9	Sold \$87 merchandise for cash.
	12	Purchased \$115 store supplies for cash.
	12	Paid Les Petits Enfants for the Mar. 2 purchases less the discount and the return.
	14	Purchased \$1 850 merchandise from Gumboots Ltd.; terms 2/10, n/30.
	16	Paid \$295 freight charges on the Mar. 14 purchases.
	18	Received payment from M. Tompkins for the Mar. 8 transaction less the discount.
	19	Sold \$169 merchandise for cash.
	22	Owner invested \$3 500 additional cash in the business.
	24	Sold \$875 merchandise to R. Ouellette; terms 2/10, n/30.
	25	Paid \$92 delivery charges for the merchandise sold on Mar. 24.
	26	Received \$115 merchandise returned by R. Ouellette; issued a credit memo.
	27	Sold \$215 merchandise to S. Butler; terms 2/10, n/30.
	28	Sold \$129 merchandise for cash.
	30	Received payment from B. Comeau for the Mar. 2 transaction.
	31	Owner withdrew \$1 100 for personal living expenses.
	31	Paid employee salaries for the month, \$1 800.

Record the above transactions in the general journal. (Ignore PST and GST for the above journal entries.)

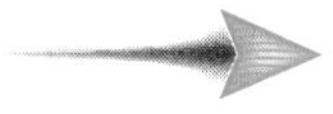

UNIT 15 Sales and Goods and Services Tax

Learning Objectives

After reading this unit, discussing the applicable review questions, and completing the applications exercises, you will be able to do the following:

1. **CALCULATE** Goods and Services Tax on sales.
2. **CALCULATE** sales tax on retail sales.
3. **JOURNALIZE** transactions involving Provincial Sales Tax and federal Goods and Services Tax.

INTRODUCING SALES TAX

In Canada, both federal and most provincial governments impose sales tax. The companies that sell taxable items become, by law, agents for the government for the collection of sales tax. A customer pays sales tax to a company and the company sends the money to the government. Manufacturers, wholesalers, and most retailers are required to register with the federal government to collect the national Goods and Services Tax. Retailers are also required to register with their provincial governments to receive a Provincial Sales Tax licence. In most provinces, retailers collect both Provincial Sales Tax and federal Goods and Services Tax.

The Federal Goods and Services Tax

The federal Goods and Services Tax (GST) is a simple concept that becomes more complex in actual practice. For the purposes of this text, only the basic GST principles and introductory accounting procedures will be discussed.

The Goods and Services Tax is a 7-percent tax charged on most sales of service and merchandise made within Canada. Manufacturers, wholesalers, and retailers of both merchandise and services must add the tax to the selling price of each item sold.

Goods or Services Selling Price	$100.00
7% GST	7.00
Total Cost	$107.00

A number of items such as basic groceries, prescription drugs, health and dental services, day-care services, residential rents, and educational services are exempt or free from GST.

The GST is collected by businesses who are registered with Revenue Canada to collect the tax, and the tax is then forwarded to the federal government. To register for GST or HST (see page 225 for a description of HST), you are required to fill out a Request for Business Number (BN) form, shown in Figure 7-13 on pages 216–217.

How Does the GST Work?

A product can be bought and sold by several businesses before you, the consumer, actually purchase the item. For example, a mountain bike is purchased by a wholesaler from the manufacturer. The wholesaler sells the bike to a retailer who in turn sells the bike to you. Each of these businesses must add the 7-percent GST to the selling price. However, the federal government receives only 7 percent of the *final* sales price. How is that possible? It's possible because the business sends the federal government only the difference between GST collected and GST paid. A business collects the 7-percent GST on the sales price of all goods and services sold. Before remitting or sending the tax collected to the federal government, the business deducts all GST paid to other businesses when purchasing goods and services. This deduction is called an *input tax credit*. The input tax credit ensures that the federal government is not receiving more than 7 percent GST on the final sales price of the goods or service that you purchase. Let's follow the mountain bike through each step and see how the GST system actually works.

Mountain Bike

	SALES PRICE	GST COLLECTED	GST INPUT TAX CREDIT	AMOUNT REMITTED
Materials sold to Manufacturer	$100	$ 7	$ 0	$ 7
Mountain bike sold to Wholesaler	$400	$28	($7)	$21
Mountain bike sold to Retailer	$500	$35	($28)	$ 7
Mountain bike sold to Customer	$700	$49	($35)	$14
Total GST remitted to Federal Government				$49

In the example shown above, the retailer sold the mountain bike for $700 plus $49 Goods and Services Tax. The retailer, however, sent only $14 ($49 GST minus $35 input tax credit) to the federal government. This represented the amount of GST collected from the customer minus the amount paid on the purchase of the bike from the wholesaler. The federal government received in total 7 percent, or $49, in GST from all the businesses who were involved in getting the product to the final consumer. In this chapter we will discuss the basic accounting procedures used by retailers to record the federal Goods and Services Tax as well as Provincial Sales Tax.

FIGURE 7–13
Request for a Business Number (BN)

Revenue Canada Revenu Canada

REQUEST FOR A BUSINESS NUMBER (BN)

BN: FOR OFFICE USE ONLY

Complete this form if you have a new business and you need to apply for a Business Number (BN). If you are a sole proprietor with more than one business, your BN will apply to all your businesses. **All businesses have to complete Parts A and F.** For more information, see the pamphlet called *The Business Number and Your Revenue Canada Accounts.*

- To apply for a GST/HST account, complete Part B.
- To apply for a payroll deductions account, complete Part C.
- To apply for an import/export account, complete Part D.
- To apply for a corporate income tax account, complete Part E.

Part A - General information

A1 Identification of business (For a corporation, enter the name and address of the head office.)

Name

Language ☐ English ☐ French

Operating, trading, or partnership name (if different from name above): If you have more than one business or if your business operates under more than one name, enter the name(s) here. If you need more space, include the information on a separate piece of paper.

Business address — Postal or zip code

Mailing address (if different from business address) — Postal or zip code

Contact person (If you choose to name a contact for your account, see our pamphlet for more information.)

First name	Last name	Language	Title	Telephone number	Fax number
		☐ English ☐ French		( )	( )

Financial institution – Enter the name and address of the branch you use for your business transactions.

A2 Client ownership type

☐ **Individual** If so, are you: ☐ a sole proprietor? ☐ a foster parent? ☐ a domestic employer?

☐ **Partnership**

☐ **Other** Are you incorporated? ☐ Yes ☐ No (All corporations have to provide a copy of the certificate of incorporation or amalgamation.)

Check the box that best describes your type of operation.

☐ Charity ☐ Union ☐ Association ☐ Financial institution ☐ University/school ☐ Municipal government

☐ Society ☐ Hospital ☐ Non-profit ☐ Religious body ☐ Trust ☐ None of the above

Enter the following information for the sole proprietor, domestic employer, or foster parent. Also enter this information for the partner(s), corporate director(s), or officer(s) of your business. If you need more space, include the information on a separate piece of paper.

First name	Last name		Home telephone number ( )	Home fax number ( )
Title		Social insurance number	Work telephone number ( )	Work fax number ( )
First name	Last name		Home telephone number ( )	Home fax number ( )
Title		Social insurance number	Work telephone number ( )	Work fax number ( )

A3 Major commercial activity

Clearly describe your major business activity.

Specify up to three main products that you mine, manufacture, or sell, or services you provide or contract. Also, please estimate the percentage of revenue that each product or service represents.

______ %

______ %

______ %

A4 Requestor information (Complete this area if you are registering for a BN on behalf of a client.)

Your name (please print) — Your company's name (please print) — Year Month Day

RC1 E (98) (Ce formulaire existe en français.) 3417 Canada

A5 GST/HST information

Do you plan to sell or provide goods or services in Canada? Yes ☐ No ☐
If *no*, you **cannot** register for GST/HST.
If you *export*, you may be deemed to be selling or providing goods or services in Canada. See our pamphlet for details.

Will your annual **worldwide** GST/HST taxable sales (including those of any associates) be more than $30,000, or $50,000 if you are a public service body? Yes ☐ No ☐
Are you a non-resident who solicits orders in Canada for prescribed goods to be sent by mail or courier and whose worldwide GST/HST taxable sales will be more than $30,000? Prescribed goods include printed materials such as books, newspapers, periodicals, and magazines. Yes ☐ No ☐

If yes to either of the above questions, you **must** register for GST/HST.

Do you operate a taxi or limousine service? Yes ☐ No ☐
Are you a non-resident who charges admission directly to audiences at activities or events in Canada? Yes ☐ No ☐
If *yes* to either of the above, you **must** register for GST/HST, even if your worldwide GST/HST taxable sales will be $30,000 or less.

Are all the goods or services you sell or provide exempt from GST/HST? Yes ☐ No ☐
If *yes*, you **cannot** register for GST/HST. See our pamphlet for an explanation of exempt goods and services.

Do you wish to register voluntarily? Yes ☐ No ☐
See our pamphlet for more information.

Part B – GST/HST account information

Complete sections B1 to B5 if you need a BN GST/HST account.

Do you want us to send you GST/HST information? ☐ Yes ☐ No

B1 GST/HST account identification (Check box ☐ if same as in Part A1 on page 1.)

Mailing address for GST/HST purposes

c/o

Account name (enter name to which we should address correspondence.)

Address

Postal or zip code

Contact person (If you choose to name a contact for your account, see our pamphlet for more information.)

First name

Last name

Language ☐ English ☐ French

Title

Telephone number ( )

Fax number ( )

B2 Filing information

Enter the fiscal year-end of your business. Month Day

Estimate your annual GST/HST taxable sales in Canada (including those of any associates in Canada).

☐ $30,000 or less
☐ more than $30,000 to $200,000
☐ more than $200,000 to $500,000
☐ more than $500,000 to $1,000,000
☐ more than $1,000,000 to $6,000,000
☐ more than $6,000,000

Enter the effective date of registration for GST/HST purposes. Year Month Day

B3 Election respecting your reporting period

If your estimated total annual GST/HST taxable sales and revenues are $500,000 or less, you will be assigned **an annual reporting period.** If your estimated total annual GST/HST sales and revenues are more than $500,000 to $6,000,000, you will be assigned **a quarterly reporting period.** If you have more than $6,000,000 in taxable sales and revenues, you **must** file monthly. If you wish to file more frequently than your assigned period, please check one of the following boxes: ☐ Quarterly ☐ Monthly
You cannot elect to file less frequently than your assigned reporting period.

B4 Type of operation

01 ☐ Government, municipality
02 ☐ Registered charity (provide your registration no.)
03 ☐ Qualifying non-profit organization
04 ☐ Listed financial institution
05 ☐ University, school board, hospital
06 ☐ Joint venture operator (not a partnership)
07 ☐ Non-resident who charges admission directly to spectators or attendees
08 ☐ Non-resident who carries on commercial activities in Canada
09 ☐ Taxi or limousine operator
99 ☐ None of the above

B5 Province or territory (Check the boxes below to indicate the provinces or territories in which you carry on commercial activities or maintain a permanent establishment.)

	Commercial activity	Permanent establishment
Alberta	☐	☐
British Columbia	☐	☐
Manitoba	☐	☐
New Brunswick	☐	☐
Newfoundland	☐	☐
Northwest Territories	☐	☐
Nova Scotia	☐	☐
Ontario	☐	☐
Prince Edward Island	☐	☐
Quebec	☐	☐
Saskatchewan	☐	☐
Yukon Territory	☐	☐

Source: Reproduced with permission of the Minister of Public Works and Government Services Canada.

Provincial Sales Tax

All provinces, except Alberta, impose a sales tax on retail sales. The tax is charged on the price of goods sold to consumers. In most provinces, the tax is charged only on tangible commodities, although a few services (such as telephone service) are taxed. Such items as food, drugs, children's clothes, school supplies, and farm equipment are exempt from sales tax in many provinces. Provincial Sales Tax (PST) is charged in addition to GST collected by the federal government. It can be calculated on the base price only or on the base price plus GST (see page 219).

In Ontario, exempt items include food products, children's clothes, books, and shoes with a value under $30. The PST on accommodations, for example, hotel and motel rooms, is 5 percent. The PST on liquor is 10 percent.

Each province determines the rate of PST to be charged. These rates change from time to time. At the time of writing, these rates were in effect:

Alberta	0%
British Columbia	7%
Manitoba	7%
New Brunswick	8%
Newfoundland	8%
Nova Scotia	8%
Ontario	8%
Prince Edward Island	10%
Quebec	7.5%
Saskatchewan	7%

A retailer who sells taxable items is required by law to collect the PST. Each retailer in Ontario is issued a retail sales tax vendor's permit by the provincial government, and similar licences or permits are issued by the other provinces. In Figure 7-14, on page 219, the permit number is shown on the remittance form.

The retailer collects the tax when goods are sold to consumers. The retailer then sends the tax to the provincial government. This is usually done each month for the previous month's collection. Figure 7-14 is the form completed in Ontario by retailers when sales tax is remitted to the government.

Provincial Sales Tax Exemptions

Figure 7-15 on page 220 illustrates an invoice for a sale of paper. Notice the sales tax exempt stamp on the invoice. The buyer, Wilco Printers, uses the paper to produce items that it prints, such as greeting cards. The paper becomes part of the greeting cards. PST is charged only when the cards are sold. It would be unfair to collect tax on the paper and then again on the cards. That would result in paper being taxed twice: once as paper and then a second time as part of the cards. When Wilco ordered the paper, it indicated that the paper was exempt from provincial tax by supplying sales tax licence numbers. The numbers have been placed on the invoice by the seller, Buntin Reid, to indicate the material is exempt from sales tax because this is not the final (end) sale of the paper.

Ministry of Revenue Ontario — Retail Sales Tax Branch — P.O. Box 620, 13 King St. West, Oshawa, Ontario L1H 8E9

CUSTOMERS COPY

TELLER STAMP HERE

KEEP THIS PORTION FOR YOUR FILE

Make cheque or money order payable in Canadian funds to the TREASURER OF ONTARIO for the full amount of Tax due and payable.

Payment may be made at your Chartered bank in Ontario free of charge. See back of form for instructions.

10 Tax Amount Paid $ 955. 17

This is your District Office Address and Telephone Numbers: 2203 Yonge Street, Toronto, Ontario, M5P 6H6, 489-1864

This Return covers the period From To

RETURN DUE DATE ▶

Permit No. 316 590 12

TEAR HERE

Ministry of Revenue Ontario — Retail Sales Tax Branch — P.O. Box 620, 13 King St. West, Oshawa, Ontario L1H 8E9

FORWARD THIS PORTION WITH PAYMENT

TELLER STAMP HERE

Return Due Date

This Return covers the period From December 1 To December 31

Permit No. 316 590 12

Registered Vendor – Retail Sales Tax Return

		Dollars	Cents
1	Total Sales in Ontario	12 568	00
2	Total Collectible on Sales	1 005	44
3	Tax on Purchases for Own Consumption		
4	Sub Total (2+3)	1 005	44
5	Current Penalty (10% of 4) Maximum $1,000.00		
6	Sub Total (4+5)	1 005	44
7	Compensation	50	27
8	Sub Total (6 7)	955	17
9	Adjustment + − (See Back)		
10	Tax Amount Paid (Net Total of 8 and 9)	955	17

Certification - To the best of my knowledge and belief the statements on both sides of the Return are certified to be correct.

Signature J. Priddle Title Treasurer

Date 31/ 15 /-- Telephone ( ) 588-2160

FOR OFFICE USE ONLY PDC DO FC CI NS

TR 101 DO NOT WRITE OR STAMP BELOW THIS LINE 0336J (83-09)

FIGURE 7-14

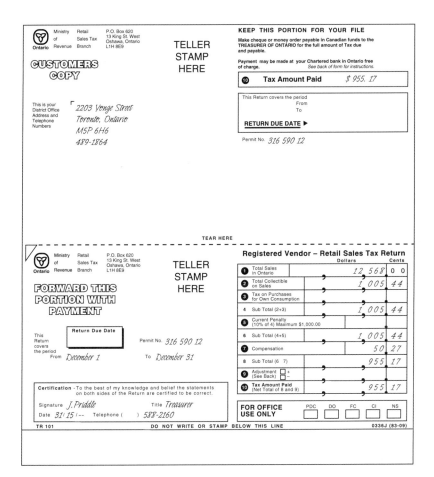

Retail sales tax return used by retailers to pay the Ontario government

Source: Publications Ontario, Ministry of Revenue.

Calculating GST and PST

When you purchased your mountain bike in the previous example, you saw that the selling price was $700 plus $49 GST. In all provinces, except Alberta, the final amount you will have to pay for the bike will also include PST. How much would you finally pay in a province where the PST is 8 percent?

Calculation of GST and PST

Mountain Bike Selling Price (base price)	$700.00
Goods and Services Tax (0.07 × $700)	49.00
	$749.00
Provincial Sales Tax (0.08 × $700)	56.00
Final Price to Customer	$805.00

This method of calculating sales tax eliminates the problem of paying tax on tax since both GST and PST are calculated as a percentage of the base price.

Some provinces calculate PST as a percentage of the base price plus GST. Using the example above, the new figures are:

Calculation of GST and PST

Mountain Bike Selling Price (base price)	$700.00
Goods and Services Tax (0.07 × $700)	49.00
	$749.00
Provincial Sales Tax (0.08 × $749)	59.92
Final Price to Customer	$808.92

Notice that the final price to the customer is higher when this method is used.

Each province can decide which method will be used to calculate PST. At the time of writing, British Columbia, Saskatchewan, Manitoba, and Ontario calculate PST on base price only, while New Brunswick, Newfoundland, and Nova Scotia pay HST, which includes PST on the bare price alone. The other provinces calculate PST on base price plus GST.

FIGURE 7–15

Sales tax licence numbers are required for sales tax exemption

THE PAPER HOUSE

BUNTIN REID PAPER
Division of Domtar Inc.
800 King Street West, Toronto, Ontario M5V 1N8 364-1351
BRANCHES:
501 Talbot St. Box 515, London, ON. N6A 2S4 432-8365
2730 Lancaster Rd., Ottawa, ON. K1B 4S4 731-8410

Wilco Printers
1825 Valentine Road
Scarborough, Ontario
M1P 4A3

INVOICE DATE
Dec. 22, 2001

INVOICE NO.

TERMS	PROV. SALES TAX	ORDER NO.	SLMN NO.	ACCOUNT NO.	CUSTOMER ORDER NO.
2/10, n/30	31659012	04153	72	20-596-5072	1209

ITEM NO.	DESCRIPTION	QUANTITY SHEETS OR UNITS	NET MASS	CODE	UNIT PRICE	CODE	AMOUNT
45984	Offset white 1 m × 1.5 m	7 000	910	1	$61.60/ per 1 000	3	$431.20

SALES TAX EXEMPT

Special terms for this invoice: n/30

CODE 1. KG 2. HUNDRED 3. THOUSAND 4. EACH 5. LITRE
SEE BACK OF INVOICE FOR ITEMS
FORM NO. B10(05/79)

INVOICE

CREDIT

INVOICE AMOUNT $431.20
E. & O.E.
CREDIT AMOUNT

GST and PST Payable Accounts

As a retailer, Warrendon Sports is responsible for collecting both the GST and PST from customers. The accounting system must include the accounts necessary to record both GST collected from customers and GST paid to suppliers (input tax credits) in order to calculate the correct amount to remit to the federal government. Remember, Warrendon will remit GST collected minus GST paid. In addition, an account is required to record the PST collected in order to remit the tax to the provincial government. This sounds complicated, but the ledger requires only three new accounts: PST Payable, GST Payable, and GST Refundable. Why are two GST accounts necessary? You must have information on GST collected and paid by your firm.

GST Collected	–	GST Paid	=	Net GST Owed
GST Payable	–	GST Refundable	=	GST Due to Federal Government

How would Warrendon Sports record the sale of the mountain bike in the previous example? The selling price was $700, the GST at 7 percent was $49, and the PST was $56 calculated on the base price. The customer paid a total of $805 cash for the bike. Warrendon would record the following journal entry:

Jan. 18	Cash	805	
	Sales		700
	GST Payable		49
	PST Payable		56
	Cash sale of bike.		

PST Payable

The amount of sales tax collected is owed to the provincial government. The sales tax collected during the month is credited in the PST Payable (or Sales Tax Payable) account. This account is a liability. It increases when taxable goods are sold and taxes are collected. It decreases when the seller of taxable goods sends the tax to the provincial government.

PST Payable account is a liability account.

PST Payable

Debit	Credit		
	Jan.	3	73.43
		4	35.62
		6	55.62
		9	41.74
		10	31.50
		~~	~~~
		31	43.65
			1 243.62

PST Payable

Debit Decrease	Credit Increase
Debit the account when sales tax is remitted to the government.	Credit the account when taxable goods are sold and taxes are collected.

At the end of the month, the amount of tax collected is calculated. In January, Warrendon collected $1 243.62 in PST and must remit this amount to the Provincial Treasurer. (Note: In some provinces, the remittance is made to the Minister of Finance. You should check the title for your province.) When the cheque is issued, the following journal entry is made:

Feb. 15	PST Payable	1 243.62	
	Cash		1 243.62
	Cheque 299 to Provincial Treasurer for January sales tax collections.		

Recording Sales Tax Commission

Several provinces pay commission to companies in return for the collection of sales tax. For example, in New Brunswick, a company receives 2 percent commission on the first $250 of tax it collects and 1 percent on amounts over $250. British Columbia pays a commission of 3 percent on the first $2 500 of tax collected and 1 percent on amounts over $2 500. In Ontario, the retailer receives $16 when the tax sent to the government is between $20 and $400. On tax amounts over $400, the retailer receives 5 percent on the tax remitted (see line 7, "Compensation," in Figure 7-14 on page 219). A maximum of $1 500 is available in any one year.

The commission earned by a company is usually recorded in an account entitled Miscellaneous Revenue or Sales Tax Commission.

On June 15, Western Supply Ltd. of Vancouver, British Columbia, has a balance of $300 in its PST Payable account. This balance represents retail tax collected from customers in May. When Western Supply remits the tax to the provincial government, it keeps a 3-percent commission of $9 (0.03 × 300 = 9). The entry, in General Journal form, to record the payment to the government and the commission earned is:

Jun. 15	PST Payable	300	
	Cash		291
	Sales Tax Commission		9
	To remit May sales tax and to record commission earned.		

GST Payable

The amount of Goods and Services Tax collected is also a liability. It is owed to the federal government. The amount of GST collected during the month is credited to the GST Payable account.

Is this the amount of tax that is sent to the federal government? No. The retailer remits GST collected *minus* GST paid. How does Warrendon record GST paid (input tax credit) on goods or services purchased for the business?

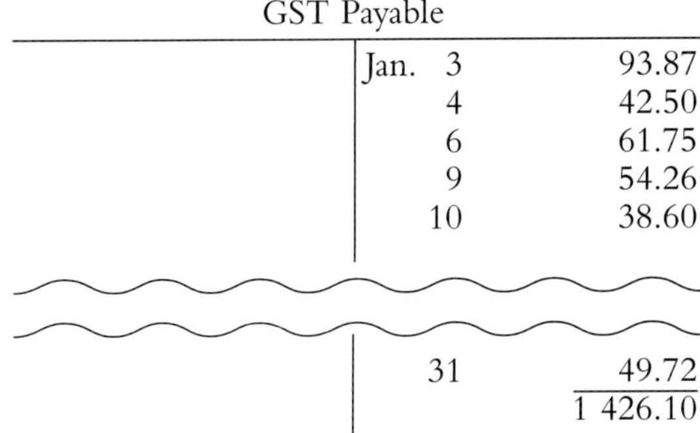

GST Payable

	Jan. 3	93.87
	4	42.50
	6	61.75
	9	54.26
	10	38.60
	31	49.72
		1 426.10

GST Input Tax Credit

Unit 14 of this chapter introduced the new accounts used by a merchandising company. You learned that the Purchases account is used to record the cost of merchandise bought for resale. In order to simplify the introduction of these accounts, GST was not included in the discussion. The following example will show the effect of GST on how the purchase of merchandise is recorded. When Warrendon Sports purchased the mountain bike from a wholesaler, it received the following purchase invoice.

FIGURE 7-16
Cash purchase of merchandise

Mountain Bike Limited
1035 Quay Street North
Vancouver, BC
V4J 6B7

Date: January 1, 2001
Sold To: Warrendon Sports
2579 Base Line Road
Ottawa, ON K2H 7B3

Item:	67 Mountain Bike
Quantity:	1
Price:	$500.00
GST:	35.00
Total Due:	$535.00

Terms of Sale: Cash

What is the amount recorded in the Purchases account? The $500 cost price. Why is the $35 GST not recorded as part of the cost price? As you learned earlier, the retailer deducts the GST paid to suppliers from the GST collected from the consumer before remitting the tax to the federal government. Therefore, Warrendon receives an input tax credit for the $35 GST paid to Mountain Bike Limited. How will Warrendon record the invoice shown in Figure 7-16? The journal entry will be:

Jan. 1	Purchases	500.00	
	GST Refundable	35.00	
	Cash		535.00
	Cash purchase of mountain bike.		

The amount of GST paid to suppliers is debited to the GST Refundable account.

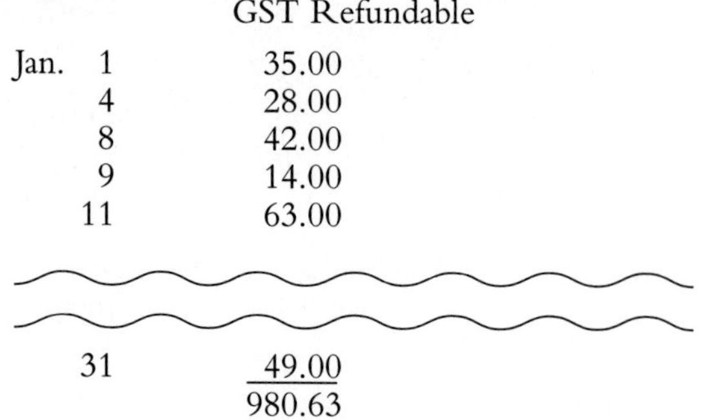

GST Refundable	
Jan. 1	35.00
4	28.00
8	42.00
9	14.00
11	63.00
31	49.00
	980.63

The GST Refundable account is a *contra liability account* since it reduces the amount of a liability. The GST Payable account balance ($1426.10) is reduced by the balance in the GST Refundable account ($980.63) in order to determine the net amount owed to the federal government ($445.47). This amount is forwarded to the federal government.

GST Refundable

	Debit	Credit
Jan. 1	35.00	
4	28.00	
8	42.00	
9	14.00	
11	63.00	
31	49.00	
	980.63	

GST Payable

Debit		Credit
	Jan. 3	93.87
	4	42.50
	6	61.75
	9	54.26
	10	38.60
	31	49.72
		1 426.10

The GST Payable account balance is forwarded to the Receiver General of the federal government monthly, quarterly, or annually, depending on the size of the business.

		Debit	Credit
Jan. 31	GST Payable	1 426.10	
	GST Refundable		980.63
	Cash		445.47
	January GST remitted.		

In the event the GST paid to suppliers exceeds the GST collected from customers, the business is able to apply for a refund from the federal government.

Recording GST for a Service Business

The Goods and Services Tax also applies to services sold and purchased. A service business would follow the same basic accounting procedures you have just learned for a merchandising business. The business collects GST from its customers on the sale of the service, deducts GST paid to suppliers, and remits the difference to the federal government.

Harmonized Sales Tax

The Harmonized Sales Tax (HST) is a tax that applies the GST and PST as a single rate of 15% to taxable supplies in the provinces of Newfoundland, Nova Scotia, and New Brunswick. The HST operates in the same way as GST and combines the federal 7% GST with an 8% PST. Accounting entries for HST are similar to those outlined for GST and PST.

Calculation of HST	
Mountain bike selling price (base price)	$700.00
Harmonized Sales Tax (0.15 × $700)	105.00
Final Price to Customer	$805.00

Provinces have the option of collecting their own PST or using the harmonized method. In most cases, where the business has sales of less than $200 000 (including GST/PST), a business may use this method.

Optional GST System for Small Business

Small business has the option of using a "quick method" of collecting GST. Businesses eligible to use this method are determined by their total sales as shown in Figure 7-17 on page 226. This method requires the small business owners to collect GST, but does not require them to keep track of input tax credits in order to calculate the amount of tax to remit. In most cases, where the business has sales of less than $200 000 (including GST/PST), a business may use this method. They simply multiply their sales by the percentage specified in the chart shown in Figure 7-17.

For example, if Warrendon Sports' yearly sales were under $200 000, it could calculate GST in the following way:

Calculation of GST Payable

Quarterly Sales (Jan.–Mar.)

Quantity Sales	×	Percentage Rate		
$50 000	×	0.03	=	$1 500

Warrendon simply remits $1 500 GST to the Receiver General at the end of March. This method removes the burden of setting up and recording the collection and payment of GST for small business.

GST, PST, and Cash Discounts

A sale of $500 worth of merchandise is made on account to J. Woodsworth. The GST at 7–percent is $35, making a total of $535. PST at 8–percent on $500 is $40. The total amount of the sale is $575. The terms of sale are 2/10, n/30.

Suppose that Woodsworth pays for the merchandise within 10 days in order to take advantage of the 2-percent cash discount. A question arises concerning the amount of the discount. Should it be 2 percent of the merchandise only ($500), or should it be 2 percent of the total owing ($575)? There are arguments for both alternatives. In actual practice, it is generally accepted that the customer is allowed to take a discount of 2 percent of $575, which is $11.50 (0.02 × 575 = 11.50).

FIGURE 7–17

GST rules for small business *(Changes to tax rates can be found on the official Canada Customs and Revenue Agency web site, http://www.rc.gc.ca.)*

Sample Quick Method Percentages

ELIGIBLE BUSINESS GROUPS	MAXIMUM ANNUAL TAXABLE SALES (INCLUDING GST)	PERCENTAGE
Manufacturers and Services (Examples: sawmills, body shops, electricians, barbers/hair-stylists, construction contractors, repair shops, food service providers)	$200 000	5%
Retailers and Wholesalers (Examples: clothing and shoe stores, stores selling less than 25% basic groceries)	$200 000	2.5%

REVIEW QUESTIONS

UNIT

1. What is the amount of the GST?
2. Is the full amount of GST collected by a business from customers remitted to the federal government? Explain the term "input tax credit."
3. What is the amount of your province's PST? Has it changed since this text was published?
4. What type of account (asset, liability, revenue, or expense) is the PST Payable account?
5. What does it mean if a product is exempt from sales tax?
6. A sale of merchandise costing $200 is made with terms of net 30. GST is 7 percent and PST is 8 percent calculated on the base price. What accounts are debited and credited in recording this transaction?
7. A customer buys $60 worth of merchandise on credit. GST is 7 percent and PST is 9 percent calculated on the base price. The merchandise is defective and is returned by the customer. A credit invoice is issued.
   (a) Record this sales return in General Journal form for a seller who uses a Sales Returns and Allowances account.
   (b) Record the same transaction in General Journal form for a seller who does not use a Sales Returns and Allowances account.
8. On November 10, your company received an invoice with terms 2/10, n/30, for $550, plus $38.50 GST, plus $44 PST.
   (a) By what date must the invoice be paid to take advantage of the discount?
   (b) Will the discount be taken on the $500 or on $632.50?

9. A service is provided for $200 cash. The GST is 7 percent and the PST is 11 percent calculated on the base price plus GST. What accounts are debited and credited?

10. A taxable item is sold for $478 cash. The GST is 7 percent and the PST is 10 percent on the base price plus GST.

    (a) Calculate the taxes and the total received from the customer.
    (b) What accounts are debited and credited to record the sale?

11. A company collected $510 in PST during March. What is the journal entry required to record the cheque issued to the Provincial Treasurer in order to remit the PST? (Assume there is a 4-percent commission paid by the government.)

17. Complete the chart shown below in your notebook.

    (a) Calculate PST on the base amount of the sale.
    (b) Calculate PST on the base amount of the sale plus GST.

Amount of Sale	GST (7%)	PST (8%)	PST on Total
$ 125.00	?	?	?
7.95	?	?	?
725.00	?	?	?
4 500.00	?	?	?

18. Prepare General Journal entries for the following retail sales:

    (a) Sold goods for $150 to R. Shadbar, terms net 30, GST $10.50, PST $12. Total $172.50.
    (b) Sold goods for $300, GST $21, PST $24, terms 2/10, n/30.
    (c) Received $172.50 cash from R. Shadbar.

19. Following is a PST Payable account:

PST Payable

	Date	Amount
	Apr. 5	80
	12	54
	19	77
	30	115

    (a) How much should be remitted to the provincial government for the month of April?
    (b) In General Journal form, prepare the entry to remit the April tax to the provincial government. Assume that the company is located in a province that does not pay a commission to companies for collecting the tax.

20. Following are GST Payable and GST Refundable accounts:

GST Payable

	Date	Amount
	May 5	85
	12	90
	19	120
	29	73

GST Refundable

Date	Amount	
May 4	55	
11	110	
20	85	
30	70	

(a) How much should be remitted to the federal government for the month of May?
(b) In General Journal form, prepare the entry to remit the May tax to the federal government.

21. (a) Union Electric Supply made taxable retail sales of $4 200 during May. How much is the cheque sent to the provincial government if the PST is 8 percent and Union Electric is allowed a commission of 3 percent for collecting the PST?
(b) Prepare the journal entry to record the payment.

22. (a) During June, Union Electric Supply made sales of $5 000, of which $900 was paid for non-taxable items. How much is remitted to the provincial government if the PST is 6 percent and the company's commission is 3 percent?
(b) Prepare the journal entry to record the payment.

23. Record the following source documents on page 307 of a General Journal:

Aug. 1 Cash register tape shows sales of $945, GST $66.15, PST $75.60.

2 Cheque received from C. Ballard for $583 to pay Invoice 803.

2 Cheque received from L. Noble for $317.52 to pay Invoice 799, $324 less $6.48 discount.

4 Cheque received from K. Engel, the owner, for $3 700 as an additional investment in the business.

7 Bank credit memo, $10 500 for a bank loan that was deposited in the company bank account.

8 Cheque received from C. Drago for $548.80 to pay Invoice 805, $560 less $11.20 discount.

9 Cash Sales Slips 940 to 955 for $2 155 plus $150.85 GST and $172.40 PST.

24. Record the following source documents on page 193 of a General Journal:

Nov. 1 Cheque received for $4 300 from the owner, C. Black, as a further investment in the business.

2 Cash Sales Slips 340 to 355 for $975 plus 6 percent PST on base price and 7 percent GST.

3 Cheques received:
From A. Derouin, $372 on account;
From V. Williams, $428.26 to pay Invoice 6061 for $437 less $8.74 discount.

5 Cheque received from A. Derouin for $749.70 to pay Invoice 6059 for $765 less $15.30 discount.

5 Cash Sales Slips 356 to 382 for $3 250 plus 6 percent PST on base price and 7 percent GST.

UNIT 16 Bank Credit Cards

Learning Objective

After reading this unit, discussing the applicable review questions, and completing the applications exercises, you will be able to do the following:

1. **EXPLAIN** the accounting procedures and **PREPARE** the journal entries for bank credit cards.

BANK CREDIT CARDS

Many merchandising enterprises accept bank credit cards rather than, or in addition to, extending credit to their customers. Credit card companies such as MasterCard and Visa supply an accounts receivable service to businesses. Since both MasterCard and Visa are operated by banking institutions, their cards are called *bank credit cards.*

Why People Use Credit Cards

Two examples are given below to show why consumers and businesses use bank credit cards.

Cindy Hutton has just purchased a sweater from Giselle's Boutique and uses her MasterCard to pay for her purchase. Like many other people, Cindy uses a bank credit card to do much of her shopping. Why do people use credit cards instead of paying with cash or by cheque? Cindy prefers to shop using a credit card for the following reasons:

- She does not have to carry large amounts of cash with her.
- She can buy things even if she does not have cash at the time she wishes to make a purchase.
- There are some businesses that do not accept personal cheques and others that demand several items of identification before accepting cheques.
- Cindy's card is accepted internationally when Cindy travels. She can obtain cash advances up to a set limit. As well, Cindy simply finds it more convenient to use a credit card. Figure 7-18 below shows the credit card form completed by the store clerk for Cindy's purchase. The form is known as a *sales draft* or *sales slip.*

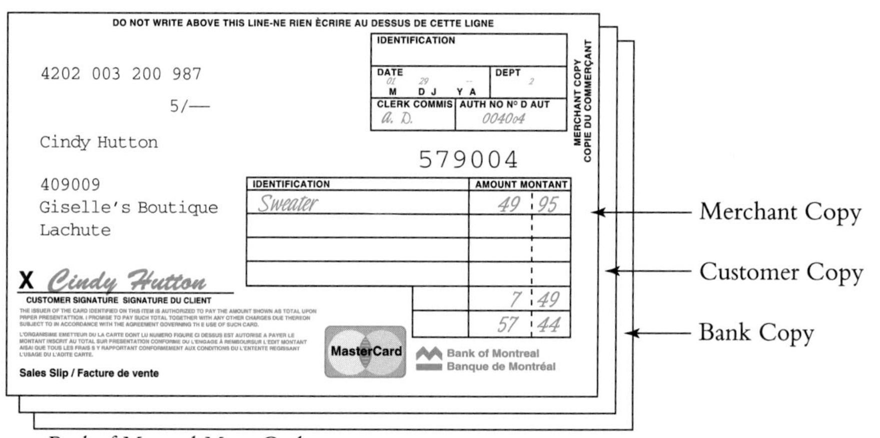

DO NOT WRITE ABOVE THIS LINE-NE RIEN ÈCRIRE AU DESSUS DE CETTE LIGNE

4202 003 200 987

5/—

Cindy Hutton

409009
Giselle's Boutique
Lachute

IDENTIFICATION

DATE M D J Y A	DEPT
01 29 --	2
CLERK COMMIS	**AUTH NO Nº D AUT**
a. D.	0040o4

579004

MERCHANT COPY
COPIE DU COMMERÇANT

IDENTIFICATION	AMOUNT MONTANT
Sweater	49 95
	7 49
	57 44

X Cindy Hutton
CUSTOMER SIGNATURE SIGNATURE DU CLIENT

THE ISSUER OF THE CARD IDENTIFIED ON THIS ITEM IS AUTHORIZED TO PAY THE AMOUNT SHOWN AS TOTAL UPON PRPER PRESENTATTION. I PROMISE TO PAY SUCH TOTAL TOGETHER WITH ANY OTHER CHARGES DUE THEREON SUBJECT TO IN ACCORDANCE WITH THE AGREEMENT GOVERNING TH E USE OF SUCH CARD.

L'ORGANISME EMETTEUR DU LA CARTE DONT LU NUMERO FIGURE CI DESSUS EST AUTORISE A PAYER LE MONTANT INSCRIT AU TOTAL SUR PRESENTATION CONFORME OU L'ENGAGE À REMBOURSUR L'EDIT MONTANT AISAI QUE TOUS LES FRAIS S Y RAPPORTANT CONFORMEMENT AUX CONDITIONS DU L'ENTENTE REGISSANT L'USAGE DU L'ADITE CARTE.

Sales Slip / Facture de vente

Source: Bank of Montreal MasterCard.

FIGURE 7-18
MasterCard sales slip

Completing the Credit Card Form

Let's follow the steps in completing the credit card form.

(1) Cindy gives the clerk the credit card. The clerk checks the expiry date on the card to make sure that it is still a valid card. Then the clerk checks the number on the card against an "update list" of stolen or lost cards to ensure that the card does belong to Cindy. The list also contains numbers of cards that have been cancelled. This process is often done electronically by passing the card through a scanning slot on the top or side of the authorization machine.
(2) The clerk then makes sure that the amount of the sale does not exceed the floor limit assigned to the store by MasterCard. The floor limit is a maximum amount assigned to the store for a credit card sale. Any credit card sale that exceeds the limit requires an authorization from MasterCard. The authorization is obtained by telephone or authorization machine by the sales clerk before the sale is completed.
(3) The clerk completes the sales draft form and then runs it through an imprint machine. This machine prints the company's name and Cindy's name and credit card number on the form.
(4) Cindy is asked to sign the form. The signature is checked against the sample signature on the credit card.
(5) Cindy is given a copy of the sales draft form. The store keeps two copies of the sales draft form.

Cindy leaves the store with her sweater without having paid out any cash for it. She will not have to pay until she receives a statement from the bank credit card company (see Figures 7-19 and 7-20 on pages 231 and 232). This is another reason why she uses a bank credit card. If she is able to pay the statement on time, she will not have to pay any interest. Depending on when a statement is issued, MasterCard allows up to 21 days from the date on the statement to pay, after which interest is charged. Cindy is very careful to pay her balance owing by the due date in order to avoid the interest charges.

Credit Card Fees

Many of the credit card companies impose a fee for using the credit card. The fee may be a separate charge for each transaction or a monthly or yearly fee for using the card. All credit card companies generally charge interest on balances that have not been paid within 15 to 30 days of the statement.

Figure 7-19 is the statement received from MasterCard by Cindy. It is a summary of a month's purchases and indicates that the new balance owing is $275.34. The date of the statement is 02/04/01 and the payment due date is 02/29/01. Cindy's cheque for $275.34 must reach the MasterCard accounts office by 02/29/01 if she is to avoid interest on the balance.

The previous example illustrates why and how a consumer uses a bank credit card. In the next section, we will examine how and why a business uses the services of a bank credit card company such as Visa or MasterCard.

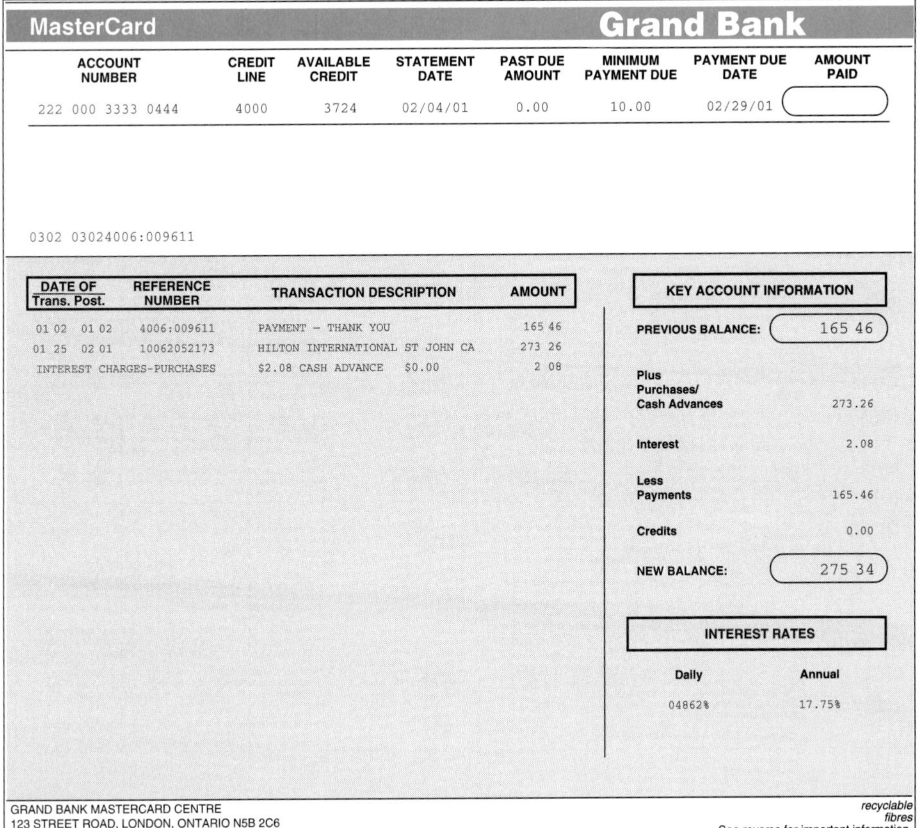

MasterCard **Grand Bank**

ACCOUNT NUMBER	CREDIT LINE	AVAILABLE CREDIT	STATEMENT DATE	PAST DUE AMOUNT	MINIMUM PAYMENT DUE	PAYMENT DUE DATE	AMOUNT PAID
222 000 3333 0444	4000	3724	02/04/01	0.00	10.00	02/29/01	

0302 03024006:009611

DATE OF Trans. Post.	REFERENCE NUMBER	TRANSACTION DESCRIPTION	AMOUNT
01 02 01 02	4006:009611	PAYMENT – THANK YOU	165 46
01 25 02 01	10062052173	HILTON INTERNATIONAL ST JOHN CA	273 26
INTEREST CHARGES-PURCHASES		$2.08 CASH ADVANCE $0.00	2 08

KEY ACCOUNT INFORMATION

PREVIOUS BALANCE:	165 46
Plus Purchases/ Cash Advances	273.26
Interest	2.08
Less Payments	165.46
Credits	0.00
NEW BALANCE:	275 34

INTEREST RATES

Daily	Annual
04862%	17.75%

GRAND BANK MASTERCARD CENTRE
123 STREET ROAD, LONDON, ONTARIO N5B 2C6

recyclable fibres
See reverse for important information.

FIGURE 7-19
Monthly MasterCard statement

Why Businesses Use Bank Credit Cards

Giselle's Boutique uses the services provided by both Visa and MasterCard. It does so for the following reasons:

- Many people have either Visa or MasterCard credit cards and will shop at stores that accept these cards.
- The store receives its money from credit card sales from the bank as soon as the sales draft forms are deposited in the bank.
- There is no risk of bad debts. The credit card company guarantees payment to the store.
- The store does not have to have an accounts receivable system to record sales to customers and does not have to worry about collecting amounts from customers.

The credit card companies provide a guaranteed, immediate collection service to companies. In return for the service, the companies pay a percentage of each sale to the bank credit card company.

FIGURE 7–20

Back of MasterCard statement

About your Statement	
Transaction date	- The date shown for each item should be the date on which the transaction occurred. If this date is not available, the date of posting to your account will be shown.
Posting date	- This is the date the item was posted to your account.
Statement period	- The statement period is normally one month ending on the statement date as shown on the front of your statement.
Reference number	- This number helps us trace each of your transactions in our files. Please provide the reference number if you are enquiring about a specific transaction on your statement.
Description	- The description provides the name and location where the transaction took place. Any payments, adjustments or interest/charges are also described here.
International transactions	- Transactions made outside Canada are converted to Canadian dollars at our MasterCard conversion rate in effect on the date the item is posted to your account. This rate may differ from the one in effect on the date of your transaction.
About our Interest/Charges	
Advances through merchants. (Purchases)	- There is **no** interest charged on **advances through merchants** when we receive **payment in full** at our payment centre **by the due date** as shown on the front of this statement. If payment in full is not received by that date, interest is charged on each transaction from the date it was posted until payment in full is posted to your MasterCard Account.
Direct (Cash) advances	- **Interest is charged on direct advances from the date of the advance until payment in full is received at our payment centre.**
Interest calculation	- When your balance is made up of advances for which you have previously been billed and/or current direct advances, this becomes your "interest-bearing balance". **As such you can minimize your interest by paying us as early as possible.**
Interest rate	- Interest on "interest-bearing" balances is calculated at a daily rate. The applicable daily rate, and such rate expressed as an annual rate, are shown on the front of this statement.
About your Payment	
Payment application	- Your payment is applied to items posted to your account, in the following order: a) to interest then service charges b) to the following previously billed items: - direct advances - interest-bearing advances through merchants and debit adjustments. - non-interest-bearing advances through merchants and debit adjustments c) and then to items which have not been previously billed but which have been posted to your account before your payment was posted, in the same order as above
Payment due date	- This is the date by which payment must be received to keep your account in good standing. This date is shown on the front of this statement under **"Payment due by".**
Minimum payment	- Please refer to the front of this statement for the **minimum payment** amount. - A balance of $10 or less is to be paid in full.

Relevé	
Date de la transaction	- La date inscrite vis-à-vis de chaque article correspond à la date à laquelle la transaction a été effectuée. Lorsque cette date n'est pas connue, le relevé fait mention de la date d'inscription de la transaction à votre compte.
Date d'inscription	- Date d'inscription de la transaction à votre compte.
Période couverte par le relevé	- Période normalement d'un mois se terminant à la date du relevé figurant au recto.
Numéro de référence	- Ce numéro nous permet de retrouver chacune de vos transactions gardées dans nos dossiers. Pour toute demande de renseignements sur une transaction figurant sur votre relevé, veuillez mentionner le numéro de référence.
Description	- Cette zone comprend le nom et l'emplacement de l'établissement où la transaction a été effectuée. Les paiements, les rectifications, l'intérêt et les frais y sont également décrits.
Transactions effectuées à l'étranger	- Les transactions effectuées à l'extérieur du Canada sont converties en dollars canadiens à notre taux MasterCard en vigueur à la date où l'écriture est passée à votre compte. Ce taux peut différer du taux en vigueur à la date de votre transaction.
Intérêt/Frais	
Avances de commerçants (Achats)	- **Aucun intérêt** n'est imputé sur **les avances de commerçants** lorsque le **paiement intégral des avances** parvient à notre centre de paiement **à la date d'échéance** indiquée au recto du présent relevé . Si nous n'avons pas reçu le paiement intégral à cette date, l'intérêt est imputé sur chaque transaction à partir de la date d'inscription de la transaction jusqu'à l'inscription à votre compte MasterCard du paiement intégral.
Avances directes (en espèces)	- **L'intérêt sur les avances directes est imputé à partir de la date de l'avance jusqu'à la date de réception du paiement intégral à notre centre de paiement.**
Calcul de l'intérêt	- Lorsque votre solde comprend des avances facturées antérieurement ou des avances directes courantes, il est qualifié de "solde portant intérêt". **Ainsi, vous pouvez réduire vos frais d'intérêt en nous payant le plus tôt possible.**
Taux d'intérêt	- L'intérêt sur les soldes rémunérés se calcule selon un taux quotidien. Le taux courant et son équivalent annuel figurent au recto du présent relevé.
Paiement	
Imputation du paiement	- Votre paiement s'applique aux articles inscrits à votre compte dans l'ordre suivant : a) aux intérêts et ensuite aux frais de service b) aux articles suivants imputés antérieurement : - avances directes - avances de commerçants portant intérêt et débits de rajustement. - avances de commerçants ne portant aucun intérêt et débits de rajustement. c) aux articles qui n'ont pas été imputés antérieurement mais qui ont été inscrits à votre compte avant l'inscription de votre paiement, dans l'ordre précédemment indiqué.
Échéance du paiement	- Il s'agit de la date à laquelle vous devez avoir remis votre paiement afin que votre compte demeure en règle. Cette date est indiquée à la rubrique **Échéance** au recto du présent relevé.
Paiement minimum	- Le **paiement minimum** est indiqué au recto du présent relevé. - Un solde de $10 ou moins doit être réglé intégralement.

Accounting Example for Bank Credit Card Transactions

In this example, we will use the Visa credit card and the Men's Wear Shop to illustrate accounting procedures for bank credit card transactions.

FIGURE 7-21

Visa sales recap form

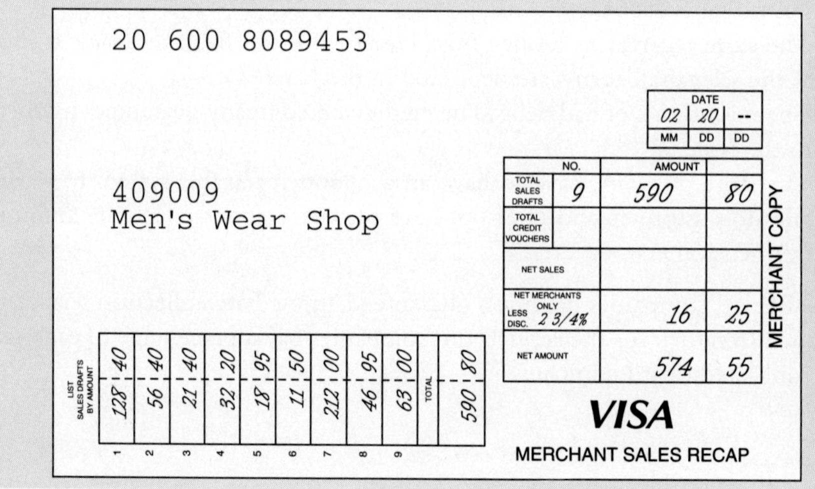

20 600 8089453

DATE: 02 | 20 | -- (MM DD DD)

409009
Men's Wear Shop

	NO.	AMOUNT	
TOTAL SALES DRAFTS	9	590	80
TOTAL CREDIT VOUCHERS			
NET SALES			
NET MERCHANTS ONLY LESS DISC. 2 3/4%		16	25
NET AMOUNT		574	55

LIST SALES DRAFTS BY AMOUNT

1	2	3	4	5	6	7	8	9	TOTAL
128 40	56 40	21 40	32 20	18 95	11 50	212 00	46 95	63 00	590 80

MERCHANT COPY

VISA

MERCHANT SALES RECAP

Sales Recap Form

At the end of the day, the store accountant prepares a merchant sales recap form (Figure 7-21). This is a summary of all the sales drafts for the day. Figure 7-21 is the recap form from February 20 and lists nine Visa sales drafts and a total of $590.80 (which includes GST and PST).

The Visa sales drafts are treated as cash and are taken to the bank and deposited at the end of the day. The bank receives the deposit and increases the balance in the account of the Men's Wear Shop. The store accountant then prepares an accounting entry to record the sales. The entry is:

Feb. 20	Cash	574.55	
	Visa Discount Expense	16.25	
	GST Payable		35.96
	PST Payable		41.10
	Sales		513.74
	To record Visa credit card sales.		

Although no cash has changed hands, the store has received its money — it was placed in the store's bank account by the bank.

Bank Fees

In return for providing instant cash for sales made, the bank charges the store a fee. The fee is calculated at the time of deposit. On the recap summary sheet (Figure 7-21), the fee is $16.25. The store treats this fee as an expense.

The amount of the fee charged by the bank credit card company is based on the average volume of credit card sales and the average draft size. The fee paid by the Men's Wear Shop is 2 3/4 percent of credit card sales. This is the rate for a business with an average monthly volume of $5 000 to $12 499, and an average draft size of $50 to $99.99. Figure 7-22 illustrates the service charges paid to Visa by merchants:

FIGURE 7-22
Table of Visa service charges

SAMPLE VISA MEMBER DISCOUNT SCHEDULE

	AVERAGE DRAFT SIZE			
Average Monthly Volume	**Under $30.00**	**$30.00 to $49.99**	**$50.00 to $99.99**	**$100.00 and over**
	%	%	%	%
$ 1 – $ 999	5 1/2	4 1/2	3 1/2	3 1/2
1 000 – 2 499	4 3/4	4	3 1/2	2 3/4
2 500 – 4 999	4 1/2	3 3/4	3	2 3/4
5 000 – 12 499	4 1/2	3 1/2	2 3/4	2 1/2
12 500 – 19 999	4	3 1/2	2 1/2	2 1/2
20 000 – 29 999	3 3/4	3	2 1/2	2 1/2
30 000 – 49 999	3 1/2	2 3/4	2 1/2	2
50 000 – 74 999	3 1/2	2 3/4	2	2
75 000 – 149 999	3	2 1/2	2	2
150 000 – 299 999	2 1/2	2 1/2	2	2
300 000 – and over	2	2	2	2

Merchant Statement

In the example described above, the merchant deposited the bank credit card sales drafts each day and deducted the Visa fee from the deposit each day. Some banks use the monthly statement method of charging the fee to the merchant.

FIGURE 7-23
Merchant statement

THE BANK OF NOVA SCOTIA
VISA CENTRE MERCHANT STATEMENT

WESTERN MOTOR INN
11503 FORT RD., N.W.
EDMONTON, AB. T5B 4G1

MERCHANT NO. 589
STATEMENT DATE Feb. 28, 2000

DATE	DEPOSIT AMOUNT	ADJUSTMENTS	CODE	REFERENCE NO.
01/29	$ 553.76			2 51301045
02/01	822.69			2 57109132
02/03	754.83			2 57109142
02/06	901.64			2 58240108
02/10	711.40			2 62300040
02/10	873.60			2 62300050
02/17	706.38			2 75223840
02/17	489.13			2 70301295
02/17	884.45			2 70301305
02/17	1,066.69			2 70301315
02/20	489.15			2 75223831
02/24	799.06			2 76246395
02/24	731.51			2 76246405
02/25	982.96			2 76246385

TOTALS $10,767.25 + $0.00 = $10,767.25 NET SALES

BRANCH TRANSIT	ACCOUNT NO.	CHAIN NO.	DISCOUNT RATE	CURRENT DISCOUNT
1072	23-00214	0	2.750%	$296.10

NUMBER & AMOUNT OF SALES DRAFTS		NUMBER & AMOUNT OF CREDITS	
125	$10,767.25	0	$0.00

CARRY FORWARD AMOUNT		UNCLEARED ADJUSTMENTS		CURRENT DISCOUNT		STATEMENT TOTAL
0.00	–	0.00	+	$296.10	=	$296.10

The statement illustrated in Figure 7-23 was received by the Western Motor Inn in Edmonton from its bank. It is called the merchant statement. Once a month, the statement is sent by the Visa bank to the merchant. The statement provides a summary of the Visa deposits made each day, the total deposits, and the fee charged by Visa for the month's transactions. The fee charged for the month covered in Figure 7-23 is $296.10. This accounting entry is made on the books of the Western Motor Inn to record the Visa service fee:

Feb. 28	Visa Discount Expense Cash To record the Visa discount fee for February.	296.10	 296.10

Can you see the advantage of using the monthly statement method as compared to the daily method for recording the fee?

Credit Cards

Visa, MasterCard, and other credit cards have a preset spending limit. In many cases, there is no annual fee but a minimum payment is due each month. Interest is charged on the balance. For more information on credit cards see page 229.

Charge Cards

American Express and other charge cards are designed for customers who pay the balance each month. They have no preset spending limit and no interest since there is no balance. There is, in most cases, an annual fee charged to the client.

MOVING TOWARD A PAPERLESS ECONOMY

Electronic Commerce

Electronic commerce (e-commerce) refers to the conduct of business activities (production, distribution, purchasing, sales, banking, and other transactions) by means of advanced communication and computer technologies. E-commerce is an important vehicle for business to fully participate in the global economy. It allows consumers, like you, to more easily purchase products and services from around the world. Companies that are networked for e-commerce are able to develop products, receive orders, communicate with suppliers, arrange production, and service customers with no delays. Participation in e-commerce is becoming a competitive necessity for businesses of all size.

Electronic Banking

The Canadian Bankers Association estimates that over 85-percent of banking transactions are done electronically. The most popular forms of electronic banking are automated banking machines (ATMs) and direct payment cards. Over 97 percent of Canadian ATMs belong to the Interac network; Interac Direct Payment is a service that allows customers to use their client cards to pay for purchases at retail outlets. Electronic banking also features telephone banking and PC/Internet banking services 24 hours per day. All services require account holders to use a personal password and a client card number.

Debit Cards

Financial institutions have introduced debit, or direct payment, cards, which eliminate the need to write cheques to pay for merchandise. The debit card requires account holders to have a Personal Identification Number (PIN) and a client card number to access the service.

Debit cards are part of a system that transfers funds between parties electronically rather than by paper cheques. The exchange of cash using this system is called *electronic funds transfer* (EFT). This method is already used by many employers to deposit employees' pay directly into their bank accounts while withdrawing from the employer's account. The same type of system allows customers to present a debit card to a retailer rather than write a cheque to pay for goods purchased. The debit card is inserted into the retailer's computer terminal which is connected to the bank. The funds to pay for the purchased goods are automatically transferred out of the customer's account, and into the store's account. The cards can be used in two ways: on-line, where the cost of the purchase is immediately deducted, or off-line, where the buyer signs a sales receipt and funds are deducted one or two days later.

This system eliminates the cost of processing the paper cheque and removes the risk of bad cheques for the retailer. Implementation of this system moves us closer to the "paperless society" where there is little need to carry cash or cheques.

Stored-value Cards

These cards are usually issued in amounts of $25–$100 and replace cash. Owners swipe the card through phones or computer terminals; when the money has been spent, the owners can then throw them away or reload them with value.

Smart Cards

This card has a microchip and can perform many functions at the same time. Field tests have used the card as photo ID, door key, credit, and ATM card. Smart cards have had a slow start because they require new merchant terminals.

Electronic Cash Cards

Electronic Cash Cards (e-cash cards) are a form of smart card. A sum of money (generally a maximum of $500) is transferred from your bank account to an electronic card. This transfer can take place at an ATM. The e-cash card is used like cash for everyday expenses. The card is swiped through a point-of-sale terminal for retailers, vending machines, telephones, and personal computers for shopping on the Internet. You replenish your card with cash value from your bank account when the original amount is used. These cards are different from debit cards, where cash is withdrawn from your account at the point of sale in the exact amount required to cover the purchase price of the item. The major e-cash card providers are Mondex, Exact, and Visa Cash.

Point-of-Sale Terminals

Electronic banking provides a number of payment options for customers and direct deposit of the funds to the bank account of the business. Retail outlets use point-of-sale (POS) terminals to allow customers to pay by credit card or direct payment card. Of course, many customers still prefer to pay cash for some purchases. The merchant receives a recap form at the end of the day listing the amount deposited automatically to the merchant's account as a result of transactions processed through the POS terminal. For example, the ABC Co. end-of-day recap form shows:

Sales	**January 15, 2001**
Visa	$12 357.10
MasterCard	11 550.30
Direct Payment	11 780.70
Total	$35 688.10

Remember, this deposit represents only the sales processed through the POS terminal. Total sales shown on the cash register summary for the day include both POS terminal sales plus sales paid with actual cash and cheques. These cheques and cash must also be deposited in the bank daily. Total sales for the day for ABC Co. would be:

POS Sales	$35 688.10
Cash/Cheque Sales	9 430.20
Total Sales	$45 118.30

The ABC Co. bank statement would show two deposits for January 15. What would they be? A point-of-sale (direct) deposit of $35 688.10 and a regular deposit of $9 430.20. Can you see the advantage for the retailer?

ACCOUNTING TERMS

Cost of Goods Sold The total of all costs involved in purchasing the merchandise to be sold.

Credit Card Discount Expense The fee paid by a merchant for using the services of a credit card company.

Delivery Expense An account used to record the cost of delivering merchandise to customers.

E-commerce Conduct of business activities by means of advanced communication and computer technologies.

Goods and Services Tax A tax charged on the sale of most goods and services in Canada.

Goods and Services Tax Payable An account used to record GST collected and GST paid by a business for a period of time. The balance is paid to the federal government.

Harmonized Sales Tax A tax that applies at a single rate the combined GST and PST in a province.

Input Tax Credit A credit for GST paid on business purchases.

Manufacturing Company A company that makes a product.

Merchandise Goods bought for resale in a merchandising business.

Merchandise Inventory The total dollar value of goods on hand for sale.

Merchandising Company A company that sells a product.

Net Purchases Purchases – Purchases Returns and Allowances – Purchases Discounts.

Net Sales Sales – Sales Returns and Allowances – Sales Discounts.

Periodic Inventory Method The actual amount of inventory on hand is determined by physical count when financial statements are prepared.

Perpetual Inventory Method A record is kept for each item in inventory, and the balance is updated continuously as items are bought or sold.

Provincial Sales Tax A tax charged on the price of goods sold to consumers.

Purchases Discount Cash discount received off the purchase price in return for early payment of the invoice.

Purchases Returns and Allowances An account used to record the return of merchandise previously purchased for resale.

Purchases An account used to record the cost of merchandise purchased for resale.

Sales An account used to record the cash and credit sales of merchandise by the business.

Sales Discounts Cash discount given to a customer off the selling price for early payment of an invoice.

Sales Returns and Allowances An account used to record the return of merchandise by a customer.

Sales Tax Commission An amount of money earned by the retailer for collecting the sales tax on behalf of the province.

Sales Tax Payable An account used to record the sales tax collected for a period of time that is payable to the provincial government.

Schedule A supporting statement providing details of an item on a main statement.

Service Company A company that sells a service.

Terms of Sale An agreement between the buyer and seller of an item regarding the method of payment.

Transportation-in An account used to record the transportation charges incurred to bring merchandise purchased for resale to the store.

REVIEW QUESTIONS

UNIT 16

1. Why do retailers accept bank credit cards even though there is a fee charged for using this service?
2. (a) Why do consumers use bank credit cards?
   (b) What is the name of the form completed by the merchant when a sale is made to a customer who makes payment with a bank credit card?
   (c) How many copies of the form are prepared and who receives each copy?

3. Look at the MasterCard customer statement, Figure 7-19, page 231, and answer these questions:

   (a) What is the statement date?
   (b) What is the payment due date?
   (c) What is the new balance owing?
   (d) What is the minimum payment that must be made?
   (e) What is the credit limit for the customer?

4. The back of a MasterCard statement is shown in Figure 7-20, page 232. Obtain definitions for the following from the statement:

   (a) Transaction date
   (b) Payment due date
   (c) Interest calculation
   (d) Minimum payment

5. What is the name of the form completed at the end of each day that summarizes the day's bank credit card sales?

6. (a) What accounts are debited and credited by the retailer when Visa sales drafts are taken to the bank and deposited?
   (b) What accounts are debited and credited to record the fee charged by the bank?

7. What is the bank credit card fee (in percentage terms) for each of the following monthly volumes? Assume the average draft size is under $30 (refer to Figure 7-22, page 233).

   (a) $3 000
   (b) $13 000
   (c) $22 000

25. Record the following transactions in a General Journal. Use the Visa Discount Expense account to record the fee paid to Visa and the MasterCard Discount Expense account to record the MasterCard fee.

Jul. 7 Cash sales, $2 500 (sales tax exempt), GST $175.

7 Invoice 6, sale on account to S. Cox, $630, GST 7 percent, PST 6 percent on base price.

7 Visa credit card sales, $680 (not taxable), GST 7 percent.

7 MasterCard credit card sales, $1 100 (sales tax exempt), GST 7 percent.

8 Visa discount fee, $19.75.

8 MasterCard discount fee, $28.34.

26. Rivera Products offers a variety of credit terms to customers. Record the following transactions for January in a General Journal. All sales are subject to 7 percent GST and 8 percent PST.

Jan. 2 Sold merchandise to J. Coon, $1 800, terms 2/10, n/30.

4 Sold merchandise to Lee Mazilli, $450, terms EOM.

4 Paid CN the $75 ($70.09 plus $4.91 GST) delivery charges for the merchandise shipped to J. Coon.

6 Damaged merchandise was returned by J. Coon. A credit invoice was issued today for $230 (GST $14 and PST $16, $200 merchandise).

7 Received a cheque from B. Lailey for $314 in payment of her account. Since payment was received within the discount period, a $6 discount had been taken.

7 The weekly cash register tape showed cash and Visa sales of $7 530, GST $527.10, PST $602.40, total cash $8 659.50.

9 Sold merchandise to C. Corbett, $520, terms 2/10, n/30.

9 Refunded $46 to a customer who made a cash purchase on Jan. 7 (GST $2.80, PST $3.20, and $40 merchandise).

10 Received a cheque from L. Mako for $160 in full payment of his account.

14 Sales tax for the period was remitted to the provincial government. The tax collected totalled $3 900. Rivera Products was entitled to a 3-percent commission for collecting the tax.

16 Received a cheque from J. Coon in payment of the Jan. 2 invoice.

21 Cash and Visa sales for the week were $6 090, GST $426.30, PST $487.20, total cash $7 003.50.

22 A cheque was received today from C. Corbett for $586.04. A discount of $11.96 had been taken; however, the cheque had been received after the discount period. Therefore the discount was not granted.

30 Received a cheque from L. Mazilli in full payment of Jan. 4 invoice.

30 The Visa merchant statement was received today. The discount fee charged for the month of January was $357.

30 GST remittance to the Receiver General. GST Payable balance $6 839; GST Refundable balance $4 719.

Henley Rowing Supplies
Trial Balance
March 31, 2002

ACCOUNT TITLE	ACC. NO.	DEBIT	CREDIT
Cash	101	$ 6 300	
Accounts Receivable	110	2 900	
Merchandise Inventory, March 1	120	30 200	
Supplies	125	600	
Equipment	151	15 000	
Truck	152	8 000	
Furniture	153	45 000	
Accounts Payable	200		$ 2 500
PST Payable	205		400
GST Payable	206		900
GST Refundable	207	600	
Bank Loan (3 years)	210		6 500
W. Creighton, Capital	300		93 800
Sales	400		19 100
Sales Returns and Allowances	401	350	
Sales Discounts	402	50	
Purchases	500	8 300	
Purchases Returns and Allowances	501		325
Purchases Discounts	502		75
Transportation-in	503	600	
Salaries Expense	600	2 100	
Rent Expense	601	2 700	
Delivery Expense	602	300	
Miscellaneous Expense	603	475	
Visa Discount Expense	604	75	
MasterCard Discount Expense	605	50	
		$123 600	$123 600

Note: **The inventory March 31 is $24 500**

1. Use the information in the above trial balance for Henley Rowing Supplies.

   (a) Prepare a schedule of cost of goods sold.
   (b) Prepare an income statement.
   (c) Prepare a classified balance sheet.
   (d) Why does the ending inventory amount not appear on the trial balance prepared from Henley Rowing Supplies ledger on March 31?

2. Some of the account balances of Warrendon Sports for the month of May are shown on the following page.

   (a) Prepare a schedule of cost of goods sold.
   (b) Prepare an income statement.
   (c) Prepare the current asset section of the balance sheet.

Purchases Discounts	$ 25
Beginning Inventory	27 300
Purchases	9 100
Purchases Returns and Allowances	300
Transportation-in	450
Ending Inventory	30 200
Sales	21 400
Sales Returns and Allowances	350
Salaries Expense	3 400
Rent Expense	2 700
Delivery Expense	700
Other Expenses	1 700
Cash on Hand	3 500
Accounts Receivable	2 200
Supplies on Hand	500
Sales Discounts	70
Visa Discount Expense	50
MasterCard Discount Expense	75

3. Use the information in the trial balance for Warrendon Sports below.

   (a) Prepare a schedule of cost of goods sold.
   (b) Prepare an income statement.
   (c) Prepare a classified balance sheet.
   (d) Why does the ending inventory amount not appear on the trial balance prepared from Warrendon Sports' ledger on June 30?

Warrendon Sports
Trial Balance
June 30, 2002

ACCOUNT TITLE	ACC. NO.	DEBIT	CREDIT
Cash	101	$ 5 300	
Accounts Receivable	102	2 400	
Merchandise Inventory, August 1	120	30 200	
Supplies	125	600	
Furniture	150	27 000	
Equipment	151	15 000	
Truck	152	33 000	
Accounts Payable	200		$ 5 300
PST Payable	205		400
GST Payable	206		900
GST Refundable	207	300	
Bank Loan (3 years)	210		22 710
W. Creighton, Capital	300		78 000
Sales	400		22 400
Sales Returns and Allowances	401	500	
Sales Discounts	402	150	
Purchases	500	9 700	
Purchases Returns and Allowances	501		625
Purchases Discounts	502		115
Transportation-in	503	600	
Delivery Expense	601	300	
Miscellaneous Expense	602	475	
Rent Expense	603	2 200	
Salaries Expense	604	2 600	
Visa Discount Expense	605	75	
MasterCard Discount Expense	606	50	
		$130 450	$130 450

****Note:*** **The June 30 inventory is $22 700.**

CHAPTER 8

The Subsidiary Ledger System

UNIT 17 The Three-Ledger System

Learning Objectives

After reading this unit, discussing the applicable review questions, and completing the applications exercises, you will be able to do the following:

1. **EXPLAIN** the advantages of using a three-ledger system.
2. **DISCUSS** the relationship between the subsidiary ledger and a control account.
3. **VERIFY** each of the three ledgers by preparing a General Ledger trial balance, a schedule of accounts payable, and a schedule of accounts receivable.
4. **EXPLAIN** the division of labour principle and discuss its applicability to the subsidiary ledger system.

GENERAL LEDGER

As a business increases in size, the system used to record accounting data must be adapted in order to efficiently process an increasing amount of data. The General Ledger is one of the first areas that is affected by the growth of the firm.

Accounts Receivable

A growing firm normally has a rapid increase in the number of customers who purchase goods or services on account. Accounts must be kept for each customer to determine the amount owed and the date payment is due. The number of accounts receivable increases from a small number for a small firm just beginning business to a very large number for a large business. How does this affect the General Ledger? Look at Figure 8-1. The dramatic increase shown for the number of accounts receivable in the General Ledger makes it necessary to devise a more efficient system of ledger accounts.

FIGURE 8-1
Partial General Ledgers for small and large businesses

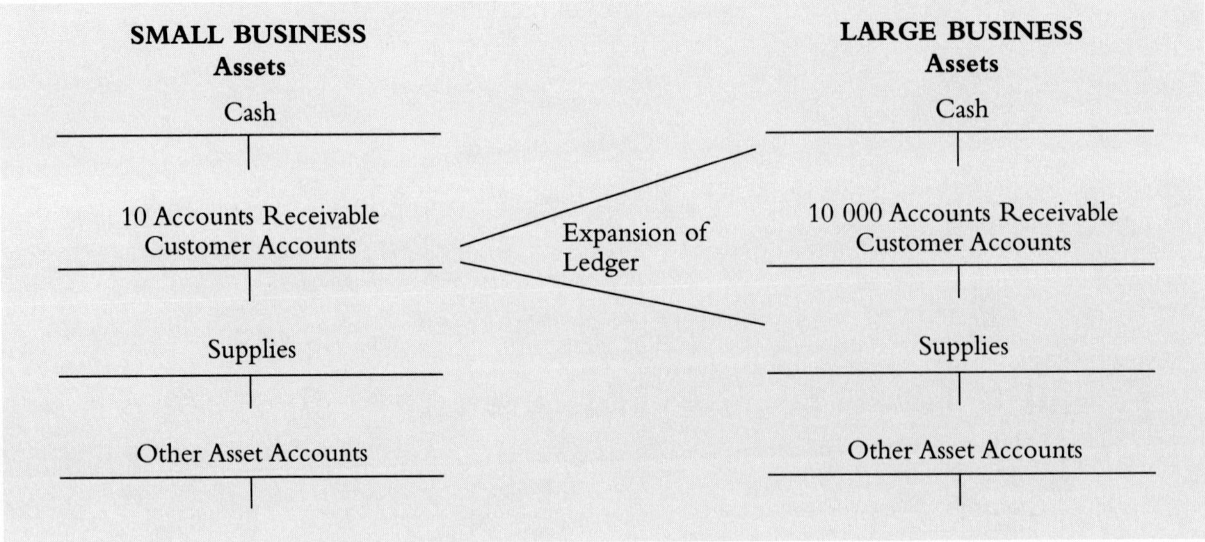

Effect on the Balance Sheet

Consider the effect of this expanded number of accounts receivable on the preparation of the balance sheet. If all the accounts receivable were listed individually on the balance sheet, it would result in a very lengthy financial statement. One of the primary objectives of financial reporting is to provide useful information to financial statement readers. The figure that interests statement readers is the total value of accounts receivable, not the value of each individual account receivable. Therefore, a total for accounts receivable would be more useful when preparing a balance sheet.

Accounts Payable

A similar situation develops in the accounts payable portion of the ledger as the business grows. The number of firms from which goods or services are purchased tends to increase as a business expands. It is necessary to keep individual accounts for each of these creditors in order to have an accurate record of the amount owed and the payment due date for each. If these data are all recorded in the General Ledger, the effect is the same as shown previously with the accounts receivable section. There would be a larger number of Accounts Payable accounts in the General Ledger and a very long balance sheet. A summary figure would be more useful on the balance sheet than a large number of individual accounts.

Adapting the General Ledger

An example using T-accounts will demonstrate how the accounting system is changed to handle this increased volume of information more efficiently and also provide the required balance sheet data. A partial ledger and trial balance for College Sales are shown in Figures 8-2 and 8-3. A small number of accounts receivable and payable are shown to demonstrate the concept. In reality, the number of these accounts could be in the thousands, but the change to the accounting system would be similar.

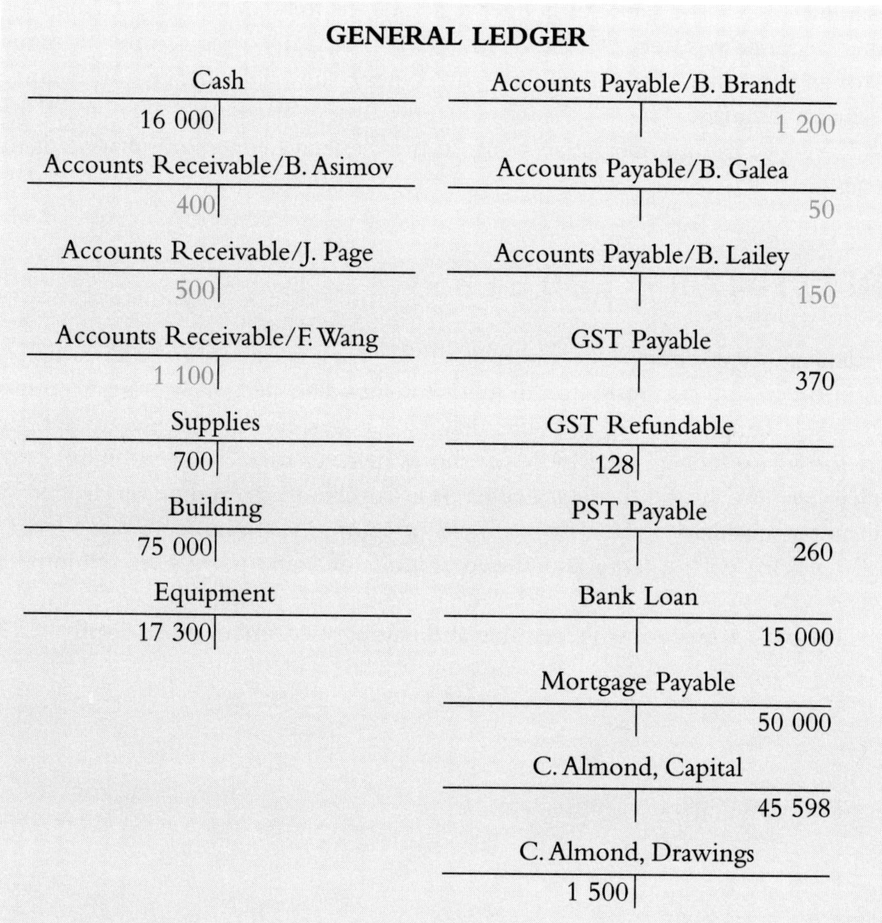

FIGURE 8-2
Partial General Ledger for College Sales

FIGURE 8-3
General Ledger trial balance for College Sales

College Sales Trial Balance September 30, 2001		
ACCOUNT TITLE	DEBIT	CREDIT
Cash	$16 000	
Accounts Receivable/B. Asimov	400	
Accounts Receivable/J. Page	500	
Accounts Receivable/F. Wang	1 100	
Supplies	700	
Building	75 000	
Equipment	17 300	
Accounts Payable/B. Brandt		$ 1 200
Accounts Payable/B. Galea		50
Accounts Payable/B. Lailey		150
GST Payable		370
GST Refundable	128	
PST Payable		260
Bank Loan		15 000
Mortgage Payable		50 000
C. Almond, Capital		45 598
C. Almond, Drawings	1 500	
	$112 628	$112 628

Figure 8-3 is the General Ledger trial balance for College Sales. Each customer account is listed separately. In a large company, there could be many customer accounts. Of course, this would make the trial balance and balance sheet very lengthy.

To reduce the number of accounts in the General Ledger, subsidiary ledgers are set up.

SUBSIDIARY LEDGERS

A subsidiary ledger is a group of accounts of one type usually organized in alphabetical order.

A *subsidiary ledger* contains accounts of similar type, usually organized in alphabetical order. The two most commonly used subsidiary ledgers are the Accounts Receivable Ledger and the Accounts Payable Ledger; however, these are not the only subsidiary ledgers used by businesses. Whenever there is a large number of similar accounts in the General Ledger, it is possible to streamline the ledger by utilizing a subsidiary ledger. An example of another common subsidiary ledger used by firms with a large and varied amount of equipment is an Equipment Ledger.

Let's look at Accounts Receivable and Payable Ledgers in more detail.

Accounts Receivable Ledger

The Accounts Receivable accounts are removed from the General Ledger and placed in a special customers' *Accounts Receivable Ledger* (see Figure 8-4 on page 248). Only the customer accounts (B. Asimov, J. Page, and F. Wang) are found in the Accounts Receivable Ledger.

The Accounts Receivable Ledger is a subsidiary ledger containing only customers' accounts in alphabetical order.

The Accounts Receivable control account replaces the individual customer accounts in the General Ledger.

The customers' accounts are replaced in the General Ledger by a single account called the *Accounts Receivable control account*. This account represents the total owing by all of the customers ($2 000) and is necessary in order that the General Ledger remain in balance. The balance in the Accounts Receivable control account should always equal the total of all of the individual customer accounts in the Accounts Receivable Ledger — that is why it is called a control account. Notice in Figure 8-4 that the balance in the Accounts Receivable control account in the General Ledger ($2 000) equals the total of the Accounts Receivable Ledger ($400 + $500 + $1 100).

Customer accounts are usually filed alphabetically in the Accounts Receivable Ledger and new accounts are inserted as required.

Accounts Payable Ledger

A business with many creditors often removes the creditors' accounts from the General Ledger and places them in alphabetical order in a subsidiary ledger called the *Accounts Payable Ledger.* The creditors' accounts are replaced in the General Ledger by an *Accounts Payable control account* (see Figure 8-4).

The Accounts Payable Ledger is a subsidiary ledger containing only creditors' accounts in alphabetical order.

The total of all of the individual creditors' accounts in the Accounts Payable Ledger ($1 200 + $50 + $150) should equal the balance of the Accounts Payable control account in the General Ledger ($1 400).

The Accounts Payable control account replaces the individual creditors' accounts in the General Ledger.

Summary

For every subsidiary ledger, there is a control account in the General Ledger. The total of the accounts in the subsidiary ledger must equal the balance of the related control account in the General Ledger.

VERIFYING THE ACCURACY OF THE LEDGERS

General Ledger Trial Balance

A trial balance is prepared to verify the mathematical accuracy of the General Ledger.

A *trial balance* is prepared to verify the mathematical accuracy of the General Ledger. The procedure to prepare the trial balance is exactly the same in the three-ledger system as in the single-ledger system we used previously. The only difference is that there is now a control account for Accounts Receivable and Accounts Payable rather than the individual Accounts Receivable accounts and Accounts Payable accounts.

FIGURE 8-4
Three-ledger system: General Ledger Accounts Receivable and Payable control accounts, Accounts Receivable Subsidiary Ledger, and Accounts Payable Subsidiary Ledger

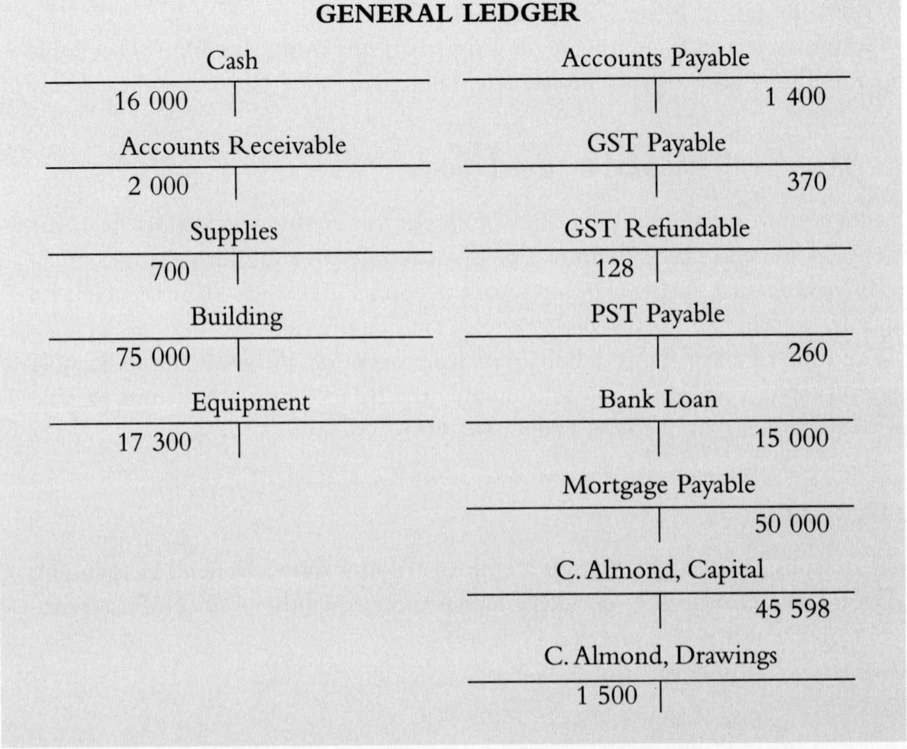

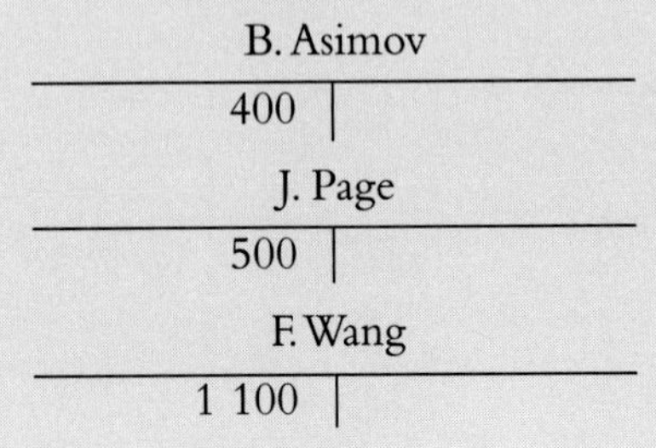

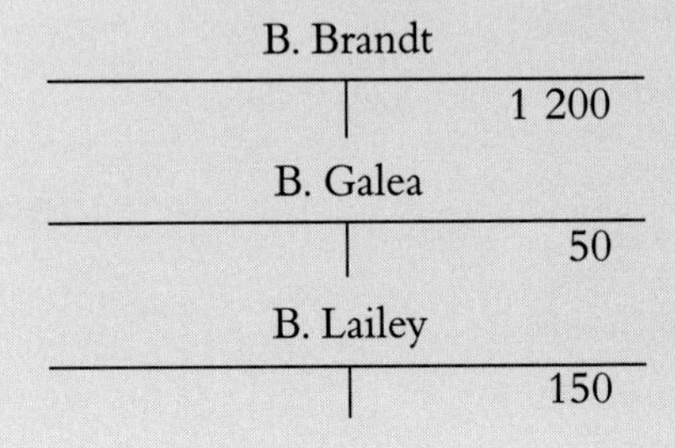

A General Ledger trial balance is shown in Figure 8-5. Notice that it contains an Accounts Receivable control account instead of individual customer accounts, and an Accounts Payable control account rather than individual creditor accounts.

FIGURE 8-5

General Ledger trial balance

College Sales
Trial Balance
September 30, 2001

ACCOUNT TITLE	DEBIT	CREDIT
Cash	$ 16 000	
Accounts Receivable	2 000	
Supplies	700	
Building	75 000	
Equipment	17 300	
Accounts Payable		$ 1 400
GST Payable		370
GST Refundable	128	
PST Payable		260
Bank Loan		15 000
Mortgage Payable		50 000
C. Almond, Capital		45 598
C. Almond, Drawings	1 500	
	$112 628	$112 628

Schedule of Accounts Receivable

The *schedule of accounts receivable* (Figure 8-6) is prepared to verify the accuracy of the Accounts Receivable Ledger. This schedule is a list of the customer accounts showing the balance of each account. The balances are totalled and must equal the value of the Accounts Receivable control account in the General Ledger in order to be correct.

A schedule of accounts receivable is prepared to prove the mathematical accuracy of the Accounts Receivable Ledger.

FIGURE 8-6

Schedule of accounts receivable

College Sales
Schedule of Accounts Receivable
September 30, 2001

B. Asimov	$1 400
J. Page	500
F. Wang	100
	$2 000 ← Equals the Accounts Receivable control account in the General Ledger

What is the total of the schedule in Figure 8-6? What is the balance of the Accounts Receivable control account in Figure 8-5?

Schedule of Accounts Payable

A schedule of accounts payable is prepared to prove the mathematical accuracy of the Accounts Payable Ledger.

A similar *schedule* or *list of accounts payable* is prepared from the subsidiary Accounts Payable Ledger. This is totalled and must equal the value of the Accounts Payable control account in the General Ledger. This verifies the correctness of the Accounts Payable Ledger.

FIGURE 8-7
Schedule of accounts payable

College Sales
Schedule of Accounts Payable
September 30, 2001

B. Brandt	$1 200
B. Galea	50
B. Lailey	150
	$1 400 ← Equals the Accounts Payable control account in the General Ledger

What is the total of the schedule in Figure 8-7? What is the balance of the Accounts Payable control account in Figure 8-4?

The College Sales example demonstrates a method of adapting or streamlining the accounting system to meet the needs of the business. Fraser Enterprises will be used throughout the remainder of the chapter to demonstrate how the concept is put into practice in an actual business.

ADVANTAGES OF SUBSIDIARY LEDGERS

There are two main advantages to using subsidiary ledgers in an accounting system:

- Division of labour
- Accounting control

Division of Labour Principle

In a small business, one employee may be able to handle all of the accounting tasks from journalizing to the preparation of the financial statements. In a larger firm that must record many business transactions each day, one person cannot handle all of the accounting work. Large firms find it necessary and more efficient to divide the work among several people, each of whom specializes in an area of accounting. Large firms identify the special accounting roles by the job titles accounts receivable clerk, accounts payable clerk, and accounting supervisor. Other companies may use other titles for these same jobs, such as junior clerk, posting clerk, senior accountant, chief accountant, or accounting manager.

Accounting Control

In a small business, the owner is involved in most of the transactions that take place. The owner can spot irregularities or errors made by employees or by other businesses with which the owner deals. A large business has a number of people involved in the handling and recording of transactions. A good accounting system controls the recording, the accuracy, and the honesty of the people involved. The control account balances in the General Ledger must equal the totals of the account balances in each of the subsidiary ledgers. When different people are responsible for each of the ledgers, they act as a check on the accuracy of one another's work.

REVIEW QUESTIONS

UNIT

1. In a larger business, why are the customer accounts removed from the General Ledger and placed in an Accounts Receivable Ledger?
2. What is the name of the account in the General Ledger that replaces all the individual customer accounts?
3. What is the name of the account in the General Ledger that replaces all the individual creditor accounts?
4. (a) What is the name of the ledger that contains only customer accounts?
   (b) What is the name of the ledger that contains only creditor accounts?
5. What is a control account? Give two examples.
6. What is a subsidiary ledger? Give two examples.
7. What are the three ledgers in a three-ledger system?
8. Give two advantages of using subsidiary ledgers.
9. From which ledger does one obtain the information required to prepare the financial statements?
10. (a) What account represents the customers in the General Ledger trial balance?
    (b) What account represents the creditors in the General Ledger trial balance?
11. (a) What is a schedule of accounts receivable?
    (b) What is a schedule of accounts payable?
12. (a) To what must the total of the schedule of accounts receivable be equal?
    (b) To what must the total of the schedule of accounts payable be equal?

UNIT 18 Accounting Systems

Learning Objectives

After reading this unit, discussing the applicable review questions, and completing the applications exercises, you will be able to do the following:

1. **PERFORM** the tasks of the accounts payable clerk, the accounts receivable clerk, and the accounting supervisor.
2. **EXPLAIN** the important principle and procedures used in a one-write system of accounting.
3. **EXPLAIN** the difference between manual and computer accounting systems.

The accounting system for a business consists of all the activities performed in order to provide the information needed to make business decisions. Managers rely on information provided by the accounting system in order to answer questions such as the following:

- Did we make a profit?
- Should we expand our business?
- Are sales increasing or decreasing?
- Are expenses increasing or decreasing?
- How efficient are the employees?
- Which products are most profitable?

Questions such as these can be answered when there is an effective accounting system to provide data. A company must record all transactions accurately. It must provide clear financial statements to its managers. If it does not, it will lose money and risk bankruptcy.

INTRODUCING FRASER ENTERPRISES

Figure 8-8 illustrates some of the parts of an accounting system. Each part is actually a subsystem. For example, the accounts receivable system consists of a series of tasks completed for all credit sales to customers.

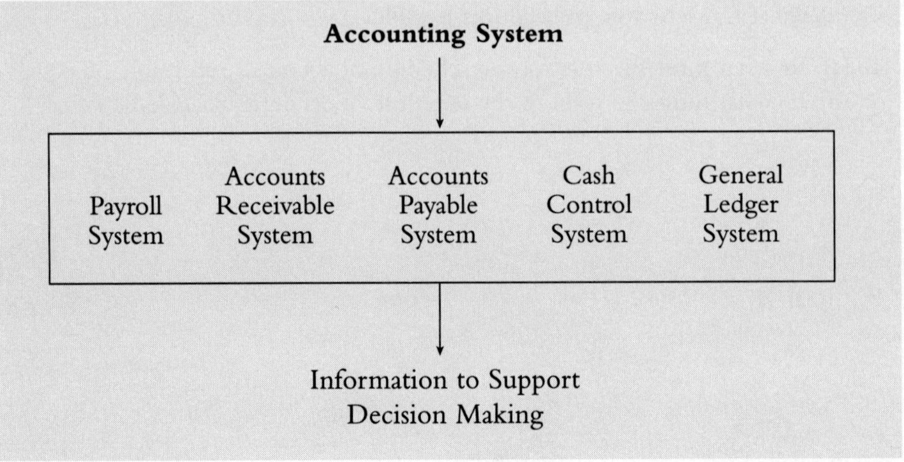

FIGURE 8-8
The accounting system provides information to management.

In this unit, part of the accounting system for a company called Fraser Enterprises will be described. The company is a wholesaler of heating and refrigeration equipment. It buys from the manufacturer and sells to companies that, in turn, sell or install the equipment. The company's head office is in Ottawa. It has branch offices in Moncton and Fredericton, New Brunswick; Halifax, Nova Scotia; and Pembroke, Sault Ste. Marie, Timmins, and Sudbury, Ontario. Among Fraser's customers are fuel oil dealers, engineering firms, and mechanical equipment firms.

PROCESSING DATA FOR THE ACCOUNTS PAYABLE SYSTEM

The five tasks listed below make up the accounts payable system for Fraser Enterprises:

Task 1: Processing purchases invoices
Task 2: Recording purchases invoices
Task 3: Paying creditors
Task 4: Updating creditors' accounts
Task 5: Preparing a schedule of accounts payable

At Fraser Enterprises, Mary Houlton, the accounts payable clerk, performs most of these tasks.

Duties of the Accounts Payable Clerk

Fraser Enterprises purchases goods and services from a number of suppliers or creditors. Mary Houlton started as a part-time data input clerk at Fraser Enterprises but, after a few months, she took over as accounts payable clerk in the Ottawa office. Now she is kept busy, full-time, just handling transactions involving accounts payable.

Figure 8-9 on page 254 is an invoice received from a creditor, Western Supply Ltd. Mary calls this a *purchase invoice* because Fraser Enterprises has purchased supplies from Western Supply Ltd. To process the invoice shown in Figure 8-9, Mary performs the accounting tasks for the accounts payable system.

A purchase invoice is a bill received from a creditor.

Task 1: Processing Purchases Invoices

Mary's first responsibility is to confirm that her company, Fraser Enterprises, ordered the goods specified in the invoice and that the total amount of the invoice is correct.

In a file of purchase orders that she maintains, Mary locates Purchase Order 683, sent out about a month before by Fraser to Western Supply Ltd. She checks to see that the order price and the invoice price are the same and that there are no mathematical errors on the invoice.

The details on the purchase invoice and purchase order must match.

Next, she must find out if the goods have actually been received. The person who receives and checks the goods completes a receiving report and sends a copy to Mary. Mary checks her file of receiving reports and locates a report showing that the goods have been received. The three documents — the purchase order, the purchase invoice, and the receiving report — are presented to a supervisor for approval before they are recorded.

Task 2: Recording Purchases Invoices

The approved invoice is returned to Mary, who records the amount owed to Western. First, Mary locates the account in the Accounts Payable Ledger and then raises the balance by entering a credit. (Remember, a liability increases on the credit side.)

The invoice, with the purchase order and receiving report attached, is now placed in a date file until it is due to be paid — which will be within the 30-day period specified on the invoice.

Task 3: Paying Creditors

When the invoice is due to be paid on February 3, Mary removes the invoice from the date file. A cheque with a copy is prepared and the original cheque is sent to the creditor.

Task 4: Updating Creditors' Accounts

Using the copy of the cheque as her source of information, Mary now decreases the balance owed to Western. It is Mary's job to maintain an accurate record of the amount owed to each creditor. She does this by recording purchases as credits and payments as debits.

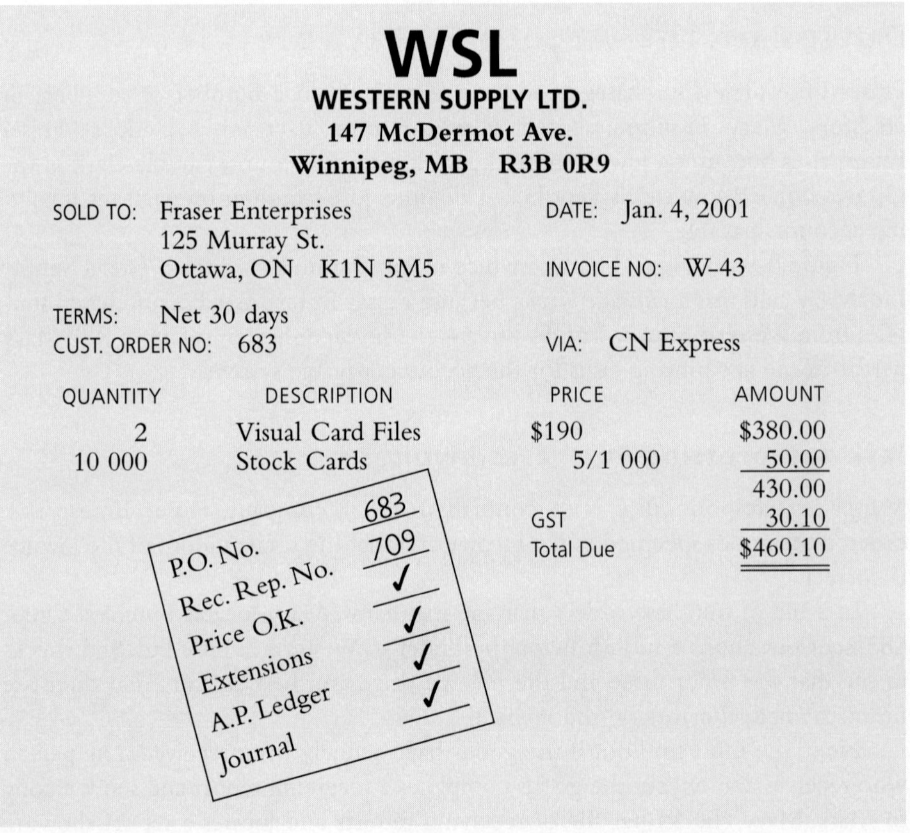

WSL
WESTERN SUPPLY LTD.
147 McDermot Ave.
Winnipeg, MB R3B 0R9

SOLD TO: Fraser Enterprises
125 Murray St.
Ottawa, ON K1N 5M5

DATE: Jan. 4, 2001

INVOICE NO: W-43

TERMS: Net 30 days
CUST. ORDER NO: 683

VIA: CN Express

QUANTITY	DESCRIPTION	PRICE	AMOUNT
2	Visual Card Files	$190	$380.00
10 000	Stock Cards	5/1 000	50.00
			430.00
		GST	30.10
		Total Due	$460.10

FIGURE 8-9
Purchase invoice received from Western Supply Ltd.

Task 5: Preparing a Schedule of Accounts Payable

Mary's job is highly specialized. She works with only one type of account — accounts payable, that is, with creditor accounts. She is responsible for the Accounts Payable Ledger. This is a ledger that contains only creditor accounts. Each month, Mary prepares a *schedule of accounts payable* as shown in Figure 8-10. This schedule is a listing of all the accounts payable with their balances. Figure 8-10, the February schedule, is a shortened version of a schedule of accounts payable. In reality, it would contain many more creditor accounts and would be several pages in length.

Fraser Enterprises
Schedule of Accounts Payable
February 28, 2001

Acme Ltd.	$ 200
Evans Co.	900
Falco Ltd.	400
Mentor Ltd.	500
	$2 000

FIGURE 8-10
Schedule of accounts payable

Mary's job as accounts payable clerk does not include journalizing the purchases invoices. This is done by the accounting supervisor who journalizes the source documents after Mary is through with them. Mary posts information directly into the Accounts Payable Ledger from the invoices and cheque copies. Figure 8-11 is a summary of Mary's duties.

Direct posting is the recording of information from source documents directly into ledger accounts.

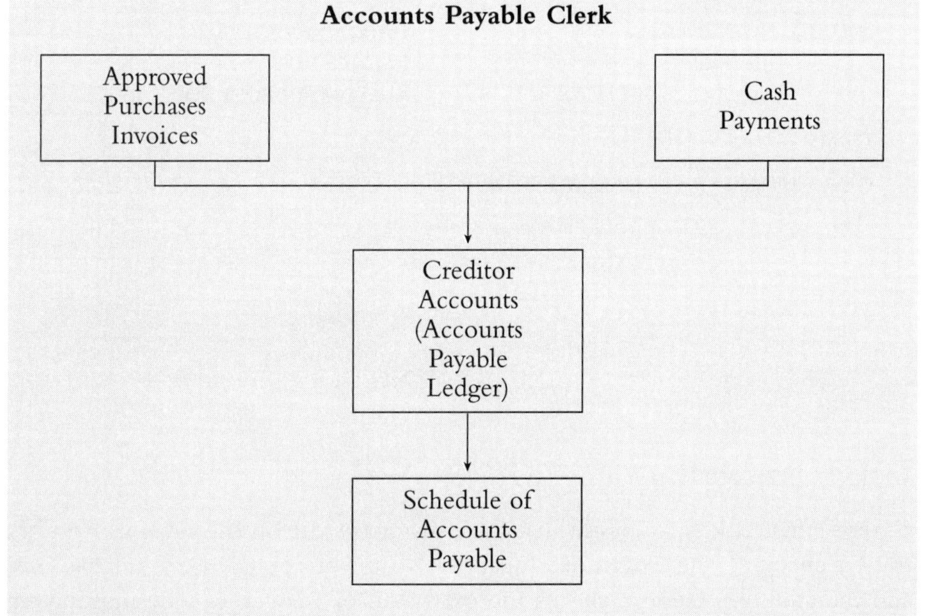

FIGURE 8-11
Duties of an accounts payable clerk

PROCESSING DATA FOR THE ACCOUNTS RECEIVABLE SYSTEM

The four tasks listed below make up the accounts receivable system for Fraser Enterprises:

Task 1: Processing sales invoices
Task 2: Recording sales invoices
Task 3: Processing cash received from customers
Task 4: Preparing a schedule of accounts receivable

Fraser Enterprises has so many customers that Mary Houlton is unable to service accounts receivable as well as accounts payable. A second accounting clerk, George Savard, handles transactions involving the customer accounts. His job title is accounts receivable clerk.

Duties of the Accounts Receivable Clerk

Figure 8-12 is a copy of a sales invoice sent to a customer, D. Meyer. When the sale was made to D. Meyer, an invoice was prepared in duplicate. The original copy was mailed to Meyer. The copy shown in Figure 8-12 was sent to George. To process the invoice shown in Figure 8-12, George performs the accounting tasks for the accounts receivable system.

FIGURE 8-12
Accounting department copy of the sales invoice sent to D. Meyer

Fraser Enterprises
125 Murray St., Ottawa, ON K1N 5M5

SOLD TO: D. Meyer
27 Lakeview Terrace
Ottawa, ON K1S 3H3

DATE: Feb. 2, 2001
INVOICE NO.: 671
CUSTOMER ORDER NO.: 43015

TERMS: Net 30 days

QUANTITY	DESCRIPTION	UNIT PRICE	AMOUNT
4	Electric Heaters, Model 8-C	$19.50	$78.00
		GST	5.46
		Total Due	$83.46

ACCOUNTING COPY

Task 1: Processing Sales Invoices

George's first task is to ensure that there are no errors on the invoice. He does this by checking the extensions (quantity × unit price), the GST calculations, and the addition. George checks the extension of Invoice 671 by multiplying the quantity (4) by the unit price ($19.50). He checks the GST by multiplying the extension ($78) by 7 percent. George then checks the addition to prove that the total ($83.46) shown on the invoice is correct.

Task 2: Recording Sales Invoices

George locates Meyer's account in the Accounts Receivable Ledger and increases the balance with a debit. (Remember, an account receivable is an asset and assets increase on the debit side.) George then initials the invoice and sends it, along with others he has processed, to his accounting supervisor.

Task 3: Processing Cash Received from Customers

When cash (currency, cheques, or money orders) is received from customers, a list is prepared showing the customers' names, the invoices being paid, and the amounts received. The money is deposited in the bank each day. George does not actually see the money but is given a list like the one in Figure 8-13.

George locates the accounts of the customers shown on the cash receipts list and reduces the balances in these accounts with credits. When George is through posting the invoices and daily cash receipts, he passes them on to the accounting supervisor for journalizing.

Fraser Enterprises
Daily Cash Receipts
Feb. 14, 2001

CUSTOMER	AMOUNT
W. Turko, Invoice 514	$ 50
C. Bard, Invoice 526	300
T. Roesler, Invoice 496	200
Total Deposited	$550

FIGURE 8-13
List of daily cash receipts

Task 4: Preparing a Schedule of Accounts Receivable

At the end of each month, George prepares a list showing the balance owed by each customer. A shortened version of this list, called the schedule of accounts receivable, is shown in Figure 8-14:

Fraser Enterprises
Schedule of Accounts Receivable
Feb 28, 2001

CUSTOMER	AMOUNT
C. Bard	$1 000
D. Meyer	700
T. Roesler	800
W. Turko	$1 000
	$3 500

FIGURE 8-14
Schedule of accounts receivable

As you will have noticed, George's job is also highly specialized. He deals with only one type of account — accounts receivable, that is, with customer accounts. A summary of George's duties is presented in Figure 8-15 on the next page.

FIGURE 8-15
Duties of an accounts receivable clerk

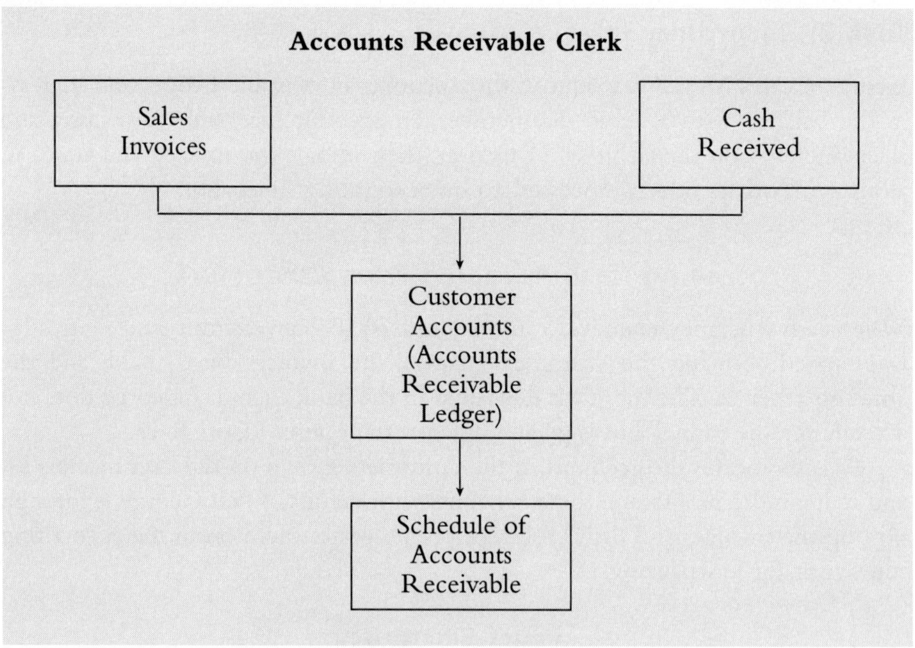

ACCOUNTING SUPERVISOR

As has been shown in the first two job descriptions, Fraser Enterprises employs two accounting clerks: the accounts payable clerk and the accounts receivable clerk. Both clerks answer to an accounting supervisor who fills a third accounting position in the department. Marni Roberts is the accounting supervisor at Fraser Enterprises. While she was going to school, Marni worked at Fraser as a part-time clerk. When she graduated from high school, she was hired as an accounts payable clerk. Several years later, Marni was promoted to the position of accounting supervisor. Her job involves the supervision of the work of the accounting clerks, the preparation of journal entries, the posting of journal entries to the General Ledger, and the preparation of a General Ledger trial balance.

Marni is given source documents after they have been posted directly to the Accounts Receivable and Accounts Payable Ledgers by George and Mary. The source documents involved are:

- Sales invoices (copies)
- List of cash receipts
- Purchases invoices
- Cheque copies

Figure 8-16 on the next page illustrates how these documents are processed by the accounting supervisor.

Preparing Journal Entries

The journal entries given under the next four headings are prepared to record the source documents sent to Marni from George and Mary.

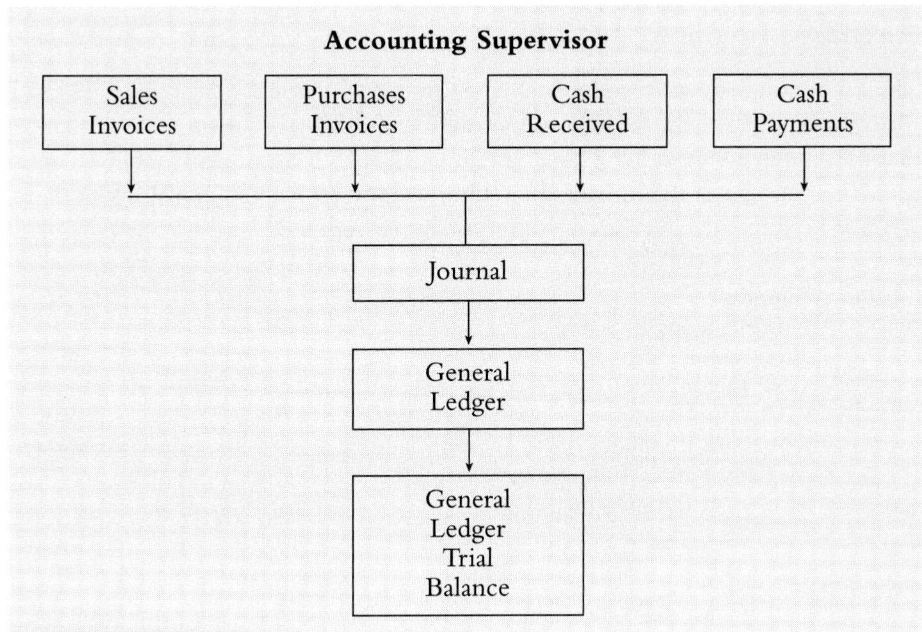

FIGURE 8-16
Documents processed by an accounting supervisor

Sales Invoices

The journal entry to record sales invoices is shown below. Notice that in this entry, individual customers are not debited. Instead, the Accounts Receivable account is debited. Also, several sales documents (Invoices 671–675) are totalled and recorded in one entry.

Feb. 4	Accounts Receivable	781.10	
	Sales		730.00
	GST Payable		51.10
	To record Invoices 671–675.		

List of Cash Receipts

The entry to record the cash received from customers is shown below. Notice that in this entry, the Accounts Receivable account is credited and not the individual customer accounts.

Feb. 4	Cash	550	
	Accounts Receivable		550
	To record cash receipts for Feb. 4.		

Purchases Invoices

The accounting supervisor's journal entry to record invoices for Supplies ($430), Miscellaneous Expense ($170), and Equipment ($700) is shown below. Notice that in this entry, several invoices are recorded. Also, the Accounts Payable account is credited instead of the individual creditor accounts. Can you explain why there are four accounts debited but only one account credited?

Feb. 4	Supplies	430	
	Miscellaneous Expense	170	
	Equipment	700	
	GST Refundable	91	
	Accounts Payable		1 391
	To record Purchases Invoices from Western Supply Ltd., Nelson Ltd., and Matheson Equipment.		

Cheque Copies

The entry to record payments to creditors is shown below. This entry records several documents (Cheques 71–73). The Accounts Payable account is debited instead of the individual creditor accounts.

Feb. 4	Accounts Payable	1 200	
	Cash		1 200
	To record Cheques 71–73.		

Posting the Journal

The General Ledger is the main ledger and contains all asset, liability, equity, revenue, and expense accounts.

Marni is also responsible for posting the journal entries to the General Ledger. When these entries have been posted to the General Ledger, the Accounts Receivable account in the General Ledger has the same balance as the total of the balances of the customer accounts in the Accounts Receivable Ledger. Remember that the sales invoices were recorded as debits in the customer accounts, and the cash amounts received were recorded as credits in the customer accounts by George, the accounts receivable clerk.

The Accounts Payable account in the General Ledger also has the same balance as the total of the balances in the creditor accounts in the Accounts Payable Ledger. Remember that the purchases invoices and cash payments (cheque copies) were recorded by Mary, the accounts payable clerk.

All the source documents have been recorded twice: once by the accounting supervisor and once by the accounting clerks. This is necessary if the balances of the control accounts in the General Ledger are to equal the total of the accounts in the subsidiary ledgers.

Preparing Other Journal Entries

The accounting supervisor is responsible for journalizing all source documents, not just those involving accounts receivable and accounts payable. Some examples of other journal entries made by Marni follow:

(1) A $200 cash sale was made:

Feb. 8	Cash	214	
	Sales		200
	GST Payable		14
	Cash sale.		

(2) The owner invested $5 000:

Feb. 8	Cash	5 000	
	D. Fraser, Capital		5 000
	Additional investment.		

(3) Cheque 74 for $200 was issued to pay the telephone bill:

Feb. 9	Telephone Expense	186.92	
	GST Refundable	13.08	
	Cash		200
	Cheque 74.		

(4) The owner withdrew $100 for personal use:

Feb. 15	D. Fraser, Drawings	100	
	Cash		100
	Cheque 75, personal use.		

Summary of Direct Posting Procedure

A summary of the direct posting procedure used by Fraser Enterprises is illustrated below.

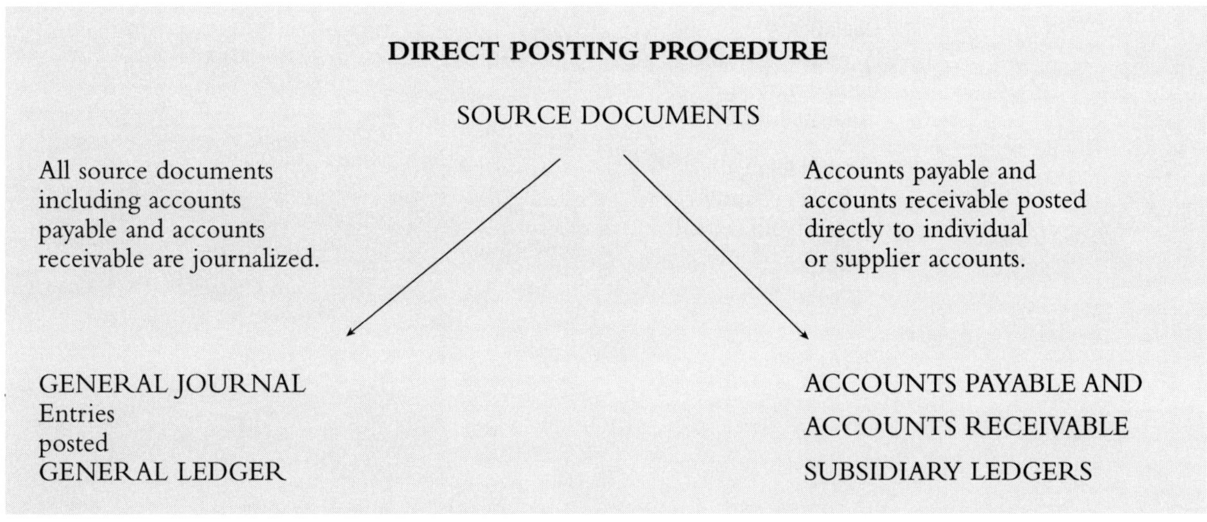

SUBSIDIARY LEDGERS SUMMARY

The three previous job descriptions have served as a basic introduction to subsidiary ledgers; a more detailed examination of the theory of subsidiary ledger accounting will now be made.

It is clear from the accounting procedures already covered in this chapter that a company like Fraser Enterprises needs more than one ledger to efficiently process and control the accuracy of its accounting data. Since Fraser Enterprises has numerous creditors and several hundred customers, it would, of course, be inconvenient to list them all on the balance sheet. Instead, the total owing by all the customers ($3 500) is indicated on the balance sheet by the Accounts Receivable account as shown in Figure 8-17 below. The total owing to all creditors ($2 000) is represented by the Accounts Payable account which is also shown in Figure 8-17. Both the Accounts Receivable and the Accounts Payable control accounts are found in the main or General Ledger.

The General Ledger is a file of all accounts used to prepare the financial statements.

In addition, the General Ledger contains all the asset, liability, equity, revenue, and expense accounts. The *General Ledger* is a file of all the accounts that are used to prepare the financial statements — both the income statement and the balance sheet.

A subsidiary ledger is a group of accounts of one type.

In order to effectively process the large number of customer and creditor account transactions, separate or *subsidiary ledgers* such as the Accounts Receivable Ledger and the Accounts Payable Ledger are used.

Before looking more closely at the two subsidiary ledgers used by Fraser Enterprises, remember that subsidiary ledgers are usually organized in alphabetical order. In the General Ledger, all accounts are numbered. For example, Cash may be number 100 and Capital may be number 300.

FIGURE 8-17
Balance sheet for Fraser Enterprises

Fraser Enterprises Balance Sheet February 28, 2001		
Assets		
Cash	$ 2 000	
Accounts Receivable	3 500	
Supplies	500	
Building	60 000	
Equipment	3 000	
Total Assets		$69 000
Liabilities and Owner's Equity		
Liabilities		
Accounts Payable	$ 2 000	
Bank Loan	20 000	
Total Liabilities		$22 000
Owner's Equity		
D. Fraser, Capital		47 000
Total Liabilities and Owner's Equity		$69 000

Accounts Receivable Ledger

In many firms like Fraser Enterprises, the Accounts Receivable accounts are removed from the General Ledger and placed in a special customers' *Accounts Receivable Ledger.* This subsidiary ledger is required to record the details of the large number of customer accounts of such businesses. Only the customer accounts are found in this Accounts Receivable Ledger.

The Accounts Receivable Ledger is a subsidiary ledger containing only customers' accounts.

The customers' accounts are replaced in the General Ledger by a single account called the *Accounts Receivable control account.* This account represents the total owing by all the customers and is necessary in order that the General Ledger remain in balance. The balance in the Accounts Receivable control account should always equal the total of all the individual customer accounts in the Accounts Receivable Ledger — that is why it is called a control account. Customer accounts are usually filed alphabetically in the Accounts Receivable Ledger and new accounts are inserted as required.

Accounts Payable Ledger

A business with many creditors often removes the creditors' accounts from the General Ledger and places them in a subsidiary ledger called the *Accounts Payable Ledger.* The creditors' accounts are replaced in the General Ledger by an *Accounts Payable control account.*

The Accounts Payable Ledger is a subsidiary ledger containing only creditors' accounts.

GENERAL LEDGER

Account	Debit	Credit
Cash	2 000	
Equipment	3 000	
Accounts Receivable	3 500	
Accounts Payable		2 000
Supplies	500	
Bank Loan		20 000
Building	60 000	
D. Fraser, Capital		47 000

ACCOUNTS RECEIVABLE LEDGER

Account	Debit	Credit
C. Bard	1 000	
D. Meyer	700	
T. Roesler	800	
W. Turko	1 000	

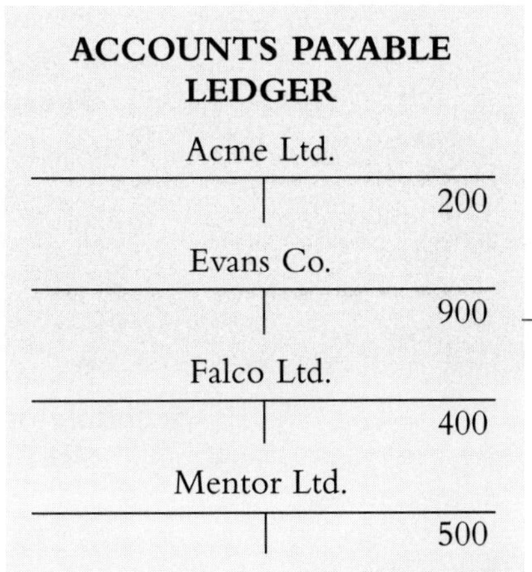

ACCOUNTS PAYABLE LEDGER

Account	Debit	Credit
Acme Ltd.		200
Evans Co.		900
Falco Ltd.		400
Mentor Ltd.		500

FIGURE 8-18
Simplified examples of the General Ledger and two subsidiary ledgers used by Fraser Enterprises

The total of all the individual creditors' accounts in the Accounts Payable Ledger should equal the balance of the Accounts Payable control account in the General Ledger. Accounts in the Accounts Payable Ledger are also organized alphabetically. Figure 8-18 shows the relationship of the three ledgers. Notice that the total of the Accounts Receivable Ledger is $3 500 ($1 000 + $700 + $800 + $1 000) and is equal to the balance in Accounts Receivable, the control account in the General Ledger. Similarly, the total of the Accounts Payable Ledger, $2 000 ($200 + $900 + $400 + $500), is equal to the balance in Accounts Payable, the control account in the General Ledger.

Proof of Accuracy of Ledgers

Each ledger should be proven to be mathematically accurate on a regular basis, for example, monthly. The proof of the accuracy of the General Ledger is a trial balance in which the debit total equals the credit total. The Accounts Receivable Ledger is proven to be correct if the total of the schedule of accounts receivable is equal to the balance of the Accounts Receivable control account in the General Ledger. Similarly, the total of the schedule of accounts payable should be equal to the balance of the Accounts Payable control account in the General Ledger. Remember this general rule:

> *For every subsidiary ledger, there is a control account in the General Ledger. The total of the accounts in the subsidiary ledger must equal the balance of the related control account in the General Ledger.*

FIGURE 8-19

Subsidiary ledger account totals must equal the balance of the related control account in the General Ledger.

Fraser Enterprises
General Ledger Trial Balance
February 28, 2001

Cash	$ 2 000	
Accounts Receivable	3 500	
Supplies	500	
Building	60 000	
Equipment	3 000	
Accounts Payable		$ 2 000
Bank Loan		20 000
D. Fraser, Capital		47 000
	$69 000	$ 69 000

Fraser Enterprises
Schedule of Accounts Receivable
February 28, 2001

C. Bard	$ 1 000
D. Meyer	700
T. Roesler	800
W. Turko	1 000
	$ 3 500

Fraser Enterprises
Schedule of Accounts Payable
February 28, 2001

Acme Ltd.	$ 200
Evans Co.	900
Falco Ltd.	400
Mentor Ltd.	500
	$ 2 000

Additional Subsidiary Ledgers

Two common examples of subsidiary ledgers have been described in this chapter. However, these are not the only subsidiary ledgers used by businesses. A *subsidiary ledger* is a ledger containing accounts of the same type with a control account replacing the individual accounts in the General Ledger. Therefore, whenever there are a large number of similar accounts in the General Ledger, it is possible to streamline the ledger by utilizing a subsidiary ledger. An example of another common subsidiary ledger used by firms with a large and varied amount of equipment is an Equipment Ledger.

JOURNALIZING BATCH TOTALS

Journalizing batch totals is a technique used to efficiently record similar transactions that are frequently repeated. Suppose a business issues 35 invoices to customers over a short period of time. For each invoice, a journal entry such as this is made by the accounting supervisor:

Feb. 5	Accounts Receivable	107	
	Sales		100
	GST Payable		7
	To record Invoice 101.		

However, rather than record this entry 35 separate times for each invoice, a total may be taken of all the invoices and this total recorded as follows:

Feb. 5	Accounts Receivable	4 494	
	Sales		4 200
	GST Payable		294
	To record Invoices 101–135 for sales on account.		

This concept of grouping source documents and recording the total is called *journalizing batch totals.* It can be applied to a variety of documents. This is the entry made when cash receipts are batched:

Journalizing batch totals is the recording of the total of a number of source documents of one type in a single journal entry.

Feb. 5	Cash	2 200	
	Accounts Receivable		2 200
	To record cash received from customers Feb. 1–5.		

Payments made to creditors may also be journalized in batches. For example, a series of cheque copies are journalized as follows:

Feb. 5	Accounts Payable	3 000	
	Cash		3 000
	Cheques 619–638.		

Purchases invoices may be grouped together as well. However, the entry to record purchases invoices may have more than one debit if different items were purchased. The following journal entry illustrates this situation:

Feb. 5	Office Supplies	500	
	Equipment	2 000	
	Heating Expense	300	
	Miscellaneous Expense	100	
	GST Refundable	203	
	Accounts Payable		3 103
	To record purchases Feb. 1–5.		

Summary of Indirect Posting Procedure

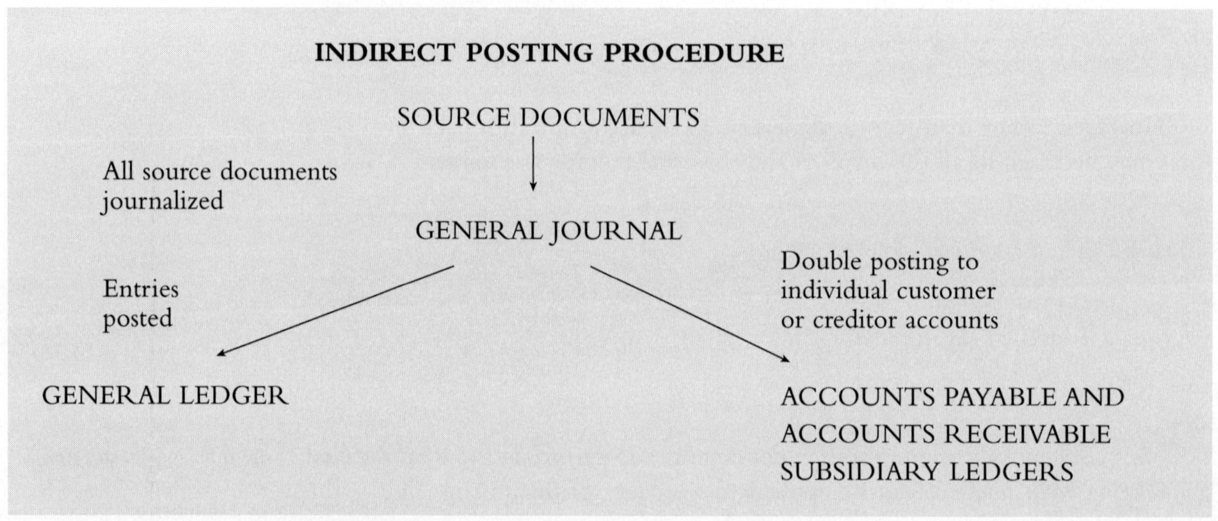

DATA COLLECTION

The information for the subsidiary ledgers can be recorded in a variety of ways depending on the size of the business. The concepts demonstrated in the manual system used by Fraser Enterprises are consistent in all systems since only the data collection method changes. These methods fall into three major categories:

- Manual system
- One-write system
- Computerized system

Manual System

A few firms record all accounting data manually. These firms may use a three-ledger system in order to have up-to-date accounts receivable and payable information. Different people specialize in recording information in the ledgers assigned to them. This system has been fully explained previously in this chapter.

One-Write System

As a business increases in size, it becomes necessary to hire additional staff to process the larger number of accounts receivable and payable. A one-write system is a method of recording accounting information that is faster than a manual system but not as sophisticated as a computerized system. It is still used in many small and medium-sized businesses to make the recording of accounts receivable and payable more efficient.

Computerized System

Most firms use computerized accounts receivable and payable software packages to improve the efficiency of recording into the subsidiary ledgers. Transactions are entered into the computer's data bank of accounting information. The accounts receivable module of the software program processes the data, updates the accounts, and provides a variety of output. The software program generates reports such as the schedule of accounts receivable, as well as a print-out of the accounts showing transaction details.

THE COMPUTERIZED SYSTEM

Up to this point, you have been doing problems and exercises manually, that is, writing by hand the solutions to assignments. As you will see, there are many tasks in accounting that are repeated. For example, sales are made and recorded every day and balance sheets are prepared every month. Such repetitive tasks are ideal for a computer. Consequently, accountants view the computer as a very helpful tool.

Computers can do the following tasks very quickly:

- Perform mathematical tasks
- Store large amounts of information
- Retrieve stored information
- Classify, sort, summarize, move, and compare information

These are all tasks routinely performed by accountants, so it makes sense for accountants to make use of the power and speed of computers. When a computer is combined with other equipment such as printers, additional terminals, and other communication devices, the resulting computer system becomes a very powerful tool.

COMPARING MANUAL AND COMPUTER ACCOUNTING

Manual Accounting Characteristics

Figure 8-20 below illustrates the steps to complete the accounting cycle. The steps are shown in the order that they are performed when accounting is done by hand, that is, manually. Each step requires that the data be rewritten.

FIGURE 8-20
Steps in a manual accounting system

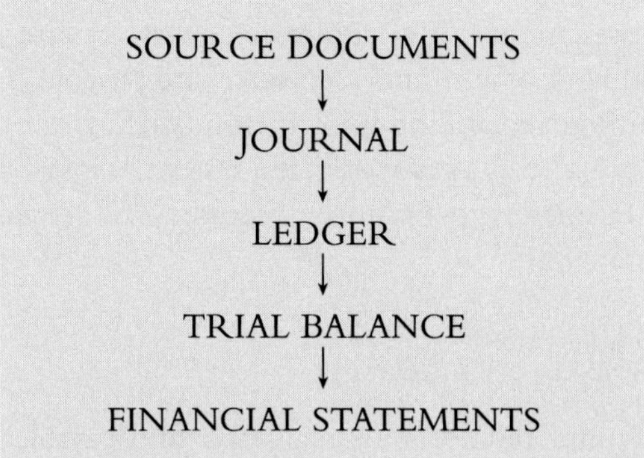

Computer Accounting Characteristics

Computers have very large storage (memory) capacities. They also have the capability to manipulate and process data in a variety of ways and with great speed. This includes the ability to handle mathematical tasks, such as calculating the balance in accounts, and to print documents.

When accounting data have been input, the computer processes the data and then provides a variety of output (reports). The nature of the processing and the output is determined by the software programs that run the computer system.

Now look at Figure 8-21. The same steps as in Figure 8-20 are illustrated in this figure, but they are listed in the order in which they are completed in a computerized accounting system.

In a computerized accounting system, the accounting cycle is reduced to just three basic steps:

(1) Inputting data
(2) Processing data
(3) Outputting data

FIGURE 8-21
Steps in a computerized accounting system

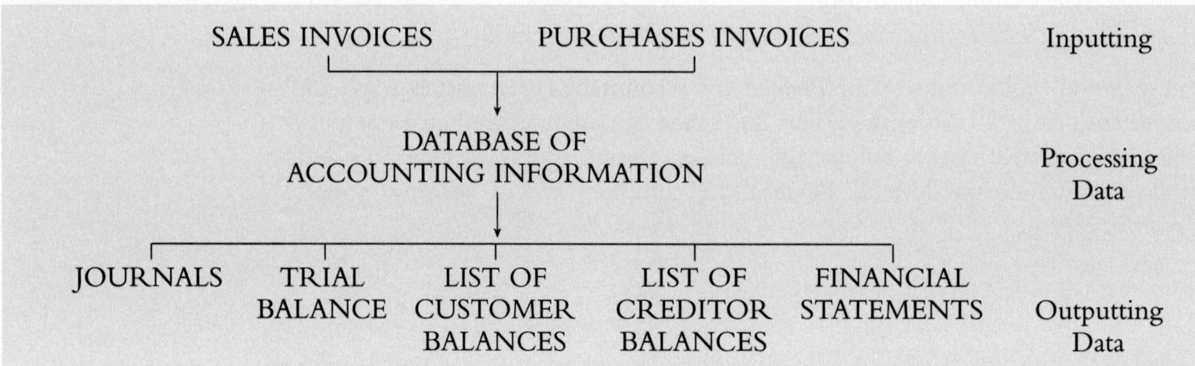

Step 1: Inputting Data

Source documents are the source of information for the computer operator. A source document is prepared for every transaction, and the information is entered into the computer system from the source document. Some companies, however, prefer to list the source documents on a data entry sheet prior to computer entry.

Step 2: Processing Data

All the information concerning transactions is stored in the computer's "memory." Here it forms a database (or data bank) of accounting information. This database of information can be manipulated (processed) in a variety of ways. The software program determines what processing will actually occur. The result of the processing can be printed as "output." It can be recalled from memory and used in a variety of ways depending on the type of output desired. The information does not have to be re-entered each time it is to be used for a report or form. Even though it has been used, it is still stored in memory and can be used again for a different report.

Step 3: Outputting Data

Output refers to the information produced by the computer. Information can be produced in a variety of ways, including printed reports, visual reports on the computer monitor, or electronic reports which can be used by computers.

As illustrated in Figure 8-21, the output can be a journal, a trial balance, ledger account information, or financial statements. The actual type and format of the report is determined by the needs of the company. Of course, a software program that is capable of producing the desired reports must be designed or purchased.

Because of the processing ability of a computer, more detailed schedules can be produced automatically. Once accounting information has been input, it becomes a database of information. Most accounting software programs are capable of producing a schedule such as the one in Figure 8-22 on page 270. Notice that it reports how old each customer's debt is. For example, the $2 100 owed by Ashburton Reinforcing has been owed for 61 to 90 days. It should have been paid within 30 days. This is valuable information and has been produced automatically by the computer.

Summary

The main difference between manual and computer accounting is the ability of the computer to store large amounts of data and to process those data in a variety of ways. The data are only entered into the system once. In a manual system, each accounting step requires that data be written and processed separately.

Information entered into a computerized accounting system forms a database of accounting information. The software program can access and process the information in the database and use it to produce a variety of output. Once information is in the database, it can be "pulled out" in a variety of ways — in the form of a journal, as ledger accounts, or as financial reports. The information does not have to be re-entered each time. In a manual accounting system, each form or report must be written individually. This means that the same information must be obtained and written out each time that a form or report is prepared.

FIGURE 8–22
Computer-prepared schedule of accounts receivable *(Courtesy Computer Associates Canada Limited)*

Universal Construction
Customer Summary, Jun. 15, 2001

	TOTAL	CURRENT	31–60	61–90	91+
24 Alberta Prefab Limited	$ 9 600.00	$ 9 600.00	—	—	—
31 Ashburton Reinforcing	2 100.00	—	—	$ 2 100.00	—
2 Asken Shopping Centre	37 472.12	7 500.00	$25 456.87	4 515.25	—
8 Bayswater School Board	10 500.00	10 500.00	—	—	—
4 Belvedere Nursing Home	6 950.00	6 450.00	—	500.00	—
23 Claridges Bakeries Ltd.	67.50	67.50	—	—	—
13 District of Slocan	599.50	599.50	—	—	—
33 Draperies Unlimited	2 550.00	—	2 550.00	—	—
21 Dunedin Development Corp.	10 576.25	2 076.25	—	8 500.00	—
18 Englhard Winery	6 000.00	—	—	6 000.00	—
15 Flannegan Hotel	8 550.00	6 050.00	—	2 500.00	—
35 Forgarty Motors	4 500.00	—	4 500.00	—	—
	$99 465.37	$42 843.25	$32 506.87	$24 115.25	—

COMPUTER SYSTEM COMPONENTS

There are two main components to a computer system — the hardware and the software. The monitor, keyboard, printer, and other metal and plastic parts of a computer system are known as *hardware.*

Computer programs are called *software.* A *program* is a set of instructions that tells the computer what to do. Computer hardware does not function without the instructions provided by software. The operator decides which instructions are to be used and then communicates the instructions to the computer system. There are several different methods used to communicate instructions to the computer system, including commands, special function keys, and selections from a menu.

ACCOUNTS RECEIVABLE APPLICATION SOFTWARE

Accounts Receivable software packages are designed to perform the routine procedures involved in journalizing and posting transactions to the subsidiary ledgers. Once accounting information has been input in either of these modules, it is combined (integrated) with information from other modules. The following example examines how the accounts receivable module is used to record transactions involving Accounts Receivable.

Selecting the Accounts Receivable Menu

When an integrated software program is loaded onto a computer, a main menu similar to the one shown in Figure 8-23 is displayed on the screen.

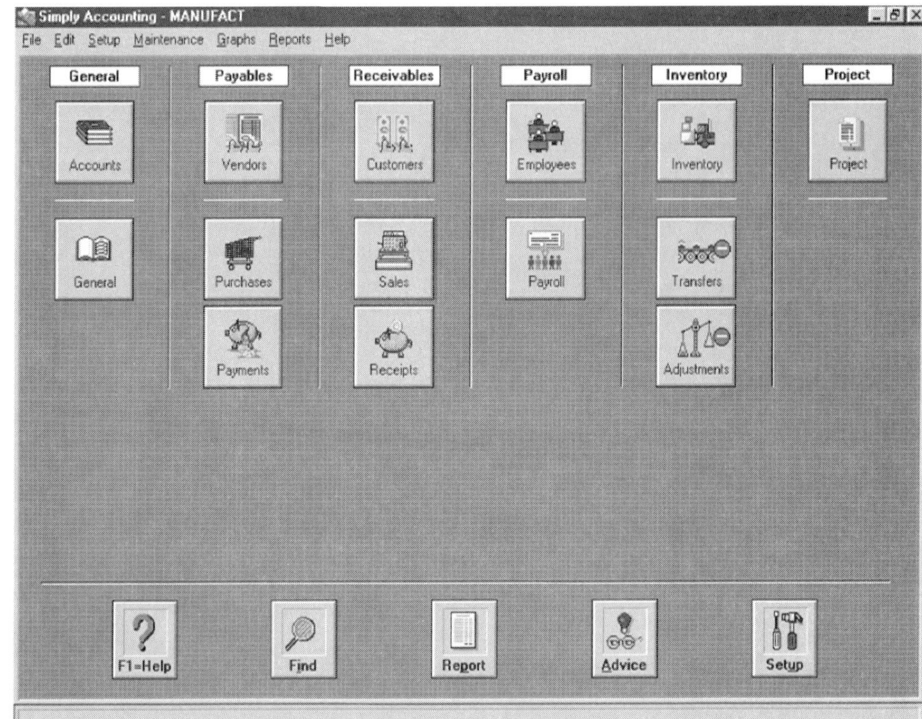

FIGURE 8-23
Main Menu

Let's assume you want to record customer transactions. First, you would locate the Receivables column in the main menu. The monitor will display a series of accounts receivable choices. There are three choices available under Receivables.

- Customers: Shows a list of current customers and allows you to add new customer lists or to modify existing ones
- Sales: Allows you to prepare sales invoices and to post sales on account to the ledger
- Receipts: Allows you to record customer payments on account and post to the ledger

Recording a Credit Sale

To record a sales invoice (a sale on credit to a customer), place your mouse pointer on Sales (Figure 8-24). When you click the mouse, the monitor will display a blank sales invoice (Figure 8-25). You have the opportunity to choose the customer name from the customer file by using the drop-down menu opposite Sold on the invoice (Figure 8-26). The drop box opens to display a customer list (Figure 8-27). When you click on a customer, Sold to/Ship to information is automatically completed. Figure 8-28 shows the invoice for Sand Sales ready to record the sales information.

FIGURE 8–24
Accounts Receivable Column

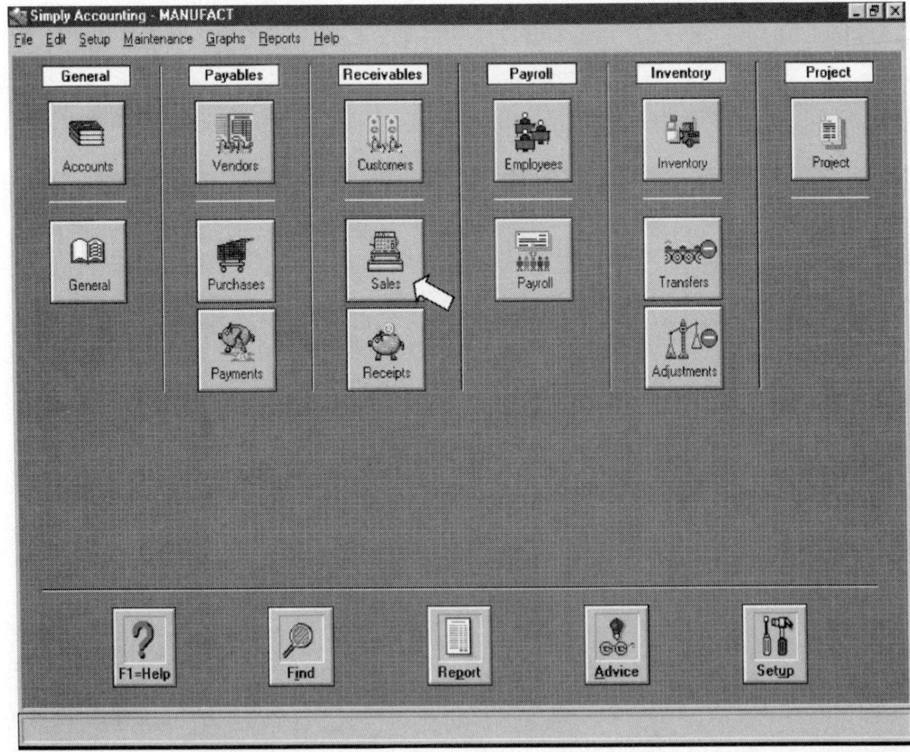

FIGURE 8–25
Sales Invoice

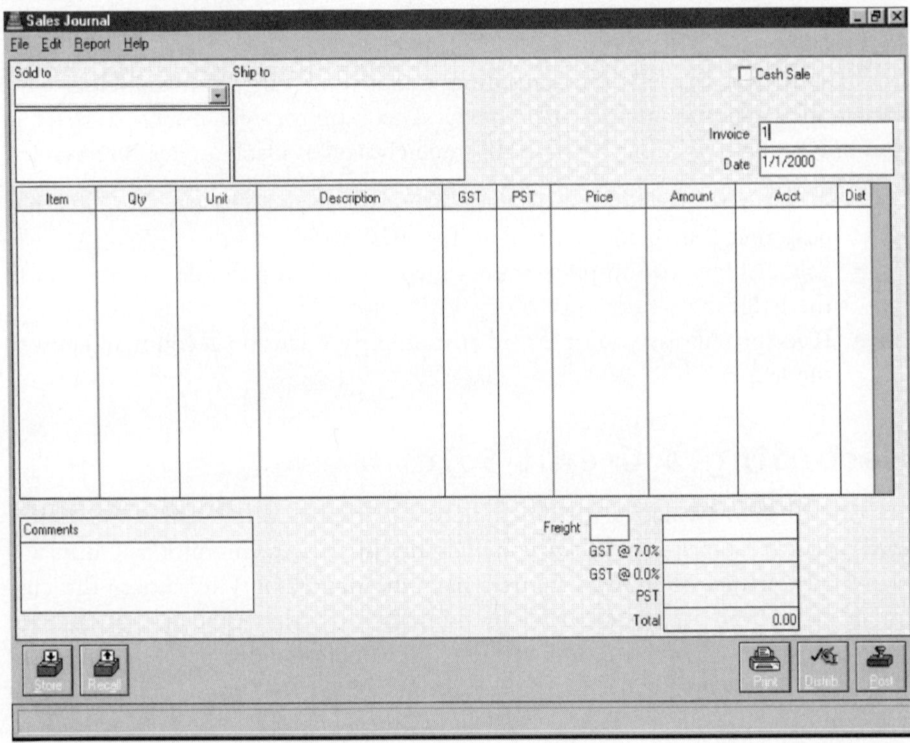

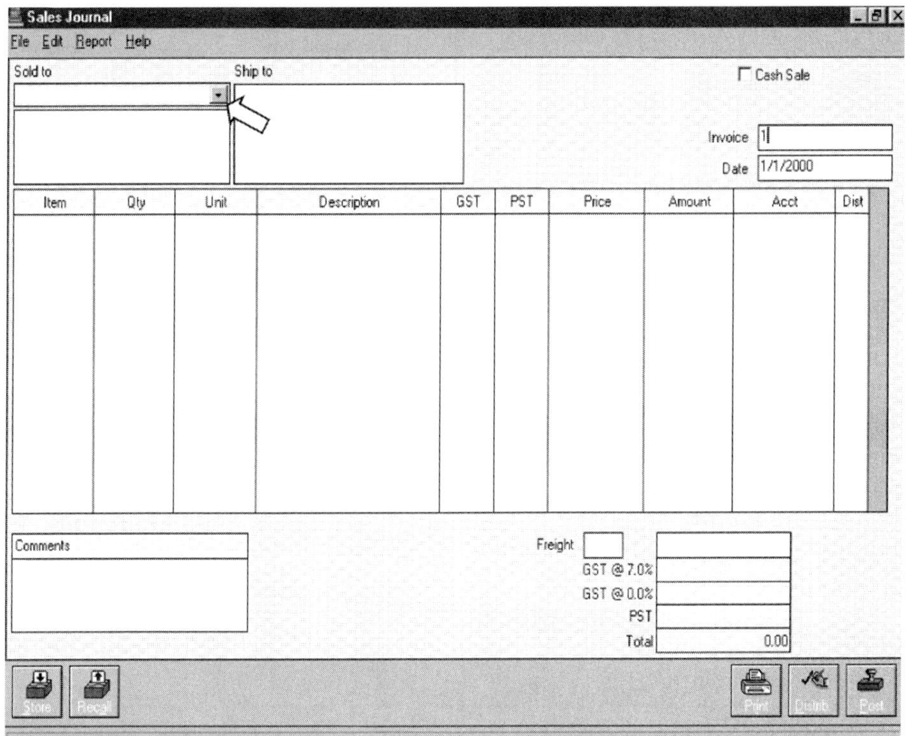

FIGURE 8–26
Drop Down Customer Menu

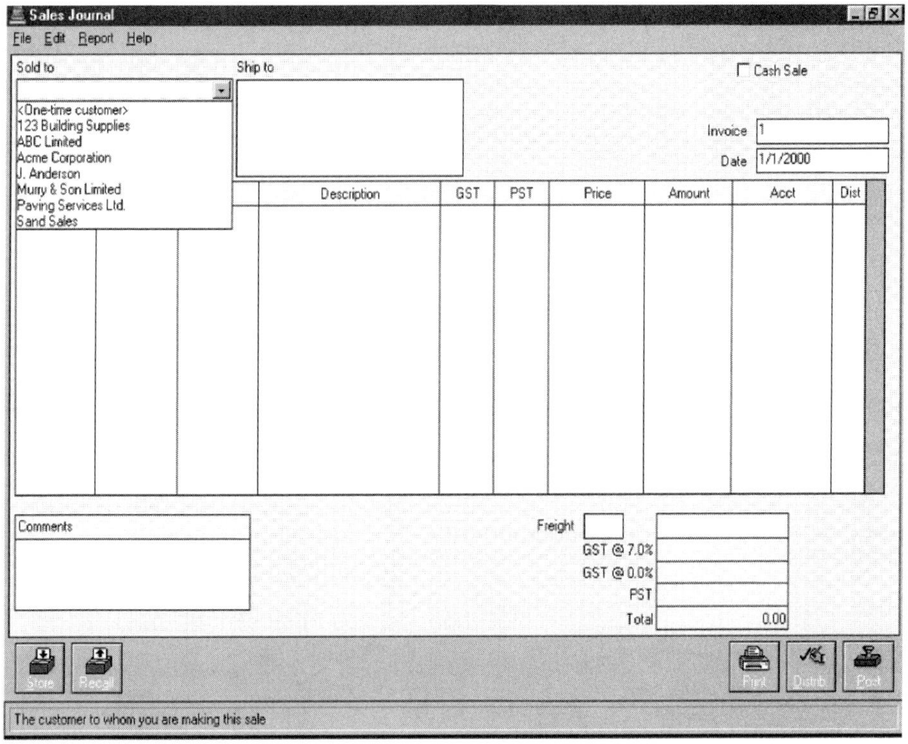

FIGURE 8–27
Customer List

FIGURE 8–28
Customer Invoice

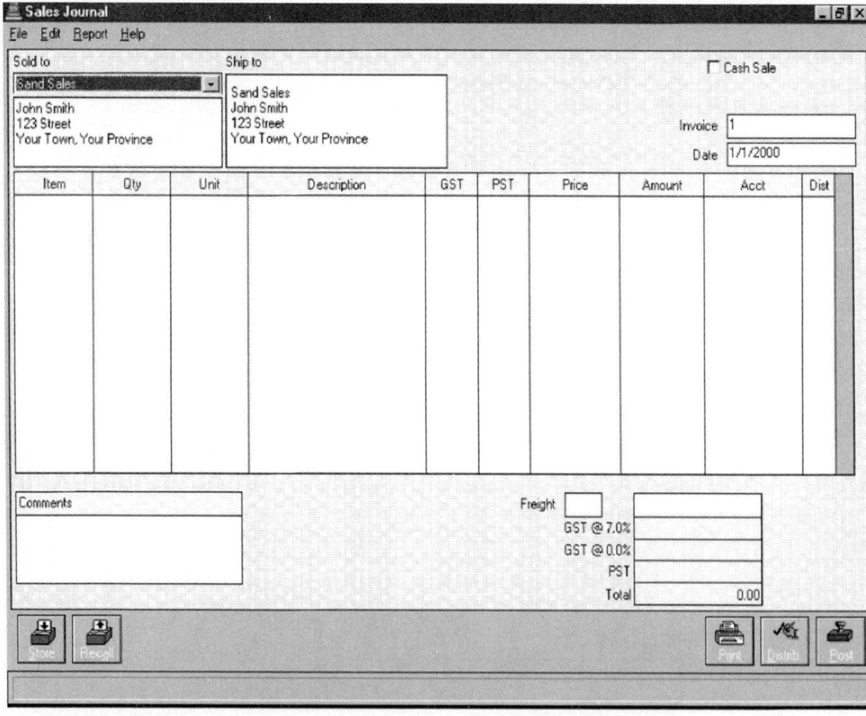

The software will prepare the journal entry and also print the invoice to be sent to the customer. Invoice details are completed as follows:

- Details regarding the items purchased by the client
- The taxes are calculated automatically

Figure 8-29 shows the completed invoice for Sand Sales. Clicking on the Printer logo will print the invoice to be mailed to the customer. Clicking on the Post box will generate the necessary journal entry and post it to the ledger. The entry is shown in Figure 8-30.

FIGURE 8–29
Completed Sales Invoice

Sales Journal
File Edit Report Help

Sold to: Sand Sales, John Smith, 123 Street, Your Town, Your Province
Ship to: Sand Sales, John Smith, 123 Street, Your Town, Your Province
Cash Sale
Invoice 1
Date 1/1/2000

Item	Qty	Unit	Description	GST	PST	Price	Amount	Acct	Dist
1	1	1	Stones	3	8.00	425.64	425.64	4040 Sales: Inven	

Comments

Freight	
GST @ 7.0%	29.79
GST @ 0.0%	
PST	34.05
Total	489.48

Store Recall Print Distrib Post

Posts (records) the entry in the related ledgers and journals

Sales Journal Entry

File Help

1/1/2000	Debits	Credits	Project
1200 Accounts Receivable	489.48	-	
2440 PST Payable	-	34.05	
2450 GST Charged On Sales	-	29.79	
4040 Sales: Inventory A	-	425.64	
	489.48	489.48	

FIGURE 8–30
Journal Entry for Sand Sales

Courtesy of ACCPAC International.

The journal entry for a credit sale to a building supply company lists the totals of the debits and credits. This ensures that for every entry the accountant has entered, debits equal credits.

When the transaction has been completely recorded, the computer will integrate the information. The accounts receivable/sales transaction data that have just been recorded will become part of the General Ledger information. Therefore, the information about sales required for the income statement will be correct. The information about assets (accounts receivable) for the balance sheet will also be correct.

USERS OF COMPUTER ACCOUNTING SYSTEMS

The number of businesses, of all sizes, using computer accounting systems will continue to increase dramatically as computer hardware and software become more affordable. Processing up-to-date accounting information is a necessity in order to make business decisions. A computer system provides the most efficient method of generating these data. Accounting personnel at all levels in a business are currently expected to exhibit proficiency in accounting procedures as well as basic understanding of computer operation and software application.

ACCOUNTING TERMS

Accounts Payable Control	Equals the value of all the individual accounts payable found in the Accounts Payable Ledger.
Accounts Payable Ledger	A ledger containing the individual accounts payable of a company.
Accounts Receivable Control	Equals the value of all the individual accounts receivable found in the Accounts Receivable Ledger.
Accounts Receivable Ledger	A ledger containing the individual accounts receivable of a company.
Control Account	An account found in the General Ledger that has a balance equal to a number of accounts found in a subsidiary ledger.
Division of Labour Principle	Divide work among several people who specialize in completing one component of the task.
One-Write Accounting System	A method of preparing two or more accounting records at the same time without having to rewrite the information.
Schedule of Accounts Payable	The individual accounts payable, found in the subsidiary ledger, are listed and totalled in order to prove they equal the Accounts Payable Control account in the General Ledger.
Schedule of Accounts Receivable	The individual accounts receivable, found in the subsidiary ledger, are listed and totalled in order to prove they equal the Account Receivable Control account found in the General Ledger.
Subsidiary Ledger	A ledger containing a group of accounts of similar type.

REVIEW QUESTIONS

UNIT

1. What source documents does an accounts payable clerk handle?
2. (a) In the Accounts Payable Ledger, what documents are entered as debits?
   (b) What documents are entered as credits in the Accounts Payable Ledger?
3. Explain what is meant by direct posting.
4. Who receives the documents after the accounts payable clerk?
5. What is the accounts receivable clerk's first task with the copies of the sales invoices?
6. Specify whether the accounts receivable clerk records:

   (a) Sales invoices as debits or credits
   (b) Cash receipts as debits or credits
7. Who gets the sales invoices and the list of cash receipts after the accounts receivable clerk?
8. List the source documents for which the accounting supervisor is responsible.
9. (a) What two accounts are always affected by a sales invoice?
   (b) What documents are entered as credits in the Accounts Payable Ledger?

10. (a) What two General Ledger accounts are always affected by a list of cash receipts?
    (b) Give an example of a journal entry resulting from a list of cash receipts.

11. (a) What account is always credited when copies of cheques issued are journalized?
    (b) Explain why the debit is not always the same when cheque copies are journalized.

12. (a) What two General Ledger accounts are always affected by copies of cheques issued on account?
    (b) Give an example of a journal entry resulting from a copy of a cheque on account.

13. What is the name given to the main ledger for a company that has more than one ledger?

14. Accounts in the General Ledger are numbered and organized in numerical sequence. How are the accounts in subsidiary ledgers usually organized?

15. What is the rule concerning the relationship between a subsidiary ledger and the General Ledger?

16. What statement or document is prepared to prove the accuracy of the General Ledger?

17. What statement or document is prepared to prove the accuracy of the Accounts Receivable Ledger?

18. Explain the process of journalizing batch totals.

19. What are the two advantages of using subsidiary ledgers?

20. What is the one-write system of accounting?

21. List three advantages of the computerized system of accounting.

22. Explain the three steps in the accounting cycle when a computerized accounting system is used by a firm.

23. What are the two basic components of a computerized accounting system?

PROBLEMS: APPLICATIONS

1. You are the accounts payable clerk for Crawford Enterprises. Your duties include recording purchases invoices in creditor accounts.

   (a) Head up the following accounts in your Accounts Payable Ledger:

   - Corbett's Service Station
   - Grant Equipment
   - Noonan Fuels Ltd.
   - Wilson Supply Ltd.

   (b) The following purchases invoices represent purchases on account made by Crawford. Record them in the Accounts Payable Ledger. The price shown is the final cost of the item and includes GST and PST.

   May 1 Noonan Fuels Ltd., No. 6931 for fuel oil, $185;
   Wilson Supply Ltd., No. K-213 for office supplies, $75;
   Grant Equipment, No. 316 for a printer/fax machine, $339.

2 Corbett's Service Station, No. 179 for gas and oil for company automobiles, $72.

3 Grant Equipment, No. 391 for filing equipment, $260;
Wilson Supply Ltd., No. K-272 for stationery, $50.

8 Corbett's Service Station, No. 225 for car repairs, $282;
Noonan Fuels Ltd., No. 6983 for furnace servicing, $40.

9 Corbett's Service Station, No. 238 for gasoline, $48;
Wilson Supply Ltd., No. K-317 for miscellaneous supplies, $36.

15 Grant Equipment, No. 421 for cheque protecting machine, $175.

2. Your duties as accounts payable clerk for Crawford Enterprises also include recording payments made to creditors. Record the following copies of cheques issued in the Accounts Payable Ledger used for exercise 1.

May 10 No. 116 to Corbett's Service Station, $72 for Invoice 179;
No. 117 to Noonan Fuels Ltd., $185 for Invoice 6931.

15 No. 118 to Wilson Supply Ltd., $75 for Invoice K-213;
No. 119 to Corbett's Service Station, $48 for Invoice 238.

20 No. 120 to Grant Equipment, $175 in part payment of Invoice 316;
No. 121 to Wilson Supply Ltd., $50 for Invoice K-272.

3. Prepare a schedule of accounts payable dated May 31 for the Accounts Payable Ledger of Crawford Enterprises. Your schedule should total $957.

4. In this exercise, you will act as the accounts receivable clerk for Crawford Enterprises. Your duties include posting sales invoices directly into the customer accounts in the subsidiary Accounts Receivable Ledger.

(a) Head up the following accounts in your Accounts Receivable Ledger:

- T. Campbell
- R. Mask
- W. Squire
- G. Thompson

(b) The following sales invoices represent sales on account made by your company to your customers. Post them directly into the Accounts Receivable Ledger. The price shown is the final cost of the item and includes GST and PST.

May 2 R. Mask, No. 76-15, total of $200;
G. Thompson, No. 76-16, $372.

3 W. Squire, No. 76-17, $625;
T. Campbell, No. 76-18, $195.

8 T. Campbell, No. 76-19, $415;
R. Mask, No. 76-20, $157.

10 W. Squire, No. 76-21, $147;
G. Thompson, No. 76-22, $235.

15 T. Campbell, No. 76-23, $430;
W. Squire, No. 76-24, $155.

5. The accounts receivable clerk's job at Crawford Enterprises includes recording money received from customers. Record the following cash receipts as credits in the customer accounts used in exercise 4.

May 15 T. Campbell, $195 for Invoice 76-18;
R. Mask, $200 for Invoice 76-15;
G. Thompson, $170 towards payment of Invoice 76-16.

18 T. Campbell, $415 for Invoice 76-19;
W. Squire, $625 for Invoice 76-17.

28 G. Thompson, $437 for Invoices 76-16 and 76-22;
W. Squire, $147 for Invoice 76-21.

6. Prepare a schedule of accounts receivable dated May 31 for the Accounts Receivable Ledger of Crawford Enterprises. Your schedule should total $742.

7. (a) How can the total of $957 for the schedule of accounts payable (exercise 3) be checked for accuracy?
(b) How can the total of $742 for the schedule of accounts receivable (exercise 6) be checked for accuracy?
(c) If your totals do not agree with $957 and $742, what does this indicate?

8. (a) As the accounts receivable clerk for Crawford Enterprises, perform the following duties:

(i) Set up the following accounts and balances in the Accounts Receivable Ledger:

- T. Campbell $430
- R. Mask 157
- W. Squire 155
- G. Thompson nil

(ii) Post the following source documents directly to the Accounts Receivable Ledger. Note: All sales are PST exempt.

June 2 Sales invoices:
W. Squire, No. 76-25, $355 (sale $331.78, plus $23.22 GST);
R. Mask, No. 76-26, $53 (sale $49.53, plus $3.47 GST).

3 Sales invoices:
R. Mask, No. 76-27, $670 (sale $626.17, plus $43.83 GST);
G. Thompson, No. 76-28, $212 (sale $198.13, plus $13.87 GST).

4 List of cash receipts:
R. Mask, $157 for Invoice 76-20;
W. Squire, $155 for Invoice 76-24.

5 Sales invoices:
T. Campbell, No. 76-29, $513 (sale $479.44, plus $33.56 GST);
R. Mask, No. 76–30, $275 (sale $257.01, plus $17.99 GST);
G. Thompson, No. 76-31, $850 (sale $794.39, plus $55.61 GST).

5 List of cash receipts:
T. Campbell, $430 for Invoice 76-23;
R. Mask, $723 for Invoices 76-26 and 76-27;
G. Thompson, $212 for Invoice 76-28.

(iii) Prepare a schedule of accounts receivable dated June 5, 2001.

(b) As the accounting supervisor for Crawford Enterprises, perform the following duties:

(i) Set up the following accounts and balances in the General Ledger as at June 1:

101	Cash	$2 109
110	Accounts Receivable	742
206	GST Payable	0
400	Sales	0

(ii) Journalize on page 35 the source documents received from the accounts receivable clerk in part (a) of this exercise.

(iii) Post the journal to the General Ledger.

(iv) Compare the Accounts Receivable control account with the schedule of accounts receivable prepared in part (a).

9. (a) As the accounts payable clerk for Crawford Enterprises, perform the following duties:

(i) Set up the following accounts and balances dated June 1 in the Accounts Payable Ledger:

- Corbett's Service Station $282
- Grant Equipment 599
- Noonan Fuels Ltd. 40
- Wilson Supply Ltd. 36

(ii) Post the following source documents directly to the Accounts Payable Ledger:

Jun. 9 Purchases invoices:
Wilson Supply Ltd., No. K-597 for office forms, $86.92, GST $6.08, total $93;
Grant Equipment, No. 480 for an office copier, $1 195.33, GST $83.67, total $1 279.

10 Purchases invoices:
Corbett's Service Station, No. 447 for gas and oil, $104.67, GST $7.33, total $112;
Noonan Fuels Ltd., No. 7340 for fuel oil, $81.31, GST $5.69, total $87.

11 Cheque copies:
No. 122 to Corbett's Service Station, $282 for Invoice 225;
No. 123 to Grant Equipment, $164 for the balance of Invoice 316.

13 Purchases invoices:
Corbett's Service Station, No. 470 for towing the car and recharging the battery, $126.17, GST $8.83, total $135;
Wilson Supply Ltd., No. K-673 for stationery, $73.83, GST $5.17, total $79.

13 Cheque copies:
No. 124 to Grant Equipment, $435 for Invoices 391 and 421;
No. 125 to Noonan Fuels Ltd., $40 for Invoice 6983;
No. 126 to Corbett's Service Station, $112 for Invoice 447.

(iii) Prepare a schedule of accounts payable dated June 15, 2001.

(b) As the accounting supervisor for Crawford Enterprises, perform the following duties:

(i) Set up the following accounts and balances on June 9 in the General Ledger:

101	Cash	$5 750
103	Office Supplies	0
110	Office Equipment	0
200	Accounts Payable	957
206	GST Payable	0
207	GST Refundable	0
600	Car Expense	0
601	Heating Expense	0

(ii) Journalize on page 36 the source documents received from the accounts payable clerk.

(iii) Post the above to the General Ledger.

(iv) Compare the Accounts Payable control account with the schedule of accounts payable prepared in part (a) of this exercise.

10. Presented below is the accounts receivable subsidiary ledger for Mike's Service Centre and the accounts payable subsidiary ledger for Autoparts Supply Store.

Accounts Receivable Ledger

ACCOUNT Mike's Service Centre

DATE		PARTICULARS	P.R.	DEBIT	CREDIT	DR. CR.	BALANCE
2001							
Jun.	1	Invoice 111-1		212.00		DR.	212.00
	5	For Invoice 109-1			184.00	DR.	28.00
	8	Invoice 112-1		187.00		DR.	215.00
	10	For Invoice 111-1			212.00	DR.	3.00

Accounts Payable Ledger

ACCOUNT Autoparts Supply Store

DATE		PARTICULARS	P.R.	DEBIT	CREDIT	DR. CR.	BALANCE
2001							
Jun.	1	Forwarded				CR	550.00
	2	Invoice 692			339.00	CR.	889.00
	4	Cheque 63 for Invoice 690		550.00		CR.	339.00
	7	Invoice 693			154.00	CR	493.00

Describe each transaction that has been posted to the subsidiary ledgers. Ignore any taxes.

1. Source documents for some of the transactions of Carlo's TV Repairs are shown on pages 283 to 284. Source documents for other transactions are listed on page 286. The accounts and balances in the three ledgers for Carlo's TV Repairs are as follows:

Carlo's TV Repairs
Schedule of Accounts Receivable
May 3, 2000

B. Dover	$ 287.40
Drive-Inn Motor Hotel	1 356.70
L. Malyk	642.30
	$2 286.40

Carlo's TV Repairs
General Ledger Trial Balance
May 3, 2000

ACCOUNT TITLE	ACC. NO.	DEBIT	CREDIT
Cash	101	$ 7 118.60	
Accounts Receivable	110	2 286.40	
Repair Parts	140	2 470.00	
Equipment	151	25 000.00	
Truck	155	18 000.00	
Accounts Payable	200		$ 2 119.63
GST Payable	206		0
PST Payable	207		0
C. Amato, Capital	300		52 755.37
C. Amato, Drawings	301	0	
Sales	400		0
Truck Expense	602	0	
Rent Expense	604	0	
		$54 875.00	$54 875.00

Carlo's TV Repairs
Schedule of Accounts Payable
May 3, 2000

Electronic Suppliers	$1 849.67
Melvyn's Body Repairs	0
Poulin's Service Station	269.96
	$2 119.63

In this exercise, you will perform the duties of three different employees of Carlo's TV Repairs:

- Accounts receivable clerk
- Accounts payable clerk
- Accounting supervisor

(a) Open the three ledgers and record the balances.
(b) In the Accounts Receivable Ledger, record the appropriate source documents given on May 4 and May 5; then prepare a schedule of accounts receivable.
(c) In the Accounts Payable Ledger, record the appropriate source documents and other transactions given on May 5; then prepare a schedule of accounts payable.
(d) Record all source documents in the journal on page 47; post to the General Ledger; and prepare a trial balance of the General Ledger.

Invoice
Carlo's TV Repairs
1750 Elgin Street, Winnipeg, Manitoba R3E 1C3

Date: May 4, 2000
Inv. No.: 2450
Terms: Net 30 days

Sold to:

Drive-Inn Motor Hotel
1460 River Road
Winnipeg, Manitoba
R2M 3Z8

RE: TVs in rooms 107 and 214

Labour	$157.40
Parts	211.12
	368.52
GST	25.80
PST on Parts	16.89
	$411.21

AMOUNT OF THIS INVOICE: $411.21

Invoice
Carlo's TV Repairs
1750 Elgin Street, Winnipeg, Manitoba R3E 1C3

Date: May 4, 2000
Inv. No.: 2451
Terms: Net 30 days

Sold to:

B. Dover
141 Dynes Road
Winnipeg, Manitoba
R2J 0Z8

RE: G.E. B/W TV

Labour	$ 50.64
Parts	87.30
	137.94
GST	9.66
PST on Parts	6.98
	$154.58

AMOUNT OF THIS INVOICE: $154.58

Daily Cash Receipts
May 4, 2000

CUSTOMER			INVOICE	AMOUNT
L. Malyk			2340	$ 642.30
Drive-Inn Motor Hotel			2355	1 375.00
Cash Sales:	Sales	1 287.74		
	GST	90.14		1 377.88
				$3 395.18

Invoice
Carlo's TV Repairs
1750 Elgin Street, Winnipeg, Manitoba R3E 1C3

Date: May 4, 2000
Inv. No.: 2452
Terms: Net 30 days

Sold to:

L. Malyk
543 Kilburn Street
Winnipeg, Manitoba
R2B 1B1

RE: Sony Colour TV

Labour	$74.71
Parts	175.10
	249.81
GST	17.49
PST on Parts	14.01
	$281.31

AMOUNT OF THIS INVOICE: $281.31

Montreal
Toronto
Winnipeg
Vancouver

Electronic Suppliers
147 Industrial Blvd., Winnipeg, Manitoba R2W 0J7
Tel.: 475-6643 Terms: Net 15 days

SOLD TO
Carlo's TV Repairs
1750 Elgin Street
Winnipeg, Manitoba R3E 1C3

SHIP TO
Same

PST No.	Date Invoiced	Inv. No.
435 70913	05/05/00	9875

Quantity	Description	Unit Price	Amount
2	X780 Speakers	$257.89	$515.78
		GST	36.10
		Pay this amount	$551.88

Melvyn's Body Repairs
4765 Borden Road, Winnipeg, Manitoba R2C 3C6
Telephone: 422-7368

Name: Carlo's TV Repairs
Address: 1750 Elgin Street
Winnipeg, Manitoba
R3E 1C3
Inv. No. 74709
Terms: Net 30 days

Make: GMC Truck
Date: May 5, 2000
Licence: A-4597

Quantity	Description	Unit Price	Amount
1	Fender	$1 380.49	$1 380.49
4	Brackets	13.25	53.00
			1 433.49
	Labour		625.41
			2 058.90
	GST		144.12
	Pay this amount		$2 203.02

ELECTRONIC SUPPLIERS				CHEQUE 576
Date	Item	Amount	Discount	Net Amount
Apr. 15	Inv. 9621	$203.76		
17	Inv. 9632	514.83		$718.59

POULIN'S SERVICE STATION				CHEQUE 577
Date	Item	Amount	Discount	Net Amount
Apr. 10	Inv. B-376	$ 24.50		
15	Inv. B-437	209.76		
20	Inv. B-533	35.70		$269.96

COCHRAN REALTIES				CHEQUE 578
Date	Item	Amount	Discount	Net Amount
Apr. 30	Rent for May	$1 500.00		
	GST	105.00		$1 605.00

Source Documents for Other Transactions:

May 5 Sales invoices:
No. 2453, to Drive-Inn Motor Hotel, $278.18, GST $19.47, total $297.65;
No. 2454, to L. Malyk, $87.51, GST $6.13, total $93.64.

Daily cash receipts:
B. Dover, $235.60 on account;
Cash sales $2 100.73, GST $147.05, total $2 247.78.

Purchases invoices:
Electronic Suppliers, No. 9778, $276.30 for parts ($258.22 sale, plus $18.08 GST);
Poulin's Service Station, No. B-675, $168.42 for a tune-up on the truck ($157.40, plus $11.02 GST).

Cheque copies:
No. 579 to Melvyn's Body Repairs, $1 400 on account;
No. 725 to C. Amato, the owner, $725 for personal use.

2. In this exercise, you are the accounting clerk for Entrepreneurial Educators International, which uses the indirect posting procedure.

   (a) Set up the accounts in the General Ledger from the following March 1 information:

101	Cash	$ 3 575	
110	Accounts Receivable	8 500	
120	Merchandise Inventory	22 000	
130	Office Supplies	1 275	
151	Furniture and Equipment	17 000	
200	Accounts Payable		$6 250
205	PST Payable		1 975
206	GST Payable		1 560
207	GST Refundable	1 350	
300	G. Rolanski, Capital		27 415
400	Sales		42 000
500	Purchases	20 000	
600	Rent Expense	5 500	
607	Office Expense	0	
		$79 200	$79 200

(b) The Accounts Receivable Ledger contains the following accounts and balances on March 1. Open the ledger.

K. Lancks	$ 4 800
K. Mullane	3 700
	$8 500

(c) The Accounts Payable Ledger contains the following accounts and balances on March 1. Open the accounts.

A. Dunn	$2 350
R. Teshima	2 100
M. Ziraldo	1 800
	$6 250

(d) Record the entries below on page 45 of a general journal.
(e) Post the entries to the General and Subsidiary Ledgers using the indirect posting method.
(f) Prepare a trial balance, accounts receivable summary, and accounts payable summary on March 7.

Mar. 1 Purchases invoice:
No. 302 from M. Ziraldo for merchandise $1 050 plus $73.50 GST.

2 Cheque copy No. 252 to R. Teshima $1 300, partial payment of account.

2 Cash purchase of office supplies from Beatties Stationery $120 plus $8.40 GST. Cheque copy No. 253.

3 Sales invoices:
K. Mullane No. 1515, $500 plus 7 percent GST and 8 percent PST;
K. Lancks No. 1516, $785 plus GST and PST.

4 Purchases invoices:
No. C475 from A. Dunn for merchandise $1 150 plus $80.50 GST;
No. 15147 from R. Teshima for merchandise $2 300 plus $161 GST.

5 Cash sales for week $4 500, plus $315 GST and $360 PST.

6 Paid rent for the month $2 000 plus GST. Cheque copy No. 254.

6 Cheques received from K. Lancks ($3 500) and K. Mullane ($2 800) in partial payment of their accounts.

3. The accounts and balances in the three ledgers for Mullane Consulting Services are as follows:

Mullane Consulting Services
Schedule of Accounts Receivable
February 28, 2002

A. Battista Ltd.	$1 250
S. Morgan & Co.	1 600
L. Quinn Inc.	185
M. Wong	2 250
	$5 285

Mullane Consulting Services
Schedule of Accounts Payable
February 28, 2002

Dustbane Enterprises	$1 190
Matheson Office Supplies	1 195
Potter's Texaco	0
Underwood Equipment Ltd.	1 470
	$3 855

Mullane Consulting Services
Trial Balance
February 28, 2002

ACCOUNT TITLE	ACC. NO.	DEBIT	CREDIT
Cash	100	$9 500	
Accounts Receivable	101	5 285	
Office Supplies	103	500	
Equipment	113	14 000	
Automobile	114	23 000	
Accounts Payable	200		$ 3 855
PST Payable	205		0
GST Payable	206		0
GST Refundable	207	0	
K. Mullane, Capital	300		48 430
K. Mullane, Drawings	301	0	
Fees Income	400		0
Cleaning Expense	500	0	
Car Expense	501	0	
		$52 285	$52 285

In this exercise, you are the accounting clerk for Mullane Consulting Services. Mullane Consulting Services uses an indirect posting procedure.

(a) Open three ledgers and record the balances from the preceding information.

(b) Perform the accounting clerk's job by journalizing all of the source documents and posting to the ledgers. Then prepare the March 31 trial balance and appropriate schedules.

Note: PST is charged on the base price only.

Mar. 1 Sales invoices:
No. 309, L. Quinn, $450 plus 7 percent GST, 8 percent PST;
No. 310, M. Wong, $300 plus 7 percent GST, 8 percent PST;
No. 311, A. Battista Ltd., $200 plus 7 percent GST, 8 percent PST;
No. 312, S. Morgan & Co., $500 plus 7 percent GST, 8 percent PST.

3 List of cash receipts:
$230, L. Quinn Inc.;
$850, S. Morgan & Co.

5 Purchases invoices:
Dustbane Enterprises, No. F-301, $130 plus 7 percent GST for cleaning office;
Potter's Texaco, No. 498, $140 plus 7 percent GST for repairs for the company automobile;
Underwood Equipment Ltd., No. 189, $300 plus 7 percent GST, 8–percent PST for equipment.

8 Sales invoices:
No. 313, L. Quinn Inc., $200, plus 7 percent GST, 8 percent PST;
No. 314, S. Morgan & Co., $450, plus 7 percent GST, 8 percent PST.

10 Cheque copies:
No. 471, $130 to Dustbane Enterprises;
No. 472, $560 to Underwood Equipment Ltd.

15 Purchases invoices:
Dustbane Enterprises, No. F-396, $130 plus 7 percent GST for cleaning office;
Matheson Office Supplies, No. M-201, $65 plus 7 percent GST, 8 percent PST for office supplies;
Potter's Texaco, No. 569, $70 plus 7 percent GST for repairs to the company car and $40 for gasoline for Mullane's family car, total $114.90.

17 List of cash receipts:
$1 230 from A. Battista Ltd.;
$850 from S. Morgan & Co.;
$1 050 from M. Wong;
$2 140 received from providing services to two customers for cash ($2 000 plus $140 GST).

20 Cheque copies:
No. 473, $149.80 to Potter's Texaco, on account;
No. 474, $430 to Matheson Office Supplies, on account;
No. 475, $650 to K. Mullane for personal use.

24 List of cash receipts:
$250, A. Battista Ltd.;
$517.50, L. Quinn Inc.;
$345 received from cash services ($300 sale plus $21 GST plus $24 PST).

31 Cheque copies:
No. 476, $438.20 to Dustbane Enterprises;
No. 477, $114.90 to Potter's Texaco.

31 Sales invoices:
No. 315, $500 to A. Battista Ltd., plus 7 percent GST, 8 percent PST;
No. 316, $285 to L. Quinn Inc., plus 7 percent GST, 8 percent PST.

31 Purchases invoice:
No. 800, $60 for gas for company car, Potter's Texaco.

CHAPTER 9

The Special Journal System

UNIT 19 A Multi-Column Journal System

Learning Objectives

After reading this unit, discussing the applicable review questions, and completing the applications exercises, you will be able to do the following:

1. **RECORD** transactions in a multi-column journal.
2. **PROVE** the accuracy of a multi-column journal by balancing its totals.
3. **FORWARD** totals in a multi-column journal.

In Chapter 8, you learned that many business enterprises use subsidiary ledgers as well as a General Ledger. The use of more than one ledger provides:

- Division of labour
- Accounting control

In this chapter, you will learn that there are several different *multi-column journal systems* that provide similar and additional accounting advantages and benefits.

INTRODUCING THE COLUMNAR JOURNAL

Examine the General Journal in Figure 9-1. GST and PST have been omitted to simplify the example. The small sampling of seven journal entries requires 28 lines of space. Notice that recording of the entries involves writing certain words and account names over and over. How many times is Cash written? Sales? Imagine how many entries involving Cash, Sales, Purchases, and other frequently used accounts a large business would have!

A multi-column journal, called a columnar journal, is used for demonstration purposes in this unit. A few small businesses may still use this system, but the more advanced special journal system discussed later in this chapter is used most frequently in business.

The same seven transactions are shown in a columnar journal in Figure 9-2, on page 292. Only seven lines are required to record the same transactions in the columnar journal.

Examine the first entry for cash sales. Notice that there is a special column for cash debits and a special column for sales credits. The words "cash" and "sales" do not have to be written by the accountant in recording this transaction. Only the date, explanation, and amount need to be written — a considerable saving of time and space.

A columnar journal is a journal that has special columns for accounts that are used often in recording transactions.

FIGURE 9-1
Two-column General Journal

GENERAL JOURNAL — PAGE 17

DATE	PARTICULARS	P.R.	DEBIT	CREDIT
2001				
Nov. 1	Cash		520.00	
	Sales			520.00
	Cash sales tickets 781–799.			
1	Accounts Receivable/E. Marano		239.60	
	Sales			239.60
	Invoice B-601, n/30.			
4	Cash		603.70	
	Sales			603.70
	Cash sales tickets 800-819			
4	Purchases		1 900.00	
	Accounts Payable/Acme Ltd.			1 900.00
	Invoice K-206, merchandise, n/30.			
5	Accounts Receivable/A. Komar		416.00	
	Sales			416.00
	Invoice B-602, n/30.			
5	Purchases		841.00	
	Cash			841.00
	Cheque 16239, merchandise.			
8	Cash		1 250.00	
	Sales			1 250.00
	Cash sales tickets 820–839.			

FIGURE 9-2

Columnar journal

COLUMNAR JOURNAL — **PAGE 26**

DATE	ACCOUNT OR EXPLANATION	REF. NO.	CASH DEBIT	CASH CREDIT	P.R.	OTHER ACCOUNTS DEBIT	OTHER ACCOUNTS CREDIT	ACCOUNTS RECEIVABLE DEBIT	ACCOUNTS RECEIVABLE CREDIT	SALES CREDIT	GST REFUND. DEBIT	GST PAYABLE CREDIT	PST PAYABLE CREDIT	PUR-CHASES DEBIT	ACCOUNTS PAYABLE DEBIT	ACCOUNTS PAYABLE CREDIT
2001																
Nov. 1	Tickets	781–799	520.00							520.00						
1	E. Marano, n/30	B-601						239.60		239.60						
4	Tickets	800–819	603.70							603.70						
4	Acme Ltd., n/30	K-206												1 900.00		1 900.00
5	A. Komar, n/30	B-602						416.00		416.00						
5	Cheque	16239		841.00										841.00		
8	Tickets	820–839	1 250.00							1 250.00						

FIGURE 9-3

Transactions recorded in a columnar journal

COLUMNAR JOURNAL — **PAGE 13**

DATE	ACCOUNT OR EXPLANATION	REF. NO.	CASH DEBIT	CASH CREDIT	P.R.	OTHER ACCOUNTS DEBIT	OTHER ACCOUNTS CREDIT	ACCOUNTS RECEIVABLE DEBIT	ACCOUNTS RECEIVABLE CREDIT	SALES CREDIT	GST REFUND. DEBIT	GST PAYABLE CREDIT	PST PAYABLE CREDIT	PUR-CHASES DEBIT	ACCOUNTS PAYABLE DEBIT	ACCOUNTS PAYABLE CREDIT
2001																
Feb. 1	Cash sale	193	345.00							300.00		21.00	24.00			
3	A. Walker, n/30	175						230.00		200.00		14.00	16.00			
6	D. Dodd, n/30	176	100.00					360.00		400.00		28.00	32.00			
9	Office Supplies	135				150.00										
	Office Equipment	135		856.00		650.00					56.00					
13	National Wholesale	B-117									28.00			400.00		428.00
16	Rent Expense	171		642.00		600.00					42.00					
18	Telephone Expense	172		101.65		95.00					6.65					
20	A. Walker		216.00						216.00							
24	Butler Mfg.	173		749.00							49.00			700.00		
28	G. LePensée, Drawings	174		100.00		100.00										

The columnar journal is designed so that there are special columns for accounts used often by a business. If a transaction involves an account for which a special column is not provided, the Other Accounts columns are used. The columnar journal is also known as a *combination* or a *synoptic journal.*

The number of columns in a columnar journal is determined by the types of transactions a company has. Ultimately, of course, the number of columns has to be limited by the size of the journal page. However, it is not uncommon to have 13 or 15 columns in a columnar journal.

Another feature of the columnar journal is the provision of a reference number column. It is located next to the explanation section. It is used to record the source document numbers, such as cheque numbers and invoice numbers.

Recording Transactions in a Columnar Journal

The recording of transactions in a columnar journal is illustrated by the transaction examples given below. Read each example and examine the corresponding entry in Figure 9-3, on page 292, which is a completed columnar journal containing these transactions. The advantages of this journal will be evident to you.

Transaction 1: Cash Sale

Feb. 1 Sold merchandise for cash, $300 plus 7 percent GST and 8 percent PST, Cash Sales Slip 193.

In General Journal form, the entry would be:

Feb. 1	Cash	345.00	
	Sales		300.00
	GST Payable		21.00
	PST Payable		24.00
	Cash Sales Slip 193.		

Compare this with the entry in the columnar journal, Figure 9-3. An explanation of the transaction is written in the account or explanation column; the source document number 193 is shown in the reference number column; the amount $345 is entered in the cash debit column; $300 is entered in the sales credit column, $21 in the GST payable credit column, and $24 in the PST payable credit column. The transaction requires only one line and very little writing compared to recording the same entry in a General Journal.

Most transactions require only one line when recorded in a columnar journal.

Transaction 2: Sale on Account

Feb. 3 Sales Invoice 175 to A. Walker, $200 plus 7 percent GST and 8 percent PST, terms n/30.

Look at the entry in Figure 9-3. The name of the customer and the terms of the sale are shown in the account or explanation column; the invoice number 175 is recorded in the reference number column; $230 is entered in accounts receivable debit, $200 in sales credit, $14 in GST payable credit, and $16 in PST payable credit.

Transaction 3: Sale with a Down Payment

Feb. 6 Sales Invoice 176 to D. Dodd, $400 plus 7 percent GST and 8 percent PST. Received $100 cash, balance of $360 to be paid in 30 days.

Although this transaction involves four accounts, the entry is done on one line in the columnar journal. In Figure 9-3, locate the debit to cash of $100, the debit to accounts receivable of $360, the credit to sales of $400, the credit to GST payable of $28, and the credit to PST payable of $32.

Transaction 4: Cash Purchase of Supplies and Equipment

Feb. 9 Cheque 135 for $856 to E.T. Wilson Ltd., payment for office supplies $150, office equipment $650, and $56 GST.

The columnar journal does not have special columns for office supplies or office equipment. Therefore, the other accounts section is used. To identify which accounts change, the account titles Office Supplies and Office Equipment are written on separate lines in the account or explanation column. The amount debited is written on the same line in the Other Accounts debit column. In Figure 9-3 this transaction is recorded using two lines.

Additional Transactions

A sampling of transactions is listed below. Examine them and decide how you would record them in a columnar journal. Check your ideas with Figure 9-3.

Feb. 13 Received Purchase Invoice B-117 from National Wholesale, $400 plus $28 GST, on account.
16 Cheque 171 to Royal Real Estate, $600 plus $42 GST, for rent.
18 Cheque 172, $95 plus $6.65 GST, for telephone bill.
20 Received $216 from A. Walker on account.
24 Cheque 173 to Butler Mfg., $700 plus $49 GST, for cash purchase of merchandise.
28 Cheque 174 to G. LePensée, the owner, $100 for personal use.

Special Sections of the Columnar Journal – Summary

Account or Explanation Column

When a transaction causes a change in a customer or a creditor account, the name of the customer or creditor is shown in the account or explanation column.

Other Accounts Section

The Other Accounts columns are used to record transactions involving accounts for which special columns have not been provided in the columnar journal.

When a transaction includes a debit or a credit for which there is not a special column in the columnar journal, the Other Accounts section is used. The account title is written in the account or explanation column so that the entry may be posted to that account in the General Ledger.

Reference Number Column

A number column is located next to the account or explanation column. This column is used to record, for referencing purposes, the number of the source document from which the transaction was recorded. For a sale on account, the number of the sales invoice is recorded in the number column. For other transactions, the cheque number, purchase invoice number, or credit invoice number is shown.

B BALANCING THE COLUMNAR JOURNAL

The debit totals should equal the credit totals on each page of the columnar journal.

If transactions have been recorded properly, the debits should equal the credits on every page of the columnar journal. To determine this, at the bottom of each page and at the end of the month, the totals of each column are shown. This is known as *balancing* the journal. The process may also be called cross-balancing. Balancing, or *cross-balancing,* a columnar journal determines if the debits equal the credits on a particular journal page. If the debit column totals equal the credit column totals, that particular page of the journal is in balance. If a calculator is used to prove the totals, the tape may be attached to the journal as proof that the page balances. The steps to be followed in balancing a columnar journal are described below.

Balancing, or cross-balancing, a columnar journal page determines if the debit totals equal the credit totals.

Steps in Balancing the Columnar Journal

The following steps are illustrated in the columnar journal in Figure 9-4 on page 267:

(1) Rule a single line across all money columns below the last line used.
(2) Add the columns. Write the totals in pencil at the foot of each column.
(3) Add the debit column totals and the credit column totals.
(4) If the debit totals equal the credit totals, write the column totals in ink at the bottom of each column. Write the debit and credit totals in the account or explanation column.
(5) Rule double lines across the date and all money columns.

Locating Errors in the Columnar Journal

If the journal totals do not balance, a recording error may have been made. Errors may be located by following this procedure:

- Start on the first line and check to see if there are equal debits and credits on each line.
- Recheck all addition.
- Then follow the locating errors steps given in Chapter 4.

Forwarding Page Totals

When a page of a journal is filled, it should be balanced and the totals carried forward to the next page. The word "Forwarded" is written in the account or explanation column on the same line as the totals. On the next journal page, the date, including the year and the month, is written on the first line. The word "Forwarded" is written on the first line in the account or explanation column and the totals are written in the money columns. For example, if column totals were being forwarded on Feb. 14, the first line on the new journal page would appear as follows:

COLUMNAR JOURNAL

DATE	ACCOUNT OR EXPLANATION	REF. NO.	CASH DEBIT	CASH CREDIT	P.R.	OTHER ACCOUNTS DEBIT	OTHER ACCOUNTS CREDIT
2001 Feb. 14		Forwarded	661.00	2 448.65	✓	1 595.00	

Totals are carried forward in this manner until the end of the month. At that time, the journal is balanced and the totals for the entire month are posted to the General Ledger.

Totals on each page are carried forward until the end of the month.

FIGURE 9-4
Balancing the columnar journal

COLUMNAR JOURNAL **PAGE 13**

DATE	ACCOUNT OR EXPLANATION	REF. NO.	CASH DEBIT	CASH CREDIT	P.R.	OTHER ACCOUNTS DEBIT	OTHER ACCOUNTS CREDIT	ACCOUNTS RECEIVABLE DEBIT	ACCOUNTS RECEIVABLE CREDIT	SALES CREDIT	GST REFUND. DEBIT	GST PAYABLE CREDIT	PST PAYABLE CREDIT	PUR-CHASES DEBIT	ACCOUNTS PAYABLE DEBIT	ACCOUNTS PAYABLE CREDIT
2001																
Feb. 1	Cash sale	193	345.00							300.00		21.00	24.00			
3	A. Walker, n/30	175						230.00		200.00		14.00	16.00			
6	D. Dodd, n/30	176	100.00					360.00		400.00		28.00	32.00			
9	Office Supplies	135				150.00										
	Office Equipment	135		856.00		650.00					56.00					
13	National Wholesale	B-117									28.00			400.00		428.00
16	Rent Expense	171		642.00		600.00					42.00					
18	Telephone Expense	172		101.65		95.00					6.65					
20	A. Walker		216.00						216.00							
24	Butler Mfg.	173		749.00							49.00			700.00		
28	G. LePensée, Drawings	174		100.00		100.00										
	Debits = $4 127.65		661.00	2 448.65		1 595.00		590.00	216.00	900.00	181.65	63.00	72.00	1 100.00		428.00
	Credits = $4 127.65															

1. How many lines does it take to record an ordinary entry in a General Journal? How many lines does it generally take to record an entry in a columnar journal?
2. What is another name for a columnar journal?
3. When is an account given its own column in a columnar journal?
4. Why does it take two lines to record the February 9 entry in Figure 9-3 in a columnar journal?
5. When is a debit or a credit amount recorded in the Other Accounts section of a columnar journal?
6. How is a columnar journal balanced?
7. How are page totals forwarded in a columnar journal?
8. What procedure is followed if a columnar journal page does not balance?

PROBLEMS: APPLICATIONS

1. (a) Journalize the June transactions for Costello Enterprises in a columnar journal on page 13. All sales are subject to 7 percent GST and 8 percent PST.

Jun.	1	Issued Cheque 76 for $1 100, plus $77 GST, to pay the June rent.
	1	Cash sales slips totalled $395, plus $27.65 GST, all sales tax exempt.
	5	Sales invoices, terms n/30: No. 171, M. Swords, $75; No. 172, W. Kranz, $210; No. 173, J. Moore, $130.
	5	Purchased merchandise for $750, plus $52.50 GST, from Tanyss Trading, Invoice B-316, terms n/30.
	8	Bought office supplies for $75, plus $5.25 GST, issued Cheque 77.
	10	Cash purchase of merchandise for $340, plus $23.80 GST, Cheque 78.
	13	Paid $370, plus $25.90 GST, to *The Star* for advertising, Cheque 79.

(b) Total, balance, and rule the journal.

2. (a) Continue to journalize transactions for Costello Enterprises in the columnar journal, page 14. Forward the totals from page 13 in exercise 1.

Jun.	15	Received cheques from customers: M. Swords, $86.25 for Invoice 171; J. Moore, $149.50 for Invoice 173.
	17	Purchased merchandise for $350, plus $24.50 GST, from National Wholesale, terms 1/10, n/30.
	19	Cash sales slips totalled $500, GST $35, PST $40, total cash received $575.
	22	Issued Cheque 80 to Tanyss Trading for $300 on account.
	22	The owner, P. Costello, invested an additional $4 000 in the business.

23 Sales invoices, terms 2/10, n/30:
No. 174, M. Swords $200;
No. 175, L. Usher $730.

25 Issued Cheque 81 for $3 800 to pay the month's wages.

26 Received Credit Invoice N-170 for goods returned to National Wholesale, $75 + $5.25 GST.

26 Issued Cheque 82 to National Wholesale as partial payment for invoice of Jun. 17, less credit invoice of Jun. 26. Amount of cheque $185.38; amount of discount taken $1.87.

29 Cheque received for $241.50 from W. Kranz.

30 Issued Cheque 83 for $95, plus $6.65 GST, to pay Utilities Expense for the month.

(b) Total, balance, and rule the journal.

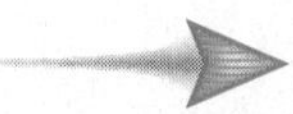

UNIT 20 Posting the Multi-Column Journal

Learning Objectives

After reading this unit, discussing the applicable review questions, and completing the applications exercises, you will be able to do the following:

1. **RECORD** credit invoices in a columnar journal.
2. **POST** the columnar journal.
3. **EXPLAIN** advantages of using a columnar journal.
4. **EXPLAIN** disadvantages of using a columnar journal.

METHODS OF POSTING

Direct Posting to the Subsidiary Ledgers

Many businesses post to the subsidiary Accounts Receivable and Payable Ledgers directly from source documents on a daily basis. The source documents are then batch journalized in the columnar journal. This method is known as *direct posting.*

Posting to All Ledgers from the Journal

If the direct posting method is not used, source documents are entered into the columnar journal and then the individual accounts receivable and payable entries are posted to the Subsidiary Accounts Receivable and Payable Ledgers daily. Amounts in the other accounts columns are posted individually to the General Ledger on a monthly basis. As illustrated in Figure 9-5 on page 300, there are three basic steps in posting to the subsidiary ledgers and the General Ledger from the columnar journal.

Step 1: Post Accounts Receivable and Payable

Each day, the individual accounts receivable and payable are posted to the subsidiary ledgers to update the customer and creditor accounts. As each amount is posted, a check mark (✓) is placed in the posting reference column of the journal. A check mark is used since the accounts receivable and payable are in alphabetical order rather than numbered.

The amounts in the Accounts Receivable and Accounts Payable columns are posted daily to the subsidiary ledgers.

Step 2: Post the Other Accounts Section

At the end of the month, the amounts in the Other Accounts section are posted individually to the General Ledger. The names of the accounts to which postings are made are found in the account or explanation column. As the postings are made, the account numbers are shown in the posting reference column of the columnar journal.

Amounts in the Other Accounts columns are posted individually.

Step 3: Post the Column Totals

At the end of the month, all column totals except the Other Accounts columns are posted to the General Ledger. As each column total is posted, the number of the account is written in brackets under each total.

All column totals except the Other Accounts totals are posted to the General Ledger.

FIGURE 9–5

Posting the columnar journal

COLUMNAR JOURNAL

PAGE 13

DATE	ACCOUNT OR EXPLANATION	REF. NO.	CASH DEBIT	CASH CREDIT	P.R.	OTHER ACCOUNTS DEBIT	OTHER ACCOUNTS CREDIT	ACCOUNTS RECEIVABLE DEBIT	ACCOUNTS RECEIVABLE CREDIT	SALES CREDIT	GST REFUND. DEBIT	GST PAYABLE CREDIT	PST PAYABLE CREDIT	PUR-CHASES DEBIT	ACCOUNTS PAYABLE DEBIT	ACCOUNTS PAYABLE CREDIT
2001																
Feb. 1	Cash sale	193	345.00							300.00		21.00	24.00			
3	A. Walker, n/30	175			✓			230.00		200.00		14.00	16.00			
6	D. Dodd, n/30	176	100.00		✓			360.00		400.00		28.00	32.00			
9	Office Supplies	135			125	150.00										
	Office Equipment	135		856.00	151	650.00					56.00					
13	National Wholesale	B-117			✓						28.00			400.00		428.00
16	Rent Expense	171		642.00	610	600.00					42.00					
18	Telephone Expense	172		101.65	612	95.00					6.65					
20	A. Walker		216.00		✓				216.00							
24	Butler Mfg.	173		749.00	✓						49.00			700.00		
28	G. LePensée, Drawings	174		100.00	302	100.00										
	Debits = $4 127.65		661.00	2 448.65		1 595.00		590.00	216.00	900.00	181.65	63.00	72.00	1 100.00		428.00
	Credits = $4 127.65		(100)	(100)				(110)	(110)	(400)	(206)	(206)	(205)	(500)		(200)

Step 3: Post all column totals except the Other Accounts columns monthly to the General Ledger. Place the account numbers in brackets under the totals to indicate the totals have been posted.

Step 2: Post each individual entry in the Other Accounts columns at the end of the month to the General Ledger. Place the account number in the P.R. column to indicate the amount has been posted.

Step 1: Post accounts receivable and payable daily to customer and creditor accounts in the Accounts Receivable Ledger or the Accounts Payable Ledger. Indicate the amount has been posted by placing a ✓ in the P.R. column provided.

POSTING REFERENCES IN THE LEDGER

The page number of the columnar journal is written in the posting reference column of the accounts. For example, C13 indicates that a posting was made from page 13 of the columnar journal. Figure 9-6 shows the Cash account after the amounts have been posted from the columnar journal.

GENERAL LEDGER						NO. 100
DATE	PARTICULARS	P.R.	DEBIT	CREDIT	DR. CR.	BALANCE
2001						
Feb. 1	Forwarded	✓			DR.	11 000.00
28		C13	661.00		DR.	11 661.00
28		C13		2 448.65	DR.	9 212.35

FIGURE 9-6
Cash account after posting the columnar journal totals

POSTING CONTROL ACCOUNTS

In Chapter 8, the relationship between a subsidiary ledger and a control account was demonstrated. As you know, the Accounts Receivable control account equals the value of all the individual accounts found in the Accounts Receivable Ledger. A similar relationship exists between the Accounts Payable control account and the Accounts Payable Ledger. When the columnar journal is posted, the subsidiary ledger accounts are posted on a daily basis in order to have current information in the customer and creditor accounts. However, the control accounts are posted along with the other General Ledger accounts at the end of the month in order to save time in posting.

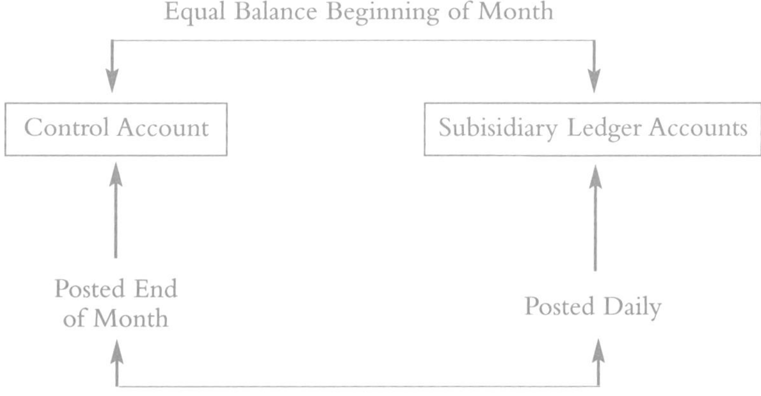

If you prepared a schedule of accounts from the subsidiary ledger during the month, would it necessarily balance with the control account? The control account would not equal the subsidiary ledger amounts during the month since the individual accounts are posted daily while the control account is only updated at the month's end. This should not present a problem, however, since the individualized customer or creditor accounts contain current amounts at all times. Any errors will be found at the end of the month when the schedules of subsidiary ledger accounts are compared with the control account balances.

RECORDING CREDIT INVOICES IN THE COLUMNAR JOURNAL

There are two methods of recording credit invoices in the columnar journal. These are the *circling method* and *using the Other Accounts section*. The sample transactions below illustrate the two methods.

Recording A Sales Return

The following transaction illustrates how a credit invoice for a sales return is recorded.

Sample Transaction

Feb. 28 D. Dodd returned $100 worth of merchandise. Credit Invoice 613 was issued for $100, plus $7 GST and $8 PST.

In General Journal form, this transaction would be recorded as follows:

Feb. 28	Sales Returns and Allowances	100	
	GST Payable	7	
	PST Payable	8	
	Accounts Receivable/D. Dodd		115
	Credit Invoice 613.		

Using the Other Accounts Section

One method of recording a credit invoice in the columnar journal is to use the Other Accounts section. The three debits (Sales Returns and Allowances $100, GST Payable $7, and PST Payable $8) are recorded in the Other Accounts debit column. This is done because the PST payable column in the journal is a credit column. GST Payable is recorded directly in the appropriate column. Figure 9-7, on page 304, illustrates the use of the Other Accounts section to record a credit invoice for a sales return.

Using the Circling Method

In the circling method, the Sales Returns and Allowances debit of $100 is recorded in the Other Accounts section; the PST Payable debit of $8 is entered and circled in the PST payable column; the GST Payable debit of $7 is entered in the GST payable debit column; and the $115 credit is entered in the accounts receivable credit column. The circling method is illustrated in Figure 9-8 on page 304.

To determine the total of a column when using the circling method, do the following:

- Add the uncircled items in the column.
- Subtract the circled items.
- Enter the result as the column total.

Circled items are subtracted from the total of the uncircled items to determine column totals.

In Figure 9-8, the uncircled items in the PST payable column total $72 ($24 + $16 + $32). The column total of $64 is arrived at by subtracting the $8 circled item from $72.

Recording a Purchase Return

The following transaction illustrates how a credit invoice for a purchase return is recorded both in General Journal form and in the columnar journal (see Figure 9-9 on page 304).

Sample Transaction

Feb. 28 Received Credit Invoice N-15 from National Wholesale, $53.50, plus $3.75 GST, for merchandise returned to them earlier in the month.

In General Journal form, the entry is:

Feb. 28	Accounts Payable/National Wholesale	57.25	
	Purchases Returns and Allowances		53.50
	GST Refundable		3.75
	Credit Invoice N-15.		

In the columnar journal, in Figure 9-9, this transaction is recorded using the Other Accounts credit column, and the GST refundable debit column with the amount circled. The $3.75 is circled because it is a credit entry in a debit column.

ADVANTAGES OF THE COLUMNAR JOURNAL

There are two main advantages to using the columnar journal:

- Posting is reduced compared to the posting of a two-column journal.
- The use of special columns saves time and space in recording transactions.

One of the major advantages of a columnar journal is the reduction in the amount of posting to the General Ledger. The use of special columns makes it possible to post only the column totals to the accounts. For example, in Figure 9-5 there are three transactions in the cash debit column, yet only one posting is made to the debit side of the Cash account in the ledger. Only the total debit is posted. There are five entries in the cash credit column, yet only one posting (the total) is required.

The use of special columns greatly reduces the amount of posting and is an important advantage of the columnar journal compared to the two-column General Journal.

DISADVANTAGES OF THE COLUMNAR JOURNAL

There are three disadvantages to using the columnar journal:

- The multi-column journal may be cumbersome and inconvenient to use.
- The risk of error is increased by the large number of columns (i.e., the danger of putting the amounts in the wrong columns).
- The use of the columnar journal is restricted to a business with relatively few transactions which can be recorded by one person.

FIGURE 9-7
Using the Other Accounts section

COLUMNAR JOURNAL — PAGE 13

DATE	ACCOUNT OR EXPLANATION	REF. NO.	CASH DEBIT	CASH CREDIT	P.R.	OTHER ACCOUNTS DEBIT	OTHER ACCOUNTS CREDIT	ACCOUNTS RECEIVABLE DEBIT	ACCOUNTS RECEIVABLE CREDIT	SALES CREDIT	GST REFUND. DEBIT	GST PAYABLE CREDIT	PST PAYABLE CREDIT	PUR-CHASES DEBIT	ACCOUNTS PAYABLE DEBIT	ACCOUNTS PAYABLE CREDIT
2001																
Feb. 28	Sales Returns & Allow.	613				100										
	GST Payable					7										
	PST Payable	613				8										
	D. Dodd	613							115							

FIGURE 9-8
Using the circling method

COLUMNAR JOURNAL — PAGE 13

DATE	ACCOUNT OR EXPLANATION	REF. NO.	CASH DEBIT	CASH CREDIT	P.R.	OTHER ACCOUNTS DEBIT	OTHER ACCOUNTS CREDIT	ACCOUNTS RECEIVABLE DEBIT	ACCOUNTS RECEIVABLE CREDIT	SALES CREDIT	GST REFUND. DEBIT	GST PAYABLE CREDIT	PST PAYABLE CREDIT	PUR-CHASES DEBIT	ACCOUNTS PAYABLE DEBIT	ACCOUNTS PAYABLE CREDIT
2001																
Feb. 1	Cash sale	193	345							300		21	24			
3	A. Walker, n/30	175						230		200		14	16			
4	D. Dodd, n/30	176	100					360		400		28	32			
28	Sales Returns & Allow.					100						(7)	(8)			
	D. Dodd								115							
			445			100		590	115	900		56	64			

FIGURE 9-9
Recording a purchase return requires two lines

COLUMNAR JOURNAL — PAGE 13

DATE	ACCOUNT OR EXPLANATION	REF. NO.	CASH DEBIT	CASH CREDIT	P.R.	OTHER ACCOUNTS DEBIT	OTHER ACCOUNTS CREDIT	ACCOUNTS RECEIVABLE DEBIT	ACCOUNTS RECEIVABLE CREDIT	SALES CREDIT	GST REFUND. DEBIT	GST PAYABLE CREDIT	PST PAYABLE CREDIT	PUR-CHASES DEBIT	ACCOUNTS PAYABLE DEBIT	ACCOUNTS PAYABLE CREDIT
2001																
Feb. 28	National Wholesale	N-15									(3.75)				57.25	
	Pur. Returns & Allow.	N-15					53.50									

ACCOUNTING TERMS

Circling Method	A method of recording credit invoices.
Columnar Journal	A multi-column journal that has separate columns for accounts that are used often in recording transactions.
Combination Journal	Another name for a columnar journal.
Cross-Balancing	The debit column totals equal the credit column totals in the journal.
Direct Posting	Posting the subsidiary ledgers directly from the source documents.
Forwarding	Transferring column totals from the bottom of a page in the columnar journal to the top of the next page.
Reference Number Column	Used to record the source document number for the transaction.
Synoptic Journal	Another name for a columnar journal.

REVIEW QUESTIONS

1. (a) When is the columnar journal balanced?
   (b) When is the columnar journal posted?
2. List the three basic steps followed in posting the columnar journal.
3. What columnar journal totals are not posted?
4. For which columns in the columnar journal are the entries posted individually?
5. When column totals have been posted, where are the posting references shown in the journal?
6. Give two advantages and three disadvantages of the columnar journal.
7. When a credit invoice is recorded for a sales return, which accounts are debited and credited?
8. When a credit invoice is recorded for a purchase return, which accounts are debited and credited?
9. When there is a circled item in a column, how is the total of that column determined?
10. Which method of posting would you recommend for a company that has a very large number of accounts receivable and payable — the direct posting method or posting the transactions from the columnar journal to the subsidiary ledgers? Give reasons for your answer.

PROBLEMS: APPLICATIONS

CHAPTER 9

3. The trial balance for the Outdoor Life Shop is shown below.

Outdoor Life Shop
Trial Balance
May 1, 2001

ACCOUNT TITLE	ACC. NO.	DEBIT	CREDIT
Cash	101	$12 300	
Accounts Receivable	110	1 756	
Store Supplies	126	6 551	
Accounts Payable	200		$ 4 407
PST Payable	205		
GST Payable	206		
GST Refundable	207		
L. Flynn, Capital	300		16 200
Sales	400		
Purchases	500		
Transportation on Purchases	503		
Advertising Expense	600		
Salaries Expense	604		
		$20 607	$20 607

(a) Record the following documents on page 47 of a columnar journal; then total, balance, and rule the journal.

May 1 Sales invoices issued:
No. 703 to K. Prentice, $450, plus $31.50 GST and $36 PST;
No. 704 to Sheridan, $376, plus $26.32 GST, no PST;
No. 705 to C. Mathers, $185, plus $12.95 GST and $14.80 PST.

2 Purchases invoices received:
Northern Wholesalers, $2 576, plus $180.32 GST, for merchandise;
CCKK TV $378, plus $26.46 GST, for TV advertising;
Robinson Trucking, $156, plus $10.92 GST, for transportation of merchandise from Northern Wholesalers.

3 List of cash receipts from:
Sheridan, $613;
C. Mathers, $346;
L. Flynn, the owner, $2 000 extra investment.

4 Copies of cheques issued:
No. 931 for $900 for employees' weekly salaries;
No. 932 for $1 270 to Northern Wholesalers, on account;
No. 933 for $175 to Robinson Trucking, on account.

(b) Open a General Ledger.
(c) Post the journal to the ledger on May 4.
(d) Prepare a trial balance.

4. Continue the accounting procedures for the Outdoor Life Shop.

(a) Set up an Accounts Receivable Ledger and an Accounts Payable Ledger with the balances shown in the schedules below.
(b) Post the subsidiary ledgers from the columnar journal.

(c) Prepare a schedule of accounts receivable and a schedule of accounts payable. Check your totals with the control accounts in the General Ledger for exercise 3.

Outdoor Life Shop
Schedule of Accounts Receivable
May 1, 2001

C. Mathers	$ 346
K. Prentice	735
Sheridan	675
	$1 756

Outdoor Life Shop
Schedule of Accounts Payable
May 1, 2001

CCKK TV	$ 532
Northern Wholesalers	3 573
Robinson Trucking	302
	$4 407

5. Librock Enterprises' General Journal contains the following entries:

GENERAL JOURNAL **PAGE 38**

DATE	PARTICULARS	P.R.	DEBIT	CREDIT
2000				
Mar. 1	Cash		226.00	
	Sales			200.00
	GST Payable			14.00
	PST Payable			12.00
	Cash register summary.			
2	Accounts Receivable/H. Hume		339.00	
	Sales			300.00
	GST Payable			21.00
	PST Payable			18.00
	Sales Invoice 301, n/30.			
3	Sales Returns and Allowances		50.00	
	PST Payable		3.00	
	GST Payable		3.50	
	Cash			56.50
	Cash Refund Slip 29.			
8	Cash		428.00	
	Sales			400.00
	GST Payable			28.00
	Tax-exempt sale on account.			
9	Sales Returns and Allowances		100.00	
	PST Payable		6.00	
	GST Payable		7.00	
	Accounts Receivable/H. Hume			113.00
	Credit Invoice 63.			
10	Cash		226.00	
	Accounts Receivable/H. Hume			226.00
	Cash received on account.			

(a) How many lines are used to record the six entries in this journal (including spaces)?

(b) How many lines would be used to record the same six transactions in a columnar journal?

6. (a) Record the following transactions for Crawford Enterprises on page 26 of a columnar journal; then total, balance, and rule the journal. All sales are non-taxable, terms n/30.

Mar. 2 Sales invoices:
Invoice 76-25 to W. Squire, $355 + $24.85 GST;
Invoice 76-26 to R. Mask, $370 + $25.90 GST.

5 Cash sales slips:
No. 69 to No. 85, for the week, total $12 970 + $907.90 GST.

9 Purchases invoices:
Wilson Supply, Invoice K-297, for $987 + $69.09 GST, terms n/30;
Grant Ltd., Invoice 491, for $650 + $45.50 GST, terms n/30.

10 Cash receipts:
R. Mask, $1 250 for Invoice 76-20;
W. Squire, $1 550 for Invoice 76-24.

10 Credit invoice issued:
No. CI-16 for $300 + $21 GST to T. Campbell for goods returned (goods were sold to Campbell on Feb. 15).

12 Cheques issued:
No. 122 to Corbett's for $1 600 in payment of Invoice 225;
No. 123 to Grant Ltd. for $5 900 in payment of Invoice 420;
No. 124 to the *Citizen* for advertising, $380 + $26.60 GST.

12 Cash receipts:
W. Squire, $379.85 for Invoice 76-25.

15 Sales invoices:
T. Campbell, Invoice 76-27 for $510 + $35.70 GST;
R. Mask, Invoice 76-28 for $670 + $46.90 GST;
G. Thompson, Invoice 76-29 for $1 490 + $104.30 GST.

15 Credit invoice received:
No. G-280 from Grant Ltd., for $250 (+ GST $17.50) worth of defective merchandise on Invoice 491, dated Mar. 9.

20 Cheque issued:
No. 125 for $175 + $12. 25 GST to Roadway Transport Ltd. for transportation on purchases of merchandise.

25 Purchases invoices:
Wilson Supply, Invoice K-320, $130 + $9.10 GST for office supplies, n/30;
Noonan Ltd., Invoice 610, $250 + $17.50 GST for merchandise, n/30.

26 Bank credit memo:
Bank loan for $12 500 has been deposited by the bank in Crawford Enterprises' account.

27 Cheques issued:
No. 126 for $3 500 to pay for a vacation trip for the P. Crawford family;

No. 127 to City Hydro, $160 + $11.20 GST for the company's hydro bill.

31 Sales invoice:
Invoice 76-30 to W. Squire for $790 + $55.30 GST.

(b) Open a General Ledger and post the columnar journal. The March 1 account balances are shown in the trial balance below.

(c) Prepare a trial balance dated March 31.

Crawford Enterprises
Trial Balance
March 1, 2002

ACCOUNT TITLE	ACC. NO.	DEBIT	CREDIT
Cash	100	$17 500	
Accounts Receivable	110	5 700	
Office Supplies	125	8 000	
Equipment	151	60 000	
Accounts Payable	200		$ 8 140
GST Payable	206		
GST Refundable	207		
Bank Loan	210		
P. Crawford, Capital	300		83 060
P. Crawford, Drawings	301		
Sales	400		
Sales Returns and Allowances	401		
Sales Discounts	402		
Purchases	500		
Purchases Returns and Allowances	501		
Purchases Discounts	502		
Transportation on Purchases	503		
Advertising Expense	600		
Utilities Expense	605		
		$91 200	$91 200

7. Continue the accounting procedures for Crawford Enterprises.

(a) Set up Accounts Receivable and Accounts Payable Ledgers with the balances shown in the schedules below.

(b) Post the accounts receivable and accounts payable source documents directly to the customer and credit accounts in the subsidiary ledgers.

(c) Prepare schedules of accounts receivable and accounts payable. Check your totals with the control accounts in exercise 6.

Crawford Enterprises
Schedule of Accounts Receivable
March 1, 2002

T. Campbell	$2 900
R. Mask	1 250
W. Squire	1 550
G. Thompson	0
	$5 700

Crawford Enterprises
Schedule of Accounts Payable
March 1, 2002

Corbett's Service Station	$1 600
Grant Ltd.	5 900
Noonan Ltd.	400
Wilson Supply	240
	$8 140

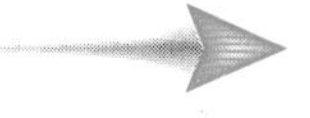

UNIT 21 Purchases Journal

Learning Objectives

After reading this unit, discussing the applicable review questions, and completing the applications exercises, you will be able to do the following:

1. **EXPLAIN** the purpose of a purchase requisition, purchase order, purchase invoice, and receiving report.
2. **DISCUSS** the process of matching documents in order to approve purchases invoices.
3. **EXPLAIN** the importance of filing invoices in a date file according to the date on which terms of sale indicate that payment is due.
4. **RECORD** transactions in a Purchases Journal.
5. **BALANCE** and post a Purchases Journal.
6. **RECORD** purchases returns.

INTRODUCING SPECIAL JOURNALS

In Chapter 8 and Units 19 and 20, you learned about accounting systems and procedures that made use of the principles of division of labour and specialization.

Chapter 8 described the three-ledger system used by large companies that have many customers and creditors. Units 19 and 20 of this chapter described the columnar journal, which made use of special columns to efficiently journalize and post transactions. Now you will learn that *several* special multi-column journals may be used in a manual accounting system by companies that have many repetitive transactions.

A large percentage of the transactions that you recorded previously fall into four major categories:

Category	Transaction
1	Purchases of goods or services on account
2	Sales of goods or services on account
3	Receipt of cash
4	Payment of cash

These four types of transactions represent the majority of financial events happening in a business. When there are too many transactions to record in one columnar journal, several specialized columnar journals are used.

A special journal system uses separate journals for similar transactions that recur frequently.

A special journal is used for each type of repetitive transaction. For example, a *Purchases Journal* is used to record all purchases on account (credit purchases). A *Sales Journal* is used to record credit sales. *Cash Receipts* and *Cash Payments Journals* are used to record cash received and cash payments. In addition, a General Journal is used to record transactions that do not fit into these major categories as well as the end-of-period adjusting and closing entries.

Different people are assigned to record transactions in each of the special journals. Thus, as you can see, the five-journal system makes use of the principles of division of labour and specialization.

The chart below is a summary of the major categories of transactions, the source documents for these transactions, and the special journal into which each will be journalized.

In this chapter, we will examine the use of each of the special journals listed in the chart below. You will find many similarities in the journalizing and posting procedures for these journals when compared to the columnar journal used earlier in the chapter. This will reduce the time needed for you to become familiar with these tasks.

Transactions	Common Source Documents	Journals Used
Purchases on account Sales of goods on account	Purchases invoices Sales invoices	Purchases Journal Sales Journal
Cash receipts	Bank credit memos Cash sales slips Cash register slips List of cheques received in the mail	Cash Receipts Journal
Cash payments	Bank debit memos Cheque copies or stubs	Cash Payments Journal
Other transactions	Credit invoices End-of-period entries Memo — correcting entries	General Journal

PURCHASING SYSTEMS

Before examining the recording and posting procedures for a Purchases Journal, it is important to understand the purchasing system as a whole. Many documents and company departments are involved in a purchasing system. This is necessary in order to efficiently divide the work load among a number of people and to control human error and possible dishonesty. Purchasing systems differ from business to business. Warrendon Sports is used in the examples that follow to illustrate standard principles used by many businesses.

Ordering Goods

Figure 9-10 illustrates the steps that are usually followed when buying goods:

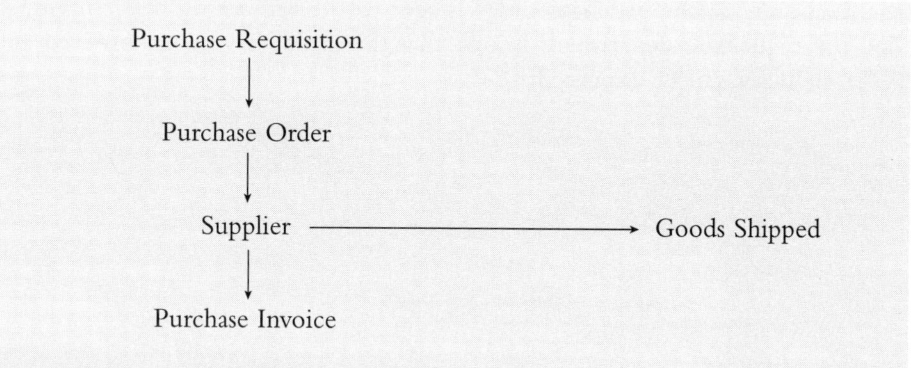

FIGURE 9-10
Steps followed in a typical purchasing system

A purchase requisition is a form sent to the purchasing department requesting that goods or services be ordered.

Purchase Requisition

An employee wishing to purchase goods or services completes a request form called a *purchase requisition*. After it is approved by a supervisor, this form is sent to the purchasing department. Figure 9-11 is an example of a purchase requisition.

FIGURE 9-11
Example of a purchase requisition

WARRENDON SPORTS
2579 Base Line Road
Ottawa, ON K2H 7B3

PURCHASE REQUISITION **DATE** July 31, 2001

TO PURCHASING DEPARTMENT Please Purchase the Following No. R-72 **DATE NEEDED** Sep. 1

QUANTITY	STOCK NO.	DESCRIPTION
30		Dolphin clear goggles
30		Olympian clear goggles
12		Assorted earplugs
6		Size 1–4 swim wings

REQUISITIONED BY Anita Rizini **APPROVED** Warren Creighton

Purchase Order

A purchase order is a form prepared by the buyer and sent to the seller. It describes the items the buyer wants to purchase.

It is the responsibility of the purchasing department to acquire the best quality items at the best price. When a supplier has been selected, a *purchase order* is prepared and sent to the supplier. When both the buyer and the seller agree on the terms of the purchase, the purchase order becomes a legal contract. Warrendon Sports uses the purchase order shown in Figure 9-12 on page 313.

Figure 9-13 on page 313 shows where each copy of the purchase order is sent. The original is sent to the supplier. The receiving department is sent a copy of the purchase order so that it will know that goods have been ordered and will accept *only* the goods ordered. The accounting department receives a copy of the purchase order so that it will pay only for the goods that have been ordered. The purchasing department retains a copy for its records, and the final copy of the purchase order is sent to the requesting department, so that the requesting department knows that the goods have been ordered and when delivery can be expected.

WARRENDON SPORTS
2579 Base Line Road
Ottawa, ON K2H 7B3

NO. 4151 **PURCHASE ORDER**

STORE: 2579 Base Line Road
❑ Tel: 684-1287
Fax: 684-5381

FACTORY: 5 Melrose Avenue
❑ Tel: 729-7100
Fax: 729-7288

DATE August 4, 2001

TO: Speedquip Ltd.
SHIP TO: Warrendon Sports
2579 Base Line Road,
Ottawa, ON K2H 7B3

Please supply the following by date specified.

REQUIRED BY September 1
SHIP BY Parcel Post

QUANTITY	DESCRIPTION
30	Dolphin clear goggles
30	Olympian clear goggles
12	Assorted earplugs
6	Size 1–4 swim wings

PST Licence No. 41902211
GST Registration No. R119282106

PER *Warren Creighton*

FIGURE 9-12
Example of a purchase order

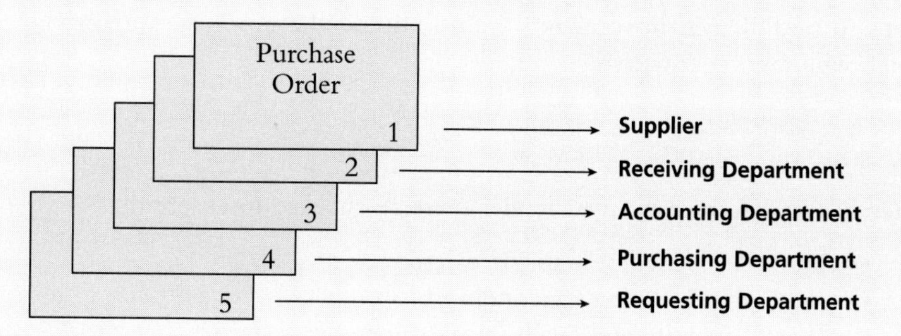

FIGURE 9-13
Distribution of purchase order and copies

Purchase Invoice

After the goods have been shipped, the seller sends an *invoice* or bill to the buyer. Figure 9-14 on the next page is the invoice received by Warrendon Sports. This invoice lists the items shipped to Warrendon that were ordered on August 4 (Figure 9-12).

An invoice is a form sent by the seller to the buyer. It lists the costs of the items shipped, along with details of the shipment.

The information in the columns headed Quantity Ordered, Quantity Shipped, Stock Number/Description, Unit Price, and Amount must be carefully checked and are subject to further detailed controls in Warrendon's purchasing system.

FIGURE 9-14
Example of a purchase invoice

Speedquip Ltd. 992 St. Mary's Rd., Winnipeg, MB R2M 3S3 Phone: 204-256-3489 Fax: 204-256-7531 **INVOICE**

SOLD TO	SHIPPED TO	
Warrendon Sports Ltd. 2579 Base Line Road Ottawa, Ontario K2H 7B3	Same	NO. 307 DATE Sep. 1, 2001 YOUR ORDER NO. 4151

Our Order No.	Salesperson	Terms	F.O.B.	Date Shipped	Shipped Via
52876	Brown	Net 30 Days	Winnipeg	Aug. 15, 2001	Parcel Post

QUANTITY ORDERED	QUANTITY SHIPPED	STOCK NUMBER/DESCRIPTION	UNIT PRICE	AMOUNT
30	30	Dolphin clear goggles	$4.80	$144.00
30	30	Olympian clear goggles	5.10	153.00
12	12	Assorted earplugs	0.90	10.80
6	6	Size 1–4 swim wings	1.80	10.80
				318.60
		Goods and Services Tax 7%		22.30
		Total Due		$340.90

2% added to overdue accounts

White — Customer's Copy / Pink — Office Copy / Canary — Commission Copy / Green — Salesperson's Copy / Blue — Shipping Copy

Paying for Purchases

To this point, the system for ordering goods from a supplier has been shown. The steps to be followed in receiving the goods and the procedures for paying for them will now be discussed.

Receiving Report

Merchandise received from a supplier must be checked to ensure that:

- Goods received were actually ordered
- Goods are in satisfactory condition
- Correct quantity and quality were shipped

A receiving report is a form that lists and describes all goods received.

The person receiving and checking the goods completes a *receiving report* (Figure 9-15) and sends a copy to the purchasing department. Remember that a copy of the purchase order was initially sent to the receiving department when the goods were ordered. This purchase order copy is used to determine if the goods received were in fact ordered.

Some firms do not use a receiving report. Instead, the receiver will check off each item on the purchase order when it is received. The receiver then initials the purchase order copy and sends it to the purchasing department.

WARRENDON SPORTS

2579 Base Line Road
Ottawa, ON K2H 7B3

RECEIVING REPORT

FROM: Speedquip Ltd.

NO. R-312
DATE Sep. 5, 2001
P.O. NO. 4151

VIA **PREPAID** **COLLECT**

STOCK NO.	QUANTITY	DESCRIPTION	UNIT PRICE
	30	Dolphin clear goggles	
	30	Olympian clear goggles	
	12	Assorted earplugs	
	6	Size 1–4 swim wings	

CHECKED BY R. Lee ENTERED IN STORE'S LEDGER BY H. Kwan

FIGURE 9-15
Example of a receiving report

Matching Process

Before an invoice is approved or recorded, it is checked and compared to the purchase order and the receiving report. This comparison is necessary to ensure that what was ordered was received, and what was charged for was ordered and received. Usually, the matching process is the responsibility of the purchasing department. If the three documents match, the invoice is approved and sent to the accounting department.

The matching process is the comparison of the purchase order, purchase invoice, and receiving report.

Approved Invoice

The accounting department receives the invoice and supporting documents from the purchasing department and checks their mathematical accuracy. Each *extension* is checked and the amounts are added to verify the total of the invoice.

An extension is the quantity multiplied by the unit price.

The account to be debited is indicated on the invoice. An accounting clerk then journalizes and posts the transaction. For example, the journal entry for the Speedquip invoice is:

Sep. 5	Purchases	318.60	
	GST Refundable	22.30	
	Accounts Payable/Speedquip Ltd.		340.90
	Invoice 307, net 30 days.		

Payment on the Due Date

After journalizing, the approved invoice is placed in a date file according to the date on which payment is to be made. On that day, the invoice is taken from the file and a cheque is prepared and sent to the supplier. The payment is then journalized and posted. The journal entry to record the payment of the Speedquip invoice is:

Oct. 3	Accounts Payable/Speedquip Ltd.	340.90	
	Cash		340.90
	Invoice 307.		

FIGURE 9-16
Typical steps followed when paying an invoice

Figure 9-16 illustrates the steps followed when paying an invoice:

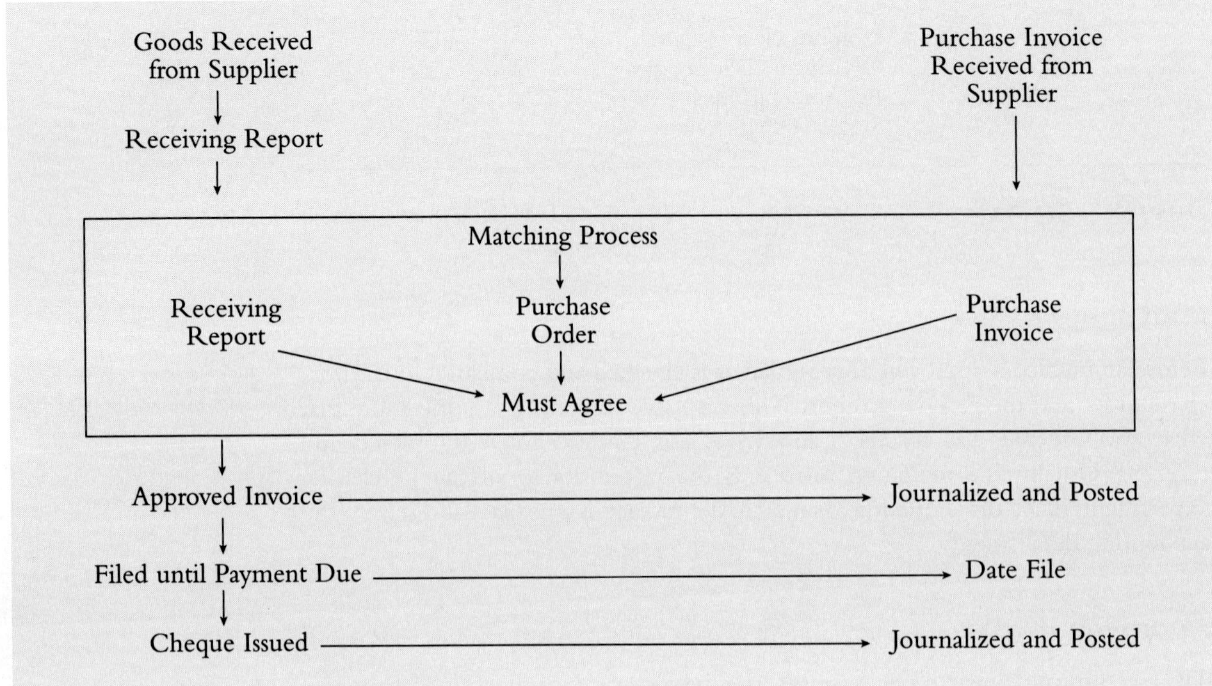

INTRODUCING THE PURCHASES JOURNAL

A Purchases Journal is a special journal used to record all purchases on account.

A business that makes many purchases on account uses a Purchases Journal instead of a General Journal to record such purchases. When invoices are received, they are approved and then recorded in the Purchases Journal:

Purchases Invoices ⟶ Invoices Approved ⟶ Purchases Journal

Journalizing Purchases on Account

As you know, an invoice received for items purchased on account is called a *purchase invoice.* After the purchase invoice has been approved, it is journalized. On September 5, approved invoices for the following transactions were received by the accounting department of Warrendon Sports.

Purchases Transactions

Sep. 5 Invoice 307 dated Sep. 1 from Speedquip Ltd., $318.60 for merchandise, GST $22.30, terms n/30.

5 Invoice W184 dated Sep. 4 from Evans & Kert, $50 for office supplies, GST $3.50, terms n/30.

5 Invoice 3871 dated Sep. 2 from Tops Service Centre, $70 for repairs to the company automobile, GST $4.90, terms n/30.

5 Invoice B-519 dated Sep. 1 from Ontario Hydro, $195 for the August hydro bill, GST $13.65, terms EOM.

5 Invoice 193 dated Sep. 1 from Cooper Bros., $500 for merchandise, GST $35, terms n/30.

Figure 9-17, below, shows these transactions recorded in a General Journal.

FIGURE 9-17
Transactions recorded in a General Journal

GENERAL JOURNAL					PAGE 17
DATE		PARTICULARS	P.R.	DEBIT	CREDIT
2001					
Sep.	5	Purchases		318.60	
		GST Refundable		22.30	
		Accts. Pay./Speedquip Ltd.			340.90
		Invoice 307, merchandise, n/30.			
	5	Supplies		50.00	
		GST Refundable		3.50	
		Accts. Pay./Evans & Kert			53.50
		Invoice W184, n/30.			
	5	Car Expense		70.00	
		GST Refundable		4.90	
		Accts. Pay./Tops Service Centre			74.90
		Invoice 3871, n/30.			
	5	Utilities Expense		195.00	
		GST Refundable		13.65	
		Accts. Pay./Ontario Hydro			208.65
		Invoice B-519, EOM.			
	5	Purchases		500.00	
		GST Refundable		35.00	
		Accts. Pay./Cooper Bros.			535.00
		Invoice 193, merchandise, n/30.			

Figure 9-18 on page 319 shows the same invoices recorded in a Purchases Journal. Compare the recording of the five invoices in the General Journal with the recording procedures followed in the Purchases Journal. How many lines does each transaction require in the General Journal and in the Purchases Journal? In the recording of these invoices, which journal requires less writing? Why do you think there are special columns headed Purchases Debit and Utilities Expense Debit? When is the Other Accounts Debit section used?

Special columns are provided for accounts that are used frequently.

Note that only purchases on account appear in the Purchases Journal. Cash purchases would be recorded in the Cash Payments Journal.

Special Column Headings

In the Purchases Journal in Figure 9-18, columns are headed Purchases Debit, GST Refundable Debit, Accounts Payable Credit, Utilities Expense Debit, and Other Accounts Debit. The Accounts Payable Credit column is required for every transaction in the Purchases Journal. Merchandise is purchased frequently and that is why there are special columns for Purchases Debit and GST Refundable Debit in the journal. A special column is headed Utilities Expense Debit because, for this particular company, the Utilities Expense account is involved in many transactions. Another company might use this column for Supplies or Delivery Expense or any other account used in repetitive transactions.

The other accounts debit section is used to record debits to accounts other than Purchases or Utilities Expense. Notice that the account title must be shown as well as the name of the creditor when the other accounts section is used.

Balancing the Purchases Journal

Since the Purchases Journal in Figure 9-18 has five money columns, it is quite possible to record part of an entry in the wrong column. To locate errors of this type before they are transferred to the ledger in the posting process, each page of the Purchases Journal is balanced. The total of the debit columns must equal the total of the credit columns.

These steps should be followed when balancing a Purchases Journal:

(1) Rule a single line across all money columns below the last line used.
(2) Add the columns; put totals in as pencil footings.
(3) Where there is more than one of each, add all the debit column totals and all the credit column totals.
(4) If the debit totals equal the credit totals, write the column totals in ink at the bottom of each column. Write the debit and credit totals in the creditor column.
(5) Rule double lines across the date and all money columns.

Figure 9-19 illustrates the balancing process for page 16 of the Purchases Journal. The Purchases Journal is balanced at the end of each page and at the end of each month. Note that additional transactions have been posted to the journal in addition to the five transactions already covered. This is done to give the Purchases Journal a more realistic appearance.

Locating Errors

If the journal does not balance:

- Start on the first line and check to see if there are equal debit and credit amounts on each line.
- Recheck all addition.
- Follow the locating error steps given in Chapter 4.

Forwarding Totals

When a page of a journal is filled, it should be balanced and the totals carried forward to the next page. Follow the forwarding procedures described earlier in this chapter.

FIGURE 9-18
Transactions recorded in a Purchases Journal

PURCHASES JOURNAL — PAGE 16

DATE		REF. NO.	CREDITOR	TERMS	P.R.	PURCHASES DEBIT	GST REFUND. DEBIT	ACCOUNTS PAYABLE CREDIT	UTILITIES EXPENSE DEBIT	OTHER ACCOUNTS ACCOUNT	P.R.	DEBIT
2001												
Sep.	5	307	Speedquip Ltd.	n/30		318.60	22.30	340.90				
	5	W184	Evans & Kert	n/30			3.50	53.50		Supplies		50.00
	5	3871	Tops Service Centre	n/30			4.90	74.90		Car Expense		70.00
	5	B-519	Ontario Hydro	EOM			13.65	208.65	195.00			
	5	193	Cooper Bros.	n/30		500.00	35.00	535.00				

FIGURE 9-19
Balancing the Purchases Journal

PURCHASES JOURNAL — PAGE 16

DATE		REF. NO.	CREDITOR	TERMS	P.R.	PURCHASES DEBIT	GST REFUND. DEBIT	ACCOUNTS PAYABLE CREDIT	UTILITIES EXPENSE DEBIT	OTHER ACCOUNTS ACCOUNT	P.R.	DEBIT
2001												
Sep.	5	307	Speedquip Ltd.	n/30		318.60	22.30	340.90				
	5	W184	Evans & Kert	n/30			3.50	53.50		Supplies		50.00
	5	3871	Tops Service Centre	n/30			4.90	74.90		Car Expense		70.00
	5	B-519	Ontario Hydro	EOM			13.65	208.65	195.00			
	5	193	Cooper Bros.	n/30		500.00	35.00	535.00				
	6	419	Hall Fuel	n/30			14.00	214.00	200.00			
	9	801	Coles Ltd.	n/30			.70	10.70		Miscellaneous Expense		10.00
	10	331	Speedquip Ltd.	n/30		200.00	14.00	214.00				
	11	207	Cooper Bros.	n/30		40.00	2.80	42.80				
	12	H-719	CN Express	n/15			8.05	123.05		Trans. on Purchases		115.00
	16	3461	City Water Dept.	EOM			25.20	385.20	360.00			
	18	219	Cooper Bros.	n/30		900.00	63.00	963.00				
	20	W220	Evans & Kert	n/30			6.79	103.79		Supplies		97.00
	23	231	Cooper Bros.	n/30		120.00	8.40	128.40				
	27	3904	Tops Service Centre	n/30			3.15	48.15		Car Expense		45.00
	30	379	Speedquip Ltd.	n/30		400.00	28.00	428.00				
			Debits = $3 874.04			2 478.60	253.44	3 874.04	755.00			387.00
			Credits = $3 874.04									

POSTING TO THE LEDGERS

The main advantage of using the Purchases Journal is that it reduces the recording workload since only one line is needed for most transactions. In contrast, three lines of writing are required when transactions are recorded directly in the General Journal.

Further efficiencies are achieved in the posting process. The posting procedure is the same as for the columnar journal used earlier in this chapter, and the efficiencies achieved in journalizing and posting transactions are the same. On the following pages, the steps involved in posting from the Purchases Journal to the Accounts Payable Ledger and the General Ledger will be described. Figure 9-20, on page 321, will illustrate the complete posting process for the Purchases Journal. First, however, we will briefly review the methods of posting to the subsidiary ledgers.

Methods of Posting to the Subsidiary Ledgers

As explained earlier in the chapter, there are two methods commonly used to post columnar journals to the subsidiary ledgers.

Direct Posting

In this method, source documents are posted *directly* to the subsidiary ledgers. Different people can be assigned the duties of journalizing transactions and updating the subsidiary ledgers. A company with a large number of transactions involving customers and creditors would use this direct posting system.

Companies with a columnar Purchases Journal usually use the direct posting method for recording source documents in the subsidiary ledgers. Purchases invoices are recorded directly into the Accounts Payable Ledger. Sales invoices are recorded directly into the Accounts Receivable Ledger. Division of responsibility is made possible since different accounting personnel can be used to perform these tasks.

Posting from the Journal

Another posting method is to enter transactions in the journal and *then* to post the entries from the journal to the ledger accounts. This method is used by companies who wish to use special journals but do not have enough transactions to have separate people working on the journals and the ledgers. In Unit 20, this method was demonstrated for the columnar journal. It will also be used here for the Purchases Journal.

FIGURE 9-20
Balancing the Purchases Journal

PURCHASES JOURNAL — **PAGE 16**

DATE		REF. NO.	CREDITOR	TERMS	P.R.	PURCHASES DEBIT	GST REFUND. DEBIT	ACCOUNTS PAYABLE CREDIT	UTILITIES EXPENSE DEBIT	OTHER ACCOUNTS ACCOUNT	P.R.	DEBIT
2001												
Sep.	5	307	Speedquip Ltd.	n/30	✓	318.60	22.30	340.90				
	5	W184	Evans & Kert	n/30	✓		3.50	53.50		Supplies	125	50.00
	5	3871	Tops Service Centre	n/30	✓		4.90	74.90		Car Expense	613	70.00
	5	B-519	Ontario Hydro	EOM	✓		13.65	208.65	195.00			
	5	193	Cooper Bros.	n/30	✓	500.00	35.00	535.00				
	6	419	Hall Fuel	n/30	✓		14.00	214.00	200.00			
	9	801	Coles Ltd.	n/30	✓		0.70	10.70		Miscellaneous Expense	614	10.00
	10	331	Speedquip Ltd.	n/30	✓	200.00	14.00	214.00				
	11	207	Cooper Bros.	n/30	✓	40.00	2.80	42.80				
	12	H-719	CN Express	n/15	✓		8.05	123.05		Trans. on Purchases	503	115.00
	16	3461	City Water Dept.	EOM	✓		25.20	385.20	360.00			
	18	219	Cooper Bros.	n/30	✓	900.00	63.00	963.00				
	20	W220	Evans & Kert	n/30	✓		6.79	103.79		Supplies	125	97.00
	23	231	Cooper Bros.	n/30	✓	120.00	8.40	128.40				
	27	3904	Tops Service Centre	n/30	✓		3.15	48.15		Car Expense	613	45.00
	30	379	Speedquip Ltd.	n/30	✓	400.00	28.00	428.00				
			Debits = $3 874.04			2 478.60	253.44	3 874.04	755.00			387.00
			Credits = $3 874.04			(500)	(206)	(200)	(615)			

Posting the Purchases Journal to the Accounts Payable Ledger

Step 1

Each day, post each entry in the accounts payable credit column of the Purchases Journal to the Accounts Payable Ledger. In the following example, Speedquip Ltd.'s account is credited with $340.90 on September 5. P16 is written in the posting reference column of the account to indicate the journal and page number of the posting:

ACCOUNTS PAYABLE LEDGER ACCOUNT Speedquip Ltd.						
DATE	**PARTICULARS**	**P.R.**	**DEBIT**	**CREDIT**	**DR. CR.**	**BALANCE**
2001 Sep. 5		P16		340.90	CR.	340.90

Posting from the Purchases Journal to the Accounts Payable Ledger is done daily in order to keep the balances in the creditors' accounts up-to-date.

Step 2

Place a check mark (✓) in the posting reference column of the Purchases Journal opposite each creditor (e.g., Speedquip Ltd.) to indicate that the amount has been posted to the subsidiary ledger account (see Figure 9-20 on page 321).

Posting the Purchases Journal to the General Ledger

Step 1

At the end of the month, post the individual transactions in the other accounts section to the General Ledger, writing the Purchases Journal page number and abbreviation in the posting reference column of the accounts. Show the ledger account number in the posting reference column of the other accounts section (see Figure 9-20).

Step 2

At the end of the month, post the totals of each column to the appropriate account in the General Ledger, again writing the Purchases Journal page number and abbreviation in the posting reference column of the accounts. The account numbers are shown in brackets under each total (see Figure 9-20). The other accounts total is not posted. The following example shows the Purchases account in the General Ledger after the purchases debit column total from the Purchases Journal has been posted.

GENERAL LEDGER						
ACCOUNT Purchases					No. 500	
DATE	PARTICULARS	P.R.	DEBIT	CREDIT	DR. CR.	BALANCE
2001 Sep.30		P16	2 478.60		DR.	2 478.60

General Posting Procedure for Special Journals

The posting procedure described for the Purchases Journal is used for all of the special journals in this chapter. A summary of this procedure follows.

Step 1

Do the following:

(1) Each day, post all the individual entries in the accounts payable or accounts receivable columns to the accounts in the subsidiary ledgers.
(2) Place the journal abbreviation and page number in the posting refer ence column of each account (e.g., P16, S17, CR 37, CP14, J10).
(3) Place a check mark (✓) in the first posting reference column in the journal beside each item to indicate that the item has been posted.

Step 2

Do the following:

(1) At the end of the month, post the individual items in the other accounts section to the relevant accounts in the General Ledger.
(2) Place the journal abbreviation and page number in the posting reference column of each account.
(3) Place the account number in the posting reference column of the other accounts section to indicate that posting of the entry is complete.

Step 3

Do the following:

(1) At the end of the month, post all column totals (except the other accounts total) to the relevant accounts in the General Ledger.
(2) Place the journal abbreviation and page number in the posting reference column of each account.
(3) Place the account number in brackets under the total in the journal to indicate that it has been posted.

CREDIT INVOICES

A credit invoice is the source document used to record the return of goods by a customer.

Occasionally, a buyer will return goods to the seller. This causes changes on the books of both the buyer and the seller. The source document prepared as a record of the transaction is the *credit invoice.*

The seller prepares the credit invoice and sends it to the buyer. The seller decreases the amount owed by the buyer. When the buyer receives the credit invoice, the buyer decreases the amount owed to the seller.

Recording Credit Invoices

Credit invoices may be recorded in several ways, depending on the information required by the company and the number of credit invoices to be processed:

(1) Credit invoices may be recorded in the General Journal. This method will be used to complete the exercises in the rest of this chapter.
(2) Credit invoices may be recorded in the Purchases Journal. The circling method can be used, or special columns can be set up in the Purchases Journal for purchases returns.
(3) A special account, the Purchases Returns and Allowances account, may be used to record returns. A Purchases Returns and Allowances account will be used to complete the exercises in this chapter.

The following sample transactions will be used to illustrate the recording of credit invoices in the buyer's books.

Transaction for a Purchase on Account

Mar. 4 Purchased merchandise from Shannon Ltd., Invoice 322, terms n/30, $500 on account, GST $35.

This transaction was recorded in the Purchases Journal in the normal way.

Transaction for a Purchase Return

Mar. 10 Returned unacceptable goods worth $100 plus $7 GST to Shannon Ltd. from merchandise purchased Mar. 4. Shannon issued Credit Invoice C-40 for $107.

The various methods of recording this $107 credit invoice are described below.

Using the General Journal

If the General Journal is used, the credit invoice is recorded as follows:

Mar. 10	Accounts Payable/Shannon Ltd.	✓/200	107	
	Purchases Returns and Allowances	501		100
	GST Refundable	207		7
	To record Credit Invoice C-40.			

When this transaction is posted, the $107 debit is posted to the Accounts Payable control account in the General Ledger and to Shannon Ltd. in the Accounts Payable Ledger. A check mark (✓) is used to show the posting to the subsidiary ledger account, while the account number 200 indicates that the General Ledger has been posted. Both the credit of $100 to the Purchases Returns and Allowances account and the $7 credit to the GST Refundable account are posted in the General Ledger.

Can you explain why the $107 debit is posted twice — once to the control account and once to Shannon's account?

Using the Purchases Journal: Special Columns

The Purchases Journal can have special columns added for accounts payable debit and purchases returns and allowances credit. A company would use these two additional columns when it had many credit invoices to be recorded. Credit invoices would then be recorded as illustrated in Figure 9-21 on page 326.

Using the Purchases Journal: Circling Method

If special columns are not used, credit invoices can be recorded in the Purchases Journal using the circling method. Any item circled is subtracted when the columns are totalled. Circling is a method of indicating that an item is to be treated as a debit, and not as a credit. This method is illustrated for the Shannon transaction in Figure 9-22 on page 326.

ADVANTAGES OF THE PURCHASES JOURNAL

There are four advantages to using a Purchases Journal. They are:

- Most entries require only one line in a Purchases Journal.
- Posting is reduced.
- Explanations are eliminated.
- Division of labour and responsibilities is possible.

FIGURE 9-21
Purchases Journal with special columns for Purchases Returns and Allowances credit and Accounts Payable debit

PURCHASES JOURNAL — **PAGE 30**

DATE	REF. NO.	CREDITOR	TERMS	P.R.	PURCHASES DEBIT	GST REFUND. DEBIT	ACCOUNTS PAYABLE CREDIT	ACCOUNTS PAYABLE DEBIT	PURCH. RET. & ALL. CREDIT	OTHER ACCOUNTS ACCOUNT	OTHER ACCOUNTS P.R.	OTHER ACCOUNTS DEBIT
2001												
Mar. 4	322	Shannon Ltd.	n/30		500	35	535					
10	C-40	Shannon Ltd.				(7)		107	100			

FIGURE 9-22
Purchases Journal showing the circling method. The circled amounts are subtracted when the columns are totalled.

PURCHASES JOURNAL — **PAGE 16**

DATE	REF. NO.	CREDITOR	TERMS	P.R.	PURCHASES DEBIT	GST REFUND. DEBIT	ACCOUNTS PAYABLE CREDIT	UTILITIES EXPENSE DEBIT	OTHER ACCOUNTS ACCOUNT	OTHER ACCOUNTS P.R.	OTHER ACCOUNTS DEBIT
2001											
Mar. 4	322	Shannon Ltd.	n/30		500	35	535				
10	C-40	Shannon Ltd.			(100)	(7)	(107)				
		Totals			400	28	428				

1. Answer the following questions about the purchase requisition shown in Figure 9-11:

   (a) Who requested the merchandise?
   (b) Who is the supervisor?
   (c) Why is it necessary to have the supervisor sign the purchase requisition?

2. What factors does the purchasing department consider before issuing the purchase order?

3. Answer the following questions about the purchase order shown in Figure 9-12:

   (a) What company was chosen to supply the goods?
   (b) Why do each of the following receive a copy of the purchase order:

      (i) Receiving department?
      (ii) Accounting department?
      (iii) Purchasing department?
      (iv) Requesting department?

4. Explain the term "matching process" and indicate what three documents are matched.

5. What department is responsible for matching the documents?

6. What supporting documents are attached to the purchase invoice?

7. What types of transactions are recorded in the Purchases Journal?

8. Explain the steps followed in posting the Purchases Journal. (Assume direct posting is not used.)

9. What is a credit invoice?

10. What is a special journal system?

11. Which accounts are debited and credited when recording a credit invoice for goods returned (purchase return) in the General Journal?

8. Lynn Halliwell owns Superior Electrical Services. Her firm uses a Cash Receipts Journal (CRJ), Cash Payments Journal (CPJ), Purchases Journal (PJ), Sales Journal (SJ), and General Journal (J). Indicate which journal should be used to record each of the following transactions:

   (a) Purchase of a new printer by paying one-third in cash and the remainder on account
   (b) Purchase of equipment for cash
   (c) Return of merchandise by a customer for a credit to her account
   (d) Return of merchandise by a customer for a cash refund
   (e) Receipt of a cheque from a customer in payment of an outstanding account
   (f) Sale of merchandise for cash
   (g) Payment of the employees' salaries for the week
   (h) Purchase of equipment on account
   (i) Sale of merchandise on account
   (j) Adjusting entry to record supplies expense for the period

9. (a) Record the following approved invoices in a Purchases Journal.
   (b) Total, balance, and rule the Purchases Journal.

Jan. 3 Purchased merchandise for $1 500 from Cavers Ltd., GST $105, Invoice 554 dated Dec. 30, terms n/30.

4 Purchased office supplies for $163 from Beatties, GST $11.41, Invoice W12 dated Jan. 3, terms n/30.

4 Purchased merchandise for $750 from Beamer Bros., GST $52.50, Invoice 7 dated Jan. 2, terms n/30.

5 Purchased office equipment for $750 from Grand Ltd., GST $52.50, Invoice 6-110 dated Jan. 2, terms n/30.

10. (a) Set up the following accounts and balances for May 1 in the partial General Ledger for Discount Stores:

101	Cash	$ 3 500	
110	Accounts Receivable	6 900	
125	Office Supplies	1 340	
200	Accounts Payable		$ 4 520
206	GST Payable		750
207	GST Refundable	500	
300	K. Duncan, Capital		14 670
501	Purchases	7 000	
503	Transportation on Purchases	240	
606	Truck Expense	460	
		$19 940	$19 940

(b) Set up the following accounts and balances on May 1 in the Accounts Payable Ledger for Discount Stores:

Canadian Tire	$ 375
Graham Wholesalers	3 470
Whitman Stationers	535
Williams Trucking	140
	$4 520

(c) Enter the following approved purchases invoices on page 73 of a Purchases Journal for Discount Stores; then total, balance, and rule the journal.

May 4 Merchandise from Graham Wholesalers for $576, GST $40.32.

5 Office supplies from Whitman Stationers for $135, GST $9.45.

6 Gas and oil used in the truck from Canadian Tire for $35, GST $2.45.

7 Transportation of merchandise from Williams Trucking for $47, GST $3.29.

8 Merchandise from Graham Wholesalers for $2 348, GST $164.36.

(d) Post the Purchases Journal to the General Ledger.

(e) Prepare a trial balance for the General Ledger.
(f) Post the relevant source documents directly to the Accounts Payable Ledger.
(g) Prepare a schedule of accounts payable. Check your total with the control account, 200, in the General Ledger.

11. (a) In a Purchases Journal for B & M Furniture, enter the approved purchases invoices given below. Assign page 214 to the Purchases Journal. Use the partial chart of accounts given below to determine the accounts affected.
(b) Total, balance, and rule the Purchases Journal.
(c) Describe how you would post this journal if all postings to the accounts in both the General Ledger and Accounts Payable Ledger are made from the Purchases Journal.

115	Prepaid Insurance	501	Purchases
121	Office Equipment	505	Transportation on Purchases
201	Accounts Payable	609	Delivery Expense
207	GST Refundable	639	Miscellaneous Expense

May 3 Carter and Wilson, insurance agents, $3 450 plus $241.50 GST for the insurance premium on the building and contents.

4 Thornhill's Service Centre, $310 plus $21.70 GST for delivery truck repairs.

4 Teak Manufacturers, $9 756 plus $682.92 GST for dining room furniture.

5 McCall's Stationers, $289 plus $20.23 GST for a new filing cabinet for the office.

7 Thornhill's Service Centre, $580 plus $40.60 GST for repairs to one of the delivery trucks.

7 Rick's Towing Service, $40 plus $2.80 GST for towing a delivery truck to Thornhill's Service Centre.

9 Ray's Landscaping, $75 plus $5.25 GST for lawn care.

10 Teak Manufacturers, $7 527 plus $526.89 GST for living room furniture.

11 Enders Ltd., $4 375 plus $306.25 GST for the purchase of five refrigerators.

11 Hi-Way Trucking, $750 plus $52.50 GST for freight charges on the refrigerator shipment.

12. (a) In a Purchases Journal for the Pro-Cycle Shop, enter the approved invoices given below. Assign page 133 to the journal. Use the following trial balance to determine the accounts affected:

Pro-Cycle Shop Trial Balance September 30, 2000			
101	Cash	$10 400	
110	Accounts Receivable	9 800	
125	Supplies	1 500	
151	Office Equipment	30 000	
200	Accounts Payable		$ 5 000
206	GST Payable		715
207	GST Refundable	400	
300	K. Paul, Capital		55 085
301	K. Paul, Drawings	0	
500	Purchases	7 000	
503	Transportation on Purchases	500	
600	Delivery Expense	700	
601	Advertising Expense	200	
607	Repairs and Maintenance Expense	300	
		$60 800	$60 800

Oct. 1 Fifteen bicycles from CCM Ltd. for $2 250, GST $157.50.

3 Tires and tubes from Dunlop Tires for $477, CST $33.39.

4 Repairs to the main entrance by Coastal Glass for $125, GST $8.75.

4 Transportation of the bicycles received on October 1, $125 from Hi-Way Transport, GST $8.75.

5 Gas and oil used in the delivery truck during June, $187.50 from Craig's Service Station, GST $13.13.

8 Advertising space, $430 from the *Daily News,* GST $30.10.

(b) Total, balance, and rule the Purchases Journal.

(c) Assign page 134 to the next journal page and bring the totals forward from page 133; then continue by recording the following approved invoices:

Oct. 9 Repairs to the owner's (K. Paul's) cottage, $1 697.02 plus GST from Denver Contractors.

9 Bicycle accessories from CCM Ltd. for $862, GST $60.34.

10 A new computer from Jason's Ltd. for $2 685, GST $187.95.

10 Ten bicycles from Mountain Bike Manufacturers for $2 960, GST $207.20.

11 Paper bags, wrapping paper, and other store supplies from Carter Supplies for $167, GST $11.69.

(d) Set up a General Ledger and post the Purchases Journal.

(e) Prepare a trial balance.

(f) Describe the procedure you would prefer to use to post the Accounts Payable Ledger. Why do you prefer this method to other methods available?

13. The following is a partial chart of accounts for Electronics Unlimited of Vancouver.

100	Cash	501	Purchases
121	Office Equipment	502	Transportation on Purchases
201	Accounts Payable	503	Purchases Returns and Allowances
205	PST Payable	604	Delivery Expense
206	GST Payable	610	Building Repairs Expense
207	GST Refundable		

(a) On page 37 of a Purchases Journal, record the approved purchases invoices for Electronics Unlimited shown on the following pages.
(b) Record credit invoices in a General Journal.
(c) Total, balance, and rule the Purchases Journal.

BANNEX LTD.
1493 Bridge Road, Toronto, ON M6A 1Z5
Phone 594-6655 Fax 594-8731

SOLD TO Electronics Unlimited
795 Beaver Drive
Vancouver, BC
V7N 3H6

INVOICE 17493
DATE Feb. 3, 2001
TERMS Net 30 days

QUANTITY	DESCRIPTION	UNIT PRICE	TOTAL
5	Spools of #10 copper wire	$23.50	$117.50
		GST	8.23
		Total Due	$125.73

Received March 2

Received by	BK
Price O.K.	✓
Account	501
Payment O.K.	CD

Sales Tax Exempt

White and Turner
Heating Contractors
for all your heating supplies
497 Albion Rd., Vancouver, BC V7A 3E4

Sold to Electronics Unlimited
795 Beaver Drive
Vancouver, BC
V7N 3H6

Invoice No. 86B743
Date Feb. 4, 2001
Terms 2/10, n/30

Stock No.	Description	Quantity	Price	Amount
N-21-2	2 cm x 3 m pipes	7	$4.50	$31.50
R-63-47	Boxes #3 washers	2	0.75	1.50
			Subtotal	33.00
			GST	2.31
			PST	1.98
			Total	$37.29

Cash ❑
Charge ❑

Received by	BK
Price O.K.	✓
Account	510
Payment O.K.	CD

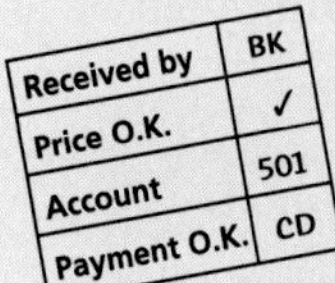

EVC Limited

1793 Pennfield Drive, Victoria, BC V8B 6M2

To	Electronics Unlimited 795 Beaver Drive Vancouver, BC V7N 3H6	**Invoice No.**	E-437073
		Terms	Net 30 days F.O.B.
		Your Order No.	7434
		Ship Via	WCT
		Date Shipped	Feb. 28, 2001
		Date of Inv.	March 1

Quantity	Description	Unit Price	Amount
20	EVC 40 Speakers	$109	$2 180.00
10	EVC 50 Speakers	129	1 290.00
10	SP-743-H Receivers	133	1 330.00
5	SP-843-H Receivers	152	760.00
		Sub Total	5 560.00
		GST	389.20
		Total	$5 949.20

Sales Tax Exempt

WEST COAST TRANSPORT

Vancouver	Seattle	Los Angeles
73 Commissioner Rd.	1890 Industrial Rd.	734 Green Street
Vancouver, BC	Seattle, WA	Los Angeles, CA
Canada V7R 3T6	U.S.A. 92000-8191	U.S.A. 96300-9852
Phone (604) 937-4370	Phone (206) 347-8650	Phone (213) 474-8503
Fax (604) 937-4819	Fax (206) 347-9190	Fax (213) 474-8888

Shipper:
EVC Limited
1793 Pennfield Drive
Los Angeles, CA 96430-5893

Consignee:
Electronics Unlimited
795 Beaver Drive
Vancouver, BC V7N 3H6

Prepaid **Collect X**

Date March 1, 2001 **Terms:** Net 30 **Inv. No.** W.B 74343

No. of Containers	Mass	Rate	Amount
45 boxes	300 kg	$0.40/kg	$120.00
		GST	8.40
		Total	$128.40
		Pay this Amount	$128.40

Received by BK
Price O.K. ✓
Account 502
Payment O.K. CD

Same Day Delivery

LOCAL DELIVERIES

475 Dynes Road
Vancouver, BC V7E 3R1
Phone 837-4390

Invoice No. 657
Terms Net 30
Date March 7, 2001

Charge
Electronics Unlimited
795 Beaver Drive
Vancouver, BC
V7N 3H6

Deliver to
Mr. K. Stafford
473 Elm Street
Vancouver, BC
V6L 2L4

Description		Amount
4 boxes		$100.00
	GST	7.00
	Total	$107.00

Received March 9

Received by	BK
Price O.K.	✓
Account	503
Payment O.K.	CD

Jonsson

Office Specialties Ltd.
63 Main Street, Vancouver, BC V6A 2S2 Phone 343-7512 Fax 343-1817
For All Your Office Needs

Sold to
Electronics Unlimited
795 Beaver Drive
Vancouver, BC
V7N 3H6

Our Invoice No. 73B4973
Your Order No. 7440
Terms 2/10, n/30
Date Shipped March 7, 2001
Date of Inv. March 7, 2001

Quantity	Description	Unit Price	Amount
1	Printer PX585	$465.64	$465.64
		GST	32.59
		PST	27.94
		Pay this amount	$526.17

Received March 9

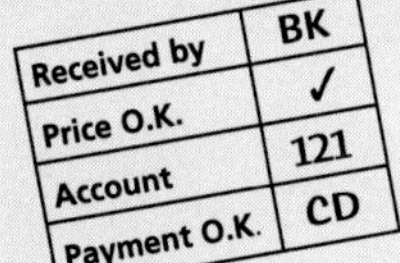

EVC
Limited
1793 Pennfield Drive, Victoria, BC V8B 6M2

TO:	Electronics Unlimited 795 Beaver Drive Vancouver, BC V7N 3H6	**Credit No.** March 7, 2001	1396

We credit your account as specified below

Re: Inv. #E-437073, dated March 1, 2001

1 SP-743-H Receiver	$133.00
1 SP-843-H Receiver	152.00
Sub Total	$285.00
GST	19.95
	$304.95

CREDIT MEMORANDUM

UNIT 22 Sales Journal

Learning Objectives

After reading this unit, discussing the applicable review questions, and completing the applications exercises, you will be able to do the following:

1. **RECORD** sales invoices in a Sales Journal.
2. **RECORD** credit invoices.
3. **TOTAL,** balance, and post a Sales Journal.
4. **EXPLAIN** the purpose of a customer statement.
5. **DISCUSS** the cycle billing method of preparing statements.

In this unit, the system for processing sales of goods on account will be discussed as well as the recording and posting procedures for a Sales Journal.

PROCEDURES FOR SALES INVOICES

For each credit sale, a source document called a *sales invoice* is prepared. This document, commonly called a *bill,* is the seller's evidence that a transaction occurred. The sales invoice in Figure 9-23 was prepared by Warrendon Sports:

FIGURE 9-23
Sales invoice

WARRENDON SPORTS

2579 Base Line Road
Ottawa, ON K2H 7B3
Tel: 684-1287 Fax: 684-5381

INVOICE **Order No.**

Sold To
High School of Commerce
300 Rochester Street
Ottawa, ON K1R 7N4

Ship To
Same

Date Oct. 15, 2001 **Invoice No.** 105 **Terms** Net 30 days **Cash** **Charge**

Quantity	Description	Unit Price	Amount
3	Volleyballs, vinyl specials	$19.65	$58.95
		GST (7%)	4.13
		PST (8%)	4.72
		Total Due	$67.80

GST Registration No. R119282106

See if you can answer the following questions about the invoice in Figure 9-23:

- Who is the seller?
- Who is the buyer?
- What is the total to be paid by the customer and when must it be paid?
- How are the $58.95, $4.13, and $4.72 calculated?

Four copies of the invoice are normally prepared and are distributed as shown in Figure 9-24.

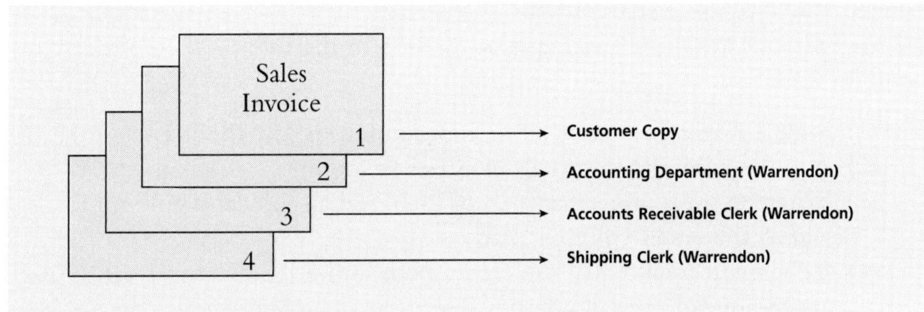

FIGURE 9-24
Distribution of sales invoice copies

INTRODUCING THE SALES JOURNAL

Earlier in this chapter, you learned that a Purchases Journal is used to record purchases of goods and services on credit. The use of special columns saves time and effort in recording and posting purchases.

For the same reasons, the *Sales Journal* is used to record sales on account (credit sales) by companies that make many such sales.

In a Sales Journal, each transaction requires only one line. Look at Figure 9-25, the Sales Journal for Warrendon Sports. Notice that in some of the transactions the customer is charged PST, while in others there is no PST. This is because some of the sales involve non-taxable items.

This Sales Journal in Figure 9-25 has been correctly balanced and posted. The steps involved in both these procedures will now be described.

FIGURE 9-25
Sales Journal for Warrendon Sports showing correct balancing and posting procedures

SALES JOURNAL **PAGE 17**

DATE	INV. NO.	CUSTOMER	TERMS	P.R.	ACCOUNTS REC. DEBIT	SALES CREDIT	GST PAYABLE CREDIT	PST PAYABLE CREDIT
2001								
Jul. 5	71	K. Roessler	n/30	✓	115.00	100.00	7.00	8.00
7	72	C. Bard	n/30	✓	345.00	300.00	21.00	24.00
8	73	M. Wong	n/30	✓	80.25	75.00	5.25	
12	74	G. Saikeley	n/30	✓	481.50	450.00	31.50	
13	75	K. Rice	n/30	✓	805.00	700.00	49.00	56.00
15	76	C. Bard	n/30	✓	690.00	600.00	42.00	48.00
		Debits = $2 516.75			2 516.75	2 225.00	155.75	136.00
		Credits = $2 516.75			(110)	(400)	(206)	(205)

Balancing the Sales Journal

If transactions have been recorded correctly, the total of the debit columns should equal the total of the credit columns.

At the bottom of each page and at the end of the month, these procedures are followed:

(1) Rule a single line across all money columns below the last line used.
(2) Add the columns; put totals in as pencil footings.
(3) Where there is more than one of each, add all the debit column totals and all the credit column totals.
(4) If the debit totals equal the credit totals, write the column totals in ink at the bottom of each column. Write the debit and credit totals in the customer column.
(5) Rule double lines across the date and all money columns.

Look again at Figure 9-25 to see an example of a Sales Journal that has been balanced. If the month has not ended, the totals are carried forward to the next page. At the end of the month, the totals are posted to the General Ledger.

Posting the Sales Journal

The use of a Sales Journal reduces the amount of posting to be done. There are only two steps followed in posting the Sales Journal. The amounts in the accounts receivable debit column are posted daily to the customer accounts in the Accounts Receivable Ledger and the four totals are posted to the General Ledger at the end of the month. The posting is similar to the posting of the Purchases Journal and is done as follows:

(1) Each day, post the entries in the accounts receivable debit column to the customer accounts in the Accounts Receivable Ledger. Write the Sales Journal page number and abbreviation in the posting reference column of each account. Enter a check mark (✓) in the posting reference column of the journal opposite each customer.
(2) At the end of the month, post the journal totals to the Accounts Receivable account, the Sales account, the GST Payable account, and the PST Payable account in the General Ledger. Enter the Sales Journal page number and abbreviation in the posting reference column of the accounts. Write the account numbers below the totals in the Sales Journal (see Figure 9-25).

RECORDING CREDIT INVOICES

When goods are returned by a customer, a credit invoice is prepared and sent to the customer. Four methods are used to record sales returns on the books of the seller. They are:

(1) In the General Journal, using a Sales Returns and Allowances account and recording the credit invoices as debits in that account
(2) In the General Journal, decreasing the Sales account with a debit
(3) In the Sales Journal, recording the return in the sales returns and allowances debit column and decreasing the GST Payable, PST Payable, and Accounts Receivable accounts using the circling method
(4) In the Sales Journal, using the circling method to decrease the Sales, GST Payable, PST Payable, and Accounts Receivable accounts

The circling method is illustrated in Figure 9-26.

FIGURE 9-26
Circled items representing sales returns are subtracted from uncircled items.

SALES JOURNAL **PAGE 17**

DATE	INV. NO.	CUSTOMER	TERMS	P.R.	ACCOUNTS REC. DEBIT	SALES CREDIT	GST PAYABLE CREDIT	PST PAYABLE CREDIT
2001								
Jul. 5	71	K. Roessler	n/30		115.00	100.00	7.00	8.00
7	72	C. Bard	n/30		345.00	300.00	21.00	24.00
8	73	M. Wong	n/30		80.25	75.00	5.25	
12	74	G. Saikeley	n/30		481.50	450.00	31.50	
13	75	K. Rice	n/30		805.00	700.00	49.00	56.00
15	76	C. Bard	n/30		690.00	600.00	42.00	48.00
21	C-12	C. Bard			(57.50)	(50.00)	(3.50)	(4.00)
		Debits = $2 459.25			2 459.25	2 175.00	152.25	132.00
		Credits = $2 459.25						

If the circling method (see Figure 9-26) is not used and if the Sales Journal does not have special columns to accommodate a sales return transaction, then the transaction is recorded in the General Journal. An example follows:

Jul. 21	Sales Returns and Allowances	401	50.00	
	GST Payable	206	3.50	
	PST Payable	205	4.00	
	Accounts Receivable/C. Bard	110/✓		57.50
	Credit Invoice C-12 for goods returned.			

Note: As you have seen previously, the $57.50 must be posted to both the Accounts Receivable in the General Ledger and to the C. Bard account in the Accounts Receivable Ledger to maintain the equality of the control account and the subsidiary ledger.

Each of the exercises in this chapter will state the company's accounting policy for recording credit invoices.

STATEMENT OF ACCOUNT

Suppose a company has a customer by the name of J. Clarke, and another named J. Clark. A sale of $100 to J. Clarke was incorrectly posted to J. Clark's account. In the seller's Accounts Receivable Ledger, J. Clarke's account balance would be $100 too low and J. Clark's account balance would be $100 too high. How would this error be discovered?

A statement of account is a form sent to customers showing charges, amounts credited, and the balance of an account.

To locate errors of this type, many companies send a *statement of account* to their customers (see Figure 9-27). At regular periods, usually every month, a copy of the debits and credits in customer accounts is mailed to every customer. In effect, a copy of the account is sent to the customer. The statement of account serves two purposes, as explained on the following page.

FIGURE 9-27
Statement of account sent each month by Renfrew Printing to its customers. It shows the balance forwarded from the previous month and the transactions for the current month.

Renfrew Printing

COMMERCIAL PRINTING • BOOK PRINTING • PHOTOCOPIES • RUBBER STAMPS
173 Raglan Street South, Renfrew, ON K7V 1R2
Tel (613) 432-6449 Fax (613) 432-1147

TO MacKillican & Associates
252 Raglan Street S.
Renfrew, ON K7V 1R1

MONTH OF October 2001
AMOUNT OF REMITTANCE $

PLEASE RETURN THIS PART WITH YOUR REMITTANCE

IN ACCOUNT WITH **PLEASE KEEP THIS PART**

DATE	PARTICULARS	DEBIT	CREDIT	BALANCE
Oct. 1	PREVIOUS BALANCE FORWARD			$263.20
15	5 000 #10 Envelopes	$321.82		585.02

2% PER MONTH (24% PER ANNUM) INTEREST CHARGED ON OVERDUE ACCOUNTS

PLEASE PAY LAST AMOUNT IN THIS COLUMN

- It enables a customer to compare his or her records with those of the seller and thus to locate errors.
- It reminds a customer of the balance owing.

The statement of account may be prepared by hand or by computer.

Cycle Billing

A company that has only a few customers usually sends a statement of account to each customer at the end of the month.

A company with a large number of customers may find it impossible to prepare all the statements at the end of the month. A more efficient method of handling the preparation of the statements is to distribute the work evenly over the month. Statements are prepared and mailed to groups of customers at different times of the month. Figure 9-28 illustrates how the work is scheduled.

In *cycle billing,* the records of transactions (source documents such as invoices and cash receipt lists) for someone like J. Clarke would be accumulated from the date of the last statement. These transactions would be entered in the customer's account and the statement of account would be prepared on the 6th day of each month. The statement of account for Resticon Ltd. would be prepared on the 21st day of each month.

Cycle billing is a method of spreading over the month the work of preparing and mailing statements to customers.

FIGURE 9-28
Cycle billing

Cycle Billing Schedule

INITIAL OF CUSTOMER'S LAST NAME	INCLUDES TRANSACTIONS UP TO	DAY OF THE MONTH ON WHICH STATEMENT IS PREPARED
A–E	5th	6th
F–L	13th	14th
M–R	20th	21st
S–Z	29th	30th

SUMMARIZING THE SYSTEM FOR RECORDING SALES

Earlier in this text, you learned that a system is a series of steps followed to complete a task. In this unit, you learned the system for recording sales. Figure 9-29 on the next page summarizes that system.

FIGURE 9-29
Complete system for recording sales

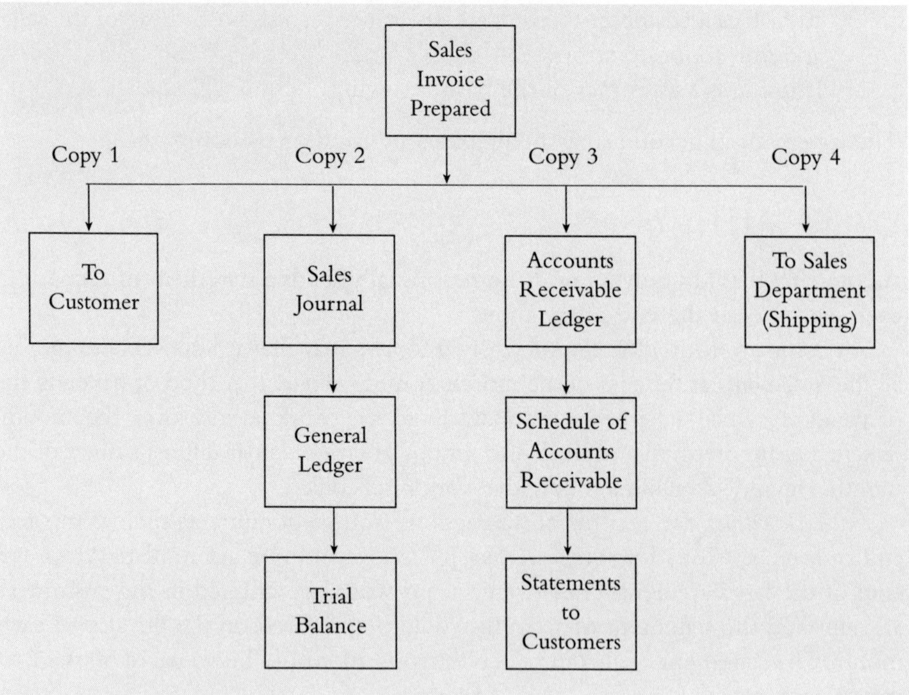

REVIEW QUESTIONS

UNIT 22

1. What source document is prepared for a credit sale?
2. In which special journal is a credit sale recorded?
3. There is a $100 entry circled in a Sales Journal's accounts receivable debit column. Should the $100 be posted as a debit or as a credit to the customer's account?
4. To which ledger are copies of a sales invoice posted when a company uses direct posting?
5. (a) What is a statement of account?
   (b) What two purposes are served by the statement of account?
6. Explain the cycle billing method of preparing customer statements.

PROBLEMS: APPLICATIONS

CHAPTER 9

14. (a) Answer the following questions about the invoice shown on the next page.
    (i) Who is the seller?
    (ii) Who is the customer?
    (iii) What is the date of the invoice?
    (iv) What are the terms of sale?
    (v) What is the last day for payment?
    (vi) How was the $66 calculated?
    (vii) Why is PST not added to the invoice?

    (b) Assuming you are the seller, record the entry for the invoice on the following page in General Journal form.

kid bindery

132 Railside Road, Don Mills, ON M3A 1B8 Phone 449-5565/Fax 449-7516

Wilco Printers
1825 Valentine Road
Scarborough, ON M1R 3C5

Invoice 14973 **Date** 1/15/02
Docket no. 3100
Terms......net 30 days
Customer's order no.

QUANTITY	DESCRIPTION	PRICE	PER	TOTAL
110 000	Rectangular labels, 45 mm x 330 mm	$0.60	1 000	$66.00
			GST 7%	4.62
			Total Due	$70.62

Provincial Sales Tax Exempt

GST NO. S22621120
Prov. Lic. 31659012

15. You are employed by Tanyss Wholesale Ltd., which sells merchandise to retailers. There is no PST on the sales because the retailer is not the end user of the merchandise, but resells it to the public.

    (a) Record the following invoices on page 71 of a Sales Journal:

    Apr. 3 No. 171 to Bayridge Ltd., terms n/15, amount $271.75, GST $19.02.

    7 No. 172 to Dacon Corp., terms 1/10, n/30, amount $633.98, GST $44.38.

    15 No. 173 to Frontenac Enterprises, terms 1/10, n/30, amount $247, GST $17.29.

    22 No. 174 to Bayridge Ltd., terms n/15, amount $165, GST $11.55.

    30 No. 175 to Fillion Co., terms n/15, amount $83.25, GST $5.83.

    (b) Total, balance, and rule the journal.

16. Ryan Enterprises does not use a Sales Returns and Allowances account. Its accounting policy is to record returns and allowances in the Sales Journal using the circling method. All sales are n/30 and are subject to 7 percent GST and 8 percent PST calculated on the base price.

    (a) Record the following invoices in a Sales Journal:

    Feb. 4 Sales Invoice 816, R. Dunlop, $550.

    5 Sales Invoice 817, R.T. Greer, $280.

    7 Credit Invoice 67, R.T. Greer, $30.

    11 Sales Invoice 818, M. Stewart, $775.

15 Sales Invoice 819, R. Ingall, $98.

18 Sales Invoice 820, R. Nakheeda, $250.

19 Sales Invoice 821, M. Wong, $95.

21 Sales Invoice 822, R. Ingall,, $180.

23 Credit Invoice 68, R. Ingall, $75.

25 Sales Invoice 823, J.R. Smoke, $450.

(b) Total, balance, and rule the Sales Journal.

17. You are an accounting clerk for Doretas, a high-fashion boutique. Sales invoices are recorded in a Sales Journal and credit invoices in a General Journal. A Sales Returns and Allowances account is used to record credit invoices. Terms of sale for all sales on account are n/30. GST of 7 percent is charged on all sales. PST of 8 percent is calculated on the base price plus GST.

(a) Record the sales invoices listed below on page 37 of the Sales Journal and the credit invoices on page 22 of the General Journal.

Apr. 2 Sales Invoice 201 to L. Matheson, amount $70.

3 Credit Invoice C-41 to L. Matheson, goods returned $40.

5 Sales Invoice 202 to M. Conway, amount $100.

9 Sales Invoice 203 to C.L. Ramsay, amount $49.50.

12 Sales Invoice 204 to E. Revell, amount $200.

13 Credit Invoice C-42 to E. Revell, goods returned $80.

15 Sales Invoice 205 to L. Matheson, amount $19.95.

16 Sales Invoice 206 to M. Conway, amount $28.75.

20 Sales Invoice 207 to E. Revell, amount $79.

22 Sales Invoice 208 to C.L. Ramsay, amount $89.

23 Sales Invoice 209 to M. Conway, amount $99.

24 Credit Invoice C-43 to M. Conway, goods returned $99.

29 Sales Invoice 210 to C.L. Ramsay, amount $140.

(b) Total, balance, and rule the Sales Journal.
(c) Open an Accounts Receivable Ledger and post the source documents to the customer accounts from the journal. You require these customer accounts: M. Conway, L. Matheson, C.L. Ramsay, and E. Revell.
(d) Prepare a schedule of accounts receivable. Compare your total to the General Ledger control account (see (g) below).
(e) Open General Ledger accounts: Accounts Receivable 102, PST Payable 205, GST Payable 206, Sales 410, and Sales Returns and Allowances 411.
(f) Post the transactions in the General Journal to the General Ledger. Post the totals of the Sales Journal to the General Ledger.
(g) Prepare a General Ledger trial balance.

18. Fernwood Industries Ltd. does not use a Sales Returns and Allowances account. It is their accounting policy to record returns and allowances in the Sales Journal using the circling method. All sales are n/30 and are subject to 7 percent GST and 6 percent PST on the base price.

(a) Record the following on page 19 of the Sales Journal.

May	4	Sales Invoice 116, P. Weitz, $800.
	5	Sales Invoice 117, M.A. Rowe, $518.
	7	Credit Invoice 5, M.A. Rowe, $48.
	11	Sales Invoice 118, V.P. Remple, $687.
	15	Sales Invoice 119, C.D. Nguyen, $375.
	18	Sales Invoice 120, L.S. Chan, $800.
	19	Sales Invoice 121, C.D. Nguyen, $85.
	21	Sales Invoice 122, P.M. Garcia, $613.
	22	Sales Invoice 123, A.V. Joe, $950.
	23	Credit Invoice 6, A.V. Joe, $50.
	25	Sales Invoice 124, B.D. Wongsam, $330.
	27	Sales Invoice 125, F.O. Bhatia, $250.

(b) Total, balance, and rule the Sales Journal.

UNIT 23 Cash Receipts Journal

Learning Objectives

After reading this unit, discussing the applicable review questions, and completing the applications exercises, you will be able to do the following:

1. **RECORD** cash received in the Cash Receipts Journal.
2. **BALANCE** and post the Cash Receipts Journal.

In the special journal system, all money received is recorded in the Cash Receipts Journal. The items considered to be money — that is, cash receipts — include cheques, money orders, bills, and coins.

INTRODUCING THE CASH RECEIPTS JOURNAL

Figure 9-30 on page 345 is a Cash Receipts Journal with seven money columns. There are debit columns for cash and sales discounts and credit columns for accounts receivable, sales, GST payable, and PST payable. There is also an Other Accounts credit column, which is used to record credits to any account for which a column is not provided.

Most transactions require only one line. However, an occasional compound transaction requires two lines. When the other accounts column is used, the name of the account must be shown in the customer or account column. Similarly, the account name must be shown when an entry is made in the accounts receivable column. Additional columns may be added to the journal if a particular account is used frequently.

The Cash Receipts Journal is totalled and balanced at the bottom of each journal page and at the end of the month as shown in Figure 9-30. The procedure followed in balancing and posting is the same as the procedure for the Sales or Purchases Journals. The following points regarding posting are illustrated by Figure 9-30:

(1) Accounts receivable are posted to the Accounts Receivable Ledger daily. A check mark in the posting reference column indicates that an entry has been posted to the customer's account.
(2) Other accounts column entries are posted individually at the end of the month to the General Ledger. A number in the posting reference column indicates that an entry has been posted and gives the account number.
(3) Column totals are posted to the General Ledger at the end of the month. A number in brackets under a column indicates that a total has been posted and gives the account number.

RECORDING SOURCE DOCUMENTS FOR CASH RECEIPTS

Cash Receipts from Customers

Source documents for two transactions involving cash received from customers are shown recorded in Figure 9-30. We will examine each of them.

Cheque Received for Payment on Account

A credit sale was made by Warrendon Sports to the High School of Commerce on October 15. The terms of the sale were net 30 days. This meant that a cheque should be received by Warrendon Sports by November 14, 30 days from the invoice date.

The cheque received by Warrendon Sports is shown in Figure 9-31 on page 346. Notice that this cheque is different from the personal cheques used by most individuals. It is called a *voucher cheque* and contains two parts:

- Cheque
- Attached statement describing the purpose of the payment

When the cheque is received, it is recorded in the Cash Receipts Journal as shown in Figure 9-30. Cash is debited $67.80 and the customer's account is decreased with a credit of $67.80. Notice that the credit is written in the accounts receivable credit column and the customer's name is shown in the section next to the date. As with many transactions in special journals, the recording procedure is completed on one line.

FIGURE 9-30
Cash Receipts Journal after balancing and posting

CASH RECEIPTS JOURNAL **PAGE 37**

DATE	REF. NO.	CUSTOMER OR ACCOUNT	P.R.	CASH DEBIT	SALES DISCOUNTS DEBIT	ACCOUNTS REC. CREDIT	SALES CREDIT	GST PAYABLE CREDIT	PST PAYABLE CREDIT	OTHER ACCOUNTS CREDIT
2001										
Nov. 14		Forwarded		3 110.60		1 955.00	1 000.00	75.60	80.00	
14		H.S. of Commerce	✓	67.80		67.80				
14		W. Mulvihill	✓	601.40	18.60	620.00				
16	71			26.75			25.00	1.75		
20		W. Creighton, Capital	300	2 000.00						2 000.00
30		Bank Interest Earned	420	75.00						75.00
		Debits = $5 900.15		5 881.55	18.60	2 642.80	1 025.00	77.35	80.00	2 075.00
		Credits = $5 900.15		(100)	(410)	(102)	(400)	(206)	(221)	

FIGURE 9-31
Voucher cheque

HIGH SCHOOL OF COMMERCE
300 Rochester St.
Ottawa, Ontario K1R 7N4

CURRENT ACCOUNT
CHEQUE NUMBER 75039
Oct. 15, 2001

PAY TO THE ORDER OF Warrendon Sports -------------------------------- $67.80

SUM OF Sixty-seven------------------------------------- 80/100 DOLLARS

THE ROYAL BANK OF CANADA
1517 Woodward Ave.
Ottawa, ON K1Z 7W5

L. McKillican
HIGH SCHOOL OF COMMERCE

61428 003 124 5802

(Detach and retain this statement)

THE ATTACHED CHEQUE IS IN PAYMENT OF ITEMS LISTED BELOW

DATE	ITEM	AMOUNT	DISCOUNT	NET AMOUNT
Oct. 15	Invoice 105	$67.80		$67.80

Cheque Received for Account Payment Less Sales Discount

Cash discounts are offered to encourage early payment of customer account balances.

You have learned that sellers offer discounts to customers to encourage early payment of account balances. When sales are being made, the buyer and seller agree on payment terms. When the final details of a sale have been completed, both parties should understand clearly when and how payment is to be made. The payment terms should appear on the purchase invoice, the sales invoice, and the monthly statement. Any penalty for late payment should also be clearly outlined on the sale documents.

Figure 9-30 on page 345 shows how the receipt of a cheque for the payment of a sales invoice less a sales discount is recorded in the Cash Receipts Journal. On November 14, a customer, M. Mulvihill, paid $601.40, being $620 less a cash discount of $18.60 ($620 × 0.03 = $18.60) for paying the invoice within 10 days. The customer's account is credited for the full amount of the invoice, $620. The credit of $620 is recorded in the Accounts Receivable credit column. The sales discount of $18.60 is recorded in the Sales Discounts debit column. The cash received, $601.40, is recorded in the Cash debit column.

Other Cash Receipts

As well as money received from customers paying the balances in their accounts, cash is received from the following types of transactions:

- Cash sales to customers
- Owner investments
- Cash refunds received for purchases returns
- Interest earned on bank accounts and other investments
- Miscellaneous sources

Source documents for three transactions of this type are shown recorded in Figure 9-30. Each will be examined.

Cash Sales Slip

A $25 non-provincial sales tax cash sale is made by Warrendon to a customer on November 16. The customer pays for the item and receives Cash Sales Slip 71, which describes the transaction and serves as proof of payment. Cash sales slips are prenumbered and the number of the slip is often recorded in the reference number column of the journal. This transaction is shown in the Cash Receipts Journal in Figure 9-30. Notice that for this cash sale it is not necessary to show anything in the customer or account column.

Cheque Received for New Investment

On November 20, W. Creighton, the owner of Warrendon Sports, uses a personal cheque to invest an additional $2 000 in the business. Figure 9-30 shows the entry made to record the cheque in the Cash Receipts Journal. Cash is debited $2 000. The credit to the Capital account is recorded in the Other Accounts credit column because there is no column entitled Capital Credit.

Bank Credit Memorandum

A *bank credit memorandum (memo)* is a source document received from a bank when the bank adds money to a customer's account. Warrendon received a bank credit memo for $75 on November 30. It indicated that $75 interest had been earned and added by the bank to Warrendon's account. The $75 is recorded on the debit side of the Cash account (an asset increasing), and on the credit side of the Bank Interest Earned account.

A bank credit memo indicates an increase in a bank account.

Bank Interest Earned is a revenue account. It increases Capital, and that is why interest received is recorded on the credit side of the Bank Interest Earned account. This transaction is shown in T-accounts below:

Bank Interest Earned is a revenue account and has a credit balance.

Cash			
Nov. 30	75		

Bank Interest Earned			
		Nov. 30	75

This transaction represents money received; therefore, it is recorded in the Cash Receipts Journal (see Figure 9-30). The $75 debit to the Cash account is placed in the cash debit column. The $75 credit to the Bank Interest Earned account is entered in the other accounts credit column.

1. What source document is prepared for a cash sale?
2. What is a voucher cheque?
3. What is the purpose of the voucher that is attached to the voucher cheque?
4. Does a bank credit memo indicate that a company's bank account has increased or decreased?

19. Record the following source documents in a General Journal:

Oct. 23 Cash sales slip for $25 plus $1.50 PST plus $1.75 GST.

23 Cheque received from the owner, B. McAdam, for $3 500 as an additional investment in the business.

23 Bank credit memo from the Bank of Montreal showing that $87 in interest has been added to the bank account.

23 Cheque received from M. Mulvihill for $196 to pay Invoice 405 of $200 less 2 percent discount allowed. Invoice date September 21. Invoice terms 2/10, n/30.

23 Cheque received from T. Davis for $275 to pay Invoice 399, no discount.

24 Cash sales slip for $160 plus $9.60 PST plus $11.20 GST.

20. (a) Record the following source documents on page 191 of a Cash Receipts Journal:

Jun. 1 Cash register tape shows sales of $2 465 plus $172.55 GST and $197.20 PST.

2 Cheque received from C. Ballard for $618 to pay Invoice 803, $618 dated April 1. Terms: n/30.

2 Cheque received from L. Noble for $317.52 to pay Invoice 799, $324 less 2 percent discount. Invoice dated April 30. Terms: n/30.

3 Bank credit memo, $145 for interest deposited into the bank account.

4 Cheque received from K. Engel, the owner, for $3 800 as an additional investment in the business.

7 Bank credit memo, $10 500 for a bank loan that was deposited in the company bank account.

8 Cheque received from C. Drago for $548.80 to pay Invoice 805, $560 less 2 percent discount. Invoice dated May 15. Terms: n/30.

9 Cash Sales Slips 940 to 955 for $2 875 plus $201.25 GST and $230 PST.

10 Cash register tape for sales of $1 890 plus $132.30 GST and $151.20 PST.

11 Money order received from C. Tierney for $875.14 to pay Invoice 810, $893 less 2 percent discount. Invoice dated May 20. Terms: n/30.

(b) Total, balance, and rule the Cash Receipts Journal.

(c) Describe how you would post this journal if this firm did not use a direct posting system for customer accounts.

21. (a) Record the source documents given below on page 193 of a Cash Receipts Journal.
    (b) Total, balance, and rule the Cash Receipts Journal.
    (c) Set up a General Ledger and an Accounts Receivable Ledger for September 1 with the following accounts and balances; then post the Cash Receipts Journal.

Cash	101	1 400	
Accounts Receivable	102	3 949	
PST Payable	205		350
GST Payable	206		400
C. Black, Capital	301		15 000
Sales	401		0
Sales Discounts	402	0	

Schedule of Accounts Receivable September 1, 2002

A. Derouin	$2 576
B. Jennings	426
V. Williams	947
	$3 949

Sep. 1 Cheque received for $4 100 from the owner, C. Black, as a further investment in the business.

2 Cash Sales Slips 340 to 355 for $975 plus $68.25 GST and $78 PST.

3 Cheques received:
$875 from A. Derouin on account;
$428.26 from V. Williams to pay Invoice 6061 for $437, Invoice dated August 26. Terms: 2/10, n/30.

4 Bank credit memo for $426 the bank collected for us from B. Jennings on account.

5 Cheque received from A. Derouin for $749.70 to pay Invoice 6059 for $765. Invoice dated August 25. Terms: 2/10, n/30.

5 Cash Sales Slips 356 to 382 for $3 250 plus $227.50 GST and $260 PST.

22. (a) Record the following source documents on page 705 of a Cash Receipts Journal.

Nov. 1 Bank credit note of $5 000 for a bank loan that was approved and deposited in the bank account.

3 Cheques received:
$344.96 from K. Bandy to pay Invoice 756 for $352 dated October 24, terms 2/10, n/30;
$463.54 from L. Kessba to pay Invoice 754 for $473 dated October 23, terms 2/10, n/30.

4 Cash register tape showing $1 325 in sales plus $106 PST plus $92.75 GST.

5 Bank credit memo, $58 for interest earned.

5 Money order received from C. Taylor for $742 to pay Invoice 601 dated October 4, terms: EOM.

(b) Total, balance, and rule the Cash Receipts Journal.

(c) Set up a General Ledger and an Accounts Receivable Ledger with the following accounts and balances; then post the Cash Receipts Journal.

Account	No.	Debit	Credit
Cash	101	6 500	
Accounts Receivable	103	2 453	
PST Payable	205		310
GST Payable	206		-0-
Bank Loan	207		-0-
Sales	401		-0-
Sales Discounts	402	-0-	
Bank Interest Earned	403		-0-

Schedule of Accounts Receivable November 1, 2001

K. Bandy	$ 730
L. Kessba	473
C. Taylor	1 250
	$2 453

UNIT 24 Cash Payments Journal

Learning Objectives

After reading this unit, discussing the applicable review questions, and completing the applications exercises, you will be able to do the following:

1. **RECORD** payments, including refunds, in the Cash Payments Journal.
2. **BALANCE** and post the Cash Payments Journal.

So far in this chapter, special columnar journals for purchases, sales, and cash receipts have been described. Now the recording of cash payments in a special journal called the *Cash Payments Journal* will be discussed.

MAKING CASH PAYMENTS

Payment By Cheque

A basic accounting principle is that all payments, except very small ones, should be made by cheque. Each cheque should be authorized. Documents such as receiving reports and approved invoices should be available to support the issuing of the cheque.

Cheque Requisition

In many companies, a cheque request form is completed before a cheque is issued. This form is called a *cheque requisition*. The cheque requisition is accompanied by all of the documents related to the transaction, because the person with the responsibility to authorize the issuing of a cheque may wish to trace the entire history of the transaction.

Voucher Cheque

Many firms use the voucher form of a cheque as shown in Figure 9-32 below. The cheque is prepared with three copies. Copy 1 is the cheque sent to the creditor. Copy 2 is kept and is used by the accounting department as the source document for the journal entry. Copy 3 is filed with the invoice. Notice that the cheque in Figure 9-32 requires two signatures. Many firms require two people to sign all cheques so that there is some control over the cash (see Cash Control).

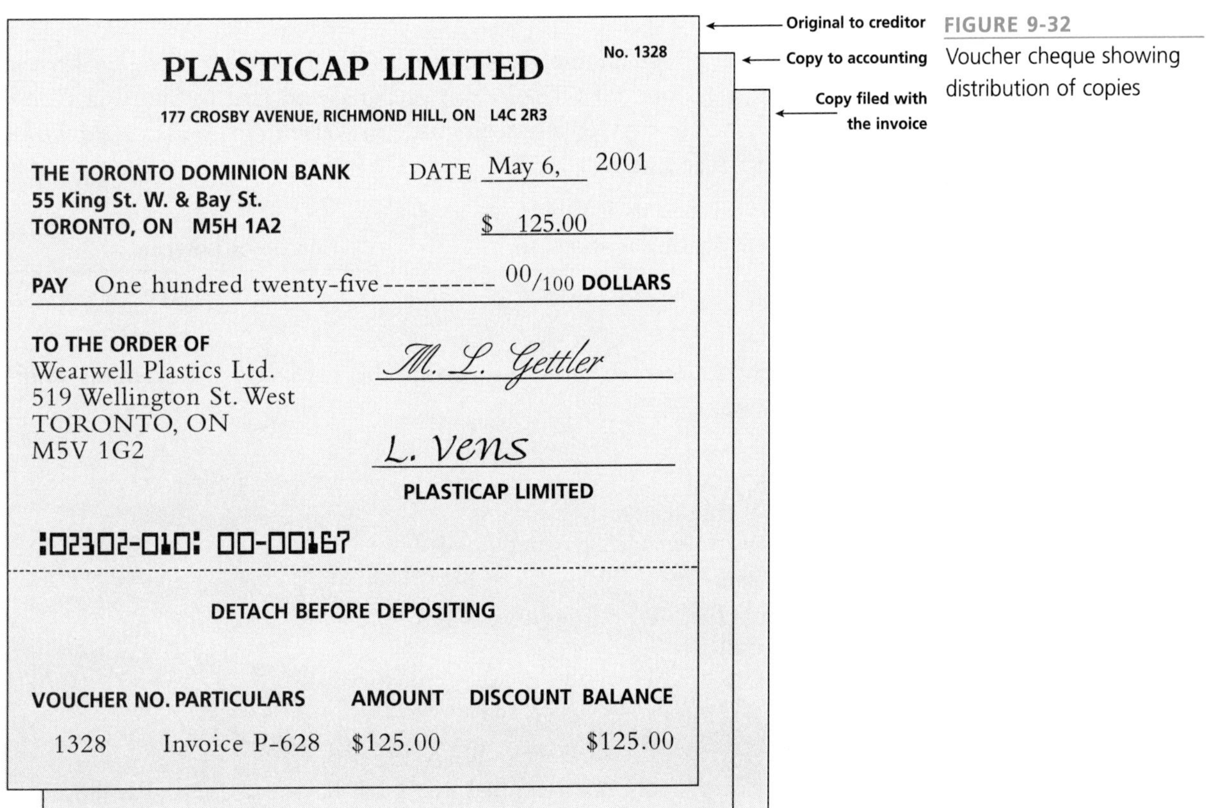
No. 1328

PLASTICAP LIMITED

177 CROSBY AVENUE, RICHMOND HILL, ON L4C 2R3

THE TORONTO DOMINION BANK
55 King St. W. & Bay St.
TORONTO, ON M5H 1A2

DATE May 6, 2001

$ 125.00

PAY One hundred twenty-five ---------- 00/100 DOLLARS

TO THE ORDER OF
Wearwell Plastics Ltd.
519 Wellington St. West
TORONTO, ON
M5V 1G2

M. L. Gettler

L. Vens

PLASTICAP LIMITED

:02302-010: 00-00167

DETACH BEFORE DEPOSITING

VOUCHER NO.	PARTICULARS	AMOUNT	DISCOUNT	BALANCE
1328	Invoice P-628	$125.00		$125.00

FIGURE 9-32
Voucher cheque showing distribution of copies

INTRODUCING THE CASH PAYMENTS JOURNAL

The Cash Payments Journal is used to record all payments.

Because of the large number of payments made, many companies record their cheques in a Cash Payments Journal. Special columns are provided for accounts that are used often. In the Cash Payments Journal in Figure 9-33 on page 353, special columns are headed Cash Credit, Accounts Payable Debit, GST Refundable Debit, Purchases Debit, and Purchases Discounts Credit. The Other Accounts debit column is provided for those accounts that do not fit into the special columns. Source documents for various transactions involving cash payments are shown recorded in Figure 9-33. In the following section, each will be examined.

Recording Source Documents for Cash Payments

Cheque Issued for Account Payment Less Purchase Discount

On November 4, Warrendon Sports received Purchase Invoice 4918 for $500 worth of basketballs, plus $35 GST, from Sporting Goods Ltd. Terms of sale on the invoice were 2/15, n/30. The invoice was checked for accuracy and since the order was received in good condition, the invoice was passed for payment. The invoice was recorded in Warrendon's books as shown by the following T-accounts:

Purchases		Accounts Payable/ Sporting Goods Ltd.		GST Refundable	
Nov. 4 500			Nov. 4 535	Nov. 4 35	

The invoice was placed in the date file in a folder dated November 19. On November 19, a cheque for $524.30 was prepared and sent to Sporting Goods Ltd. From the cheque copy, entries were made in Warrendon's books as shown by the following T-accounts:

Cash		Accounts Payable/ Sporting Goods Ltd.		Purchases Discounts	
	Nov. 19 524.30	Nov. 19 535.00	Nov. 4 535.00		Nov. 19 10.70

In General Journal form, the entries shown in these two sets of T-accounts would appear as follows:

Date	Account	Debit	Credit
Nov. 4	Purchases	500.00	
	GST Refundable	35.00	
	Accts. Payable/Sporting Goods Ltd.		535.00
	Invoice 4918, terms 2/15, n/30.		
19	Accts. Payable/Sporting Goods Ltd.	535.00	
	Cash		524.30
	Purchases Discounts		10.70
	Invoice 4918, less discount.		

The Purchases Discounts account is a negative cost account.

This payment on account was recorded in a Cash Payments Journal as illustrated in Figure 9-33.

FIGURE 9-33
Cash Payments Journal

CASH PAYMENTS JOURNAL PAGE 26

DATE	CH. NO.	CREDITOR OR ACCOUNT	P.R.	CASH CREDIT	ACCOUNTS PAYABLE DEBIT	GST REFUNDABLE DEBIT	PURCHASES DEBIT	PURCHASES DISCOUNTS CREDIT	OTHER ACCOUNTS DEBIT
2001									
Nov. 19	326	Sporting Goods Ltd.		524.30	535.00			10.70	
20	DM	Bank Interest Expense		150.00					150.00
22	327	Sylvia Post		109.25					
		Sales Returns & Allow.							95.00
		PST Payable							7.60
		GST Payable							6.65

Bank Debit Memo

A bank debit memo indicates a decrease in a customer's bank account.

A *bank debit memo* indicates a decrease in a bank account. On November 20, Warrendon Sports received a bank debit memo from the Bank of Nova Scotia. The memo indicated that $150 had been deducted from Warrendon's bank account for the monthly interest on their bank loan.

The $150 is an expense, and must be recorded in the Bank Interest Expense account. In Figure 9-33, the debit to Bank Interest Expense is placed in the Other Accounts debit column and the credit is entered in the Cash Credit column.

Cheque Issued for Refund on Cash Sale with GST and PST

On November 20, Sylvia Post purchased a pair of tennis shoes for $65 and a racquet for $95. She paid a total of $184 cash for her purchases, which included GST of $11.20 (0.07 × 160 = 11.20) and PST of $12.80 (160 × 0.08 = 12.80). The seller, Warrendon Sports, recorded the sales as follows:

Nov. 20 Cash	184.00	
Sales		160.00
GST Payable		11.20
PST Payable		12.80
To record a cash sale.		

Sylvia was unhappy with the quality of the racquet and returned it on November 22. She received Cheque 327 for $109.25 as a cash refund. The cheque consisted of $95 plus $6.65 GST (0.07 × 95 = 6.65) and PST of $7.60 (95 × 0.08 = 7.60) for a total of $109.25.

This refund cheque affected the books of Warrendon Sports as shown by the following T-accounts:

Cash	
Nov. 20 184.00	Nov. 22 109.25

Sales Returns & Allowances	
Nov. 22 95.00	

PST Payable	
Nov. 22 7.60	Nov. 20 12.80

GST Payable	
Nov. 22 6.65	Nov. 20 11.20

The refund cheque of $109.25 is recorded in the cash credit column of the Cash Payments Journal (Figure 9-33, page 325). The sale amount, $95, is debited to Sales Returns and Allowances using the other accounts debit column. Since Warrendon Sports refunded the $6.65 GST and the $7.60 PST to Sylvia, it no longer owes this amount to the government. Therefore, Warrendon decreased its liability to the government by debiting GST Payable $6.65 and PST Payable $7.60 in the Other Accounts debit column of the journal. Notice that the entry on November 22 in Figure 9-33 requires four lines because the journal does not have a Sales Returns and Allowances debit column, a PST Payable debit column, or a GST Payable debit column.

Recording Transactions in a Cash Payments Journal

The transactions shown in Figure 9-34 on page 356 provide examples of a number of common cash payment transactions that occur in business. See if you can trace them to the journal from the list of sample transactions.

Sample Transactions

May 1 Issued Cheque 101 for $535 to Tanyss Trading for cash purchase of merchandise, $500 plus $35 GST.
3 Issued Cheque 102 for $149 to Speedquip Ltd. for Invoice B-231 dated Apr. 2.
8 Issued Cheque 103 for $75 to Len's Service Centre to pay for repairs to the company automobile (repairs $70.09, GST $4.91).
12 Issued Cheque 104 for $200 to Willson's Ltd. as partial payment of account.
15 Issued Cheque 105 for $500 to *The Star* for advertising ($467.29 plus $32.71 GST).
17 Issued Cheque 106 for $220 to Angelo's Masonry to pay for a patio at the home of the owner, B. McAdam.
22 Issued Cheque 107 for $49 to Evans & Kert for the cash purchase of supplies (supplies $45.79, GST $3.21).
23 Issued Cheque 108 for $127 to the Provincial Treasurer for last month's PST collections.
25 Issued Cheque 109 for $288.90 to Willson's Ltd. for cash purchase of merchandise (merchandise $270, GST $18.90).
28 Issued Cheque 110 for $343 to Tanyss Trading in payment of Invoice 673 (amount of invoice $350, discount taken $7).
31 Issued Cheque 111 for $3 400 for monthly salaries.
31 Issued Cheque 112 for $300 to Receiver General for GST remittance.

Balancing and Posting the Cash Payments Journal

Procedures similar to those used with the other special journals are followed when balancing and posting the Cash Payments Journal:

(1) Each page is totalled and balanced. Page totals are carried forward if the month has not ended.
(2) At the end of each month, the journal is totalled, balanced, and ruled; it is then posted.
(3) Entries in the Accounts Payable debit column are posted daily to the creditor accounts in the Accounts Payable Ledger.
(4) The Other Accounts debit column entries are posted individually at the end of each month.
(5) The column totals are posted to the General Ledger at the end of the month.
(6) The Other Accounts column total is not posted.

FIGURE 9-34

Recording transactions in a Cash Payments Journal

CASH PAYMENTS JOURNAL **PAGE 44**

DATE		CH. NO.	CREDITOR OR ACCOUNT	P.R.	CASH CREDIT	ACCOUNTS PAYABLE DEBIT	GST REFUNDABLE DEBIT	PURCHASES DEBIT	PURCHASES DISCOUNTS CREDIT	OTHER ACCOUNTS DEBIT
2001										
May	1	101	Tanyss Trading		535.00		35.00	500.00		
	3	102	Speedquip Ltd.		149.00	149.00				
	8	103	Car Repairs Expense		75.00		4.91			70.09
	12	104	Willson's Ltd.		200.00	200.00				
	15	105	Advertising Expense		500.00		32.71			467.29
	17	106	B. McAdam, Drawings		220.00					220.00
	22	107	Supplies Expense		49.00		3.21			45.79
	23	108	PST Payable		127.00					127.00
	25	109	Willson's Ltd.		288.90		18.90	270.00		
	28	110	Tanyss Trading		343.00	350.00			7.00	
	31	111	Salaries Payable		3 400.00					3 400.00
	31	112	GST Payable		300.00					300.00

SUMMARY OF DIRECT POSTING TO THE SUBSIDIARY LEDGERS

Figures 9-35 and 9-36 summarize the procedures followed when source documents are posted directly to the subsidiary ledgers. Figure 9-35 shows how transactions involving customers are posted directly from the source documents to the customer accounts in the Accounts Receivable Ledger. Transactions involving creditors are posted directly to the accounts in the Accounts Payable Ledger.

FIGURE 9-35
Direct posting to the subsidiary ledgers

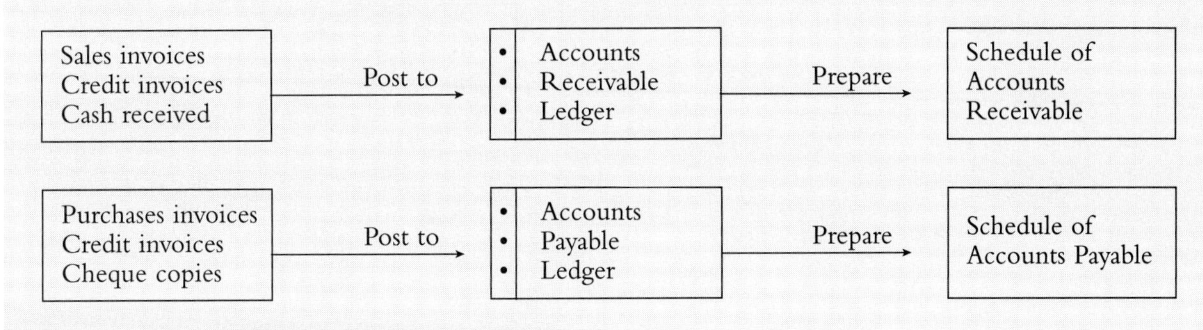

The same transactions are entered in the journals and then posted to the General Ledger. Figure 9-36 illustrates how this is done:

FIGURE 9-36
Posting to the General Ledger

SUMMARY OF THE SPECIAL JOURNAL SYSTEM

Since many business transactions are similar in nature, journals may be specially designed to handle the recording of transactions that occur frequently. The following special journals are used by many firms:

- Purchases Journal: Used for recording purchases on account
- Sales Journal: Used for recording sales of merchandise on account
- Cash Receipts Journal: Used for recording all cash received
- Cash Payments Journal: Used for recording all payments of cash

The special journal system is summarized in Figure 9-37 on page 358.

FIGURE 9-37
Special journal system

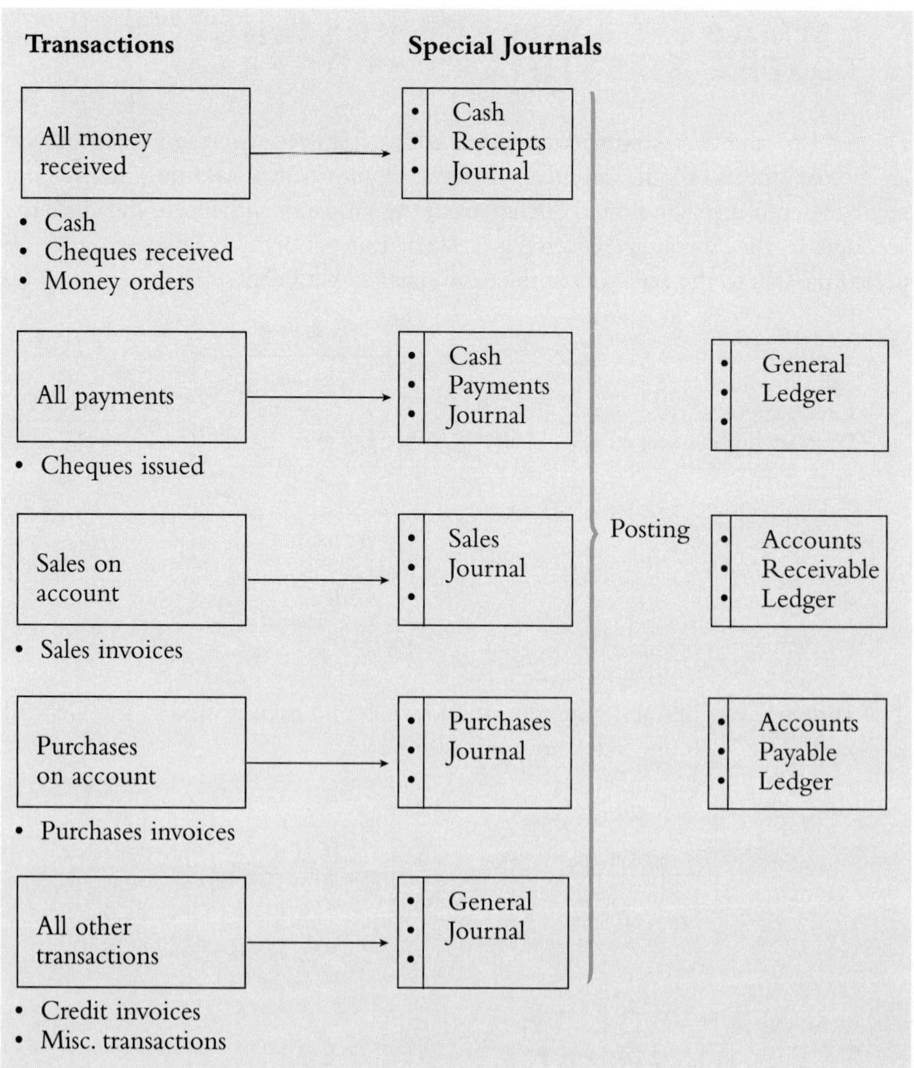

ACCOUNTING TERMS

Bank Credit Memo A memorandum from the bank indicating an increase in a bank account.

Bank Debit Memo A memorandum from the bank indicating a decrease in a bank account.

Cash Payments Journal Special journal used to record cash payments.

Cash Receipts Journal Special journal used to record cash received.

Credit Invoice Source document used to record the return of goods by a customer.

Cycle Billing Method of spreading over the month the work of preparing and mailing statements to customers.

Due Date The date on which payment is to be made.

Matching Process for Purchases Comparing of purchase order, purchase invoice, and receiving report before payment is made.

Purchase Discount A discount earned by the purchaser for early payment of an account.

Purchase Invoice	Form sent to the buyer from the seller showing costs of items shipped, along with details of the shipment.
Purchase Order	A form prepared by the buyer and sent to the seller containing the details regarding the goods to be purchased.
Purchase Requisition	A form sent to the purchasing department requesting that goods or services be ordered.
Purchases Journal	Special journal used to record purchases on account.
Receiving Report	Form listing all goods received.
Sales Discount	A discount allowed to a customer for early payment of an account.
Sales Invoice	A source document prepared by the seller with the information regarding a credit sale.
Sales Journal	Special journal used to record credit sales.
Special Journal System	Uses separate journals for similar transactions that recur frequently.
Statement of Account	Form sent to customer showing charges, amounts credited, and the balance of the account.

1. (a) What is a cheque requisition?
   (b) What is a voucher cheque?
2. Are purchases discounts recorded as debits or credits? Why?
3. Does a bank debit memo indicate that the bank account has increased or decreased?
4. Should the PST Payable account be increased or decreased when a customer returns goods on which tax has been charged?
5. Is anything other than a cheque number recorded in the cheque number column of the Cash Payments Journal?
6. Briefly describe the types of transactions recorded in each of the following:
   (a) Sales Journal
   (b) Cash Receipts Journal
   (c) Purchases Journal
   (d) Cash Payments Journal
   (e) General Journal
7. Superior Electrical Services uses a five-journal accounting system. Answer the following questions regarding their system:
   (a) In which journal will you find the closing entries?
   (b) Which journal will contain the fewest entries?
   (c) If Accounts Payable and Accounts Receivable Ledgers are used, explain how transactions are posted to these ledgers. (Assume a direct posting system is not used.)
   (d) When are transactions usually posted to the General Ledger?
   (e) Which journals contain information that must be posted to the Accounts Receivable control account?

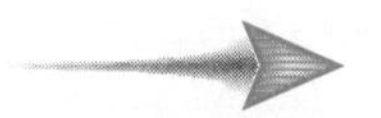

23. (a) Using the accounts below, record the following documents on page 319 of a Cash Payments Journal:

Aug. 1 Cheque 1890, $725 to K. Bellamy for a week's salary.

3 Cheque 1891, $950 to P. Meikle, the owner, for personal use.

5 Bank debit memo, $15.25 for service charges.

6 Cheque 1892, $833 to General Distributors for $850 less $17 discount.

6 Cheque 1893, $90.10 to Bill's Service Centre on account.

7 Bank debit memo, $450 for monthly payment on the bank loan.

9 Cheque 1894, $4 410 to Electronic Wholesalers, for $4 500 invoice less $90 discount.

(b) Total, balance, and rule the Cash Payments Journal.

(c) Set up a General Ledger and an Accounts Payable Ledger for August 1 with the following accounts and balances; then post the Cash Payments Journal.

No.	Account	Debit	Credit
101	Cash	18 493	
200	Accounts Payable		9 458
210	Bank Loan		25 000
300	P. Meikle, Drawings	0	
502	Purchases Discounts		0
600	Salaries Expense	0	
615	Bank Charges Expense	0	

Schedule of Accounts Payable August 1, 2002

Bill's Service Centre	$ 145
Electronic Wholesalers	7 056
General Distributors	2 257
	$9 458

24. (a) Record the following source documents on page 109 of a Cash Payments Journal:

Dec. 3 Cheque 705, $2 600 plus GST to Clark Realtors for the December rent.

3 Cheque 706, to Colonial Manufacturers for Invoice 17849 for $14 500 less one-percent discount. Invoice dated November 23. Terms: 1/10, n/30.

4 Bank debit memo M85192 for $29.50 for bank charges.

6 Refund Cheque 707, $179.40 to C. Bartoli, a customer, for a $156 coffee table (returned today) plus $12.48 PST and $10.92 GST.

6 Cheque 708 for Invoice 11529 for $4 275 to Dupuis Cabinets on account. Invoice dated November 10. Terms: n/30.

7 Cheque 709 to General Electric for Invoice B8521 for $7 561 less discount. Invoice dated November 27. Terms: 2/10, n/30.

8 Cheque 710, $800 to L. Colby for personal use.

(b) Total, balance, and rule the Cash Payments Journal.
(c) Set up a General Ledger and Accounts Payable Ledger with the accounts and balances below; then post the Cash Payments Journal.

No.	Account	Debit	Credit
101	Cash	41 453.72	
202	Accounts Payable		35 696.67
205	PST Payable		0
206	GST Payable		0
207	GST Refundable	1 126.10	
302	L. Colby, Drawings	13 490.44	
403	Sales Returns and Allowances	2 376.49	
503	Purchases Discounts		6 273.91
600	Rent Expense	28 600.00	
613	Bank Charges Expense	1 875.95	

Schedule of Accounts Payable December 1, 2001

Colonial Manufacturers	$14 500.00
Dupuis Cabinets	9 400.23
General Electric	11 796.44
	$35 696.67

PROBLEMS: CHALLENGES

1. The accounting system of Brockcounty Kennels includes a General Journal, four special journals, a General Ledger, and two subsidiary ledgers. All credit sales have terms of n/30. GST of 7 percent is charged on all sales of service or merchandise. PST of 8 percent calculated on the base price is charged on pet food sales only. Grooming is performed only on a cash basis. The firm's chart of accounts appears on page 363.

(a) Enter the June transactions given below in the five journals used by Brockcounty Kennels.
(b) Total, balance, and rule the journals.
(c) Show how the postings would be made by placing the ledger account numbers and check marks in the appropriate columns of the journals. Brockcounty Kennels does not use a direct posting system to the subsidiary ledgers.

Jun. 1 The owner, S. Robson, deposited $2 000 in the firm's bank account as a further personal investment in the business.

3 Purchased additional grooming equipment from Jayco Supplies ($2 897.20 + $202.80 GST), paying $1 000 cash and agreeing to pay the remaining $2 100 EOM.

4 Signed an agreement with J. Johnson to train and exhibit her dog at a price of $250 per month, plus expenses, to be billed at the end of each month.

4 Sold dog food worth $85, plus taxes, to Greenlane Kennels on account, Invoice 874.

6 Received $175, plus $12.25 GST, cash for boarding W. Szpilewski's dog for the past three weeks.

7 Purchased a load of Joy Dog Food for resale, $2 400, plus $168 GST, terms n/30.

7 Sold two bags of dog food for cash, $78 plus taxes.

7 Grooming income for the week was $780, plus $54.60 GST, per cash sales slips.

9 Billed M. Kennedy $300, plus $21 GST, for training her dog for the past month, Invoice 875.

10 Greenland Kennels returned one bag of feed for credit, $36 plus taxes. Credit Invoice 73 was issued today.

12 Purchased supplies for $75, plus $5.25 GST, cash.

13 Purchased dog food for use in our kennel for $700, plus $49 GST, from Purina on account.

14 Grooming income for the week was $910, plus $63.70 GST, per cash sales slip.

15 Received payment from Greenlane Kennels for the Jun. 4 purchase less returns.

15 Sold $250, plus taxes, worth of pet food to Casey's Kennel on account, Invoice 876.

15 Purchased additional fencing materials for the kennel from Lincoln Farm Supply, $450, plus $31.50 GST, on 30-day account.

16 Received a credit invoice today from Joy Dog Food for $100 worth of damaged goods, plus $7 GST, which we had returned previously.

16 Billed Grousehaven Kennels $1 000, plus $70 GST, for the monthly training fee, Invoice 877.

18 Billed B. Iannizzi $52, plus $3.64 GST, for boarding his dog for four days, Invoice 878.

19 Received $490 from P. Partington in payment of training fee previously billed.

21 Grooming revenue for the week $650, plus $45.50 GST.

22 Purchased dog food for resale from Beatrice Foods, $1 450, plus $101.50 GST, on 30-day account.

22 Paid the freight charges on the Beatrice shipment, $63, plus $4.41 GST, cash.

23 Paid Purina $3 100 on account.

24 Sold an old set of grooming clippers to P. Dolynski for $175 on account. The clippers were recorded in the Grooming Equipment account at a cost of $250.

26 Borrowed $2 500 from the bank and signed a note payable.

28 Sold pet food to Brookfield Kennels, $375, plus taxes, on account, Invoice 879.

28 Grooming fees for the week, $1 050, plus $73.50 GST, cash.

29 Paid the monthly salaries, $1 275 cash.

30 Paid Jayco Supplies in full for the Jun. 3 purchase.

30 Sold pet food to P. Partington, $83, plus taxes, on account, Invoice 880.

30 Received $321 from M. Kennedy in payment of her account.

100	Cash	301	S. Robson, Drawings
110	Accounts Receivable	302	Income Summary
120	Merchandise Inventory	410	Pet Food Sales
125	Supplies	420	Grooming Revenue
126	Feed Supply	430	Boarding Revenue
135	Prepaid Insurance	440	Training Revenue
150	Building	450	Interest Earned
153	Kennel Fencing	475	Sales Returns & Allow.
155	Furniture and Fixtures	500	Purchases
158	Grooming Equipment	525	Purchases Returns & Allow.
160	Land	550	Transportation-in
200	Accounts Payable	600	Salaries Expense
205	PST Payable	601	Taxes Expense
206	GST Payable	602	Supplies Expense
207	GST Refundable	603	Insurance Expense
210	Bank Loan	604	Interest Expense
250	Mortgage Payable	605	Feed Expense
300	S. Robson, Capital	606	Loss on Sale of Equip.

2. Studio 21 offers terms of 2/10, n/30 to credit customers. All sales are exempt from PST. A chart of accounts (showing only those accounts necessary for this exercise) appears on page 365, and schedules of accounts receivable and payable as of April 30 appear on page 365.

(a) Record the May transactions given below in the following journals:
- Sales Journal
- Purchases Journal
- Cash Receipts Journal
- Cash Payments Journal
- General Journal

(b) Total, balance, and rule all special journals.
(c) Indicate how the postings would be made to the General Ledger by placing the ledger account numbers in the appropriate places in the journals.
(d) Post to the subsidiary ledgers.
(e) Prepare schedules of accounts receivable and payable as of May 30. The control accounts in the General Ledger on this date show Accounts Receivable $9 178.80 and Accounts Payable $7 150.

May 1 Purchased merchandise from W. Hagadorn Inc. for $15 000 ($14 018.69 plus $981.31 GST). Invoice 39187 dated today with terms 2/15, n/30.

4 Issued Cheque 232 for $21 000 to W. Hagadorn Inc. for an April purchase, Invoice 38714. No discount was taken.

4 Sold merchandise to A. Akmel, $5 607.48 plus GST, Invoice 275.

5 Sold merchandise for cash, $9 200 plus GST.

7 Received a Credit Invoice C1826 from W. Hagadorn Inc. for returned merchandise valued at $1 000 ($934.58 plus $65.42 GST).

9 Issued Cheque 233 for $160.50 ($150 plus $10.50 GST) to A. Wing for merchandise returned today.

10 Purchased merchandise from K. Lee & Associates for $7 500 plus $525 GST. Invoice 4499 dated May 8 with terms 2/10, n/30.

11 Sold merchandise to G. Alvarez for $7 943.93 plus GST, Invoice 276.

13 Received payment from A. Akmel to pay her account in full.

14 Issued Credit Invoice 78 to G. Alvarez for $706.20 ($660 plus $46.20 GST).

15 Sold excess equipment for $12 149.53 plus GST to Tieche Co. A cash down payment of $3 000 was received with the remainder due on a promissory note in 60 days. The equipment originally cost $12 500.

17 Received a cheque from G. Alvarez for $15 300 for an April sale.

19 Purchased a one-year liability insurance policy from Royal Insurance for $887.85 plus $62.15 GST on account.

20 Paid K. Lee and Associates, Cheque 234.

22 Paid W. Hagadorn Inc. for the May 1 purchase less returns, Cheque 235.

23 Received $4 000 on account from G. Alvarez.

24 Purchased new equipment for $32 710.18 plus $2 289.72 GST. Paid 10 percent down (Cheque 236) and signed a promissory note with Avco Finance for the remainder.

25 Sold merchandise to A. Akmel, $5 500 plus GST, on account, Invoice 277.

26 Purchased merchandise from K. Lee and Associates, $5 794.39 plus $405.61. Invoice dated today with terms 2/10, n/30.

28 Paid the $3 600 monthly mortgage payment, of which $1 500 was interest expense, Cheque 237.

30 Paid the monthly office salaries, $7 900, Cheque 238.

30 Issued Credit Invoice 79 to A. Akmel, $467.29 plus $32.71 GST, for goods returned today.

30 Purchased merchandise from Dupont Services, $1 680 plus $117.60 GST, Cheque 239.

100	Cash	475	Sales Returns & Allow.
120	Accounts Receivable	480	Sales Discounts
125	Notes Receivable	500	Purchases
130	Supplies	525	Purchases Returns & Allow.
135	Prepaid Insurance	550	Purchases Discounts
160	Equipment	555	Transportation-in
200	Accounts Payable	601	Salaries Expense
206	GST Payable	602	Supplies Expense
207	GST Refundable	603	Insurance Expense
210	Notes Payable	604	Loss on Sale of Equipment
220	Mortgage Payable	605	Interest Expense
400	Sales		

Schedule of Accounts Receivable April 30, 2002

G. Alvarez	$15 300.00
A. Akmel	10 750.00
	$26 050.00

Schedule of Accounts Payable April 30, 2002

W. Hagadorn Inc.	$21 000.00
K. Lee & Associates	12 000.00
	$33 000.00

3. The cash receipts and cash payments journals are presented below. Certain transactions in each of the journals have been incorrectly recorded, and there are other errors as well; each journal contains five errors. However, each journal has at least one correct entry.

CASH RECEIPTS JOURNAL

DATE	REF. NO.	CUSTOMER OR ACCOUNT	P.R.	CASH CREDIT	SALES DISC. DEBIT	ACCOUNTS REC. CREDIT	SALES CREDIT	PST PAYABLE CREDIT	OTHER ACCOUNTS CREDIT
2003									
Jul. 2	1	Bank Loan	210	8 000		8 000			
3	2	Lynch, Capital	301	2 500					2 500
5	71	A. Butler	✓	392	8		400		
7	3	Land	160	41 000					41 000
8		Cash Register Tape		3 162.50			2 750	220	
				(100)	(410)	(102)	(400)	(221)	

CASH PAYMENTS JOURNAL

DATE	REF. NO.	CUSTOMER OR ACCOUNT	P.R.	CASH CREDIT	ACCOUNTS PAYABLE DEBIT	GST REFUND CREDIT	PURCHASE DEBIT	PURCHASES DISC. CREDIT	OTHER ACCOUNTS CREDIT
2003									
Jul.2	74	Salaries Expense	600	475	475				
5		Bank Charges Expense	615	14.25					14.25
6	75	Remo Ltd.	✓	490	500		10		
7	76	Purina	✓	795	795				
8	77	Lynch, Drawings	300	850			850		
		Debits = $874.25 Credits = $4 394.25		2 624.25	1 770		860		14.25
				(100)	(200)	(500)	(207)	(550)	

(a) Identify the errors in each of the journals.

(b) Identify the correct transaction(s) in each of the journals.

INTEGRATIVE 2 ACTIVITY

THE SPECIAL JOURNAL SYSTEM

Marcov's Furniture

Elizabeth Marcov, owner of Marcov's Furniture, has exclusive rights of distribution for the products of Teak Manufacturers and of General Appliances Ltd. The store has been operating successfully for a number of years. The accounting system includes three ledgers and five journals. The journals are:

- Purchases Journal
- Sales Journal
- Cash Receipts Journal
- Cash Payments Journal
- General Journal

The General Journal is used for returns and allowances and for correcting entries.

On January 10, the balances in the General Ledger accounts are as shown in the trial balance on page 368.

The balances in the subsidiary ledger accounts are shown in the two schedules below.

Marcov's Furniture
Schedule of Accounts Receivable
January 10, 2001

A. Bartoli	$ 4 687.35
D. Crankshaw	390.47
L. Larivierre	491.60
M. St. Amour	3 673.38
S. Walli	1 374.28
	$10 617.08

Marcov's Furniture
Schedule of Accounts Payable
January 10, 2001

Campbell Heating	$	493.70
CKNH TV		767.00
General Appliances Ltd.		5 358.61
Hi-Way Transport		478.90
Teak Manufacturers		6 798.50
Welland Motors Ltd.		653.35
		$14 550.06

Marcov's Furniture Trial Balance January 10, 2001			
Account Title	**Acc. No.**	**Debit**	**Credit**
Cash	101	$ 27 678.50	
Accounts Receivable	110	10 617.08	
Merchandise Inventory	120	255 673.84	
Buildings	150	230 768.00	
Office Equipment	151	4 763.35	
Fixtures	152	11 342.89	
Trucks	153	24 897.88	
Land	160	75 000.00	
Accounts Payable	200		14 550.06
Sales Tax Payable	205		5 369.90
GST Payable	206		4 872.10
GST Refundable	207	2 772.10	
Bank Loan	210		15 765.31
Mortgage on Building	250		103 575.35
E. Marcov, Capital	300		501 819.08
E. Marcov, Drawings	301	1 700.00	
Sales	400		13 658.73
Sales Returns and Allowances	401	146.51	
Purchases	500	9 105.82	
Purchases Returns and Allowances	501		97.33
Transportation on Purchases	502	278.85	
Salaries Expense	600	2 376.51	
Truck Repairs Expense	601	138.64	
Heating Expense	602	173.56	
Utilities Expense	603	78.53	
Bank Charges Expense	604	45.20	
Advertising Expense	605	2 150.60	
		$659 707.86	$659 707.86

Part A

1. Open the five journals.
2. Open the ledgers and record the January 10 balances.
3. In the appropriate journals, record the transactions given below — both those shown in source documents and those listed. Prepare one batch entry for each day's cash sales.

Jan. 13 ***Cash Sales Invoice 7339, shown on page 369.***

Jan. 13 ***Other cash sales invoices:***
No. 7340, $299.96 plus sales tax and GST;
No. 7342, $83.98 plus sales tax and GST;
No. 7343, $119.98 plus sales tax and GST;
No. 7344, $1 355.74 plus sales tax and GST.

MARCOV'S FURNITURE **INVOICE 7339**

359 Portage Ave.
Ottawa, ON
K2A 7N9 **Order No.____**

Sold D. Mitchell
19 Oakwood Ave.
Gloucester, ON
K2E 5B4

Ship to: Same

Date Jan. 13, 2001
Terms Cash
Cash X **Charge**

Quantity	Description	Unit Price	Amount
1	Washing Machine	$650.95	$650.95
1	Dryer	$549.49	549.49
		Subtotal	1 200.44
		GST	84.03
		Sales Tax (8%)	96.04
		Pay this Amount	$ 1 380.51

Jan. 13 Charge Sales Invoice 7341 to L. Larivierre (on account), $649.90 plus sales tax and GST.

13 Cash received, $300 from A. Bartoli.

13 Cheque 345 issued: merchandise $445.10 + $31.18 GST.

No. 345	
BALANCE	27 678.50
DEP.	3 135.10
TOTAL	30 813.60
CHEQUE	476.58
BAL.	30 337.02
PAY TO:	Elgin Cabinets
on account	
SUM OF	$476.58

MARCOV'S FURNITURE **NO. 345**
359 Portage Ave.
Ottawa, ON
K2A 7N9 **January 13, 2001**

PAY TO THE ORDER OF **Elgin Cabinets** **$ 476.58**

SUM OF **Four hundred and seventy-six** 58/100 DOLLARS

THE BANK OF NOVA SCOTIA
Preston & Norman Branch
Ottawa, ON K1R 7V7

⑆70276-002⑆81720⑈00

Jan. 14 Cheques issued:
No. 346 to Hi-Way Transport, $359 on account;
No. 347 to Bell Canada, $126.79 + $8.88 GST = $135.67.

14 Cash sales invoices:
No. 7345, $530 plus sales tax and GST;
No. 7346, $164.98 plus sales tax and GST;
No. 7348, $549.98 plus sales tax and GST;
No. 7349, $239.98 plus sales tax and GST.

14 Charge sales invoices (on account):
No. 7347 to M. St. Amour, $574.98 plus sales tax and GST;
No. 7350 to D. Crankshaw, $356.90 plus sales tax and GST.

14 *Purchases invoices:*
From Welland Motors Ltd., for truck repairs, $220.22 + $15.41 GST = $235.63;
From Campbell Heating, for fuel, $528.64 + $37 GST = $565.64.

14 *Correcting entry:*
An error was made on January 3 in recording an amount of $57.53 to the Fixtures account when it should have been recorded in the Office Equipment account. Record a correcting entry.

15 *Credit Invoice 3470 received from Teak Manufacturers, $35 + $2.45 GST overcharge on Invoice 110985.*

15 *Cash sales invoices:*
No. 7352, $609.50 plus sales tax and GST;
No. 7353, $79.96 plus sales tax and GST;
No. 7354, $499.98 plus sales tax and GST;
No. 7355, $419.98 plus sales tax and GST;
No. 7356, $799.98 plus sales tax and GST.

15 *Charge Sales Invoice 7351 to S. Walli (on account), $359.98 plus sales tax and GST.*

15 *Cash receipts:*
From M. St. Amour, $350 on account;
From D. Crankshaw, $120 on account.

15 *Purchases invoices:*
From General Appliances Ltd., for merchandise, $2 567.56 + $179.73 GST = $2 747.29;
From Hi-Way Transport, for transportation on merchandise, $467.50 + $32.73 GST = $500.23.

Jan. 15 *Cheques issued:*
No. 348 to the Provincial Treasurer, $4 265.14 for sales tax collected in December;
No. 349 to Teak Manufacturers, $1 567.50 on account;
No. 350 to CKNH TV $450 on account.

16 *Credit Invoice 175 issued:*

MARCOV'S FURNITURE — **CREDIT INVOICE 175**

359 Portage Ave.
Ottawa, ON
K2A 7N9

Sold L. Larivierre
4935 rue Champlain
Ottawa, ON
K1C 3P1

Date Jan. 16, 2001

Quantity	Description	Unit Price	Amount
4	Chairs	$ 80.00	$ 320.00
		GST	22.40
		PST	25.60
		Total Credit	$ 368.00
	Overcharge on Invoice 7341		

Jan. 16 Cash sales invoices:
No. 7357, $209.50 plus sales tax and GST;
No. 7359, $549.98 plus sales tax and GST;
No. 7361, $355 plus sales tax and GST;
No. 7362, $322 plus sales tax and GST;
No. 7363, $79.98 plus sales tax and GST.

16 Charge sales invoices (on account):
No. 7358 to A. Bartoli, $289.98 plus sales tax and GST;
No. 7360 to M. St. Amour, $539.98 plus sales tax and GST.

16 Cash receipts:
From L. Larivierre, $250 on account;
From S. Walli, $95 on account.

16 Purchases invoices:
From CKNH TV, $1 200 + $84 GST = $1 284 for advertising;
From Teak Manufacturers, $1 563.69 + $109.46 sales tax = $1 673.15 for merchandise.

16 Cheques issued:
No. 351 to Welland Motors Ltd., $450 on account.
No. 352 to Bank of Nova Scotia, $2 000 payment on the bank loan;
No. 353 to Commercial Realtors, $1 500 payment on the mortgage.

17 Bank debit memo for $54 received for bank charges.

17 Cash sales invoices:
No. 7364, $298.98 plus sales tax and GST;
No. 7365, $74.95 plus sales tax and GST;
No. 7367, $599.98 plus sales tax and GST;
No. 7368, $239.98 plus sales tax and GST;
No. 7369, $209.98 plus sales tax and GST.

17 Charge Sales Invoice 7366 to D. Crankshaw (on account), $408.96 plus sales tax and GST.

17 Purchases invoices:
From Hi-Way Transport, $367.50 + $25.73 GST = $393.23 for transportation of merchandise.
From Welland Motors Ltd., $198 + $13.86 GST = $211.86 for truck repairs.

17 Cheques issued:
No. 354 to E. Marcov, the owner, $1 450 for personal use;
No. 355 to General Appliances Ltd., $3 600 on account;
No. 356 to Campbell Heating, $493.70 on account;
No. 357 to Receiver General of Canada for GST collected, $2 100.

Part B

1. Total, balance, and rule the journals.
2. Post the journals to the subsidiary ledgers and the General Ledger.
3. Prepare schedules for the subsidiary ledgers.
4. Prepare a trial balance for the General Ledger.

Part C

1. Prepare a schedule of cost of goods sold and an income statement for the two weeks ended January 17, 2001. The January 17 merchandise inventory is $257 931.12.
2. Prepare a balance sheet dated January 17, 2001.

Part D

1. Design one columnar journal that could replace all five journals and be used to record transactions for Marcov's Furniture.
2. Which journal system is more appropriate for Marcov's Furniture — the five-journal system or the single columnar journal you have designed? Give reasons for your answer.

Part E — Optional — Computer Accounting

1. Complete this project with a computer, following these instructions:

   (a) Prepare a chart of accounts with appropriate computer numbers for each account.
   (b) Record the transactions (manually) on data entry sheets.
   (c) Input the transactions (manually) on data entry sheets.
   (d) Print the following:
   - Journal (or special journals, if possible, depending on the capability of your software program)
   - General Ledger
   - Accounts Receivable and Payable Ledgers
   - Trial balance
   - Customer statements
   - Financial statements
   - Closing entries
   - Post-closing trial balance

CHAPTER 10

Cash Control and Banking

UNIT 25 Cash Control

Learning Objectives

After reading this unit, discussing the applicable review questions, and completing the applications exercises, you will be able to do the following:

1. **EXPLAIN** the purpose and importance of the internal control system of a business.
2. **DISCUSS** the importance of cash control, and **EXPLAIN** why the tasks of handling and recording cash are separated for control purposes.
3. **EXPLAIN** why source documents are prenumbered. **PREPARE** a daily cash proof and record shortages or overages. **DEPOSIT** cash receipts daily.
4. **DISCUSS** why cash payments should be made by cheque.
5. **ESTABLISH** and **MAINTAIN** a petty cash fund to pay small bills.

Internal accounting control is used to protect assets and to ensure the reliability of records and statements.

The internal control system of a business refers to the method and procedures used to:

(1) Protect the assets from waste, loss, theft, and fraud
(2) Ensure reliable accounting records
(3) Ensure accurate and consistent application of the firm's policies
(4) Evaluate the performance of departments and personnel

These components of an effective internal control system can be divided into administrative controls and accounting controls. *Administrative controls* normally relate to components (3) and (4). They increase the efficiency of the business and ensure company policies are followed. *Accounting controls* relate to components (1) and (2). They protect assets and ensure the reliability of accounting records and statements.

Accountants must be familiar with both administrative and accounting controls. Proper internal control ensures that the accounting system is dependable and efficient and provides security for the resources of the business.

Cash includes cheques, money orders, bills, and coins.

In this chapter, we will discuss one portion of the accounting control system of a business — the need for control of cash. We will examine a number of procedures that are used to protect this important asset, as well as methods of keeping accurate cash records. It should be understood that the term "cash" includes cheques, money orders, bills, and coins.

IMPORTANCE OF CASH CONTROL

Leslie Ho works for Finest Flowers Ltd. One of Leslie's duties is to handle cash sales. When a customer buys merchandise for cash, a cash sales slip is completed in duplicate. One copy is given to the customer and the second is placed in the cash register with the money received from the sale. Leslie is often left alone in the store and has learned that a sale can be made, a cash sales slip given to the customer, the duplicate copy destroyed, and the money placed in Leslie's pocket instead of in the company's cash register.

This story is an example of why all companies, both large and small, require accounting systems that provide control over dishonesty and error.

Because of the ease with which cash may be lost or stolen and errors may be made in counting cash, systems are needed that give effective control over all cash received and all payments made. No two businesses operate in exactly the same way. Some have many cash sales every day while others have only a few. It is the accountant's task to design a system that suits the particular needs of a company. The system should effectively control cash, but it should not be overly complicated or expensive to operate.

In the case of Finest Flowers, the solution can be as simple as prenumbering all the sales slips and having Leslie's supervisor check them periodically to ensure that none are missing. Cash is involved in a large portion of the transactions of a business and therefore presents opportunities for errors to occur. Cash is also an attractive target for theft and fraud. Therefore, control of cash is very important to the owner or manager of the enterprise.

CASH CONTROL PROCEDURES

A business owned and operated by one person or by a small family has little need for control procedures. However, as a company grows and employs an increasing number of people, it is often necessary to pass on to others those tasks that include financial responsibilities. This makes it necessary to control theft, fraud, and errors made by people within the company. As well, control procedures can result in more efficient use of employee time. There are a number of established accounting procedures that have been designed to provide internal control over cash. In this chapter, we will discuss the eight cash control procedures listed here:

- Procedure 1: Separation of Duties
- Procedure 2: Immediate Listing of Cash Receipts
- Procedure 3: Daily Cash Proof
- Procedure 4: Daily Deposit of Cash
- Procedure 5: Payment by Cheque
- Procedure 6: Petty Cash Procedures
- Procedure 7: Periodic Audit
- Procedure 8: Monthly Bank Reconciliation

Procedure 1: Separation of Duties

A key component of all control systems is the separation of duties of employees. In order to discourage fraud and theft as well as to ensure the accuracy of accounting data, the duties of the accounting personnel should be arranged so that one employee verifies the accuracy of another employee's work. In a cash control system, it is important that the employee responsible for preparing and depositing the cash in the bank not be the employee responsible for recording the cash receipts. This provides a verification of the cash recorded and minimizes the chance of theft since both employees would have to work together to remove cash from the company. The recording function should be divided among employees also, where possible, to provide additional verification of accuracy of the records and protection for the asset. You have already seen this type of division of duties where the work of the accounts receivable clerk is verified by the accounting supervisor, who compares the schedule of accounts receivable total to the control account in the General Ledger. The importance of this control procedure for both cash receipts and cash payments will be demonstrated throughout this chapter.

Different people should carry out the task of recording cash received and the task of actually handling the cash.

CONTROL OF CASH RECEIPTS

The accounting controls in Procedures 2, 3, and 4 ensure the accuracy of cash receipts.

Procedure 2: Immediate Listing of Cash Receipts

Cash receipts consist of cash received at the time of the sale, over the counter, and cheques received by mail, in payment of accounts receivable.

Cash Sales

All cash should be recorded as soon as it is received.

Cash registers or terminals are usually used to record cash sales as they occur. The cash register should be set up to allow the customer to see the amount being recorded. The customer assists with the control system by preventing an error in recording a cash sale and by preventing the employee from ringing in a lower amount than that charged to the customer and then pocketing the difference. The cash register tape provides a total of the cash sales for the day. It is compared to the actual cash receipts by the manager, supervisor, or owner when preparing the daily cash proof. This allows a person other than the cashier to verify the accuracy of the cash.

This procedure follows the concept of separation of duties explained previously. In addition, the immediate recording of the sale by the cash register eliminates the possibility of cash being stolen and the sale remaining unrecorded.

Computerized cash register systems provide additional accounting controls by verifying prices and updating inventory records.

Prenumbered Sales Slips

In many businesses, a prenumbered, multiple-copy sales slip is prepared for each cash sale. One copy is given to the customer and two are kept on file in the business. At the end of the day, the sales slips are totalled and compared to the cash register tape and the actual cash on hand. One set of sales slips is forwarded with the cash to the person responsible for making a bank deposit. The other set is forwarded to the accounting department to act as a source document to record the cash sales for the day.

If all documents are prenumbered, all of them must be accounted for. It is therefore impossible for the sales clerk to destroy a cash sales slip and pocket the money, since it would mean that one of the numbered slips would be destroyed. If a sales slip is spoiled or cancelled, it must be marked *void* and kept with the rest of the day's source documents. The principle of prenumbering documents is applied to many forms. For example, cheques, sales invoices, and petty cash vouchers are all prenumbered. This ensures that every document is accounted for.

Cancelled sales slips are marked void and are kept on file.

Cash Received by Mail

The employee who opens the mail should prepare a list of the cheques received. One copy of this list, along with the cheques, is forwarded to the person responsible for making the daily deposit. The second copy is sent to the accounting department to act as a source document to record these cash receipts. In some firms, a third copy is kept on file for future reference by the employee opening the mail.

These procedures ensure a separation in duties between the employees handling the cash and the employees recording the cash receipts. This is important in order to verify the accounting records and to prevent theft.

Procedure 3: Daily Cash Proof

Each day, the owner or supervisor should balance the cash received against the source documents used to record the cash transactions. By preparing this proof daily, any major shortages or overages can be dealt with immediately. In the case of Brighton Cleaners, a daily cash proof form is completed by the owner of the business, E. Plata. This form is shown in Figure 10-1.

Introducing the Cash Short and Over Account

As Figure 10-1 illustrates, the cash is counted and a $150 cash float (change fund) is removed from the cash and kept for the next day's business. On June 6, the cash is short $3. Since the company has lost funds, an expense must be recorded in an expense account called *Cash Short and Over.*

The Cash Short and Over account is used to record shortages and overages of cash.

FIGURE 10-1

Daily cash proof showing a cash shortage

DAILY CASH PROOF

DATE Jun. 6 2001	
TOTAL CASH	$1 344.80
LESS CASH FLOAT	150.00
TOTAL DEPOSITED	$1 194.80
SALES SLIPS NO.s 706 to 785	$1 197.80
CASH SHORT	3.00
or	
CASH OVER	
AUTHORIZED E. Plata	

The daily cash proof is the source document for a journal entry to record the day's sales. For June 6, the journal entry is:

Jun. 6	Cash	1 194.80	
	Cash Short and Over	3.00	
	Sales		1 197.80
	To record Sales Slips 706 to 785.		

FIGURE 10-2
Daily cash proof showing a cash overage

DAILY CASH PROOF

DATE Jun. 7 2001	
TOTAL CASH	$1 366.73
LESS CASH FLOAT	150.00
TOTAL DEPOSITED	$1 216.73
SALES SLIPS NO.s 786 to 861	$1 212.73
CASH SHORT	
or	
CASH OVER	4.00
AUTHORIZED E. Plata	

The daily cash proof for the next day, June 7, is shown in Figure 10-2. Notice that the total cash deposited is $4 more than it should be according to the cash sales slips. In this entry, the overage is recorded as a credit to Cash Short and Over. The journal entry for June 7 is:

Jun. 7	Cash	1 216.73	
	Sales		1 212.73
	Cash Short and Over		4.00
	To record Sales Slips 786 to 861.		

Cash shortages are recorded as debits in the Cash Short and Over account.

Cash overages are recorded as credits in the Cash Short and Over account.

These two journal entries may be summarized as follows. In the daily cash proof in Figure 10-1, the cash is short by $3. This shortage represents a loss to the company and is charged as a debit (a decrease in owner's equity) to the Cash Short and Over account. If the cash is over (see Figure 10-2), the amount is recorded in the same Cash Short and Over account. However, an overage is recorded as a credit (an increase in owner's equity).

When an income statement is prepared, the Cash Short and Over account may appear in either the revenue or the expense section. It appears in the revenue section if the account has a credit balance or the overages have been greater than the shortages. It appears in the expense section if the account has a debit balance or the shortages have been greater than the overages.

Some companies prefer to use a separate section at the bottom of the income statement for miscellaneous items such as cash short and over. This section, called Other Income and Expenses, includes such items as bank interest earned, cash short and over, and gain or loss on sale of assets. The use of this section clearly indicates how much of the net income comes from the regular operations of the business and how much comes from miscellaneous sources.

Cash Short and Over Policy

A company that handles a lot of cash transactions and prepares a daily cash proof is faced with a problem. What should be done about shortages and overages? There are several possibilities, including these:

- Absorb all shortages and overages.
- Deduct shortages from the cashier's pay.

Many companies prefer to keep all shortage information from the cashier. The daily cash proof is prepared by someone from the accounting office. Shortages and overages are absorbed by the company and are not mentioned to the cashier, unless they are frequent and fairly large. If this occurs, the situation is discussed with the cashier. Retraining may be necessary. If errors still continue on a large scale, the cashier may be transferred or dismissed.

Procedure 4: Daily Deposit of Cash

Each day, the total cash receipts of the business (cash sales and cheques received) should be deposited in the bank. Therefore, no large amounts of money (which could be stolen) are kept on the premises. No bills should be paid out of these funds. Thus, the amount of the deposit each day will be the same as the amount recorded in the Cash Receipts Journal by the accounting department. This allows a further verification of the records by the company's bank when the bank sends the bank statement at the end of the month. After completing the daily cash proof (see Figure 10-1), E. Plata, the owner of Brighton Cleaners, completes the deposit slip shown in Figure 10-3. The cash is deposited in the bank. A copy of the deposit slip is kept by the company.

FIGURE 10-3
Bank deposit slip

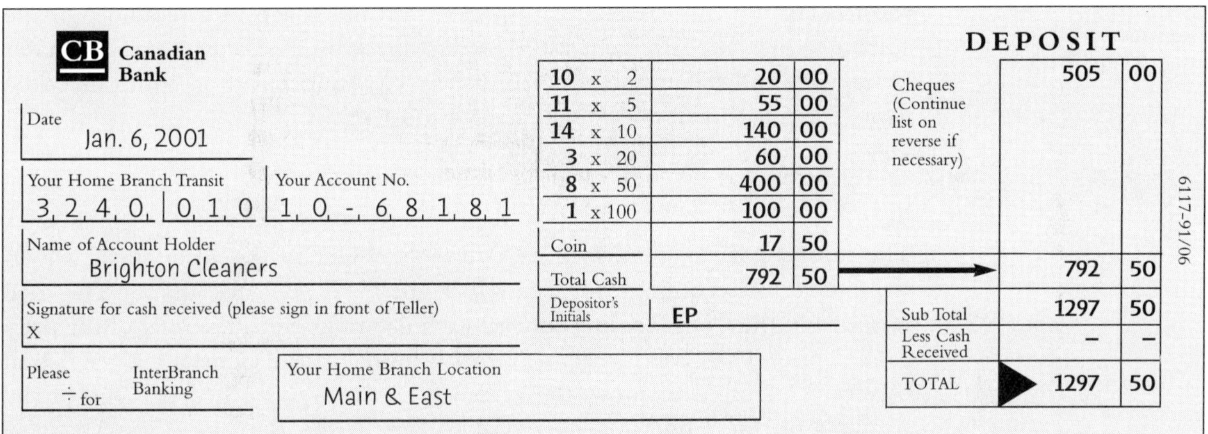

CB Canadian Bank

Date: Jan. 6, 2001

Your Home Branch Transit: 3, 2, 4, 0, 0, 1, 0

Your Account No.: 1, 0, -, 6, 8, 1, 8, 1

Name of Account Holder: Brighton Cleaners

Signature for cash received (please sign in front of Teller): X

Please ÷ for InterBranch Banking

Your Home Branch Location: Main & East

10 x 2	20	00
11 x 5	55	00
14 x 10	140	00
3 x 20	60	00
8 x 50	400	00
1 x 100	100	00
Coin	17	50
Total Cash	792	50
Depositor's Initials	EP	

DEPOSIT

Cheques (Continue list on reverse if necessary)	505	00
	792	50
Sub Total	1297	50
Less Cash Received	–	–
TOTAL	1297	50

6117-91/06

Fraser Enterprises' Cash Receipts Control System

The example of Fraser Enterprises, a large wholesaler of heating and refrigeration equipment, is used to demonstrate the cash control procedures we have discussed to this point. The principle of separation of duties is used by Fraser Enterprises to control and record cash receipts. Each day, a list of all cash received is prepared by the mail clerk. This list shows the name of the customer, the amount received, and the invoice that is being paid. Two copies of the list are prepared. They are sent to the accounting department where the money received is recorded.

The actual cash is taken to the bank each day by the office manager. Cheques received are endorsed using a restrictive endorsement stamp as shown in Figure 10-4. This endorsement ensures that the cheque is deposited in the company account. It cannot be cashed by anyone. A duplicate deposit slip is prepared, and one copy is kept by the bank. The second copy, signed by the bank teller, is kept by the company.

FIGURE 10-4
Restrictive endorsement stamp on the back of a cheque

DEPOSIT TO THE CREDIT OF
FRASER ENTERPRISES
The Bank of Nova Scotia
Carlingwood & Woodroffe Branch
Ottawa, Ontario
K2A 3T3

Using the List of Cash Received

When the two copies of the list of cash received are sent to the accounting department, one copy goes to the accounts receivable clerk for posting and the other copy goes to the accountant for journalizing.

Duties of the Accounts Receivable Clerk

From the list of cash received, the accounts receivable clerk posts to the customer accounts. Each account is lowered with a credit. Once every week, the accounts receivable clerk prepares a schedule of accounts receivable. This is a list showing the amount owed by each customer and the total owed by all the customers as a group.

Once a month, a statement is sent to each customer. The statement shows the balance, charges, and credits for cash received, and it acts as a reminder of the amount owing. The statement also is used to check on the accuracy of both Fraser Enterprises' and the customer's records. The customer is sure to complain if the balance owing shown on the statement is too high!

Duties of the Accountant

The second copy of the list of cash receipts is sent to the accountant, who is responsible for recording cash received in the Cash Receipts Journal. The total recorded in the Cash Receipts Journal each day must equal the total of the daily bank deposit. The Cash Receipts Journal is posted to the General Ledger. A trial balance is prepared to prove the accuracy of the General Ledger. One of the accounts on the General Ledger trial balance is the *Accounts Receivable control account*. The balance in this account must equal the total of the schedule of accounts receivable prepared by the accounts receivable clerk.

Control Features

In the system just described, four people are involved in the cash receipts procedures. One person prepares the deposit and another takes the money to the bank. The duty of recording the receiving of cash is handled by two other people. The duties are *separated*. Figure 10-5 illustrates all these tasks that have been described.

FIGURE 10-5

The duties of depositing and recording cash received are carried out by four people — the mail clerk, the office manager, the accounts receivable clerk, and the accountant.

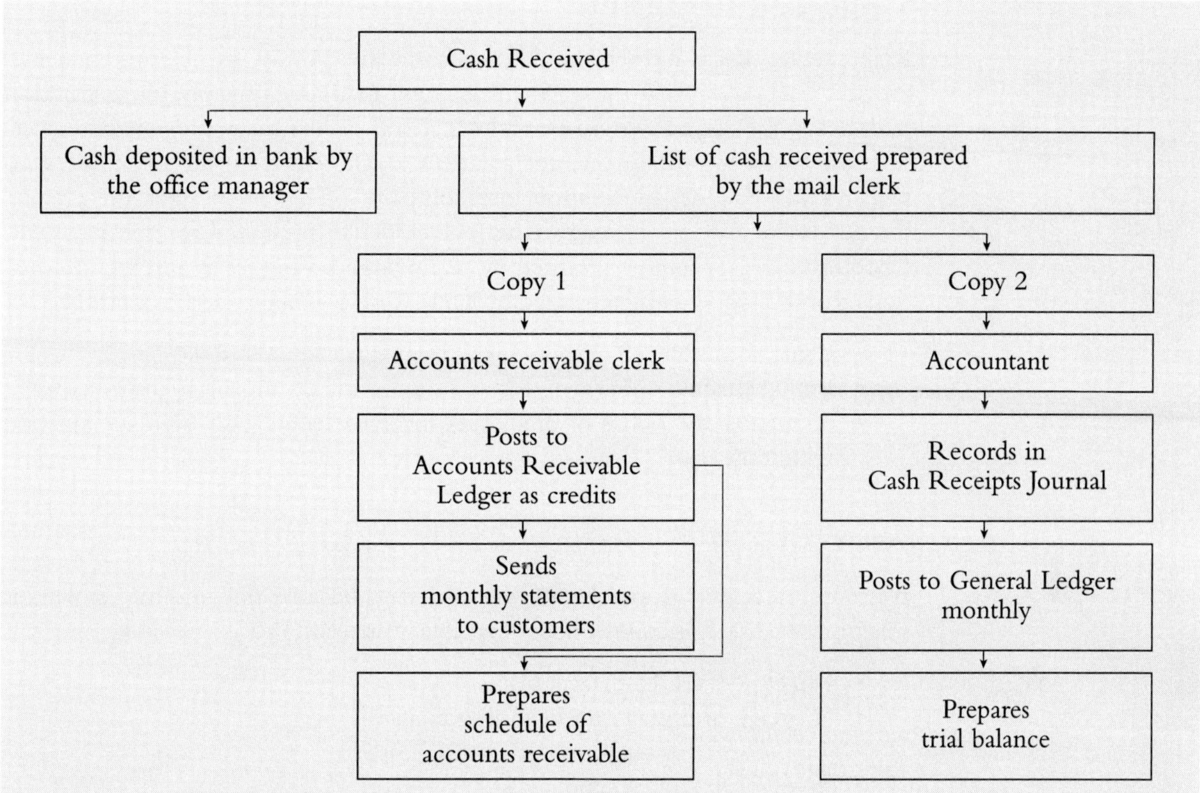

The separation of duties shown in Figure 10-5 has several built-in control features:

- The entries in the Cash Receipts Journal each day should equal the total of the day's bank deposit.
- The customer should discover any errors in the customer account when the statement is sent out.
- The total of the schedule of accounts receivable should always equal the balance of the Accounts Receivable control account in the General Ledger trial balance.

The separation of duties concept is observed by most large companies. The separation is more difficult to achieve in small businesses because there are fewer employees. It is important for the owner of the enterprise to become involved in order to achieve the necessary controls.

CONTROL OF CASH PAYMENTS

Although most people think of protecting cash receipts when discussing control procedures, it is just as important to control cash payments. Procedures 5 and 6 are important parts of a cash payment control system.

Procedure 5: Payment by Cheque

All cash payments should be made by cheque. The exception is small bills paid out of petty cash as discussed in Procedure 6. Cheques are prenumbered and spoiled cheques should be marked *void*. Therefore, all cheques can be accounted for at any time. It is important that company cheques be kept in a safe place to prevent theft.

Supporting Documents

Each cheque that is written should be accompanied by an invoice or voucher to provide verification that the payment is being made legitimately. The separation of duties in the control system for cash payments occurs when the person responsible for approving the invoice for payment is different from the employee who prepares the cheque. In addition, the company official who signs the cheque should do so only when there is proper evidence presented for the payment. Cheque-signing machines are used by many large businesses as an extra precaution against cheques being changed by hand. Cash payments can be controlled by:

- Using prenumbered cheques for all payments
- Issuing cheques only when there are supporting documents to justify payment
- Separating the duties of employees involved in the cash payment function within the firm

Procedure 6: Petty Cash Procedures

It is often necessary to make a payment by cash because the amount involved is small or because a cheque is not acceptable. For example:

- Parcel post COD charge: $1.50
- Shortage of postage on incoming mail: 50¢.
- Taxi charge for a rush order of supplies: $15
- Payment for office supplies: $12

The petty cash fund is an amount of cash used to make small payments.

To meet these situations, a small amount of cash is kept on hand. This *petty cash fund* is given to one person, the petty cashier, to maintain. The petty cashier usually has no connection with the accounting system of the company.

Setting Up the Petty Cash Fund

To establish the petty cash fund, a cheque is issued and given to the petty cashier. The cheque is cashed and the money is usually kept in a petty cash box.

When a petty cash fund is established, this journal entry is made:

Jan. 2	Petty Cash	100	
	Cash		100
	Cheque 171 to set up a petty cash fund.		

The Petty Cash account is a current asset.

The Petty Cash account debited in this entry is found in the General Ledger. It is an asset and appears in the current assets section of the balance sheet.

Making Payments

The petty cashier is the only person who handles petty cash. Payments made must be authorized by a properly supporting *petty cash voucher* (Figure 10-6 below)

The petty cash voucher is a signed authorization for small payments.

Petty cash vouchers are kept in the petty cash box with the remaining cash. Because they have been signed by the party receiving the cash payment, the vouchers prove that legitimate, authorized payments have been made.

Proving the Petty Cash

Suppose a petty cashier starts with $100 cash in the petty cash fund. At any time, the petty cash can be proven by adding the total of the cash in the box to the total of the vouchers in the box. Cash plus vouchers should always equal $100.

Replenishing the Petty Cash Fund

When the petty cash fund runs low, it must be replenished. The petty cashier presents the vouchers and a summary of all payments to the accountant. The vouchers prove that authorized payments have been made. The accountant then issues a cheque equal to the total of the vouchers. The petty cashier cashes the cheque and places the money in the petty cash box. This brings the petty cash fund back to its original amount. This process will now be examined in detail.

Replenishing the petty cash fund means bringing the total currency on hand up to the original amount.

Suppose that on January 23, the petty cashier notes that there is only $12 cash left in the petty cash fund. Along with this cash are eight vouchers for payments made. Since the original amount of the fund was $100 and there is only $12 left, the payment vouchers should total $88.

FIGURE 10-6
Petty cash voucher

Petty Cash Voucher

No. 36

Date Jun. 29, 2001

Amount $14.95

For Pens and staples

Charge to	Office Expense	$13.97
	GST Refundable	.98

Approved by B. Mallet

Received by A. Hodgson

The petty cashier adds the eight vouchers; they total $88. This means that there were no errors in handling the petty cash. The vouchers are then used to prepare the summary below.

Petty Cash Summary
January 2 to January 23, 2001

K. Martin, Drawings	$ 20.00
Office Expense	23.25
Delivery Expense	17.00
Miscellaneous Expense	22.00
GST Refundable	5.75
Total Payments	$ 88.00
Cash on hand	12.00
Total of fund	$100.00
Cheque request: $88	
Number of vouchers: 8	

The eight vouchers and the summary are then presented to the accountant. The accountant checks to see that all payments are supported by numbered, signed vouchers and that all the vouchers have been accounted for. Then a replenishing cheque for $88 is issued by the accountant and given to the petty cashier. This journal entry is made by the accountant:

2001			
Jan. 23	K. Martin, Drawings	20.00	
	Office Expense	23.25	
	Delivery Expense	17.00	
	Miscellaneous Expense	22.00	
	GST Refundable	5.75	
	Cash		88.00
	Cheque 207 to replenish petty cash, vouchers 1–8.		

A journal entry similar to this one is made each time the petty cash fund is replenished. The accounts to be debited are determined by referring to the vouchers and the summary submitted by the petty cashier. Notice that expense accounts are debited each time the fund is replenished. The Petty Cash account is used only when the fund is established or the size of the fund is changed.

The petty cashier cashes the $88 cheque, obtaining a variety of denominations of bills, and places the cash in the petty cash box. When this $88 is placed in the petty cash box, the total cash is increased to $100. (Remember, there was a $12 cash balance before the fund was replenished.)

The petty cash fund is replenished in the way that has been described whenever it runs low. In addition to replenishing petty cash when needed, the fund is also normally replenished at the end of the fiscal period whether the fund is low or not. This is necessary in order to provide current expense account balances for financial statement preparation.

Petty Cash Guidelines

The petty cashier is usually given a set of guidelines like the following:

- The amount of the fund is $100.
- An approved voucher is required for every payment.
- Replenish the fund when the cash level reaches $10.
- The maximum for any one payment is $15.
- Approved vouchers must be presented to the accountant when requesting a replenishing cheque.

Changing the Size of the Petty Cash Fund

At some point, the office manager may find that the petty cash fund is constantly running out of money during the month and may therefore want to increase the size of the fund. If the fund were to be increased to $150, the journal entry at the time of replenishing (using the previous example) would be as follows:

2001			
Jan. 23	K. Martin, Drawings	20.00	
	Office Expense	23.25	
	Delivery Expense	17.00	
	Miscellaneous Expense	22.00	
	GST Refundable	5.75	
	Petty Cash	50.00	
	Cash		138.00
	Cheque 207 to replenish petty cash, vouchers 1–8, and to increase fund.		

Notice that this entry *does* contain a debit to the Petty Cash account as well as to the expense accounts. This is due to the fact that the amount of the fund has been increased. How would you decrease the original fund to $75 if you found it was too large? Here is an example:

2001			
Jan. 23	K. Martin, Drawings	20.00	
	Office Expense	23.25	
	Delivery Expense	17.00	
	Miscellaneous Expense	22.00	
	GST Refundable	5.75	
	Cash		63.00
	Petty Cash		25.00
	Cheque 207 to replenish petty cash, vouchers 1–8, and to decrease fund.		

In this example, the fund is only replenished with enough cash to reach the new value of $75. Petty cash is credited since the amount of the fund is being decreased.

REVIEW QUESTIONS

1. What is the purpose of an internal control system?
2. Explain the difference between administrative controls and accounting controls.
3. Why is control of cash necessary?
4. What items are included when cash control is discussed?
5. What type of business must consider cash control systems?
6. What is the first principle of cash control?
7. How can the customer assist in the control of cash when an over-the-counter cash sale is made?
8. What is the purpose of prenumbering source documents?
9. What should be done with cancelled or voided cash sales slips in a prenumbered system?
10. What is a cash float?
11. The day's cash total is $583.39. The sales slips total $582.13. Is the cash short or over and by how much?
12. (a) Is a cash shortage recorded as a debit or a credit in the Cash Short and Over account?
    (b) How is an overage recorded?
13. The Cash Short and Over account has a debit balance of $19 at the end of a fiscal period. Is this considered a revenue or an expense? Does it increase or decrease net income?
14. Who receives the two copies of the deposit slip?
15. When all the day's cash receipts are deposited, both the company's records and the bank's record show the cash the company has received on that day. How is this an advantage for the company?
16. Give an advantage of making all payments by cheque.
17. How is a separation of duties achieved when making cash payments by cheque?
18. What is the purpose of a petty cash fund?
19. How does the petty cash voucher prove that a legitimate payment was made?
20. One cash control procedure states that all payments must be made by cheque. Explain how the petty cash fund is designed so that this principle is followed.
21. What type of account is Petty Cash?
22. Some of the following practices contribute to a strong cash control system and some weaken the system. Identify each as a strength or weakness and explain your reasons.
    (a) Any cash shortage or overage in the daily cash proof is added to or removed from petty cash.
    (b) All cash receipts are deposited daily.
    (c) Cheques are issued for all cash payments other than petty cash disbursements.
    (d) All payments under $175 are made through the petty cash fund.
    (e) Cheques received through the mail are listed and recorded by the accounts receivable clerk.

1. The change fund for Brighton Cleaners consists of:

BILLS	COINS
1 × $20	3 × $2
1 × $10	5 × $1
2 × $ 5	23 × 25¢
	20 × 10¢
	20 × 5¢
	25 × 1¢

The cash on hand for Brighton Cleaners consists of:

BILLS	COINS
3 × $20	18 × $2
12 × $10	39 × $1
20 × $ 5	40 × 25¢
	29 × 10¢
	41 × 5¢
	26 × 1¢

The calculator tape of the day's cash sales slips for Brighton Cleaners consists of:

Date: May 10, 2001
Cash Sales Slips: 934-997
Total: $314.59

(a) Remove the $60 change fund from the cash on hand and prepare a deposit slip for account no. 91835-09.
(b) Prepare the daily cash proof.

2. Prepare the journal entry to record the daily cash proofs prepared for exercise 1.

3. A petty cash fund was established with $100. At present, the petty cash box contains:

Bills	Coins	Vouchers
1 × $10	1 × $1	6 totalling $40.27
2 × $ 5	2 × $2	

Have any errors been made in the handling of the petty cash?

4. Mechanical Services Ltd. decides to establish a petty cash fund. The office supervisor is chosen to be responsible for petty cash. The accountant issues Cheque 171 for $100 on Sep. 1 and gives it to the supervisor to establish the fund. Record the $100 cheque in a General Journal.

5. On March 17, a summary of vouchers in a petty cash box shows:

Office Expense	$ 41.50
G. Le Pensée, Drawings	40.00
Donations Expense	15.00
Miscellaneous Expense	14.50
Total	$111.00

In a General Journal form, record the $111 cheque issued by the accountant to replenish the petty cash fund.

6. On September 7, Print-O-Matic Ltd. decided to begin using a petty cash fund. A cheque for $125 was issued and cashed. The $125 cash was given to the receptionist who was to act as petty cashier. The receptionist/petty cashier was told to obtain authorized vouchers for all payments. The petty cash was to be replenished when the balance in the cash box reached $25. When this happened, a summary of vouchers was to be prepared and given to the accountant.

(a) Record the $125 cheque to establish the fund on September 7.
(b) On September 19, this summary was prepared:
Prepare the entry to replenish the petty cash.

Delivery Expense	$ 49.90
Miscellaneous Expense	20.40
Office Expense	24.10
GST Refundable	6.60
Total	$101.00

(c) It was decided to increase the amount of the petty cash fund from $125 to $175. A cheque for $50 was issued. Record this cheque.

7. If only one cheque were issued in 6(b) and (c) to both replenish and increase the fund, how would the cheque be recorded in a General Journal?

8. September 30 was the end of the fiscal year for Print-O-Matic. The following summary of vouchers from the petty cash fund was prepared:

Office Expense	$ 55.34
Miscellaneous Expense	21.83
Delivery Expense	21.25
S. Kerrigan, Drawings	30.00
GST Refundable	7.16
	$135.58

(a) Record the cheque issued to replenish the petty cash fund on September 30.
(b) Why was the fund replenished even though it still contained a substantial amount of cash?

UNIT 26 Checking Cash Records

Learning Objectives

After reading this unit, discussing the applicable review questions, and completing the applications exercises, you will be able to do the following:

1. **EXPLAIN** audit, bank debit memo, bank credit memo, NSF cheque, cancelled cheque, outstanding cheque, and reconciliation statement.
2. **PREPARE** a reconciliation statement.
3. **PREPARE** journal entries involving banking transactions.

CONCLUDING CASH CONTROL PROCEDURES

In Unit 25, we examined the first six cash control procedures. Now, in this unit, we will look at the two concluding procedures.

Procedure 7: Periodic Audit

Periodically, a check or an *audit* is made to determine that all cash is properly accounted for. Any system, no matter how complicated or foolproof, can break down. Those involved in the system can devise ways to break the system. People can get together and contrive to defraud a company. The periodic — often unannounced — audit is designed to thwart such attempts.

An audit is a periodic check on the accuracy of an accounting system.

An auditor, employed either by the company or by an outside accounting firm, is given the task of checking the company records. Transactions are traced from their source documents to their posting in the ledgers. Invoices and deposit slips are checked for accuracy. As you learned when studying Procedure 2, prenumbered documents should be used to record cash. However, if a check is not made to ensure that all documents and cash are accounted for, the system breaks down.

EXAMINING THE BANKING CONNECTION

Procedure 8 will involve making sure that a company's record of its money agrees with the bank's record of the company's money. This requires an understanding of the banking connection or, in other words, an understanding of the relationship between a bank and its depositors. What is the relationship between the bank and a company or person who deposits money? Do banks follow the same accounting rules and the same theory of debits and credits as everyone else? The following example is a good illustration of the banking connection. *Note:* GST and PST have been excluded from these transactions in order to simplify the examples.

Renfrew Printing makes cash sales of $1 500 and deposits the $1 500 in a savings account at the Bank of Nova Scotia. In the books of Renfrew Printing, the following occurs, as shown in T-account form:

Renfrew Printing's Books

Cash		Sales	
1 500			1 500

Through this transaction, Renfrew Printing has more money: its Cash account increases (debit) and its Sales account increases (credit). When the Bank of Nova Scotia receives the deposit, its books also change as shown by the following T-accounts:

Bank of Nova Scotia's Books

Cash		Renfrew Printing	
1 500			1 500

Through this transaction, the Bank of Nova Scotia has more money: its asset Cash increases (debit). The bank *owes* this $1 500 to Renfrew Printing; in other words, Renfrew Printing is an account payable on the bank's books. At any time, the depositor can demand the money owing and withdraw cash from the account. The bank records the debt by placing a credit of $1 500 in the liability account, Renfrew Printing.

Transactions Involving the Bank's Source Documents

Some of the bank's source documents are the same as those of other companies. For example, banks receive purchase invoices and write cheques. The source document that is evidence that a depositor has withdrawn money from the bank is the *withdrawal slip.* The *deposit slip* is the source document proving that money was deposited by a depositor. Two other source documents commonly used by banks are the *bank credit memo* and the *bank debit memo.* Transactions involving these two documents follow.

Bank Debit Memo

A bank debit memo is a source document indicating a decrease in a depositor's account.

To give notice of a service charge of $22.50 for cashing cheques on Renfrew Printing's account, the Bank of Nova Scotia issues the debit memo shown in Figure 10-7. As shown in the T-accounts following Figure 10-7, the bank deducts the $22.50 by debiting Renfrew's account. Remember, a liability decreases on the debit side.

FIGURE 10-7

A bank debit memo is the source document prepared when the bank decreases a customer's account.

THE BANK OF NOVA SCOTIA

26189-57 June 10, 2001

Account Number Date

DEBIT Service charge for month $22.50

Authorized by C.S. Checked by H.G. Entry made by M.G.

This slip must be initialled by an authorized signing officer.

Bank of Nova Scotia's Books

Renfrew Printing	
22.50	1 500.00

A depositor's account is a liability of the bank. Service charges decrease the liability of the bank.

When the depositor, Renfrew Printing, receives the debit memo, the following changes are made in its books:

Renfrew Printing's Books

Cash		Bank Charges	
1 500	22.50	22.50	

Since this transaction is a payment, it is recorded in the Cash Payments Journal of Renfrew Printing.

Bank Credit Memo

If Renfrew Printing has a savings account, it will earn interest which is periodically calculated by the bank. Suppose interest amounting to $67.39 has been earned by Renfrew Printing. This means that the bank owes Renfrew more money and the bank will increase the amount in its liability account, Renfrew Printing.

Bank of Nova Scotia's Books

Renfrew Printing	
22.50	1 500.00
	67.39

A bank credit memo (Figure 10-8) is completed and serves to instruct the bank's clerk to increase the Renfrew account. A copy of the memo is sent to Renfrew to inform the company that its bank account has been increased.

A bank credit memo is a source document indicating an increase in a depositor's account.

THE BANK OF NOVA SCOTIA

June 10, 2001
Date

CREDIT Renfrew Printing
$67.39 Interest earned on term deposit.
Deposit to Renfrew Printing's account 26189-57.

C. Smith

FIGURE 10-8
A bank credit memo is the source document prepared when the bank increases a customer's account.

When the depositor, Renfrew Printing, receives the credit memo, it will change its accounts as follows:

Renfrew Printing's Books

Cash		Interest Earned	
1 500.00	22.50		67.39
67.39			

This transaction represents cash received and is recorded in the Cash Receipts Journal. After the debit and credit transactions, what is the balance in the bank's liability account, Renfrew Printing? What is the balance in Renfrew Printing's Cash account?

A company's Cash account should, theoretically, always have the same balance as the bank's record of the company's bank account. However, in actual practice this is rarely the situation. We will now look at Procedure 8 to see what is done to determine if the bank's records agree with the depositor's records.

Procedure 8: Monthly Bank Reconciliation

Personal Chequing Account Reconciliation

Pat and Bob Hunter are a young couple striving to make ends meet. Because they are making payments on their new home and on furniture, they have little money left over for savings. Several months ago, they received telephone calls from their insurance company and the company holding their house mortgage. Both companies said that the cheques given to them by Pat and Bob were NSF — that is, the cheques had been returned by the bank with the explanation that there were *not sufficient funds* in the Hunters' account to cash the cheques.

An NSF cheque is one that cannot be paid because there are not sufficient funds in the account of the person who wrote the cheque.

The Hunters were quite upset because, according to their records, there was enough money in their bank account to cover the cheques. They called the bank and suggested that the bank had made an error. They were right. Somehow, the combined deposit for both their pay cheques had ended up in someone else's account! Do banks make errors? Of course they do! People who work in banks are human and can make mistakes just like anyone else. Can you remember instances of banks making errors in your own or your family's bank account? The Hunters felt good about discovering this error in their account because it demonstrated that they kept a good record of their bank account balance. Let's look at their account records for the month of July. This will illustrate how the Hunters always check the accuracy of the bank's records by observing Procedure 8.

Cancelled cheques are cheques that have been cashed by the bank.

The Hunters have a joint personal chequing account at the Bank of Nova Scotia. They use this account to make payments for their personal expenses such as mortgage payments, utilities, and charge accounts. Every month, the bank sends them a bank statement and returns their cancelled cheques. At the end of July, the Hunters received from the bank the bank statement shown in Figure 10-9 on page 392. According to the bank statement, the Hunters' balance was $277.76. Enclosed with the bank statement were four *cancelled cheques,* numbered 73, 74, 75, and 76 (Figure 10-10 on page 393).

The cheque book provided to the Hunters by the bank included cheque record pages as shown in Figure 10-11. These provided the Hunters with a record of cheques written, deposits made, and the balance. According to their cheque record, the Hunters had a July balance of $533.48. Which was correct — the bank statement balance of $277.76, the Hunters' balance of $533.48, or neither?

FIGURE 10-9
Bank statement received by the Hunters

THE BANK OF NOVA SCOTIA

Pat and Bob Hunter
675 Willow Place, Apt. 702
Ottawa, ON
K1R 6W3

ACCOUNT NUMBER
21830-42

STATEMENT OF	FROM	TO	PAGE
Personal Chequing Account	Jul. 1, 2001	Jul. 31, 2001	1

DESCRIPTION	DEBITS	CREDITS	DATE M	DATE D	BALANCE
Balance forward			07	01	486.79
Deposit		900.00	07	02	1,386.79
Cheque 73	12.84		07	05	1,373.95
Cheque 74	386.29		07	09	987.66
Cheque 75	499.00		07	15	488.66
Cheque 76	200.00		07	17	288.66
SC	10.90		07	29	277.76

NO. OF DEBITS	TOTAL AMOUNT OF DEBITS	NO. OF CREDITS	TOTAL AMOUNT OF CREDITS	NO. OF ENCLOSURES
5	1,109.03	1	900.00	4

FIGURE 10-10
Cancelled cheques enclosed with bank statement

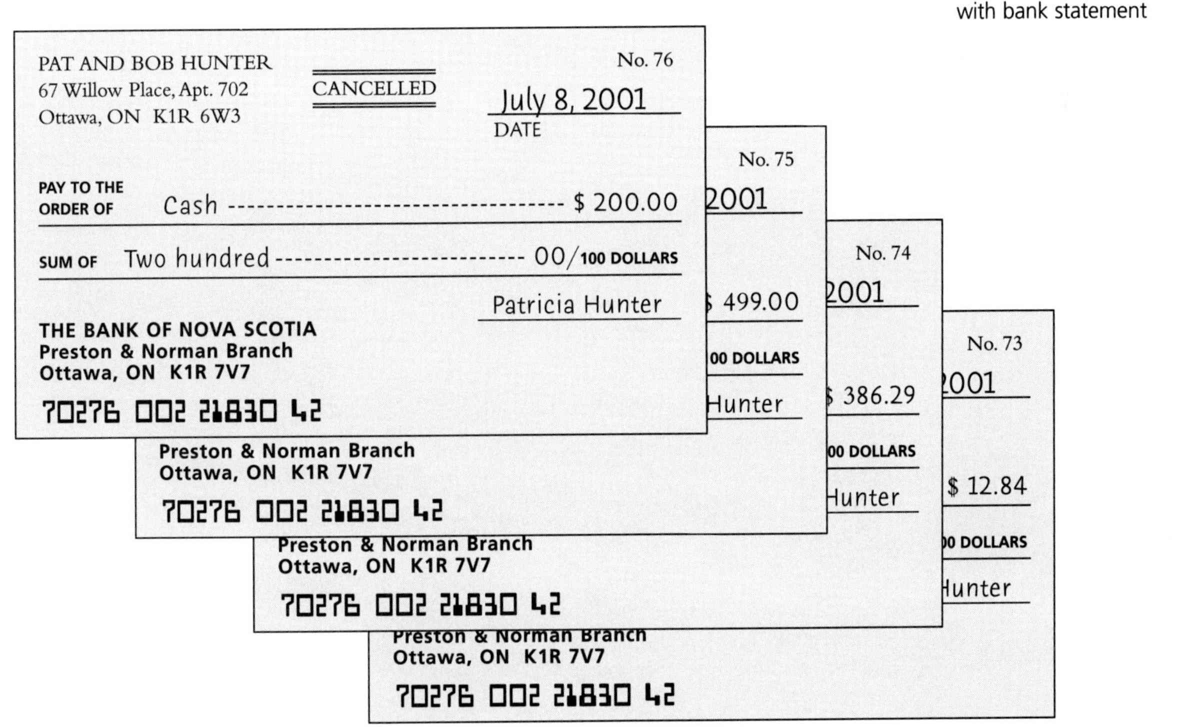

PAT AND BOB HUNTER
67 Willow Place, Apt. 702
Ottawa, ON K1R 6W3
CANCELLED
No. 76
July 8, 2001
DATE
PAY TO THE ORDER OF Cash $ 200.00
SUM OF Two hundred 00/100 DOLLARS
Patricia Hunter
THE BANK OF NOVA SCOTIA
Preston & Norman Branch
Ottawa, ON K1R 7V7
70276 002 21830 42
No. 75
No. 74
No. 73
$ 499.00
$ 386.29
$ 12.84

Preparing the Personal Bank Reconciliation Statement

To determine the correct balance, the Hunters did the following:

Outstanding cheques are cheques issued but not yet cashed.

(1) In their cheque record (Figure 10-11), they ticked off (✓) each of the cancelled cheques returned by the bank. The three unticked cheques were outstanding; that is, they were cheques that had been issued but had not yet been cashed by the bank. Cheques 72, 77, and 78 were outstanding.

(2) They matched and ticked off the deposits on the bank statement with deposits in their cheque book record. The last deposit of $400 was not shown in the bank statement — probably because the statement was being prepared and mailed before the Hunters made the deposit.

A reconciliation statement is a statement that brings into agreement the bank's records with the depositor's records.

(3) They looked for items that appeared on the bank statement but not on their records. The Hunters then prepared a *reconciliation statement* (Figure 10-12), which brought their records into agreement with the bank's records. This statement indicated that their correct balance was $522.58.

(4) After preparing the reconciliation statement, the Hunters record the service charges on their cheque record. They did this by recording the $10.90 SC (service charge) in the Amount of Cheque column on their cheque record. Their new balance in the cheque record was then $522.58.

FIGURE 10-11
Page from the Hunters' cheque book showing their record of banking transactions

CHEQUE NO.	DATE	DESCRIPTION OF TRANSACTION	AMOUNT OF CHEQUE		✓	AMOUNT OF DEPOSIT		BALANCE	
	Jul. 1	Balance forward						486	79
	2	Deposit			✓	900	00	1 386	79
72	3	MasterCard	48	60				1 338	19
73	3	Bell Canada	12	84	✓			1 325	35
74	3	Central Mortgage Corp.	386	29	✓			939	06
75	5	CIAG Insurance	499	00	✓			440	06
76	8	Cash	200	00	✓			240	06
77	23	The Bay	62	08				177	98
78	29	Exxon Ltd.	44	50				133	48
	31	Deposit				400	00	533	48

FIGURE 10-12
Bank reconciliation statement prepared by the Hunters

Pat and Bob Hunter
Bank Reconciliation Statement
July 31, 2001

Bank statement balance		$277.76
Add: Unrecorded deposit of July 31		400.00
		677.76
Less: Outstanding cheques		
No. 72	$48.60	
No. 77	62.08	
No. 78	44.50	155.18
Correct bank balance		$522.58
Cheque record balance		$533.48
Less: Service charges		10.90
Correct cheque book balance		$522.58

People like the Hunters wisely prepare monthly bank reconciliation statements. This ensures that their records and the bank's records agree. Reconciliation statements will bring to light errors made by the bank or by the depositor. Companies follow similar procedures.

Business Current Account Reconciliation

Fraser Enterprises has a current account with the Bank of Nova Scotia. Each month, the bank sends a statement to Fraser Enterprises and encloses cancelled cheques that were paid out of Fraser's account. The company accountant compares the bank statement balance with the balance in Fraser's books. A reconciliation statement is then prepared to bring the two into agreement. Figure 10-13 is the bank statement received by Fraser Enterprises. It shows a balance of $1 999.12 on June 30. Figure 10-14 on pages 397 and 398 is the company's cash records. The Cash account shows a balance of $3 251.02 on June 30. Which of the two balances is correct — the bank's or Fraser's? Or is neither correct?

FIGURE 10-13
Bank statement received by Fraser Enterprises

THE BANK OF NOVA SCOTIA

Fraser Enterprises
125 Murray St.
Ottawa, ON
K1N 5M5

ACCOUNT NUMBER
31924-06

STATEMENT OF	FROM	TO	PAGE
Current Account	Jun. 1, 2001	Jun. 30, 2001	1

DESCRIPTION	DEBITS	CREDITS	DATE M	DATE D	BALANCE
Balance forward			06	01	780.22
Deposit		395.00 ✓	06	02	1,175.22
Cheque 171	75.00 ✓		06	05	
Deposit		1,200.00 ✓	06	05	2,300.22
Cheque 172	149.50 ✓		06	10	2,150.72
RI	50.00		06	12	
SC	20.00		06	12	
Deposit		250.00 ✓	06	12	2,330.72
Cheque 174	675.00 ✓		06	19	
Cheque 175	1,500.00 ✓		06	19	
Deposit		1,800.00 ✓	06	19	1,955.72
Cheque 176	29.60 ✓		06	28	1,926.12
SC	22.00		06	30	
CM		95.00	06	30	1,999.12

NO. OF DEBITS	TOTAL AMOUNT OF DEBITS	NO. OF CREDITS	TOTAL AMOUNT OF CREDITS	NO. OF ENCLOSURES
7	2,521.10	5	3,740.00	6

Preparing the Business Bank Reconciliation Statement

To determine the correct balance, a bank reconciliation statement is prepared. This statement will bring the bank's balance into agreement with the company's balance in order to determine the true or correct cash balance. These procedures are followed in preparing the bank reconciliation statement:

Subtract outstanding cheques.

(1) Prepare a list of the outstanding cheques. This is done by ticking off in the Cash Payments Journal all the cancelled cheques returned by the bank (see Figure 10-14). Unticked cheques are outstanding; they have not been cashed by the bank. The cancelled cheques are also ticked off on the bank statement debits column (see Figure 10-13). The outstanding cheques (in the case of Fraser Enterprises, Nos. 173, 177, and 178) are subtracted from the bank statement balance on the reconciliation statement to bring the bank's balance into agreement with the company's balance (see Figure 10-15).

Add outstanding deposits.

(2) Compare the deposits shown in the cash debit column of the Cash Receipts Journal (see Figure 10-14) with those shown in the credits column of the bank statement (see Figure 10-13). Tick off the deposits on both records. Deposits not recorded on the bank statement are added to the bank statement balance on the reconciliation statement (refer to the $2 200 unrecorded June 30 deposit in Figure 10-15).

Add credit memos. Subtract debit memo.

(3) Locate all unticked items on the bank statement. Add unticked items in the credits column to the company's record of the cash balance (on the cheque book stub). In this case, CM, or credit memo, indicates that $95 in interest must be added. Subtract the unticked items in the debits column of the bank statement from the company's record of the cash balance (on the cheque book stub). Two items must be subtracted in this example: SC (service charges) of $42 and RI of $50. RI stands for returned item and in this case is a not-sufficient-funds cheque. *Note:* The $20 service charge under the RI is the bank charge for the NSF cheque. For more information on NSF cheques, see page 400.

(4) Journal entries to adjust the company's Cash account to reflect the unticked items on the bank statement are prepared after the bank reconciliation statement. Adjust both the bank's and the company's balance for any obvious errors. For example, cheque amounts could have been recorded incorrectly or arithmetic errors might have been made. If you have problems in understanding whether the bank's or the company's balance should be adjusted on a bank reconciliation statement, here are a couple of rules to follow:

- Adjust the balance of whomever makes a mistake (the company or the bank).
- Adjust the balance of whomever is last to know about an adjustment (e.g., NSF cheque).

FIGURE 10-14
Fraser Enterprises' cash records

CASH RECEIPTS JOURNAL **PAGE 21**

DATE	REF. NO.	CUSTOMER OR ACCOUNT	P.R.	CASH DEBIT	SALES DISCOUNTS DEBIT	ACCOUNTS REC. CREDIT	SALES CREDIT	GST PAYABLE CREDIT	PST PAYABLE CREDIT	OTHER ACCOUNTS CREDIT
2001										
May 31		Deposit		395.00 ✓						
		May total		1 175.22						
Jun. 5				1 200.00 ✓						
12				250.00 ✓						
19				1 800.00 ✓						
30				2 200.00						
				5 450.00						
				(101)						

Deposits made in June

CASH PAYMENTS JOURNAL — **PAGE 32**

DATE	CH. NO.	CREDITOR OR ACCOUNT	P.R.	CASH CREDIT	ACCOUNTS PAYABLE DEBIT	GST REFUNDABLE DEBIT	PURCHASES DEBIT	PURCHASES DISCOUNTS CREDIT	OTHER ACCOUNTS DEBIT
2001									
Jun. 1	171			75.00 ✓					
4	172			149.50 ✓					
11	173			50.00					
16	174			675.00 ✓					
17	175			1 500.00 ✓					
26	176			29.60 ✓					
27	177			68.10					
28	178			827.00					
				3 374.20					
				(101)					

Cheques written in June

ACCOUNT Cash — **NO. 101**

DATE	PARTICULARS	P.R.	DEBIT	CREDIT	DR. CR.	BALANCE
May 31	Forwarded	✓			DR.	1 175.22
Jun. 30	Cash Receipts	CR21	5 450.00		DR.	6 625.22
30	Cash Payments	CP32		3 374.20	DR.	3 251.02

Cash account in the General Ledger

Fraser Enterprises Bank Reconciliation Statement June 30, 2001		
Bank statement balance		$1 999.12
Add: Unrecorded June 30 deposit		2 200.00
		4 199.12
Less: Outstanding cheques		
No. 173	$50.00	
No. 177	68.10	
No. 178	827.00	945.10
Correct bank balance		$3 254.02
Cash balance per ledger		$3 251.02
Add: Interest earned (CM)		95.00
		$3 346.02
Less: Service charges	$42.00	
RI (NSF cheque)	50.00	92.00
Correct cash balance		$3 254.02

FIGURE 10-15
Bank reconciliation statement prepared by Fraser Enterprises

Figure 10-15 is the bank reconciliation statement prepared after completing the preceding four steps. It shows that the correct Cash account balance is $3 254.02.

Journal Entries After Bank Reconciliation

After the reconciliation statement has been prepared, the company's Cash account balance must be brought up-to-date. Remember, Figure 10-14 showed that, according to the company's Cash account, the cash balance was $3 251.02. However, the correct balance is $3 254.02, as shown on the reconciliation statement. The company's Cash account is brought up-to-date by preparing journal entries for any unrecorded items brought to light by the reconciliation statement. A journal entry decreasing cash is made for items such as service charges, NSF cheques, and interest charged. A journal entry increasing cash is made for an item such as interest earned that was added by the bank.

Service Charges

The bank has deducted $42 for service charges; therefore, the company should record an expense and decrease its cash. The following entry is made:

Jun. 30	Bank Service Charges	42	
	Cash		42
	To record bank service charges.		

The following section outlines the procedures for recording NSF cheque service charges.

NSF Cheques

An *NSF cheque* is usually a customer's cheque that has been deposited by the company but cannot be cashed by the bank because there are not sufficient funds in the customer's bank account. Since the bank cannot collect from the writer of the cheque, it will deduct the amount of the cheque from Fraser Enterprises' account. The company will charge the amount plus the bank service charge back to its customer's account as an account receivable and will try to collect the amount. This entry is made:

Jun. 30	Accounts Receivable/G. Symons	70	
	Cash		70
	NSF cheque ($50) and bank charges ($20) charged back to G. Symons.		

Interest Earned

Fraser Enterprises has earned $95 interest on a term deposit. Since the bank has added the $95 to Fraser Enterprises' bank account, the company must now prepare a journal entry to record the $95. The following entry is made to record the revenue earned and to increase the Cash account:

Jun. 30	Cash	95	
	Interest Earned		95
	To record interest earned on a term deposit.		

Interest Expense

In addition to the entries described above, it is sometimes necessary to record interest expense deducted from a company's bank account. Suppose a company has a bank loan and $120 interest is paid each month. When the bank deducts interest for the loan from the company's bank account, this entry is made on the company's books:

Jun. 30	Interest Expense	120	
	Cash		120
	To record interest on the bank loan deducted by the bank.		

SUMMARY

In this chapter, you have learned eight procedures that are used to ensure that a firm has a proper accounting system in place to control cash:

- Procedure 1: Separation of Duties
- Procedure 2: Immediate Listing of Cash Receipts
- Procedure 3: Daily Cash Proof
- Procedure 4: Daily Deposit of Cash
- Procedure 5: Payment by Cheque
- Procedure 6: Petty Cash Procedures
- Procedure 7: Periodic Audit
- Procedure 8: Monthly Bank Reconciliation

ACCOUNTING TERMS

Accounting Controls	Procedures used to protect assets and ensure reliable accounting records.
Administrative Controls	Procedures used to ensure application of company policies and evaluate performance.
Audit	Verification of the accuracy of company records.
Bank Credit Memo	Source document indicating an increase in a depositor's account.
Bank Debit Memo	Source document indicating a decrease in a depositor's account.
Bank Reconciliation	Statement that brings into agreement the depositor's records and the bank's records.
Cancelled Cheque	Cheque that has been cashed by the bank.
Cash Proof	Verifies cash on hand equals cash sales slips for the day.
Cash Short and Over	An account used to record the amount of cash over or under the cash proof total each day.
NSF Cheque	A cheque that cannot be cashed because there are not sufficient funds in the account of the person who wrote the cheque.
Outstanding Cheque	Cheque that has not been cashed by the bank.
Petty Cash Fund	A small amount of cash kept on hand to make small payments.
Petty Cash Voucher	A signed authorization for petty cash payments.
Prenumbered Sales Slip	Multiple-copy sales slip prepared for each cash sale.
Replenishing Petty Cash	Bringing the total currency on hand up to the original amount.
Separation of Duties	Duties of employees should be arranged so that one employee verifies the work of another employee.

REVIEW QUESTIONS

1. Explain the role of the auditor.
2. Jan O'Dacre has a savings account with the Toronto-Dominion bank. In which section of its ledger will the bank locate O'Dacre's account — the asset, liability, owner's equity, revenue, or expense section?
3. Will a debit memo increase or decrease the balance of a depositor's account?
4. Will a credit memo increase or decrease the balance of a depositor's account?
5. In which journal is a bank credit memo recorded? A bank debit memo?
6. What is an NSF cheque?
7. What is a bank statement?
8. What is a cancelled cheque?
9. What is an outstanding cheque?

10. Some cheques that have been issued will not appear on the bank statement. Explain how such a situation can happen.
11. Some deposits that have been recorded in the depositor's records may not appear on the bank statement. Explain how such a situation can happen.
12. Give examples of certain items that appear on a bank statement but not on the depositor's records.
13. A bank reconciliation statement brings into agreement two sets of records. What are they?
14. Who prepares the bank reconciliation statement, the bank or the depositor?
15. When a company prepares a bank reconciliation statement, to what is the balance on the bank statement compared?
16. What is the General Journal entry to record a customer's cheque returned NSF?
17. Does cash control mean anything more than procedures used to prevent losses from fraud or theft? Explain.

9. Record the following transactions in a General Journal for I. Noren Rowing Machines Ltd.:

Nov. 7 Cash sales slips totalled $3 295 + $230.65 GST. Cash was deposited.

7 Issued Sales Invoice 87-B to A. Michaels, terms 3/15, n/30, amount $2 000, non-taxable, GST $140.

8 Received bank credit memo for $260 interest earned by the company.

9 Received bank debit memo for $25, plus $1.75 GST, for the annual charge for a safety deposit box.

15 Received cheque from A. Michaels, $2 075.80 for Invoice 87-B less $64.20 discount. Cheque was deposited.

30 Received bank debit memo for $21.00 for service charges on current account.

10. Record the following transactions in a General Journal for I. Noren Rowing Machines Ltd.:

Dec. 1 Received bank credit memo for a $15 000 loan granted and deposited in the company account, term two months, interest at 12 percent payable monthly.

31 Received bank debit memo for $150 deducted from the company account for interest on the loan.

Jan. 31 Received bank debit memo for $15 150 deducted from the company account ($15 000 repayment of the bank loan, $150 interest on the loan).

11. Below are the types of reconciling items found on the bank reconciliation:

    (a) added to the book balance
    (b) deducted from the book balance
    (c) added to the bank balance
    (d) deducted from the bank balance
    (e) omitted from the reconciliation

    ____ 1. The bank statement included $40 in monthly service charges.

    ____ 2. A $500 deposit made by Casey, Inc. on June 30 did not appear on the bank statement.

    ____ 3. The bookkeeper discovered an error. A $300 cheque disbursement was recorded as $30.

    ____ 4. The bank statement indicated an EFT collection of a note receivable of $1 200 with interest of $75.

    ____ 5. Cheques 405 and 406 were not among the cancelled cheques returned by the bank.

    ____ 6. The bank had charged Casey's account for a cheque written by Casay Ltd., and included it among the cancelled cheques.

    ____ 7. Included in the cancelled cheques returned by the bank were cheques 381 and 390, which had been outstanding on May 31.

    ____ 8. The bank statement included an NSF cheque from Remo Ltd., in the amount of $450.

    ____ 9. A May 31 deposit, which was included as a deposit in transit on the May 31 bank reconciliation, was recorded by the bank on June 2.

    ____ 10. A $600 deposit was recorded by the bookkeeper as $6 000.

    Tasks required:

    (a) For each of the above items taken from the records of Casey, Inc., put a letter in the space provided which identifies the treatment it would receive on the June 30 bank reconciliation.
    (b) Circle the letters that would require an adjustment on the books of Casey, Inc.

12. At the end of August, Pat and Bob Hunter have a balance of $1 240 in their cheque record. The statement received from their bank shows a balance of $1 574.75. The bank statement contains a deduction of $10.60 for service charges. A comparison of the cheques issued in the Hunters' cheque record and the cheques cashed on the statement indicates that Cheque 72 for $48.60, Cheque 86 for $250, and Cheque 89 for $46.75 are outstanding. Prepare a bank reconciliation statement dated August 31.

13. At September 30, Pat and Bob Hunter have a balance of $865.84 in their cheque record. The bank statement shows a balance of $1 578.40. The bank statement contains a service charge deduction of $12.54 and a deposit made on September 15 for $379. This deposit is not recorded in the Hunters' cheque record. Cheque 92 for $48.60, Cheque 94 for $110, and Cheque 95 for $187.50 are outstanding. Prepare the September reconciliation statement.

14. (a) Prepare the November reconciliation statement for C. Tucker Painting Contractors using the following information:

Company Records:

- Cash account balance is $1 990.11.
- These cheques are recorded in the Cash Payments Journal but not on the bank statement:
  No. 161 $49.50 No. 170 $150 No. 176 $75
- A deposit for $400 was recorded in the Cash Receipts Journal on November 30 but did not appear on the bank statement.

Bank Statement:

- Bank statement balance is $1 839.86.
- Bank service charges of $24.75 are shown on the bank statement.

(b) In a General Journal, record any entries required to bring the company records up-to-date.

15. (a) Prepare the December reconciliation statement for C. Tucker Painting Contractors using the following information:

- Cash account balance is $2 090.51.
- Bank statement balance is $1 684.51.
- These cheques were recorded in the Cash Payments Journal but did not appear on the bank statement:
  No. 186 $87 No. 193 $297.30 No. 199 972.30
- A deposit for $1 910 dated December 31 was recorded in the Cash Receipts Journal but did not appear on the bank statement.
- Service charges of $27.25 are shown on the bank statement.
- A cheque for $37.50 has been cashed (correctly) by the bank but was incorrectly recorded in the company's Cash Payments Journal as $375.50. The cheque was issued for the purchase of office supplies.
- An NSF cheque for $143.35 appeared on the bank statement as a returned item. It was deducted by the bank. It had been received from J. Barkley and was recorded in the company's Cash Receipts Journal. A bank charge of $20 was levied.

(b) In a General Journal, record any entries required to bring the company records up-to-date.

1. Record the following selected transactions in a General Journal for The Sundowner:

Mar. 1 Established a petty cash fund by issuing Cheque 178 for $125.

5 Cash sales slips for the week totalled $2 400. PST on taxable sales was $84, GST was $168. Total cash $2 652.

5 The cash proof indicated a shortage of $1.63.

8 Issued Cheque 179 for $795 + $55.65 GST for a cash purchase of merchandise from Carswell Ltd.

10 Issued sales invoices (all sales tax exempt, terms 2/10, n/30):
No. 818, $500 + $35 GST = $535 to Warrendon Ltd.;
No. 819, $79.80 + $5.59 GST = $85.39 to Tisi and Zotta;
No. 820, $465 + $32.55 GST = $497.55 to J. Mocson & Sons;
No. 821, $720 + $50.40 GST = $770.40 to L. Gojmerac.

12 Cash sales slips for the week totalled $1 700. PST was $53, GST $119. Total $1 872.

15 Replenished the petty cash. Issued Cheque 180.
Summary of petty cash vouchers:

Office Expense	$33
Advertising Expense	47
Postage Expense	29
GST Refundable	6

15 Received a cheque for $83.68 from Tisi & Zotta in payment of Invoice 819 less $1.71 discount.

16 The cash proof indicated that cash was over by $2.27.

19 Received a bank debit memo for $83.68 plus $10 service charge. Tisi & Zotta's cheque was returned NSF.

20 Purchased merchandise on account from Finlays Inc., $1 115 + $78.05 GST, terms 30 days.

20 Received a cheque for $487.60 from J. Mocson & Sons in payment of Invoice 820 less $9.95 discount.

29 The monthly bank reconciliation was prepared. The bank statement included a debit of $28.00 for bank service charges.

2. The following data have been gathered for LMML Consulting, Inc.:

(a) The July 31 bank balance was $4 000.
(b) The bank statement included $65 in service charges.
(c) There was an EFT deposit of $900 on the bank statement for the monthly rent from a tenant.
(d) Cheques 541 and 543 for $205 and $320, respectively, were not among the cancelled cheques returned with the statement.
(e) The July 31 deposit of $350 did not appear on the bank statement.
(f) The bookkeeper had erroneously recorded a $50 cheque as $500. The cheque was written to an office supply store as a payment on account.

(g) Included with the cancelled cheques was a cheque written by LMML Contractors, Ltd., for $200, which was deducted from LMML Consulting's account.
(h) The bank statement also included an NSF cheque written by Multimedia, Ltd., for a $460 payment on account.
(i) The cash account showed a balance of $3 200 on July 31.

Tasks required:

(a) Prepare the July 31, 2002, bank reconciliation for LMML Consulting, Inc.
(b) Prepare the necessary journal entries.

3. M. Monroe Ltd. has a current account with the Bank of Nova Scotia. The October bank statement that follows was sent to M. Monroe Ltd. by the bank.

Bank Statement:

THE BANK OF NOVA SCOTIA

M. Monroe Ltd.
575 Goulding St.
Winnipeg, MB
R3G 2S3

ACCOUNT NUMBER
81720-00

STATEMENT OF	FROM	TO	PAGE
Current Account	Sep. 30, 2001	Oct. 31, 2001	1

DESCRIPTION	DEBITS	CREDITS	DATE M	DATE D	BALANCE
Balance forward			09	30	2,690.50
Deposit		700.00	10	01	3,390.50
Deposit		200.00	10	05	3,590.50
Cheque 301	200.00		10	08	3,390.50
Deposit		75.00	10	10	3,465.50
Cheque 303	1,200.00		10	15	2,265.50
Deposit		225.00	10	19	2,490.50
Deposit		600.00	10	22	3,090.50
Cheque 304	50.00		10	23	3,040.50
Cheque 305	17.00		10	28	3,023.50
SC	22.25		10	29	3,001.25
RI	75.00		10	31	2,926.25
DM	20.00		10	31	2,906.25

NO. OF DEBITS	TOTAL AMOUNT OF DEBITS	NO. OF CREDITS	TOTAL AMOUNT OF CREDITS	NO. OF ENCLOSURES
6	1,584.25	5	1,800.00	5

Cheques:

The bank also sent the following four cancelled cheques — Nos. 301, 303, 304, and 305 — and an NSF cheque for $75 which had been deposited by M. Monroe Ltd. The NSF cheque was from Bloom & Co. Inc., a customer of M. Monroe Ltd. A bank debit memo for $20 (NSF charge) was also sent.

CANCELLED

M MONROE LTD.
575 Goulding St.
Winnipeg, MB R3G 2S3

301 Oct. 1, 2001
No. Date

PAY TO THE ORDER OF Malcolm Enterprises ------------------------------ $ 200.00

SUM OF Two hundred --------------------------------- 00/100 DOLLARS

M. Monroe
M. MONROE LTD.

THE BANK OF NOVA SCOTIA
319 Graham Ave.
Winnipeg, MB R3C 2Y5

CANCELLED

M MONROE LTD.
575 Goulding St.
Winnipeg, MB R3G 2S3

303 Oct. 15, 2001
No. Date

PAY TO THE ORDER OF Salaries -- $ 1,200.00

SUM OF One thousand two hundred----------------- 00/100 DOLLARS

THE BANK
319 Graha
Winnipeg,

CANCELLED

M MONROE LTD.
575 Goulding St.
Winnipeg, MB R3G 2S3

304 Oct. 16, 2001
No. Date

PAY TO THE ORDER OF T. Clements -- $ 50.00

SUM OF Fifty-- 00/100 DOLLARS

CANCELLED

M MONROE LTD.
575 Goulding St.
Winnipeg, MB R3G 2S3

305 Oct. 23, 2001
No. Date

PAY TO THE ORDER OF Clayton Ltd. --------------------------------------- $ 17.00

SUM OF Seventeen ---------------------------------- 00/100 DOLLARS

M. Monroe
M. MONROE LTD.

THE BANK OF NOVA SCOTIA
319 Gra
Winnipe

PURSUANT TO CLEARING RULES THIS ITEM
MAY NOT BE CLEARED AGAIN UNLESS CERTIFIED

BLOOM & CO. INC.
99 Jefferson Ave.
Winnipeg, MB R2V 0M2

576 Oct. 8, 2001
No. Date

PAY TO THE ORDER OF M. Monroe Ltd.------------------------------------ $ 75.00

SUM OF Seventy-five --------------------------------- 00/100 DOLLARS

A. Bloom
BLOOM & CO. INC.

THE BANK OF NOVA SCOTIA
9 Keewatin St.,
Winnipeg, MB R3E 3B6

Company Records:

The cash records kept by M. Monroe Ltd. are illustrated below:

CASH RECEIPTS JOURNAL — PAGE 14

DATE	REF. NO.	CUSTOMER OR ACCOUNT	P.R.	CASH DEBIT	SALES DISCOUNTS DEBIT	ACCOUNTS REC. CREDIT	SALES CREDIT	GST PAYABLE CREDIT	PST PAYABLE CREDIT	OTHER ACCOUNTS CREDIT
2001										
Oct. 1		Cash Sales		700.00						
5		J. Bentley		200.00						
10		Bloom & Co. Inc.		75.00						
19		T. Gabriel		225.00						
22		Cash Sales		600.00						
31		Cash Sales		450.00						
				2 250.00						
				(101)						

CASH PAYMENTS JOURNAL — PAGE 17

DATE	CH. NO.	CREDITOR OR ACCOUNT	P.R.	CASH CREDIT	ACCOUNTS PAYABLE DEBIT	GST REFUND-ABLE DEBIT	PURCHASES DEBIT	PURCHASES DISC. CREDIT	OTHER ACCOUNTS CREDIT
2001									
Oct. 1	301	Purchases		200.00					
8	302	A. Baker		100.00					
15	303	Salaries		1 200.00					
16	304	T. Clements		50.00					
23	305	Supplies		17.00					
24	306	Aster Ltd.		250.00					
30	307	Purchases		170.00					
				1 987.00					
				(101)					

ACCOUNT Cash — NO. 101

DATE	PARTICULARS	P.R.	DEBIT	CREDIT	DR. CR.	BALANCE
2001						
Oct. 1	Forwarded	✓			DR.	2 690.50
31	Cash Receipts	CR14	2 250.00		DR.	4 940.50
31	Cash Payments	CP17		1 987.00	DR.	2 953.50

Tasks Required:

(a) Prepare the bank reconciliation statement dated October 31, 2001.

(b) Prepare the necessary journal entries.

CHAPTER 11

Completing the Accounting Cycle for a Merchandising Company

UNIT 27 Adjusting the Books

Learning Objectives

After reading this unit, discussing the applicable review questions, and completing the applications exercises, you will be able to do the following:

1. **EXPLAIN** why adjustments are necessary.
2. **PREPARE** the adjustment for bad debts using the income statement method and the balance sheet method.
3. **PREPARE** entries for uncollectible accounts.
4. **PREPARE** adjustments for accrued expenses.
5. **PREPARE** adjustments for accrued revenue.

In Chapter 6, you were introduced to the accounting procedures performed at the end of the fiscal period for a service business. These included adjustments, financial statements, adjusting and closing entries, and the post-closing trial balance. A service business, Management Consultant Services, was used to explain the adjusting and closing procedures. Adjustments were prepared for prepaid expenses such as supplies and prepaid rent and to record amortization expense on capital assets.

A service company sells a service.

A merchandising company sells merchandise.

You will remember that a *service business* sells a service to its customers. For example, a movie theatre sells entertainment; a dentist sells a dental health service.

A *merchandising company* sells merchandise to its customers. For example, a clothing store sells clothes; a sporting goods store sells sports equipment.

A merchandising firm must prepare adjustments for the same reason that a service company must — so that the financial statements will be accurate. Adjustments to prepaid expense accounts and amortization on capital assets are similar to those prepared for a service business. However, additional adjustments are necessary for merchandising companies. These include adjusting the Merchandise Inventory account and recording purchases of merchandise at the end of the fiscal period.

Bad debts are uncollectible amounts owed by customers.

Some new adjustments that apply to both service and merchandising companies will be outlined in this chapter. These are the adjustment for bad debts and the adjustments for recording, at the end of the accounting periods, amounts that have not yet been recorded.

INTRODUCING THE BAD DEBTS ADJUSTMENT

Selling on credit is necessary for most companies.

Almost all companies and many consumers buy on credit at some time. They buy when they need or desire goods, and they pay when they have cash or according to the terms of sale. Our economy relies heavily on credit — there are more credit sales made than cash sales. In many product areas, a business cannot survive if it does not offer customers the opportunity to *buy now and pay later*. Unfortunately, however, sometimes customers do not pay — and this can mean problems for a company making credit sales.

Accounting Problems Caused by Bad Debts

Bad debts expense is the loss due to uncollectible accounts.

Accounting problems arise when customers do not pay their debts and the resulting loss of revenue becomes a *bad debts expense* for the company. Let us take, as an example, two consecutive years in the business affairs of Fraser Enterprises.

Suppose that, in 2000, Fraser Enterprises makes sales worth $1 320 000. The net income for the year is $155 575. If in the next year, 2001, customers default on 2000 sales worth $10 000, the net income of $155 575 will be incorrect. It includes sales of $10 000 for which money will never be received. A more accurate net income figure is $145 575.

In Figure 11-1, an expense of $10 000, from the Bad Debts Expense account, has been included in the expense section of Fraser Enterprises' income statement for 2000. This results in an adjusted net income for the year of $145 575, which is more accurate than the $155 575 figure.

FIGURE 11-1
Income statement for 2000

Fraser Enterprises Income Statement For the Year Ended December 31, 2000		
Revenue		
Sales		$1 320 000
Cost of Goods Sold		
Cost of Goods Sold (per schedule)		1 016 000
Gross Profit		304 000
Operating Expenses		
Bad Debts Expense	$ 10 000	
Other Expenses	148 425	
Total Expenses		158 425
Net Income		$145 575

The inclusion of the $10 000 expense for bad debts is based on an important Generally Accepted Accounting Principle — the matching principle. The matching principle states that expenses for an accounting period should be matched against the revenue produced during the accounting period. If the $10 000 bad debts expense were not included, the proper total for the expenses would not be matched against revenue for the 2000 accounting period.

Figure 11-2 shows part of the balance sheet for 2000. The Accounts Receivable figure of $153 000 includes the $10 000 in credit sales that will never be paid by customers.

When the balance sheet was prepared at the end of 2000, the business hoped to collect all $153 000 of the accounts receivable. However, during 2001, $10 000 worth of the accounts receivable proved to be uncollectible. The $153 000 amount for the Accounts Receivable account in Figure 11-2 is therefore not accurate. A figure of $143 000 more correctly describes the value of the Accounts Receivable.

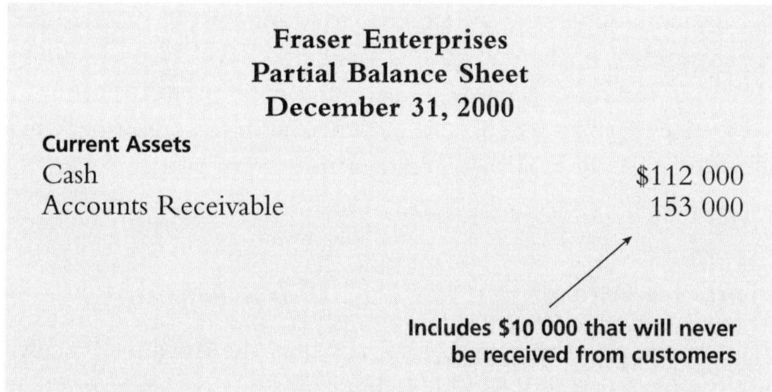

Fraser Enterprises Partial Balance Sheet December 31, 2000	
Current Assets	
Cash	$112 000
Accounts Receivable	153 000

Includes $10 000 that will never be received from customers

FIGURE 11-2
Partial balance sheet for 2000

It is the accountant's task to prepare financial statements that are as accurate as possible. For this reason, an adjustment of $10 000 is required at the end of 2000 to establish the correct value for the Accounts Receivable account on the balance sheet and for the expenses on the income statement.

From past experience, the accountant knows that despite anything a business does, there will be bad debts. Some customers will not, or cannot, pay their debts. However, the accountant does not know which customers will not pay, nor does the accountant know the exact amount that will not be paid. Past experience only indicates that there will be a loss due to bad debts.

In our example, the accountant for Fraser Enterprises knows, based on past experience, that about $10 000 worth of credit sales will become uncollectible. However, the accountant does not know which customers will not pay their bills until quite some time into the next accounting period, or even later. Therefore, using past experience as a guide, the accountant prepares an adjustment for bad debts to improve the accuracy of the financial statements.

Preparing the Adjustment for Bad Debts

Based on the estimated bad debts for 2000, the accountant prepares this adjustment before preparing the 2000 financial statements:

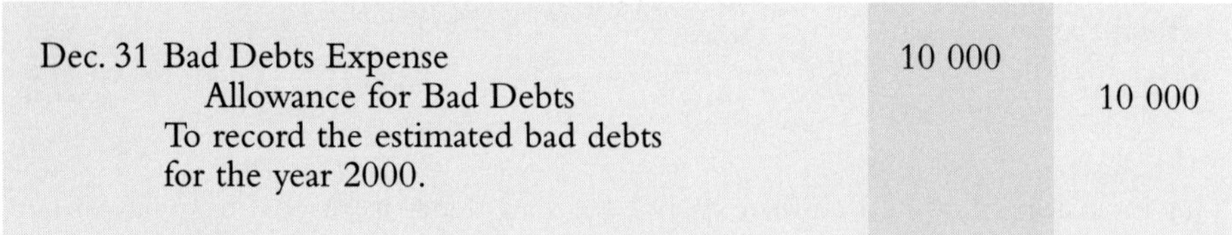

Dec. 31	Bad Debts Expense	10 000	
	Allowance for Bad Debts		10 000
	To record the estimated bad debts for the year 2000.		

The effect of this entry is shown here in T-account form:

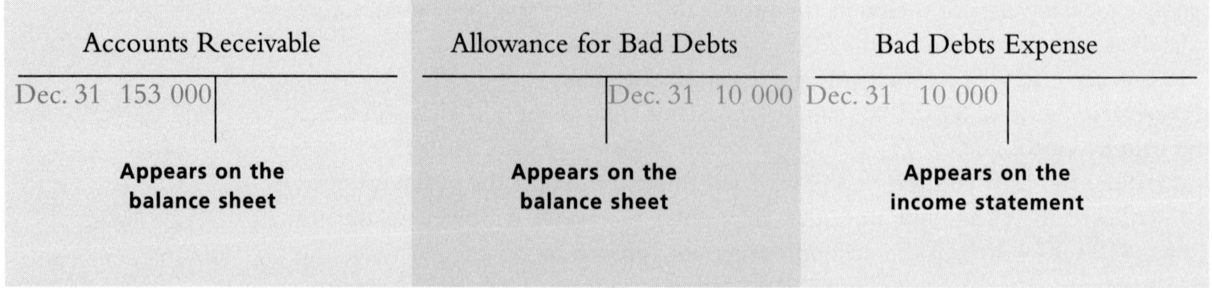

Examining the Bad Debts Expense Account

Bad Debts Expense appears as an expense account on the income statement as shown in Figure 11-1. At the end of the fiscal period, Bad Debts Expense is closed into the Income Summary account. During the fiscal period, there is no balance in the Bad Debts Expense account. It is opened with the adjustment made at the end of the fiscal period. It is then reduced to a zero balance when the closing entries are prepared.

Examining the Allowance for Bad Debts Account

The partial balance sheet in Figure 11-2 contains the Account Receivable control account with a balance of $153 000. Fraser Enterprises estimates that $10 000 worth of the Accounts Receivable balance will become bad debts. Why is the asset Accounts Receivable not credited $10 000 when the adjustment is made?

This is not done because it is not known which customer balances will become uncollectible. Therefore, it is not possible to credit any customer in the Accounts Receivable Ledger. Furthermore, it is not possible to credit the Accounts Receivable control account in the General Ledger because the control account must always be equal to the total of the individual customer balances in the Accounts Receivable Ledger. This is why the Allowance for Bad Debts account is credited instead with the estimated uncollectible amount.

The Allowance for Bad Debts account appears in the asset section of the balance sheet, as shown in Figure 11-3, but it is considered to be a contra account or a valuation account. As explained earlier in the text, a contra account reduces the value of the account that it describes. The Allowance for Bad Debts account is used to determine a realistic valuation for the Accounts Receivable account. The accounts used to record the accumulated amortization on various assets are also considered to be valuation or contra accounts. Examples of such accounts are shown later in this chapter in Figure 11-12.

FIGURE 11-3
Partial balance sheet with Allowance for Bad Debts included

Fraser Enterprises Partial Balance Sheet December 31, 2000		
Current Assets		
Cash		$112 000
Accounts Receivable	$153 000	
Less: Allowance for Bad Debts	10 000	143 000

ESTIMATING BAD DEBTS EXPENSE

A company may use any one of several methods for estimating bad debts expense. Whichever method is used must be consistently followed. The two methods commonly used — the income statement method and the balance sheet method — are described below.

Using the Income Statement Method

The income statement method is based on the question: "How much of this year's sales will become bad debts?" This is how it works. The accountant examines the bad debt losses in previous years. If, for instance, the losses have consistently been about 1 percent of net sales, then 1 percent is used for the adjustment. If sales are $1 320 000 and sales returns are $30 000, the net sales are $1 290 000. Since 1 percent of 1 290 000 is $12 900, this is the amount used for the adjustment. This entry is made:

The income statement method of estimating bad debts uses a percentage of net sales.

Dec. 31 Bad Debts Expense	12 900	
Allowance for Bad Debts		12 900
To record bad debts at 1 percent of net sales.		

Using the Balance Sheet Method

Many companies examine their customer accounts in order to estimate the value of the uncollectible balances. This method is known as the *balance sheet method* because it uses the asset Accounts Receivable as a basis for estimating the bad debts expense. In order to determine the value of the uncollectible accounts, it is necessary to prepare an accounts receivable *age analysis* as shown in Figure 11-4. This is a listing of all customers, showing the balance owed by each customer. It also shows how long the balance has been owed.

The balance sheet method uses a percentage of accounts receivable as a basis for estimating bad debts expense.

FIGURE 11-4

Age analysis prepared for accounts receivable

Accounts Receivable Age Analysis
December 31, 2000

CUSTOMER	BALANCE OF ACCOUNTS RECEIVABLE	CURRENT ACCOUNTS RECEIVABLE	1–30 DAYS OVERDUE	31–60 DAYS OVERDUE	61–90 DAYS OVERDUE	90+ DAYS OVERDUE
Axon	$ 400	$ 400				
Bell	200	50	$ 50	$ 100		
Clark	2 600	2 600				
Dervin	800				$ 800	
Elichuk	600	600				
All Others	148 400	96 450	21 700	9 100	11 750	$9 400
Total	$153 000	$100 100	$21 750	$9 200	$12 550	$9 400

The age analysis tells a company manager which customer balances have not been paid for various time periods. With this information, a manager can decide when to stop giving credit to a customer or when to start collection proceedings against a customer.

At the end of a fiscal period, the age analysis is used to determine the amount required for the bad debts expense adjustment. Here is how it is done. For each age group, the accountant estimates a percentage loss. For example, past experience might indicate that 50 percent of all debts over 90 days past due will be uncollectible. Figure 11-4 shows that an amount of $9 400 is over 90 days old. Therefore, $4 700 (0.50 × 9 400 = 4 700) will probably be uncollectible. In a similar way, estimates are made for each of the age groups. Figure 11-5 shows the percentage considered uncollectible for each group and the total amount of estimated bad debts. The total of $10 000 shown in Figure 11-5 is the amount required in the Allowance for Bad Debts account and is used to prepare the adjustment.

FIGURE 11-5

Estimated amount of accounts receivable that will become bad debts

Estimated Bad Debts
For the Year 2000

AGE OF ACCOUNTS	AMOUNT	PERCENTAGE ESTIMATED TO BE UNCOLLECTIBLE	BAD DEBTS ESTIMATE
Current	$100 100	1%	$ 1 000
1–30 days	21 750	4%	870
31–60 days	9 200	10%	920
61–90 days	12 550	20%	2 510
90+ days	9 400	50%	4 700
Total	$153 000		$10 000

Net realizable accounts receivable is Accounts Receivable less estimated bad debts.

Accounts Receivable less estimated bad debts is often referred to as *net realizable accounts receivable.*

Balance Sheet Method Steps

The following three steps are completed when using the balance sheet method of estimating the amount of bad debts:

- **Step 1:** Prepare an accounts receivable age analysis. A list of all customers is prepared (see Figure 11-4) showing the balance owed by each customer. The amounts owed by each customer are classified according to how long they have been owed. The normal terms of payment are net 30 days. This means the customer must pay the invoice amount within 30 days from the invoice date. Let's look at one customer as an example.

In Figure 11-4, Bell owes $200. This represents several different sales to Bell. Of the $200 owing, $50 is current. That means $50 worth of merchandise was bought on credit and 30 days from the invoice date have not elapsed. However, Bell does have another $150 in the overdue columns. Of this $150 owing, $50 is for an invoice that is 1 to 30 days overdue. This means Bell has not paid the amount within the normal terms of payment. Bell also has $100 that is 31 to 60 days overdue. In summary, Bell owes $200 represented by more than one sale or invoice. One invoice is overdue 1 to 30 days; another invoice is overdue 31 to 60 days; another invoice is current and is not overdue.

- **Step 2:** Estimate a percentage loss.
- **Step 3:** Prepare the adjusting entry.

Previous Balance in the Allowance for Bad Debts Account

When using the balance sheet method of estimating bad debts, any existing balance in the contra account (Allowance for Bad Debts) *must* be considered. For example, suppose the age analysis indicates an estimate for bad debts of $10 000, but there is already a credit balance of $50 in the Allowance for Bad Debts account. The $50 credit balance of actual bad debts occurring during the period is less than the estimate (Allowance for Bad Debts $9 500 – $9 450 Accounts Receivable written off = $50 balance). A credit of only $9 950 is required to attain the balance of $10 000 for this period in the Allowance for Bad Debts account. This would be the adjusting entry:

When using the balance sheet method of estimating debts expenses, any existing balance in the Allowance for Bad Debts account must be considered.

Dec. 31	Bad Debts Expense		9 950	
	Allowance for Bad Debts			9 950
	To increase the Allowance account to $10 000.			
	Previous *credit* balance	50		
	Adjustment	9 950		
	New balance	10 000		

The result of the adjusting entry in T-account form would appear as follows:

Bad Debts Expense

Debit		Credit	
Dec. 31	9 950		

Appears on the income statement

Allowance for Bad Debts

Debit		Credit	
		Balance	50
		Dec. 31	9 950
		New balance	10 000

Appears on the balance sheet

When using the income statement method of estimating bad debts, the previous balance in the Allowance for Bad Debts account is ignored.

Where does the $50 beginning balance in the Allowance for Bad Debts account originate? It could be caused by a collection of an account previously written off or by an overestimate of bad debts from the last accounting period. Remember, the adjustment for bad debts is an estimate only. It is usually impossible to estimate the exact amount of the bad debts. There will generally be a debit or a credit balance in the Allowance account. When using the balance sheet method of adjusting bad debts, the previous balance must be considered. With the income statement method, it is ignored. The reason for this is that the income statement method identifies "new" bad debts based on "new" credit sales, whereas the balance sheet method estimates "cumulative" bad debts based on all accounts receivable.

It is possible to have a debit balance in the Allowance for Bad Debts account. This occurs when the actual amount of bad debts for the period exceeds the estimated allowance. Suppose the age analysis indicates an estimate of $10 000 for bad debts. There is an existing debit balance of $100 in the Allowance for Bad Debts account. An adjustment of $10 100 is necessary. This is the entry:

2000				
Dec. 31	Bad Debts Expense		10 100	
	Allowance for Bad Debts			10 100
	To increase the Allowance account to $10 000.			
	Previous *debit* balance	100		
	Adjustment, credit	10 100		
	New balance, credit	10 000		

WRITING OFF UNCOLLECTIBLE ACCOUNTS

Three accounts are involved in the adjustment for bad debts: Accounts Receivable, Allowance for Bad Debts, and Bad Debts Expense. The first two accounts appear in the asset section on the balance sheet. The third, Bad Debts Expense, is an expense on the income statement. It is closed at the end of the fiscal period. At the beginning of the new fiscal period, these three accounts will appear in T-account form as follows:

Accounts Receivable

Debit		Credit	
Dec. 31	153 000		

Appears on the balance sheet

Allowance for Bad Debts

Debit		Credit	
		Balance	50
		Dec. 31	9 950
		2001	
		New balance	10 000

Appears on the balance sheet as a contra asset account

Bad Debts Expense

Debit		Credit	
Dec. 31	9 950	Dec. 31	9 950

Appears on the income statement

What does a company do when it determines that it will never be able to collect a debt owed by a customer? Examine the following system used by Fraser Enterprises. Suppose that after several months, a customer of Fraser Enterprises, J. Wilson, declares bankruptcy. By March 12, it is clearly determined that the $750 owed by J. Wilson will never be collected. The following entry is made:

2001			
Mar. 12	Allowance for Bad Debts	750	
	Accounts Receivable/J. Wilson		750
	To write off J. Wilson's account as uncollectible.		

Notice that in this entry, the Bad Debts Expense account is not used. The loss is written off against the Allowance for Bad Debts account which was set up in expectation of, or to allow for, such losses. Remember that a total of $10 000 was recorded in the Bad Debts Expense account when the adjustment was made. To record the $750 loss in the Bad Debts Expense account would be wrong because this would mean the expense would be recorded twice: once in the adjustment and once in the write-off. After J. Wilson's account is written off, the T-accounts would appear as follows:

Accounts Receivable

Debit	Credit
Dec. 31 153 000	

Allowance for Bad Debts

Debit	Credit
2001	
Mar. 12 750	Dec. 31 10 000

Accounts Receivable/J. Wilson

Debit	Credit
	2001
Balance 750	Mar. 12 750

This account now closed

Bad Debts Expense

Debit	Credit
Dec. 31 9 950	Dec. 31 9 950

No change in this account

During the year, write-off entries are made whenever it is certain that a debt is uncollectible. At the end of the year, there will probably be a balance in the Allowance for Bad Debts account. It is almost impossible to be exactly correct in estimating a year's uncollectible accounts. When the next fiscal period ends, the balance in the Allowance for Bad Debts account must be considered if the balance sheet method of adjusting for bad debts is used. The income statement method ignores any such balance.

Payment of an Account Receivable Previously Written Off

Sometimes an account that was assumed uncollectible and was written off is unexpectedly collected. Such payments are termed *recovery of bad debts.* When this occurs, it is necessary to make two entries.

In the previous example, J. Wilson's account was written off on March 12. On June 1, Wilson unexpectedly pays Fraser Enterprises the full amount ($750). Two entries are made. The first one records the debt in the customer's account again and re-establishes the amount in the Allowance for Bad Debts account:

2001			
Jun. 1	Accounts Receivable/J. Wilson	750	
	Allowance for Bad Debts		750
	To set up previously written-off account.		

The second entry records the money received and decreases the customer's account:

2001			
Jun. 1	Cash	750	
	Accounts Receivable/J. Wilson		750
	Received payment in full.		

After the entries have been posted, J. Wilson's account appears as below:

Accounts Receivable/J. Wilson

	Debit date	Debit	Credit date	Credit	
	2000		2001		
Original sale →	Dec. 10	750	Mar. 12	750	← **Account written off**
	2001				
Sale rerecorded →	Jun. 1	750	Jun. 1	750	← **Payment received**

Now that we have looked at the adjustment for bad debts, we will examine two other adjustments, called accrued expenses and accrued revenue.

INTRODUCING ACCRUED EXPENSES

Accrued expenses are expenses that have been incurred but not yet recorded in the books.

Adjusting entries are required for any expenses that are owed but not yet recorded. These are called *accrued expenses.* They have been incurred but not journalized and posted to the General Ledger. Interest owed but not recorded is an example.

Accrued Interest

Suppose $100 000 was borrowed by Fraser Enterprises from a bank on October 1 and is to be repaid in six months, on March 31. Interest at 9 percent is charged by the bank. The following entry is made when the money is borrowed:

Oct. 1	Cash	100 000	
	Bank Loan		100 000
	Borrowed $100 000 for six months at 9 percent interest.		

On December 31, at the end of the fiscal period, the bank is owed three months' interest. This amount owing is an expense and should be on the income statement. The interest figure for three months is $2 250. This amount must be shown in an account called Interest Expense. The adjustment necessary is:

Dec. 31	Interest Expense	2 250	
	Interest Payable		2 250
	To record October, November, and December interest (100 000 × 0.09 × 3/12 = 2 250).		

After this entry has been posted, the Interest Expense, Bank Loan, and Interest Payable accounts appear as follows:

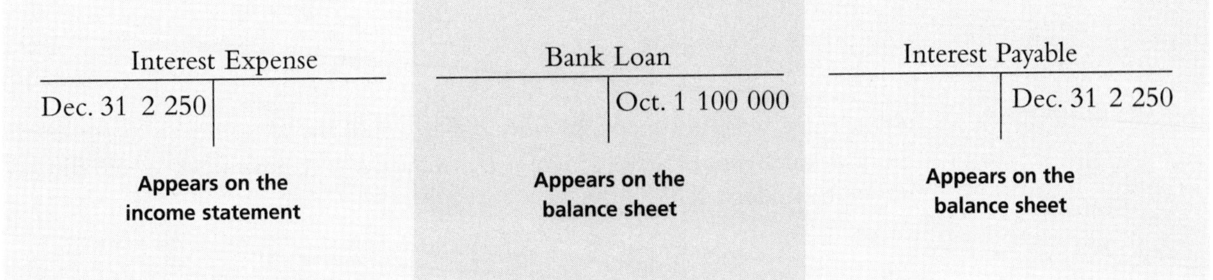

What would be wrong with the financial statements if this adjustment were not made? Which accounting principle would be violated if these expenses were not recorded at the end of the accounting period? First of all, the expenses would be too low and this would cause the net income to be $2 250 too high. Because net income would be overstated, the final owner's equity total would also be too high. A mismatch would have occurred between the expenses and revenue for the period.

Such an error would be a result of not matching all the expenses of a period with the revenue for that period. If the interest was not recorded until it was paid in the next accounting period, the net income in this fiscal period would be too low. By how much would the net income be incorrect during the second fiscal period? The expenses in the next fiscal period would be too high and this would cause the net income to be $2 250 too low. Can you explain why the owner's equity would be correct at the end of the second fiscal period even though the income statement was incorrect? Failure to record the expense in the first instance would result in an overstatement of net income of $2 250 while recording too high an expense in the second instance would result in an understatement of net income of $2 250. The total net income added to the owner's equity over the two fiscal periods would be correct even though both income statements were incorrect.

Accrued Salaries

A second example of unrecorded accrued expenses is salaries earned but not yet paid. The most common reason for accrued salaries is that the financial period end does not match a payday. The following is another reason for accrued salaries.

Fraser Enterprises pays a commission to its sales staff of 10 percent of their monthly sales. The commission is paid the following month for the previous month's sales. In December, the sales staff made sales of $50 000. The commission of $5 000 ($0.10 \times 50\ 000 = 5\ 000$) is paid at the end of January. However, since it was earned in December, the amount of commission should be part of the financial statements prepared in December. This adjustment is necessary:

Dec. 31	Salaries Expense	5 000	
	Salaries Payable		5 000
	To record December commissions owing to sales staff.		

When this entry is posted, the accounts appear as follows:

Salaries Expense			Salaries Payable	
Dec. 31	110 000		Dec. 31	5 000
31	5 000			
Balance	115 000			

If this entry were not made, by how much would the expenses be understated? By how much would the net income be overstated? By how much would the liabilities be understated?

INTRODUCING ACCRUED REVENUE

Accrued revenue is revenue earned during the fiscal period but not yet recorded in the books.

Accrued revenue is revenue that has been earned but not recorded. Here is an example.

Fraser Enterprises purchased a three-year guaranteed investment certificate worth $10 000 from its bank. The certificate earns interest at the rate of 9 percent, or $900, a year. The interest (a total of $2 700) will be received at the end of three years. However, $900 in interest is actually earned each year, as illustrated:

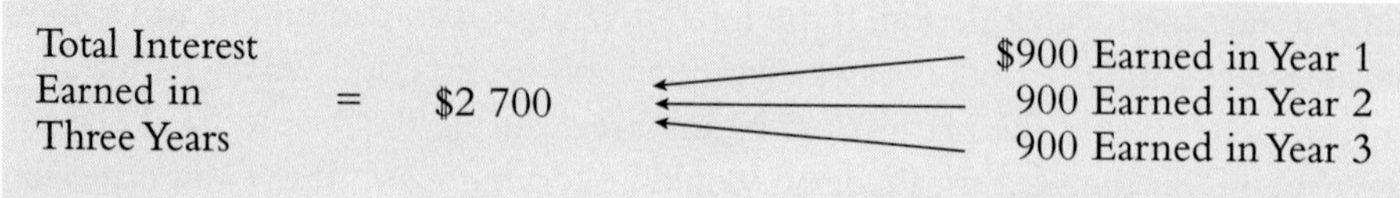

Since $900 interest is earned at the end of Year 1, that interest should be recorded as revenue and should be included in the income statement for Year 1. If it is not recorded, there would be a mismatch between revenue and expenses. Some of the revenue for the year ($900) would not be matched against the expenses for the year. To avoid that error, this adjustment is made:

Dec. 31	Interest Receivable	900	
	Interest Revenue		900
	To record one year's interest on the guaranteed investment certificate.		

SUMMARY OF ACCRUED ADJUSTMENTS

Adjusting entries are necessary for accrued revenue and for accrued expenses so that the financial statements will be accurate. This is in agreement with the matching principle. If accrued expenses are not recorded, there will be a mismatch between expenses and revenue and the following will occur:

- Expenses will be too low.
- Net income will be overstated.
- Liabilities will be too low.
- Owner's equity will be too high.

If accrued revenue is not recorded, the following will occur:

- Revenue will be too low.
- Net income will be understated.
- Assets will be too low.
- Owner's equity will be understated.

1. Explain the difference between a service company and a merchandising company.
2. On which financial statements do the following two accounts appear:

   (a) Bad Debts Expense?
   (b) Allowance for Bad Debts?

3. (a) What is the General Journal entry to record estimated bad debts?
   (b) Name the financial statement on which each account in the entry from (a) would appear.
   (c) Which of the two accounts in (a) are closed at the end of the fiscal period?
4. (a) Name the two methods of estimating bad debts.
   (b) Which method takes into consideration the previous balance in the Allowance for Bad Debts account?
5. What is the General Journal entry to write off an uncollectible account?
6. When is an account written off as uncollectible?
7. What is the adjusting entry to record interest owed but not recorded?
8. What is the adjusting entry to record salaries owed to employees?
9. Define accrued expenses and give two examples.
10. Define accrued revenue and give two examples.

1. At the end of the fiscal period, December 31, Boutique Anne Marie has a balance of $13 000 in the Accounts Receivable account. The Allowance for Bad Debts account has a zero balance. It is estimated that the bad debts will be $275.

   (a) Prepare the adjusting entry to record the estimated bad debts of $275.
   (b) Copy the T-accounts that follow. Post the adjusting entry to your own T-accounts.

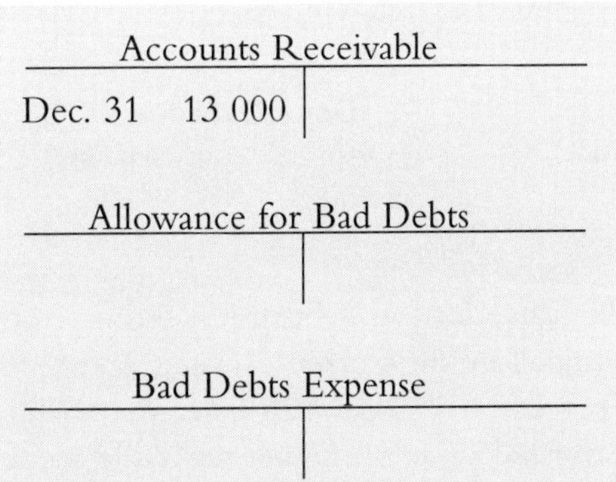

   (c) How much will appear on the income statement for Bad Debts Expense?
   (d) Show how Accounts Receivable and Allowance for Bad Debts will appear on the balance sheet.

2. Dave Taylor's Marina has a balance of $18 500 in the Accounts Receivable account. The Allowance for Bad Debts account has a zero balance. The estimated amount for bad debts is $750.

(a) Prepare the adjusting entry to record the estimated bad debts for December 31.
(b) How much will appear in the income statement for Bad Debts Expense?
(c) Show how Accounts Receivable and Allowance for Bad Debts will appear on the balance sheet.

3. The three companies in the following description all use the income statement method of estimating bad debts. For each, prepare the adjusting entry.

(a) Company A: Net sales were $135 000. Bad debts are estimated to be 1 percent of net sales.
(b) Company B: Net sales were $210 000. Bad debts are estimated to be 0.5 percent of net sales.
(c) Company C: Net sales were $280 000. Bad debts are estimated to be 0.5 percent of net sales.

4. For each of the following cases, give the adjusting entry for bad debts if the balance sheet method of estimating bad debts is being used.

(a) Estimated bad debts: $11 250; balance in the Allowance for Bad Debts account: $215 credit.
(b) Estimated bad debts: $47 600; balance in the Allowance for Bad Debts account: $1 070 debit.

5. (a) Copy the T-accounts that follow:

Accounts Receivable		Allowance for Bad Debts		Bad Debts Expense	
Dec. 31 235 000			Dec. 31 1 875		

(b) An age analysis shows that $3 125 worth of the Accounts Receivable account is estimated to be uncollectible. Journalize and post the necessary adjusting entry.

6. The accounts receivable age analysis for the Gaylor Trading Company on December 31, 2001 shows the following totals:

		Days Overdue			
Balance	**Current**	**1–30**	**31–60**	**61–90**	**90+**
$110 700	$78 600	$18 700	$5 700	$3 200	$4 500

(a) Calculate the allowance for bad debts if it is estimated that the following percentages are uncollectible: Current, 1.5 percent; 1–30 days, 7 percent; 31–60 days, 15 percent; 61–90 days, 25 percent; over 90 days, 45 percent.
(b) Calculate the estimated value of the net realizable accounts receivable.

7. (a) Copy the T-accounts that follow:

Accounts Receivable		Allowance for Bad Debts		Bad Debts Expense	
Dec. 31 20 000			Dec. 31 315		

(b) Record these transactions in a General Journal on page 29 and post the entries to the T-accounts:

Jan. 17 Write off L. Doresco's account of $95 as uncollectible. Doresco has gone out of business.

25 Write off C. Rosenblatt's account of $190 as uncollectible. Rosenblatt has left town and cannot be located.

30 An age analysis shows that $500 worth of the Accounts Receivable account is estimated to be uncollectible. Prepare the necessary adjusting entry. Use the balance sheet method, remembering that the balance in the Allowance for Bad Debts account must be considered.

Feb. 28 C. Rosenblatt's cheque for $190 was received in payment of her account previously written off.

8. Journalize these transactions in a General Journal:

May 1 No entry is required. The balance in the Allowance for Bad Debts account is $150 credit.

9 Write off Joyce Turner's account of $85 as uncollectible.

23 Write off E. McKurcher's account of $145 as uncollectible.

30 The age analysis indicates that $225 is required in the Allowance for Bad Debts account. The balance sheet method is being used. Prepare the adjusting entry.

9. (a) Copy the T-accounts that follow:

Bank Loan		Interest Payable		Interest Expense	
	Dec. 31 60 000				

(b) At the end of the fiscal period, $600 interest has accrued. Prepare the adjusting entry to record the $600 interest.

(c) Post the adjusting entry to the T-accounts.

10. For each of the following cases, give the adjusting entry for interest owing:

(a) Interest for twelve months of $2 400, to be paid on June 30. Date of adjustment: February 28.

(b) Interest for nine months of $2 125, to be paid on September 30. Date of adjustment: June 30.

(c) Interest for six months of $3 768, to be paid on March 31. Date of adjustment: January 31.

11. For each of the following cases, give the adjusting entry for interest owing:

    (a) Loan of $6 000 for one year at an annual interest rate of 7 percent to be repaid on March 31. Date of adjustment: August 31.
    (b) Loan of $12 000 for six months at an annual interest rate of 8 percent, to be repaid on October 31. Date of adjustment: June 30.

12. (a) Copy the T-accounts that follow:

Salaries Expense			Salaries Payable	
Dec. 31	29 000			

    (b) At the end of the fiscal period, $1 080 is owed to the employees. Prepare the adjusting entry to record the salaries owing.
    (c) Post the adjusting entry to the T-accounts.

13. For each of the following cases, give the adjusting entry for salaries owing:

    (a) Sales staff receive a 5 percent commission on their monthly sales. In May, they sold $35 000 worth of goods for which they are to be paid on June 30. The date of the adjustment is May 31.
    (b) The total earnings of all hourly employees is $3 500 per day, excluding Saturdays and Sundays. They are paid every Friday. What will the adjusting entry be if the financial statements are prepared at the end of the working day on Wednesday?

14. At the end of the fiscal period, W. Pollock, a lawyer, had completed $8 200 worth of work for clients, but had not yet prepared the invoices.

    (a) Prepare the journal entry to record the information.
    (b) Post the entry to T-accounts for April 30.

UNIT 28 Adjustments and the Work Sheet

Learning Objectives

After reading this unit, discussing the applicable review questions, and completing the applications exercises, you will be able to do the following:

1. **RECORD** the beginning and ending inventory on a work sheet.
2. **RECORD** adjustments on a work sheet.
3. **COMPLETE** a work sheet for a merchandising company.

In the first unit of this chapter, you learned how to prepare adjustments for bad debts, accrued expenses, and accrued revenue. These adjustments were described in General Journal form. In this unit, the work sheet will be used to plan the adjustments for a merchandising company.

RECORDING ADJUSTMENTS ON THE WORK SHEET

The accountant for Campbell Enterprises has prepared the trial balance for the fiscal period ended December 31, 2000. It is shown on the work sheet in Figure 11-6 on page 426. The following information is used to prepare the adjustments on the work sheet:

- The age analysis indicates that a balance of $2 000 is required in the Allowance for Bad Debts account.
- Supplies worth $2 000 are left at the end of the year.
- Amortization is recorded using the declining-balance method. The equipment amortizes 20 percent and the building 5 percent per year.
- Interest of $225 is owed on the bank loan.
- Salaries of $1 200 are owed to the employees.

Analysis of the Work Sheet Adjustments

Adjustment for Bad Debts

Campbell Enterprises uses the balance sheet method for estimating bad debts. The age analysis indicates that $2 000 is required in the Allowance for Bad Debts account. Since there is already a credit balance, an adjustment of $1 950 is made. Bad Debts Expense is added to the work sheet and is debited $1 950. A credit of $1 950 is written on line 3 opposite Allowance for Bad Debts. The debit and credit amounts in the adjusting columns are coded (a). The adjustments are coded to provide easy identification of the debit and credit portions of the entry.

Adjustment for Prepaid Expenses

As you may recall, prepaid expenses such as prepaid rent, prepaid insurance, and supplies must be adjusted on the work sheet.

FIGURE 11-6
Completed work sheet for a merchandising business

Campbell Enterprises, Work Sheet
For the Year Ended December 31, 2000

	ACCOUNT TITLE	ACC. NO.	TRIAL BALANCE DEBIT	TRIAL BALANCE CREDIT	ADJUSTMENTS DEBIT	ADJUSTMENTS CREDIT	INCOME STATEMENT DEBIT	INCOME STATEMENT CREDIT	BALANCE SHEET DEBIT	BALANCE SHEET CREDIT	
1	Cash	101	112 000						112 000		1
2	Accounts Receivable	110	53 000						53 000		2
3	Allowance for Bad Debts	111		50		(a) 1 950				2 000	3
4	Merchandise Inventory, January 1	120	90 000				90 000	86 000	86 000		4
5	Supplies	125	4 500			(b) 2 500			2 000		5
6	Building	150	160 000						160 000		6
7	Accum. Amort. — Building	151		48 200		(c) 5 590				53 790	7
8	Equipment	160	23 000						23 000		8
9	Accum. Amort. — Equipment	161		10 200		(d) 2 560				12 760	9
10	Accounts Payable	200		23 450						23 450	10
11	PST Payable	205		2 130						2 130	11
12	GST Payable	206		1 870						1 870	12
13	GST Refundable	207	640						640		13
14	Bank Loan	210		10 000						10 000	14
15	Mortgage Payable	250		88 000						88 000	15
16	S. Campbell, Capital	300		200 640						200 640	16
17	S. Campbell, Drawings	301	8 000						8 000		17
18	Sales	400		320 000				320 000			18
19	Purchases	500	110 000				110 000				19
20	Advertising Expense	600	5 000				5 000				20
21	General Expense	601	4 000				4 000				21
22	Salaries Expense	602	120 000		(f) 1 200		121 200				22
23	Utilities Expense	603	7 400				7 400				23
24	Insurance Expense	604	7 000				7 000				24
25			704 540	704 540							25
26	Bad Debts Expense	605			(a) 1 950		1 950				26
27	Supplies Expense	606			(b) 2 500		2 500				27
28	Amort. Expense — Building	607			(c) 5 590		5 590				28
29	Amort. Expense — Equipment	608			(d) 2 560		2 560				29
30	Interest Expense	609			(e) 225		225				30
31	Interest Payable	215				(e) 225				225	31
32	Salaries Payable	220				(f) 1 200				1 200	32
33					14 025	14 025	357 425	406 000	444 640	396 065	33
34	Net Income						48 575			48 575	34
35							406 000	406 000	444 640	444 640	35
36											36

Note: **(1) Adjustments coded with letters for easy identification. (2) Opening inventory extended to income statement debit column. (3) Ending inventory extended to income statement credit and balance sheet debit columns.**

An inventory of supplies shows a $2 000 total for supplies on hand at the end of the year. The Supplies account on the work sheet has a $4 500 balance. An adjustment of $2 500 is required. Supplies Expense is added to the work sheet and is debited $2 500, the amount of the supplies used. Supplies (line 5) is credited $2 500. This adjustment is coded (b).

Adjustment for Amortization

The declining-balance method of amortizing fixed assets is used by Campbell Enterprises.

The building amortizes at the rate of 5 percent per year on the declining balance which is now $111 800 (160 000 - 48 200 accumulated amortization = 111 800). Amortization Expense — Building is added to the work sheet and debited $5 590 (111 800 × 0.05 = 5 590). Accumulated Amortization — Building is credited $5 590 (line 7). The adjustment is coded (c).

The declining balance of the Equipment account is $12 800 (23 000 - 10 200 accumulated amortization = 12 800). The rate of amortization is 20 percent per year. Amortization Expense — Equipment is added to the work sheet and debited $2 560 (0.20 × 12 800 = 2 560). Accumulated Amortization — Equipment is credited $2 560 (line 9). This adjustment is coded (d).

Adjustment for Accrued Interest

Three months' interest is owed on the bank loan and amounts to $225 (10 000 × 0.09 × 3/12 = 225). Both Interest Expense and Interest Payable are added to the work sheet. The $225 adjustment is coded (e).

Adjustment for Accrued Salaries

The salaries adjustment is made to record the $1 200 owed to the employees. Salaries is debited $1 200. Salaries Payable is added to the work sheet and is credited $1 200. The adjustment is coded (f).

Adjustment for Merchandise Inventory — Perpetual Inventory System

Under the perpetual inventory system discussed in Chapter 7, the Merchandise Inventory account is continually adjusted as merchandise is bought and sold during the accounting period. What entry may be required to ensure the accuracy of the inventory account at the end of the accounting period? As you learned in Chapter 7, an entry may be required to record the difference between the physical inventory (counting and pricing the inventory) taken at the end of the fiscal period and the Merchandising Inventory ledger account.

Calculation:			
Dec. 31	Merchandise Inventory (Ledger Balance)	$76 000	
	Physical Inventory	75 450	
	Inventory Shortage	$ 550	
Journal Entry:			
Dec. 31	Inventory Shortage	550	
	Merchandise Inventory		550
	To adjust the balance of Merchandise Inventory to equal physical inventory.		

Inventory Shortage is an expense account and is shown on the income statement.

The entries required to adjust inventory for a firm, like Campbell Enterprises, that uses a periodic inventory system are somewhat different.

Adjustment for Merchandise Inventory — Periodic Inventory System

The Merchandise Inventory account shows the cost of goods on hand at a specific date.

The work sheet in Figure 11-6 contains the Merchandise Inventory account with a January balance of $90 000. This means that at the beginning of the fiscal period, there were goods on hand that cost $90 000. During the year, merchandise was sold and the sales transactions were recorded in the Sales account. Merchandise was purchased when it was required and recorded in the Purchases account.

At the end of the year, the Merchandise Inventory account must be adjusted since it contains the cost of the merchandise on hand at the beginning of the year, January 1. This figure is incorrect. It has changed because of sales and purchases of merchandise during the year. The Merchandise Inventory must be adjusted so that it contains the value of the inventory on hand at the end of the year (December 31). This value is obtained by taking a physical inventory at the end of the fiscal year. This adjustment will now be examined in greater detail.

E EXAMINING THE MERCHANDISE INVENTORY ADJUSTMENT

In line with the periodic inventory method used to date in the examples given in this book, entries were not made in the Campbell Enterprises Merchandise Inventory account during the accounting period. At the end of the accounting period, an adjustment is needed to update the balance of the Merchandise Inventory account. We will look first at the steps involved in making this adjustment and at the journal entries required.

Steps in Inventory Adjustment

Three steps are completed in adjusting the Merchandise Inventory account.

Step 1: Determine the Value of the Inventory

At the end of the fiscal period, a physical count called taking an inventory is made of merchandise on hand. This results in a new dollar amount of $86 000 for the Merchandise Inventory account. This is the actual value of the merchandise on hand.

Step 2: Prepare the Closing Entry for Merchandise Inventory

An entry is made to remove the beginning inventory figure. This is necessary because the beginning merchandise value has been replaced by the end-of-the-year inventory figure of $86 000. This entry is made to close out the beginning inventory to the Income Summary account:

Dec. 31	Income Summary	90 000	
	Merchandise Inventory		90 000
	To close the beginning inventory into the Income Summary account.		

Step 3: Prepare the Entry to Record the Value of the Inventory

This entry is made to record the new inventory figure:

Dec. 31	Merchandise Inventory	86 000	
	Income Summary		86 000
	To record the ending inventory.		

This entry is necessary because the inventory on hand at the end of the year is an asset and must be recorded.

The Merchandise Inventory account now appears as follows:

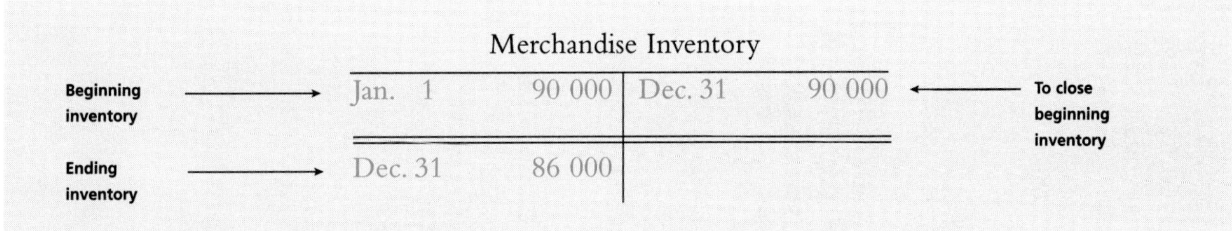

The balance of the Merchandise Inventory account is now $86 000, the value of the ending inventory. When the financial statements are prepared, Merchandise Inventory of $86 000 will appear in the current assets section of the balance sheet.

The Income Summary T-account follows. Note that it has a debit and a credit in it as a result of the inventory adjustments:

Income Summary

Dec. 31	90 000	Dec. 31	86 000

The beginning inventory of $90 000 is on the left, or expenses and cost side, of the Income Summary account. The new inventory figure of $86 000 (the cost of goods not yet sold) is on the revenue side. The debit of $90 000 and the credit of $86 000 were recorded on the work sheet shown earlier in Figure 11-6.

Two entries involving inventory have been described. One entry reduces the Merchandise Inventory account to zero by transferring the beginning inventory to the Income Summary account. The other entry records the ending inventory in the Merchandise Inventory account.

FIGURE 11-7
Transfer the beginning inventory balance of $90 000 from the trial balance section to the debit column of the income statement section of the work sheet.

Campbell Enterprises, Work Sheet
For the Year Ended December 31, 2000

	ACCOUNT TITLE	ACC. NO.	TRIAL BALANCE DEBIT	TRIAL BALANCE CREDIT	ADJUSTMENTS DEBIT	ADJUSTMENTS CREDIT	INCOME STATEMENT DEBIT	INCOME STATEMENT CREDIT	BALANCE SHEET DEBIT	BALANCE SHEET CREDIT	
1	Cash	101	112 000						112 000		1
2	Accounts Receivable	110	53 000						53 000		2
3	Allowance for Bad Debts	111		50		(a) 1 950				2 000	3
4	Merchandise Inventory, January 1	120	90 000				90 000				4
5	Supplies	125	4 500			(b) 2 500			2 000		5

FIGURE 11-8
Record the new inventory of $86 000 in the credit column of the income statement section of the work sheet.

Campbell Enterprises, Work Sheet
For the Year Ended December 31, 2000

	ACCOUNT TITLE	ACC. NO.	TRIAL BALANCE DEBIT	TRIAL BALANCE CREDIT	ADJUSTMENTS DEBIT	ADJUSTMENTS CREDIT	INCOME STATEMENT DEBIT	INCOME STATEMENT CREDIT	BALANCE SHEET DEBIT	BALANCE SHEET CREDIT	
1	Cash	101	112 000						112 000		1
2	Accounts Receivable	110	53 000						53 000		2
3	Allowance for Bad Debts	111		50		(a) 1 950				2 000	3
4	Merchandise Inventory, January 1	120	90 000				90 000	86 000			4
5	Supplies	125	4 500			(b) 2 500			2 000		5

FIGURE 11-9
Record the new inventory of $86 000 in the debit column of the balance sheet section of the work sheet.

Campbell Enterprises, Work Sheet
For the Year Ended December 31, 2000

	ACCOUNT TITLE	ACC. NO.	TRIAL BALANCE DEBIT	TRIAL BALANCE CREDIT	ADJUSTMENTS DEBIT	ADJUSTMENTS CREDIT	INCOME STATEMENT DEBIT	INCOME STATEMENT CREDIT	BALANCE SHEET DEBIT	BALANCE SHEET CREDIT	
1	Cash	101	112 000						112 000		1
2	Accounts Receivable	110	53 000						53 000		2
3	Allowance for Bad Debts	111		50		(a) 1 950				2 000	3
4	Merchandise Inventory, January 1	120	90 000				90 000	86 000	86 000		4
5	Supplies	125	4 500			(b) 2 500			2 000		5

Beginning Inventory and Ending Inventory value required to calculate Cost of Goods Sold on the income statement

Ending Inventory value required for the balance sheet

Recording the Inventory Adjustment on the Work Sheet

The two entries that have just been described explain how the Merchandise Inventory account is adjusted at the end of the accounting period. This adjustment can be organized on a work sheet before the journal entries are made. Figures 11-7, 11-8, and 11-9 on page 430 illustrate, in three steps, the recording of the adjustment on a work sheet:

- **Step 1:** Transfer the beginning inventory ($90 000) to the debit column of the income statement section. This $90 000 figure is the cost of merchandise sold, which is an asset. This is why it is recorded as a debit and why it decreases the net income (see Figure 11-7 on page 430).
- **Step 2:** Record the new inventory ($86 000) in the credit column of the income statement section (see Figure 11-8 on page 430). This is the cost of inventory not sold yet.
- **Step 3:** Record the new inventory ($86 000) in the debit column of the balance sheet section. This records the ending inventory as an asset at cost (see Figure 11-9 on page 430).

Trace the three steps described above through Figures 11-7, 11-8, and 11-9. Rather than preparing separate entries to adjust Merchandise Inventory, the account is adjusted as part of the closing entry procedure discussed in the next unit.

COMPLETING THE WORK SHEET

The individual amounts on the trial balance are then transferred to either the income statement section or the balance sheet section of the work sheet. The columns are totalled and the net income is determined. Then, the work sheet columns are balanced and double ruled.

Look again at Figure 11-6 to see the completed work sheet for Campbell Enterprises. The major difference between this work sheet and that of a service company is the addition of the Purchases and Merchandise Inventory accounts. The Purchases account is transferred to the income statement section. As regards the Merchandise Inventory account, the new inventory value is shown in the debit column of the balance sheet section and in the credit column of the income statement section. The old, or beginning, inventory value is shown in the debit column of the income statement section.

REVIEW QUESTIONS

UNIT 28

1. Where is the beginning inventory figure found on the work sheet?
2. Why is the inventory figure in the trial balance section of the work sheet different from the inventory figure in the balance sheet section of the work sheet?
3. How is the ending inventory determined?
4. What is the General Journal entry to set up the new inventory value at the end of the fiscal period?
5. What is the General Journal entry to close the beginning inventory?
6. How is the inventory adjustment shown on the work sheet?
7. What are the major differences between a work sheet for a service business and a work sheet for a merchandising business?

PROBLEMS: APPLICATIONS

CHAPTER 11

15. (a) A business uses the perpetual inventory system. At the end of its fiscal period, March 31, the Merchandise Inventory ledger account has a balance of $93 350. On March 31, the physical inventory taken (counting and pricing) amounts to $91 825. Record the journal entry necessary to ensure the accuracy of the balance in the Merchandise Inventory ledger account.
    (b) Another business uses the periodic inventory system. At the end of its fiscal period, February 28, the Merchandise Inventory ledger account has a balance of $112 700. After taking an inventory, the physical count is $94 600. Record the journal entries necessary to adjust the balance in the Merchandise Inventory ledger account.

16. The first four columns of Murray Hunt Enterprises' work sheet for the year appears below. Complete the work sheet in your workbook. The December 31 inventory was determined to be $5 800.

ACCOUNT TITLE	ACC. NO.	TRIAL BALANCE DEBIT	TRIAL BALANCE CREDIT	ADJUSTMENTS DEBIT	ADJUSTMENTS CREDIT
Cash	101	280			
Accounts Receivable	110	1 920			
Merchandise Inventory, December 1	120	6 800			
Unexpired Insurance	130	580			(b)240
Store Equipment	160	2 300			
Accum. Amortization — Store Equip.	161		620		(a) 260
Accounts Payable	200		2 880		
PST Payable	205		352		
GST Payable	206		308		
GST Refundable	207	210			
M. Hunt, Capital	300		6 620		
M. Hunt, Drawings	301	1 800			
Sales	400		52 800		
Sales Returns & Allowances	401	1 600			
Sales Discounts	402	1 200			
Purchases	500	36 000			
Purchases Returns & Allowances	501		1 600		
Purchases Discounts	502		800		
Transportation-in	508	900			
Advertising Expense	600	5 390			
Rent Expense	601	2 800			
Salaries Expense	602	4 200			
		65 980	65 980		
Amortization Expense — Store Equip.	603			(a) 260	
Insurance Expense	604			(b) 240	
				500	500

17. From the year-end trial balance shown below and the following additional information, prepare a work sheet. Set up your own account names and numbers.

Additional Information:

- Merchandise Inventory, December 31, valued at $51 000.
- Supplies on hand, December 31, valued at $1 800.
- The Allowance for Bad Debts account must be increased to $600 using the balance sheet method.
- Store Fixtures amortize 20 percent per year using the declining-balance method.
- Interest owing but unrecorded, $750.
- Salaries owing to employees, $1 350.

Jeans Unlimited
Trial Balance
December 31, 2000

ACCOUNT TITLE	ACC. NO.	DEBIT	CREDIT
Cash	100	$ 13 530	
Accounts Receivable	102	30 000	
Allowance for Bad Debts	103		$ 50
Merchandise Inventory, January 1	120	60 000	
Supplies	131	5 000	
Store Fixtures	141	15 000	
Accum. Amortization — Store Fixtures	142		7 300
Accounts Payable	200		9 000
PST Payable	205		1 730
GST Payable	206		1 520
GST Refundable	207	470	
Bank Loan	221		8 000
L. Steeves, Capital	300		51 225
L. Steeves, Drawings	301	19 000	
Sales	400		260 000
Purchases	500	80 000	
Advertising Expense	610	8 000	
Office Expense	611	4 000	
Store Expense	612	9 000	
Rent Expense	613	14 000	
Salaries Expense	614	80 000	
Interest Expense	615	825	
		$338 825	$338 825

18. Prepare a work sheet for Vashti Ali Stores using the trial balance on page 434 and the following additional information.

Additional Information:

- Merchandise Inventory, December 31, valued at $5 100.
- Supplies on hand valued at $450.
- Insurance expired, $1 200.
- Building amortizes 5 percent and Equipment 20 percent per year.
- Bad debts are recorded at 1 percent of net credit sales.

Vashti Ali Stores Trial Balance December 31, 2003			
ACCOUNT TITLE	ACC. NO.	DEBIT	CREDIT
Cash	100	$ 3 800	
Accounts Receivable	102	8 000	
Merchandise Inventory, January 1	120	21 000	
Supplies	121	1 700	
Prepaid Insurance	122	2 000	
Land	140	40 000	
Building	141	120 000	
Equipment	143	35 000	
Accounts Payable	200		$ 13 700
PST Payable	205		1 800
GST Payable	206		1 640
GST Refundable	207	560	
Mortgage Payable	210		50 000
P. Kanani, Capital	300		139 920
P. Kanani, Drawings	301	8 500	
Sales	400		195 000
Sales Returns & Allowances	401	1 000	
Sales Discounts	402	300	
Purchases	500	95 000	
Transportation on Purchases	501	7 000	
Purchases Returns & Allowances	502		3 300
Purchases Discounts	503		3 000
Salaries Expense — Selling	610	30 000	
Salaries Expense — Administrative	611	20 000	
Delivery Expense	612	7 000	
General Expense	613	2 000	
Property Tax Expense	614	5 500	
		$408 360	$408 360

19. Masako Ichikawa formed Ichikawa Engineering Supply on January 1, 2002. At year-end, the trial balance on page 435 was prepared. Prepare an eight-column work sheet for Ichikawa Engineering Supply using the trial balance and the additional information given. Set up any additional accounts you require. Choose appropriate account names and numbers.

Additional Information:

- Merchandise Inventory, December 31, valued at $43 000.
- Cost of insurance that expired during the year, $720.
- Supplies on hand, $840.
- Building amortizes 5 percent and Equipment 20 percent per year.
- Interest to date on the bank loan, $325.
- Salaries and wages owing at the end of the year, $875.
- Property taxes accrued but unpaid, $1 200.
- An Allowance for Bad Debts account must be set up with bad debts recorded at 1 percent of gross sales.

Ichikawa Engineering Supply Trial Balance December 31, 2002			
ACCOUNT TITLE	ACC. NO.	DEBIT	CREDIT
Cash	101	$ 6 680	
Accounts Receivable	110	23 000	
Merchandise Inventory, January 1	120	72 000	
Supplies	126	2 840	
Unexpired Insurance	127	1 080	
Land	140	140 000	
Building	150	200 000	
Equipment	155	24 000	
Accounts Payable	200		$ 54 600
PST Payable	205		2 540
GST Payable	206		2 225
GST Refundable	207	1 320	
Bank Loan	210		25 000
M. Ichikawa, Capital	300		340 235
M. Ichikawa, Drawings	301	18 000	
Sales	400		388 000
Sales Returns & Allowances	401	7 000	
Sales Discounts	402	1 000	
Purchases	500	232 000	
Purchases Returns & Allowances	501		4 000
Purchases Discounts	502		1 600
Transportation-in	503	9 640	
Advertising Expense	601	11 510	
Delivery Expense	602	3 500	
Salaries and Wages Expense	603	59 230	
Property Tax Expense	604	5 400	
		$818 200	$818 200

UNIT 29 Financial Statements

Learning Objectives

After reading this unit, discussing the applicable review questions, and completing the applications exercises, you will be able to do the following:

PREPARE the following for a merchandising company:

- Schedule of cost of goods sold
- Classified income statement
- Classified balance sheet
- Adjusting, closing, and reversing entries

MERCHANDISING BUSINESS USING A PERIODIC INVENTORY SYSTEM

Once the work sheet has been completed, financial statements are prepared. These include the schedule of cost of goods sold, the income statement, and the balance sheet. The financial statements may also include a separate statement of owner's equity. If such a statement is used, the complete equity calculation is not included in the owner's equity section of the balance sheet. Examples of this situation were shown in Chapter 5 in Figures 5-9 and 5-10.

PREPARING THE SCHEDULE OF COST OF GOODS SOLD

The first statement prepared is the schedule of cost of goods sold. The cost information used to prepare this schedule is found in the income statement section of the work sheet. The cost information used by Campbell Enterprises includes Merchandise Inventory — beginning and ending inventories — and Purchases. Other cost accounts that appear in the schedule of cost of goods sold of some merchandising companies are:

- Transportation on Purchases
- Purchases Returns and Allowances
- Purchases Discounts

Campbell Enterprises uses a periodic inventory system. The schedule of cost of goods sold for the year 2000 is shown in Figure 11-10:

FIGURE 11-10
Schedule of cost of goods sold for Campbell Enterprises

Campbell Enterprises Schedule of Cost of Goods Sold For the year ended December 31, 2000		
Merchandise Inventory, January 1	$ 90 000	
Add: Purchases	110 000	
Total Cost of Merchandise	200 000	
Less: Merchandise Inventory, December 31	86 000	
Cost of Goods Sold		$114 000

PREPARING THE INCOME STATEMENT

Now that the cost of goods sold figure has been determined from the schedule of cost of goods sold, the income statement can be prepared. Figure 11-10 reveals that the goods sold during the year cost $114 000. This figure is now used on the income statement (Figure 11-11) to determine the gross profit. The items in the revenue and expenses sections of the income statement are obtained from the work sheet.

Classified Income Statement

The grouping of accounts using a standardized format is an aid to those who examine and interpret financial statements. Owners, managers, creditors, and government officials examine the financial statements of a variety of companies. Their task is made easier by the use of standard or classified financial statements.

The income statement shown in Figure 11-11 is a classified statement. There are three main sections in a classified income statement: revenue, cost of goods sold, and operating expenses. Two separate categories may be found in the expenses sections of merchandising companies: administrative expenses and selling expenses, illustrated in Figure 11-11.

FIGURE 11-11
Income statement for Campbell Enterprises

Campbell Enterprises Income Statement For the Year Ended December 31, 2000			
Revenue			
Sales			$320 000
Cost of Goods Sold			
Cost of Goods Sold (per schedule)			114 000
Gross Profit			206 000
Operating Expenses			
Administrative Expenses			
Amortization Expense — Building	$ 5 590		
Amortization Expense — Equipment	2 560		
Interest Expense	225		
General Expense	4 000		
Office Salaries Expense	81 200		
Office Supplies Expense	1 500		
Office Insurance Expense	4 000		
Utilities Expense	7 400		
Total Administrative Expenses		$106 475	
Selling Expenses			
Advertising Expense	$ 5 000		
Bad Debts Expense	1 950		
Salespersons' Salaries Expense	40 000		
Sales Supplies Expense	1 000		
Sales Insurance Expense	3 000		
Total Selling Expenses		50 950	
Total Operating Expenses			157 425
Net Income			$ 48 575

Administrative Expenses

Money spent in the general operation of a business is usually classified as an administrative expense. This would include expenses involved in the operation of the business office and all departments other than sales. Office salaries, office supplies, and building maintenance are a few examples.

Selling Expenses

Money spent for the direct purpose of selling goods is classified as a selling expense. Some examples include salespersons' salaries, advertising, deliveries, and sales supplies.

Allocating Responsibility for Expenses

Classifying expenses as administrative or selling expenses provides a detailed breakdown of where the money is being spent. It also allows the top management of a company to allocate responsibility for the spending of money. For example, if the sales manager is held responsible for all selling expenses, it is the responsibility of the sales manager to justify the spending of money for all the selling expenses. The responsibility for administrative expenses may be allocated to someone in the same manner. A person such as an office manager may be held responsible for controlling the administrative expenses.

Some expenses may be allocated as both selling and administrative expenses. For example, Insurance Expense may be incurred on behalf of both the office and the sales departments. Amortization may have to be divided between the administrative and the sales sections. It is the accountant's task to determine a fair basis for allocating the expense. For example, if the office occupies 30 percent of the building, then 30 percent of the amortization on the building would be charged as an administrative expense. If the remaining 70 percent is occupied by the sales sections, then 70 percent of the amortization on the building would be charged as a selling expense.

PREPARING THE BALANCE SHEET OR STATEMENT OF FINANCIAL POSITION

Statement of financial position is another name for a balance sheet.

Another name for a balance sheet is a *statement of financial position.* The data required for the balance sheet are found in the balance sheet section of the work sheet. The balance sheet for Campbell Enterprises is shown in Figure 11-12 on page 439. Notice how Capital is updated in the equity section. The additional investments and the difference between the Net Income and Drawings are added to the Capital account.

Classified Balance Sheet or Statement of Financial Position

The balance sheet shown in Figure 11-12 is also a classified statement. As was said previously in regard to the income statement, it is much easier for users to examine and interpret such standard or classified financial statements.

Current assets are listed in order of liquidity.

Order of liquidity is the order in which current assets can be converted into cash.

Capital assets are listed in order of longest life first.

As you learned in Chapter 5, Unit 10, assets are divided into two sections on a classified balance sheet — *current* and *capital* (sometimes called Plant and Equipment or Property, Plant, and Equipment) — as shown in Figure 11-12. The current assets are listed in order of liquidity, that is, in the order in which they will be converted into cash. The capital assets that have the longest life are listed first in the capital assets section.

Current Assets	**Capital Assets**
Cash	Land
Accounts Receivable	Building
Merchandise Inventory	Equipment
Prepaid Expenses	

FIGURE 11-12
Balance sheet for Campbell Enterprises

Campbell Enterprises Balance Sheet December 31, 2000			
ASSETS			
Current Assets			
Cash		$112 000	
Accounts Receivable	$ 53 000		
Less: Allowance for Bad Debts	2 000	51 000	
Merchandise Inventory		86 000	
Supplies		2 000	
Total Current Assets			$251 000
Capital Assets			
Building	160 000		
Less: Accumulated Amortization	53 790	106 210	
Equipment	23 000		
Less: Accumulated Amortization	12 760	10 240	
Total Capital Assets			116 450
Total Assets			$367 450
LIABILITIES AND OWNER'S EQUITY			
Current Liabilities			
Accounts Payable		$ 23 450	
Salaries Payable		1 200	
PST Payable		2 130	
GST Payable		1 870	
GST Refundable		(640)	
Interest Payable		225	
Bank Loan		10 000	
Total Current Liabilities			$ 38 235
Long-Term Liabilities			
Mortgage Payable			88 000
Total Liabilities			126 235
Owner's Equity			
S. Campbell, Capital, January 1		100 640	
Add: New Investment for Year	$100 000		
Add: Net Income for Year	48 575		
Less: S. Campbell, Drawings	(8 000)		
Increase in Capital		140 575	
S. Campbell, Capital, December 31			241 215
Total Liabilities and Owner's Equity			$367 450

Liabilities are also divided into two sections — *current* and *long-term*. Current liabilities are those that will be paid within one year. They are listed according to maturity, that is, in the order in which they will be paid. Long-term liabilities are those that have a due date longer than one year. They are also listed according to maturity.

Current liabilities are listed according to maturity.

Long-term liabilities are listed according to maturity.

Current Liabilities	**Long-Term Liabilities**
Accounts Payable	Bank Loan (3 years)
Salaries Payable	Mortgage Payable (25 years)
Interest Payable	
Bank Loan (6 months)	

FIGURE 11-13
Adjusting entries in the General Journal

PREPARING JOURNAL ENTRIES

The adjustments on the work sheet are recorded in the General Journal and then posted to the General Ledger.

Adjusting Entries

You have learned that adjusting entries are required so that the adjustments made on the work sheet will become part of the permanent records. When the adjustments on the work sheet are coded with letters such as (a), (b), (c), etc., the preparation of the adjusting entries is made quite simple. The adjusting entries made for Campbell Enterprises are shown in the General Journal in Figure 11-13 below. See if you can trace these entries back to the work sheet (see Figure 11-6).

GENERAL JOURNAL — PAGE 33

DATE		PARTICULARS	P.R.	DEBIT	CREDIT
2000					
Dec.	31	Bad Debts Expense		1 950	
		Allowance for Bad Debts			1 950
		To record estimated bad debts according to age analysis.			
	31	Supplies Expense		2 500	
		Supplies			2 500
		To record supplies used.			
	31	Amortization Expense — Building		5 590	
		Accum. Amortization — Building			5 590
		To record amortization at 5 percent using declining-balance method.			
	31	Amortization Expense — Equipment		2 560	
		Accum. Amortization — Equipment			2 560
		To record amortization at 20 percent using declining-balance method.			
	31	Interest Expense		225	
		Interest Payable			225
		To record three months' interest owed on bank loan.			
	31	Salaries Expense		1 200	
		Salaries Payable			1 200
		To record salaries owed to employees.			

Closing Entries

Closing entries are required to prepare the ledger for the next fiscal period and to update the owner's Capital account. The revenue, expense, and cost of goods sold accounts are closed into the Income Summary account. The Income Summary and Drawings accounts are closed into the Capital account. Four basic closing entries are prepared as follows:

(1) Close the credits from the income section of the work sheet.
(2) Close the debits from the income section of the work sheet.
(3) Close the Income Summary account into the Capital account.
(4) Close the Drawings account into the Capital account.

Included in these entries are two entries involving the adjustment for the Merchandise Inventory account. One entry closes the beginning inventory amount and the other records the ending inventory amount in the Merchandise Inventory account.

The General Journal in Figure 11-14 contains the closing entries prepared from the work sheet (see Figure 11-6). Can you trace each entry back to the work sheet? What effect does the credit of $90 000 have on the Merchandise Inventory account? What effect does the debit of $86 000 have on the Merchandise Inventory account?

FIGURE 11-14
Closing entries in the General Journal

GENERAL JOURNAL				PAGE 34
DATE	PARTICULARS	P.R.	DEBIT	CREDIT
2000				
Dec. 31	Merchandise Inventory		86 000	
	Sales		320 000	
	Income Summary			406 000
	To record the new inventory			
	and to close the Sales account.			
31	Income Summary		357 425	
	Merchandise Inventory			90 000
	Purchases			110 000
	Advertising Expense			5 000
	General Expense			4 000
	Salaries Expense			121 200
	Utilities Expense			7 400
	Insurance Expense			7 000
	Bad Debts Expense			1 950
	Supplies Expense			2 500
	Amortization Expense — Building			5 590
	Amortization Expense— Equipment			2 560
	Interest Expense			225
	To close the inventory account,			
	the cost of goods sold accounts,			
	and the expense accounts.			
31	Income Summary		48 575	
	S. Campbell, Capital			48 575
	To transfer the year's net income to			
	the Capital account.			
31	S. Campbell, Capital		8 000	
	S. Campbell, Drawings			8 000
	To close the Drawings account.			

FIGURE 11-15
Partial General Ledger showing some of the ledger accounts after posting of adjusting and closing entries

ACCOUNT Merchandise Inventory NO. 120

DATE		PARTICULARS	P.R.	DEBIT	CREDIT	DR. CR.	BALANCE
2000							
Jan.	1	Beginning balance	✓	90 000		DR.	90 000
Dec.	31	To close	J34		90 000		0
	31	To record new inventory	J34	86 000		DR.	86 000

ACCOUNT S. Campbell, Capital NO. 300

DATE		PARTICULARS	P.R.	DEBIT	CREDIT	DR. CR.	BALANCE
2000							
Jan.	1	Balance	✓			CR.	100 640
Jun.	30	New Investment	J18		100 000	CR.	200 640
Dec.	31	Net Income	J34		48 575	CR.	249 215
	31	Drawings	J34	8 000		CR.	241 215

ACCOUNT S. Campbell, Drawings NO. 301

DATE		PARTICULARS	P.R.	DEBIT	CREDIT	DR. CR.	BALANCE
2000							
Dec.	31	Balance	✓			DR.	8 000
	31	To close	J34	8 000			0

ACCOUNT Income Summary NO. 302

DATE		PARTICULARS	P.R.	DEBIT	CREDIT	DR. CR.	BALANCE
2000							
Dec.	31	Merch. Inventory and Sales	J34		406 000	CR.	406 000
	31	Merch. Inv., Costs and Exp.	J34	357 425		CR.	48 575
	31	Net Income to Capital	J34	48 575			0

ACCOUNT Sales NO. 400

DATE		PARTICULARS	P.R.	DEBIT	CREDIT	DR. CR.	BALANCE
2000							
Dec.	31	Balance	✓			CR.	320 000
	31	To close	J34	320 000			0

POSTING TO THE LEDGER

The adjusting and closing entries in the General Journal are posted to the General Ledger. After this is done, the revenue, expense, and cost of goods sold accounts, as well as the Drawings account, will have zero balances. They will be ready to receive the revenue, expense, and cost of goods sold transactions for the new fiscal period. The Merchandise Inventory account will contain the new inventory figure. The Capital account will be updated. It will contain the new balance, which takes into consideration the operating results for the fiscal period.

In Figure 11-15 on page 442, several of the General Ledger accounts are shown after the adjusting and closing entries have been posted. Notice that the Sales account is prepared for the next fiscal period. It has a zero balance and has been ruled closed. The Merchandise Inventory account has been closed and re-opened. It contains the new inventory of $86 000. The Capital account has a balance of $241 215, the same as the new Capital amount on the balance sheet in Figure 11-12.

PREPARING THE POST-CLOSING TRIAL BALANCE

A final proof is required to ensure that the General Ledger is in balance to start the new fiscal period. Figure 11-16 shows the trial balance prepared after the closing entries have been posted. It contains only asset, liability, and equity accounts. All the revenue, expense, and cost of goods sold accounts have been closed and do not have to be shown on the last trial balance.

FIGURE 11-16
Post-closing trial balance proving the accuracy of the recording process in preparation for the new fiscal period

Campbell Enterprises
Post-Closing Trial Balance
December 31, 2000

ACCOUNT TITLE	ACC. NO.	DEBIT	CREDIT
Cash	100	$112 000	
Accounts Receivable	102	53 000	
Allowance for Bad Debts	103		$ 2 000
Merchandise Inventory	120	86 000	
Supplies	131	2 000	
Building	140	160 000	
Accumulated Amortization — Building	141		53 790
Equipment	142	23 000	
Accumulated Amortization — Equipment	143		12 760
Accounts Payable	200		23 450
Interest Payable	201		225
Salaries Payable	202		1 200
PST Payable	205		2 130
GST Payable	206		1 870
GST Refundable	207	640	
Bank Loan	221		10 000
Mortgage Payable	231		88 000
S. Campbell, Capital	300		241 215
		$436 640	$436 640

EXAMINING REVERSING ENTRIES

Earlier in this chapter, you learned how to adjust accrued expenses. The example used was $225 interest, which was owed on a bank loan. The loan was for six months. At the end of the fiscal period, three months' interest of $225 was owed but had not been recorded because it was not due to be paid until March 31. The following T-accounts illustrate the adjusting and closing entries made on December 31:

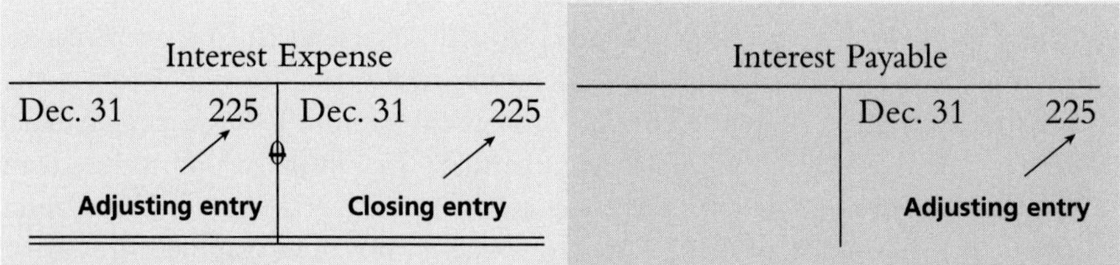

On March 31, payment was made to the bank for six months' interest of $450. This covered the full period of the loan, October 1 to March 31. When this entry was made, Interest Expense was debited $450 and Cash was credited $450 as shown here:

Interest Expense			
Dec. 31	225	Dec. 31	225
Mar. 31	450		

Cash			
		Mar. 31	450

But there is a dilemma here. Can you see it? How much interest on this loan had already been recorded in December?

Because of the adjusting entry, the interest for October 1 to December 31 ($225) was recorded twice — once when the adjustment was made and again when the interest was actually paid to the bank in March. A total of $675 ($225 + $450) has been recorded in the Interest Expense account. The actual amount of the interest is $450. This double recording of interest is avoided by the use of a *reversing entry.*

On January 3, the first working day after the end of the fiscal period, this reversing entry is made:

Date	Account	Debit	Credit
Jan. 3	Interest Payable	225	
	Interest Expense		225
	To reverse the adjusting entry of Dec. 31.		

The effect of this entry is shown in the following T-accounts:

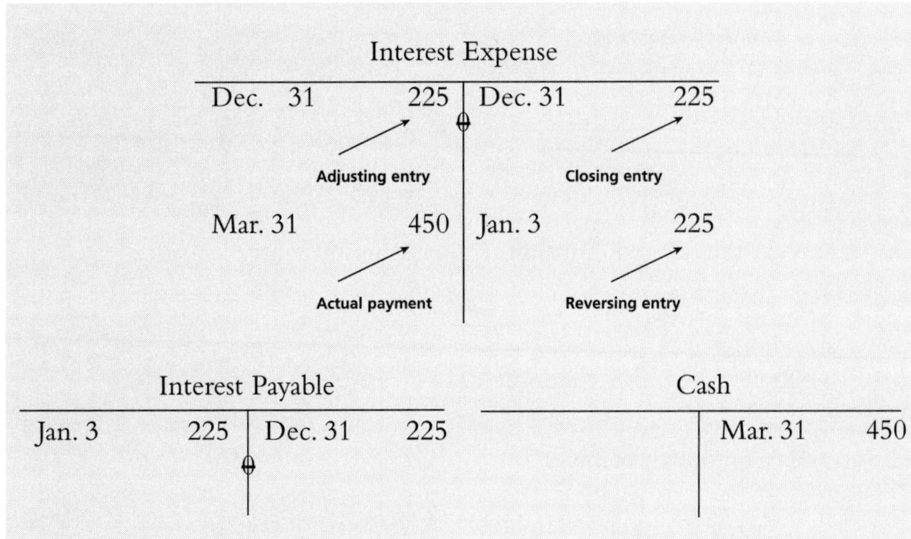

Notice that the reversing entry of January 3 has the effect of allocating half of the actual interest paid to the new fiscal period and half to the previous fiscal period. This is correct and results in the correct matching of expenses and revenue for each fiscal period.

Other Reversing Entries

Reversing entries are required for all accrued expense and accrued revenue adjustments. Earlier in this chapter, an adjusting entry for salaries owed ($1 200) was explained. The adjusting entry is shown in these T-accounts:

Salaries Expense

Dec. 31	1 200		

Salaries Payable

		Dec. 31	1 200

This entry was necessary because sales commissions are paid the month after they have been earned. The closing entries resulted in the following:

Salaries Expense

Dec. 31	1 200	Dec. 31	1 200

The following reversing entry was made on January 3. This entry was necessary to avoid a double recording of the sales commissions:

Jan. 3	Salaries Payable	1 200	
	Salaries Expense		1 200
	To reverse the adjusting entry of Dec. 31.		

The accounts now appear as follows:

Salaries Expense				Salaries Payable			
Dec. 31	1 200	Dec. 31	1 200	Jan. 31	1 200	Dec. 31	1 200
		Jan. 3	1 200				

On January 31 the sales commissions are paid and this entry is made:

Jan. 31	Salaries Expense	1 200	
	Cash		1 200
	To pay December commissions.		

The accounts are shown below:

Salaries Expense				Cash			
Dec. 31	1 200	Dec. 31	1 200			Jan. 31	1 200
Jan. 31	1 200	Jan. 3	1 200				

The reversing entry avoids double recording of the $1 200. Similar reversing entries are prepared on the first working day of the new fiscal period for all accrued expense and revenue adjustments.

Reversing entries could be avoided by debiting the payable account when payment is made in the new fiscal period. However, this is *not* done; with a number of accruals and payments spread out over months, it would be easy to forget to handle the transactions correctly. To avoid errors and reliance on one person's memory, it is standard accounting practice to use the reversing entry procedure.

COMPLETING THE ACCOUNTING CYCLE

You have now learned the final steps in the accounting cycle for a merchandising company. Figure 11-17 on page 447 summarizes the complete accounting cycle and illustrates all the tasks completed during the accounting period.

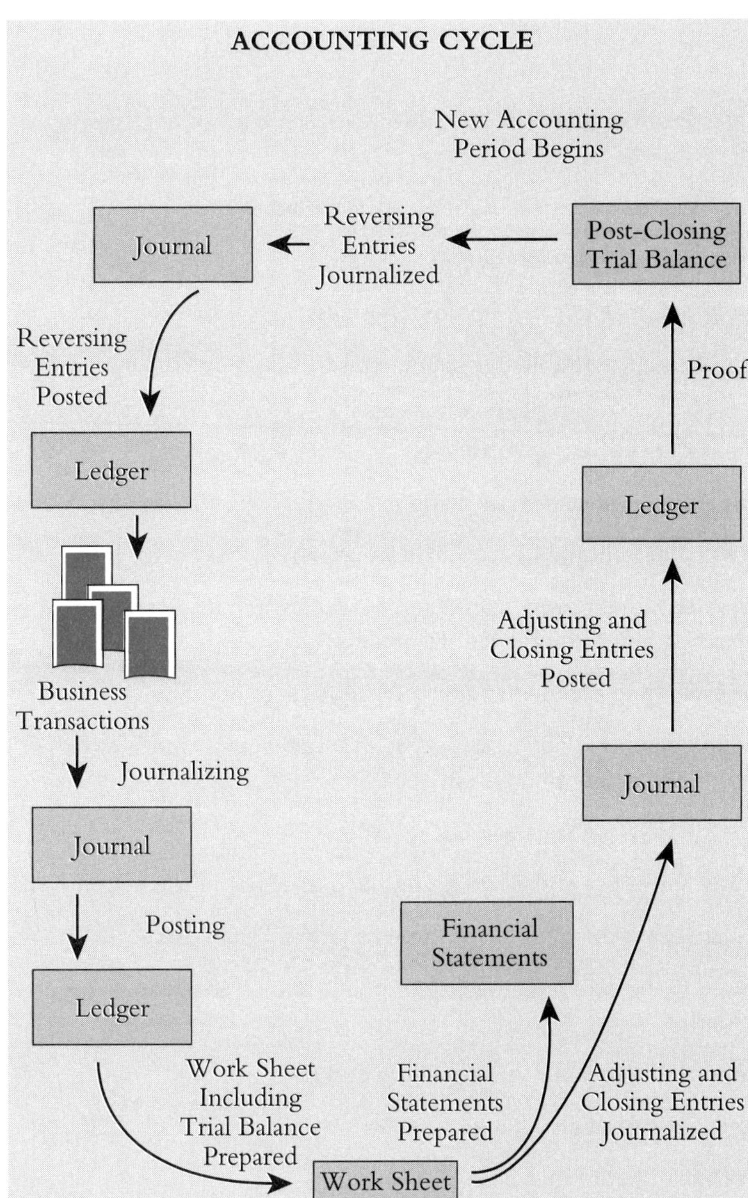

FIGURE 11-17

The accounting cycle is a continuous process.

ACCOUNTING TERMS

Accounts Receivable Age Analysis A listing of all customers' balances and how long each balance has been owed.

Accrued Expenses Expenses that have been incurred but not yet recorded.

Accrued Revenue Revenue earned but not yet recorded.

Administrative Expenses Money spent in the general operation of a business.

Allowance for Bad Debts A contra asset account used to determine a realistic value for Accounts Receivable on the balance sheet.

Bad Debts Uncollectible amounts owed by customers.

Bad Debts Expense Loss of revenue due to uncollectible accounts.

Balance Sheet Method A method using a percentage of accounts receivable.

Classified Statements Financial statements that group accounts in a standard format as an aid to those who examine and interpret the statements.

Income Statement Method A method of estimating bad debts using a percentage of net sales.

Matching Principle Expenses for an accounting period should be matched against the revenue produced during the accounting period.

Merchandising Company Sells merchandise to its customers.

Merchandise Inventory An account that shows the cost of goods on hand at a specific date.

Reversing Entries Entries necessary to make accurate adjustments to accrued revenue.

Schedule of Cost of Goods Sold A schedule used to indicate how the cost of goods sold on the balance sheet was determined.

Selling Expenses Money spent for the direct purpose of selling goods.

Service Company Sells a service to its customers.

Uncollectible Accounts Accounts receivable that cannot be collected.

REVIEW QUESTIONS

UNIT

1. What is the purpose of classifying financial statements?
2. What are the two classes into which operating expenses may be divided?
3. What are the five separate sections on a classified balance sheet?
4. Explain why reversing entries are necessary.
5. Which adjusting entries require reversing entries?
6. Explain how the closing entries result in the Merchandise Inventory account being both closed and opened.

20. (a) Prepare schedules of cost of goods sold for each of the following companies. The fiscal period is the month of August 2001.

Company A

Beginning Merchandise Inventory	$19 000
Purchases	60 000
Transportation on Purchases	1 200
Purchases Returns and Allowances	3 000
Ending Merchandise Inventory	12 000

Company B

Beginning Merchandise Inventory	$50 000
Purchases	83 000
Transportation on Purchases	4 900
Duty	6 000
Purchases Returns and Allowances	4 100
Purchases Discounts	1 800
Ending Merchandise Inventory	47 000

Company C

Beginning Merchandise Inventory	$ 75 000
Purchases	125 000
Transportation on Purchases	5 000
Sales Discounts	5 600
Sales Returns and Allowances	7 800
Purchases Returns and Allowances	7 500
Ending Merchandise Inventory	85 000

(b) Which inventory system do Companies A, B, and C use?

21. (a) Shown below is a list of expenses. Divide the list into two sections — administrative expenses and selling expenses. Insurance, Utilities, Telephone, and Amortization — Building are all divided 75 percent to selling expenses and 25 percent to administrative expenses.
(b) What is the total of the selling expenses and the total of the administrative expenses?
(c) What is the net income if the gross profit is $44 000?
(d) What are net sales if the cost of goods sold is $38 000?

Expenses

Advertising	$3 500
Utilities	1 200
Salaries — Office	8 100
Delivery	6 000
Office Supplies (used)	630
Insurance	300
Amortization — Building	2 800
Amortization — Truck	1 000
Store Supplies (used)	970
Telephone	200

22. (a) Prepare a classified income statement for exercise 17 on page 433 Jeans Unlimited classifies Bad Debts Expense as a selling expense and allocates Supplies Expense, Rent Expense, Amortization Expense, and Salaries Expense 70 percent to selling expenses and 30 percent to administrative expenses.
    (b) Prepare a classified balance sheet.
    (c) Journalize the adjusting and closing entries.
    (d) Post the adjusting and closing entries.
    (e) Prepare a post-closing trial balance.

23. The following adjustments were prepared on December 31. In a General Journal, prepare the reversing entries that would be made on January 3.

2001				
Dec.	31	Interest Expense	410	
		Interest Payable		410
		To record interest owed but not yet paid.		
	31	Salaries Expense	2 350	
		Salaries Payable		2 350
		To record salaries owed to workers but not yet paid.		

24. A company pays its workers every two weeks. The next payday is January 4. Employees are owed (but have not been paid) $1 800 for work in December.

    (a) Prepare the adjusting entry to record salaries owing.
    (b) Prepare the reversing entry.

25. Prepare the necessary reversing entries for Ichikawa Engineering Supply in exercise 19 on page 434.

26. At the end of the fiscal period, a company has earned, but not received, interest of $1 550 on a long-term deposit. Prepare the adjusting and reversing entries. The accounts involved are Interest Receivable and Interest Income.

PROBLEMS: CHALLENGES

1. Using the work sheet completed for Vashti Ali Stores in exercise 18 on page 433:

    (a) Prepare an income statement.
    (b) Prepare a statement of owner's equity.
    (c) Prepare a classified balance sheet.
    (d) Journalize on page 18 the adjusting, closing, and reversing entries.

2. The following accounts and balances appear on The General Store's partial work sheet as of September 30, 2002, the end of its fiscal year.
   (a) Without completing the work sheet, prepare an income statement.
   (b) Prepare a classified balance sheet.

Note: Inventory on hand September 30 is $20 800. All operating expenses are summarized in the General Expenses account.

ACCOUNT TITLE	TRIAL BALANCE DEBIT	TRIAL BALANCE CREDIT	ADJUSTMENTS DEBIT	ADJUSTMENTS CREDIT
Cash	$ 13 500			
Accounts Receivable	8 900			
Inventory, October 1	38 300			
Store Supplies	2 800			$ 1 900
Land	55 000			
Building	135 000			
Accumulated Amortization — Building		$ 18 000		6 000
Store Equipment	43 000			
Accumulated Amortization — Store Equipment		7 000		3 500
Accounts Payable		6 700		
Interest Payable				1 500
Salaries Payable				2 850
PST Payable		1 427		
GST Payable		1 877		
GST Refundable	1 150			
Property Tax Payable				1 750
Mortgage Payable		115 000		
M. Tompkins, Capital		108 346		
M. Tompkins, Drawings	28 000			
Sales		226 500		
Sales Returns and Allowances	4 500			
Sales Discounts	3 100			
Purchases	83 000			
Purchases Returns and Allowances		2 800		
Purchases Discounts		4 100		
Transportation on Purchases	6 400			
Selling Expenses	37 500		$ 2 850	
General Expenses	25 800		1 900	
Amortization Expense — Billing			6 000	
Amortization Expense — Store Equipment			3 500	
Property Tax Expense			1 750	
Interest Expense	5 800		1 500	
Totals	$ 491 750	$ 491 750	$17 500	$17 500

INTEGRATIVE ACTIVITY 3

THE ACCOUNTING CYCLE

Metro Sales Co.

INTRODUCTION

Integrative Activity 3 takes you through the accounting cycle for a merchandising company.

On May 1, T. Clements started a business called Metro Sales Co. Clements went to a public accounting firm, J. Kisel and Associates, and obtained recommendations for an accounting system for the new business. Kisel recommended a columnar journal and a three-ledger system (General Ledger, Accounts Payable Ledger, and Accounts Receivable Ledger). It was also recommended that Metro Sales use a periodic inventory system and that the accounts shown below be set up in the General Ledger. (Notice that the chart of accounts contains six sections and the accounts commonly used by merchandising companies.) Clements has further engaged Kisel and Associates to make recommendations concerning a computerized accounting system and to set up a system of internal accounting control for Metro Sales Co.

General Ledger Accounts

100	Cash	400	Sales
101	Petty Cash	401	Sales Returns and Allowances
110	Accounts Receivable	402	Sales Discounts
120	Merchandise Inventory	500	Purchases
125	Office Supplies	501	Purchases Returns and Allow.
126	Prepaid Insurance	502	Purchases Discounts
150	Equipment	503	Transportation on Purchases
151	Accum. Amortization — Equip.	600	Advertising Expense
200	Accounts Payable	601	Delivery Expense
205	PST Payable	602	Accounting Fees Expense
206	GST Payable	603	Miscellaneous Expense
207	GST Refundable	604	Rent Expense
210	Salaries Payable	605	Salaries Expense
300	T. Clements, Capital	606	Telephone Expense
301	T. Clements, Drawings	607	Utilities Expense
302	Income Summary		

Part A

The May transactions are given after Part D. Your first task is to record the transactions in the subsidiary ledgers as follows:

1. Post sales invoices, cash received, and credit invoices issued directly into the customer accounts in the Accounts Receivable Ledger. Open accounts as required.
2. Post purchase invoices, cheques issued, and credit invoices received directly into the Accounts Payable Ledger. Open accounts as required.
3. On May 31 prepare schedules for each of the subsidiary ledgers.

Part B

1. Record the May transactions in the columnar journal in your work book. You will note that Metro Sales records GST collected as well as the input tax credits. Therefore, GST Refundable DR. and GST Payable CR. columns are included in the journal.
2. Total, balance, and rule the columnar journal.
3. Post the columnar journal to the General Ledger.
4. Prepare a General Ledger trial balance on work sheet paper.

Part C

Complete the work sheet and prepare financial statements using the following information:

- Equipment amortizes 30 percent per year.
- One month of the 12-month insurance policy has expired.
- At the end of the month, there was $70 worth of supplies on hand.
- The ending inventory is $1 450.

Part D

1. Journalize the adjusting and closing entries in a General Journal and post.
2. Prepare a post-closing trial balance.
3. Record the adjusting entries.
4. Print the financial statements and ledgers.
5. Record the closing entries.
6. Print the General Ledger and the post-closing trial balance.

May Transactions

May 1 T. Clements invested $30 000 and started Metro Sales Co.

2 Cheque copies:
No. 1 to J. Kisel, C.A., $1 500 plus $105 GST for organizing an accounting system;
No. 2 to Dot Personnel, $1 000 plus $70 GST for hiring services (Miscellaneous Expense);
No. 3 to Maxwell Realty Ltd., $2 000 plus $140 GST for May rent;

3 No. 4 to Lambton Mfg. Ltd., $3 500 plus $245 GST for a cash purchase of merchandise;
No. 5 to *Daily Express*, $450 plus $31.50 GST for advertising.

3 Purchase invoices:
Burford Supply, T-5986, $1 700 plus $119 GST for merchandise, terms net 60 days;
Willson's Ltd., 9324, $250 plus $17.50 GST for letterhead, business forms, and miscellaneous office supplies, terms net 30 days;
Halton Interiors, 4438, $9 000 plus $630 GST for office equipment and furnishings, terms: three equal payments, May 15, May 31, and June 30;
Stevensville Mfg. Ltd., SM7955, $2 000 plus $140 GST for merchandise, terms 2/10, n/30.

4 Cash sales:
Sales Invoices 1 to 4, $3 250 plus 7 percent GST, plus 8 percent PST, total $3 737.50.

5 Sales invoices (terms 2/10, n/30 for all sales on account):
No. 5, $200 to J. Barnes, plus $14 GST, plus 8 percent PST $16;
No. 6, $300, plus 7 percent GST, plus 8 percent PST, to M. Charters;
No. 7, $1 200, plus GST, plus PST, to A. Falcone;
No. 8, $140, plus GST, plus PST, to L. Parrish.

8 Purchase invoices:
Bell Canada, 4987321, $90 plus $6.30 GST for installation services;
CP, H4836, $120 plus $8.40 GST for transportation on merchandise purchases;
Jenkins Enterprises, 3952, $2 900 plus $203 GST for merchandise, terms 3/10, n/60.

9 Credit invoices received:
Burford Supply, C-8924, $120 for defective merchandise, plus $8.40 GST, total credit $128.40;
Halton Interiors, C-5558, $250 allowance off the price of scratched furnishings plus $17.50 GST, total credit $267.50.

10 Cash sales:
Sales Invoices 9 to 12, $2 400, plus GST, plus PST.

11 Credit invoice issued:
No. C-1 to M. Charters, $115 for $100 worth of merchandise returned, $8 PST, $7 GST.

12 Sales invoices:
No. 13 to L. Becker, $1 200, plus GST, plus PST;
No. 14 to T. Gabriel, $5 000, plus GST, plus PST;
No. 15 to M. Charters, $2 200, plus GST, plus PST.

12 Cheque copies:
No. 6 to Bell Canada, $96.30 on account;
No. 7 to CP, $128.40 on account;
No. 8 to Halton Interiors, $3 210 on account;
No. 9 to Stevensville Mfg., $2 097.20 for invoice of May 3 less 2 percent discount.

15 Purchase invoice:
Stevensville Mfg., SM8347, $275 for merchandise, GST $19.25, terms 2/10, n/30.
Cheque copies:

15 No. 10, $1 800 for a 12-month comprehensive business insurance policy to Metropolitan Life;
No. 11, $100 to establish a petty cash fund.

15 Cash received from customers:
J. Barnes $225.40 for May 5 invoice less 2 percent cash discount;
L. Parrish, $157.78 for May 5 invoice less 2 percent cash discount.

16 Sales invoices:
No. 16 to L. Becker, $4 000, plus GST, plus PST;
No. 17 to T. Gabriel, $650, plus GST, plus PST;
No. 18 to M. Braganolo, $940, plus GST, plus PST;
No. 19 to N. Lumsden, $895, plus GST, plus PST.

18 Cheque copies:
No. 12 for $126 plus $8.82 GST to pay for an invoice received today from Mac's Delivery Service, terms, cash;
No. 13 for $500 to T. Clements for personal use;
No. 14 for $3 009.91 to Jenkins Enterprises for May 8 invoice, less 3 percent cash discount.

19 Cash sales:
Sales Invoices 20 to 26, $3 170, plus GST, plus PST.

22 Purchases invoices:
CP, H5981, $79 for transportation on purchases of merchandise plus $5.53 GST;
Willson's Ltd., 9947 $46 for office supplies, plus $3.22 GST.

24 Credit invoice issued:
No. C-2 to N. Lumsden, $45, plus GST, plus PST, for defective merchandise.

25 Cheque copy:
No. 15 for $93 to replenish petty cash.
Summary of petty cash vouchers:
Office Supplies $35; Miscellaneous Expenses $33;
T. Clements, Drawings $20; GST $5.

25 Sales invoices:
No. 27 to J. Barnes, $798, plus GST, plus PST;
No. 28 to T. Gabriel, $240, plus GST, plus PST.

30 Cheque copies:
No. 16 for $3 210 to Halton Interiors on account;
No. 17 for $1 500 to T. Clements for personal use.

30 Purchases invoices:
Bell Canada, 4988412, $39, plus $2.73 GST, plus $3.12 PST;
City Light and Power, D4941, $185, plus $12.95 GST for hydro bill;
Daily Express, 8348, $870, plus $60.90 GST for newspaper advertising.

31 Cheque No. 18 for $261.50 to the Receiver General for Canada for the GST payment.

CHAPTER 12

Payroll Accounting

UNIT 30 Paying Employees

Learning Objectives

After reading this unit, discussing the applicable review questions, and completing the applications exercises, you will be able to do the following:

1. **SPECIFY** three compulsory deductions.
2. **LIST** five voluntary deductions.
3. **DETERMINE** a net claim code for income tax deduction purposes.
4. **EXPLAIN** the purpose of the social insurance number.
5. **OUTLINE** the benefits and services provided by Canada Pension Plan, Employment Insurance, health insurance, registered pension plans, credit unions, group insurance, and extended health service.
6. **CALCULATE** net earnings.
7. **SPECIFY** the five pay periods and the six payment plans used by businesses.
8. **DEFINE** payroll, compulsory deductions, voluntary deductions, TD1 form, gross earnings, statement of earnings and deductions, and net earnings.

All companies pay their employees a wage or a salary and have a payroll accounting procedure as part of the accounting system. The word *payroll* means a list (*roll*) of employees and the money (*pay*) to be given to them. Thus you can see the origin of the phrase "being on the payroll."

A payroll is a list of employees and the amount of money to be paid to them.

The type of accounting procedures used by a company to prepare the payroll depends on the number of employees, the type of equipment available, the complexity of the payroll, and the number of people available in the accounting department.

Payroll procedures may be performed manually or using a computer system. Some companies prefer to buy a payroll service from an accounting firm or from a bank. Such businesses do the payroll work for other companies and charge a fee for providing the service.

EMPLOYMENT LAWS

Companies are required by law to keep certain payroll records, to prepare payroll reports, and to provide each employee with a "statement of earnings and deductions." There are both federal and provincial laws governing the paying of employees. One of these is the *Employment Standards Act.*

Provincial Laws

All provinces have an *Employment Standards Act.* These provincial laws govern:

- Minimum wages
- Hours of work
- Statutory holidays
- Vacation pay
- Overtime
- Many other employment practices

Provincial ministries of labour or departments of labour administer these acts. One of their tasks is to investigate employee complaints of unfair treatment.

These laws ensure that all employees receive fair treatment. For example, all employees must receive the statutory holidays which are: New Year's Day, Good Friday, Victoria Day, Canada Day, Labour Day, Thanksgiving, and Christmas. The acts also set out the payroll records that must be kept and give provincial government auditors the authority to inspect company records.

Federal Laws

A number of federal laws impose payroll requirements on employers and affect the pay received by all employees. The federal laws include the *Income Tax Act,* the *Canada Pension Act,* the *Employment Insurance Act,* and the *Workers' Compensation Act.* The example of M. Lostracco used in this chapter will illustrate how all workers are affected by the federal laws.

EARNINGS

A statement of earnings and deductions is provided to all employees and shows how net earnings are determined.

M. Lostracco is an employee of Western Systems, a computer consulting firm located in Vancouver. Lostracco earns a salary of $800 a week as a supervisor. However, the paycheque received by Lostracco for one week's pay is for $576.59. The cheque is shown in Figure 12-1. Notice that it also includes a pay statement showing employee earnings and payroll deductions.

If Lostracco earns $800 and receives only $576.59, what happens to the difference of $223.41? Does the company keep it? Of course not! The $223.41 deducted from Lostracco's cheque by the employer is passed on to other agencies for Lostracco. For example, $175.70 is sent to the federal government to pay Lostracco's personal income tax; $19.20 is paid out for employment insurance; and $28.51 is paid out for the Canada Pension Plan.

FIGURE 12-1
Paycheque with statement of employee earnings and deductions

Pay statement

STATEMENT OF EMPLOYEE EARNINGS AND PAYROLL DEDUCTIONS

EMP. NO.	REGULAR	OVERTIME	TOTAL GROSS EARN.	CPP	EI	INC. TAX	HLTH.	GR. INS.	OTHER	TOTAL DEDUCTIONS	NET EARNINGS	TOTAL CPP TO DATE	CH. NO.	PAY PERIOD ENDING
	GROSS EARNINGS			DEDUCTIONS										
1620	100.00		800.00	28.51	19.20	175.70	0			223.41	576.59	484.67	3821	May 7, 2001

MISCELLANEOUS DEDUCTIONS

1 PENSION ______
2 BONDS ______
3 UNION ______
4 ______
5 ______

WESTERN SYSTEMS
7389 Jasper Cres.
Vancouver, BC V5P 3S3

PAYROLL ACCOUNT CHEQUE NO. 3821
DATE May 7, 2001

PAY TO THE ORDER OF M. Lostracco ---------------------- $ 576.59

SUM OF Five hundred and seventy-six ---------- 59/100 DOLLARS

THE BANK OF NOVA SCOTIA
3549 Hudson St.
Vancouver, BC V6H 3A4

Harry Lock
WESTERN SYSTEMS

Cathy M. Drummond
WESTERN SYSTEMS

Cheque

DEDUCTIONS

Deductions are amounts subtracted from an employee's gross earnings.

The items deducted from an employee's pay are called *payroll deductions*. Some deductions are *compulsory* — they apply to all workers. Others are voluntary on the part of the employee.

Compulsory Deductions

Compulsory payroll deductions include income tax, Canada Pension Plan, and Employment Insurance.

Employers are required by law to make three payroll deductions for their employees:

- Personal income tax
- Employment Insurance contributions
- Canada Pension Plan contributions

In some provinces, health insurance is also a compulsory deduction. In Ontario, however, employers must pay an Employer Health Tax rather than deduct premiums from employees.

Employers may also have collective agreements (contracts) with unions that require union dues to be deducted from the employees' earnings. The union dues are then forwarded to the union by the company.

Voluntary Deductions

There are a large number of deductions that an employee may ask the employer to make. These include:

- Charitable donations
- Payments to a credit union
- Group life insurance payments
- Purchase of government bonds
- Extended health insurance premiums
- Private pension plan contributions

These deductions are made by the company if *an employee requests that they be made.* They are then forwarded to the appropriate agency by the company. In effect, the company is handling the payment of some of the employee's personal bills.

EXAMINING COMPULSORY DEDUCTIONS

Canada Pension Plan

Every employee who is over 18 and under 70 years of age and working in Canada (with minor exceptions) must contribute to the Canada Pension Plan (CPP). The amount of the contribution is 3.9 percent of the employee's salary to a maximum yearly contribution of $1 329.90. Upon retirement, anyone who has contributed will receive a pension at the age of 65. A reduced pension is available to those who retire at an earlier age. In the event of death, the contributor's dependants receive a pension.

Federal legislation requires that the employer also make contributions to the Canada Pension Plan on behalf of each employee. The employer contributes an amount equal to the employee's contribution (3.9 percent). Thus, both the employee and the employer are paying for the employee's future pension. Once a month, the company sends all the employees' deductions along with the employer's share to the federal government. In effect, the business is acting as a collection agent for the government and also helping to finance the Canada Pension Plan benefits for the employee.

In Quebec, the province has organized the Quebec Pension Plan. It is operated in much the same way as the Canada Pension Plan.

Employment Insurance

Employment insurance is designed to provide income to those workers who become unemployed through no fault of their own. Most workers in Canada must contribute to the employment insurance fund. Benefits are received only when a person becomes unemployed. This means that those workers who are fortunate enough never to be unemployed will contribute to the fund but will not receive payments from it.

With minor exceptions, all full-time employees are required to make employment insurance payments. The employer makes payroll deductions from the employees' earnings and forwards the money to the federal government. The maximum yearly employee contribution is $936.00.

The employer must also contribute to the employment insurance fund on behalf of employees. The employer must contribute 1.4 times the amount deducted for each employee. For example, since Lostracco's employment insurance premium is $19.20, the employer must contribute $26.88 (1.4 × $19.20) on behalf of Lostracco.

Employment Insurance and the Record of Employment

A form called the Record of Employment must be completed and given to an employee who leaves employment. This form is used to decide if a person is eligible for employment insurance benefits, the amount of the benefits, and how long the person can collect benefits. In effect, it is the employee's proof that contributions have been made and that the employee is entitled to receive benefits from the employment insurance fund. The Record of Employment form must be issued by the employer within five days of the stoppage in employment.

Personal Income Tax

The *Income Tax Act* requires that employers deduct an amount for income tax from each employee's earnings each payday. Once a month, the employer must send the amounts deducted to the federal government. Through these deductions, workers pay their income tax to the government on a regular basis.

A T1 is the income tax return completed each year by taxpayers.

Each year before April 30, Canadians must complete a personal income tax return. This form, called the T1, is used to determine the amount of income tax for which each person is responsible. The total amount payable is compared to the amount the employee has already paid through payroll deductions each payday. The result may be a refund (money back) for the employee if the payroll deductions were too large or an extra amount owing if the payroll deductions were too low.

The amount of tax payable is determined in two steps.

Step 1: Calculation of Taxable Income

The amount of taxable income is determined by the amount of income earned minus deductions. Allowable deductions include payments made for items such as registered pension plan contributions, child care expenses, and union dues.

Income – (Registered Pension Plan Contributions +
Child Care Expenses + Union Dues) = Taxable Income

Step 2: Calculation of Income Tax

The amount of tax payable is determined by subtracting non-refundable tax credits from the amount of tax owing on taxable income. Non-refundable tax credits for items such as dependants, CPP or EI contributions, and tuition reduce the amount of federal income tax payable. They are called non-refundable because, if these credits are more than your federal income tax, the difference is not refunded to you.

To determine an employee's credits, the employer is required to have each employee complete a *Personal Tax Credits Return* (TD1 form), or when there is a new change of credits. This form is used to determine a person's tax credits, which affect the amount of income tax paid. Tax credits are amounts of income on which income tax is not paid. Therefore, a person with a number of credits (e.g., for spouse or infirm dependants) pays less income tax than a person with few credits. Figures 12-2 and 12-3 on pages 462 and 463 show the TD1 form completed by M. Lostracco. You will notice that the employee lists all personal credits to arrive at a net claim code. For Lostracco, the net claim code is 1. This code is used by the employer to determine the tax deduction to be made each payday.

A TD1 form shows an employee's claim for non-refundable tax credits. It must be completed by all employees when credits change.

EXAMINING VOLUNTARY DEDUCTIONS

Group Life Insurance

Many companies provide a group life insurance plan for their employees. Because of the large number of people joining the plan, the insurance companies provide a group discount rate. The amount paid by each employee is determined by the amount of insurance requested and the age of the employee. For example, an employee who decides to purchase $50 000 worth of life insurance for a premium of 25 cents per $1 000 per month, would pay $12.50. The $12.50 is deducted from earnings by the employer and sent to the insurance company for the employee.

Credit Union

A *credit union* is a non-profit banking organization operated by the employees of a company or organization. A credit union is similar to a banking institution. It receives deposits from members and gives interest on the deposits. Funds contributed by the employees are lent to other members who pay interest on money borrowed. The expenses of a credit union are low because it is operated by its own members, facilities are often provided by the employer, and bad debts on loans are rare since loans are made only to the members who are all employed workers. Credit unions provide many banking services including:

- Loans
- Chequing accounts
- Savings accounts
- Mortgages
- Registered retirement savings plans

FIGURE 12-2
Personal Tax Credit
TD1 form (side 1)

Canada Customs and Revenue Agency | Agence des douanes et du revenu du Canada

PERSONAL TAX CREDITS RETURN

See the instructions on page 2 for completing this return.

Last name (capital letters)	Usual first name and initials	Employee number
LOSTRACCO	MARY W.	1620
Address	For non-residents only – country of permanent residence	Social insurance number
19 QUEEN'S QUAY		457638529
VANCOUVER, BC — Postal code: V5K 6A4		Date of birth (Year/Month/Day): 1969 08 14

Basic personal amount – Everyone can claim $7,131 as the basic personal amount. If you choose not to claim this amount or if you are a non-resident, see section 1 on page 3.	$7131	1
Spousal amount – You may be able to claim an amount for supporting your spouse if you are married or have a common-law spouse. See section 2 on page 3.	Ø	2
Equivalent-to-spouse amount – You may be able to claim an equivalent-to-spouse amount if you are single, divorced, separated, or widowed. See section 3 on page 3.	Ø	3
Amount for infirm dependants age 18 or older – You may be able to claim an amount for infirm dependants age 18 or older if they are related to you. See section 4 on page 3.	Ø	4
Pension income amount – You can claim your eligible pension income or $1,000, whichever amount is less. See section 5 on page 4.	Ø	5
Age amount – You can claim an amount if you will be 65 or older at the end of the year and your estimated net income from all sources for the year will be $25,921 or less. See section 6 on page 4.	Ø	6
Tuition and education amounts (full-time) – You can claim your tuition fees and $200 for each month you are enrolled as a full-time student. See section 7 on page 4.	Ø	7
Tuition and education amounts (part-time) – You can claim your tuition fees and $60 for each month you are studying in a part-time course that qualifies for the education deduction. See section 8 on page 4.	Ø	8
Disability amount – You can claim $4,233 if you are claiming the disability amount by using Form T2201, *Disability Tax Credit Certificate*. See section 9 on page 4.	Ø	9
Caregiver amount – You may be able to claim an amount if you take care of your parent or grandparent age 65 or older or an infirm dependant age 18 or older who lives with you. See section 10 on page 4.	Ø	10
Amounts transferred from your spouse or dependants – You can transfer any of the following amounts that your spouse or dependants do not need to reduce their federal income tax to zero.		
Age amount – See item 11 on page 4.	Ø	11
Pension income amount – See item 12 on page 4.	Ø	12
Disability amount – See item 13 on page 4.	Ø	13
Tuition and education amounts – See item 14 on page 4.	Ø	14
Total personal tax credit amounts. Add lines 1 to 14.	$7131	

See the claim codes on page 2 to determine which claim code applies to you. Enter this code in box **A**. If the total of all your personal tax credit amounts is more than your total employment income from all sources for the year, your claim code is "E". | 1 | **A**

Additional tax to be deducted – If you receive other income, you may want to have more tax deducted from each pay. By doing this, you may not have to pay as much tax when you file your income tax return. To choose this option, state the amount of additional tax you want to have deducted from each pay. To change this deduction later, you have to complete a new personal tax credits return. $ Ø

I certify that the information given in this return is, to the best of my knowledge, correct and complete.

Signature M. Lostracco Date 01/01/2000

TD1 E (00) (Ce formulaire existe en français.) 0500 Canada

FIGURE 12-3
Personal Tax Credit TD1 form (side 2)

Instructions for completing your personal tax credits return

page 2

Complete this return if you have a new employer or payer, and you will receive one or more of the following types of income:

- salary, wages, commissions, pensions, or any other remuneration; or
- Employment Insurance benefits.

You **do not** have to file a new return every year unless your marital status changes or you expect a change in your personal credits for that year. Complete a new return no later than seven days after the change.

If you make regular spousal support payments, or if you regularly contribute to a registered retirement savings plan (RRSP) during the year, you can reduce the amount of tax to be withheld from your income. To make this request, you have to write to any tax services office for a letter of authority. You do not need a letter of authority if your employer deducts RRSP contributions from your salary.

If you receive non-employment income, such as a pension or Old Age Security, and you want to have extra tax deducted at source, you can complete Form TD3, *Request for Income Tax Deduction on Non-Employment Income*, or complete the "Additional tax to be deducted" section on page 1.

If you need help, ask your employer or payer, or call your tax services office. You can find the telephone number in the Government of Canada section of your telephone book.

After you complete this return, give pages 1 and 2 to your employer. Keep the confidential calculations on pages 3 and 4 for your records.

It is an offence to file a false return.

Deduction for living in a prescribed zone (e.g., Yukon, Nunavut, or Northwest Territories)

If you live in **Yukon, Nunavut, the Northwest Territories**, or another prescribed zone for more than six months in a row, beginning or ending this year, you can claim:

- $7.50 for each day that you live in the prescribed zone; or
- $15 for each day that you live in the prescribed zone, if during that time you live in a dwelling that you maintain, and you are the only person living in that dwelling who is claiming this deduction. $ ______

For more information, get Form T2222, *Northern Residents Deductions*, and the publication called *Northern Residents Deductions – Places in Prescribed Zones* from Internet at **www.ccra-adrc.gc.ca**, or by calling 1-800-959-2221.

Additional information for employers who use computer payroll programs. (Optional)

If you reside in one of the provinces indicated below and your employer uses a computer payroll program, the following information will be used to calculate your provincial tax and surtax reduction. If you do not reside in one of these provinces, you do not need to fill in this box.

If you reside in **Ontario**, **Manitoba**, **Saskatchewan**, or **British Columbia**, enter the number of dependants you have under 18 years old at the end of the year. ☐

Notes

- For **Ontario**, **Manitoba**, and **Saskatchewan** residents, only the spouse with the higher net income can claim for a dependant.
- For **Ontario**, **Manitoba**, or **British Columbia** residents, do not include a child claimed for the equivalent-to-spouse amount on line 3 on page 1.

Claim codes

Total claim amount	Claim code	Total claim amount	Claim code
No claim amount	0	$13,458.01 – 15,039	6
Minimum $7,131	1	$15,039.01 – 16,621	7
$7,131.01 – 8,712	2	$16,621.01 – 18,202	8
$8,712.01 – 10,294	3	$18,202.01 – 19,784	9
$10,294.01 – 11,877	4	$19,784.01 – 21,368	10
$11,877.01 – 13,458	5	$21,368.01 and over (Manual calculation required by employer)	X

No tax withholding required	E

FIGURE 12-4
Personal Tax Credit
TD1 form (side 3)

page 3

1. Basic personal amount

Everyone can claim $7,131 as the basic personal amount.
- If you choose to claim this amount, **enter $7,131** on line 1 on page 1.
- If you choose not to claim this amount (e.g., when you have more than one employer or payer and you have already claimed the basic personal amount), **enter 0** in box **A** on page 1. Do not complete sections 2 to14.

If you want additional tax to be deducted, complete the appropriate section on page 1.

If you are a non-resident, and you are including 90% or more of your annual world income when determining your taxable income in Canada, you can claim certain personal amounts. If you are including less than 90% of your annual world income, **enter 0** in box **A** on page 1. If you are not sure about your non-resident status, or need more information, call any tax services office or the International Tax Services Office.

2. Spousal amount

You may be able to claim an amount for supporting your spouse if you are **married** or have a **common-law spouse.**

Generally, a common-law spouse is a person of the opposite sex with whom you live in a common-law relationship for any continuous period of at least 12 months, including any period of separation (due to a breakdown in the relationship) of less than 90 days. It can also be a person of the opposite sex with whom you live in a common-law relationship and who is the natural or adoptive parent of your child. If you are not sure about your marital status, or need more information, call any tax services office.

If you marry during the year, your spouse's net income for the year includes the income earned before and during the marriage.

If your spouse's net income for the year will be:
- $6,661 or more, you cannot make a claim; enter 0 on line 2 on page 1;
- $606 or less, enter $6,055 on line 2 on page 1; or
- more than $606 but less than $6,661, complete the following calculation:

Base amount		**$6,661**
Minus: Spouse's net income	–	
Enter this amount on line 2 on page 1.	=	

3. Equivalent-to-spouse amount

You may be able to claim an equivalent-to-spouse amount if you are **single**, **divorced**, **separated**, or **widowed**, and you support a dependant who is:
- under 18, your parent or grandparent, or mentally or physically infirm;
- related to you by blood, marriage, or adoption; and
- living with you, in Canada, in a home that you maintain (a dependant may live away from home while attending school).

If your equivalent-to-spouse claim is for an infirm dependant age 18 or older, you may be able to claim an amount in section 4. Otherwise, any person you claim here cannot be claimed again in section 4.

If your dependant's net income for the year will be:
- $6,661 or more, you cannot make a claim; enter 0 on line 3 on page 1;
- $606 or less, enter $6,055 on line 3 on page 1; or
- more than $606 but less than $6,661, complete the following calculation:

Base amount		**$6,661**
Minus: Dependant's net income	–	
Enter this amount on line 3 on page 1.	=	

4. Amount for infirm dependants age 18 or older

You may be able to claim an amount for each infirm dependant age 18 or older who has a physical or mental infirmity and who is your or your spouse's:

- child or grandchild; or
- parent, grandparent, brother, sister, aunt, uncle, niece, or nephew, who resides in Canada.

You have to complete a separate calculation for each infirm dependant you have.

If your dependant's net income for the year will be:
- $7,131 or more, you cannot make a claim; enter 0 on line 4 on page 1; or
- less than $7,131, complete the following calculation:

Base amount		**$7,131**
Minus: Dependant's net income	–	
If more than $2,353, enter $2,353.		
Minus: Equivalent-to-spouse amount claimed for this dependant in section 3	–	
Enter this amount on line 4 on page 1.	=	

5. Pension income amount

Eligible pension income includes pension payments received from a pension plan or fund as a life annuity, and foreign pension payments. It does not include payments from the Canada Pension Plan or Quebec Pension Plan, Old Age Security, guaranteed supplements, or lump-sum withdrawals from a pension fund.

If you receive an eligible pension income, you can claim your eligible pension income or $1,000, whichever amount is **less**.

Enter this amount on line 5 on page 1. ____________

FIGURE 12-5
Personal Tax Credit
TD1 form (side 4)

page 4

6. Age amount

If you will be 65 or older at the end of the year and your estimated net income from all sources for the year will be:
- $49,134 or more, you cannot make a claim; enter 0 on line 6 on page 1;
- $25,921 or less, enter $3,482 on line 6 on page 1; or
- more than $25,921, but less than $49,134, complete the calculation.

Maximum age amount		$3,482	1
Annual estimated net income	________		2
Minus: Base amount	– **$25,921**		3
Line 2 minus line 3	= ________		4
Multiply the amount on line 4 by 15%.		– ________	5
Line 1 minus line 5. (If negative, enter 0.) Enter this amount on line 6 on page 1.		= ________	6

7. Tuition and education amounts (full-time)

Enter your tuition fees for courses you will take in the year, to attend a university, college, or an institution that the Minister of Human Resources Development has certified. ________

Add $200 for each month in the year that you will be enrolled full-time in a qualifying educational program at a university, college, or a school offering job retraining courses or correspondence courses. + ________

Subtotal = ________

Subtract any scholarships, fellowships, or bursaries you will receive in the year (do not report the first $500). – ________

Enter the amount on line 7 on page 1. (If the amount is negative, **enter 0**.) = ________

8. Tuition and education amounts (part-time)

Enter your tuition fees that are more than $100 in total for part-time courses you will take in the year at a designated educational institution. ________

Add $60 for each month in the year that you will be enrolled in a course that will last at least 3 consecutive weeks and involve a minimum of 12 hours of course time per month at a designated educational institution. You cannot claim both the part-time and full-time education tax credit in the same month. + ________

Enter this amount on line 8 on page 1. = ________

9. Disability amount

Enter $4,233 if you are severely impaired, mentally or physically, and are claiming the disability amount by using Form T2201, *Disability Tax Credit Certificate*. Such an impairment has to markedly restrict your daily living activities. The impairment has to last, or be expected to last, for a continuous period of at least 12 months.

Enter this amount on line 9 on page 1. ________

10. Caregiver amount

If you take care of your parent or grandparent age 65 or older, or an infirm dependant age 18 or older, **who lives with you** in a home that you maintain, and your dependant's net income for the year will be:
- $13,853 or more, you cannot make a claim; enter 0 on line 10 on page 1; or
- less than $13,853, complete the calculation.

You cannot claim this amount if you or anyone else is claiming an **infirm dependant amount** for the dependant.

You have to complete a separate calculation for each qualified dependant.

Base amount	$13,853	1
Minus: Dependant's net income	– ________	2
Line 1 minus line 2. If more than $2,353, enter $2,353.	= ________	3
Minus: equivalent-to-spouse amount claimed in section 3 for this dependent	– ________	4
Line 3 minus line 4. (If negative, enter 0.) Enter this amount on line 10 on page 1.	= ________	5

If any other person also contributes to the support of the dependant, the combined amount that you and that other person claim cannot be more than the amount on line 5.

Amounts transferred from your spouse or dependants

You can transfer any of the following amounts that your spouse or dependants do not need to reduce their federal income tax to zero.

11. **Age amount** – If your spouse will be 65 or older this year, you can claim any unused balance of the age amount, to a maximum of **$3,482**. Enter this amount on line 11 on page 1. ________

12. **Pension income amount** – If your spouse receives eligible pension income, you can claim any unused balance of the pension income amount, to a maximum of **$1,000**. Enter this amount on line 12 on page 1. ________

13. **Disability amount** – If your spouse or dependant qualifies for the disability amount, you can claim the unused balance of their disability amount, to a maximum of **$4,233** for each person. Enter this amount on line 13 on page 1. ________

14. **Tuition and education amounts (full or part-time)** – If you are supporting a spouse, child, or grandchild attending a university, college, or certified educational institution, you can claim the unused balance of their tuition and education amounts, to a maximum of **$5,000** for each person. Enter this amount on line 14 on page 1. ________

Source: Reproduced with permission of the Minister of Public Works and Government Services Canada.

Deposits to the credit union, or payments on loans granted by the credit union, may be made through payroll deductions. The employer deducts the appropriate amounts from the employees' earnings and transfers them to the credit union for the employees.

Health Insurance

In Canada, there is *universal health coverage.* This means that everyone is able to obtain health insurance. Each province operates its own health plan. The benefits provided by provincial health insurance plans include:

- Payment of doctors' fees for required services
- Hospital expenses

The cost to the public for this insurance varies from province to province. Many companies pay part or all of the health insurance premium as a fringe benefit for their employees. Often this is part of a contract negotiated with the union. The portion of the monthly premium paid by the company is an expense of operating the business and is recorded in an account called Health Insurance Expense or in an account called Payroll Expense. In Ontario, the public does not pay directly for health insurance. Employers pay an Employer Health Tax, which will be explained later in this chapter.

In provinces where employees pay part or all of the premium, the premium is deducted from earnings by the employer and is sent to the provincial health plan organization.

Extended Health Insurance Plans

Provincial health plans do not pay for all health services. Many employees like to have additional health insurance provided by insurance companies. The premiums for additional health insurance are deducted from the employees' earnings by the employer and sent to the appropriate insurance organization.

Extended health plans provide benefits not covered by provincial plans such as:

- Cost of prescription drugs
- Special medical services and supplies
- Semi-private or private hospital accommodation
- Home care nursing

Registered Pension Plans

Employees of some companies can voluntarily join a private pension plan. This plan provides pension benefits to the employee upon retirement. The pension is in addition to the benefits the employee would receive from the Canada Pension Plan.

While working, the employee contributes to the private pension plan through payroll deductions. The employer sends the money deducted to the insurance company. Usually, the employer makes a matching contribution on behalf of the employee.

Private pension plans are usually registered with the federal government. Contributions made to a registered pension plan (RPP) are an eligible income tax deduction. Each year when completing their personal income tax returns (T1), employees are allowed to deduct, for income tax purposes, the payments made to an RPP. This lowers the amount of income tax to be paid by the worker.

GOVERNMENT REQUIREMENTS

In order to receive benefits from employment insurance and the Canada Pension Plan, a person must have contributed to the plans. The contributions are recorded using each person's social insurance number (SIN).

Social Insurance Number

The recording of contributions is much more efficiently done by SIN than by name. Can you imagine how many *Jack Chins, Mary Smiths,* or *Maurice Leblancs* there are in Canada? By assigning numbers to each person, the possibilities of error due to similarities in names is eliminated. Revenue Canada, Taxation also uses the SIN to handle the tax records of Canadians.

Books and Records

Every person carrying on a business in Canada is required by law to keep records and accounts for income tax, Canada Pension Plan, and employment insurance purposes. The records must contain enough information to determine the correct payroll deductions. On request, the records must be made available to officers of Revenue Canada, Taxation. Normally, the records must be kept for a minimum of six years. Written permission of the Minister of National Revenue is required before records are destroyed.

CALCULATING NET EARNINGS

The net earnings for an employee are determined as follows:

Gross Earnings – Deductions = Net Earnings

Net earnings is the balance remaining after deductions have been subtracted from gross earnings.

In M. Lostracco's case:

$800 – $223.41 = $576.59

The deductions of $223.41 are as follows:

Gross earnings are the total earnings of an employee before deductions.

Canada Pension Plan	$ 28.51
Employment Insurance	19.20
Income Tax	175.70
Total Deductions	$223.41

Let's examine the calculation of each of these deductions.

Canada Pension Plan Deduction

Lostracco's employer consults the Revenue Canada, Taxation booklet, Payroll Deductions Tables, to get the CPP deduction. Figure 12-6 on page 468 is a page from this booklet. It indicates that the CPP contribution required on weekly earnings of $800 is $28.51. *Note:* Taking 3.9 percent of an employee's earnings will not give the same figures as on the CPP chart. The reason for this is that there is a basic yearly exemption (currently $3 500).

FIGURE 12-6

CPP Contribution Table

Canada Pension Plan Contributions — Cotisations au Régime de pensions du Canada

Weekly (52 pay periods a year) — Hebdomadaire (52 périodes de paie par année)

Pay Rémunération From - De	To - À	CPP RPC	Pay Rémunération From - De	To - À	CPP RPC	Pay Rémunération From - De	To - À	CPP RPC	Pay Rémunération From - De	To - À	CPP RPC
510.25	510.50	17.28	528.72	528.96	18.00	547.18	547.42	18.72	565.64	565.88	19.44
510.51	510.76	17.29	528.97	529.22	18.01	547.43	547.68	18.73	565.89	566.14	19.45
510.77	511.01	17.30	529.23	529.47	18.02	547.69	547.94	18.74	566.15	566.40	19.46
511.02	511.27	17.31	529.48	529.73	18.03	547.95	548.19	18.75	566.41	566.65	19.47
511.28	511.53	17.32	529.74	529.99	18.04	548.20	548.45	18.76	566.66	566.91	19.48
511.54	511.78	17.33	530.00	530.24	18.05	548.46	548.71	18.77	566.92	567.17	19.49
511.79	512.04	17.34	530.25	530.50	18.06	548.72	548.96	18.78	567.18	567.42	19.50
512.05	512.29	17.35	530.51	530.76	18.07	548.97	549.22	18.79	567.43	567.68	19.51
512.30	512.55	17.36	530.77	531.01	18.08	549.23	549.47	18.80	567.69	567.94	19.52
512.56	512.81	17.37	531.02	531.27	18.09	549.48	549.73	18.81	567.95	568.19	19.53
512.82	513.06	17.38	531.28	531.53	18.10	549.74	549.99	18.82	568.20	568.45	19.54
513.07	513.32	17.39	531.54	531.78	18.11	550.00	550.24	18.83	568.46	568.71	19.55
513.33	513.58	17.40	531.79	532.04	18.12	550.25	550.50	18.84	568.72	568.96	19.56
513.59	513.83	17.41	532.05	532.29	18.13	550.51	550.76	18.85	568.97	569.22	19.57
513.84	514.09	17.42	532.30	532.55	18.14	550.77	551.01	18.86	569.23	569.47	19.58
514.10	514.35	17.43	532.56	532.81	18.15	551.02	551.27	18.87	569.48	569.73	19.59
514.36	514.60	17.44	532.82	533.06	18.16	551.28	551.53	18.88	569.74	569.99	19.60
514.61	514.86	17.45	533.07	533.32	18.17	551.54	551.78	18.89	570.00	570.24	19.61
514.87	515.12	17.46	533.33	533.58	18.18	551.79	552.04	18.90	570.25	570.50	19.62
515.13	515.37	17.47	533.59	533.83	18.19	552.05	552.29	18.91	570.51	570.76	19.63
515.38	515.63	17.48	533.84	534.09	18.20	552.30	552.55	18.92	570.77	571.01	19.64
515.64	515.88	17.49	534.10	534.35	18.21	552.56	552.81	18.93	571.02	571.27	19.65
515.89	516.14	17.50	534.36	534.60	18.22	552.82	553.06	18.94	571.28	571.53	19.66
516.15	516.40	17.51	534.61	534.86	18.23	553.07	553.32	18.95	571.54	571.78	19.67
516.41	516.65	17.52	534.87	535.12	18.24	553.33	553.58	18.96	571.79	572.04	19.68
516.66	516.91	17.53	535.13	535.37	18.25	553.59	553.83	18.97	572.05	572.29	19.69
516.92	517.17	17.54	535.38	535.63	18.26	553.84	554.09	18.98	572.30	572.55	19.70
517.18	517.42	17.55	535.64	535.88	18.27	554.10	554.35	18.99	572.56	572.81	19.71
517.43	517.68	17.56	535.89	536.14	18.28	554.36	554.60	19.00	572.82	573.06	19.72
517.69	517.94	17.57	536.15	536.40	18.29	554.61	554.86	19.01	573.07	573.32	19.73
517.95	518.19	17.58	536.41	536.65	18.30	554.87	555.12	19.02	573.33	573.58	19.74
518.20	518.45	17.59	536.66	536.91	18.31	555.13	555.37	19.03	573.59	573.83	19.75
518.46	518.71	17.60	536.92	537.17	18.32	555.38	555.63	19.04	573.84	574.09	19.76
518.72	518.96	17.61	537.18	537.42	18.33	555.64	555.88	19.05	574.10	574.35	19.77
518.97	519.22	17.62	537.43	537.68	18.34	555.89	556.14	19.06	574.36	574.60	19.78
519.23	519.47	17.63	537.69	537.94	18.35	556.15	556.40	19.07	574.61	574.86	19.79
519.48	519.73	17.64	537.95	538.19	18.36	556.41	556.65	19.08	574.87	575.12	19.80
519.74	519.99	17.65	538.20	538.45	18.37	556.66	556.91	19.09	575.13	575.37	19.81
520.00	520.24	17.66	538.46	538.71	18.38	556.92	557.17	19.10	575.38	575.63	19.82
520.25	520.50	17.67	538.72	538.96	18.39	557.18	557.42	19.11	575.64	575.88	19.83
520.51	520.76	17.68	538.97	539.22	18.40	557.43	557.68	19.12	575.89	576.14	19.84
520.77	521.01	17.69	539.23	539.47	18.41	557.69	557.94	19.13	576.15	576.40	19.85
521.02	521.27	17.70	539.48	539.73	18.42	557.95	558.19	19.14	576.41	576.65	19.86
521.28	521.53	17.71	539.74	539.99	18.43	558.20	558.45	19.15	576.66	576.91	19.87
521.54	521.78	17.72	540.00	540.24	18.44	558.46	558.71	19.16	576.92	577.17	19.88
521.79	522.04	17.73	540.25	540.50	18.45	558.72	558.96	19.17	577.18	577.42	19.89
522.05	522.29	17.74	540.51	540.76	18.46	558.97	559.22	19.18	577.43	577.68	19.90
522.30	522.55	17.75	540.77	541.01	18.47	559.23	559.47	19.19	577.69	577.94	19.91
522.56	522.81	17.76	541.02	541.27	18.48	559.48	559.73	19.20	577.95	578.19	19.92
522.82	523.06	17.77	541.28	541.53	18.49	559.74	559.99	19.21	578.20	578.45	19.93
523.07	523.32	17.78	541.54	541.78	18.50	560.00	560.24	19.22	578.46	578.71	19.94
523.33	523.58	17.79	541.79	542.04	18.51	560.25	560.50	19.23	578.72	578.96	19.95
523.59	523.83	17.80	542.05	542.29	18.52	560.51	560.76	19.24	578.97	579.22	19.96
523.84	524.09	17.81	542.30	542.55	18.53	560.77	561.01	19.25	579.23	579.47	19.97
524.10	524.35	17.82	542.56	542.81	18.54	561.02	561.27	19.26	579.48	579.73	19.98
524.36	524.60	17.83	542.82	543.06	18.55	561.28	561.53	19.27	579.74	579.99	19.99
524.61	524.86	17.84	543.07	543.32	18.56	561.54	561.78	19.28	580.00	580.24	20.00
524.87	525.12	17.85	543.33	543.58	18.57	561.79	562.04	19.29	580.25	580.50	20.01
525.13	525.37	17.86	543.59	543.83	18.58	562.05	562.29	19.30	580.51	580.76	20.02
525.38	525.63	17.87	543.84	544.09	18.59	562.30	562.55	19.31	580.77	581.01	20.03
525.64	525.88	17.88	544.10	544.35	18.60	562.56	562.81	19.32	581.02	581.27	20.04
525.89	526.14	17.89	544.36	544.60	18.61	562.82	563.06	19.33	581.28	581.53	20.05
526.15	526.40	17.90	544.61	544.86	18.62	563.07	563.32	19.34	581.54	581.78	20.06
526.41	526.65	17.91	544.87	545.12	18.63	563.33	563.58	19.35	581.79	582.04	20.07
526.66	526.91	17.92	545.13	545.37	18.64	563.59	563.83	19.36	582.05	582.29	20.08
526.92	527.17	17.93	545.38	545.63	18.65	563.84	564.09	19.37	582.30	582.55	20.09
527.18	527.42	17.94	545.64	545.88	18.66	564.10	564.35	19.38	582.56	582.81	20.10
527.43	527.68	17.95	545.89	546.14	18.67	564.36	564.60	19.39	582.82	583.06	20.11
527.69	527.94	17.96	546.15	546.40	18.68	564.61	564.86	19.40	583.07	583.32	20.12
527.95	528.19	17.97	546.41	546.65	18.69	564.87	565.12	19.41	583.33	583.58	20.13
528.20	528.45	17.98	546.66	546.91	18.70	565.13	565.37	19.42	583.59	583.83	20.14
528.46	528.71	17.99	546.92	547.17	18.71	565.38	565.63	19.43	583.84	584.09	20.15

Employee's maximum CPP contribution for the year 2000 is $1329.90 La cotisation maximale de l'employé au RPC pour l'année 2000 est de 1329,90 $ B-7

Canada Pension Plan Contributions — Cotisations au Régime de pensions du Canada

Weekly (52 pay periods a year) — Hebdomadaire (52 périodes de paie par année)

Pay Rémunération From - De	To - À	CPP RPC	Pay Rémunération From - De	To - À	CPP RPC	Pay Rémunération From - De	To - À	CPP RPC	Pay Rémunération From - De	To - À	CPP RPC
584.10	584.35	20.16	602.56	602.81	20.88	621.02	621.27	21.60	639.48	639.73	22.32
584.36	584.60	20.17	602.82	603.06	20.89	621.28	621.53	21.61	639.74	639.99	22.33
584.61	584.86	20.18	603.07	603.32	20.90	621.54	621.78	21.62	640.00	640.24	22.34
584.87	585.12	20.19	603.33	603.58	20.91	621.79	622.04	21.63	640.25	640.50	22.35
585.13	585.37	20.20	603.59	603.83	20.92	622.05	622.29	21.64	640.51	640.76	22.36
585.38	585.63	20.21	603.84	604.09	20.93	622.30	622.55	21.65	640.77	641.01	22.37
585.64	585.88	20.22	604.10	604.35	20.94	622.56	622.81	21.66	641.02	641.27	22.38
585.89	586.14	20.23	604.36	604.60	20.95	622.82	623.06	21.67	641.28	641.53	22.39
586.15	586.40	20.24	604.61	604.86	20.96	623.07	623.32	21.68	641.54	641.78	22.40
586.41	586.65	20.25	604.87	605.12	20.97	623.33	623.58	21.69	641.79	642.04	22.41
586.66	586.91	20.26	605.13	605.37	20.98	623.59	623.83	21.70	642.05	642.29	22.42
586.92	587.17	20.27	605.38	605.63	20.99	623.84	624.09	21.71	642.30	642.55	22.43
587.18	587.42	20.28	605.64	605.88	21.00	624.10	624.35	21.72	642.56	642.81	22.44
587.43	587.68	20.29	605.89	606.14	21.01	624.36	624.60	21.73	642.82	643.06	22.45
587.69	587.94	20.30	606.15	606.40	21.02	624.61	624.86	21.74	643.07	643.32	22.46
587.95	588.19	20.31	606.41	606.65	21.03	624.87	625.12	21.75	643.33	643.58	22.47
588.20	588.45	20.32	606.66	606.91	21.04	625.13	625.37	21.76	643.59	643.83	22.48
588.46	588.71	20.33	606.92	607.17	21.05	625.38	625.63	21.77	643.84	644.09	22.49
588.72	588.96	20.34	607.18	607.42	21.06	625.64	625.88	21.78	644.10	644.35	22.50
588.97	589.22	20.35	607.43	607.68	21.07	625.89	626.14	21.79	644.36	644.60	22.51
589.23	589.47	20.36	607.69	607.94	21.08	626.15	626.40	21.80	644.61	644.86	22.52
589.48	589.73	20.37	607.95	608.19	21.09	626.41	626.65	21.81	644.87	645.12	22.53
589.74	589.99	20.38	608.20	608.45	21.10	626.66	626.91	21.82	645.13	645.37	22.54
590.00	590.24	20.39	608.46	608.71	21.11	626.92	627.17	21.83	645.38	645.63	22.55
590.25	590.50	20.40	608.72	608.96	21.12	627.18	627.42	21.84	645.64	645.88	22.56
590.51	590.76	20.41	608.97	609.22	21.13	627.43	627.68	21.85	645.89	646.14	22.57
590.77	591.01	20.42	609.23	609.47	21.14	627.69	627.94	21.86	646.15	646.40	22.58
591.02	591.27	20.43	609.48	609.73	21.15	627.95	628.19	21.87	646.41	646.65	22.59
591.28	591.53	20.44	609.74	609.99	21.16	628.20	628.45	21.88	646.66	646.91	22.60
591.54	591.78	20.45	610.00	610.24	21.17	628.46	628.71	21.89	646.92	647.17	22.61
591.79	592.04	20.46	610.25	610.50	21.18	628.72	628.96	21.90	647.18	647.42	22.62
592.05	592.29	20.47	610.51	610.76	21.19	628.97	629.22	21.91	647.43	647.68	22.63
592.30	592.55	20.48	610.77	611.01	21.20	629.23	629.47	21.92	647.69	647.94	22.64
592.56	592.81	20.49	611.02	611.27	21.21	629.48	629.73	21.93	647.95	648.19	22.65
592.82	593.06	20.50	611.28	611.53	21.22	629.74	629.99	21.94	648.20	648.45	22.66
593.07	593.32	20.51	611.54	611.78	21.23	630.00	630.24	21.95	648.46	648.71	22.67
593.33	593.58	20.52	611.79	612.04	21.24	630.25	630.50	21.96	648.72	648.96	22.68
593.59	593.83	20.53	612.05	612.29	21.25	630.51	630.76	21.97	648.97	649.22	22.69
593.84	594.09	20.54	612.30	612.55	21.26	630.77	631.01	21.98	649.23	649.47	22.70
594.10	594.35	20.55	612.56	612.81	21.27	631.02	631.27	21.99	649.48	649.73	22.71
594.36	594.60	20.56	612.82	613.06	21.28	631.28	631.53	22.00	649.74	649.99	22.72
594.61	594.86	20.57	613.07	613.32	21.29	631.54	631.78	22.01	650.00	650.24	22.73
594.87	595.12	20.58	613.33	613.58	21.30	631.79	632.04	22.02	650.25	650.50	22.74
595.13	595.37	20.59	613.59	613.83	21.31	632.05	632.29	22.03	650.51	650.76	22.75
595.38	595.63	20.60	613.84	614.09	21.32	632.30	632.55	22.04	650.77	651.01	22.76
595.64	595.88	20.61	614.10	614.35	21.33	632.56	632.81	22.05	651.02	651.27	22.77
595.89	596.14	20.62	614.36	614.60	21.34	632.82	633.06	22.06	651.28	651.53	22.78
596.15	596.40	20.63	614.61	614.86	21.35	633.07	633.32	22.07	651.54	651.78	22.79
596.41	596.65	20.64	614.87	615.12	21.36	633.33	633.58	22.08	651.79	652.04	22.80
596.66	596.91	20.65	615.13	615.37	21.37	633.59	633.83	22.09	652.05	652.29	22.81
596.92	597.17	20.66	615.38	615.63	21.38	633.84	634.09	22.10	652.30	652.55	22.82
597.18	597.42	20.67	615.64	615.88	21.39	634.10	634.35	22.11	652.56	652.81	22.83
597.43	597.68	20.68	615.89	616.14	21.40	634.36	634.60	22.12	652.82	653.06	22.84
597.69	597.94	20.69	616.15	616.40	21.41	634.61	634.86	22.13	653.07	653.32	22.85
597.95	598.19	20.70	616.41	616.65	21.42	634.87	635.12	22.14	653.33	653.58	22.86
598.20	598.45	20.71	616.66	616.91	21.43	635.13	635.37	22.15	653.59	653.83	22.87
598.46	598.71	20.72	616.92	617.17	21.44	635.38	635.63	22.16	653.84	654.09	22.88
598.72	598.96	20.73	617.18	617.42	21.45	635.64	635.88	22.17	654.10	654.35	22.89
598.97	599.22	20.74	617.43	617.68	21.46	635.89	636.14	22.18	654.36	654.60	22.90
599.23	599.47	20.75	617.69	617.94	21.47	636.15	636.40	22.19	654.61	654.86	22.91
599.48	599.73	20.76	617.95	618.19	21.48	636.41	636.65	22.20	654.87	655.12	22.92
599.74	599.99	20.77	618.20	618.45	21.49	636.66	636.91	22.21	655.13	655.37	22.93
600.00	600.24	20.78	618.46	618.71	21.50	636.92	637.17	22.22	655.38	655.63	22.94
600.25	600.50	20.79	618.72	618.96	21.51	637.18	637.42	22.23	655.64	655.88	22.95
600.51	600.76	20.80	618.97	619.22	21.52	637.43	637.68	22.24	655.89	656.14	22.96
600.77	601.01	20.81	619.23	619.47	21.53	637.69	637.94	22.25	656.15	656.40	22.97
601.02	601.27	20.82	619.48	619.73	21.54	637.95	638.19	22.26	656.41	656.65	22.98
601.28	601.53	20.83	619.74	619.99	21.55	638.20	638.45	22.27	656.66	656.91	22.99
601.54	601.78	20.84	620.00	620.24	21.56	638.46	638.71	22.28	656.92	657.17	23.00
601.79	602.04	20.85	620.25	620.50	21.57	638.72	638.96	22.29	657.18	657.42	23.01
602.05	602.29	20.86	620.51	620.76	21.58	638.97	639.22	22.30	657.43	657.68	23.02
602.30	602.55	20.87	620.77	621.01	21.59	639.23	639.47	22.31	657.69	657.94	23.03

 Employee's maximum CPP contribution for the year 2000 is $1329.90 La cotisation maximale de l'employé au RPC pour l'année 2000 est de 1329,90 $

Canada Pension Plan Contributions | **Cotisations au Régime de pensions du Canada**

Weekly (52 pay periods a year) | Hebdomadaire (52 périodes de paie par année)

Pay Rémunération From - De	To - À	CPP RPC	Pay Rémunération From - De	To - À	CPP RPC	Pay Rémunération From - De	To - À	CPP RPC	Pay Rémunération From - De	To - À	CPP RPC
657.95	658.19	23.04	676.41	676.65	23.76	694.87	695.12	24.48	713.33	713.58	25.20
658.20	658.45	23.05	676.66	676.91	23.77	695.13	695.37	24.49	713.59	713.83	25.21
658.46	658.71	23.06	676.92	677.17	23.78	695.38	695.63	24.50	713.84	714.09	25.22
658.72	658.96	23.07	677.18	677.42	23.79	695.64	695.88	24.51	714.10	714.35	25.23
658.97	659.22	23.08	677.43	677.68	23.80	695.89	696.14	24.52	714.36	714.60	25.24
659.23	659.47	23.09	677.69	677.94	23.81	696.15	696.40	24.53	714.61	714.86	25.25
659.48	659.73	23.10	677.95	678.19	23.82	696.41	696.65	24.54	714.87	715.12	25.26
659.74	659.99	23.11	678.20	678.45	23.83	696.66	696.91	24.55	715.13	715.37	25.27
660.00	660.24	23.12	678.46	678.71	23.84	696.92	697.17	24.56	715.38	715.63	25.28
660.25	660.50	23.13	678.72	678.96	23.85	697.18	697.42	24.57	715.64	715.88	25.29
660.51	660.76	23.14	678.97	679.22	23.86	697.43	697.68	24.58	715.89	716.14	25.30
660.77	661.01	23.15	679.23	679.47	23.87	697.69	697.94	24.59	716.15	716.40	25.31
661.02	661.27	23.16	679.48	679.73	23.88	697.95	698.19	24.60	716.41	716.65	25.32
661.28	661.53	23.17	679.74	679.99	23.89	698.20	698.45	24.61	716.66	716.91	25.33
661.54	661.78	23.18	680.00	680.24	23.90	698.46	698.71	24.62	716.92	717.17	25.34
661.79	662.04	23.19	680.25	680.50	23.91	698.72	698.96	24.63	717.18	717.42	25.35
662.05	662.29	23.20	680.51	680.76	23.92	698.97	699.22	24.64	717.43	717.68	25.36
662.30	662.55	23.21	680.77	681.01	23.93	699.23	699.47	24.65	717.69	717.94	25.37
662.56	662.81	23.22	681.02	681.27	23.94	699.48	699.73	24.66	717.95	718.19	25.38
662.82	663.06	23.23	681.28	681.53	23.95	699.74	699.99	24.67	718.20	718.45	25.39
663.07	663.32	23.24	681.54	681.78	23.96	700.00	700.24	24.68	718.46	718.71	25.40
663.33	663.58	23.25	681.79	682.04	23.97	700.25	700.50	24.69	718.72	718.96	25.41
663.59	663.83	23.26	682.05	682.29	23.98	700.51	700.76	24.70	718.97	719.22	25.42
663.84	664.09	23.27	682.30	682.55	23.99	700.77	701.01	24.71	719.23	719.47	25.43
664.10	664.35	23.28	682.56	682.81	24.00	701.02	701.27	24.72	719.48	719.73	25.44
664.36	664.60	23.29	682.82	683.06	24.01	701.28	701.53	24.73	719.74	719.99	25.45
664.61	664.86	23.30	683.07	683.32	24.02	701.54	701.78	24.74	720.00	720.24	25.46
664.87	665.12	23.31	683.33	683.58	24.03	701.79	702.04	24.75	720.25	720.50	25.47
665.13	665.37	23.32	683.59	683.83	24.04	702.05	702.29	24.76	720.51	720.76	25.48
665.38	665.63	23.33	683.84	684.09	24.05	702.30	702.55	24.77	720.77	721.01	25.49
665.64	665.88	23.34	684.10	684.35	24.06	702.56	702.81	24.78	721.02	721.27	25.50
665.89	666.14	23.35	684.36	684.60	24.07	702.82	703.06	24.79	721.28	721.53	25.51
666.15	666.40	23.36	684.61	684.86	24.08	703.07	703.32	24.80	721.54	721.78	25.52
666.41	666.65	23.37	684.87	685.12	24.09	703.33	703.58	24.81	721.79	722.04	25.53
666.66	666.91	23.38	685.13	685.37	24.10	703.59	703.83	24.82	722.05	722.29	25.54
666.92	667.17	23.39	685.38	685.63	24.11	703.84	704.09	24.83	722.30	722.55	25.55
667.18	667.42	23.40	685.64	685.88	24.12	704.10	704.35	24.84	722.56	722.81	25.56
667.43	667.68	23.41	685.89	686.14	24.13	704.36	704.60	24.85	722.82	723.06	25.57
667.69	667.94	23.42	686.15	686.40	24.14	704.61	704.86	24.86	723.07	723.32	25.58
667.95	668.19	23.43	686.41	686.65	24.15	704.87	705.12	24.87	723.33	733.32	25.78
668.20	668.45	23.44	686.66	686.91	24.16	705.13	705.37	24.88	733.33	743.32	26.17
668.46	668.71	23.45	686.92	687.17	24.17	705.38	705.63	24.89	743.33	753.32	26.56
668.72	668.96	23.46	687.18	687.42	24.18	705.64	705.88	24.90	753.33	763.32	26.95
668.97	669.22	23.47	687.43	687.68	24.19	705.89	706.14	24.91	763.33	773.32	27.34
669.23	669.47	23.48	687.69	687.94	24.20	706.15	706.40	24.92	773.33	783.32	27.73
669.48	669.73	23.49	687.95	688.19	24.21	706.41	706.65	24.93	783.33	793.32	28.12
669.74	669.99	23.50	688.20	688.45	24.22	706.66	706.91	24.94	793.33	803.32	28.51
670.00	670.24	23.51	688.46	688.71	24.23	706.92	707.17	24.95	803.33	813.32	28.90
670.25	670.50	23.52	688.72	688.96	24.24	707.18	707.42	24.96	813.33	823.32	29.29
670.51	670.76	23.53	688.97	689.22	24.25	707.43	707.68	24.97	823.33	833.32	29.68
670.77	671.01	23.54	689.23	689.47	24.26	707.69	707.94	24.98	833.33	843.32	30.07
671.02	671.27	23.55	689.48	689.73	24.27	707.95	708.19	24.99	843.33	853.32	30.46
671.28	671.53	23.56	689.74	689.99	24.28	708.20	708.45	25.00	853.33	863.32	30.85
671.54	671.78	23.57	690.00	690.24	24.29	708.46	708.71	25.01	863.33	873.32	31.24
671.79	672.04	23.58	690.25	690.50	24.30	708.72	708.96	25.02	873.33	883.32	31.63
672.05	672.29	23.59	690.51	690.76	24.31	708.97	709.22	25.03	883.33	893.32	32.02
672.30	672.55	23.60	690.77	691.01	24.32	709.23	709.47	25.04	893.33	903.32	32.41
672.56	672.81	23.61	691.02	691.27	24.33	709.48	709.73	25.05	903.33	913.32	32.80
672.82	673.06	23.62	691.28	691.53	24.34	709.74	709.99	25.06	913.33	923.32	33.19
673.07	673.32	23.63	691.54	691.78	24.35	710.00	710.24	25.07	923.33	933.32	33.58
673.33	673.58	23.64	691.79	692.04	24.36	710.25	710.50	25.08	933.33	943.32	33.97
673.59	673.83	23.65	692.05	692.29	24.37	710.51	710.76	25.09	943.33	953.32	34.36
673.84	674.09	23.66	692.30	692.55	24.38	710.77	711.01	25.10	953.33	963.32	34.75
674.10	674.35	23.67	692.56	692.81	24.39	711.02	711.27	25.11	963.33	973.32	35.14
674.36	674.60	23.68	692.82	693.06	24.40	711.28	711.53	25.12	973.33	983.32	35.53
674.61	674.86	23.69	693.07	693.32	24.41	711.54	711.78	25.13	983.33	993.32	35.92
674.87	675.12	23.70	693.33	693.58	24.42	711.79	712.04	25.14	993.33	1003.32	36.31
675.13	675.37	23.71	693.59	693.83	24.43	712.05	712.29	25.15	1003.33	1013.32	36.70
675.38	675.63	23.72	693.84	694.09	24.44	712.30	712.55	25.16	1013.33	1023.32	37.09
675.64	675.88	23.73	694.10	694.35	24.45	712.56	712.81	25.17	1023.33	1033.32	37.48
675.89	676.14	23.74	694.36	694.60	24.46	712.82	713.06	25.18	1033.33	1043.32	37.87
676.15	676.40	23.75	694.61	694.86	24.47	713.07	713.32	25.19	1043.33	1053.32	38.26

Employee's maximum CPP contribution for the year 2000 is $1329.90 La cotisation maximale de l'employé au RPC pour l'année 2000 est de 1329,90 $

Employment Insurance Premiums — Cotisations à l'assurance-emploi

Insurable Earnings Rémunération assurable From - De	To - À	EI premium Cotisation d'AE	Insurable Earnings Rémunération assurable From - De	To - À	EI premium Cotisation d'AE	Insurable Earnings Rémunération assurable From - De	To - À	EI premium Cotisation d'AE	Insurable Earnings Rémunération assurable From - De	To - À	EI premium Cotisation d'AE
480.21	480.62	11.53	510.21	510.62	12.25	540.21	540.62	12.97	570.21	570.62	13.69
480.63	481.04	11.54	510.63	511.04	12.26	540.63	541.04	12.98	570.63	571.04	13.70
481.05	481.45	11.55	511.05	511.45	12.27	541.05	541.45	12.99	571.05	571.45	13.71
481.46	481.87	11.56	511.46	511.87	12.28	541.46	541.87	13.00	571.46	571.87	13.72
481.88	482.29	11.57	511.88	512.29	12.29	541.88	542.29	13.01	571.88	572.29	13.73
482.30	482.70	11.58	512.30	512.70	12.30	542.30	542.70	13.02	572.30	572.70	13.74
482.71	483.12	11.59	512.71	513.12	12.31	542.71	543.12	13.03	572.71	573.12	13.75
483.13	483.54	11.60	513.13	513.54	12.32	543.13	543.54	13.04	573.13	573.54	13.76
483.55	483.95	11.61	513.55	513.95	12.33	543.55	543.95	13.05	573.55	573.95	13.77
483.96	484.37	11.62	513.96	514.37	12.34	543.96	544.37	13.06	573.96	574.37	13.78
484.38	484.79	11.63	514.38	514.79	12.35	544.38	544.79	13.07	574.38	574.79	13.79
484.80	485.20	11.64	514.80	515.20	12.36	544.80	545.20	13.08	574.80	575.20	13.80
485.21	485.62	11.65	515.21	515.62	12.37	545.21	545.62	13.09	575.21	575.62	13.81
485.63	486.04	11.66	515.63	516.04	12.38	545.63	546.04	13.10	575.63	576.04	13.82
486.05	486.45	11.67	516.05	516.45	12.39	546.05	546.45	13.11	576.05	576.45	13.83
486.46	486.87	11.68	516.46	516.87	12.40	546.46	546.87	13.12	576.46	576.87	13.84
486.88	487.29	11.69	516.88	517.29	12.41	546.88	547.29	13.13	576.88	577.29	13.85
487.30	487.70	11.70	517.30	517.70	12.42	547.30	547.70	13.14	577.30	577.70	13.86
487.71	488.12	11.71	517.71	518.12	12.43	547.71	548.12	13.15	577.71	578.12	13.87
488.13	488.54	11.72	518.13	518.54	12.44	548.13	548.54	13.16	578.13	578.54	13.88
488.55	488.95	11.73	518.55	518.95	12.45	548.55	548.95	13.17	578.55	578.95	13.89
488.96	489.37	11.74	518.96	519.37	12.46	548.96	549.37	13.18	578.96	579.37	13.90
489.38	489.79	11.75	519.38	519.79	12.47	549.38	549.79	13.19	579.38	579.79	13.91
489.80	490.20	11.76	519.80	520.20	12.48	549.80	550.20	13.20	579.80	580.20	13.92
490.21	490.62	11.77	520.21	520.62	12.49	550.21	550.62	13.21	580.21	580.62	13.93
490.63	491.04	11.78	520.63	521.04	12.50	550.63	551.04	13.22	580.63	581.04	13.94
491.05	491.45	11.79	521.05	521.45	12.51	551.05	551.45	13.23	581.05	581.45	13.95
491.46	491.87	11.80	521.46	521.87	12.52	551.46	551.87	13.24	581.46	581.87	13.96
491.88	492.29	11.81	521.88	522.29	12.53	551.88	552.29	13.25	581.88	582.29	13.97
492.30	492.70	11.82	522.30	522.70	12.54	552.30	552.70	13.26	582.30	582.70	13.98
492.71	493.12	11.83	522.71	523.12	12.55	552.71	553.12	13.27	582.71	583.12	13.99
493.13	493.54	11.84	523.13	523.54	12.56	553.13	553.54	13.28	583.13	583.54	14.00
493.55	493.95	11.85	523.55	523.95	12.57	553.55	553.95	13.29	583.55	583.95	14.01
493.96	494.37	11.86	523.96	524.37	12.58	553.96	554.37	13.30	583.96	584.37	14.02
494.38	494.79	11.87	524.38	524.79	12.59	554.38	554.79	13.31	584.38	584.79	14.03
494.80	495.20	11.88	524.80	525.20	12.60	554.80	555.20	13.32	584.80	585.20	14.04
495.21	495.62	11.89	525.21	525.62	12.61	555.21	555.62	13.33	585.21	585.62	14.05
495.63	496.04	11.90	525.63	526.04	12.62	555.63	556.04	13.34	585.63	586.04	14.06
496.05	496.45	11.91	526.05	526.45	12.63	556.05	556.45	13.35	586.05	586.45	14.07
496.46	496.87	11.92	526.46	526.87	12.64	556.46	556.87	13.36	586.46	586.87	14.08
496.88	497.29	11.93	526.88	527.29	12.65	556.88	557.29	13.37	586.88	587.29	14.09
497.30	497.70	11.94	527.30	527.70	12.66	557.30	557.70	13.38	587.30	587.70	14.10
497.71	498.12	11.95	527.71	528.12	12.67	557.71	558.12	13.39	587.71	588.12	14.11
498.13	498.54	11.96	528.13	528.54	12.68	558.13	558.54	13.40	588.13	588.54	14.12
498.55	498.95	11.97	528.55	528.95	12.69	558.55	558.95	13.41	588.55	588.95	14.13
498.96	499.37	11.98	528.96	529.37	12.70	558.96	559.37	13.42	588.96	589.37	14.14
499.38	499.79	11.99	529.38	529.79	12.71	559.38	559.79	13.43	589.38	589.79	14.15
499.80	500.20	12.00	529.80	530.20	12.72	559.80	560.20	13.44	589.80	590.20	14.16
500.21	500.62	12.01	530.21	530.62	12.73	560.21	560.62	13.45	590.21	590.62	14.17
500.63	501.04	12.02	530.63	531.04	12.74	560.63	561.04	13.46	590.63	591.04	14.18
501.05	501.45	12.03	531.05	531.45	12.75	561.05	561.45	13.47	591.05	591.45	14.19
501.46	501.87	12.04	531.46	531.87	12.76	561.46	561.87	13.48	591.46	591.87	14.20
501.88	502.29	12.05	531.88	532.29	12.77	561.88	562.29	13.49	591.88	592.29	14.21
502.30	502.70	12.06	532.30	532.70	12.78	562.30	562.70	13.50	592.30	592.70	14.22
502.71	503.12	12.07	532.71	533.12	12.79	562.71	563.12	13.51	592.71	593.12	14.23
503.13	503.54	12.08	533.13	533.54	12.80	563.13	563.54	13.52	593.13	593.54	14.24
503.55	503.95	12.09	533.55	533.95	12.81	563.55	563.95	13.53	593.55	593.95	14.25
503.96	504.37	12.10	533.96	534.37	12.82	563.96	564.37	13.54	593.96	594.37	14.26
504.38	504.79	12.11	534.38	534.79	12.83	564.38	564.79	13.55	594.38	594.79	14.27
504.80	505.20	12.12	534.80	535.20	12.84	564.80	565.20	13.56	594.80	595.20	14.28
505.21	505.62	12.13	535.21	535.62	12.85	565.21	565.62	13.57	595.21	595.62	14.29
505.63	506.04	12.14	535.63	536.04	12.86	565.63	566.04	13.58	595.63	596.04	14.30
506.05	506.45	12.15	536.05	536.45	12.87	566.05	566.45	13.59	596.05	596.45	14.31
506.46	506.87	12.16	536.46	536.87	12.88	566.46	566.87	13.60	596.46	596.87	14.32
506.88	507.29	12.17	536.88	537.29	12.89	566.88	567.29	13.61	596.88	597.29	14.33
507.30	507.70	12.18	537.30	537.70	12.90	567.30	567.70	13.62	597.30	597.70	14.34
507.71	508.12	12.19	537.71	538.12	12.91	567.71	568.12	13.63	597.71	598.12	14.35
508.13	508.54	12.20	538.13	538.54	12.92	568.13	568.54	13.64	598.13	598.54	14.36
508.55	508.95	12.21	538.55	538.95	12.93	568.55	568.95	13.65	598.55	598.95	14.37
508.96	509.37	12.22	538.96	539.37	12.94	568.96	569.37	13.66	598.96	599.37	14.38
509.38	509.79	12.23	539.38	539.79	12.95	569.38	569.79	13.67	599.38	599.79	14.39
509.80	510.20	12.24	539.80	540.20	12.96	569.80	570.20	13.68	599.80	600.20	14.40

Yearly maximum insurable earnings are $39,000
Yearly maximum employee premiums are $936

Le maximum annuel de la rémunération assurable est de 39 000 $
Le cotisation maximal annuelle de l'employé est de 936 $ C-5

FIGURE 12-7
EI Premium Table

Employment Insurance Premiums — Cotisations à l'assurance-emploi

Insurable Earnings / Rémunération assurable From - De	To - À	EI premium / Cotisation d'AE	Insurable Earnings / Rémunération assurable From - De	To - À	EI premium / Cotisation d'AE	Insurable Earnings / Rémunération assurable From - De	To - À	EI premium / Cotisation d'AE	Insurable Earnings / Rémunération assurable From - De	To - À	EI premium / Cotisation d'AE
600.21	600.62	14.41	630.21	630.62	15.13	660.21	660.62	15.85	690.21	690.62	16.57
600.63	601.04	14.42	630.63	631.04	15.14	660.63	661.04	15.86	690.63	691.04	16.58
601.05	601.45	14.43	631.05	631.45	15.15	661.05	661.45	15.87	691.05	691.45	16.59
601.46	601.87	14.44	631.46	631.87	15.16	661.46	661.87	15.88	691.46	691.87	16.60
601.88	602.29	14.45	631.88	632.29	15.17	661.88	662.29	15.89	691.88	692.29	16.61
602.30	602.70	14.46	632.30	632.70	15.18	662.30	662.70	15.90	692.30	692.70	16.62
602.71	603.12	14.47	632.71	633.12	15.19	662.71	663.12	15.91	692.71	693.12	16.63
603.13	603.54	14.48	633.13	633.54	15.20	663.13	663.54	15.92	693.13	693.54	16.64
603.55	603.95	14.49	633.55	633.95	15.21	663.55	663.95	15.93	693.55	693.95	16.65
603.96	604.37	14.50	633.96	634.37	15.22	663.96	664.37	15.94	693.96	694.37	16.66
604.38	604.79	14.51	634.38	634.79	15.23	664.38	664.79	15.95	694.38	694.79	16.67
604.80	605.20	14.52	634.80	635.20	15.24	664.80	665.20	15.96	694.80	695.20	16.68
605.21	605.62	14.53	635.21	635.62	15.25	665.21	665.62	15.97	695.21	695.62	16.69
605.63	606.04	14.54	635.63	636.04	15.26	665.63	666.04	15.98	695.63	696.04	16.70
606.05	606.45	14.55	636.05	636.45	15.27	666.05	666.45	15.99	696.05	696.45	16.71
606.46	606.87	14.56	636.46	636.87	15.28	666.46	666.87	16.00	696.46	696.87	16.72
606.88	607.29	14.57	636.88	637.29	15.29	666.88	667.29	16.01	696.88	697.29	16.73
607.30	607.70	14.58	637.30	637.70	15.30	667.30	667.70	16.02	697.30	697.70	16.74
607.71	608.12	14.59	637.71	638.12	15.31	667.71	668.12	16.03	697.71	698.12	16.75
608.13	608.54	14.60	638.13	638.54	15.32	668.13	668.54	16.04	698.13	698.54	16.76
608.55	608.95	14.61	638.55	638.95	15.33	668.55	668.95	16.05	698.55	698.95	16.77
608.96	609.37	14.62	638.96	639.37	15.34	668.96	669.37	16.06	698.96	699.37	16.78
609.38	609.79	14.63	639.38	639.79	15.35	669.38	669.79	16.07	699.38	699.79	16.79
609.80	610.20	14.64	639.80	640.20	15.36	669.80	670.20	16.08	699.80	700.20	16.80
610.21	610.62	14.65	640.21	640.62	15.37	670.21	670.62	16.09	700.21	700.62	16.81
610.63	611.04	14.66	640.63	641.04	15.38	670.63	671.04	16.10	700.63	701.04	16.82
611.05	611.45	14.67	641.05	641.45	15.39	671.05	671.45	16.11	701.05	701.45	16.83
611.46	611.87	14.68	641.46	641.87	15.40	671.46	671.87	16.12	701.46	701.87	16.84
611.88	612.29	14.69	641.88	642.29	15.41	671.88	672.29	16.13	701.88	702.29	16.85
612.30	612.70	14.70	642.30	642.70	15.42	672.30	672.70	16.14	702.30	702.70	16.86
612.71	613.12	14.71	642.71	643.12	15.43	672.71	673.12	16.15	702.71	703.12	16.87
613.13	613.54	14.72	643.13	643.54	15.44	673.13	673.54	16.16	703.13	703.54	16.88
613.55	613.95	14.73	643.55	643.95	15.45	673.55	673.95	16.17	703.55	703.95	16.89
613.96	614.37	14.74	643.96	644.37	15.46	673.96	674.37	16.18	703.96	704.37	16.90
614.38	614.79	14.75	644.38	644.79	15.47	674.38	674.79	16.19	704.38	704.79	16.91
614.80	615.20	14.76	644.80	645.20	15.48	674.80	675.20	16.20	704.80	705.20	16.92
615.21	615.62	14.77	645.21	645.62	15.49	675.21	675.62	16.21	705.21	705.62	16.93
615.63	616.04	14.78	645.63	646.04	15.50	675.63	676.04	16.22	705.63	706.04	16.94
616.05	616.45	14.79	646.05	646.45	15.51	676.05	676.45	16.23	706.05	706.45	16.95
616.46	616.87	14.80	646.46	646.87	15.52	676.46	676.87	16.24	706.46	706.87	16.96
616.88	617.29	14.81	646.88	647.29	15.53	676.88	677.29	16.25	706.88	707.29	16.97
617.30	617.70	14.82	647.30	647.70	15.54	677.30	677.70	16.26	707.30	707.70	16.98
617.71	618.12	14.83	647.71	648.12	15.55	677.71	678.12	16.27	707.71	708.12	16.99
618.13	618.54	14.84	648.13	648.54	15.56	678.13	678.54	16.28	708.13	708.54	17.00
618.55	618.95	14.85	648.55	648.95	15.57	678.55	678.95	16.29	708.55	708.95	17.01
618.96	619.37	14.86	648.96	649.37	15.58	678.96	679.37	16.30	708.96	709.37	17.02
619.38	619.79	14.87	649.38	649.79	15.59	679.38	679.79	16.31	709.38	709.79	17.03
619.80	620.20	14.88	649.80	650.20	15.60	679.80	680.20	16.32	709.80	710.20	17.04
620.21	620.62	14.89	650.21	650.62	15.61	680.21	680.62	16.33	710.21	710.62	17.05
620.63	621.04	14.90	650.63	651.04	15.62	680.63	681.04	16.34	710.63	711.04	17.06
621.05	621.45	14.91	651.05	651.45	15.63	681.05	681.45	16.35	711.05	711.45	17.07
621.46	621.87	14.92	651.46	651.87	15.64	681.46	681.87	16.36	711.46	711.87	17.08
621.88	622.29	14.93	651.88	652.29	15.65	681.88	682.29	16.37	711.88	712.29	17.09
622.30	622.70	14.94	652.30	652.70	15.66	682.30	682.70	16.38	712.30	712.70	17.10
622.71	623.12	14.95	652.71	653.12	15.67	682.71	683.12	16.39	712.71	713.12	17.11
623.13	623.54	14.96	653.13	653.54	15.68	683.13	683.54	16.40	713.13	713.54	17.12
623.55	623.95	14.97	653.55	653.95	15.69	683.55	683.95	16.41	713.55	713.95	17.13
623.96	624.37	14.98	653.96	654.37	15.70	683.96	684.37	16.42	713.96	714.37	17.14
624.38	624.79	14.99	654.38	654.79	15.71	684.38	684.79	16.43	714.38	714.79	17.15
624.80	625.20	15.00	654.80	655.20	15.72	684.80	685.20	16.44	714.80	715.20	17.16
625.21	625.62	15.01	655.21	655.62	15.73	685.21	685.62	16.45	715.21	715.62	17.17
625.63	626.04	15.02	655.63	656.04	15.74	685.63	686.04	16.46	715.63	716.04	17.18
626.05	626.45	15.03	656.05	656.45	15.75	686.05	686.45	16.47	716.05	716.45	17.19
626.46	626.87	15.04	656.46	656.87	15.76	686.46	686.87	16.48	716.46	716.87	17.20
626.88	627.29	15.05	656.88	657.29	15.77	686.88	687.29	16.49	716.88	717.29	17.21
627.30	627.70	15.06	657.30	657.70	15.78	687.30	687.70	16.50	717.30	717.70	17.22
627.71	628.12	15.07	657.71	658.12	15.79	687.71	688.12	16.51	717.71	718.12	17.23
628.13	628.54	15.08	658.13	658.54	15.80	688.13	688.54	16.52	718.13	718.54	17.24
628.55	628.95	15.09	658.55	658.95	15.81	688.55	688.95	16.53	718.55	718.95	17.25
628.96	629.37	15.10	658.96	659.37	15.82	688.96	689.37	16.54	718.96	719.37	17.26
629.38	629.79	15.11	659.38	659.79	15.83	689.38	689.79	16.55	719.38	719.79	17.27
629.80	630.20	15.12	659.80	660.20	15.84	689.80	690.20	16.56	719.80	720.20	17.28

Yearly maximum insurable earnings are $39,000 — Le maximum annuel de la rémunération assurable est de 39 000 $

C-6 Yearly maximum employee premiums are $936 — Le cotisation maximal annuelle de l'employé est de 936 $

Employment Insurance Premiums — Cotisations à l'assurance-emploi

Insurable Earnings / Rémunération assurable From - De	To - A	EI premium / Cotisation d'AE	Insurable Earnings / Rémunération assurable From - De	To - A	EI premium / Cotisation d'AE	Insurable Earnings / Rémunération assurable From - De	To - A	EI premium / Cotisation d'AE	Insurable Earnings / Rémunération assurable From - De	To - A	EI premium / Cotisation d'AE
720.21	720.62	17.29	750.21	750.62	18.01	780.21	780.62	18.73	810.21	810.62	19.45
720.63	721.04	17.30	750.63	751.04	18.02	780.63	781.04	18.74	810.63	811.04	19.46
721.05	721.45	17.31	751.05	751.45	18.03	781.05	781.45	18.75	811.05	811.45	19.47
721.46	721.87	17.32	751.46	751.87	18.04	781.46	781.87	18.76	811.46	811.87	19.48
721.88	722.29	17.33	751.88	752.29	18.05	781.88	782.29	18.77	811.88	812.29	19.49
722.30	722.70	17.34	752.30	752.70	18.06	782.30	782.70	18.78	812.30	812.70	19.50
722.71	723.12	17.35	752.71	753.12	18.07	782.71	783.12	18.79	812.71	813.12	19.51
723.13	723.54	17.36	753.13	753.54	18.08	783.13	783.54	18.80	813.13	813.54	19.52
723.55	723.95	17.37	753.55	753.95	18.09	783.55	783.95	18.81	813.55	813.95	19.53
723.96	724.37	17.38	753.96	754.37	18.10	783.96	784.37	18.82	813.96	814.37	19.54
724.38	724.79	17.39	754.38	754.79	18.11	784.38	784.79	18.83	814.38	814.79	19.55
724.80	725.20	17.40	754.80	755.20	18.12	784.80	785.20	18.84	814.80	815.20	19.56
725.21	725.62	17.41	755.21	755.62	18.13	785.21	785.62	18.85	815.21	815.62	19.57
725.63	726.04	17.42	755.63	756.04	18.14	785.63	786.04	18.86	815.63	816.04	19.58
726.05	726.45	17.43	756.05	756.45	18.15	786.05	786.45	18.87	816.05	816.45	19.59
726.46	726.87	17.44	756.46	756.87	18.16	786.46	786.87	18.88	816.46	816.87	19.60
726.88	727.29	17.45	756.88	757.29	18.17	786.88	787.29	18.89	816.88	817.29	19.61
727.30	727.70	17.46	757.30	757.70	18.18	787.30	787.70	18.90	817.30	817.70	19.62
727.71	728.12	17.47	757.71	758.12	18.19	787.71	788.12	18.91	817.71	818.12	19.63
728.13	728.54	17.48	758.13	758.54	18.20	788.13	788.54	18.92	818.13	818.54	19.64
728.55	728.95	17.49	758.55	758.95	18.21	788.55	788.95	18.93	818.55	818.95	19.65
728.96	729.37	17.50	758.96	759.37	18.22	788.96	789.37	18.94	818.96	819.37	19.66
729.38	729.79	17.51	759.38	759.79	18.23	789.38	789.79	18.95	819.38	819.79	19.67
729.80	730.20	17.52	759.80	760.20	18.24	789.80	790.20	18.96	819.80	820.20	19.68
730.21	730.62	17.53	760.21	760.62	18.25	790.21	790.62	18.97	820.21	820.62	19.69
730.63	731.04	17.54	760.63	761.04	18.26	790.63	791.04	18.98	820.63	821.04	19.70
731.05	731.45	17.55	761.05	761.45	18.27	791.05	791.45	18.99	821.05	821.45	19.71
731.46	731.87	17.56	761.46	761.87	18.28	791.46	791.87	19.00	821.46	821.87	19.72
731.88	732.29	17.57	761.88	762.29	18.29	791.88	792.29	19.01	821.88	822.29	19.73
732.30	732.70	17.58	762.30	762.70	18.30	792.30	792.70	19.02	822.30	822.70	19.74
732.71	733.12	17.59	762.71	763.12	18.31	792.71	793.12	19.03	822.71	823.12	19.75
733.13	733.54	17.60	763.13	763.54	18.32	793.13	793.54	19.04	823.13	823.54	19.76
733.55	733.95	17.61	763.55	763.95	18.33	793.55	793.95	19.05	823.55	823.95	19.77
733.96	734.37	17.62	763.96	764.37	18.34	793.96	794.37	19.06	823.96	824.37	19.78
734.38	734.79	17.63	764.38	764.79	18.35	794.38	794.79	19.07	824.38	824.79	19.79
734.80	735.20	17.64	764.80	765.20	18.36	794.80	795.20	19.08	824.80	825.20	19.80
735.21	735.62	17.65	765.21	765.62	18.37	795.21	795.62	19.09	825.21	825.62	19.81
735.63	736.04	17.66	765.63	766.04	18.38	795.63	796.04	19.10	825.63	826.04	19.82
736.05	736.45	17.67	766.05	766.45	18.39	796.05	796.45	19.11	826.05	826.45	19.83
736.46	736.87	17.68	766.46	766.87	18.40	796.46	796.87	19.12	826.46	826.87	19.84
736.88	737.29	17.69	766.88	767.29	18.41	796.88	797.29	19.13	826.88	827.29	19.85
737.30	737.70	17.70	767.30	767.70	18.42	797.30	797.70	19.14	827.30	827.70	19.86
737.71	738.12	17.71	767.71	768.12	18.43	797.71	798.12	19.15	827.71	828.12	19.87
738.13	738.54	17.72	768.13	768.54	18.44	798.13	798.54	19.16	828.13	828.54	19.88
738.55	738.95	17.73	768.55	768.95	18.45	798.55	798.95	19.17	828.55	828.95	19.89
738.96	739.37	17.74	768.96	769.37	18.46	798.96	799.37	19.18	828.96	829.37	19.90
739.38	739.79	17.75	769.38	769.79	18.47	799.38	799.79	19.19	829.38	829.79	19.91
739.80	740.20	17.76	769.80	770.20	18.48	799.80	800.20	19.20	829.80	830.20	19.92
740.21	740.62	17.77	770.21	770.62	18.49	800.21	800.62	19.21	830.21	830.62	19.93
740.63	741.04	17.78	770.63	771.04	18.50	800.63	801.04	19.22	830.63	831.04	19.94
741.05	741.45	17.79	771.05	771.45	18.51	801.05	801.45	19.23	831.05	831.45	19.95
741.46	741.87	17.80	771.46	771.87	18.52	801.46	801.87	19.24	831.46	831.87	19.96
741.88	742.29	17.81	771.88	772.29	18.53	801.88	802.29	19.25	831.88	832.29	19.97
742.30	742.70	17.82	772.30	772.70	18.54	802.30	802.70	19.26	832.30	832.70	19.98
742.71	743.12	17.83	772.71	773.12	18.55	802.71	803.12	19.27	832.71	833.12	19.99
743.13	743.54	17.84	773.13	773.54	18.56	803.13	803.54	19.28	833.13	833.54	20.00
743.55	743.95	17.85	773.55	773.95	18.57	803.55	803.95	19.29	833.55	833.95	20.01
743.96	744.37	17.86	773.96	774.37	18.58	803.96	804.37	19.30	833.96	834.37	20.02
744.38	744.79	17.87	774.38	774.79	18.59	804.38	804.79	19.31	834.38	834.79	20.03
744.80	745.20	17.88	774.80	775.20	18.60	804.80	805.20	19.32	834.80	835.20	20.04
745.21	745.62	17.89	775.21	775.62	18.61	805.21	805.62	19.33	835.21	835.62	20.05
745.63	746.04	17.90	775.63	776.04	18.62	805.63	806.04	19.34	835.63	836.04	20.06
746.05	746.45	17.91	776.05	776.45	18.63	806.05	806.45	19.35	836.05	836.45	20.07
746.46	746.87	17.92	776.46	776.87	18.64	806.46	806.87	19.36	836.46	836.87	20.08
746.88	747.29	17.93	776.88	777.29	18.65	806.88	807.29	19.37	836.88	837.29	20.09
747.30	747.70	17.94	777.30	777.70	18.66	807.30	807.70	19.38	837.30	837.70	20.10
747.71	748.12	17.95	777.71	778.12	18.67	807.71	808.12	19.39	837.71	838.12	20.11
748.13	748.54	17.96	778.13	778.54	18.68	808.13	808.54	19.40	838.13	838.54	20.12
748.55	748.95	17.97	778.55	778.95	18.69	808.55	808.95	19.41	838.55	838.95	20.13
748.96	749.37	17.98	778.96	779.37	18.70	808.96	809.37	19.42	838.96	839.37	20.14
749.38	749.79	17.99	779.38	779.79	18.71	809.38	809.79	19.43	839.38	839.79	20.15
749.80	750.20	18.00	779.80	780.20	18.72	809.80	810.20	19.44	839.80	840.20	20.16

Yearly maximum insurable earnings are $39,000 — Le maximum annuel de la rémunération assurable est de 39 000 $

Yearly maximum employee premiums are $936 — Le cotisation maximal annuelle de l'employé est de 936 $

C-7

Employment Insurance Premiums — Cotisations à l'assurance-emploi

Insurable Earnings / Rémunération assurable From - De	To - À	EI premium / Cotisation d'AE	Insurable Earnings / Rémunération assurable From - De	To - À	EI premium / Cotisation d'AE	Insurable Earnings / Rémunération assurable From - De	To - À	EI premium / Cotisation d'AE	Insurable Earnings / Rémunération assurable From - De	To - À	EI premium / Cotisation d'AE
840.21	840.62	20.17	870.21	870.62	20.89	900.21	900.62	21.61	930.21	930.62	22.33
840.63	841.04	20.18	870.63	871.04	20.90	900.63	901.04	21.62	930.63	931.04	22.34
841.05	841.45	20.19	871.05	871.45	20.91	901.05	901.45	21.63	931.05	931.45	22.35
841.46	841.87	20.20	871.46	871.87	20.92	901.46	901.87	21.64	931.46	931.87	22.36
841.88	842.29	20.21	871.88	872.29	20.93	901.88	902.29	21.65	931.88	932.29	22.37
842.30	842.70	20.22	872.30	872.70	20.94	902.30	902.70	21.66	932.30	932.70	22.38
842.71	843.12	20.23	872.71	873.12	20.95	902.71	903.12	21.67	932.71	933.12	22.39
843.13	843.54	20.24	873.13	873.54	20.96	903.13	903.54	21.68	933.13	933.54	22.40
843.55	843.95	20.25	873.55	873.95	20.97	903.55	903.95	21.69	933.55	933.95	22.41
843.96	844.37	20.26	873.96	874.37	20.98	903.96	904.37	21.70	933.96	934.37	22.42
844.38	844.79	20.27	874.38	874.79	20.99	904.38	904.79	21.71	934.38	934.79	22.43
844.80	845.20	20.28	874.80	875.20	21.00	904.80	905.20	21.72	934.80	935.20	22.44
845.21	845.62	20.29	875.21	875.62	21.01	905.21	905.62	21.73	935.21	935.62	22.45
845.63	846.04	20.30	875.63	876.04	21.02	905.63	906.04	21.74	935.63	936.04	22.46
846.05	846.45	20.31	876.05	876.45	21.03	906.05	906.45	21.75	936.05	936.45	22.47
846.46	846.87	20.32	876.46	876.87	21.04	906.46	906.87	21.76	936.46	936.87	22.48
846.88	847.29	20.33	876.88	877.29	21.05	906.88	907.29	21.77	936.88	937.29	22.49
847.30	847.70	20.34	877.30	877.70	21.06	907.30	907.70	21.78	937.30	937.70	22.50
847.71	848.12	20.35	877.71	878.12	21.07	907.71	908.12	21.79	937.71	938.12	22.51
848.13	848.54	20.36	878.13	878.54	21.08	908.13	908.54	21.80	938.13	938.54	22.52
848.55	848.95	20.37	878.55	878.95	21.09	908.55	908.95	21.81	938.55	938.95	22.53
848.96	849.37	20.38	878.96	879.37	21.10	908.96	909.37	21.82	938.96	939.37	22.54
849.38	849.79	20.39	879.38	879.79	21.11	909.38	909.79	21.83	939.38	939.79	22.55
849.80	850.20	20.40	879.80	880.20	21.12	909.80	910.20	21.84	939.80	940.20	22.56
850.21	850.62	20.41	880.21	880.62	21.13	910.21	910.62	21.85	940.21	940.62	22.57
850.63	851.04	20.42	880.63	881.04	21.14	910.63	911.04	21.86	940.63	941.04	22.58
851.05	851.45	20.43	881.05	881.45	21.15	911.05	911.45	21.87	941.05	941.45	22.59
851.46	851.87	20.44	881.46	881.87	21.16	911.46	911.87	21.88	941.46	941.87	22.60
851.88	852.29	20.45	881.88	882.29	21.17	911.88	912.29	21.89	941.88	942.29	22.61
852.30	852.70	20.46	882.30	882.70	21.18	912.30	912.70	21.90	942.30	942.70	22.62
852.71	853.12	20.47	882.71	883.12	21.19	912.71	913.12	21.91	942.71	943.12	22.63
853.13	853.54	20.48	883.13	883.54	21.20	913.13	913.54	21.92	943.13	943.54	22.64
853.55	853.95	20.49	883.55	883.95	21.21	913.55	913.95	21.93	943.55	943.95	22.65
853.96	854.37	20.50	883.96	884.37	21.22	913.96	914.37	21.94	943.96	944.37	22.66
854.38	854.79	20.51	884.38	884.79	21.23	914.38	914.79	21.95	944.38	944.79	22.67
854.80	855.20	20.52	884.80	885.20	21.24	914.80	915.20	21.96	944.80	945.20	22.68
855.21	855.62	20.53	885.21	885.62	21.25	915.21	915.62	21.97	945.21	945.62	22.69
855.63	856.04	20.54	885.63	886.04	21.26	915.63	916.04	21.98	945.63	946.04	22.70
856.05	856.45	20.55	886.05	886.45	21.27	916.05	916.45	21.99	946.05	946.45	22.71
856.46	856.87	20.56	886.46	886.87	21.28	916.46	916.87	22.00	946.46	946.87	22.72
856.88	857.29	20.57	886.88	887.29	21.29	916.88	917.29	22.01	946.88	947.29	22.73
857.30	857.70	20.58	887.30	887.70	21.30	917.30	917.70	22.02	947.30	947.70	22.74
857.71	858.12	20.59	887.71	888.12	21.31	917.71	918.12	22.03	947.71	948.12	22.75
858.13	858.54	20.60	888.13	888.54	21.32	918.13	918.54	22.04	948.13	948.54	22.76
858.55	858.95	20.61	888.55	888.95	21.33	918.55	918.95	22.05	948.55	948.95	22.77
858.96	859.37	20.62	888.96	889.37	21.34	918.96	919.37	22.06	948.96	949.37	22.78
859.38	859.79	20.63	889.38	889.79	21.35	919.38	919.79	22.07	949.38	949.79	22.79
859.80	860.20	20.64	889.80	890.20	21.36	919.80	920.20	22.08	949.80	950.20	22.80
860.21	860.62	20.65	890.21	890.62	21.37	920.21	920.62	22.09	950.21	950.62	22.81
860.63	861.04	20.66	890.63	891.04	21.38	920.63	921.04	22.10	950.63	951.04	22.82
861.05	861.45	20.67	891.05	891.45	21.39	921.05	921.45	22.11	951.05	951.45	22.83
861.46	861.87	20.68	891.46	891.87	21.40	921.46	921.87	22.12	951.46	951.87	22.84
861.88	862.29	20.69	891.88	892.29	21.41	921.88	922.29	22.13	951.88	952.29	22.85
862.30	862.70	20.70	892.30	892.70	21.42	922.30	922.70	22.14	952.30	952.70	22.86
862.71	863.12	20.71	892.71	893.12	21.43	922.71	923.12	22.15	952.71	953.12	22.87
863.13	863.54	20.72	893.13	893.54	21.44	923.13	923.54	22.16	953.13	953.54	22.88
863.55	863.95	20.73	893.55	893.95	21.45	923.55	923.95	22.17	953.55	953.95	22.89
863.96	864.37	20.74	893.96	894.37	21.46	923.96	924.37	22.18	953.96	954.37	22.90
864.38	864.79	20.75	894.38	894.79	21.47	924.38	924.79	22.19	954.38	954.79	22.91
864.80	865.20	20.76	894.80	895.20	21.48	924.80	925.20	22.20	954.80	955.20	22.92
865.21	865.62	20.77	895.21	895.62	21.49	925.21	925.62	22.21	955.21	955.62	22.93
865.63	866.04	20.78	895.63	896.04	21.50	925.63	926.04	22.22	955.63	956.04	22.94
866.05	866.45	20.79	896.05	896.45	21.51	926.05	926.45	22.23	956.05	956.45	22.95
866.46	866.87	20.80	896.46	896.87	21.52	926.46	926.87	22.24	956.46	956.87	22.96
866.88	867.29	20.81	896.88	897.29	21.53	926.88	927.29	22.25	956.88	957.29	22.97
867.30	867.70	20.82	897.30	897.70	21.54	927.30	927.70	22.26	957.30	957.70	22.98
867.71	868.12	20.83	897.71	898.12	21.55	927.71	928.12	22.27	957.71	958.12	22.99
868.13	868.54	20.84	898.13	898.54	21.56	928.13	928.54	22.28	958.13	958.54	23.00
868.55	868.95	20.85	898.55	898.95	21.57	928.55	928.95	22.29	958.55	958.95	23.01
868.96	869.37	20.86	898.96	899.37	21.58	928.96	929.37	22.30	958.96	959.37	23.02
869.38	869.79	20.87	899.38	899.79	21.59	929.38	929.79	22.31	959.38	959.79	23.03
869.80	870.20	20.88	899.80	900.20	21.60	929.80	930.20	22.32	959.80	960.20	23.04

Yearly maximum insurable earnings are $39,000 — Le maximum annuel de la rémunération assurable est de 39 000 $

Yearly maximum employee premiums are $936 — Le cotisation maximal annuelle de l'employé est de 936 $

FIGURE 12-8
Tax Deduction Table

Ontario — Ontario
Federal and Provincial Tax Deductions — **Retenues d'impôt fédéral et provincial**
Weekly (52 pay periods a year) — **Hebdomadaire (52 périodes de paie par année)**

Pay / Rémunération	If the employee's claim code from the TD1(E) form is / Si le code de demande de l'employé selon le formulaire TD1(F) est										
	0	1	2	3	4	5	6	7	8	9	10
From / De - Less than / Moins de		Deduct from each pay / Retenez sur chaque paie									
471. - 479.	105.40	73.10	69.55	62.40	55.20	48.05	40.90	33.75	26.55	18.65	9.50
479. - 487.	107.20	74.90	71.30	64.15	57.00	49.80	42.65	35.50	28.35	20.90	11.75
487. - 495.	108.95	76.65	73.05	65.90	58.75	51.60	44.45	37.25	30.10	22.95	14.00
495. - 503.	110.70	78.40	74.85	67.70	60.50	53.35	46.20	39.05	31.85	24.70	16.25
503. - 511.	112.45	80.20	76.60	69.45	62.30	55.10	47.95	40.80	33.65	26.45	18.50
511. - 519.	114.25	81.95	78.35	71.20	64.05	56.90	49.70	42.55	35.40	28.25	20.75
519. - 527.	116.00	83.70	80.15	72.95	65.80	58.65	51.50	44.30	37.15	30.00	22.85
527. - 535.	117.75	85.50	81.90	74.75	67.55	60.40	53.25	46.10	38.95	31.75	24.60
535. - 543.	119.55	87.25	83.65	76.50	69.35	62.15	55.00	47.85	40.70	33.55	26.35
543. - 551.	121.30	89.00	85.45	78.25	71.10	63.95	56.80	49.60	42.45	35.30	28.15
551. - 559.	123.05	90.75	87.20	80.05	72.85	65.70	58.55	51.40	44.20	37.05	29.90
559. - 567.	124.85	92.55	88.95	81.80	74.65	67.45	60.30	53.15	46.00	38.85	31.65
567. - 575.	126.85	94.55	90.95	83.80	76.65	69.50	62.30	55.15	48.00	40.85	33.65
575. - 583.	129.60	97.30	93.75	86.55	79.40	72.25	65.10	57.90	50.75	43.60	36.45
583. - 591.	132.35	100.05	96.50	89.35	82.15	75.00	67.85	60.70	53.50	46.35	39.20
591. - 599.	135.10	102.85	99.25	92.10	84.95	77.75	70.60	63.45	56.30	49.15	41.95
599. - 607.	137.90	105.60	102.00	94.85	87.70	80.55	73.35	66.20	59.05	51.90	44.70
607. - 615.	140.65	108.35	104.80	97.60	90.45	83.30	76.15	68.95	61.80	54.65	47.50
615. - 623.	143.40	111.10	107.55	100.40	93.20	86.05	78.90	71.75	64.55	57.40	50.25
623. - 631.	146.15	113.90	110.30	103.15	96.00	88.80	81.65	74.50	67.35	60.15	53.00
631. - 639.	148.95	116.65	113.05	105.90	98.75	91.60	84.40	77.25	70.10	62.95	55.75
639. - 647.	151.70	119.40	115.85	108.65	101.50	94.35	87.20	80.00	72.85	65.70	58.55
647. - 655.	154.45	122.15	118.60	111.45	104.25	97.10	89.95	82.80	75.60	68.45	61.30
655. - 663.	157.20	124.95	121.35	114.20	107.05	99.85	92.70	85.55	78.40	71.20	64.05
663. - 671.	160.00	127.70	124.10	116.95	109.80	102.65	95.45	88.30	81.15	74.00	66.80
671. - 679.	162.75	130.45	126.90	119.70	112.55	105.40	98.25	91.05	83.90	76.75	69.60
679. - 687.	165.50	133.20	129.65	122.50	115.30	108.15	101.00	93.85	86.65	79.50	72.35
687. - 695.	168.25	136.00	132.40	125.25	118.10	110.90	103.75	96.60	89.45	82.25	75.10
695. - 703.	171.05	138.75	135.15	128.00	120.85	113.65	106.50	99.35	92.20	85.05	77.85
703. - 711.	173.80	141.50	137.95	130.75	123.60	116.45	109.30	102.10	94.95	87.80	80.65
711. - 719.	176.55	144.25	140.70	133.55	126.35	119.20	112.05	104.90	97.70	90.55	83.40
719. - 727.	179.30	147.05	143.45	136.30	129.10	121.95	114.80	107.65	100.50	93.30	86.15
727. - 735.	182.15	149.85	146.30	139.10	131.95	124.80	117.65	110.50	103.30	96.15	89.00
735. - 743.	185.00	152.70	149.10	141.95	134.80	127.65	120.45	113.30	106.15	99.00	91.80
743. - 751.	187.80	155.55	151.95	144.80	137.65	130.45	123.30	116.15	109.00	101.85	94.65
751. - 759.	190.70	158.40	154.80	147.65	140.50	133.35	126.15	119.00	111.85	104.70	97.50
759. - 767.	193.55	161.30	157.70	150.55	143.35	136.20	129.05	121.90	114.75	107.55	100.40
767. - 775.	196.45	164.15	160.60	153.40	146.25	139.10	131.95	124.75	117.60	110.45	103.30
775. - 783.	199.35	167.05	163.45	156.30	149.15	141.95	134.80	127.65	120.50	113.35	106.15
783. - 791.	202.20	169.90	166.35	159.20	152.00	144.85	137.70	130.55	123.35	116.20	109.05
791. - 799.	205.10	172.80	169.20	162.05	154.90	147.75	140.60	133.40	126.25	119.10	111.95
799. - 807.	207.95	175.70	172.10	164.95	157.80	150.60	143.45	136.30	129.15	121.95	114.80
807. - 815.	210.85	178.55	175.00	167.80	160.65	153.50	146.35	139.20	132.00	124.85	117.70
815. - 823.	213.75	181.45	177.85	170.70	163.55	156.40	149.20	142.05	134.90	127.75	120.55
823. - 831.	216.60	184.35	180.75	173.60	166.40	159.25	152.10	144.95	137.80	130.60	123.45
831. - 839.	219.50	187.20	183.65	176.45	169.30	162.15	155.00	147.80	140.65	133.50	126.35
839. - 847.	222.40	190.10	186.50	179.35	172.20	165.00	157.85	150.70	143.55	136.40	129.20
847. - 855.	225.25	192.95	189.40	182.25	175.05	167.90	160.75	153.60	146.40	139.25	132.10
855. - 863.	228.15	195.85	192.25	185.10	177.95	170.80	163.60	156.45	149.30	142.15	134.95
863. - 871.	231.00	198.75	195.15	188.00	180.85	173.65	166.50	159.35	152.20	145.00	137.85
871. - 879.	233.90	201.60	198.05	190.85	183.70	176.55	169.40	162.20	155.05	147.90	140.75
879. - 887.	236.80	204.50	200.90	193.75	186.60	179.40	172.25	165.10	157.95	150.80	143.60
887. - 895.	239.65	207.35	203.80	196.65	189.45	182.30	175.15	168.00	160.80	153.65	146.50
895. - 903.	242.55	210.25	206.65	199.50	192.35	185.20	178.05	170.85	163.70	156.55	149.40
903. - 911.	245.40	213.15	209.55	202.40	195.25	188.05	180.90	173.75	166.60	159.40	152.25

This table is available on diskette (TOD). Vous pouvez obtenir cette table sur disquette (TSD). D-3

Employment Insurance Deduction

The same booklet contains a section on employment insurance. Figure 12-7 on pages 471 – 474 shows that the maximum EI premium deduction required on gross weekly earnings of $800 is $19.20. Notice, however, that maximum premium deduction for the year is $936.00. According to the table, Lostracco's EI contribution on a weekly salary of $800 is $19.20. Once the year-to-date deduction reaches $936.00, no more is deducted.

Income Tax Deduction

Lostracco's income tax deduction for the week is determined by referring again to the Payroll Deductions Tables and using the taxable earnings amount and the net claim code from the TD1 form. Figure 12-8 on page 475 shows that for taxable earnings of $800 and with a net claim code of 1, the income tax deduction is $175.70.

Taxable earnings are the earnings that remain after non-taxable deductions. Taxable earnings are used to determine the amount of income tax that will be deducted.

When an employee contributes to an RPP or pays union dues, the contribution reduces taxable earnings. To find the taxable earnings for employees who have these deductions, the calculation is:

Taxable Earnings = Gross Earnings – (Registered Pension Plan Contributions + Union Dues + Other Authorized Deductions [Alimony Payments, Living Away From Home Deductions, Child Care, etc.])

Would Lostracco's income tax deduction change if she had paid union dues or made an RPP contribution during the pay period? Yes, it would, since the income tax deduction is based on taxable earnings.

Example:

Gross Earnings	–	RPP	–	Union Dues	=	Taxable Earnings
$800	–	$50.00	–	$14.50	=	$735.50

Figure 12-8 shows the income tax deduction for taxable earnings of $735.50 at net claim code 1 is $152.70. Therefore Lostracco's tax deduction is reduced as a result of having approved income tax deductions.

Net Earnings

Lostracco's cheque, Figure 12-1, was for net earnings of $576.59. This figure was arrived at as follows:

Gross Earnings	–	Deductions	=	Net Earnings
$800	–	$223.41	=	$576.59

PAYROLL ACCOUNTING PROCEDURES

Lostracco is paid a salary of $800 for a work period of one week. There are several other pay periods used.

Pay Periods

Payrolls are prepared for different time periods such as:

- Weekly: Every week, or 52 times a year.
- Bi-weekly: Every two weeks, or 26 times a year.
- Monthly: Every month, or 12 times a year.
- Semi-monthly: Twice a month, or 24 times a year.

Payment Plans

A variety of payment plans are used by companies. Lostracco is paid on a salary basis.

Salary

The employee's earnings are a set amount for a stated period of time. The salary is an amount for a week, a month, or a year, for example, $1 000 a week, $4 250 a month, or $52 000 a year. A common practice is to hire on a yearly basis and then to pay the worker according to one of the pay periods described above.

Hourly Rate

In this plan, workers are paid an hourly rate for each hour worked. An employee working at the rate of $12 an hour who works 40 hours a week would earn $480 (before deductions).

Commission

Sales personnel are often paid on a commission basis. Their earnings are determined by the amount of sales they make. The gross earnings for a person who gets a 4-percent commission and has sales of $15 000 are $600 ($15 000 × 0.04 = $600).

Combination of Salary and Commission

It is more common to see a combination of a set minimum salary plus a commission on sales. An employee might receive a base salary of $300 a week plus a 2-percent commission on sales. If the week's sales are $10 000, the employee receives a total of $600 ($300 + 0.02 × $15 000 = $600).

Piece Rate

Manufacturing companies often use the piece rate method. To provide an incentive to workers, payment is based on the number of units the worker produces. If an employee is paid $1.75 per unit and completes 350 units, the earnings are $612.50.

Overtime

Provincial laws require that extra pay be given after a certain number of hours have been worked in a week. For example, if 40 hours were the maximum number of hours at regular pay, an employee who worked more than that would receive extra pay for the time worked over 40 hours.

Suppose a person earns $9/h for the first 40 hours worked each week, plus time and one-half for overtime. The overtime hours are paid at the rate of $13.50/h, the regular rate of $9 plus one-half, $4.50, which totals $13.50. If the person works 48 hours in the week, a total of $468 would be earned. The earnings are calculated as follows:

$ 9.00	×	40	=	$360.00
13.50	×	8	=	108.00
				$468.00

Overtime regulations are set by the provincial governments and by agreements between the employer and the employees.

REVIEW QUESTIONS UNIT 30

1. What does the word "payroll" mean?
2. List three federal laws that affect payroll accounting procedures.
3. (a) What are the two parts of Lostracco's cheque in Figure 12-1?
   (b) What is the purpose of the pay statement?
4. What are the compulsory deductions in your province?
5. List five voluntary deductions.
6. (a) Who must contribute to the Canada Pension Plan?
   (b) What percentage of gross earnings must be contributed by employees?
   (c) If all the employees of a company together made CPP contributions of $436.70 in the week, what must the company also contribute?
7. (a) Who must pay employment insurance premiums?
   (b) If all of the employees of a company together paid EI premiums of $313.25, what is the amount of the premium paid by the company?
8. (a) What is a TD1 form?
   (b) Explain why Lostracco's net claim code is 1.
   (c) What is a non-refundable tax credit?
9. (a) What are the gross earnings?
   (b) What are the net earnings?
   (c) What are the deductions?
   (d) What is Lostracco's take-home pay?
   (e) For which deductions must the employers also make a contribution? How much is the contribution of the employer?
10. What purpose is served by the SIN?
11. Describe five commonly used pay periods.

12. Describe four of the six payment methods.

13. What benefits or services are provided by the following:
    (a) Provincial health insurance
    (b) Extended health insurance
    (c) Canada Pension Plan
    (d) Employment insurance
    (e) Group life insurance
    (f) Credit unions
    (g) Registered pension plans

Note: Where necessary, use either current payroll deduction booklets or the tables given on pages 468–475 to complete the exercises in this chapter.

PROBLEMS: APPLICATIONS

1. (a) Calculate each week's gross earnings for Agnes Davis, a salesperson who earns a 5-percent commission on weekly sales.

WEEK	SALES
1	$10 152.60
2	13 420.33
3	12 366.29
4	14 986.50

   (b) Calculate the total sales and commission for the four weeks.

2. What are Nancy Koosman's gross earnings if she receives a 3.5-percent commission and had sales of $24 230 during the week?

3. Motoko Haslam is paid a basic salary of $280 plus 2.5-percent commission on sales. The sales made for four weeks are shown below:

WEEK	SALES
1	$23 570
2	25 450
3	29 610
4	19 375

   (a) Calculate gross earnings for each week.
   (b) Calculate total earnings for the month.
   (c) If Motoko had received a straight commission of 5 percent of sales, what would the month's commission be?
   (d) Which method would you prefer — salary and commission or commission only? Why?

4. Ulla Eckhardt works for a firm producing electronic components. She is paid according to the number of components she assembles. Calculate Eckhardt's gross earnings for each day of the week if she is paid $1.74 for each assembly.

Day	No. of Components
Monday	70
Tuesday	74
Wednesday	81
Thursday	87
Friday	75

5. Determine the gross earnings for each of the following employees:

Name	Hourly Rate	Hours
C. Giamberardino	$13.20	40
C. Murphy	9.60	39
D. Kimura	15.25	40
R. Trites	14.75	38

6. If each employee in exercise 5 works four hours of overtime in addition to the regular hours, and is paid time and one-half for each hour of overtime, what are the gross earnings for each?

7. Charmaine Hooper, a welder, is paid on a piece-rate basis. She receives $3.95 for each sheet metal part produced. What are her earnings for each day and for the week?

Day	Number Produced
Monday	42
Tuesday	57
Wednesday	65
Thursday	51
Friday	47

8. Lois Belincki is paid at the rate of $7.50/h and time and one-half for overtime. Any work over eight hours in one day is considered overtime. Calculate her week's gross earnings if she worked the following hours:

Day	Hours
Monday	8.00
Tuesday	7.50
Wednesday	10.00
Thursday	7.75
Friday	8.00

9. During the month of July, Veronica Drepko's gross earnings were as follows:

Week	Gross Earnings
1	$687.50
2	703.27
3	671.45
4	684.92

Calculate the CPP and EI premium for the month of July.

10. (a) Charles Mazer contributes $22 per week to the company pension plan and $10 per week to union dues. Calculate his taxable earnings in July if his gross earnings for the four weeks were as follows:

Week	Gross Earnings
1	$690.25
2	715.80
3	739.45
4	710.75

(b) Mazer's net claim code for income tax deduction purposes is 6. Calculate the income tax deduction for each week in July.
(c) Calculate the CPP and EI premiums that Mazer pays each week.
(d) As well as the deductions that you have calculated in parts (a), (b), and (c), Mazer also has the following weekly deductions: group life insurance for $30 000 at a premium of 15¢ per $1 000. In the fourth week, he chose to buy a Canada Savings Bond at $50 per week. Calculate his total deductions and his net earnings for the four weeks.

11. Grace Trumball contributes $11.25 per week to her company's pension plan. She also has the following weekly deductions: group life insurance for $25 000 at a cost of 17¢ per $1 000; union dues $6.75. Her net claim code for tax purposes is 1. Her gross earnings in March were as follows:

Week	Gross Earnings
1	$730.40
2	792.80
3	761.50
4	728.62

(a) Calculate the taxable earnings and income tax payable.
(b) Calculate the CPP contributions and the EI premium.
(c) Calculate net earnings.

12. Use the TD1 form shown in Figures 12.2, 12-3, 12-4, and 12-5 to determine the net claim code for each of the following:

(a) Richard Rancourt has one dependent, 21 years old. The dependent attends college for eight months of the year, earns $6 000 per year, and pays tuition fees of $2 400.
(b) Gerald Ouellette has a dependent spouse who earns no income.
(c) Pat Brophy is a university student for eight months of the year and pays tuition of $4 050. This year Pat receives a scholarship for $1 250.
(d) B. Falconer is 66 years old, has a dependent spouse, and receives a $21 000 pension.

13. Refer to exercise 12. Use this year's TD1 form to determine the net claim code for each person.

UNIT 31 Payroll Records and Journal Entries

Learning Objectives

After reading this unit, discussing the applicable review questions and completing the applications exercises, you will be able to do the following:

1. **COMPLETE** and **PROVE** the accuracy of a Payroll Journal.
2. **EXPLAIN** the purpose of the employee's earnings record.
3. **PREPARE** the four basic types of payroll entries in the General Journal.
4. **DESCRIBE** the process of remitting payroll deductions to the federal government.
5. **DEFINE** Payroll Journal, T4, employee's earnings record, Employer Health Tax, and workers' compensation.

IMPLEMENTING PAYROLL PROCEDURES

Various forms and procedures are used for payroll. We will begin this unit by examining them.

Using the Payroll Journal

In order to determine the amount to be paid to employees (net earnings), a number of calculations are necessary. The deductions of each employee must be listed, totalled, and subtracted from gross earnings. These calculations are performed on an accounting form called a *Payroll Journal,* which is sometimes called a Payroll Register.

A Payroll Journal is the form used to record gross earnings, deductions, and net earnings for all of a firm's workers.

A Payroll Journal records the payroll details for employees for each pay period. It shows the gross earnings, deductions, and net earnings. It is a form that helps the payroll accountant to organize the calculation of the payroll. An example is shown in Figure 12-9 on page 483. Notice in Figure 12-9 how the totals of the Payroll Journal are balanced as a form of mathematical proof of accuracy. Two separate proofs are prepared to avoid errors:

(1) Gross Earnings − Total Deductions = Net Earnings

(2) Gross Earnings − Individual Deduction Totals = Net Earnings

Using the Employee's Earnings Record

On or before April 30 each year, Canadians must file their income tax returns with the federal government. In order to complete an income tax return, an employee must know how much he or she earned and the amounts of payroll deductions withheld by the employer throughout the year. To provide this information, the federal government requires all employers to give their employees a Statement of Remuneration Paid form, commonly called a *T4 slip.* The employer must provide the T4 slip to all employees by February 28. An example is shown in Figure 12-10 on page 486.

A T4 slip provides an employee with the total earnings and deductions for the year.

FIGURE 12-9
Completed Payroll Journal

COMPANY NAME WESTERN SYSTEMS

PAY PERIOD ENDING MAY 7, 2001

PAYROLL JOURNAL

PAGE

EMPL. NO.	NAME OF EMPLOYEE	NET CLAIM CODE	GROSS EARNINGS	NON-TAXABLES		TAXABLE EARNINGS	OTHER DEDUCTIONS					TOTAL DEDUC-TIONS	NET EARNINGS
				RPP*	UNION DUES		INCOME TAX	CPP	EI	HEALTH INS.	GROUP INS.		
1617	Barlow, J.	7	900 00			900 00	170.85	32.41	21.60			224.86	675.14
1618	Campbell, K.	2	750 00			750 00	151.95	26.56	18.00			196.51	553.49
1619	Campbell, R.	1	600 00			600 00	105.60	20.78	14.40			140.78	459.22
1620	Lostracco, M.	1	800 00			800 00	175.70	28.51	19.20			223.41	576.59
1621	Palmer, R.	7	550 00			550 00	49.60	18.83	13.20			81.63	468.37
1622	Smyth, P.	8	800 00			800 00	129.15	28.51	19.20			176.86	623.14
			4400 00			4400 00	782.85	155.60	105.60			1044.05	3355.95

* The term Registered Pension Plan (RPP) identifies deductions payable to a pension plan provided by the employer.

Proof 1

Gross Earnings	$	4400.00
Less: Total Deductions		1044.05
Net Earnings	$	3355.95

Proof 2

Gross Earnings	$		$ 4400.00
Less: CPP		155.60	
EI		105.60	
Income Tax		782.85	1044.05
Net Earnings			$ 3355.95

An employee's earnings record is a record of all of the payroll information for an employee for one year.

The T4 slip in Figure 12-10 shows the employee's gross earnings and all deductions that will affect the personal income tax calculations. In order to prepare the T4 slip, an employer must keep cumulative totals of the employee's earnings and deductions. The totals are kept on a form called an *employee's earnings record.*

The employee's earnings record provides all of the information required for the preparation of the T4 slip. Figure 12-11 on page 487 shows the earnings record for M. Lostracco. Notice which figures are transferred from this form to the T4 slip in Figure 12-10.

At the present time, every worker in Canada is required to pay 3.9 percent of contributory earnings, to a maximum of $1 329.90 yearly, to the Canada Pension Plan. Many employees will have paid their total year's premium of $1 329.90 before the end of the year. For this reason, a special column is used on the earnings record to accumulate the CPP premiums. When the total reaches $1 329.90 for the year, the employee will no longer have the CPP deduction made. At the year's end, the earnings record is totalled and balanced. Similarly, EI contributions have a maximum of $936.00. When the EI maximum is reached, there are no further deductions.

Paying Employees

Generally, employers use one of three methods to pay employees:

(1) Cash
(2) Cheque
(3) Bank, credit union, or trust company deposit.

Paying by Cash

Although this method is not preferred by employers, it is sometimes necessary to pay by cash because of agreements with employees or in remote areas where banks are not readily available.

Paying by Cheque

Many companies prefer to pay by cheque. To simplify the end-of-month bank reconciliations, a separate payroll bank account is opened at the bank. Each month, a cheque is written on the regular account. The amount of this cheque is exactly the total required to pay all of the employees. This cheque is deposited in the special payroll bank account. The entry to record this cheque is:

May 28	Salaries Payable	30 000	
	Cash		30 000
	To transfer funds to the payroll bank account for the Mar. 28 payroll.		

Next, cheques are issued to each employee. These cheques have the pay statements attached and are usually identified as payroll cheques by the words "payroll account" printed on the cheque face. When workers cash their cheques, the bank will cash them from the company's special payroll account. If all of the workers cash their cheques, the special payroll account balance will be reduced to zero.

Paying by Deposit

Many companies and employees prefer the deposit method. In this case, a bank provides a payroll service to companies. The employer gives the bank a list of employees, showing the amount earned by each. In return for a fee, the bank pays the employees by depositing the money in their accounts in various banks, credit unions, or trust companies.

The deposit method frees the employer from having to prepare pay cheques or having to handle cash when paying employees. Employees like this system because money is placed directly in their accounts. No matter which method is used, provincial labour laws require that each employee receive a statement (like the one shown at the beginning of the chapter in Figure 12-1) outlining gross earnings, deductions, and net pay. Why do you think this law was passed?

Remitting Deductions

Once a month, the employer must remit the deductions taken from the employee's wages and salaries to the proper agencies. Income tax, CPP, and EI deductions must be sent to the Receiver General for Canada by the 15th of the following month. Canada Customs and Revenue Agency supplies companies with the official remittance form, PD7AR, which is used to send deductions to Canada Customs and Revenue Agency. Other deductions, such as union dues and life insurance premiums, etc., must also be remitted to the appropriate agencies.

RECORDING THE PAYROLL

Up to this point, we have described the procedures for determining and keeping track of the earnings and deductions for employees. Now, we will examine the recording of the payroll information in the accounting system.

Payroll involves expenses, liabilities, and payment of funds. Therefore, journal entries must be made to record these items so that the accounts and financial statements will be accurate. There are four basic types of payroll entries in the General Journal:

- **Step 1:** Make an entry to record the Salaries Expense and the payroll liabilities for each pay period. The figures for this entry are taken from the Payroll Journal.
- **Step 2:** Make an entry to record the payment to workers for each pay period.
- **Step 3:** Make entries to record the employer's share of CPP and EI premiums for each pay period.
- **Step 4:** Make entries to remit the payroll deductions to the government and other agencies. These entries are made once a month.

All of these entries will now be examined.

FIGURE 12-10

Statement of remuneration paid (T4)

Revenue Canada / Revenu Canada

T4

STATEMENT OF REMUNERATION PAID
ÉTAT DE LA RÉMUNÉRATION PAYÉE

For departmental use / Réservé au Ministère: 001735

Employer's name – Nom de l'employeur	WESTERN SYSTEMS
Year / Année	2001
VOID / ANNULÉ	
14 Employment income / Revenus d'emploi	41600.00
22 Income tax deducted / Impôt sur le revenu retenu	9136.40
54 Business Number / Numéro d'entreprise	131157070RP001
10 Province of employment / Province d'emploi	
16 Employee's CPP contributions / Cotisations de l'employé au RPC	1329.90
24 EI insurable earnings / Gains assurables d'AE	39000.00
12 Social insurance number / Numéro d'assurance sociale	452638529
28 Exempt – Exemption: CPP/QPP (RPC/RRQ), EI (AE)	
29 Employment Code / Code d'emploi	
17 Employee's QPP contributions / Cotisations de l'employé au RRQ	
26 CPP/QPP pensionable earnings / Gains donnant droit à pension - RPC/RRQ	34100.00
18 Employee's EI premiums / Cotisations de l'employé à l'AE	936.00
44 Union dues / Cotisations syndicales	
20 RPP contributions / Cotisations à un RPA	
46 Charitable donations / Dons de bienfaisance	
52 Pension adjustment / Facteur d'équivalence	
50 RPP or DPSP registration number / N° d'agrément d'un RPA ou d'un RPDB	

Employee's name and address – Nom et adresse de l'employé

Surname – Nom de famille	LOSTRACCO
First name – Prénom	MARY
Initial – Initiale	H
Address – Adresse	19 QUEEN'S QUAY, VANCOUVER
Postal code – Code postal	V5K 6A4

Other Information (see the back) / Autres renseignements (voir au verso)

Box / Case | Amount / Montant | Box / Case | Amount / Montant

Box / Case | Amount / Montant | Box / Case | Amount / Montant | Box / Case | Amount / Montant | Box / Case | Amount / Montant

T4 (98) 3769

Revenue Canada / Revenu Canada

T4

STATEMENT OF REMUNERATION PAID
ÉTAT DE LA RÉMUNÉRATION PAYÉE

For departmental use / Réservé au Ministère: 001735

Employer's name – Nom de l'employeur	
Year / Année	
VOID / ANNULÉ	
14 Employment income / Revenus d'emploi	
22 Income tax deducted / Impôt sur le revenu retenu	
54 Business Number / Numéro d'entreprise	
10 Province of employment / Province d'emploi	
16 Employee's CPP contributions / Cotisations de l'employé au RPC	
24 EI insurable earnings / Gains assurables d'AE	
12 Social insurance number / Numéro d'assurance sociale	
28 Exempt – Exemption: CPP/QPP (RPC/RRQ), EI (AE)	
29 Employment Code / Code d'emploi	
17 Employee's QPP contributions / Cotisations de l'employé au RRQ	
26 CPP/QPP pensionable earnings / Gains donnant droit à pension - RPC/RRQ	
18 Employee's EI premiums / Cotisations de l'employé à l'AE	
44 Union dues / Cotisations syndicales	
20 RPP contributions / Cotisations à un RPA	
46 Charitable donations / Dons de bienfaisance	
52 Pension adjustment / Facteur d'équivalence	
50 RPP or DPSP registration number / N° d'agrément d'un RPA ou d'un RPDB	

Employee's name and address – Nom et adresse de l'employé

Surname – Nom de famille

First name – Prénom | Initial – Initiale

Address – Adresse

Postal code – Code postal

Other Information (see the back) / Autres renseignements (voir au verso)

Box / Case | Amount / Montant | Box / Case | Amount / Montant

Box / Case | Amount / Montant | Box / Case | Amount / Montant | Box / Case | Amount / Montant | Box / Case | Amount / Montant

T4 (98) 3769

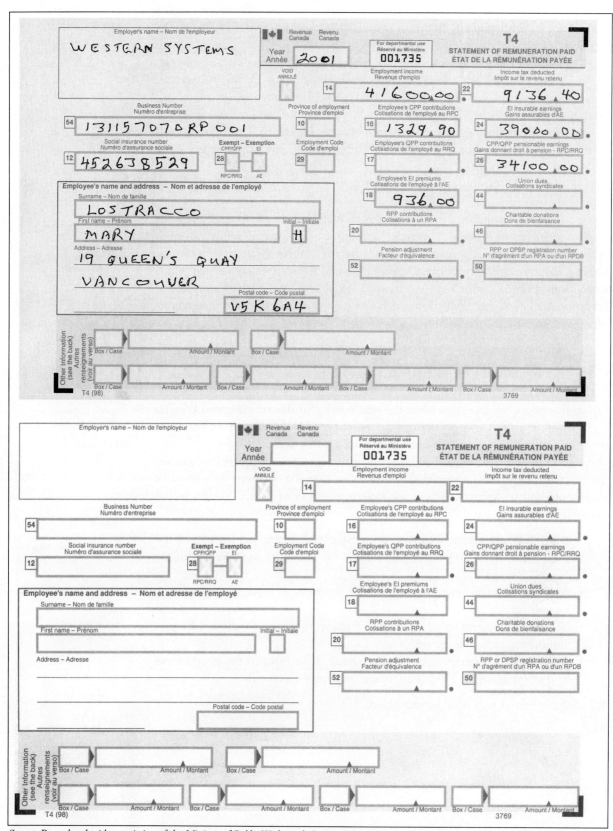

Source: Reproduced with permission of the Minister of Public Works and Government Services.

FIGURE 12-11
Employee's earnings record

EMPLOYEE EARNINGS RECORD FOR THE YEAR 2001

NAME Lostracco, M.	DEPARTMENT Info. Tech.	DATE EMPLOYED 06/01/96
ADDRESS 19 Queen's Quay	POSITION Supervisor	DATE TERMINATED
Vancouver, B.C. V5K 6A4	SOCIAL INS. NO. 452-638-529	NO. OF DEPENDANTS 0
TELEPHONE 825-6621	SALARY $800/week	NET CLAIM CODE 1

EMP. NO.	REGULAR OVERTIME	GROSS EARNINGS	DEDUCTIONS					TOTAL DEDUCTIONS	NET EARNINGS	TOTAL EI TO DATE	CH. NO.	PAY PERIOD ENDING
			CPP	EI	INC. TAX	GR. INS.	OTHER					
1620	19 200.00	19 200.00	684.24	460.80	4 216.80			5 361.84	13 838.16	460.80		Jan.-Jun.
	800.00	800.00	28.51	19.20	175.70			223.41	576.59	480.00		Jul. 5
	800.00	800.00	28.51	19.20	175.70			223.41	576.59	499.20		12
	800.00	800.00	28.51	19.20	175.70			223.41	576.59	518.40		19
	800.00	800.00	28.51	19.20	175.70			223.41	576.59	537.60		26
	800.00	800.00	28.51	19.20	175.70			223.41	576.59	556.80		Aug. 2

Step 1: Record the Salaries Expense and Payroll Liabilities

The first entry involves recording the total Salaries Expense and the amounts owed to the employees, government, and other agencies, such as insurance companies.

The figures for the entry come from the Payroll Journal, Figure 12-9 on page 483:

May 7	Salaries Expense	4 400.00	
	CPP Payable		155.60
	EI Payable		105.60
	Income Tax Payable		782.85
	Salaries Payable		3 355.95
	To record the May 7 payroll.		

This first entry records the deductions held back from the employees and recorded as liabilities on the books of the employer. As you will see, these amounts must be paid out once a month, and until they are paid are debts owed by the employer. The first entry also records the figures for a liability account called *Salaries Payable.* This is the amount owed to the workers and is a liability until the workers are paid.

Step 2: Record the Payment to Employees

The second entry is made when the employees are paid. In the previous entry, a credit was entered in the Salaries Payable account to record the liability to the employees. When the employees are paid, this liability is cancelled:

May 7	Salaries Payable	3 355.95	
	Cash		3 355.95
	Payment of May 7 payroll.		

Step 3: Record the Employer's Payroll Expenses

As you learned earlier, the employer is required to contribute to the Canada Pension Plan and to the employment insurance fund on behalf of employees. *For CPP, the employer must contribute an amount equal to that contributed by employees. For EI, the employer's contribution is 1.4 times the employee premiums.*

In the case of Western Systems (Figure 12-9), the employees' CPP contribution is $155.60; therefore, the employer's contribution is $155.60. The employees' EI contribution is $105.60; therefore, the employer's EI contribution is $147.84 (1.4 × $105.60).

The company records its contribution to CPP in an expense account called CPP Expense. This account is debited for the employer's contribution to CPP. The company's contribution to EI is debited to an expense account called EI Expense. The entries for Western Systems are as follows:

May 7	CPP Expense	155.60	
	CPP Payable		155.60
	To record the employer's contribution to CPP.		
7	EI Expense	147.84	
	EI Payable		147.84
	To record the employer's contribution to EI.		

Employer Health Tax

In Ontario, all employers must pay an Employer Health Tax (EHT) calculated at a graduated tax rate on total gross payroll. This tax replaces employee contributions to provincial health care plans.

Employer Health Tax Rates

The rate of EHT is determined by the total annual gross earnings of employees during the year. The chart in Figure 12-12 shows the earnings categories and applicable rates:

FIGURE 12-12
Employer Health Tax rates

Tax Rates

APPLICATION The amount of tax payable is a percentage of the total annual remuneration paid by employers during a calendar year. The tax is calculated by multiplying the total amount of remuneration paid in a year by the tax rate applicable to that amount of remuneration.

The tax rate on total remuneration is graduated, ranging from 0.98% to 1.95%, with the highest rate applying in those cases where total annual remuneration paid by the employer exceeds $400 000.

RATES Ranges of remuneration and applicable tax rates are outlined below:

TOTAL ONTARIO ANNUAL REMUNERATION	RATE
up to and including $200 000	0.98%
$200 001, up to and including $230 000	1.101%
$230 001, up to and including $260 000	1.223%
$260 001, up to and including $290 000	1.344%
$290 001, up to and including $320 000	1.465%
$320 001, up to and including $350 000	1.586%
$350 001, up to and including $380 000	1.708%
$380 001, up to and including $400 000	1.829%
over $400 000	1.95%

Quebec calculates EHT on the basis of a flat rate of 3.45 percent of the gross payroll amount, while the Manitoba EHT is based on the following schedule:

Gross Payroll	Rate
Less than $600 000	0%
$600 000 – $1 200 000	4.5%
Over $1 200 000	2.25%

Employer Health Tax Calculation

Employer Health Tax is calculated by multiplying the appropriate rate found in the chart on the previous page by the total gross earnings for the period. Western Systems' gross earnings can be found on the Payroll Journal (Figure 12-9). The gross earnings are \$4 400 per week. Western Systems has an annual payroll between \$200 001 and \$230 000 (\$4 400 × 52 weeks = \$228 800). Can you find the appropriate EHT rate in the chart in Figure 12-12? Western Systems' rate is 1.101 percent. Therefore, the Employer Health Tax owing is \$4 400 × 0.01101 = \$48.44 for this pay period. The following entry is made to record the EHT for the pay period.

May 7	Employer Health Tax Expense	48.44	
	Employer Health Tax Payable		48.44
	To record EHT for May 7 payroll.		

The entries just described to record and pay the payroll and to record the employer's payroll expenses are made each pay period and posted to the General Ledger. The partial ledger in Figure 12-13 on page 491 shows the entries in the accounts relating to payroll after four pay periods have been posted in May. Notice that CPP Payable and EI Payable include entries for both the employees' and employer's contributions.

Step 4: Record the Payment of Payroll Deductions

Once a month, the employer's contributions and deductions withheld from employees are forwarded to the appropriate agencies. The payment is recorded with the entries illustrated below. The entries are made on the 15th of the following month and record the remittance of the deductions for all the pay periods of the previous month. The amounts are obtained from the ledger accounts shown in Figure 12-13.

The first entry shown records the payment of money to the federal government. The amounts include both the employee and employer contributions to CPP and EI and the employees' income tax deductions:

June 15	CPP Payable	1 244.80	
	EI Payable	1 013.76	
	Income Tax Payable	3 131.40	
	Cash		5 389.96
	To record the payment of the May payroll deductions to the Receiver General.		

The next entry shown records the payment to the Provincial Treasurer for the Employer Health Tax when remittance is made monthly.

June 15	Employer Health Tax Payable	193.76	
	Cash		193.76
	To record the payment of Employer Health Tax to the Provincial Treasurer.		

Other payroll liabilities are also paid once a month. Similar entries are made for union dues, life insurance, health care plans in provinces that require employee contributions, and other payroll liabilities, if applicable.

Figure 12-14, on the next page, illustrates the ledger accounts after the June 15 entries have been posted. The debts owed to the federal and provincial governments have been paid, and these liability accounts are reduced to zero.

FIGURE 12-13
Partial General Ledger showing the May payroll entries recorded in the payroll accounts

PARTIAL GENERAL LEDGER

Cash					101
May	1	30 000.00	May	7	3 355.95
				14	3 355.95
				21	3 355.95
				28	3 355.95

Employee Health Tax Payable					223
			May	7	48.44
				14	48.44
				21	48.44
				28	48.44
					193.76

CPP Payable					220
			May	7	155.60
				7	155.60
				14	155.60
				14	155.60
				21	155.60
				21	155.60
				28	155.60
				28	155.60
					1 244.80

Salaries Payable					224
May	7	3 355.95	May	7	3 355.95
	14	3 355.95		14	3 355.95
	21	3 355.95		21	3 355.95
	28	3 355.95		28	3 355.95
		13 423.80			13 423.80

Salaries Expense					620
May	7	4 400.00			
	14	4 400.00			
	21	4 400.00			
	28	4 400.00			
		17 600.00			

EI Payable					221
			May	7	105.60
				7	147.84
				14	105.60
				14	147.84
				21	105.60
				21	147.84
				28	105.60
				28	147.84
				28	1 013.76

CPP Expense					621
May	7	155.60			
	14	155.60			
	21	155.60			
	28	155.60			
		622.40			

EI Expense					622
May	7	147.84			
	14	147.84			
	21	147.84			
	28	147.84			
		591.36			

Income Tax Payable					222
			May	7	782.85
				14	782.85
				21	782.85
				28	782.85
					3 131.40

Employer's Health Tax Expense					623
May	7	48.44			
	14	48.44			
	21	48.44			
	28	48.44			
		193.76			

FIGURE 12-14

Partial General Ledger after the June 15 entries have been posted

PARTIAL GENERAL LEDGER

Cash — 101

Date	Debit	Date	Credit
May 1	30 000.00	May 7	3 355.95
		14	3 355.95
		21	3 355.95
		28	3 355.95
		June 15	5 389.96
		15	193.76

Employer's Health Tax Payable — 223

Date	Debit	Date	Credit
June 15	193.76	May 7	48.44
		14	48.44
		21	48.44
		28	48.44
	193.76		193.76

CPP Payable — 220

Date	Debit	Date	Credit
June 15	1 244.80	May 7	155.60
		7	155.60
		14	155.60
		14	155.60
		21	155.60
		21	155.60
		28	155.60
		28	155.60
	1 244.80		1 244.80

Salaries Payable — 224

Date	Debit	Date	Credit
May 7	3 355.95	May 7	3 355.95
14	3 355.95	14	3 355.95
21	3 355.95	21	3 355.95
28	3 355.95	28	3 355.95
	13 423.80		13 423.80

Salaries Expense — 620

Date	Debit	Date	Credit
May 7	4 400.00		
14	4 400.00		
21	4 400.00		
28	4 400.00		
	17 600.00		

EI Payable — 221

Date	Debit	Date	Credit
June 15	1 013.76	May 7	105.60
		7	147.84
		14	105.60
		14	147.84
		21	105.60
		21	147.84
		28	105.60
		28	147.84
	1 013.76	28	1 013.76

CPP Expense — 621

Date	Debit	Date	Credit
May 7	155.60		
14	155.60		
21	155.60		
28	155.60		
	622.40		

EI Expense — 622

Date	Debit	Date	Credit
May 7	147.84		
14	147.84		
21	147.84		
28	147.84		
	591.36		

Income Tax Payable — 222

Date	Debit	Date	Credit
June 15	3 131.40	May 7	782.85
		14	782.85
		21	782.85
		28	782.85
	3 131.40		3 131.40

Employer's Health Tax Expense — 623

Date	Debit	Date	Credit
May 7	48.44		
14	48.44		
21	48.44		
28	48.44		
	193.76		

SOME CONCLUDING POINTS ABOUT PAYROLL

Workers' Compensation

All provinces provide an insurance plan for the protection of workers who suffer personal injuries or occupational diseases related to their jobs. Compensation is paid to injured workers from a fund administered by a provincial Workers' Compensation Board. Employers supply the money for the fund. The amount paid by an employer varies according to the type of business and its accident record.

In return for providing money to the fund, the employer is relieved of liability for injuries suffered by workers. The amount of compensation received by an injured worker is based on the average salary earned while working. The employer's payment to the fund is an expense of operating the business. When premiums are paid, this entry is made:

Jun. 30	Workers' Compensation Expense	150	
	Cash		150
	To pay semi-annual premium to Workers' Compensation Board.		

Payroll Ledger Accounts

Payroll accounting involves a number of expense accounts. For example, Wages Expense is the account used for earnings of hourly rated workers. Salaries Expense is used for the earnings of salaried employees.

Several expense accounts are used to record employers' contributions required by various laws. These include CPP Expense, EI Expense, and Workers' Compensation Expense. Rather than use these individual accounts, some companies prefer to use one account called Payroll Expense. This account is used for all employer payments such as the employer's share of CPP, EI, EHT, and other insurances. A sample entry using the Payroll Expense account follows:

Jun. 30	Payroll Expense	369	
	CPP Payable		85
	EI Payable		99
	Workers' Compensation Payable		50
	Group Insurance Payable		45
	Employer Health Tax Payable		90
	To record the employer's payroll expenses.		

FIGURE 12-15
Summary of payroll procedures

SUMMARY OF PROCEDURES

Figure 12-15 illustrates the payroll accounting procedures covered in this chapter.

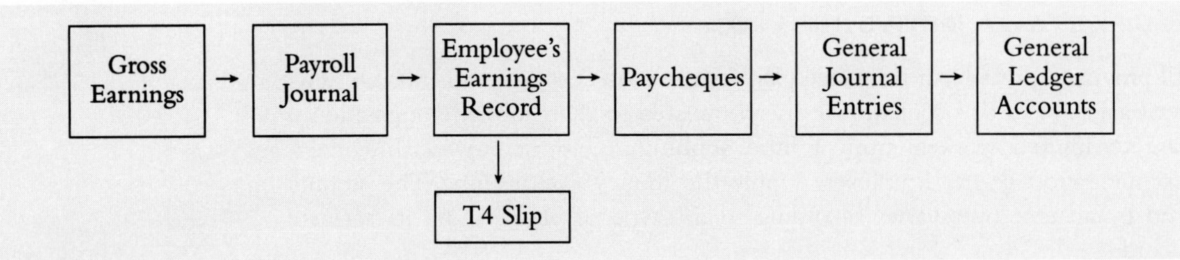

ACCOUNTING TERMS

Canada Pension Plan All employees over 18 and under 71 contribute a percentage of their earnings during their working years and receive a pension at age 65.

Compulsory Deductions Personal income tax, Employment Insurance, and Canada Pension Plan contributions are deductions required by law.

Deductions Employer Health Tax Items deducted from an employee's pay. A graduated health tax, payable by Ontario employers, which is based on total gross payroll.

Employment Insurance Employees contribute a percentage of their earnings while employed to a fund that is designed to provide income to those workers who later become unemployed.

Employment Standards Act Provincial laws governing the paying of employees.

Health Insurance Each province has its own version of health insurance plans and all citizens are covered for basic health services that they require.

Net Earnings Gross earnings minus deductions.

Payroll A list of employees and the amount of pay earned.

Payroll Journal Records gross earnings, deductions, and net earnings for each employee for all pay periods.

Personal Income Tax A percentage of personal income remitted to the federal and provincial governments.

TD1 A form completed annually by employees to determine personal tax credits.

T4 A statement of remuneration provided yearly to employees showing gross earnings and deductions that offset personal income tax calculations.

Tax Credit Credits for items such as dependent children, CPP and EI contributions, and tuition reduce the amount of federal income tax payable.

Taxable Income Income earned minus allowable deductions such as pension contributions.

Workers' Compensation An insurance plan provided by provinces for the protection of workers injured on the job.

1. Explain how a Payroll Journal is proven to be mathematically correct.
2. Pat has just completed a Payroll Journal and the totals balance; yet there is an error in the journal. How can this happen?
3. When must the employer remit payroll deductions to the federal government?
4. Which payroll deductions are remitted to the federal government?
5. To whom is the cheque made payable when deductions are remitted to the government?
6. What form is completed when remitting to the federal government?
7. What is the purpose of the employee's earnings record?
8. Describe the four basic types of payroll entries in the General Journal.
9. (a) What insurance compensates workers injured on the job?
   (b) Who pays the premiums for this insurance?
10. What single expense account may be used instead of CPP Expense, EI Expense, and Workers' Compensation Expense?
11. How is Ontario's Employer Health Tax calculated?

Note: Where necessary, use either current payroll deduction booklets or the tables given previously on pages 468–475 to complete the exercises in this chapter.

14. D. Houston Ltd. has six employees on the salary payroll.

(a) Record the following information in a Payroll Journal.

EMP. NO.	NAME	NET CLAIM CODE	GROSS EARNINGS	CO. PENSION
103	Jaswinder Singh	8	$780.00	$19.50
104	Bill Strahan	1	740.00	19.50
105	Linda Lo	10	660.00	19.50
106	Lesley Durvan	4	710.00	19.50
107	Stan Trudeau	9	660.00	19.50
108	Tracey St. James	1	660.00	19.50

(b) Determine the taxable earnings and the income tax deduction for each employee.
(c) Determine the CPP and EI deductions for each employee.
(d) Calculate the net earnings for each employee.
(e) Balance the Payroll Journal.

15. The payroll information for Maingot Manufacturers for the week ended March 24 is shown on the following page. Every employee also pays union dues of $7.25 weekly and has $30 000 worth of group life insurance for which 12¢ per $1 000 is contributed weekly.

(a) Record the payroll in a Payroll Journal, determining the CPP contributions, EI premiums, and income tax deductions.
(b) Total and prove the Payroll Journal.

EMP. NO.	NAME	NET CLAIM CODE	GROSS EARNINGS
101	P. Dagenais	4	$660.00
102	L. Rasmussen	8	680.00
103	C. Hayashi	1	780.00
104	T. Chan	6	660.00
105	F. Brammel	9	710.00
106	C. Lazzari	3	740.00

16. The payroll information for Western Distributors for the week ended August 18 follows:

EMP. NO.	NAME	NET CLAIM CODE	GROSS EARNINGS	CO. PENSION
201	T. Fong	1	$665.75	$2.13
202	A. Hjelt	9	681.91	2.34
203	A. Covington	6	707.34	2.59
204	C. Amato	1	723.70	2.64
205	P. Surat	4	692.41	2.41
206	S. Betterworth	7	673.56	2.27

Every employee also pays union dues of $9 weekly and has $35 000 worth of group life insurance for which 15¢ per $1 000 is contributed weekly.

(a) Record the payroll in a Payroll Journal; determine CPP, EI, and income tax.
(b) Total and prove the Payroll Journal.

17. The Payroll Journal for the pay period ended September 22 showed the following totals: gross earnings $5 783.20; CPP contributions, $104.09; EI premiums, $62.70; federal income tax, $983.14; health insurance, $132; union dues, $142.50; net earnings, $4 358.77. Prepare journal entries to record:

(a) The payroll
(b) The paying of the employees
(c) The employer's share of the CPP contributions and EI premiums.

18. The Payroll Journal for the pay period ended July 21 showed the following totals: gross earnings, $46 793.55; CPP contributions, $842.28; EI premiums, $495; registered pension plan, $1 544.19; income tax, $7 954.90; union dues, $1 325.25; group insurance, $797.53; net earnings, $33 834.40. The Employer Health Tax is $912.47. Prepare journal entries on page 10 to record:

(a) The payroll
(b) The paying of the employees
(c) The employer's share of the CPP contributions and EI premiums and Employer Health Tax.

19. Refer to the completed Payroll Journal for exercise 14, D. Houston Ltd.

(a) Prepare the journal entry on page 8 to record the payroll on May 24.
(b) Prepare the entry to pay the employees.
(c) Prepare the entry to record the company's share of CPP and EI.
(d) Prepare the entry to record the EHT of $46.35

20. Presented below are selected data from the August 15 payroll register for Darwin and Goodall Manufacturers. Some amounts have been intentionally omitted.

Gross earnings	$22 412
Deductions	
CPP	578
EI	637
Income Tax	(a)
Group Insurance	265
Registered Pension Plan	706
Total Deductions	(b)
Net Pay	15 483
Accounts debited	
Office Salaries	11 875
Shop Wages	(c)

(a) Calculate the missing amounts.
(b) Calculate the company's share of CPP and EI.
(c) Prepare the journal entry to record the payroll.
(d) Prepare the journal entry to record the company's share of CPP and EI.
(e) Prepare the journal entry to pay the employees on August 22.

1. Delmonte Manufacturing pays its salaried employees once a month. The Payroll Journal at the end of June for these employees is shown on the following page. Prepare journal entries on page 27 to record:

   (a) The payroll at the end of June
   (b) The employer's share of the CPP contributions and the EI premiums
   (c) The cheques to pay the employees
   (d) The remittance to Clarica for group insurance
   (e) The remittance to Clarica for the pension
   (f) The remittance to the Provincial Treasurer for the Employer Health Tax if the rate is 1.344 percent.

2. Refer to the completed Payroll Journal for exercise 16, Western Distributors.

   (a) Prepare the journal entry to record the payroll.
   (b) Prepare the entry to pay the employees.
   (c) Prepare the entry to record the company's share of CPP and EI.

COMPANY NAME DELMONTE MANUFACTURING **PAYROLL JOURNAL** **PAGE 307**

PAY PERIOD ENDING JUNE 30, 2000

EMPL. NO.	NAME OF EMPLOYEE	NET CLAIM CODE	GROSS EARNINGS	NON-TAXABLES		TAXABLE EARNINGS	OTHER DEDUCTIONS					TOTAL DEDUC-TIONS	NET EARNINGS
				RPP*	UNION DUES		INCOME TAX	CPP	EI	HEALTH INS.	GROUP INS.		
65	O'Connell, P.	9	4 025.00	125.69		3 899.31	678.10	145.74	96.60		33.61	1 079.74	2 945.26
66	Dooner, C.	1	2 875.00	77.20		2 797.80	524.55	100.75	69.00		22.93	794.43	2 080.57
67	Greenspoon, L.	3	3 115.00	110.58		3 004.42	548.45	110.11	74.76		31.50	875.40	2 239.60
68	Ritcher, F.	10	3 897.00	118.72		3 778.28	610.35	140.67	93.53		35.90	999.17	2 897.83
69	Lapchinski, C.	6	4 250.00	136.70		4 113.30	842.85	154.32	102.00		29.88	1 265.75	2 984.25
70	Karklins, A.	4	4 250.00	136.70		4 113.30	904.95	154.32	102.00		29.88	1 327.85	2 922.15
			22 412.00	705.59		21 706.41	4 109.25	805.91	537.89		183.70	6 342.34	16 069.66

* The term *Registered Pension Plan* (RPP) identifies deductions payable to a pension plan provided by the employer.

Proof 1

Gross Earnings	$	22 412.00
Less: Total Deductions		6 342.34
Net Earnings	$	16 069.66

Proof 2

Gross Earnings	$		$ 22 412.00
Less: RPP		705.59	
Income Tax		4 109.25	
CPP		805.91	
EI		537.89	
Group Insurance		183.70	6 342.34
Net Earnings			$16 069.66

INTEGRATIVE ACTIVITY 4

PAYROLL ACCOUNTING

Claymore Industries

INTRODUCTION

In this activity, you will perform the duties of a payroll accountant employed by Claymore Industries and responsible for hourly rated workers. You will complete the payroll for four weeks in February and then journalize and post the entries to record the payroll. Payroll information and time cards for employees follow.

Payroll Information

Every employee pays weekly group insurance premiums of 20¢ per $1 000. Other information is given in the following table:

Emp. No.	Name	Net Claim Code	Co. Pension	Union Dues	Group Ins.
101	T.A. Means	2	$3.70	$5.50	$35 000.00
102	S.M. Tompkins	9	1.78	5.50	45 000.00
103	R.P. Lynch	6	1.80	5.50	60 000.00
104	E.A. Erdman	1	1.78	5.50	30 000.00

Time Cards for the Week of February 6, 2001 for Three Employees

NO. 101 — **Pay Period Ending Feb. 6, 2001**
NAME T. A. Means
Regular Hours — **Regular Rate** $13.80
Overtime Hours — **Overtime Rate** 20.70
Total Earnings

	MORN	NOON	NOON	NIGHT	EXTRA		
	IN	OUT	IN	OUT	IN	OUT	HOURS
M	07:58	12:01	13:00	17:00			
T	08:00	12:01	13:00	17:00	18:00	21:00	
W	07:56	12:04	13:00	17:01			
T	07:59	12:03	12:55	17:01			
F	07:58	12:02	12:56	17:02			
S							
S							

NO. 102 — **Pay Period Ending Feb. 6, 2001**
NAME S. M. Tompkins
Regular Hours — **Regular Rate** $14.50
Overtime Hours — **Overtime Rate** 21.75
Total Earnings

	MORN	NOON	NOON	NIGHT	EXTRA		
	IN	OUT	IN	OUT	IN	OUT	HOURS
M	07:59	12:01	12:59	17:01			
T	07:58	12:02	12:58	17:00	18:00	21:00	
W	08:02	12:01	13:02	17:02			
T	08:03	12:03	13:05	17:03			
F	07:59	12:01	13:00	17:05			
S							
S							

NO. 103
NAME R. P. Lynch
Regular Hours
Overtime Hours

Pay Period Ending Feb. 6, 2001

Regular Rate $14.20
Overtime Rate 21.30
Total Earnings

	MORN	NOON	NOON	NIGHT	EXTRA		
	IN	OUT	IN	OUT	IN	OUT	HOURS
M			12:50	17:01			
T	07:59	12:00	12:51	17:02			
W	07:58	12:01	12:57	17:00	17:59	21:02	
T	07:57	12:04	12:55	17:05			
F	07:56	12:05	12:50	17:04			
S							
S							

Payroll Rules

In calculating the hours worked, the following rules apply:

- Any time worked on Saturday or Sunday is paid at time and one-half.
- Any time worked after 5:00 p.m. is overtime and is paid at time and one-half. Overtime is recorded in the extra (in, out) columns of the time cards.
- Regular hours of work are 8:00 a.m. to 12:00 noon and 1:00 p.m. to 5:00 p.m. Employees lose 15 minutes' pay if they are between 2 and 15 minutes late, and 30 minutes' pay if they are between 16 and 30 minutes late.

NO. 104
NAME E. A. Erdman
Regular Hours 35.75
Overtime Hours 3.0

Pay Period Ending Feb. 6, 2001

Regular Rate $14.20
Overtime Rate 21.30
Total Earnings

	MORN	NOON	NOON	NIGHT	EXTRA		
	IN	OUT	IN	OUT	IN	OUT	HOURS
M			12:52	17:02			4.0
T	08:00	12:00	13:04	17:02			7.75
W	07:55	12:02	13:00	17:01			8.0
T	07:58	12:01	12:59	17:00	18:00	21:01	8.0/3.0
F	07:58	12:02	12:59	17:01			8.0
S					Regular		35.75
S					O.T.		3.0

Part A

1. (a) Complete the time cards and calculate the gross earnings. The time card for E.A. Erdman is done as an example.
   (b) Complete the February 6 payroll in the Payroll Journal.
   (c) Total and prove the Payroll Journal.

2. Prepare General Journal entries to record:

   (a) The payroll
   (b) The employer's share of CPP contributions, EI premiums, and EHT if the rate is 1.223 percent
   (c) The transfer of funds to the employees' bank accounts.

3. Post the General Journal entries to the General Ledger. (You may use T-accounts.) The accounts required are:

101	Cash (Balance $15 000)	216	Group Insurance Payable
210	Wages Payable	217	Union Dues Payable
211	CPP Payable	610	Wages Expense
212	EI Payable	611	CPP Expense
213	EHT Payable	612	EI Expense
214	Income Tax Payable	613	EHT Expense
215	RPP Payable		

4. For the week ended February 13, the gross earnings for the four employees are:

101	T.A. Means	$625.80
102	S.M. Tompkins	642.50
103	R.P. Lynch	593.60
104	E.A. Erdman	563.25

   (a) Complete the Payroll Journal for the week.
   (b) Total and prove the Payroll Journal.
   (c) Prepare General Journal entries to record:

      (i) The payroll
      (ii) The employer's share of CPP contributions, EI premiums, and EHT.
      (iii) Post the General Journal entries.

5. For the week ended February 20, the gross earnings for the four employees are:

101	T.A. Means	$618.40
102	S.M. Tompkins	656.50
103	R.P. Lynch	580.90
104	E.A. Erdman	578.30

   (a) Complete the Payroll Journal for the week.
   (b) Total and prove the Payroll Journal.
   (c) Prepare General Journal entries to record:

      (i) The payroll
      (ii) The employer's share of CPP contributions, EI premiums, and EHT
      (iii) The transfer of funds to the employees' bank accounts.

   (d) Post the General Journal entries.

6. For the week ended February 27, the gross earnings for the four employees are:

101	T.A. Means	$645.50
102	S.M. Tompkins	650.10
103	R.P. Lynch	610.60
104	E.A. Erdman	587.40

(a) Complete the Payroll Journal for the week.
(b) Total and prove the Payroll Journal.
(c) Prepare General Journal entries to record:

(i) The payroll
(ii) The employer's share of CPP contributions, EI premiums, and EHT
(iii) The transfer of funds to the employees' bank accounts

(d) Post the General Journal entries.

7. (a) Prepare the journal entries which would be made on March 15 to remit the February payroll deductions.
(b) Post these entries to the General Ledger and total the accounts.

Part B — Optional — Computer Accounting

Complete Payroll Journals for the weeks ended February 6 and February 13 using a computer.

Part C — Optional — Report

Prepare a written comparison of the two systems used in this project (manual and computer. Include the advantages and disadvantages of each system.

CHAPTER 13

Accounting for Partnerships and Corporations

UNIT 32 Accounting for Partnerships

Learning Objectives

After reading this unit, discussing the applicable review questions, and completing the applications exercises, you will be able to do the following:

1. **EXPLAIN** the difference between a sole proprietorship, a partnership, and a corporation.
2. **DISCUSS** the major advantages and disadvantages of each form of business organization.
3. **PREPARE** the accounting entries required to form and operate a partnership.
4. **CALCULATE** each partner's share of net income or net loss based on a variety of acceptable apportionment methods.
5. **PREPARE** closing entries for a partnership.
6. **PREPARE** financial statements for a partnership.

TYPES OF BUSINESS OWNERSHIP

In the first part of this book, most of the accounting theory involved businesses owned by one person. For example, Chapter 4 described the journal and ledger system used by K. Martin, the owner of Martin Painting Contractors. A business owned by one person is known as a *sole proprietorship.* Two other types of ownership are the partnership and the corporation.

A sole proprietorship is a business owned by one person.

SOLE PROPRIETORSHIP

The owner of a *sole proprietorship* is legally responsible for all its debts and legal obligations. Many small businesses are sole proprietorships. These include small stores, restaurants, and many service businesses such as barbershops, TV repair firms, and hairstylists.

Advantages of Proprietorships

- pride of ownership
- ease of formation and dissolution
- freedom of action
- privacy
- simplified decision making
- owner receives all the net income
- personal satisfaction
- possible tax savings

In a sole proprietorship, the proprietor has unlimited personal liability for the debts and legal obligations of the business.

Disadvantages of Proprietorships

- unlimited personal liability
- limited capital
- heavy personal responsibilities
- lack of continuity
- limited talent

Taxation and the Proprietorship

A proprietorship does not pay income tax on its net income. The owner must add the net income of the business to his or her own income and then pay personal income tax on the total. There can be a tax advantage with this form of ownership when the combined net income is quite low. However, when net income becomes fairly high, there may be a tax advantage in switching to a corporate form of ownership. This is explained in detail in Unit 33.

PARTNERSHIPS

Two or more persons may find it worthwhile to combine their talents and money to form a *partnership.* Doctors, lawyers, dentists, and small retail and service businesses are frequently owned by partners. Some of the characteristics of the partnership are exactly like those of the proprietorship except when related to transactions that directly affect the partners' equities. Because ownership rights in a partnership are divided between two or more partners, there must be a capital and withdrawals account for each partner and a division of earnings. The net income or net loss belongs to the owners, and they have *unlimited personal liability* for the debts of the business. This means there is no ceiling on the liability of a partner; thus, his or her personal property can legally be taken, if necessary, to pay these debts. The net income becomes the personal income of the individual partners for income tax purposes.

A partnership is a business owned by two or more persons.

In a partnership, the partners have unlimited personal liability for the debts and legal obligations of the business.

Advantages of Partnerships

- two or more persons are available to share the work load
- varied skills will be brought to a partnership
- access to more capital (i.e., personal savings or increased borrowing capacity)

Disadvantages of Partnerships

- debts of the business fall to both partners
- unlimited personal liability
- personality conflicts
- limited life — death of a partner immediately dissolves the partnership

CORPORATIONS

A corporation is a business owned by three or more persons and has a legal existence of its own.

Unlike a sole proprietorship or a partnership, a *corporation* has a legal existence of its own and may have many owners. However, the owners are not personally responsible for the debts and obligations of the corporation. In the partnership and proprietorship, the owners have unlimited personal liability for the business and risk the loss of their own personal assets. The owners of a corporation do not risk their personal assets but only their direct investment in the corporation. For this reason, the term *limited company* is sometimes used to describe the corporate form of ownership.

A *limited partnership* could be formed for those individuals who want to invest but are unwilling to accept the risk of unlimited liability. One class of partners must assume unlimited liability.

Advantages of the Corporate Form of Ownership

In a corporation, the owners' liability is limited to their investment in the corporation.

- limited liability
- access to more capital (i.e., selling shares)
- greater chance to borrow funds
- continuous life — a corporation does not cease if a shareholder dies
- no mutual agency — a shareholder can sell his/her shares and the business will continue to operate
- can be used to split income among family members

Disadvantages of the Corporate Form of Ownership

- complicated legal requirements to form corporations (i.e., hire a lawyer)
- high start-up costs
- complex decision-making process (i.e., hierarchy of management)
- less likely to have strong employee dedication
- corporate earnings are subject to double taxation

ACCOUNTING PROCEDURES FOR PARTNERSHIPS

Two or more persons may agree orally or in writing to establish a partnership. Each of the provinces has a *Partnership Act*, which establishes rules and regulations for partnerships. It is a general practice to prepare a written contract of partnership or "declaration of partnership." This contract outlines the rights and responsibilities of each of the parties concerned. The contract could also contain the provision for settlement in case a partner dies or a partner withdraws from the partnership. In the absence of an oral or written agreement, all profits and losses are shared among the partners on an equal basis.

The partnership agreement outlines the rights and responsibilities of the partners.

Formation of a Partnership

There are several ways in which a partnership may be formed. Five basic examples and the journal entries involved follow.

Example 1

Ron Kendall and Betty McArthur agree to contribute $20 000 each to form a partnership. A Capital account is required for each partner. The entry to open the books of Kendall and McArthur Services is:

Cash	40 000	
R. Kendall, Capital		20 000
B. McArthur, Capital		20 000
To record the investments of R. Kendall and B. McArthur.		

Example 2

J. Hill and D. Love have been operating businesses of their own. Their balance sheets are shown in Figure 13-1.

D. Love
Balance Sheet
January 1, 2001

ASSETS		LIABILITIES AND EQUITY	
Cash	12 000	Accounts Payable	4 000
Accounts Receivable	14 000	Bank Loan	20 000
Inventory	19 000	Mortgage Payable	46 000
Building	95 000	D. Love, Capital	70 000
	140 000		140 000

FIGURE 13-1
Balance sheets for J. Hill and D. Love

J. Hill
Balance Sheet
January 1, 2001

ASSETS		LIABILITIES AND EQUITY	
Cash	25 000	Accounts Payable	5 000
Accounts Receivable	15 000	J. Hill, Capital	140 000
Inventory	35 000		
Equipment	70 000		
	145 000		145 000

They decide to merge their companies and to form a partnership. A separate journal entry is made for each of the partners' contributions to the new business.

Jan. 1	Cash	25 000	
	Accounts Receivable	15 000	
	Inventory	35 000	
	Equipment	70 000	
	Accounts Payable		5 000
	J. Hill, Capital		140 000
	To record J. Hill's assets, liabilities, and capital.		

Jan. 1	Cash	12 000	
	Accounts Receivable	14 000	
	Inventory	19 000	
	Building	95 000	
	Accounts Payable		4 000
	Bank Loan		20 000
	Mortgage Payable		46 000
	D. Love, Capital		70 000
	To record D. Love's assets, liabilities, and capital.		

Example 3

W. Henry and W. Gordon operate competing businesses. Henry's firm is thriving, profitable, and uses modern equipment. Gordon's business is not as successful. Simplified versions of the accounts of the two businesses follow:

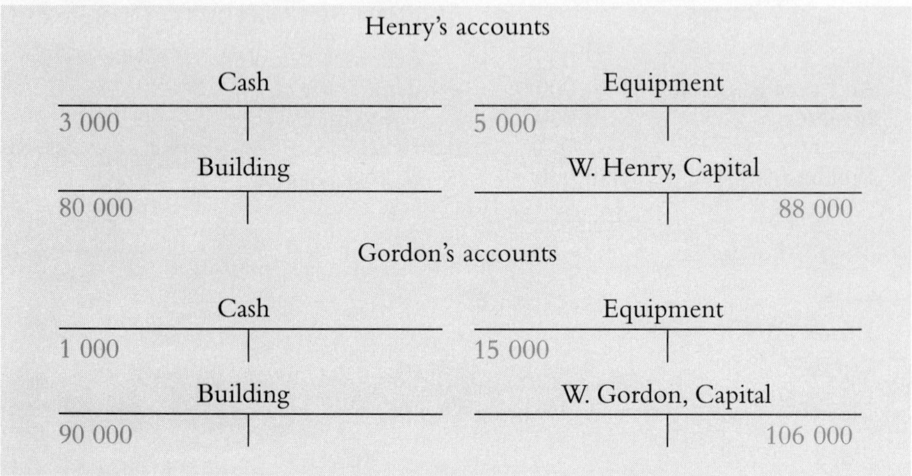

The two proprietors agree to merge their business assets with the following provision: Gordon's assets are to be devalued by $31 000 (Equipment to be decreased by $10 000 and Building by $21 000).

Two proprietorships merge to form a partnership. Assets are revalued and capital accounts are adjusted to reflect the change.

The entry to decrease the assets of the Gordon business is:

W. Gordon, Capital	31 000	
Equipment		10 000
Building		21 000
To devalue equipment and building according to partnership agreement.		

After the entry above has been posted, the two businesses close their books and a new set of books is opened for the partnership, Henry & Gordon Associates. The following two entries are made to open the partnership's books:

Cash	3 000	
Equipment	5 000	
Building	80 000	
W. Henry, Capital		88 000
To record the assets and capital of W. Henry.		

Cash	1 000	
Equipment	5 000	
Building	69 000	
W. Gordon, Capital		75 000
To record the assets and capital of W. Gordon.		

After posting this entry, the accounts of the partnership appear as follows:

Cash

	Debit	Credit
	3 000	
	1 000	
Balance	4 000	

Equipment

	Debit	Credit
	5 000	
	5 000	
Balance	10 000	

Building

	Debit	Credit
	80 000	
	69 000	
Balance	149 000	

W. Gordon, Capital

Debit	Credit
	75 000

W. Henry, Capital

Debit	Credit
	88 000

Example 4

F. Pearen, the sole owner of Pearen Security Services, decides that in order to expand his business he will take in a partner. B. Nicols invests $30 000 and becomes a partner in Pearen & Nicols Security Services. The entry to record Nicols as a partner in the firm is:

Cash	30 000	
B. Nicols, Capital		30 000
To record Nicols' investment.		

The same ledger used by Pearen Security Services will continue to be used by the new partnership. The $30 000 contributed by Nicols was deposited into the bank account of the business. The Cash account increased and a new Capital account was opened.

Example 5

A proprietor sells an interest in a business to a partner. Cash is paid to the owner personally.

Bill Dolman, the sole proprietor of Dolman TV Services, has agreed to sell part of his business. Bill's Capital account has a balance of $90 000. A. Salman has offered $45 000 to become an equal partner in the firm. Dolman accepts the offer. Dolman will personally receive the $45 000. In return he will give up half of his capital in the business. The Cash account of the business does not change since the transaction is between Dolman and Salman and not Salman and the business. The only change in the books of the business is a decrease in Dolman's capital and the addition of a second Capital account, A. Salman, Capital. The entry to record the new account is:

B. Dolman, Capital	45 000	
A. Salman, Capital		45 000
Admission of a partner to the business.		

It should be noted that this is a private exchange of money outside of the business. The assets and the total capital remain the same, but there are now two Capital accounts.

PARTNERSHIPS AND INCOME TAXES

The partners in a business pay personal income tax on their share of the partnership's net income.

As a business, a partnership does not pay income taxes on its net income. Each partner is taxed on his or her share of the partnership's net income, in addition to any income received from other sources.

Suppose the partnership of R. Kendall and B. McArthur (Example 1, page 507) earned a net income of $88 000, and the partnership agreement stipulated that the partners were to share the net income equally. The business, Kendall and McArthur Services, is not taxed. The net income is treated as personal income of the owners. Kendall must include his share of the partnership's net income ($44 000) on his personal income tax return. McArthur must include her share ($44 000) on her personal income tax return.

LEDGER ACCOUNTS OF A PARTNERSHIP

The accounts in the Ledger of a partnership are the same as those of a proprietorship except that there is one Drawings account and one Capital account for *each* partner.

Drawings Account

The Drawings account of each partner is used in the same way in a partnership as the Drawings account in a sole proprietorship. The relevant Drawings account is debited whenever assets are withdrawn by a partner from the business. Typical transactions involving Drawings accounts are:

There is a Drawings account and a Capital account for each partner in the ledger of a partnership.

- payment of salaries to partners
- withdrawal of cash or other business assets by a partner
- payments of a personal nature for a partner using partnership funds

It should be emphasized that salaries paid to partners during the year *must* be recorded in the Drawings accounts. They cannot be treated as a company expense and debited to Salaries Expense. One of the difficulties encountered by accountants is to decide if a transaction involves a legitimate business expense or should be treated as a personal withdrawal and recorded in the owner's Drawings account. Personal expenses charged to the business have the effect of lowering the net income of the business and, in the long run, the income taxes paid by the owners. By charging personal expenses to the business, owners can obtain free fringe benefits illegally.

Salaries paid to partners must be recorded in the Drawings account.

CLOSING THE PARTNERSHIP BOOKS

In a proprietorship, revenue and expense accounts are closed into an Income Summary account. The balance of the summary account would be the net income or the net loss. This balance is then transferred to the owner's Capital account. The owner's Drawings account is then closed into the Capital account.

The books of a partnership are closed in a similar way but with one difference. The balance of the Income Summary account is closed into each of the partner's Capital accounts according to the partnership agreement for dividing net income and net loss. Figure 13-2 illustrates the closing of the books when there is a net income of $90 000 to be divided equally between the two partners. In General Journal form this entry is:

Dec. 31	Income Summary	90 000	
	Partner A, Capital		45 000
	Partner B, Capital		45 000
	To divide the net income equally as per partnership agreement.		

After the net income has been transferred to the partners' Capital accounts, the partners' Drawings accounts are closed into the Capital accounts. The partners' Drawings accounts contain the salaries paid to the owners during the year as well as any other personal withdrawals. The debit balance of the Drawings accounts represents a decrease in equity and this decrease is reflected by closing the Drawings account into the Capital account with this entry:

Dec. 31	Partner A, Capital	28 000	
	Partner B, Capital	28 000	
	Partner A, Drawings		28 000
	Partner B, Drawings		28 000
	To close the Drawings accounts.		

The steps in closing the books of a partnership include:

(1) Close revenue accounts into the Income Summary account.
(2) Close expense accounts into the Income Summary account.
(3) Close the Income Summary account into the partners' Capital accounts (based on the terms of the partnership agreement).
(4) Close the partners' Drawings accounts into the partners' Capital accounts.

These steps are illustrated in Figure 13-2.

FIGURE 13-2
The partnership agreement in this example states that the net income is to be divided equally between partners A and B.

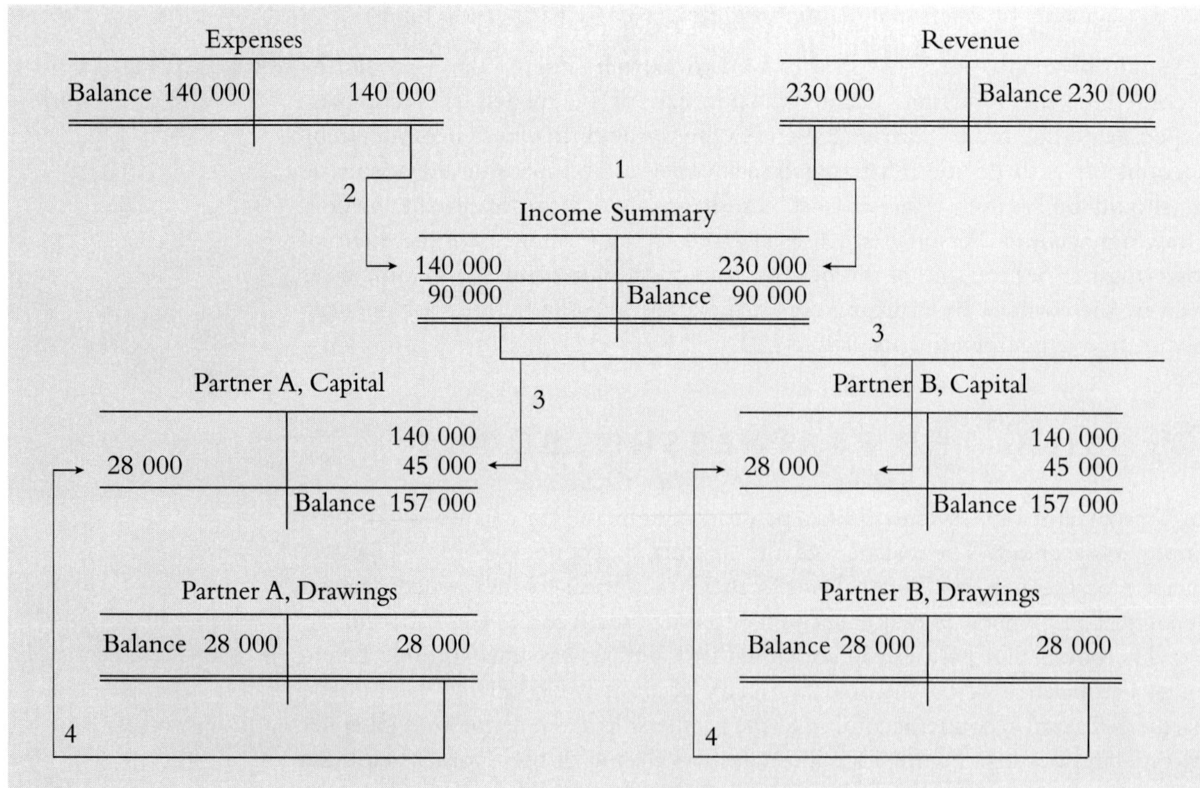

DIVIDING NET INCOME

The partnership contract states how net income or net losses are to be shared.

Partners may make any agreement they wish for the division of the partnership's net income or net loss. One of the most important clauses of the partnership contract is the one stating how these will be shared. Four factors considered by partners in coming to an agreement on the sharing of net income and net loss are:

- payment for amount of work performed
- return on capital
- amount of capital invested
- skills, talent, reputation

Payment for Amount of Work Performed

Suppose one partner is very actively engaged in running a business while another contributes money but does not work in the business. It seems fair that the working partner should be paid for the work performed. In some partnerships both partners work in the business but one has a more responsible position or puts in more hours of work than the other. In preparing the partnership agreement, the partners may consider the amount of work performed in deciding how to share the net income or net loss.

Return on Capital

If a partner invested money in government bonds, term deposits, or mortgages, interest would be earned on that money. Likewise, if a partner invests in a partnership, it seems reasonable for the partnership to receive interest on the money invested. This is especially so when one partner invests more funds in the partnership than the others. If interest is paid on all funds contributed to a partnership proportionately to all partners, the partner who invested more money would appropriately receive more interest.

Amount of Capital Invested

If partners contribute an equal amount of money, work, time, and skills to a partnership, it seems fair to distribute net income equally to the partners. However, if one of the partners contributes more money, that partner could expect to receive a greater share. Suppose one partner contributes $10 000 and another partner contributes $20 000. The second partner could demand a greater share of net income because of the larger investment.

Skills, Talent, and Reputation

Sometimes partners use factors such as skills, talents, and reputation of the owners in deciding how to share net income or net losses. It can be argued that if a net income is earned, it is because of the personal contributions of the partners. The differing levels of skills, talent, and reputation of partners may be reflected in how the partners agree to share net income or net loss.

METHODS OF DIVIDING NET INCOME OR NET LOSS

Among the many methods used to divide net income and net loss are:

- fixed ratio
- capital ratio
- salaries and remaining net income (or net loss) to partners on a fixed ratio
- interest on capital, salaries, and remaining net income (or net loss) to partners on a fixed ratio

Fixed Ratio

On forming their partnership, Kendall and McArthur (Example 1, page 507) agreed to divide net income and net loss equally. Thus 50 percent of net income will belong to Kendall and 50 percent to McArthur. They felt that a 50:50 ratio was fair since both contributed the same amount of capital, both would work full time in the business, and both had special skills to offer to the new business. At the end of a year, net income is $88 000. According to the partnership agreement, this amount is divided 50:50. When the books are closed, the division is made by the following entry:

Income Summary	88 000	
R. Kendall, Capital		44 000
B. McArthur, Capital		44 000
To divide the net income equally between the partners, per partnership agreement.		

Figure 13-3 shows how the division of net income is included on the bottom of the income statement.

FIGURE 13-3
Distribution of net income as shown on the income statement

Kendall and McArthur Services Income Statement For the Year Ended December 31, 2001		
REVENUE		
Sales		198 000
EXPENSES		
Selling Expenses	90 000	
Administrative Expenses	20 000	110 000
Net Income		88 000
Distribution of net income		
R. Kendall (50%)	44 000	
B. McArthur (50%)	44 000	88 000

Capital Ratio

The capital ratio method is used when the success of the business depends to some extent on the contribution of capital. In some businesses, such as auto dealerships, substantial investments in equipment, buildings, and merchandise are required. The capital ratio method recognizes the importance of capital to the business and divides the net income or net loss accordingly.

J. Hill and D. Love (Example 2, page 504) have invested $140 000 and $70 000, respectively, in their partnership. They agree to share net income and net loss in the ratio of their beginning capital. The ratio is determined as follows:

	Beginning Capital	Percentage of Total
J. Hill	$140 000	66.7%
D. Love	70 000	33.3%
Total	$210 000	100.0%

Hill receives 66.7 percent of any net income and Love 33.3 percent. They share net losses in the same way, that is, in the ratio of 66.7:33.3. Suppose there is net income of $100 000. The division of the net income would be calculated as follows:

		Share of Net Income
J. Hill	0.667 × 100 000	$ 66 700
D. Love	0.333 × 100 000	33 300
	Total	$100 000

The entry to record the division of net income is:

Dec. 31 Income Summary	100 000	
J. Hill, Capital		66 700
D. Love, Capital		33 300
To divide net income in the ratio of 33.3:66.7, per partnership agreement.		

The division of the net income would be shown on the bottom of the income statement as was the case in Figure 13-3.

Salaries and Remaining Profits in a Fixed Ratio

In their partnership agreement (Example 4, page 509), F. Pearen and B. Nicols agreed to the following:

- a salary of $32 000 to Pearen and $30 000 to Nicols per year
- any remaining net income after salaries to be shared 50:50

At the end of the year, there is a net income of $125 000. A special report called a *statement of distribution of net income* is prepared as shown in Figure 13-4.

Pearen & Nicols Security Services
Statement of Distribution of Net Income
December 31, 2001

Net Income to be divided			$125 000
	F. Pearen	B. Nicols	Total
Salaries	$ 32 000	$ 30 000	$ 62 000
Remaining net income shared equally (50:50)	31 500	31 500	63 000
Totals	$63 500	$61 500	$125 000

FIGURE 13-4
Statement of distribution of net income for two partners, Pearen & Nicols Security Services

The statement of distribution of net income outlines clearly to the partners how the net income is shared between them. There are two entries required in the General Ledger.

Dec. 31 Income Summary	62 000	
F. Pearen, Capital		32 000
B. Nicols, Capital		30 000
To credit partners with their net salaries, per partnership agreement.		
Dec. 31 Income Summary	63 000	
F. Pearen, Capital		31 500
B. Nicols, Capital		31 500
To divide remainder of net income on a 50:50 ratio, per partnership agreement.		

Interest, Salaries, and Fixed Ratio

In forming their partnership, W. Chong and W. Larocque agreed on the following division of net income and net loss:

- each partner to receive a $34 000 salary per year
- 10-percent interest on the beginning capital to be credited annually to each partner from net income (Chong, Capital $90 000, Larocque, Capital $120 000)
- any remaining net income or net loss after interest and salaries to be divided equally

In the last fiscal year, the partnership earned net income of $93 000. The statement of distribution of net income was prepared to divide the net income as shown in Figure 13-5.

FIGURE 13-5

Statement of distribution of net income for Chong & Larocque Enterprises

Chong & Larocque Enterprises
Statement of Distribution of Net Income
December 31, 2001

Net income to be divided			$93 000
	W. Chong	W. Larocque	Total
Salaries	$34 000	$34 000	$68 000
Interest on beginning capital 10%	9 000	12 000	21 000
Remaining net income shared equally	2 000	2 000	4 000
Total	$45 000	$48 000	$93 000

There are three entries required to record this division of net income in the General Ledger accounts.

Dec. 31	Income Summary	68 000	
	W. Chong, Capital		34 000
	W. Larocque, Capital		34 000
	To credit partners with salaries, per partnership agreement.		
Dec. 31	Income Summary	21 000	
	W. Chong, Capital		9 000
	W. Larocque, Capital		12 000
	To credit each partner with interest based on beginning capital, per partnership agreement.		
Dec. 31	Income Summary	4 000	
	W. Chong, Capital		2 000
	W. Larocque, Capital		2 000
	To divide remainder ($4 000) of net income equally, per partnership agreement.		

DIVIDING NET LOSS AND INSUFFICIENT NET INCOME

In each of the situations discussed to this point, there was a net income large enough to give each partner what was owing according to the partnership agreement. However, businesses often suffer losses or do not earn enough net income to pay the partners according to the agreement. Two examples of such situations follow.

First, J. Hill and D. Love agreed to share net income and net loss in the ratio of their beginning capital balances. This ratio was 66.7:33.3. This means that if there is a net loss, Hill absorbs 66.7 percent of the net loss and Love 33.3 percent. Suppose the partnership suffers a net loss of $8 000. The division of the net loss would be calculated as follows:

		Share of Net Loss
J. Hill	0.667 × 8 000 =	$5 336
D. Love	0.333 × 8 000 =	2 664
	Total	$8 000

The entry to record this division of the net loss is:

Dec. 31	J. Hill, Capital	5 336	
	D. Love, Capital	2 664	
	Income Summary		8 000
	To close the Income Summary account and to divide the net loss per partnership agreement.		

Second, when there is an agreement on how to allocate salary, interest, and earnings, it is normal to follow the same procedure whether allocating a loss or a profit. For example, Smyth and Maggio agree to the following provisions: Smyth would receive a salary of $25 000 plus $5 000 interest on capital while Maggio would receive $20 000 salary and $6 000 interest. They also agree to divide profits or losses equally. The distribution of a net income for the year of $10 000 is shown on the following page.

Smyth and Maggio Group
Statement of Distribution of Net Income
December 31, 2001

Net income to be divided			$10 000
	Smyth	Maggio	Total
Salaries	$25 000	$20 000	$45 000
Interest on capital	5 000	6 000	11 000
Total salaries plus interest	30 000	26 000	56 000
Remainder of net income shared equally	(23 000)	(23 000)	(46 000)
Partner's share	$7 000	$3 000	$10 000

The entry to record this division of a net income which was insufficient to meet salary and interest obligations of the partners is:

Income Summary	10 000	
Smyth, Capital		7 000
Maggio, Capital		3 000

PARTNERS' SALARIES

Journal entries involving partners' salaries are handled as follows. A debit entry is made to the partners' drawings accounts during the year each time salaries are paid to the partners and when personal withdrawals are made. Another entry is made at the end of the year when the net income or net loss is divided between the partners. For example, suppose Creaco and Costanza invest $18 000 each and become partners in a masonry business. Their partnership agreement states that they are to receive salaries and to share equally any remaining net income or net loss after salaries. Each receives a salary of $42 000 a year. Once a month, each partner receives a cheque for $3 500. At the end of the year, each partner will have received cash payments of $42 000. The following T-accounts show the entries for salaries on the debit side of the Drawings accounts.

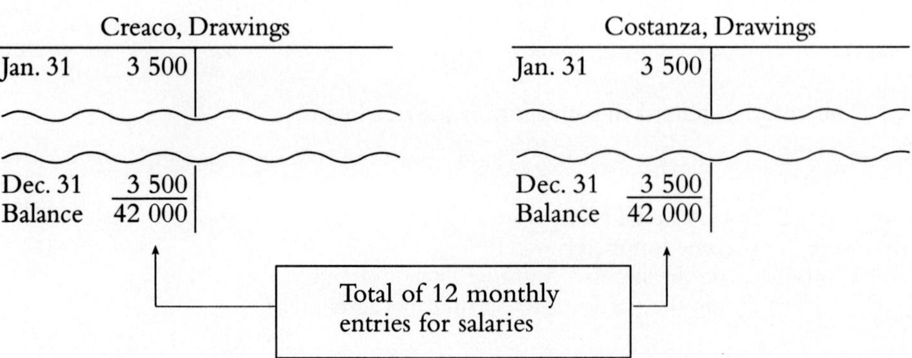

Suppose the partnership has earned a net income of $94 000 for the year. According to the partnership agreement, the partners share this $94 000 by:

- receiving salaries of $42 000 each (total $84 000)
- sharing the remainder ($10 000) equally

These entries are made to distribute the net income:

Dec. 31 Income Summary	84 000	
Creaco, Capital		42 000
Costanza, Capital		42 000
To credit each partner with $42 000 salary, per the partnership agreement.		
Dec. 31 Income Summary	10 000	
Creaco, Capital		5 000
Costanza, Capital		5 000
To distribute the remaining net income equally, per the partnership agreement.		

Finally, the Drawings accounts are closed into the Capital accounts with this entry:

Dec. 31 Creaco, Capital	42 000	
Costanza, Capital	42 000	
Creaco, Drawings		42 000
Costanza, Drawings		42 000
To close the Drawings accounts.		

See if you can understand these principles:

(1) The debits in the Drawings accounts represent actual withdrawals of cash made during the year.
(2) Each partner's share of the net income ($47 000 in this example, which is made up of $42 000 salary and $5 000 remainder) appears as a credit in each Capital account.
(3) Although each partner's share of the net income is $47 000, the partners' Capital accounts only increase by $5 000 each because they withdrew $42 000 during the year as salaries.

FINANCIAL STATEMENTS

In a partnership, the following four financial statements may be prepared:

- income statement
- statement of distribution of net income
- balance sheet
- statement of partners' equity

Income Statement

The income statement of a partnership is very similar to that of a proprietorship. However, a section may be added to the bottom to show the division of the net income or net loss (see Figure 13-3).

Statement of Distribution of Net Income

If the division of the net income or net loss is not shown on the income statement, a *statement of distribution of net income* is prepared (Figure 13-5). This is a more formal report that is prepared when there are salaries, interest, and a remainder of net income or loss to be divided.

The Balance Sheet

There are at least two people in every partnership. For every partner there is a Capital account. Each partner's capital appears in the equity section of the balance sheet, as shown in Figure 13-6.

FIGURE 13-6
Balance sheet for Holmes & Palmer Consultants

Holmes & Palmer Consultants Balance Sheet December 31, 2001			
ASSETS			
Current Assets			
Cash		$ 9 000	
Accounts Receivable		12 000	
Inventory		30 000	
Total Current Assets			$ 51 000
Capital Assets			
Building	$149 000		
Less: Accumulated Amortization	7 000	142 000	
Equipment	10 000		
Less: Accumulated Amortization	1 000	9 000	
Total Capital Assets			151 000
Total Assets			$202 000
LIABILITIES AND PARTNERS' EQUITY			
Current Liabilities			
Accounts Payable			$ 4 000
Partners' Equity			
P. Holmes, Capital		$ 85 000	
T. Palmer, Capital		113 000	198 000
Total Liabilities and Partners' Equity			$202 000

Statement of Partners' Equity

Partners are usually interested in seeing the changes in their Capital accounts from year to year. A *statement of partners' equity* is prepared to provide this information (see Figure 13-7). The information in this statement could be placed in the equity section of the balance sheet if it did not make the balance sheet unduly long.

Partners' equity is the claim of the partners against the assets of a partnership.

The statement of partners' equity is a picture of all the activity involving the partners' investments; it shows additions to the business contributed during the year; it shows all withdrawals made; it shows the share of the net income or net loss credited to each partner.

Holmes & Palmer Consultants Statement of Partners' Equity For the Year Ended December 31, 2001			
	Holmes	Palmer	Total
Capital, Jan. 1	$ 75 000	$100 000	$175 000
Add: Additional Investment	5 000	5 000	10 000
Share of Net Income	25 000	28 000	53 000
Total	$105 000	$133 000	$238 000
Less: Withdrawals	20 000	20 000	40 000
Total Capital, Dec. 31	$ 85 000	$113 000	$198 000

FIGURE 13-7
Statement of partners' equity for Holmes & Palmer Consultants

REVIEW QUESTIONS

1. Explain what is meant by the following:

   (a) sole proprietorship (b) partnership (c) corporation

2. Explain the term "unlimited personal liability."
3. If a proprietorship does not pay income tax on its net income, how does the net income get taxed?
4. How many persons may form:

   (a) a partnership? (b) a corporation?

5. Give three advantages and three disadvantages for each of the three forms of business ownership.
6. What do you think are the three main items that should be included in a partnership agreement?
7. Why might some assets be revalued when two persons combine their businesses to form a partnership?
8. Explain how income tax is paid on the income of a partnership.
9. Which account is used to record the payment of salaries to partners?
10. What accounts are debited and credited when a partner withdraws merchandise from the business for personal use?
11. In closing partnership books at the end of a fiscal period, into which account (or accounts) are the following closed:

    (a) the balance of the Income Summary account?
    (b) revenue and expenses?
    (c) the Drawings account?

12. List the four steps followed in closing the books of a partnership.
13. List four methods of dividing the net income of a partnership.
14. Chow and Wong use the ratio of beginning capital balances as their method of dividing net income. Chow's capital balance is $27 000 and Wong's is $18 000. In what ratio is the net income divided?
15. Name the four financial statements that may be prepared for a partnership.

PROBLEMS: APPLICATIONS

1. For each of the following, prepare General Journal entries to record the formation of the partnership.
   (a) D. Renshaw, J. Heward, and B. Malloy each contribute $31 000 cash to a new partnership.
   (b) S. Signer and L. Harris agree to form a new business. Signer contributes $21 000 and Harris $27 000.
   (c) S. Brucculieri and M. Scornaiencki form a partnership with Brucculieri contributing $5 000 cash, land valued at $40 000, and a building worth $90 000. Scornaiencki invests $35 000 cash and equipment worth $42 000.

2. M. Bondar and C. Church agree to join their two businesses to form a partnership. Bondar's assets and liabilities are: Cash $2 800; Accounts Receivable $2 000; Equipment $10 000; Accounts Payable $1 700. Church's assets and liabilities are: Cash $2 000; Accounts Receivable $3 000; Land, $40 000; Building $95 000; Mortgage Payable $65 000; Bank Loan $10 000. Prepare General Journal entries to set up the partnership.

3. M. Ross wishes to expand her business and agrees to take K. Golumbia in as an equal partner. M. Ross has a capital balance of $32 000. K. Golumbia contributes $32 000 cash to the business. Prepare the General Journal entry to record Golumbia's investment in the business.

4. C. DeGagne has an investment of $54 000 in a sole proprietorship. In order to share the work of running the company, he sells an equal share of the company to R. Francis. In return, he personally receives $27 000 cash from Francis. The assets of the business do not change. Prepare the General Journal entry to admit Francis as a partner.

5. Moffat and Mottola agree to join their businesses and to form a partnership.

Moffat's Accounts	
Cash	$ 9 000
Accounts Receivable	20 000
Equipment	40 000
Accounts Payable	7 000

Mottola's Accounts	
Cash	$ 3 500
Accounts Receivable	7 000
Land	40 000
Building	55 000
Equipment	19 000
Mortgage Payable	39 000

Their agreement includes the following:

- Moffat's equipment is to be reduced in value to $27 000 from the balance of $40 000.
- Mottola's building is to be increased in value to $95 000 from $55 000.
- Mottola's equipment is to be reduced in value to $9 000 from $19 000.

(a) Prepare General Journal entries to revalue assets for Moffat and for Mottola.
(b) Prepare General Journal entries to set up the partnership.

6. (a) Prepare General Journal entries to record these transactions for Ron Kendall and Betty McArthur:

May	10	McArthur withdrew cash for personal use, $250.
	20	Kendall took home merchandise worth $120.
	31	Paid salaries, $2 500 each to partners.
Jun.	15	Paid $115 for golf lessons for Kendall's daughter.
	30	Paid partners' salaries $2 500 each.
Jul.	25	Kendall invested an additional $8 000 in the business.

   (b) After closing the expense and revenue accounts, there is a credit balance of $58 000 in the Income Summary account. This net income is to be divided equally between Kendall and McArthur. Prepare the General Journal entry to close the Income Summary account and to divide the net income between the partners.
   (c) Kendall's Drawings account has a debit balance of $9 000 and McArthur's a debit balance of $12 000. Prepare the General Journal entry to close the Drawings accounts.
   (d) The next year, the firm of Kendall and McArthur Services incurs a net loss of $12 000. This is represented by a debit balance in the Income Summary account. Prepare the General Journal entry to close the Income Summary account and to divide the net loss equally.

7. (a) Stewart and Smith divide net income and net loss according to the ratio of their beginning capital balances. Stewart has a capital balance of $30 000 and Smith $60 000. What is the ratio used?
   (b) Using the ratio from part (a), how much is received by each partner if the net income is $84 000?
   (c) If Stewart and Smith incurred a net loss of $6 000, how much of the net loss would be shared by each partner?

8. Hill and Love divide net income from their partnership in the ratio of their capital. The ratio is 40:60.

   (a) The net income or net loss for each of three years follows. For each year determine how much of the net income or net loss is allocated to Hill and how much is allocated to Love.

Year 1	Net Income	$140 000
Year 2	Net Loss	90 000
Year 3	Net Income	250 000

   (b) Prepare General Journal entries to close the Income Summary account and to divide the net income or net loss each year.

9. Pearen and Nicols divide net income and net loss on the following basis:

   - Pearen's salary is $46 000 and Nicols' salary is $38 000.
   - Any remaining net income or net loss after salaries is shared equally.

(a) Prepare a statement of distribution of net income for each of these years:

Year 1	Net Income	$98 000
Year 2	Net Income	72 000
Year 3	Net Income	102 000

(b) Prepare General Journal entries to distribute the net income each year.

10. Chong and Larocque share the net income of their partnership in the following manner:

- Salaries are $48 000 each.
- Interest on beginning capital is 10 percent. Chong's capital is $70 000, Larocque's $82 000.
- Remaining net income or loss after salaries and interest is shared equally.

(a) Prepare a December 31 statement of distribution of net income for each of these years:

Year 1	Net Income	$120 000
Year 2	Net Income	78 000
Year 3	Net Loss	27 000

(b) Prepare the General Journal entries to distribute the net income or net loss each year.

11. Prepare a statement of partners' equity for Klemba and Swords on December 31 using this information:

- January 1 capital balances: Klemba $41 000; Swords $56 000.
- Additional investment: Klemba $7 500.
- Withdrawals: Klemba $21 500; Swords $26 000.
- Share of net income: Klemba $19 000; Swords $24 000.

12. Prepare a December 31 statement of partners' equity for Doyle and Durivage:

- January 1 capital balances: Doyle $28 000; Durivage $11 000.
- Additional investment: $9 000 each.
- Withdrawals: Doyle $13 500; Durivage $14 000.
- Share of net income: Doyle $27 000; Durivage $19 500.

13. Stewart and Todkill decide to form a partnership. Stewart invests $25 000 cash and Todkill $20 000 cash. They are each to receive a salary of $32 000 and interest of 15 percent on their beginning capital. The balance of the net income or net loss is to be divided in the ratio of the Capital accounts at the time of formation.

(a) Prepare the General Journal entry to record the formation.
(b) Prepare a December 31 statement of distribution of net income if the year's net income is $88 000.

UNIT 33 Accounting For Corporations

Learning Objectives

After reading this unit, discussing the applicable review questions, and completing the applications exercises, you will be able to do the following.

1. **EXPLAIN** the difference between the two types of business corporations.
2. **IDENTIFY** and discuss the types of shares and their basic rights.
3. **PREPARE** the accounting entries required to form a corporation, issue shares, and pay dividends.
4. **PREPARE** the closing entries for a corporation.
5. **PREPARE** the financial statements for a corporation.

UNLIMITED LIABILITY

The proprietorship and partnership forms of ownership, discussed in previous chapters, have several disadvantages. One of these is illustrated by the following example.

John Bowers operated a very successful business as a sole proprietorship for fifteen years. Through hard work and good management, John's company earned substantial net income for him. Over the years, John invested the money earned by his business by purchasing a cottage, two expensive cars, and several apartment buildings, which he rented out.

However, his business suddenly became unprofitable as new products and competitors caused several large losses in consecutive years. John's business was unable to pay a number of debts on time and, as a result, the business was forced into bankruptcy. To pay off his creditors, John was ordered by the court to sell his cottage and the apartment buildings. John had to do so despite the fact that the properties belonged to him, personally, and not to his business.

The proprietor of a business is personally responsible for its debts.

John was personally liable for all the business debts. He lost his business investment and some of his personal assets.

The case of John Bowers illustrates a major disadvantage of partnerships and proprietorships: unlimited liability. It also points out one of the advantages of forming a corporation. In the corporate form of ownership, an investor risks the investment in the business, but not personal assets. Limited liability is an important advantage of the corporate form of ownership. Because of this characteristic, the term *limited company* is often used instead of *corporation*. Other advantages of the corporate form of ownership were given in Unit 32.

WHAT IS A CORPORATION?

A corporation is a business that has a legal existence of its own. It is separate from its owners. Each owner is liable only for the amount of his or her investment in the business. In a partnership or proprietorship, the owners are not separate from the business. A corporation has the right to sue and can be sued by others.

Forming a Corporation

Shareholders (owners) of corporations have limited legal liability. This means each owner is only liable up to the amount of his or her investment in the company for the debts or obligations of the business.

A corporation is formed by applying to a provincial government or to the federal government for a certificate of incorporation. The application, signed by one or more persons, must include the following information:

- name and address of the corporation
- types and number of shares to be authorized for issue
- names of directors
- nature of the business to be conducted

Generally, a corporation that will do business in only one province will apply to that province for incorporation. A business that will operate in more than one province usually applies to the federal government for incorporation.

Corporation Name

Have you ever wondered why so many businesses use Limited or Ltd. in their names? The reason for this is that the corporation laws require the words "Limited," "Limitée," "Incorporated," or "Incorporée" to be part of the name. The short forms "Ltd.," "Ltée.," or "Inc." may also be used. Other requirements for the corporation name are:

- The proposed name must differ from any other Canadian business.
- The name must be acceptable to the public.
- The name must be clearly displayed on the outside of the business in all its locations and in notices and advertisements.

After the application has been accepted by the government and the incorporation fee paid, the limited company or corporation comes into existence. The persons who applied for incorporation receive a document from the government. It is called a *charter* or *certificate of incorporation* if issued by the federal government, or *letters patent* or *memorandum of association* depending on the province involved.

Once a business is incorporated, a meeting is held to elect directors of the corporation. The directors then hire people to manage the business. Shares are sold or exchanged for assets and the company is in business.

An important difference between a corporation and partnership or proprietorship is that the corporation has a continuous life or perpetual existence. Owners may change for a variety of reasons but the corporation continues under the management of employees hired by the board of directors who represent all shareholders.

TYPES OF BUSINESS CORPORATION

There are two types of business corporation:

- private corporation
- public corporation

Private Corporation

A private business corporation is limited in the number of shareholders it may have and in the way it raises its capital. It may not have more than 50 shareholders, and it must obtain its funds privately. It cannot sell shares or bonds to the public. Many small proprietorships and partnerships change their form of ownership to that of a private corporation in order to take advantage of the limited liability feature of the corporation. The owners still control and own the business and yet have protection for their personal assets.

Public Corporation

A public business corporation can have any number of shareholders. It can sell shares and bonds to the public, but it is subject to the requirements of the provincial Securities Commission.

ACCOUNTING PROCEDURES FOR CORPORATIONS

Share Certificates

Ownership of a corporation is represented by shares in the company. A person who invests in a corporation buys a portion or a share of the corporation. A share certificate is a form issued by a corporation showing the number of shares owned. The person purchasing the shares receives the share certificate and is called a *shareholder*. The terms *stock* and *stockholder* are sometimes used in place of *share* and *shareholder*.

A share certificate is a form issued by a corporation indicating the number of shares owned.

Shareholders' Equity Accounts

The books and accounts of a corporation are similar to those of proprietorships and partnerships except for differences in the equity section.

Shareholders are owners of shares in a corporation.

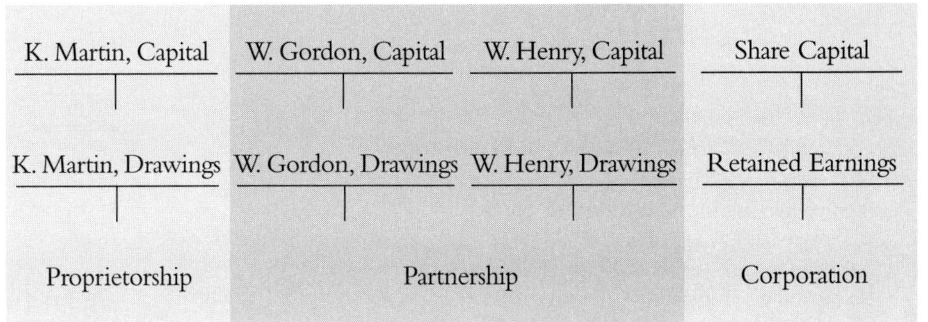

FIGURE 13-8
Owner's Equity accounts for the three types of business ownership

The Retained Earnings account is an equity account containing the balance of undistributed net income.

Figure 13-8 illustrates the different types of Owner's Equity accounts. In the corporate form of ownership, there are no Drawings accounts. The shareholders or owners of a corporation may not withdraw assets. They may, however, receive a portion of the corporate net income in the form of *dividends*. Dividends are the amount of earnings that may be declared by the board of directors for distribution to the shareholders in proportion to the number of shares owned if the year-end profits are favourable.

The equity section of a corporate balance sheet is shown in Figure 13-9. Note that in this simplified balance sheet, there are two new accounts in the equity section. The *Share Capital* account is a record of shares sold. The *Retained Earnings* account contains the balance of net income earned by the corporation after dividends have been paid.

Par-Value and No-Par-Value Shares

When a company applies to the government for the articles of incorporation, it indicates the number of shares that will be sold (authorized) and the type of share. The two types of common shares are par- and no-par-value shares. The *Canada Business Corporations* Act requires the use of no-par-value shares, while some provinces allow the use of both types of share issue. Par-value shares have a stated value, but it is important to note that this does not indicate the actual selling price of the share.

For example, a company may issue common shares with a $20 par value. This does not mean that each share is worth $20. A share is worth whatever buyers will pay for it.

Some corporations prefer to issue no-par-value shares. No-par-value shares have no stated value. These shares are recorded on the corporate books at the price for which they are sold. The par value of a share (if any) is the amount entered in the Share Capital account. It represents legal capital per share. It does not mean market value. By law, dividends may *not* be declared if the payment of the dividend causes the shareholders' equity to fall below the par value of the outstanding shares.

Journal Entries

W. Gordon and W. Henry operate a business as a partnership. In order to have the benefits of limited liability, they have applied to their provincial government for permission to incorporate their company. They have received permission to incorporate as a private corporation with 10 000 authorized shares at a no-par value of $50 per share.

FIGURE 13-9
Equity section on the Excello Corporation balance sheet

Excello Corporation Balance Sheet December 31, 2001		
ASSETS		
Cash		$ 5 000
Other Assets		100 000
Total Assets		$105 000
LIABILITIES AND SHAREHOLDERS' EQUITY		
Current Liabilities		
Accounts Payable		$ 20 000
Shareholders' Equity		
Share Capital	$45 000	
Retained Earnings	$40 000	85 000
Total Liabilities and Shareholders' Equity		$105 000

Four hundred shares are sold in the new corporation to Gordon, Henry, and several of their friends. The entry to record the issuing of the shares for cash in General Journal form is:

Feb. 1	Cash		20 000	
	Share Capital			20 000
	Sold 400 shares at $50:			
	W. Gordon	100 shares		
	W. Henry	100 shares		
	D. Thomas	75 shares		
	M. Thomas	25 shares		
	J. Bak	100 shares		
		400 shares		

Shares for Assets

W. Gordon and W. Henry turned over to the corporation the assets of their previous business in return for shares in the corporation. Equipment worth $10 000 and a building valued at $150 000 are exchanged for company shares.

Feb. 2	Equipment		10 000	
	Building		150 000	
	Share Capital			160 000
	Issued 3 200 shares for property at $50:			
	W. Gordon	1 200 shares		
	W. Henry	2 000 shares		
		3 200 shares		

The corporation, Gordon & Henry Ltd., is now formally established. Its balance sheet is shown in Figure 13-10. In the equity section of the balance sheet, it is necessary to show both the authorized shares and the value of the shares actually issued or sold.

Authorized shares are the number of shares that a company may issue according to the terms of its articles of incorporation.

FIGURE 13-10

Balance sheet for the new corporation — Gordon & Henry Ltd.

Gordon & Henry Ltd.
Balance Sheet
February 2, 2001

ASSETS		
Current Assets		
Cash		$ 20 000
Capital Assets		
Equipment	$ 10 000	
Building	150 000	160 000
Total Assets		$180 000
SHAREHOLDERS' EQUITY		
Share Capital		
Authorized 10 000 shares, no par value		
Issued 3 600 shares		$180 000

Issue of outstanding shares are the number of authorized shares that have been sold and issued to shareholders.

Organization Expenses

Organization Expense is an account used to record costs of organizing a business.

A number of expenses are incurred in organizing a corporation. These include legal fees, a fee to the government, and miscellaneous items such as share certificates and a company seal. These expenses are charged to an account called *Organization Expense*. Generally, this account is treated in one of two ways:

- as an expense charged to the first year's operations
- as an asset that is *written off* as an expense over a number of years. Each year, the balance in the account, Organization Expense, is shown after the fixed assets on the balance sheet.

The first of these two methods is used when the amount involved is small. Whichever method is followed, the entry to record organizational costs is:

Organization Expense	2 000	
Cash		2 000
Paid organizing costs.		

Corporate Net Income

The net income of a corporation increases the shareholders' equity. The decision concerning what happens to the net income is made by the board of directors. The board has several alternatives:

- distribute all of the net income to the shareholders
- leave all of the net income in the corporation
- a combination of the above — leave part of the net income in the business and distribute part to the shareholders

The shareholders do not participate directly in deciding what is done with corporate net income. However, if they are not satisfied with the decision of the board of directors, they can make their displeasure known at the annual shareholders' meeting. Every business corporation must hold a meeting of shareholders each year. At this meeting, the board of directors is elected by the shareholders. If enough shareholders are displeased with the operation of the corporation, some or all of the directors may be replaced. Elections are based on a majority vote of shareholders with one vote allowed for each share owned. Shareholders must also approve the annual report, which contains the latest set of financial statements.

DIVIDENDS

Generally speaking, the owners of a proprietorship or partnership may withdraw money from their business as they wish. The Drawings account is a record of withdrawals.

There is no opportunity for shareholders in a corporation to withdraw cash in the way that proprietors or partners do. Because of the limited liability feature of corporations, the creditors must be protected from the possibility of corporate owners withdrawing the assets and leaving no funds for the payment of corporate debts. In that event, the creditors would lose their investment since shareholders are not personally liable for the corporation's debts.

The portion of a corporation's net income distributed to the shareholder is called a *dividend*. Payment of a dividend must be approved by the Board of Directors of the corporation. Corporate laws allow dividends to be paid to owners or shareholders only out of accumulated net income. The accumulated net income is recorded in the Retained Earnings account. This account appears in the shareholders' equity section of the balance sheet (see Figure 13-9). If there is a balance in this account, dividends may be declared.

Dividends are the portion of a corporation's net income paid to the shareholders.

Dividends are paid out of retained earnings.

Closing the Books of a Corporation

The closing phase of the accounting cycle for a corporation is very similar to those of partnerships and proprietorships. The steps in closing the books include:

(1) Close Revenue and Expense accounts into the Income Summary account.

(2) Close the Income Summary account balance (which is the net income or the net loss) into the Retained Earnings account.

These steps are illustrated in Figure 13-11.

There is no change in the Share Capital account. The Retained Earnings account balance represents the accumulated net income (credit balance) or net loss (debit balance) of the corporation. It presents a historical picture of the company's profitability.

If dividends are to be paid, the Retained Earnings account must have a credit balance. Dividends may be paid in a year when the corporation has sustained a loss, as long as the net income from previous years leaves a credit balance in the Retained Earnings account.

FIGURE 13-11
Closing the books

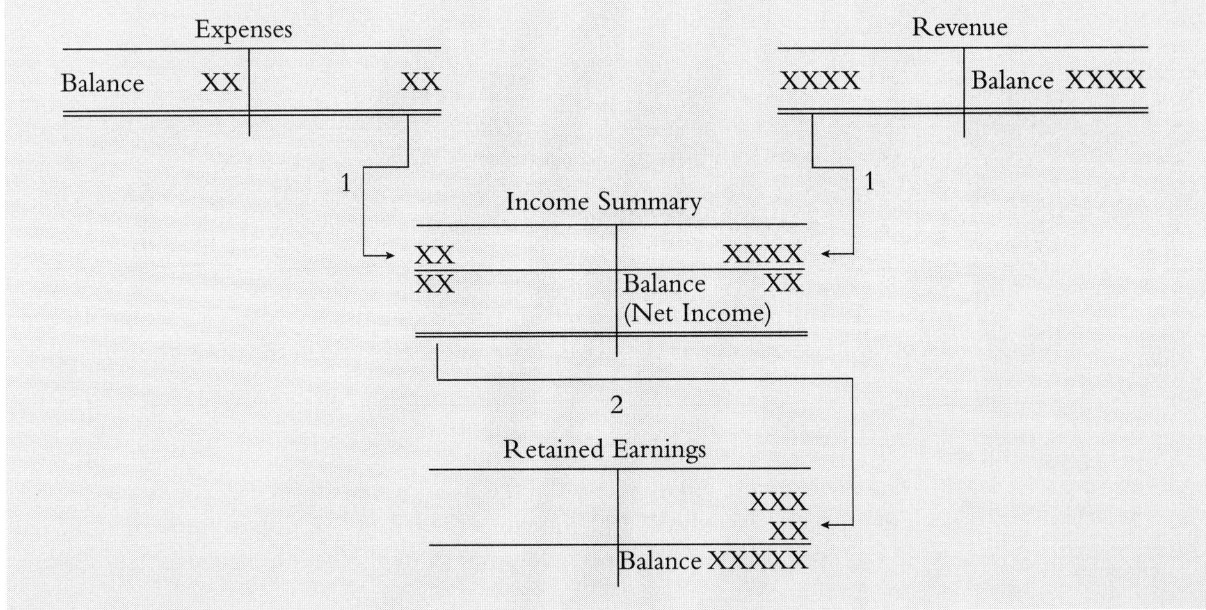

Distributing Dividends

The board of directors has decided to pay a dividend of $2 on each of the outstanding shares of Gordon & Henry Ltd. June 15 was the date that the decision was made (Date of Declaration). It was also decided that the $2 dividend would be paid to all owners of shares on record as of June 25 (Date of Record). The dividend cheques would be issued on July 10 (Date of Payment). This entry is made on June 15 to establish a liability on the corporate books:

June 15	Retained Earnings	7 200	
	Dividends Payable		7 200
	Declared a $2 dividend on the 3 600 outstanding shares.		

This entry results in a decrease in the shareholders' equity because some of the accumulated net income will be taken out of the business. The debit to Retained Earnings reduced the equity. This entry also establishes a current liability called *Dividends Payable.*

On July 10, cheques are issued to the shareholders of record on June 25. The entry to record the payment is:

July 10	Dividends Payable	7 200	
	Cash		7 200
	Issued dividend cheques to shareholders.		

The payment cancels the liability created by the previous declaration of the dividend. After several years of profitable operation, the shareholders' equity section of Gordon & Henry Ltd. appears as in Figure 13-12.

FIGURE 13-12
Shareholders' equity portion of the balance sheet

SHAREHOLDERS' EQUITY

Share Capital		
Authorized	10 000 shares, no-par-value	
Issued	3 600 shares	$180 000
Retained Earnings		90 000
		$270 000

The balance of $90 000 in retained earnings indicates that a net income has been earned and that not all the net income was distributed in the form of dividends.

Statement of Retained Earnings

The shareholders' equity section of the balance sheet shown in Figure 13-12 indicates retained earnings of $90 000 when the balance sheet was prepared at the end of the fiscal period. However, it does not show the beginning balance or changes during the year.

A *statement of retained earnings* as shown in Figure 13-13 provides a complete description of changes in retained earnings. It shows the beginning balance, net income added, dividends paid, and ending balance or retained earnings. A statement of retained earnings is prepared in addition to the income statement and the balance sheet.

Gordon & Henry Ltd. Statement of Retained Earnings December 31, 2002	
Retained Earnings, January 1, 2002	$55 200
Add: Net Income for the Year	42 560
Total	97 760
Less: Dividends	7 200
Retained Earnings, December 31, 2002	$90 560

FIGURE 13-13
The statement of retained earnings provides a complete description of changes to retained earnings.

CORPORATE INCOME TAX

A corporation has a legal existence of its own and is a taxpayer. Corporations pay income tax on their net income to the federal government (29 percent of taxable income) and to the provinces in which they earn income (9 percent to 15.5 percent, depending on the province). A special income tax rate is available to small Canadian-owned corporations. This deduction, if applicable, results in a small Canadian business paying income tax at a rate of approximately 22 percent rather than 29 percent. Special accounting procedures must be followed if the reduced rate is to be obtained.

The income tax paid by a corporation is an expense of operating the business and appears as a deduction on the income statement, as shown in Figure 13-14.

Gordon & Henry Ltd. had a net income of $56 000 *before* income taxes. This income is the difference between total revenue and total expenses. From the information on the income statement, there was a net income of $42 560 *after* taxes. This amount is the increase in the shareholders' equity as a result of the year's activity and appears on the statement of retained earnings as shown in Figure 13-13. This is the net income that a corporation reports to its shareholders. Figure 13-13 also shows that $7 200 in dividends was distributed to the shareholders during the year.

Gordon & Henry Ltd. Income Statement For the Year Ended December 31, 2002		
Revenue		
Sales		$120 000
Expenses		
Selling	$39 000	
Administrative	24 000	
Amortization	2 500	65 500
Operating Income		54 500
Other Income		
Investments		1 500
Net Income Before Income Taxes		56 000
Income Taxes		13 440
Net Income After Income Taxes		$ 42 560

FIGURE 13-14
Income statement for Gordon & Henry Ltd.

Double Taxation

A shareholder receiving a dividend from a corporation like Gordon & Henry Ltd. must add the dividend to personal income. As a result, the shareholder ends up paying income tax on this dividend. Shareholders, unlike the owners of sole proprietorships and partnerships, are not taxed directly for any profits earned by their companies. The corporation, however, pays income tax on the same income from which the shareholder received a dividend. This can be considered to be a case of double taxation: the corporation was taxed and so was the shareholder on the same net income.

To alleviate the burden of double taxation, the federal government generally taxes dividends from a taxable Canadian corporation at a reduced rate.

TYPES OF SHARES

The capital of a corporation takes the form of shares. Shares are sold for cash or exchanged for assets or for services performed for the corporation. Shares may be issued with a *par value* (a stated value) or *without par value* (see page 528). The shares may be common shares alone or a mixture of common shares and preferred shares.

Common Shares

Common shares have one vote per share but no guaranteed dividend.

The basic shares issued by a corporation are *common shares*. Each common share entitles the owner to one vote at shareholders' meetings. There is no guarantee that owners of common shares will receive a dividend since only the board of directors may decide if dividends are to be paid on common shares. The board also decides the amount of any dividend. The person or group owning a majority of common shares controls the voting at shareholders' meetings — and thus the makeup of the board of directors and how the business will be managed.

When a corporation offers additional shares for sale, it usually provides common shareholders the first opportunity to purchase the shares, often at less than the current market price. The term *rights* is used to describe the privilege of buying new shares at special prices.

Preferred Shares

Preferred shares do not have voting rights but have prior claim on assets and net income over common shares.

Sometimes a corporation, in order to attract investors and cash, offers shares with special features. These shares, called *preferred shares*, have the following advantages:

- fixed dividend
- preferred position for dividends and assets

For instance, a $2 preferred share is one that entitles the shareholder to a $2 dividend if the corporation earns a profit. A 5-percent preferred share is one that entitles the holder to a dividend of 5 percent of the par value of the share. Thus a 5-percent preferred share, par value $30, would pay a dividend of $1.50 on each preferred share. These dividends must be paid before any dividends are allocated to the common shares. In the event that a corporation dissolves or goes into bankruptcy, the holders of preferred shares have a right to the assets *before* the holders of common shares. Normally, preferred shares do *not* carry voting rights.

Other special features that may be attached to preferred shares are:

- cumulative dividends
- convertibility
- participating
- callable

Cumulative Preferred Share

A *cumulative* preferred share is a share for which the dividends build up or accumulate if they are not paid. For example, a $2 cumulative preferred shareholder might not be given the $2 dividend in a year when a loss is suffered by the corporation. However, the next year, a $4 dividend is paid before any portion of the net income is given to common shareholders.

Convertible Preferred Share

A convertible preferred share is a share that the owner may exchange for common shares at a set price. For example, the owner might be given the right to exchange each convertible preferred share for two common shares.

Callable Preferred Share

A callable preferred share gives the corporation the right to repurchase the share at a set price.

Participating Preferred Share

The shareholder of a participating preferred share has the right to share in any remaining net income along with the common shareholders. This means that the preferred shareholder receives the fixed dividend and may also share in any remaining net income after dividends have been paid to the common shareholders.

Journal Entries

Separate equity accounts are used for each class of share. The following entries record the issue of both common and preferred shares.

Jan. 2	Cash	20 000	
	Share Capital — Common		20 000
	Issued 1 000 common shares, par value $20.		
3	Cash	30 000	
	Share Capital — Preferred		30 000
	Issued 1 000, 5% preferred shares, par value $30.		

The accounts for the different classes of shares are shown below:

Share Capital — Preferred			
	Jan. 3	30 000	

Share Capital — Common			
	Jan. 2	20 000	

The shareholders' equity section of the balance sheet is shown in Figure 13-15. For each class of share, the total number of shares authorized and issued is shown.

FIGURE 13-15
Number of shares authorized and issued is shown on the balance sheet.

SHAREHOLDERS' EQUITY	
Share Capital	
Authorized	
10 000 5% preferred shares, $30 par value	
70 000 common shares, $20 par value	
Issued	
4 000 preferred shares	$ 120 000
30 000 common shares	600 000
	720 000
Retained Earnings	400 000
	$1 120 000

Dividends — Common and Preferred

The board of directors of a corporation decides if dividends are to be paid and their amount. Suppose net income is $90 000. The board of directors declares a dividend of 5 percent of the par value for preferred shares and of $1 for common shares. Since there is a total of 4 000 preferred shares outstanding at $30 each, the preferred share dividend is $1.50 per share ($30 × 5%) or a total of $6 000 ($1.50 × 4 000 shares). The dividend for the common shares amounts to $30 000 or $1 for each of the 30 000 common shares that have been issued.

The Declaration Reduces Retained Earnings

The entry to record the declaration of dividends is as follows:

Apr. 15	Retained Earnings	36 000	
	Dividends Payable — Preferred		6 000
	Dividends Payable — Common		30 000
	Dividends declared, $1 per common share and $1.50 per 5% preferred share.		

The Payment Reduces the Asset

When the dividends are paid, this entry is made:

May 1	Dividends Payable — Preferred	6 000	
	Dividends Payable — Common	30 000	
	Cash		36 000
	Issued dividend cheques		

Suppose that in the next fiscal period, the net income went down to $20 000. The board of directors decided to pay the 5-percent dividend on the preferred shares, but to pay nothing to the common shareholders. They felt that a common share dividend would put a strain on the corporation's finances by removing too much cash. They hoped that by keeping the cash in the corporation, the operations and net income would improve in the next fiscal period. An entry for $6 000 was made to record only the preferred dividend.

In the next fiscal period, the net income of the corporation increased dramatically to $200 000. The board of directors was right! The board decided to again declare a 5-percent dividend on each preferred share, but to raise the dividend on the common shares to $4. The following entry was made:

Apr. 17	Retained Earnings	126 000	
	Dividends Payable — Preferred		6 000
	Dividends Payable — Common		120 000
	Dividends declared, $4 per common share and $1.50 per 5% preferred share.		

The three examples just covered illustrate some of the differences in types of shares and dividend payments. The preferred shares have first claim on net income. Common shares may receive no dividend at all when net income is low. However, common shares may receive high dividends when net income increases significantly. It should be noted that the preferred shareholders could also miss their dividends if the directors decide that sufficient funds are not available.

Market Value of Shares

W. Gordon and W. Henry own the majority of shares in a private corporation, Gordon & Henry Ltd. The corporation has no need of additional funds and does not plan to issue more shares. Both Gordon and Henry paid $50 a share when the corporation was formed.

J. Probyn is aware of the success of the corporation and feels that Gordon & Henry Ltd. will continue to be successful in the future. She would like to invest in the company, but it is not issuing any new shares. She offers W. Gordon $83 a share for 100 of his shares. Gordon agrees and receives $8 300. He has made a gain of $33 per share, a total of $3 300 on the 100 shares sold, since he originally paid only $50 per share. This example illustrates the *market value* of a share. Market value is the price at which a buyer and seller agree to exchange shares.

Market value is the price at which buyers and sellers agree to exchange shares.

THE STOCK MARKET

The *stock market* is a place where shares in a corporation are bought and sold after they have been issued. It is a place where a shareholder who wishes to sell shares may find a buyer willing to purchase the shares. Large public corporations such as the Ford Motor Company of Canada, Inco, and John Labatt Limited know it is important to make it easy for the public to buy and sell their shares. One reason for this is that these corporations may wish to expand their operations. Expansion requires financing, which can be obtained by issuing more shares.

The stock market is a place where shares in a corporation are bought and sold after they have been issued.

To facilitate this process, large public corporations list their companies on a *stock exchange*, where shares are bought and sold. In order to be listed on a stock exchange, a corporation must follow detailed regulations and must provide the public with much information concerning the operation of the company. In Canada, there are stock exchanges in Calgary, Toronto, and Montreal. *Stockbrokers* act as agents for those who wish to buy and sell shares. The brokers arrange the sale in return for a commission on the sale. As well as handling the sale of shares between shareholders and people who wish to buy shares, stockbrokers sell large blocks of new shares for corporations in need of funds.

ACCOUNTING TERMS

Board of Directors A group of persons, elected by the shareholders, who are responsible for the operation of the corporation.

Business Corporation A legal entity owned by shareholders.

Common Shares Shares that have one vote per share but no guaranteed dividend.

Corporation A business owned by one or more persons whose liability is limited to their investment in the corporation. A corporation has a legal existence of its own.

Dividends The portion of the corporation's net income paid out of retained earnings to the shareholders.

Limited Company Term that is sometimes used to describe the corporate form of ownership.

Market Value The price at which buyers and sellers agree to exchange shares.

Officers Hired employees of a corporation who manage the day-to-day operations of the corporation.

Organization Expense An account used to record the costs incurred in organizing a corporation.

Partnership A business owned by two or more persons, each of whom has unlimited personal liability for the debts and legal obligations of the business.

Preferred Shares Shares that do not have voting rights but have prior claim on assets and net income over common shares.

Retained Earnings An equity account containing the balance of undistributed net income.

Share Capital An account that is a record of shares sold.

Shareholders Owners of shares in a corporation.

Sole Proprietorship A business owned by one person who has unlimited personal liability for the debts and legal obligations of the business.

Statement of Retained Earnings A statement that provides a complete description of changes in the Retained Earnings account.

REVIEW QUESTIONS

UNIT 33

1. Explain why limited liability is an advantage of the corporate form of ownership.
2. Explain what is meant by the phrase "a corporation has a legal existence of its own."
3. (a) Why do creditors need to know whether the company applying for credit is a corporation?
   (b) Why must the name of the corporation be clearly displayed in all its notices and advertisements?
4. The firm of Gordon & Henry Ltd. is a corporation, not a partnership. How does the public know this?
5. What is the board of directors?

6. What is the difference between a private and a public business corporation?
7. What is the name of the form that indicates that a person owns shares in a corporation?
8. Name the two main equity accounts in a corporation's Shareholders' Equity section of the balance sheet.
9. What information does the Retained Earnings account provide?
10. What is the difference between shares authorized and shares issued?
11. What account is debited to record the costs of forming a corporation?
12. What are the three options for distributing the net income of a corporation?
13. Who decides what will be done with the net income of a corporation?
14. What is the name given to the portion of a corporation's net income that is paid to the shareholders?
15. What is the name of the account that is used to record the accumulated net income of a business?
16. Into which account are the Revenue and Expense accounts of a corporation closed?
17. Into which account is the balance of the Income Summary account closed?
18. What does the balance of the Retained Earnings account represent?
19. (a) What effect do declared dividends have on the Retained Earnings account?
    (b) What effect does net income have on the Retained Earnings account?
    (c) What effect does net loss have on the Retained Earnings account?
20. What is a common share?
21. Explain three main features of common shares.
22. What are rights?
23. What is a preferred share?
24. Explain why preferred shares are generally considered to be a safer investment than common shares.
25. Explain the following terms:
    (a) cumulative preferred shares
    (b) convertible preferred shares
    (c) callable preferred shares
    (d) participating preferred shares
26. What does the par value of a share mean?
27. What is the market value of a share?
28. After a corporation has sold its shares to the public, how can a person purchase shares in that corporation?

PROBLEMS: APPLICATIONS

CHAPTER 13

14. A group of business people have received a certificate of incorporation to operate a Canadian corporation called General Distributors Ltd. They were authorized to issue 20 000 shares of $50 par value per share. Record the following in a General Journal using these accounts: Cash; Equipment; Building; Share Capital.

    Jul. 2 Sold 1 000 shares for $50 000 cash ($50 per share).

    5 Issued 600 shares to G. Devine, a founding shareholder, in return for equipment (600 × $50 = $30 000).

    6 Issued 3 000 shares to A. Galla in return for a building (3 000 × $50 = $150 000).

15. I. Grant Ltd. has been incorporated with authorized share capital of 70 000 common shares having a $20 par value. Journalize the following transactions using these accounts: Cash; Delivery Equipment; Building; Organization Expense; Share Capital.

    Apr. 1 I. Grant, F. Grant, and W. McMichael purchased 2 000 shares each for cash at par value.

    2 I. Grant was issued 700 shares in return for a new delivery van.

    3 I. Grant and F. Grant each received 8 000 shares in return for a building.

    15 A cheque for $600 was issued in payment for printing of share certificates.

    15 W. McMichael was issued 100 shares in return for legal services for incorporating the business.

16. O. Muma, a sole proprietor, has received letters patent that allow him to organize his business as a private corporation to be called Brookfield Products Ltd. The accounts of the proprietorship are exchanged for common shares in the new company. Brookfield Products Ltd. has authorized 100 000 common shares with a $100 par value per share. The accounts of the proprietorship had these balances:

ACCOUNT TITLE	ACC. NO.	DEBIT	CREDIT
Cash		19 000	
Supplies		2 500	
Equipment		25 000	
Land & Building		200 000	
O. Muma, Capital			246 500

(a) Record the journal entry to take over the accounts of the proprietorship in return for common shares:

Sep. 1 Issued shares in return for assets of the proprietorship.

(b) Record the following transactions:

Sep. 1 Issued 30 shares to D. Adams in return for legal services to set up the corporation.

10 Issued shares at par for cash:
D. Adams 70 shares,
R. Bradfield 100 shares,
J. Scobie 120 shares.

15 Paid $32 000 cash for delivery equipment.

20 Paid $5 000 cash for advertising.

17. (a) Prepare closing General Journal entries using the balances in the T-accounts below:

Expense Account	
80 000	

Revenue Account	
	112 000

Income Summary	

Retained Earnings	
	135 000

(b) Close the Expense account into the Income Summary account.
(c) Close the Revenue account.
(d) Close the Income Summary account into the Retained Earnings account.
(e) Post the journal to the T-accounts.

18. An Income Summary account has a credit balance (net income) of $70 000. Prepare the Journal entries from the following information:

- Close the Income Summary account and transfer net income into the Retained Earnings account; dividends of $38 000 are declared.
- Dividends are paid by cheque.

19. An Income Summary account has a credit balance of $75 000. Prepare the General Journal entries from the following information:

- Close the Income Summary account; dividends of $27 000 are declared.
- Dividends are paid by cheque.

20. Prepare a statement of retained earnings dated December 31, 2003 for Gordon & Henry Ltd. using the following information:

- net income for the year, $90 000
- dividends paid, $30 000
- retained earnings, beginning balance January 1, $68 000

21. Prepare the next year's (from exercise 20) statement of retained earnings dated December 31, 2004 for Gordon & Henry Ltd. using the following information:

- net income for the year, $22 000
- dividends paid, $30 000
- retained earnings, January 1, $128 000

22. Mayfair Enterprises Ltd. pays income tax at the rate of 24 percent. This year, the corporation's net income before taxes is $90 000.

    (a) What is the income tax expense for this year?
    (b) What is the net income after taxes?

23. Broadway Mfg. Ltd. was organized on April 1 with the following capital authorized:

    - 5 000, 7-percent cumulative preferred shares, par value $50
    - 100 000 common shares, par value $5

    Record the following transactions in a General Journal.

    Apr. 1 Issued 400 preferred shares for cash.
    6 Received cash for 10 000 common shares sold at par.
    10 Paid legal fees for incorporation of $2 000 by issuing common shares at par.
    15 Received title to land in exchange for 2 000 preferred shares and 10 000 common shares at par.
    20 Sold 500 preferred shares and 10 000 common shares at par for cash.

24. Prepare the shareholders' equity section of a balance sheet from the following information:

    - 150 000 common shares authorized, no par value
    - 50 000 common shares issued with a total value of $300 000
    - 10 000, 5-percent preferred shares authorized, no par value
    - 1 000 preferred shares issued with a total value of $50 000
    - retained earnings, $78 000

25. Prepare the shareholders' equity section of a balance sheet from the following:

    - 200 000 common shares authorized, $10 par value
    - issued 90 000 common shares at par
    - 30 000 preferred shares authorized, $25 par value
    - issued 10 000 perferred shares at par
    - retained earnings, $205 000

26. Prepare a statement of retained earnings and the shareholders' equity section of the balance sheet dated June 30, 2001, for Brookfield Products Ltd.

    - authorized share capital, 100 000 common shares
    - shares issued, 2 825 common shares valued at $282 500
    - retained earnings, beginning balance July 1, $75 000
    - net income for the year, $60 000

27. Broadway Mfg. Ltd. has issued 2 900, 8-percent cumulative preferred shares, par value $50.

    (a) How much is the total annual dividend on the preferred shares?
    (b) Assume no dividends were paid the first year. How much is the total of dividends owing to preferred shareholders at the end of the second year?

28. During 2001, its third year of operations, a corporation earned a net income of $71 000. Dividends of 75¢ per share were paid on the 50 000 common shares outstanding. The next year, a net loss of $37 000 was reported. No dividends were paid that year. On January 1, 2001, the balance in the retained earnings account was $38 000.
    (a) Calculate the balance in the Retained Earnings account at December 31, 2002.
    (b) Prepare the journal entry to close the Income Summary account at December 31, 2002.

PROBLEMS: CHALLENGES

1. Following is the trial balance of F. Addario and W. Box, who are partners. They share net income and net loss in the ratio of 2:1. Each receives a salary of $31 000. The ending inventory, December 31, is $51 000. Prepare:
    (a) an income statement
    (b) a statement of distribution of net income
    (c) a statement of partners' equity
    (d) a balance sheet
    (e) the closing entries

Addario & Box
Trial Balance
December 31, 2000

ACCOUNT TITLE	ACC. NO.	DEBIT	CREDIT
Cash		$ 45 000	
Accounts Receivable		22 000	
Inventory, January 1		46 000	
Equipment		40 000	
Accumulated Amortization: Equipment			$ 8 000
Accounts Payable			14 000
Addario, Capital			27 000
Box, Capital			24 000
Addario, Drawings		13 000	
Box, Drawings		12 000	
Sales			297 000
Purchases		90 000	
Transportation on Purchases		2 000	
Selling Expense		70 000	
Administrative Expense		30 000	
		$370 000	$370 000

2. Chateau Holdings Ltd. was formed with the following capitalization:
    - authorized Share Capital:
      20 000, 5-percent preferred shares, par value $30
      100 000 common shares, no par value

(a) Record the following transactions in a General Journal:

Jan. 3 Sold 10 000 common shares for $7 each. Received cash, $70 000.

4 Issued for cash, 500 preferred shares at par value.

10 Purchased equipment for $8 500 cash. Issued a cheque.

12 Paid legal fees of incorporation by issuing 100 preferred shares to the company lawyers.

15 Sold 10 000 common shares for $7 each.

16 Purchased land and a building valued at $320 000 in return for $130 000 cash, an $85 000 mortgage, and 15 000 common shares at $7 per share. Note: Land value is $80 000.

(b) Prepare T-accounts and post the General Journal entries.

3. Prepare the year's income statement for Chateau Holdings Ltd. from the adjusted trial balance that follows. Use an income tax rate of 24 percent.

Chateau Holdings Ltd.
Adjusted Trial Balance
December 31, 2003

ACCOUNT TITLE	ACC. NO.	DEBIT	CREDIT
Cash		$ 31 000	
Supplies		25 000	
Accounts Receivable		90 000	
Inventory		100 000	
Land		80 000	
Building		240 000	
Accumulated Amortization: Building			$ 20 000
Equipment		8 500	
Accumulated Amortization: Equipment			1 900
Accounts Payable			7 000
Mortgage Payable			85 000
Share Capital: Common			245 000
Preferred			18 000
Retained Earnings			100 000
Sales			347 600
Selling Expense		225 000	
Administrative Expense		25 000	
		$820 500	$824 500

4. (a) Record these General Journal entries for Chateau Holdings Ltd. Refer to exercises 2 and 3:

Nov. 1 Declared a 5-percent dividend on preferred shares, par value $30 and a $1.50 per share dividend on common shares.

25 Issued dividend cheques.

(b) Prepare closing entries for revenue and expenses including Income Tax Expense.

(c) Post the closing entries to a T-account for Income Summary.
(d) Journalize and post the entry to close the Income Summary account into the Retained Earnings account.

5. Prepare a statement of retained earnings and the shareholders' section of the Chateau Holdings Ltd. balance sheet using information from exercises 2 to 4 and the following:

   - dividends paid, $53 400
   - net income after taxes, $74 176

6. Remo Industries Inc. has 1 000 outstanding shares of 6-percent preferred shares, $30 par value, and 30 000 no-par-value common shares outstanding. Assume that the preferred shares carry the cumulative feature. During a five-year-period, the company paid out the following amounts in dividends:

1999	$0
2000	10 000
2001	15 000
2002	0
2003	12 000

No dividends were owed to the preferred shareholders prior to 1999.

(a) Set up a table using the following format to show the distribution of dividends to each class of shareholder:

Year	Preferred	Common	Total

(b) For the year 2003, what is the dividend per share that was paid to each common shareholder?

Index

Account balance, 31, 35
Accountant, 380
Accounting, 4, 19, 25
Accounting controls, 251, 374, 401
Accounting cycle, 92, 102, 114, 174, 446–447
Accounting equation, 3, 19
Accounting period, 14, 45, 64
Accounting procedures, 35
Accounting supervisor, 258–261
  cheque copies, 260
  list of cash receipts, 259
  other journal entries, 261
  posting the journal, 260
  preparing journal entries, 258–260
  purchase invoices, 260
  sales invoice, 259
Accounting systems, 19
  accounts payable system, 253–256
  accounts receivable system, 256–258
  computerized system, 267
  Fraser Enterprises, 252–253
  manual system, 267
  one-write system, 267
  purchasing systems, 311–316
Accounts, 35
  balance sheet, 25
  calculation of new balances, 31–32
  checking, 91
  recording transactions in, 28–31
  transaction analysis, 28–31
  trial balance, 32–34
Accounts payable, 6, 8, 19, 245
Accounts payable clerk, 253–256
Accounts payable control account, 247, 263, 276
Accounts payable ledger, 247, 263–264, 276
  posting purchases journal, 322
  schedule of accounts payable, 250
Accounts payable system, 253–256
Accounts receivable, 6, 8, 19
  age analysis, 448
  general ledger, 244
  previously written off, 417–418
  schedule of. *See* schedule of accounts receivable
Accounts receivable application software, 270–275
  accounts receivable menu, 271
  credit sales, 271–275
Accounts receivable clerk, 256–258, 380
Accounts receivable control account, 247, 263, 276, 380
Accounts receivable ledger, 247, 263, 276
Accounts receivable system, 256–258
Accrual basis of accounting, 48, 64
Accrued
  adjustments, 420
  expenses, 418–420, 448
  interest, 418–419, 427
  revenue, 420, 448
  salaries, 419–420, 427
Accumulated amortization, 138, 174
Accuracy, checking for, 91
Adjusted trial balance, 163, 174
Adjusting entry, 135, 161–163, 174, 440
  adjusted trial balance, 163
  posting, 162–163
Adjusting the books, 174
Adjustments, 124
  accrued, 420
  accrued interest, 427
  accrued salaries, 427
  adjusting entry, 135, 161–163
  amortization, 427
  bad debts, 425
  coding, 149
  merchandise inventory, 427–428, 428–431
  prepaid expenses, 425–426
  preparation on work sheet, 144, 145–154
  purpose of, 134
  and the work sheet, 425–428
Administrative controls, 374, 401
Administrative expenses, 437, 448
Allowance for bad debts account, 412–413, 415–416, 448
Amortization, 137–139, 174
  accumulated, 138
  adjustments, 427
  capital cost allowance, 141
  contra asset account, 139
  declining-balance method, fixed percentage, 140–141
  defined, 138
  expense, 138, 174
  and income taxes, 141
  methods of calculating, 139–141
  recording, 138
  straight-line method, 140
  total amount of amortization, 139
  valuation account, 139
Analyzing transactions. *See* transaction analysis
Approved invoice, 315
Asset accounts, 35, 164
Assets, 3, 6, 8, 19
  book value, 156
  capital, 123, 124, 128, 438
  current, 123, 124, 128, 134–135, 438
  order on balance sheet, 9
  recording balances in T-accounts, 25–26
Audit, 81, 389, 401
Authorized shares, 529
Automated banking machines (ATMs), 235

Bad debts, 410, 448
adjustment, 410–413
adjustments for, 425
expense account, 412
recovery of, 417–418
Bad debts expenses, 410–412, 448
balance sheet method, 413–416
estimating, 413–416
income statement method, 413
Balance-column account, 78, 102
Balance column form of ledger account, 78–81
DR./CR. column, 79
posting to, 79–81
Balance sheet, 3, 5–7, 19
account form of, 51
accounts, 25, 35, 63, 64
accounts payable, 6
accounts receivable, 6, 244
assets, 9
balances, 25
classified. *See* classified balance sheet
debit and credit theory, 63
equity accounts on, 49–51
liabilities, 9
mortgage payable, 6
new balances, 16
order of items, 9
owner 's equity, 125
partnerships, 520
preparation, 6–7, 438–439
preparation of financial statements from, 52–54
report form, 51–52, 65
and trial balances, 34
users of, 9–10
valuation of items, 9
and work sheet, 118–119
Balance sheet method of estimating bad debts, 413–416, 448
Bank credit cards, 229–235
accounting example for credit card transactions, 232–233
for business, 231
charge cards, 235
completion of credit card form, 230
credit cards, 235
fees, 230, 233
merchant statement, 234–235
purpose of, 229
sales recap form, 233
Bank credit memo, 347, 358, 391–392, 401
Bank debit memo, 354, 358, 390–391, 401
Bank loan, 8
Bank reconciliation, 401
Banking
bank credit memo, 391–392
bank debit memo, 390–391
business current account reconciliation, 395–399
depositor's account, 391
interest earned, 400
interest expense, 400
monthly bank reconciliation, 392–399
personal chequing account reconciliation, 392–395
service charges, 399
source documents, 390–399
Batch totals, 265–266
Board of directors, 536, 538
Book of original entry, 73, 102
Book value, 139, 156, 175
Books and records, 467
Business
balance sheet, 5–7
current account reconciliation, 395–399
financial position, 4–5
goods or services, 44
transactions. *See* business transactions
Business corporation, 538
Business entity concept, 5, 19
Business operations, types of, 184
Business ownership
corporations, 506
partnerships, 505–506
sole proprietorship, 505
Business transactions
accounting period, 14
defined, 14
introduction, 14
recording in accounts, 28–31
transaction analysis sheet, 15–16
Callable preferred share, 535
Canada Business Corporations Act, 528
Canada Pension Plan, 457, 458–459, 459, 467–470
Canadian Bankers Association, 235
Canadian Institute of Chartered Accountants (CICA), 5
Cancelled cheques, 392, 401
Capital, 19
Capital assets, 123, 124, 128, 438
Capital cost allowance, 141, 175
Capital ratio method, 514–515
Cash, 8, 194, 374
discounts, 346
overages, 378
on receipt of invoice, 194
received, 257
shortages, 378
Cash control
cash payments, 381–385
cash receipts, 376–381
cash received by mail, 376
cash sales, 376
cash short and over account, 377–378
cash short and over policy, 379
daily cash proof, 377–379
daily deposit of cash, 379
immediate listing of cash receipts, 376–377
importance of, 374
monthly bank reconciliation, 392–399
payment by cheque, 382
periodic audit, 389
petty cash procedures, 382–385
prenumbered sales slips, 376
procedures, 375
separation of duties, 375, 381
supporting documents, 382
Cash payments, 351, 381–385
Cash payments journal, 352–356, 358
balancing, 355–356
bank debit memo, 354
cheque issued for refund on cash sale, 354
posting, 355–356
recording source documents, 352–354

recording transactions, 355
Cash proof, 377–379, 401
Cash receipts
cash control, 376–381
control system, 379–381
immediate listing of, 376–377
Cash receipts journal, 343–344, 358
bank credit memo, 347
cash sales slips, 347
from customers, 344–346
new investment, 347
recording source documents, 344–347
Cash sales, 376
Cash sales slips, 96–97, 102, 347
Cash short and over account, 377–378, 401
Cash short and over policy, 379
Certificate of incorporation, 526
Charge sale, 97
Chart of accounts, 85–86, 189–190
Charter of incorporation, 526
Cheques, 99–100
cancelled, 392, 401
copies, 260
endorsement, 100
issued for refund on cash sale, 354
list of cheques received, 100
new investment, 347
NSF, 392, 400, 401
outstanding, 394, 401
paid, 99
payment by, 351
payment less sales discount, 346
payment on account, 344–346
received, 99–100
requisition, 351
restrictive endorsement, 100
voucher, 351
CICA Handbook, 5
Circling method, 302, 305, 325
Classified balance sheet, 123–125, 128
Classified income statement, 437–438
Claymore Industries, 499–503
Closing entries, 163–174, 168, 429, 440–441
Closing the books, 163–164, 175
closing expense accounts, 166, 169
closing revenue accounts, 169
closing the drawings accounts, 167
corporations, 531
income summary account, 164–165, 166–167
partnerships, 511–512
purpose of, 164
revenue accounts, 165
steps in, 165–168
updating owner's equity account, 164, 169–172
from work sheet, 168–172
C.O.D., 194
Coded adjustments, 149, 175
Columnar journal, 291–294, 305
account or explanation column, 294
advantages of, 303
balancing, 294–296
circling method, 302
credit invoices, 302–303
disadvantages of, 303–304
errors, 295
forwarding page totals, 295
other accounts section, 294
purchases returns and allowances, 303
recording transactions in, 293–294
reference number column, 294, 305
sales return, 302
special sections of, 294
Combination journal, 293, 305
Commission, 477
Common shares, 534, 538
Compound entry, 74, 102
Compulsory payroll deductions, 458–459, 459–461
Computerized system, 267, 268–269, 270, 275
Concept of objectivity, 101
Contra asset account, 139, 175
Contra liability account, 224
Contra revenue account, 192
Control account, 276, 301
Controls
accounting, 374, 401
administrative, 374, 401
cash. *See* cash control
of cash receipts, 376–381
internal accounting, 374
Convertible preferred share, 535
Corporate income tax, 533–534
Corporate net income, 530
Corporations, 506, 538
accounting procedures, 527–533
business, 538
closing the books, 531
corporate net income, 530
defined, 526
dividends. *See* dividends
forming, 526
journal entries, 528–529
name, 526
officers, 538
organization expense, 538
private, 527
retained earnings account, 528
share certificates, 527
shareholders, 526
shareholders' equity accounts, 527–528
shares for assets, 529
types of, 527
Cost of goods sold, 237
Cost of goods sold account transactions, 197–201
delivery expense, 201
purchases account, 197–198
purchases returns and allowances, 198–199
transportation on purchases, 200–201
Cost principle, 9, 19
Credit, 25, 35
balances, 27
memorandum, 193
note, 193
sale, 97
Credit card discount expense, 237
Credit cards. *See* bank credit cards
Credit invoices, 193–194, 199, 302–303, 324–325, 337–338, 358
Credit union, 461–466
Creditor, 2, 254
Cross-balancing, 305
Cumulative preferred share, 535
Current assets, 123, 124, 128, 134–135, 438
Current liabilities, 123, 125, 128, 439
Cycle billing, 339, 358

Daily cash proof, 377–379

Data collection, 266–267
Debit, 25, 35
Debit and credit theory, 34, 63–64, 190, 201–202
Debit balances, 27
Debit cards, 236
Debtors, 19
Declining-balance method, fixed percentage, 140–141, 175
Delivery expense, 201, 237
Depositor's account, 391
Direct posting, 255, 261, 299, 305, 320, 357
Dividends, 528, 530–531, 531, 532, 536–537, 538
Division of labour principle, 250, 276
Double-entry accounting, 27, 35, 61, 75
Double taxation, 534
DR./CR. column, 79
Drawings account, 48–49, 53, 64, 167, 511
Due date, 358

E-cash cards, 236
E-commerce, 235, 237
Eight-column work sheet, 145–154, 175
  completion of, 149–153
  equipment, 149
  net income, determination of, 153
  net loss, determination of, 153
  prepaid insurance, 147
  prepaid rent, 147
  preparing adjustments, 145–153
  steps in preparation of, 153
  supplies, 145–147
Electronic banking, 235
Electronic Cash Cards, 236
Electronic commerce, 235, 237
Electronic funds transfer, 236
Employee's earning record, 482–484
Employer Health Tax, 458, 489–490
Employment Insurance Act, 457, 458, 459–460, 476
Employment laws, 457
Employment Standards Act, 457
Endorsement, 100
Entrepreneur, 19
EOM, 194
Equipment, 149
Equities, 8, 19
Equity accounts, 64
Errors
  columnar journal, 295
  correction of, 90
  posting, 88
  purchases journal, 318
  transposition, 89–90, 102
  trial balance, 89–90
Expense accounts, 59
  closing, 166, 169
  double-entry accounting, 61
  reason for, 60–61
  rules of debit and credit, 59–60
  temporary accounts, 164
  transaction analysis, 61–63
Expenses, 44, 64, 137
  accrued, 418–420
  adjustments, 134
  administrative, 437, 448
  allocating responsibility for, 438
  amortization, 138, 174
  income statement, 46
  owner's equity, 60
  and owner's equity, 48
  prepaid, 124
  rules for recording, 48
  selling, 437, 448
  and work sheet, 118
Extended health insurance plans, 466

Federal laws, 457
Financial position, 19
  accounting equation, 3
  of an individual, 2–3
  balance sheet, 3
  of a business, 4–5
  calculation of, 2
  statement of. *See* balance sheet
Financial statements, 64
  classified, 448
  classified balance sheet, 123–125
  partnerships, 519–521
  preparation from balance sheet, 52–54
  preparation of, 154–156
  purpose of, 122
  schedule of cost of goods sold, 436
  statement of owner's equity, 126
  supporting statements and schedules, 126–127
Fiscal period, 45, 64
Fixed ratio method, 514, 515–517
Forwarding procedure, 86–87, 305
Fraser Enterprises, 252–253, 379–381

GAAP. *See* Generally Accepted Accounting Principles (GAAP)
General journal, 73, 78, 102
  credit invoices, 324
  posting purchases journal to, 322–323
General ledger, 262
  accounts payable, 245
  accounts receivable, 244
  adapting, 245–246
  trial balance, 248–249
Generally Accepted Accounting Principles (GAAP), 5, 19
Goods and Services Tax, 214–217, 237
  calculating, 219–221
  and cash discounts, 225
  GST payable accounts, 221, 222
  GST refundable account, 224
  Harmonized Sales Tax, 225
  how it works, 215
  input tax credit, 215, 223–224, 237
  optional for small business, 225
  payable, 237
  quick method, 226
  service business, 224
Government requirements, 467
Gross earnings, 467
Group life insurance, 461
GST payable accounts, 221, 222

Hardware, 270
Harmonized Sales Tax, 225, 237
Health insurance, 466
Hourly rate, 477

Income statement, 45, 64
  accounts, 64, 191
  accuracy of, 47–48
  classified, 437–438
  debit and credit rules for revenue and expense accounts, 59–60
  debit and credit theory, 64

expense accounts, 59–63
expenses, 46
merchandising company, 436–438
net income, 47
net loss, 47
partnerships, 516
preparation, 45–47
revenue, 46
revenue accounts, 58–63
and work sheet, 118
Income statement method of estimating bad debts, 413, 416, 448
Income summary account, 164–165, 166–167, 175
Income tax
and amortization, 141
corporate, 533–534
partnerships, 510
personal, 460–461, 476
Income Tax Act, 141, 457, 460–461, 476
Indirect posting, 266
Insufficient net income, 517–518
Insurance, prepaid, 137
Integrative activity
Claymore Industries, 499–503
Marcov's Furniture, 367–372
Metro Sales Co., 452–455
Westbrooke Cinema, 179–182
Interac Direct Payment, 235
Interest earned, 400
Interest expense, 400
Internal accounting control, 374
Inventory. *See* merchandise inventory
Inventory adjustment, 428–431, 431

Journal, 102
advantages of, 75
cash payments. *See* cash payments journal
cash receipts. *See* cash receipts journal
columnar, 291–294
combination, 293
correction of entries, 90
declining-balance method, 141
defined, 73
double-entry accounting, 75
general, 78
payroll, 482
posting the, 260
purchases. *See* purchases journal
recording procedures, 74–75
sales. *See* sales journal
sample transactions, 73–74
special, 310–311
synoptic, 293
Journal entries, 73, 102, 258–260
after bank reconciliation, 399–400
no-par-value shares, 528–529
shares, 535–536
Journalizing, 73, 102
Journalizing batch totals, 265–266

Ledger, 35
in balance, 172
balance-column form of, 78–81
defined, 26
drawings account in, 49
forwarding procedure, 86–87
opening ledger accounts, 84–85
opening the, 26–27
partnership, 510–511
posting, 78, 299
update of, 161
verifying accuracy of, 248–250, 264
Letters patent, 526
Liabilities, 3, 7, 8, 19
current, 123, 125, 128, 439
long-term, 123, 125, 128, 439
order on balance sheet, 9
recording balances in T-accounts, 26
Liability accounts, 35, 164
Limited company, 506, 525, 538
Limited partnership, 506
Liquidity, 9, 19
Liquidity order, 124, 438
List of accounts payable, 250
List of cash receipts, 259, 380
Long-term liabilities, 123, 125, 128, 439
Loss, 44–45, 64

Manual system, 267, 268
Manufacturing companies, 184, 237
Marcov's Furniture, 367–372
Market value, 537, 538
Matching principle, 47, 64, 448
Matching process, 315, 358
Maturity date rule, 9, 19
Memorandum of association, 526
Merchandise, 184, 237
Merchandise inventory, 124, 187–188, 237, 448
adjustments for, 427–428, 428–431
closing entry, 429
determining value of inventory, 428
post-closing trial balance, 443
posting to ledger, 443
Merchandise inventory account, 184
Merchandising company, 184, 238, 410, 448
chart of accounts, 189–190
credit invoices, 193–194
debit and credit rules for, 190
debit and credit theory, 201–202
determining net income, 185
income statement, 436–438
income statement accounts, 191
periodic inventory system, 436
recording cost of goods sold account transactions, 197–201
recording revenue account transactions, 191–196
revenue section of income statement, 191
sales, 191–192
sales discounts, 194–196
sales returns and allowances, 192–193
Merchant statement, 234–235
Metro Sales Co., 452–455
Monthly bank reconciliation, 392–399
Mortgage payable, 6, 8
Multi-column journal systems, 290
columnar journal. *See* columnar journal
posting, 299–300

Net 30, 194
Net balance sheet value, 139
Net earnings, 467–476, 476
Net income, 44–45, 64
determination of, 153
income statement, 47
for merchandising company, 185
partnerships, 513–517
and work sheet, 118

Net loss, 44–45, 64
determination of, 153
dividing, in partnerships, 517–518
effect of, 172–174
income statement, 47
methods of dividing, in partnerships, 513–517
recording on work sheet, 117
and work sheet, 118
Net purchase cost, 187
Net purchases, 238
Net realizable accounts receivable, 414
Net sales, 238
No-par-value shares, 528
NSF cheque, 392, 400, 401

Objectivity concept, 101, 102
Office supplies, 8
Officers, 538
On account sale, 97, 194
On credit, 194
1/10, n/30 EOM, 194
One-write system, 267, 276
Open the ledger, 35
Opening entry, 83, 102
Opening ledger accounts, 84–85
Opening the books, 81–85
ledger accounts, 84–85
opening entry, 83
Organization expense, 530, 538
Original cost, 139
Outstanding cheques, 394, 401
Overtime, 477
Owner's equity, 5, 7, 19, 125
capital account, 49
drawings account, 48–49, 53, 64
expenses, 48, 60
owner's salary, 49
and purchase discounts, 200
and revenue, 47
and sales discounts, 196
statement of, 126, 128
Owner's equity account, 35, 164, 169–172
Owner's salary, 49

Paperless economy, 235–237
Par-value shares, 528
Participating preferred share, 535
Partnership Act, 507
Partnership agreement, 507, 512
Partnerships, 505–506, 538
amount of capital invested, 513
balance sheet, 520
capital ratio method, 514–515
closing the books, 511–512
dividing net income, 512–513
dividing net loss, 517–518
drawings account, 511
financial statements, 519–521
fixed ratio method, 514, 515–517
formation of, 507–510
income statement, 519
and income taxes, 510
insufficient net income, 517–518
interest, 516–517
ledger accounts, 510–511
methods of dividing net income/loss, 513–517
payment for amount of work performed, 513
return on capital, 513
salaries, 516–517, 518–519
skills, talent and reputation, 513
statement of distribution of net income, 515, 520
statement of partners' equity, 520–521
Pay periods, 477
Paying employees, 484–485
Payment plans, 477–478
Payroll, 457
Payroll accounting
commission, 477
Employer Health Tax, 489–490
hourly rate, 477
implementing procedures, 482–485
methods for paying employees, 484–485
overtime, 477
pay periods, 477
payment plans, 477–478
payroll journal, 482
piece rate, 477
procedures, 477–478
recording payment of payroll deductions, 490
recording the payroll, 485–494
remitting deductions, 485
salary, 477
T-4 slip, 482–484
Payroll deductions, 458–459
Canada Pension Plan, 459, 467–470
compulsory, 458–459, 459–461
credit union, 461–466
employment insurance, 459–460, 476
extended health insurance plans, 466
group life insurance, 461
health insurance, 466
personal income tax, 460–461, 476
recording payment of, 490
registered pension plans, 466
remitting, 485
voluntary, 459, 461–466
Payroll journal, 482
Periodic inventory method, 187, 188, 238
Periodic inventory system, 427–428, 436
Permanent accounts, 164
Perpetual inventory method, 187, 188
Perpetual inventory system, 427–428
Personal chequing account reconciliation, 392–395
Personal equity, 3, 19
Personal income tax, 460–461, 476
Personal net worth, 2
Petty cash
account, 382
changing size of, 385
fund, 382, 401
guidelines, 385
procedures, 382–385
proving, 383
replenishing, 383–384, 401
voucher, 383, 401
Physical inventory, 188
Piece rate, 477
Point of sale terminals, 237
Post-closing trial balance, 172, 175, 443
Posting, 102
accounts receivable and payable, 299
adjusting entries, 162–163
to all ledgers from journal, 299
avoiding errors, 88

to balance column form of ledger account, 79–81
cash payments journal, 355–356
column totals, 299
control accounts, 301
direct, 255, 261, 299, 305, 320, 357
indirect, 266
journal, 260, 320–321
ledger, 78, 443
other accounts section, 299
purchases journal, 320–324
reference column, 102
references, 81
references in ledger, 301
sales journal, 337
special journals, 323
Preferred shares, 534–535, 538
Prenumbered sales slips, 376, 401
Prepaid expenses, 124, 134–137, 175
adjustments for, 425–426
current assets, 134–135
prepaid insurance, 137, 175
prepaid rent, 135–136, 175
supplies, 136
Prepaid insurance, 137, 147, 175
Prepaid rent, 135–136, 147, 175
Private corporation, 527
Profit, 44–45, 65
Provincial laws, 457
Provincial sales tax. *See* sales tax
PST payable accounts, 221–222
Purchase invoices, 99, 102, 253, 254, 260, 313–314, 359
Purchase order, 253, 312–313, 359
Purchase requisition, 312, 359
Purchases, 238, 358
Purchases account, 197–198
Purchases discounts, 187, 199–200, 238, 358
Purchases journal, 310, 316–319, 359
advantages of, 325–326
balancing, 318–319
circling method, 325
errors, 318
forwarding totals, 318
journalizing purchases on account, 316–319
posting to accounts payable ledger, 322
posting to general ledger, 322–323
posting to ledgers, 320–324
purchases transactions, 317
special column headings, 318
special columns, 325
Purchases returns and allowances, 186, 198–199, 238, 303
Purchasing systems, 311–316
approved invoice, 315
matching process, 315
ordering goods, 311–314
paying for purchases, 314–316
payment on due date, 316
purchase invoices, 313–314
purchase order, 312–313
purchase requisition, 312
receiving report, 314–315
Purpose of accounting, 4, 44

Receipt of invoice, 194
Receiving report, 314–315, 359
Recognition of costs, 198
Reconciliation statement, 394
Record of Employment, 460
Recording practices, 10–11
Recovery of bad debts, 417–418
Reference number column, 305
Registered pension plans, 466
Rent, prepaid, 135–136
Restrictive endorsement, 100
Retained earnings, 538
Retained earnings account, 528
Revenue, 44, 65
adjustments, 134
earned, 47
income statement, 46
owner's equity, 47
rules for recording, 47
and work sheet, 118
Revenue accounts, 58
closing, 165, 169
double-entry accounting, 61
reason for, 60–61
recording transactions for merchandising company, 191–196
rules of debit and credit, 59–60
temporary accounts, 164
transaction analysis, 61–63
Reversing entries, 444–446, 448

Salary
employees, 477
owner's, 49
partnerships, 516–517, 518–519
Sales, 191–192, 238
Sales discounts, 194–196, 238, 346, 359
decrease owner's equity, 196
disallowance of, 196
and sales returns, 196
terms of sale, 194–196
Sales invoice, 97–98, 99, 102, 256, 257, 259, 334–335, 359
Sales journal, 336–337, 359
balancing, 336
credit invoices, 337–338
posting, 337
Sales recap form, 233
Sales recording system, 339–340
Sales returns and allowances, 192–193, 196, 238, 302
Sales tax, 214–226
calculating, 219–221
and cash discounts, 225
commission, 238
exemptions, 218
federal. *See* Goods and Services Tax
Goods and Services Tax. *See* Goods and Services Tax
Harmonized Sales Tax, 225
licence numbers, 220
payable, 238
provincial, 218–219, 238
PST payable accounts, 221–222
recording commission, 222
Schedule, 186, 238
Schedule of accounts payable, 250, 255, 276
Schedule of accounts receivable, 126, 128, 249, 257–258, 276
schedule of cost of goods sold, 186–187, 436, 448
net purchase cost, 187
preparation of, 186–187
purchase discounts, 187
purchases returns and allowances, 186
transportation on purchases, 187
Scrap value, 138
Selling expenses, 437, 448
Selling on credit, 410

Separation of duties, 375, 381, 401
Service charges, 399
Service companies, 184, 238, 410, 448
Share capital, 538
Share certificates, 527
Shareholders, 526, 527, 538
Shareholders' equity accounts, 527–528
Shares
 callable preferred share, 535
 common, 534, 538
 convertible preferred share, 535
 cumulative preferred share, 535
 journal entries, 535–536
 market value of, 537
 no-par-value shares, 528
 par-value shares, 528
 participating preferred share, 535
 preferred, 534–535, 538
 types of, 534–536
Shares for assets, 529
Smart cards, 236
Social insurance number, 467
Software, 270
Sole proprietorship, 505, 525, 538
Source documents, 95, 102
 bank credit memo, 347
 banking, 390–399
 cash receipts, 344–347
 cash sales slips, 96–97
 cheques, 99–100
 as evidence of transactions, 101
 objectivity concept, 101
 prenumbered, 101
 purchase invoices, 99
 recording for cash payments, 352–354
 sales invoice, 97–98
Special journal system, 310–311, 323, 357–358, 359
Statement of account, 338–339, 359
Statement of distribution of net income, 515, 520
Statement of earnings and deductions, 458
Statement of financial position. *See* balance sheet
Statement of owner's equity, 126, 128
Statement of partners' equity, 520–521
Statement of Remuneration Paid, 482–484
Statement of retained earnings, 532–533, 538
Stock, 527
Stock market, 537
Stockholder, 527
Stored-value cards, 236
Straight-line method, 140, 175
Subsidiary ledgers, 246–247, 262–265, 276
 accounting control, 251
 additional, 265
 advantages of, 250–251
 division of labour principle, 250
 posting from purchases journal, 320–321
 posting to, 299, 357
Supplies, 136, 145–147
Supporting
 documents, 382
 schedule, 128
 schedules, 126–127
 statements, 126–127
Synoptic journal, 293, 305

T-4 slip, 482–484
T-accounts, 25–26, 35
 credit, 25
 debit, 25
 recording balances in, 25–26
Temporary accounts, 164
Ten-column work sheet, 154, 175
10th following, 194
Terms of sale, 194–196, 238
Three-column account, 78
Time-period principle, 45, 65
Total amount of amortization, 139
Total cost of merchandise purchased, 187
Trade-in value, 138
Transaction analysis, 35
 accounts, 28–31
 business transactions, 15–16
 expense accounts, 61–63
 major categories of transactions, 311
 revenue accounts, 61–63
 sheet, 15–16
Transportation-in, 238
Transportation on purchases, 187, 200–201
Transposition error, 89–90, 102
Trial balance, 32–34, 35, 53, 88–89
 adjusted, 163
 forms of, 89
 general ledger, 248–249
 locating errors, 89–90
 post-closing, 172, 443
2/10, n/30, 194

Uncollectible accounts, 416–418, 448
Universal health coverage, 466
Unlimited personal liability, 505, 525

Valuation
 account, 139, 175
 balance sheet items, 9
 cost principle, 9
Voluntary payroll deductions, 459, 461–466
Voucher cheque, 351

Westbrooke Cinema, 179–182
Work sheet, 114–117, 128
 and adjustments, 425–428
 see also adjustments
 balancing the, 153
 closing the books from, 168–172
 coding, 175
 completion of, 149–153
 eight-column, 145–154
 merchandise inventory adjustment, 431
 preparation of, 115–117
 preparing balance sheet from, 118–119
 preparing income statement from, 118
 recording net loss, 117
 ten-column, 154
 using the, 118–119
Workers' Compensation Act, 457
Working papers. *See* work sheet
Write-off entries, 416–418